D0944494

The French Republic
1879–1992

A History of France will, in five volumes, provide an account of 1,000 years of French history. The authors are among the most distinguished French historians, and the reception given to the first three volumes when they appeared in France in 1987 and 1988 suggests that this will be the standard history of France for many years to come.

Already published

France in the Middle Ages 987–1460
Georges Duby

Revolutionary France 1770–1880
François Furet

The French Republic 1879–1992
Maurice Agulhon

Forthcoming

Early Modern France 1460–1610
Emmanuel Le Roy Ladurie

The Ancien Régime 1610–1771
Emmanuel Le Roy Ladurie

The French Republic 1879–1992

MAURICE AGULHON

Translated by
Antonia Nevill

BLACKWELL
Oxford UK & Cambridge USA

First published as *La République* by Hachette, Paris, 1990

English edition first published 1993

Blackwell Publishers
108 Cowley Road
Oxford OX4 1JF
UK

238 Main Street, Suite 501
Cambridge, Massachusetts 02142
USA

British Library Cataloguing in Publication Data

A CIP catalogue record for this book is available from the British Library.

Library of Congress Cataloging-in-Publication Data

Agulhon, Maurice.
  [République. English]
  The French Republic: 1879–1992 / Maurice Agulhon; translated
by Antonia Nevill.
     p. cm.
  Includes bibliographical references and index.
  ISBN 0-631-17031-6
    1. France—History—Third Republic, 1870–1940. 2. France—History—20th
century. 3. France—Politics and government—1870–1940. 4. France—Politics
and government—20th century. I. Title.
DC33.A3813   1993
944.08—dc20   92-45622
                                                                                CIP

Typeset in 10 on 12 pt Plantin by Pure Tech Corporation, Pondicherry, India
Printed in Great Britain by Hartnolls Ltd, Bodmin, Cornwall

This book is printed on acid-free paper

Contents

List of Illustrations

All illustrations are courtesy of Roger-Viollet, Paris

Introduction

France was born of the course of history, and is the definition of a people. This book retraces the public and collective aspects of the many-faceted and varied life of the French people over the last century – its politics, in short. And why not? Politics was a particularly sensitive topic throughout that period.

France had long existed as nation and *Patrie* or homeland, but one may venture to say that it had never lived those roles so strongly as in the last hundred years, from which emerge the names of Jules Ferry, Clemenceau and de Gaulle, and also – why should they be any less significant – of Victor Hugo, Charles Péguy and Louis Aragon. In that period the French nation, in terms of the common consciousness of almost all its inhabitants, reached a kind of apogee. That apogee was closely interwoven with violence and conflict, and passed through two world wars. At what cost? We shall see. What is astonishing is that this high point of patriotism should have existed side by side with the continuation of the most impassioned struggles between the heirs of the Revolution and those of the Counter-Revolution. That dialectic, which could a priori be judged complex, between the presence of a national event, unanimous by its very nature, and of a stubborn political 'war of religion' deserves to be regarded as one of the main themes of this history.

From 1870 France was known officially as the 'French Republic', but to tell the truth, the Republic kept on beginning. It at last came into existence on 4 September 1870, but did not possess its constitutional laws until 1875, and the republicans did not fully hold power until 1879. That victory, which was not immediately known to be definitive, by no means put an end to the controversies surrounding the word 'Republic' and the way it was construed.

In France, the 'Republic' then designated the constitutional system, as in Switzerland or America. But unlike the term 'Republic' in the United States, in France 'Republic' evoked far more than a juridical system; it embraced a complex set of values, and for a long time was the object of opposing interpretations and rival passions. France's originality in 1880 lay in adding to all those objective political anxieties experienced by other countries an endless debate on its own history and rules of play.

The Republic of the period from 1870–1940 was the Third, which would be followed by the Fourth and Fifth. These numbered regimes disclose the remarkable nature of a legal history marked by a permanent malaise, the stubborn persistence of which shows to what extent it went beyond the strictly constitutional field. How could 'What is the Republic?' fail to be one of France's recurring questions?

All in all, France was a great and prosperous country, and notably a capitalist, industrial and modern power. The class struggle continued to develop at the end of the nineteenth century and throughout the twentieth. It gave rise to the birth of an important 'working-class movement', comparable with those of neighbouring powers, especially German and British. But there again, complexity and extremism seem to characterize the French manner of waging social combat. The strange epic of Communism cannot be reduced to controversy about the *Patrie*, or controversy about the regime, and it was never in any lasting way a product of left–right conflict – it interacted with all those elements in an eminently variable fashion. Communism, or more broadly, the revolutionary component of French history, was the passionate commitment of some, the terror of a greater number and an enigma for many. The critical attention given to it here cannot be considered excessive, since the presence of an unusual subversive force undeniably contributed to the singular nature of France throughout nearly all the period under consideration.

At the moment when the Third Republic was emerging from the years 1870–9, which had seen its painful gestation, what was the state of the regime, of national feeling, and what were the relations of citizens with one another? After a century of turmoil, the regime was becoming stabilized. Yes, to repeat a fine piece of imagery, 'the French Revolution was coming into port'.[1]

The end of the eighteenth century had seen a great and necessary revolution take place in France, but that social revolution had not been able to find its political expression. It had inaugurated little short of a century (1789–1879) of trial and error and bloody chaos before witnessing the emergence of a stable political regime.

The explanation for that chaos and the responsibility for that bloodshed still form the subject of a recently reactivated controversy. For some,[2] the difficulty lay with the radicalism of the principles of the 1789 Revolution, which forged an obstacle to the institution of an English-style constitutional monarchy in France. That radicalism would also make the distinction between the French Republic and the American Republic, to which a more religious inspiration would give better protection against the system mentality and its excesses.

[1] François Furet, *La Révolution française*, *Histoire de France*, vol. 4, Hachette, 1988, p. 517. Translated as *Revolutionary France 1770–1880*, Blackwell, 1992.
[2] Furet, *La Révolution*, passim.

For others,[3] the men of 1789 were not so radical. They had offered constitutional monarchy on a plate to Louis XVI, but he would have none of it and, indeed, did all he could, both overtly or by secret manipulation, to regain his power – that of tradition, the only one he regarded as legitimate. Worse still, the émigrés and higher clergy rejected the Revolution from the outset, well before it became 'Jacobin'. And from that resistance would arise the civil war which, in its turn, brought radicalization and its outcomes: war, dictatorship, the Terror.

In other words, the difference between the American and French way of being republican had nothing to do with the former being congenitally sensible and the latter basically extremist; it was due to the fact that, on the victory of their 'Revolution', the Americans had been free of a counter-revolutionary camp, whereas in France, the regimes which emerged from the Revolution had constantly to coexist with an ineradicable and active counter-revolutionary group.

Whatever may be read into those interpretations of the past, the fact of that division had not totally disappeared in 1870, and the wholesale slaughter of political regimes continued after that date. It is easy to understand why the Second Empire was unable to survive Sedan, or the idea of a dictatorship of Public Safety to survive the Commune, or the plan for a monarchic restoration to survive the obstinate fixation of the Comte de Chambord about the symbolic white flag. But that last episode seems particularly significant. What was there, in fact, to prevent constitutional monarchy from winning the day in its Orléanist form (liberal, tricolour, modern), unless it were the 'merging' by which the Orléanists linked their destiny with the legitimists? The fact that the royalists of both followings had carried out that merging clearly shows the requirement, or rather the need, to resort to the social weight of the legitimists? To put it plainly, in the camp of conservative France the openly counter-revolutionary sector was powerful enough to be considered essential.

In addition, one must recall, with François Furet,[4] the major, outstanding and decisive roles played by Thiers and Gambetta in the 1870s. Thiers was certainly the principal founder of the Republic in France, in that he was the first to understand that the republican form of government (in plain words, a law-based state without a hereditary monarch) could accomplish the simultaneously liberal and conservative system desired by the majority of the French middle classes (liberal system, implying modernity, the principles that had emerged from 1789, and conservative system, implying no interference with the customs and interests that had been acquired). Thiers's backing for the Republic caused his downfall on 24 May 1873, but the way in which the Duc de Broglie, under Mac-Mahon in 1873–4, guided

---

[3] Towards whom I incline, wrongly or rightly. It is all the more useful to recall this argument because it was the one that inspired the republican victors at the time, and helps in understanding their politics.

[4] See Furet, *La Révolution*, and *Revolutionary France*. I am following its final analyses, to which a brief reference is essential here.

conservative policy could only prove Thiers right: with Broglie, despite his Orléanist label, a possible 'merged' monarchy would be more likely to draw closer to a Restoration or an authoritarian Empire than to a July monarchy, and would thus be unacceptable to the liberals.

The liberal element of the Orléanist ideal had been betrayed by the reactionary nature of the politics of Moral Order. From then on, following Thiers's example, the Orléanists who had remained attached to liberty became republican in order to stay liberal, since the greater part of the monarchists had ceased to be liberals.

But, in order that the Republic should gain a good foundation from that support, those who were republican by reasoning needed to be accepted by those who were republican at heart and by conviction. That was Gambetta's stroke of genius, after Thiers's, and was just as necessary, as François Furet has so judiciously pointed out in his final analysis.

Gambetta, the herald of the Belleville democracy, but also the hero of the liberal struggle against the Empire, hero of the National Defence in the winter of 1870–1, founded the Republic by the unheroic means of 'opportunism', snatching the opportunity to form, at the very outset of the regime, a majority alliance with the moderate right.

Should we then, in the American fashion, adorn both Monsieur Thiers and Léon Gambetta with the title 'founding fathers'?

The fact is that such a title has no currency in France, and today the French Republic is proving a very ungrateful offspring towards those 'fathers'. Gambetta no longer counts among the ranks of those top people whose image and reputation survive. And if Thiers retains a place in the collective memory it is either, viewed from the right, as a too-clever-by-half, lower-middle-class parvenu or, viewed from the left, as the 'executioner of the Commune'. His erstwhile republican renown has vanished, eroded by the scorn of some and the hatred of others . . . a proof, if it were needed, that republicanism, like any other historical event, is subject to evolution.

National feeling is another extremely important factor. France in 1871 was an old nation. Men from every background met in the military profession and acknowledged the flag with its three colours as the emblem of both their calling and their ideal. That was the very deep-seated reason for the misunderstanding between the Comte de Chambord and Marshal-President Mac-Mahon. The pretender to the throne was still lingering over the idea prevalent in his childhood (1830), when the tricolour flag signified the Revolution. By contrast, the Marshal had assimilated the modern idea that the three colours were those of France and transcended parties.

Many Frenchmen felt themselves to be French, and were patriots. How many? That is a vast problem. No attempt will be made to evaluate, only to state the trend, with the claim that if patriotism then was less widespread than it would be during its peak between 1914 and 1918, it was far greater than in 1815, in the sad aftermath of Waterloo. Patriotism was gaining ground as the century progressed, and the Republic would take over and perfect the sentiment.

Without doubt, in the unclear situation of 1870–1, social fear sometimes obstructed patriotism whereas, in the heart of rural France, it might still be weak, but on the whole it did exist. In his appeals for National Defence, Gambetta obtained a response which, though far from complete, was incomparably greater than had been accorded to Napoleon in 1814 and 1815.

In its most stoutly maintained, most autonomous, perhaps most secular version – that of the left (for the right's patriotism was then usually intertwined with religious convictions) – French patriotism was linked with the concept of French greatness and its mission in life. It displayed a fairly egocentric pride. The cradle of the concepts of liberty and justice, France must show itself to be strong and influential because it was in a good cause.

However, in the days following 1871, there had to be a reappraisal of the notion that linked French patriotism to the European revolution; France had helped its fellow peoples, or its sister nations, to liberate themselves by fighting against the kings. Now, after Sadowa (1866), and still more after the Treaty of Frankfurt, the emancipated European nations did not necessarily appear in the role of accommodating little sisters; they could take on the guise of possible rivals, even enemies, when the German fatherland assumed the features of Bismarck.

Deprived of its preferential bond with the principle of nationhood, the brotherhood of peoples and the 'universal Republic', would French patriotism back away from its ideal points of reference? Not entirely . . . for happily (if one dare say so) there was Alsace, that Alsace-Lorraine wrested forcibly from France in 1871, and thanks to which national lamentation could still be seen to contain a concern for principle. In fact, the annexation was not reduced to a blunt fact, namely, Germany, being the stronger, had gained what France had lost; it also gave rise to an exchange of ideas about the matter of nationalities. Germany made its claim, in the name of what might be termed an objective interpretation of this principle: an older history and more widespread language. France preferred a subjective interpretation: those lands were French because the people had desired it so, had expressed that desire and let it be known in many ways since 1879.

France obviously believed in the legal and moral superiority of the 'French' principle of the people's right to self-determination over the 'Germanic' argument of historic right. In this way, though French patriotism after 1871 could still claim additional justification by law, it remained bound to universal values.

In the long term, France's aim would therefore be to nullify the Treaty of Frankfurt. But in the medium and short term, how was the national interest to be defined? In the years from 1871 to 1879, debate on diplomacy was combined with debate on internal policies, and in two ways: fairly clearly in relation to ultramontanism, but more gingerly in relation to the *de facto* supervision which Bismarck was imposing on France. For Catholic France, 1870 had brought not one but two disasters: French defeat and the end of the Pope's temporal power. But a French policy (diplomatic and *a fortiori* military) which might really have tried to help the Pope to recapture Rome would have set France at odds with the kingdom of Italy and, in that situation of defeat and isolation, would have created yet another enemy. It was easy for the republicans to say that their policy of accepting the *fait accompli* in Rome was the only national policy possible, and that the 'ultramontane machinations' were irresponsible and antinational. It was the Roman camp which constituted the 'foreign party'.

But the argument could backfire. For the Republic, without having the slightest sympathy for Prussia, nevertheless stayed in place partly through Bismarck's indulgence. Not that the Chancellor, on his side, had any love for the Republic, but he considered that the new German Empire needed stability in Europe, and that such stability would be better ensured if France remained governed by intelligent politicians, who had the merit of being *in situ* – Thiers obviously, and Gambetta perhaps. That convergence of interests, in its turn, gave rise to criticism. Chiefly when Bismarck had his period of anti-Catholicism with the *Kulturkampf*. The French right, and even certain passionately anti-German republican circles (Juliette Adam's salon, for instance), then came to suspect Bismarckian affinities in the anticlericalism of a Gambetta or a Jules Ferry and, ultimately, a tone that was far from French. Thus, in the matter of anticlericalism, the accusation based on supposed intent – that is to say, the suspicion of harming the national interest – could well change sides. Things were at that stage when, with the Eastern affair, the Russo-Turkish war and the Congress of Berlin, it was realized that Bismarck took a favourable view of France's starting a policy of overseas expansion which would sidetrack French forces from keeping guard on the Rhine. A possible new accusation of intent!

In 1879–80, the starting point for the present account, as the right had been removed from power it was thenceforth out of the question that dangerous provocations could result from 'ultramontane machinations'. But there was a foreboding that there could be republican ways of provoking the central empires under the pretext of not giving in to Bismarck.

Finally, a general question must clearly be asked about 1880. What was the best, and therefore the most patriotic, foreign policy? Should it be a realistic policy, keeping a 'low profile' with regard to Germany, the diplomatic equivalent of opportunist good sense in internal policies? Or a more active policy, concentrating more on the eastern frontiers, and more positive in feeling, with a hope for revenge? That choice, in any case inherently delicate, was and would for a long time be aggravated by mistrust, even slanders. For slander is easily unleashed, and that is a political fact which needs to be examined to start with: the parties found it easy to be suspicious of one another, because they disliked one another.

When the 1789 programme reached its political outcome in 1879, with the Republic, *we* know that the regime had sixty years of stability ahead of it. But its contemporaries, who by definition could not know that, could still envisage its possible overthrow. The Revolution and the subsequent civil war were not over in hearts and minds, if they were in essence over in actual fact. Above all, it should not be forgotten that, in the depths of French society, in the provinces, among the grass roots, the struggle between the conscious elements of the right (counter-revolutionary) and the left (or the Republic, it was all one then) was nearly always coloured by or wrapped up in religion. At that time no ecumenical spirit existed, and very little sceptical weariness. The 'war of religion' therefore had a bitterness which we can no longer imagine. Everyone's convictions were tinged with intransigence and passionate feelings. Whether or not to enter a place of worship, to eat or fast on Fridays, etc., were urgent and significant choices. Naturally, the uncompromising attitudes of opposing sides bred and fed one another reciprocally.

To an agnostic, a priest or devout person was a wicked hypocrite or an imbecile, or both. And it was just the same for a good Catholic in respect of an anticlerical, a 'sectarian' or a 'Freemason'. Each was the embodiment of evil for the other. The adversary was both feared and despised.

Moreover, in Paris and several other places, the Commune of spring 1871 had dug a chasm of comparable moral depth. It is scarcely an exaggeration to say that a 'Versaillais' for a 'Communard', or a 'Communard' for a God-fearing bourgeois, was some kind of monster, and first and foremost quite simply a killer.

This battle front, however, did not completely match the one preceding. The Commune had involved only a part of the left, while another part had supported Versailles. Furthermore, it was because the class struggle between Parisian workers and the 'bourgeois' society symbolized by Thiers had largely split and caused internal divisions in the camp of modernity and the Republic, that the latter's unity would be so fragile and its reunifications so ephemeral.

In short, one of the features of the French political situation in 1879 lay in those hostilities. The fact that France had institutions which were for the most part accepted, or that the French considered themselves to be all consenting members of the national community, would not be enough to dismiss the particular and incompatible attachments inspired by passions to which many of them still clung. France would soon regain Paris as its official capital but – a worrying sign – 'capitals' abroad still persisted. Indeed, for quite a strong minority, the longed-for sovereign was the one living in exile in Austria; and for another, the dearest companions were those moping in the shelter of London, Geneva or Brussels, or suffering in the penal colonies of New Caledonia.

Would the budding Republic be able to heal the still-open wounds of this nation?

PART I

Building the Republic
1879–1914

I

Ten Founding Years
1879–1889

It is not merely as a simple point of reference for the centenary of the Revolution that 1889 should be seen to mark a first stage, and a pause for an initial appraisal. It was also the year in which the regime emerged victorious from a serious and difficult challenge, which had arisen partly from the republican camp itself – Boulangism. Would it be misusing an adjective that has become commonplace to describe these years as 'decisive'? Political tendencies adopted then were influential over the span of a century, and sometimes beyond. Let us take stock. In the first place, there was a symbolic, constitutional and enduring legislative undertaking, whole sections of which still form the framework of French political life. Then there were the directions which conflict would take, clearly, on two fronts: against clericalism on the right, and against the revolutionary social movement on the extreme left. Thirdly, a certain political practice, the unwritten constitution of the parliamentary regime, which was then identified with liberty but would today be branded with the name of 'absolute Republic', to quote a title that has made its mark.[1] And lastly, looking beyond the frontiers, that other long-term orientation, the colonial empire.

Behind all this lay a coherence, 'the Republic': was it a clear doctrine or a key idea experienced more intuitively? It was really 'the Republic' as understood by Gambetta, Édouard Herriot or Pierre Mendès France which was being defined at that time. The word had a sacred ring, whether acknowledged or unavowed. It was the era when every Minister of the Interior who wished to win obedience in a serious situation, yet dared not say 'Order will be maintained' because it had an authoritarian resonance, would declare '*Republican* order will be maintained', thinking that this would immediately gain the ear of the people. A magic word, therefore, or intended to be so.

The Republic asserted itself in actions and institutions. But had that work been based on doctrine in the first place? Did a republican doctrine exist?

[1] Odile Rudelle, *La République absolue*, Publications de la Sorbonne, 1982.

Implicit, yes – nothing is achieved without a system which stems from a guiding line of thought. Explicit, no. Besides, the idea of basing a regime on an official doctrine would be scarcely in keeping with the claim to govern a secular society, in which all doctrines must exist side by side and the impartial state must watch over the peaceable nature of their relationships. The Republic scandalized many French people by denying state recognition of God, but, conversely, it never turned atheism or materialism into a state maxim.

If it had no state religion (a rejection hallowed since the July 1830 revolution), nor did the Republic have an official philosophical doctrine, not even – although it was sometimes claimed – positivism.[2] Auguste Comte's philosophy was far too harsh for the old humanism which had come from the Enlightenment and which itself formed the regime's implicit philosophical foundation. Comte would doubtless have qualified these ideal-istic postulates as 'metaphysical', which in his vocabulary was a pejorative term; besides, many descendants of positivism, from Taine to Maurras, would on the contrary soon come to nurture and rejuvenate counter-revolutionary thinking. Actually, the republicans claimed to be inspired by the philosophy of natural law (optimistic rationalism, the Enlightenment of the *philosophes*, the Rights of Man), thereby carrying on the main current of liberal thought. As for the 'ordinary' republicans (that is, all those who were not specialists in intellectual speculation), they maintained for both recent Comtism and Voltairean humanism ties of affection which only theorists held to be incompatible. The attraction of positivism worked strongly from another angle: Auguste Comte's doctrine gave backing to a confidence in science that was then totally antagonistic to the dogmatic teachings of the Roman Church. The learned irreligiousness of Comte's disciples could therefore be summoned as a reinforcement for the basic republican anticlericalism which had its origins chiefly, and more simply, in Voltaire, and in its application wished first and foremost to be seen as social and political. In the view of the majority of militants and citizens, all this doubtless counted for less than several key ideas which had emerged from the experiences of the century.

Being republican was, firstly, to show oneself a supporter of a rule which was not personal, not lifelong, not hereditary and not arbitrarily defined. That series of negations boiled down to two concrete rejections: neither monarchy nor dictatorship. In the nineteenth century, those two rejections amounted to more or less the same thing, since there was hardly any example, save in far-off South America, of an enduring personal power that had not become royal or imperial. Cromwell? He belonged to the distant past. Robespierre? On the evidence, there had been something exceptional and uncompliant about him. There remained the Caesars and the Bona-partes, who led back to the monarchic instance. But why refuse kings? After all, the British and the Belgians and several other nations had managed to

---

[2] On this point I am following Claude Nicolet's analysis in the already classic work: *L'Idée républicaine en France*, Gallimard, 1983.

make a good job of reconciling the preservation of a hereditary head of state with modernity, liberty and progress.

The answer lay in France's experience of the past hundred years, in the course of which all the constitutional monarchies, even after some liberal inclinations, had in the end turned out badly. Since 1870, the supporters of the old ruling families – Bourbons, Orléans, Bonapartes ('the conservatives' as they were called, using a loose general term, or 'the right-wingers') – had tended to merge their differences and bind themselves together in a desire for order strongly impregnated with religion (Moral Order, if given a favourable interpretation; 'clericalism', if not); in fact, making use as a means of government of an authoritarianism of the Bonapartist kind such as had reappeared in 1873 and, for a while, in 1877.[3] Here were the two systems acting as foils for each other, clericalism and Bonapartism. The direct influence of the Catholic Church on the state, the negation of the principle of secularism in society and the rejection of the philosophical neutrality of government, were designated 'clericalism'. As for 'Bonapartism', this was put forward as the exact antithesis of political liberalism. A liberal was first of all defined by his attachment to the law, placing legality above reasons of state and all alleged 'legitimacy', even popular. The dates of 18 Brumaire and 2 December, based on these latter principles, therefore embodied evil politically, as the *Syllabus* embodied evil philosophically.

Because the French monarchy, whether concerned with 'merged' royalisms or with post-1870 Bonapartism, as represented by someone like Rouher, had thus been characterized as a power with an authoritarian tone and clerical influence, the Republic became the only possible banner for the partisans of liberty and secularism. Such a realization had been decisive in the Republic's conquest of a majority of supporters.

That specifically French progression explains how the Republic, in principle a simple form of executive rule, with a head of state who was neither for life nor hereditary, came to be defined by a precise political creed of liberty and secularism – which is as much as to say, by the ideal of 1789 or, equally well, of 1830.

With the experience of the 1870s, the French concept of Republic had ended by identifying with the tradition that had come from 1789. This reminder is necessary in order to understand a paradox which may be surprising: to be 'republican', in the nineteenth century and Third Republic sense of the word, was to adhere to the great principles and the decisive Revolution of 1789, even though 1789 had preserved the king and the Republic had not been established until 1792. Thus defined by two rejections, of clericalism and Bonapartism, and by a historical reference to the Revolution, the Republic was still, across the vicissitudes of the century, bound up with two major concepts – the *Patrie* and the People.

The *Patrie*, or homeland, cannot be the monopoly of one party; in one sense this is self-evident. However, history had slightly complicated matters.

---

[3] See the preceding volume in this series, Furet, *La Révolution*.

Firstly, the France of 1789 and the Rights of Man, perceived as a beacon by many liberals and oppressed foreigners, had turned the Revolution into an event which rather flattered self-esteem, adding philosophical prestige and modern ethics to what France had already derived from the cultural influence of the *Grand Siècle*. Furthermore, the counter-revolution of 1792 and 1814 had taken the form of a war waged by foreigners against France. French patriotism was therefore somewhat imprinted with Revolution, and the revolutionary ideal bore a connotation of national pride. Thus for a long time a bond of memory was woven between Republic and *Patrie* – a bond which soon became natural, part of the mentality, although the realities were in principle heterogeneous. That bond, however, would not be without perverse effects. Since Napoleon, in his foreign policies, had acted mainly to extend the wars of the Revolution, his confrontation with foreign countries prevented republicans from being as hostile towards him as logically they should have been. The man of 18 Brumaire was also the man who humiliated kings and, even if he did not overturn all thrones, he at least caused a few of them to tremble.

To a greater or lesser extent, the same could be said about the People – that is, ordinary people – about the spirit of humanity, compassion or social justice. History played its part in creating ties which were not inevitably necessary. It is all very well to underline the theoretically humanitarian implications of the principles of 1789 (men are equal, society aims for common happiness) but nevertheless, nothing had stopped the liberty–republic–state system of law in America from evolving in a very inhumane way: equality of opportunity, but a struggle for existence; competition; people could help one another but the state must not be called upon to have special responsibilities towards those who failed. In France, history arranged things differently: the liberal revolution was able to conquer thanks only to its historical connection with the urban lower classes (chiefly Parisian) who had social aspirations that reached beyond liberalism. The year 1793 and Year II and, later, the revolutionary months of summer 1830 and spring 1848 formed the staging points of this partial amalgamation. The sons of the sansculottes, who provided the infantry in the republican battles, thereby incorporated to some extent in the republican programme elements of populist and humanitarian thinking and aspirations that were not self-evident.

Need one add that, in this manner of 'being republican', it was plain to see the spirit of that most illustrious and admired of living Frenchmen, Victor Hugo, in all its diversity and generality, with that slight vagueness that made it all the more appealing?

Victor Hugo was at that time firmly set in his final image, of patriarch, and his last role, of uncrowned King of the Republic.[4] Since 1878 he had

---

[4] The main facts about his career and role are mentioned in Furet, *La Révolution*.

been living with Juliette Drouet in a small private house at 130 rue d'Eylau. This building no longer exists; its furnishings – the last decor in the master's life – have been removed, by an accepted anachronism, to the house (museum) in the place des Vosges, where he had lived during Louis-Philippe's reign. There, next to the bed, by way of a holy object, may be seen an ornament representing the Republic, as sculpted by Clésinger for the 1878 Exhibition. In the house next door, number 132, his grandchildren Georges and Jeanne were installed, together with their mother, Alice, Charles Hugo's widow, who had remarried with the deputy Lockroy. It was the two adolescents who were most often seen in the company of the old writer, who had published *The Art of Being a Grandfather* in 1877. There is no doubt that he loved them deeply and received a great deal of affection in return. There is similarly no doubt that this image of sensibility and virtue happily coincided with the one which the era, and even the regime, expected. The robust old man's prolonged and pressing need for sexual roamings, though not entirely secret, was better dissimulated. The cerebral attack he suffered in June 1878 had scarcely diminished him. The only thing was that he wrote for less time each day, and his publications appeared at less frequent intervals.

The author of *Hernani* and *Notre-Dame de Paris*, *Les Châtiments* and *Les Contemplations*, *Les Misérables* and *La Légende des siècles* had in any case done enough to be placed without any possible competition in the front rank of living writers. People therefore thronged to the weekly receptions and frequent dinners which he gave at his home, amid his family and several old friends, such as Auguste Vacquerie and Paul Meurice. With a large household, numerous staff, right in the heart of the new *beaux quartiers*, Victor Hugo's home was the chief salon in the capital, and all those who loved not only the Republic, but simply art or literature, were determined to get themselves presented there. Visitors of all kinds: politicians and poets, veterans and novices, admirers of both sexes, the Emperor of Brazil and Sarah Bernhardt. From then on, he was visited more than he went out.

Of course, he was a senator, but he no longer had a battle to wage since the Republic had been attained, and above all since it had granted amnesty to the Communards. After that historic date, 14 July 1880, Senator Hugo might well have his seat at the extreme left of the semicircle in the Luxembourg, he was no longer a part of the radical opposition, but fairly and squarely governmental. In his 1881 will, Victor Hugo even appointed Jules Grévy, Léon Say and Léon Gambetta as the executors of his last wishes, in other words, the three presidents (of the Republic, the Senate and the Chamber)! It would appear that he was sensitive chiefly to the charm of Gambetta, with whom he showed solidarity (but Gambetta would precede him to the grave). The spirit of 1848 still lived on in the poet, with his extraordinary mixture of humanitarian idealism and French patriotism. Did not that same will stipulate that all his manuscripts should be bequeathed to the 'National Library of Paris, which will one day be the Library of the United States of Europe'!

The fervour shown to him in return by the Republic, the *Patrie* and the people is understandable. On 27 February 1881 Victor Hugo was seventy-nine years old. It was preferable to say that he had 'entered his eightieth year', with the magic of the round figure and the glamour of a still-rare longevity. And it was turned into a sort of national festival! Grévy emerged from the Élysée to bring the old master a Sèvres vase, and 600,000 Parisians, at the summons of a committee presided over by Louis Blanc, came to file past below his balcony to salute the budding octogenarian. The next day, half of the avenue d'Eylau was 'de-baptized' to become the avenue Victor Hugo. Sanctified during his lifetime – though 'sanctified' is not quite the word. Has enough attention been drawn to the fact that not for one moment did anyone consider holding his celebration on the feast day of Saint-Victor, and that the choice was made of the secular, rather pagan, rather Anglophile and not at all Catholic celebration of the anniversary of the day of his birth? Fêted by the heart of France, without a doubt, but in the completely secular fashion of the times. After that apotheosis, death would have its turn. Juliette Drouet's demise on 11 May 1883 overwhelmed Victor Hugo even more brutally than the vascular illness of 1878. He no longer wrote; his receptions, which were kept up to the very end, became more dismal affairs. He lived on for two years, dying on 22 May 1885 after several days of lung congestion. One can understand the emotion aroused in France by the death of such an exceptional man, with the added attributes of veteran and symbol. The patriarch of 'avenue Victor Hugo' was also the elected representative of the people, who had once been proscribed and had taken refuge in Guernsey. He had brought to the Third Republic a historical support somewhat comparable, all things considered, to that which the Second Empire had derived from the memory of the first Napoleon, or the Restoration from that of Henri IV. The funeral of such a man could not be other than a state affair. Before that special solemnity was reached, the principles and feelings of Hugo's Republic had been translated into some general symbolic decisions.

Indeed, at the time, certain arrangements were made which were so enduring that today they seem perfectly natural to the French, to the point where most of them have forgotten the age (recent) and the bias (left) of these fundamental acts.

The seat of government, settled at Versailles in March 1871, was re-established in Paris (June 1879). The 'Marseillaise' was chosen as the national anthem (1879) and 14 July for the national festival (1880). It was on the occasion of that first celebration that the complete amnesty granted to the Communards came into force, a gift to mark the joyous advent of a finally republican regime to rebels who had also regarded themselves as forerunners of the Republic. Those great decisions were the symbolic sign of the regime's victory over the forces of the right, and its uniting with the French Revolution. Of course, this meant the Revolution in its most liberal interpretation, that of 1789, the Tennis Court Oath, Mirabeau's address, the taking of the Bastille, but also the (irenic) Festival of the Federation – all of which can be perceived as moderate, especially today (compared with 1793), but which were felt by conservative contemporaries to have a . . . revolutionary nature.

A whole range of singular and localized symbolic acts accompanied that series of decisions. A great number of streets, squares and avenues were baptized 'of the Republic' before it became their turn to honour the soon-to-depart heroes, Gambetta or Victor Hugo. It became the custom to adorn town halls with the bust of a woman wearing a Phrygian cap – the Republic, known as 'Marianne'. It was then that those communes where republican zeal reached a frenzied climax erected in the main square a monument to the Republic (copying Paris, 1883), and the cult of raising monuments to great men who were linked with the *Patrie*, progress and liberty gained a new momentum, which good taste and ill temper soon branded with the name 'statuemania'.[5]

Two great moments were yet to mark that symbolic agenda. Frédéric Auguste Bartholdi, a sculptor truly representative of the times (was he not Alsatian, a veteran of 1870, a moderate republican and friend of Gambetta?) at last completed, thanks to a large public subscription, the gigantic *Liberty Enlightening the World*, with which a group of French liberals, as early as 1865, had decided to pay homage to Abraham Lincoln's emancipatory Republic. The head, colossal in itself, and the first part to be completed, had already been exhibited at the Universal Exhibition of 1878; the whole statue was finished and erected in Paris in 1884, dismantled and shipped to America in 1885, reassembled and finally set up at the entrance to New York harbour in October 1886. It was a potent affirmation of the community of spirit and ideals of the two great democracies. That spirit was of liberty, but also of scientific optimism, for Bartholdi's work (helped by the engineer Gustave Eiffel for its architectural assemblage) was a technical triumph and a world record in size. From 1889, replicas, of rather smaller dimensions, would spread through Paris and across France.

The other great moment was the death of Victor Hugo. It could scarcely fail to be a momentous event. But two particular circumstances outdid the sensational and the political. Firstly, being a deist and spiritualist, Victor Hugo was anticlerical and averse to all Catholic faith and practice. It was a well-known fact, and was in any case confirmed by two authentic and perfectly precise wills. No priest was summoned to his bedside, therefore, and preparations were made for a civil funeral, which the clergy and contemporary conservative opinion deemed doubly scandalous: sacrilegious and revolutionary. Two years earlier, Gambetta's death had already caused

---

[5] Maurice Agulhon, *Marianne au pouvoir, l'imagerie et la symbolique républicaines de 1880 à 1914*, Flammarion, 1989.

Paris to hold an immense and secular official funeral procession. Victor Hugo's would reinforce that triumph. Then, after the cortege, there would be the question of the tomb. Would it be a fine monument, like a hundred others, in the Père-Lachaise cemetery? Something so relatively banal did not measure up to the memory of such an extraordinary man. It was then that the republican party decided to propose the Panthéon, which would be secularized for the occasion. After all, it was quite normal; the Revolution had devoted Soufflot's church of Sainte-Geneviève to the great men in 1791; the counter-revolution had restored it to the Catholic Church in 1814; the revolution had regained it in 1830; the reaction had taken it back in 1851 . . . Re-secularization by the Republic was therefore in the nature of things; the fact that it had not taken place earlier was but one sign among many of the prudence of opportunist management.

But Victor Hugo's death helped the ruling powers to rediscover the logic of their symbols. Hastily, the necessary decrees were made. The violence of the polemic between the republican press and the royalist and clerical press was then redoubled. It was in that climate that the ceremony was planned (taking a long time, from 22 to 31 May). In the early hours of Sunday 31 May, the coffin left its resting place in the avenue Victor Hugo to be exhibited, not far away, under the Arc de Triomphe at the Étoile, a great patriotic site, at that period both Napoleonic and republican (Falguière's four-horse chariot of the Revolution, gone today, still surmounted it).

Catafalque, funeral draperies, guards of honour, the long procession of visitors paying homage . . . And furthermore, in the entire *quartier*, in the place de l'Étoile, in the great radiating avenues, in the Bois, flowed a vast and curious crowd, attracted by the erection of this grandiose temporary setting. For two days now they had come back and forth, buying and selling souvenirs, booklets, badges, everything that we would call 'gimmicks' today but which were then something of a novelty. People ate and drank as well, around the Étoile, at the stalls of an improvised fair. A whole army of pilgrims, whose huge throngs the left joyfully recorded, and whose somewhat vulgar masses the right termed 'saturnalian'.

From the Étoile, the cortege was to reach the Panthéon on Monday 1 June. The route was imposed by its very straightforwardness: Champs Élysées, Concorde, pont de la Concorde, boulevard Saint-Michel, rue Soufflot. But it had the symbolic drawback of having to pass through a number of *beaux quartiers* (Saint-Germain) and not through 'popular' areas: neither the big boulevards of the right bank, nor the squares of the Republic or the Bastille. That gave rise to fresh controversies which would, however, change nothing. Of course there would be – and there were – detachments of troops, salvos of cannon fire from the Invalides, music, orchestras. And chiefly the procession. That was to be formed in essence by delegations from 'societies'. It would be a great review of that sociability, both customary and democratic, which was then in full swing: clubs – secular, sporting, musical, masonic, philanthropic – friendly societies, town bands, sometimes with comical names, often from those little provincial backwaters, the mere mention of which made Parisians smile – a chance for further mockery. No denigration was missing, Catholic (as has been said), aesthetic (it has been suggested), revolutionary: the Guesdist avant-garde of pure socialism denounced Victor Hugo as the millionaire writer, the outmoded moralist of family and homeland, and the supporter of the bourgeois Republic. But every defamation and smear was obliterated by the hugeness of the success. Eight hours of procession, from eleven o'clock until seven in the evening, on Monday 1 June, nineteen speeches (the four main ones at the Étoile, the rest at the Panthéon), innumerable crowds the whole length of the route, at every window, on trees and rooftops – a memorable occasion, whose potency can be measured in terms of the vast number and emotional content of literary accounts and autobiographical records that it produced.

The immense Parisian homage to Victor Hugo thus for one day marginalized the resistant members of the right and the extreme left. Had it really been so unanimous? The argument over the route (the big boulevards or Saint-Germain?) had already set republicans at odds among themselves. Other conflicts of that kind had taken place. Had not the Académie française intended Maxime Du Camp, its current director, to deliver its speech of homage? The radical press had let it be known that the 'insulter of the Commune' would not be allowed to speak; Du Camp stepped down and the Académie hastily appointed Émile Augier to give the funeral oration.

Better still! By sheer coincidence, those last days of May when the funeral ceremony was being arranged were the anniversary of the crushing of the Commune. On Sunday 24 May, coming from a demonstration at the Père-Lachaise, groups of socialist and radical workers, mostly from the nearby Belleville quarter, had been beaten up by police with truncheons. On 1 June, that incident would obtain undeniably subversive applause for the Belleville societies taking part in Victor Hugo's funeral cortege. The vast cult of the poet and republican symbol, in fact, spread over an official 'Hugolatry' and a popular 'Hugolatry' so incompletely blended that the decencies due at a funeral could barely conceal their conflict. But was it not just the same with the Republic itself? By that intimate contradiction too, Hugo was well and truly its representative.

However, one cannot live by symbols, proclamations and festivals alone. Institutions were also undergoing in-depth changes, firstly on behalf of freedoms, the most important and obvious being the freedom of the press (the celebrated law of 29 July 1881, which retained only one quite legitimate restriction, the right of reply). Freedom of association was also hoped for; but as that ran up against the problem of religious *congrégations*, it would have to wait until 1901 for a general law. Dealing with the most pressing need, republican majorities at least passed the law of 1884, which confirmed and consolidated the professional trades unions' right to exist, and governments allowed clubs and societies a very wide range of freedoms in actual fact. Chiefly for that political reason the 1880s witnessed a veritable explosion of associations, which the 1901 law would merely have to ratify and formalize.

Associations and meetings, political sociability and personal sociability were also given a helping hand by another freedom law, applied to the opening of small cafés or bars (1880). The Republic that declared itself in favour of free trading in general was also conscious of how much politics, reading of newspapers and informal chatting went on in such establishments. Under former regimes morality had often served as a pretext for conservative repression to close down bistros where people shouted too loudly or thought the wrong thoughts. The new legislation thus freed cafés and bars, but at the same time made specific regulations against public drunkenness.

Lastly, the law of 1882, subsumed in the great municipal law of 1884, granted all municipal councils the right to elect a mayor (except in Paris) endowed with all the powers that are still recognized in France. Since the beginning of the century, and particularly since 1870, every swing of the pendulum towards the right had favoured the system of an appointed mayor, and every swing to the left, of an elected mayor. When it settled down, the pendulum stayed to the left as regards that key democratic institution, local government.

Despite its legal lacunae and its practical imperfections, this republican liberalism, in comparison with Moral Order and the Second Empire, to go back no further, definitely constituted a considerable improvement, and only the fact that the French think its stipulations so 'natural' prevents them from fully applauding its initial merit.

Thus 'Bonapartism' was combated with freedoms. Against 'clericalism' the republican struggle demanded secularism.

In actual fact, the essential had been achieved since the revolution of 1830: no state religion. The opportunism of the 1880s believed it could postpone the separation of Church and state, which was nevertheless logical, and preferred to make do with the Concordat, which offered the advantage of leaving the state a certain amount of hold over the clergy. However, several significant measures of principle were passed, to say nothing of the work done on state education.

From 1880 onwards, freedom to work on Sundays was granted. It was the kind of law that causes one to reflect on the interaction of social and ideological matters. In this case there was total confusion: Sunday rest represented both the subjection of a civil law to a religious commandment, and a benefit for the employee whose boss would like to force him to work continuously. The 'clerical' thus shared solidarity with the social. The 1880 Republic therefore gave priority to the secular principle (civic society did not have to depend on the Decalogue), though taking the risk of benefiting an employer who might abuse his power. Obligatory 'weekly rest days', with a purely social justification, would not be (re)introduced until 1906. In 1880 the secular–religious conflict was thus held to be more important than the employee–employer conflict.

In 1884, Naquet's law permitted divorce – another interesting debate. Marriage being indissoluble only from the Christian point of view, it was logical for the Revolution – for which it was merely a contract – to allow it to be broken and to authorize divorce; a logic which the Restoration, in 1816, prohibited, and which the secular Republic reintroduced. For it was truly a matter of philosophical logic, and not of family or sexual morality. It has been said often enough that, in practice, the morality advocated in fact by republican moralists such as Jules Ferry and his followers was not so very different from conservative morality with religious foundations. Jules Ferry, indeed, had no wish to 'destroy the family'. The 1884 law placed difficult conditions on divorce, especially for women, whose adultery was castigated far more severely than men's. The reinstitution of divorce, therefore, brought about no decline in male chauvinism. It weakened religious authority, which was the chief battle at the time. Lastly, in 1884, one constitutional revision among other more important aspects provided another opportunity of secularizing institutions by quashing the legal obligation for public prayers at the start of parliamentary sessions.

Finally, the first-rate work undertaken in public education can be ranked under the united banners of secularism and freedom.

Legislation on state education obviously claimed to be secular since it created or reinforced the opportunity for all citizens to receive an education independent of any of the religious dogmas. And, more precisely, it aimed to challenge the dominant influence of the Catholic Church. But it also wanted to be seen as a work of freedom, for at least three reasons. Firstly, to free minds from a Church which was then explicitly dogmatic and anti-liberal was to help the cause of liberty. Secondly, to instruct, to inform, to give people the means and the taste for reading, must contribute to their liberation from the restricted docility that left them, as voters, following in the wake of notables or calls to a plebiscite. Thirdly, educating people prompts them to freedom of thought and the development of all the potential of the human mind. It was certainly because the educational undertaking contained all those implications that the republicans of the 1880s pursued it so keenly; for that reason, too, the three or four succeeding generations viewed it as the most meritorious work of the Third Republic, while history still regards it as the most significant.

In broad outline, what were its provisions? The spread of elementary education dated from the distant past, a work begun by the Catholic Reformation, and progressing like an oil slick throughout the next three centuries; then in the nineteenth century, given further emphasis by Guizot's law of 1833, and by the great unacknowledged ministers of the Second Empire – Hippolyte Fortoul, Gustave Rouland, Victor Duruy. But thenceforward, thanks to a huge budgetary effort, public schooling was made free of charge (1881), which allowed it to be made compulsory (the obligation being to attend a school – not necessarily a state one – but education could be made compulsory because in every area there would always be at least one state school to which entry was free). Lastly – the third term of the celebrated triad – education had been rendered secular, like the state from which it proceeded. The faithful could send their children to a private school (called 'free' in the sense of non-state) and, in order to allow Christian schoolchildren in state schools to have religious instruction, Thursdays were left open.

Following the same line of thinking, the network of state primary schools was completed, for the last little villages and isolated hamlets, and improved in quality by a vast effort in school building, the raising of the standard of curricula and the recruitment of teachers of both sexes, of really professional standards, trained in the *Écoles normales*.

Primary education (compulsory to the age of twelve) was extended by a less complete network (broadly at canton level) of higher primary education ('upper primary schools', properly speaking, or 'complementary courses' in certain elementary primary schools) which could lead to an elementary diploma, or even to competitive recruitment examinations, among the most prized being competition for entry to the *École normale*.

It was through this channel that the 'good student from humble background and village school who would become schoolteacher in his turn' found a place, and soon became an archetypal reality. In order to recruit teachers for the upper primary schools and the *Écoles normales*, two new *Écoles normales supérieures* were established, at Saint-Cloud for men and at Fontenay-aux-Roses for women, their role intended to be similar to that played for nearly a century in training teachers for boys' secondary schools by the *École normale supérieure*, which still stood alone, and was situated in the rue d'Ulm.

There was parallelism but inequality; in standards and even more in prestige. When leftist opinion, for a long time highly favourable, turned against Jules Ferry's work, much was made of the contrast between the bourgeois side of the secondary network of *lycées* and high schools, which led only to the *baccalauréat*, which led only to higher education, which led only to top posts; and the limited, popular side of the primary channels – elementary schools, upper elementary schools, diploma, thence to minor official posts or, at a pinch, Saint-Cloud and the teaching profession restricted to the primary pyramid, nothing more.

It is true that the 1880 Republic did not undertake to provide the scholastic system with the total unification and democratization which our present day would have liked, and with which it is still wrestling. But the range of the achievements effected by the men of 1880 should put a curb on French retrospective severity. All the more so, since, even as regards democratization, this must still be borne in mind: if it was indeed unimaginable that in 1880 the son of a working man could get into a *lycée*, a rare, elitist and fee-paying establishment, if that same son was gifted, he could nevertheless obtain entry to an upper primary school and thence to some lower-middle-class position, and then a grandson – gifted in his turn – would be able to enter a *lycée*. To climb the social ladder, therefore, Jules Ferry had offered only a narrow competitive path, spread over two generations. But a narrow path does not mean a barrier; for that period it meant unblocking the way ahead.

In secondary education there were few changes in the boys' *lycée*, a sacred institution. Now, the equivalent for girls had to be created. That was effected by Camille Sée's law in 1880. Girls' *lycées*, an appropriate teaching staff and, to train them, an *École normale supérieure* for young women, known as the École de Sèvres, with the avowed intent of gradually becoming the female version of the rue d'Ulm.

As for higher education, it was secularized, or re-secularized, by the repeal of the law of 1875, which meant that the monopoly of conferring a qualification (*baccalauréat*, degree, doctorate) lay with state higher education, and that the senior examining board should be composed purely of members of the teaching profession. But studies leading to those examinations could be undertaken anywhere, since freedom of education existed at all levels.

Impressive in its scope, this legislative operation had a dual nature: as an institution, it was a fundamental work which would endure. But through the ups and downs of its development it was a political battle, enmeshed in the combat between the parties and even – as people like to say nowadays – between the different Frances.

For that great edifice had not been constructed in an atmosphere of serenity, and its 'building site' had more often than not resembled a battlefield. To say one single battlefield would not suffice, because the nascent Republic had to maintain a war on two fronts.

One, against the right, had been taken on and even planned for since the middle of the century. The other, against a revolutionary extreme left, had not been expected, and its appearance was a painful surprise, at all events for the republicans.

Before analysing them separately, as one should, it is necessary to emphasize the durable – one might almost say structural – quality of this system. Political France under the Republic was and would remain divided, not into two but into three; and not three comprising the right, the left and the centre (too facile, and misleading), but the right, the left and the extreme tip of the left which entertained the idea of a new revolution, the revolutionary workers' movement. But around 1880, and for a further decade or so, the chief front was the opposition between left and right. It revealed itself with undeniable clarity, and almost perfectly matched the antagonism of Republic–monarchy. However, the 'left' and the 'right' were used fairly infrequently to denote, in the singular, each of the two camps in public opinion and in the country at large. Those two terms stayed confined to parliamentary vocabulary: also it was more usual to say the 'left-wingers' and the 'right-wingers' with reference to groups and tendencies whose multiplicity was very noticeable in the Chamber of Deputies. That said, left–right matched the Republic–monarchy pair in the political field, and the secularism–defence-of-Catholic-primacy pair in the philosophical field; lastly, a little less clearly here because of the complexity of various issues, the left tended to favour the solutions of liberal democracy (universal suffrage, election of mayors by municipal councils, total freedom of the press), which accorded best with its overall optimism; and the right to place greater importance on the solutions of tradition and authority. Looked at in that sense, the Thiers of those last years, who backed Gambetta, upheld the electoral campaign of the '363', and whom republican Paris would solemnly accompany to the Père-Lachaise in September 1877, must be classified as 'left'. Thiers on the left? There's an assertion fit nowadays to horrify the immense majority of those on the left in this century. Nevertheless, it is strongly characteristic of an era when no link yet existed between the idea of 'left' and that of a socialist programme.

Those neat, divided categories were expressed in a rich vocabulary into which contemporaries were thoroughly initiated.

The republicans referred to themselves as 'republicans', or sometimes as the 'democracy', in a sense which curiously intermingled the social and the political, the 'democracy' of such and such a town denoting both those who had emerged from the people and those who supported the power of the people, above all when the two categories – and that was the ideal! – coincided. Recollections of ancient battles sometimes intervened in local designations: there were 'blues' in memory of 1792, or 'reds' evoking 1848, but all meaning the 'left'.

The republicans taxed their adversaries (should the chance arise) with being Bonapartists or royalists or reactionaries or – still meaning men of the right – clericals or 'whites' (the twin and antagonistic term for 'blue' or 'red' according to the region). The right had no cause to be jealous of the left when it came to vocabulary.

'Royalist' could sometimes be quite cheerfully applied to oneself, but with a somewhat provocative daring. It seems that 'conservative', more neutral and more attractive, was preferred as a sympathetic designation for that group. Naturally, when they were stressing the problem of secularism, the so-called 'clericals' avoided that epithet, as they would avoid calling their enemies 'anticlericals'; they referred to themselves as 'Catholics' or 'Christians', and to their opponents as 'sectarians' or 'ungodly'. Lastly, it still happened that polemicists of the right, without fear of seeming anti quated, pushed logic and a sense of history as far as naming the republicans 'the Revolution', recognizing in them those who were applying the principles of 1789, which were held to be bad. Therefore, for any good and educated Catholic conservative, Jules Ferry would still pass for a 'man of the Revolution', while on the extreme left appeared groups who regarded Ferry as a man of the bourgeois Republic against whom revolution should be waged: so there was Revolution and revolution.

For the republicans in government, whose point of view carries the day in this analysis, since it was their politics that dominated and must be explained, the fight against the right took priority, convinced as they were that the Republic alone could guarantee a law-based state and a modern society. The republicans included the Catholic Church in that all-embracing outlook, since the vast majority of the clergy and the more militant among the faithful supported a desire for the monarchy and its authoritarian ways, and unhesitatingly drew their inspiration from a strong spiritual intransigence that could be termed anti-liberal, or counter-revolutionary, because for them, too, it was all one. The combative measures and anticlerical ardour of Jules Ferry and his followers are incomprehensible if one forgets (as is nowadays often forgotten, on account of the subsequent changes in the Roman attitude) that they were confronting clergy who had blessed 2 December and for whom the *Syllabus* had been a staple diet.

History knows that this identification of Catholicism with evil in those two major aspects was already admitting exceptions, as history knows what happened subsequently, but the republicans did not know; they still considered themselves to be liberal by striking a blow, even without liberalism, at the enemies of liberty.

For they did strike at them, by purging the Council of State and the magistracy, whose permanent tenure of office was suspended; next, by the roundabout means of a schools law in 1880, with the famous article VII. That forbade teaching to be carried out by members of religious houses (*congrégations*) not authorized in France. Article VII opened the first great public battle sustained by the regime after its victory in 1879. There were impassioned parliamentary debates, but also reaction in the streets. For the most ardent republicans, 'Long live article VII' was for a while synonymous with 'Long live the Republic'. On the right, there were certain attempts, bordering on the illegal, at physical resistance to the closure of a school or the expulsion of the Jesuits. Details of all this are very complex, because the republicans were divided over certain points. Jules Ferry, too lukewarm for some resolute anticlericals, seemed too repressive in the eyes of moderates like Jules Simon, who persuaded the Senate to vote against article VII.

On the whole, Jules Ferry applied the policy of secularism without extreme aggressiveness, and the matter of the *congrégations* quietened down, as in times past, after some discreet negotiations. The Concordat continued to be loyally applied. Scholastic policy, in the sensitive area of the introduction of new programmes, was carried out with considerable moderation. In state primary schools, in the forefront of moral teaching, 'duties towards God' were in fact, tolerated, and the positive social morality which was taught laid much more emphasis on the rules common to all moralities than on those which might set libertarian against Christian morality. Jules Ferry, who was then abused for having instituted a morality 'without a God', is nowadays reviled by the left for having made an almost religious morality official. That is the difference between the times!

At all events, it became the habit to set Republic and Church in opposition. Naturally, at 'ground level' controversies did not enjoy the same
standards of behaviour as those which Jules Ferry, Jules Simon and Mgr
Freppel could use in parliament. Village politics often consisted of petty
spiteful in-fighting or second-rate insults; here, local versions of Homais
ridiculed the curé (if his only support came from pious old ladies); there,
God-fearing notables harassed the local schoolmaster (when the secular
camp was in the minority). Whether the argument was high-flown or low,
in the greater part of France that was the principal matter at stake, and
would continue to be so.

Whatever may be said about it, the 'war of religion' at issue here seems
difficult to reduce to the class struggle, although that viewpoint had its
theorists then. What *is* noticeable is the absence of coincidence between
generalized social conflicts in terms of class struggles and the major politico-
spiritual conflict just described. For not only did the battle waged by right
and left express itself in theoretical terms far removed from questions
of economy, but the confrontation itself failed to produce even vaguely
coherent groups of social forces in the country at large.

Certainly, it was more of a people's Republic, which explains its electoral
majority, whereas the right clearly dominated the elites of the aristocracy
and the old bourgeoisie; it claimed the 'best circles' and would continue to
do so for a long while. Yet the other side of the coin was that certain
economic powers could feel attracted to the left for other than economic
reasons (the Protestant upper middle class, leading Jewish bankers – these
were no myths), while rural people for the most part voted for the right,
even if certain of the peasantry had turned 'red' since 1848 in some regional
areas of the east, the south-east and the centre. In Paris and Lyon, the
workingman was republican but, in the majority of small towns and industrial zones, he often stayed in the moral wake of the employers, who were
themselves most frequently conservative. In the middle classes there were
as many spiritual divisions as there were social differences.

On the right, as on the left, there were theorists with convictions who, if
they were allowed to act, would know how to guide social interests towards
conciliation. On the right, a social Catholicism existed, with its doctrine
and references. It was the same on the left. The best among the opportunist
rulers, often well-off notables, were still conscious of belonging to the
bourgeoisie, but felt rather that they did not belong to the world of large
businesses or top industrial employers who had long been supporters of
Bonapartism. Their sincere sympathy for ordinary lowly people, and the
humanitarianism inherent in republican sensibility were steeped in the
optimism of progress. They believed that a more widespread culture would
make adaptation and social advancement easier, that universal suffrage –
rendered 'intelligent' by state education – would allow deputies to pass laws
fit to deal with all problems. In short, they believed that, in a climate of

liberty, civic spirit and enlightenment, insoluble social problems would cease to exist. It was a matter of time and debate. In that perspective, one can understand the law of 1884 on professional trades unions: it was not wrested from the Republic; the latter willed it in order to create a sensible means of dialogue.

Of course, neither Gambetta nor Jules Ferry would have been able to forget the bloody struggles and extreme theories experienced in the past, from June 1848 to the Commune, but they could, if need be, still attribute them to the flaws of a former time when governments were violent and the poor people crude and easily roused. For the present and the future, trust could be placed in the restorative and integrative virtues of the Republic.

Besides, the Republic was exerting itself in that direction. The coincidence between the stages in its progress towards political freedom and the march towards the rebirth of a republican workers' movement had been noteworthy.

The first Workers' Congress, which brought together employers' federations, mutual benefit societies, social studies groups and other associations, had been held in Paris in 1876, under the aegis of friends of Gambetta, and on the heels of the republican victory in the legislative elections at the beginning of the year. The second Congress, planned for autumn 1877, had been unable to take place because, owing to the crisis of 16 May, Moral Order held the government, while the left had needed to mobilize its entire forces for the electoral battle. It finally took place in Lyon in the autumn of 1878, and the third Congress met in Marseille in October 1879. Soon after, the elderly Blanqui, elected deputy for Bordeaux, was snatched by that vote from his last prison. And in 1880, Gambetta threw his weight behind complete amnesty for the Communards and managed to get the law passed by parliament.

It was hoped that the amnesty of 14 July 1880, symbolically coinciding with the new regime's first national festival, would allow the revolutionary people of Paris to return to the republican camp.

How sorely that hope was to be disappointed! Class struggles would again cut across French society, not taking up the flag of the Republic against the monarchy, but brandishing against the republican government itself the banner of a workers' movement which had been self-defined at the 1879 Congress. With hindsight, it is easy to see the reasons for that conflict, which from a Marxist viewpoint would hardly require any explanation (for a Marxist, it is the situations when struggles do *not* develop which pose a problem) but which, examined without preconceptions, merit a word of comment.

Without doubt, the first reason should be sought in the scale of the bloodbath of May 1871 in Paris. Things like that could not be erased by an amnesty: it would not bring the dead back to life, wipe out memories or resentments, the generators of political frames of mind against which no amount of reasoning could prevail. Amnesty had not, therefore, restored to France men who were inclined to rally to the Republic, but men who were ready to make use of the new freedoms to demand a social revolution. The fact that some politicians, even good republicans, after letting Thiers do what he wanted in 1871, should grant an amnesty in 1880 after several years of shillyshallying, did not really put them in a position to obtain the support of former Communards! There was too much that needed settling between them! Here, a necessary qualifying comment must be added to the earlier brief eulogy of Thiers, founder of the Republic. Yes, Thiers, the intelligent politician of 1872, 1873, then the Thiers once again in opposition under Mac-Mahon, had been a powerful aid in establishing the regime. But Thiers in spring 1871, ordering, allowing to happen, or covering up the Versailles repression, had undeniably built a fearsome fragility into the republican edifice from the very start. The cruelty of the military and the bourgeoisie at that time had lastingly undermined the Republic by compromising it and preventing it from ever receiving the total support of popular forces. The recurrent radicalism of French politics derives from that: even in the middle of the twentieth century, the Versaillais barbarity would still be used by Bolshevism as a theoretical and emotional point of argument. As for knowing the nature of that barbarity, whether it belonged to 'capitalists' or 'whites', it would take a decisive debate to reveal who, in the final analysis, should bear responsibility for that wound which has never healed over.

A second reason is less historical. The economic forces which not long before had naturally put their stake on the conservatives (coal-mining, industrialists, railway companies) did not linger in the opposition once the Republic was established. They had accepted it and even invested in it, since it had become the government in power, the head of administration and the source of laws. Large-scale capitalism would soon become republican in France, as it would perhaps have turned royalist had Henri V won; or as it had become imperial in Germany or Austria-Hungary. The tendency towards coexistence, even harmony, between the business world and the world of government had become noticeable – and commented on as such – in 1884, through the advantageous renewal of the agreements linking the state with the railway companies. Some called them 'blackguardly agreements'. Those former members of the Commune who had expected that the Republic in office would turn out to be 'bourgeois', since it had been baptized by Thiers the Versaillais, thus had their worst fears and their doctrine confirmed.

A final reason, then, and the most widely diffused: life was hard in the 1880s. Economic depression set in and there was unemployment; and in the absence of any state social provision, unemployment meant swift and profound distress. So there were various social troubles, from demonstrations to strikes, sometimes with downright criminality, and a general malaise. There were consequently clashes with the police who, though now 'republican', still retained their professional toughness, which was partly unavoidable and partly inherited from the habits of former days. Those were all minor items to be added to the increasing dossier of the Republic's 'bourgeois' character. The passions they evoked are well known: every difficulty in life, every intransigence on the part of employers, every instance of police brutality prompted thinking workers to accept, to regard as obvious, the analyses that were put to them in terms of class struggle. And every incident of violence – physical violence from the wretched unfortunates or the verbal violence of revolutionary theory – in return provoked the average bourgeois and even the average deputy to look on the worker as a rebel against whom republican order must be defended, or as an unrepentant lawbreaker who did not understand the sacred nature of the law. It is always difficult to interrupt that sort of cycle.

In 1886, when the striking miners of Decazeville threw the engineer Watrin out of the window, it became evident that the Republic's problems would not all stem from Rome! During the decade 1879–89, however, the discontent of the workers and the poor had still been only partially won over by the 'workers' parties', which had existed since Marseille, but were divided, weak, fragmented into small groups. It found expression far more in votes or demonstrations in favour of radical republicans, then Boulangists (sometimes they were the same).

In France at that time 'radical' had exactly the same meaning as it has today in English-speaking countries: someone who goes as far as he possibly can, an extremist, almost a revolutionary, in any case an exacting man, hostile to concessions. The radical republican was the opposite of the republican who made concessions in order to obtain results, one by one, classifying problems, and who was then known as an opportunist. In 1880 that dualism (radical–opportunist) was already firmly rooted. In 1875, in order to achieve the republican form of government, had not the first act of opportunism been to give in to the right on certain matters of principle, such as the maintenance of a strong presidency and the existence of an Upper Assembly?[6] As it is impossible to rule without taking account of difficulties and opponents, that is to say, without manoeuvring, government republicans would be opportunists and the radicals, distanced from the government, would very willingly become the spokesmen for the disappointed and malcontent. Originally, therefore, the criticism delivered by the radicals, Clemenceau, Rochefort and Naquet against Gambetta and his followers was that of men of principle and open combat against those of negotiation, compromise and gradualism. It was the battle of those who would have liked to found a true republican Constitution by means of a head-on victory, against those who had accepted that the Republic should worm its way in by means of constitutional concessions. Thenceforth, radical opposition would also include men who sympathized with the social and democratic aspirations of the workers and Parisian lower classes, against the government. A man like Clemenceau, for example, who harshly

---

[6] See Furet, *La Révolution.*

criticized Gambetta and Jules Ferry, but respected the memory of Blanqui and retained his friendship with Louise Michel. All the same, in his turn, twenty years later, the trials of government would sever all his links with the 'working-class movement'. Truly, an enduring propensity in French history began there. Jules Ferry, Georges Clemenceau, recalled once again, so close yet so different . . . By their very contrast, they are indeed the most outstanding examples at the opposite poles of the republican camp.

By present-day criteria, Ferry,[7] at the start of his political life, was squarely in the 'centre', or the *juste milieu*, between his opposition to the Empire and his no less firm resistance to the excesses of the Parisian people. Nevertheless, for his contemporaries, he was neither a moderate nor a waverer, but a front-line combatant on what was then the principal front: Republic, secularism – in short, liberty – against conservatism, clericalism and imposed order.

It is certainly easy to see everything that could bring the charge of moderation against him. He was a bourgeois, in the still accepted but already almost archaic meaning of the term. Provincial wealth (tile factories, lands, investments) had for two generations allowed the head of the family to be a barrister without doing much pleading in court and to devote himself to literature, the arts, 'society' and public life. Typically bourgeois again was the sharing of roles within the family, in which a gifted brother would shine as a barrister, a precocious intellectual and as a politican if he could – that was Jules – while his younger brother Charles, rather more modest, contented himself (if one can call it that) with being a banker and capitalist, and swelling an inheritance which in fact remained for the most part commonly shared. Thus Jules Ferry had always been rich without having to bother about money. Even more so since, in 1875 at the age of forty-three, through his marriage to Eugénie Risler, he had entered the vast and prosperous Alsatian family network of the Scheurer-Kestners.

The man's private life was also well and truly bourgeois, with its two clearly defined periods – a bachelor life, free, varied, even a little cynical up to his early forties, then marriage, taken seriously, not only because it was seemly but also through the blessing of a real love.

Nevertheless, that so-bourgeois marriage contained a spark of the revolutionary in that it was limited to a civil ceremony, with no concession to the religious rites and customs practised by so many indifferent people, and which many of his friends, unbelievers like himself, had amicably advised him to follow. But Jules and his wife belonged to that kind of 'religion' which in the nineteenth century still numbered adherents among the notables – philosophy (or the Enlightenment, or free-thinking, call it what you will). They did not, however, purely and simply ignore religion, nor did they despise believers, with whom they were well acquainted. Jules Ferry

---

[7] See ibid. and Jean-Michel Gaillard, *Jules Ferry*, Fayard, 1988.

respected and loved his older sister, who had been a kind of mother to him, and who was religious, even devout. But personal faith is one thing, dogmas and clergy another. Jules Ferry and his followers had an intellectual allergy towards the *Syllabus*, not forgetting the one they had, politically, with regard to the coup d'état.

This distinguished bourgeois, somewhat elitist and, in some respects, rather inflexible, had his good points, or perhaps his aspects of goodness. All his correspondence and all the evidence show him to have been affectionate and sensitive towards his sister and brother, his wife, little Abel Ferry (his nephew and adopted child), friends like Gambetta, even when they were to some extent rivals, the villagers of Foucharupt, and so on. To someone who accused him of being difficult to approach in public: 'You're like a thornbush', he is said to have replied: 'Yes, but there are roses on the inside.' I quote this rather mawkish exchange only because it was still appearing in school textbooks several decades after his death.

To tell the truth, another touch of colour is connected with him even more than the well-concealed rose in the thornbush, and that is the blue – this time openly declared – of the Vosges mountains. Drawn up in 1890, his will states: 'I want to rest in the same tomb as my father and sister, facing that blue line of the Vosges whence arises the moving cry of the vanquished to touch my faithful heart. Naturally, I want no priest to attend my funeral.' Posterity is unfair to Ferry when, of those two sentences, it recalls only 'the blue line of the Vosges', and insists always on the blue, as if that colour, attributed to a mark on a map, equally implied chauvinism or military dress, harking back to the volunteers of 1792, or in anticipation of the 'sky blue' uniform of 1915. Certainly, Jules Ferry was a patriot, a former pupil of the Strasbourg *lycée*, and Alsatian by marriage. But why, in the confidential prose of a will, should he have used a semantic artifice? Would it not be better to remember that any line of crests, seen from far away against a clear sky, show up in a darker blue, and that Jules Ferry had an artist's eye, adored nature and even did some painting?

As it happens, it was his admirers (later his detractors) who 'laid it on a bit thick' about the symbolism of that over-famous blue. More simply, Jules Ferry was without doubt a man of heart, conviction and principles, rather than one given to clever turns of phrase. That is often the way with great politicians, whom the historian sometimes has a duty to divest of their fancy attire.

Opposite him, so close yet so hostile, Georges Clemenceau.

Born in Mouilleron-en-Pareds (Vendée) in 1841, Georges Clemenceau[8] belonged to the same generation as Jules Ferry and Léon Gambetta and, like them, Ferry in particular, was a republican of old stock. The family were bourgeois (landowning and the not very lucrative practice of liberal

---

[8] J.-B. Duroselle, *Clemenceau*, Fayard, 1988.

professions) and, at least on the male side, philosophical and agnostic since the beginning of the century.

In his adolescence Georges Clemenceau had been personally traumatized by the persecutions which his father, a republican, had suffered under Napoleon III. Like Jules Ferry, all his life there would be three things to which he gave his loyalty above and beyond any hesitation or compromise: the liberal, democratic and legalist Republic, against any Bonapartism, real or supposed; secularism, against clericalism; and France. Again like Jules Ferry, as an adolescent he had not envisaged serving the state under the Empire, and after his studies at the Nantes *lycée* he turned to the (well-named) liberal professions. Ferry, as may be recalled, had chosen a more commonplace path and become a barrister. In the 1860s in Paris, medical studies were helping to disclose a rapidly advancing science, filled with practical and metaphysical hopes, and often caused agnosticism to open out into rationalism or materialism. Moreover, practising medicine could reveal to the practitioner, more easily than to any other bourgeois, the extent of the miseries that existed in the poor quarters. Would that be to seek, rather vainly perhaps, the reason that made a Clemenceau more 'radical' than a Jules Ferry? A reason is necessary, since the two men, whose ideas shared the same foundation, fought each other so bitterly. Unless it is admitted that weight must also be attached to the clashes of men engaged in a struggle for power, or to differences in mentality and sensibilities which cannot be reduced to pure intellectual ideas and are sometimes more decisive.

Personal clashes can never be totally ruled out. In 1865, his affections rejected by Hortense Kestner, Clemenceau failed to gain entry to the great Scheurer-Kestner clan, into which Jules Ferry managed to incorporate himself ten years later. Georges then went to the United States, perhaps thinking he would make his life there; he married, and the union gave him three children, but no fortune, and very quickly ended in dissension and divorce.

Before that conclusion, he had returned to France for the events of 1870.

In short, in contrast with Ferry – a convenient comparison – Georges Clemenceau had infinitely less wealth, less serenity and less stability.

With the new regime, he entered politics. He hardly practised medicine any more but acted as a deputy and journalist. For his newspapers; for his dazzling life as a virtually bachelor socialite, as a sportsman (a skilled horseman, and a good shot who was feared in duels) and as a traveller; sometimes for his family – he was in constant need of money. He led a restless life, making all kinds of associates, whose doubtful character his political enemies would naturally not miss a chance to dwell upon. All that, of course, was very Parisian, even Montmartrian. And Montmartre, around 1880 or 1890, still meant 'the people' and not just amusements. The last point in the contrast between Clemenceau and Jules Ferry is without doubt that the former felt at home in the capital, whereas the latter had a deep affinity with the provinces.

Finally, 'what was Clemenceau after' at that moment in French history? He wanted the Republic in its widest acceptance, that is, the Belleville programme of 1869,[9] therefore in the terms of the era, intransigent, radical, anti-opportunist. Without a Senate, without a presidency, without a Concordat. Without a death penalty. That extremism was not socialist, however, unless the term is used in the broad sense it had around 1848. Clemenceau stood for all the freedoms, including those of trade and industry, and of private ownership. But he also stood for the most extensive laws of social protection and public assistance. The maximum of individualism with the maximum of humanitarianism. All through legal means: the Republic, founded on the freedom of thought and universal suffrage, in principle allows all the progress that is to be desired.

So Clemenceau was not revolutionary, because he did not envisage the overthrow of the Republic so that it could be replaced by another system. Nevertheless he seemed to be – and perhaps was, in a way – for he could not accept that the Republic, on the pretext of governing, should fall in with the powerful (whether Bismarck, the bishops or the railway companies) and leave the great principles and the poor people dangling.

That desire for the absolute would make him for such a long time a pitiless critic of the republicans in government and, aided by his eloquence, a great 'toppler of ministers'. It was as if, for twenty or thirty years longer than usual, a superior vital energy within him had stood in the way of politics (in the administrative sense of the word).

Behind these major protagonists, how were the affairs of the state developing? A Chamber of Deputies with a strong republican majority had been elected for four years in October 1877, and Jules Grévy chosen as Head of State for seven years in January 1879. Contrary to expectations, the President did not summon Gambetta to form the government. The great republican leader got himself elected president of the Chamber, and the government was formed by Waddington, soon to be replaced by Freycinet and then Jules Ferry. The life and work of those early governments consisted basically in starting to put into effect the symbolic programme and principles and deal with the conflicts, all of which have been mentioned. Gambetta obviously approved of all this work, which was accomplished without his direct participation. He distinguished himself, however, by tabling the question of how the ballot was effected. The French today know very well that this is a political just as much as a technical question. The single-name ballot, by *arrondissement*, had been set up in 1875 by a rather conservative National Assembly, and was taken to be essentially a conservative system, strengthening the local, the traditional, and stressing the personal status of the deputy. Gambetta recalled that republican tradition (1792, 1848) favoured the list ballot, by *département*, where naturally more

[9] See Furet, *La Révolution*.

emphasis was placed on the political labels, ideas and programmes in the name of which the candidates had to group themselves.

He achieved nothing, however; the legislative elections of August 1881 took place with an *arrondissement* ballot, which did not prevent them from being a triumph for the Republic (or the left – it was all the same then): 467 seats to 90! The budding Republic's enthusiasm for battle and victory, which had not yet been cooled by disappointment, had produced its full effect. Gambetta's friends were elected in particularly large numbers, and the summons of the great man to the government, which Jules Grévy (who did not like him very much) had been able to put off for two years, became inevitable.

Formed on 14 November 1881, after several weeks of procrastination, Gambetta's government was overthrown in less than three months, on 30 January 1882. But the episode was as interesting as it was brief.

For a start, Gambetta had been boycotted by the other leaders whom he would have liked to unite with him in a 'great cabinet' (*grand ministère*). His team was still called the 'great cabinet', but out of mockery, as he had been able to appoint only second-rate men as his ministers. The other big names, being his rivals, had not wanted to take a place in his government, thereby acknowledging him as leader. His downfall resulted from his proposal to re-establish the list ballot: he was a victim chiefly of parliamentary jealousies and unpopularity which deserve some examination.

This was the man who in 1868 had hurled rude defiance at the Empire in the court action over the Baudin subscription;[10] who in 1870–1 had been the personification of National Defence; and who, after five years of struggle, had led the republican party to success against Moral Order. Surely he had more claim than anyone to be a respected and admired leader?

What was it about Gambetta, then, that could cause him to be ostracized? Certainly, in the field of political strategy, he embodied the strategy of opportunism more clearly and for longer than any other leader. One of the facets of his clever republicanism consisted in trying to rally men to the Republic on the basis of a common patriotic attachment, rather than keep them indefinitely at a distance because of their past; in that way he was able to attract a Miribel or a Galliffet – formerly monarchist soldiers. And on this point, as on others, opportunist strategy was combated by radical strategy. However, that was not enough to overthrow a man like Gambetta since, after all, the opportunists by far outnumbered the radicals. But not all the opportunists liked Gambetta. Some, who had acquired their electoral habits and interests in the *arrondissement*, mistrusted the list ballot. Others were wary of the personal euphoria and social blossoming of a leader who was still young and surrounded with distinction. A mistaken interpre-

---

[10] Ibid. Remember that Baudin had been killed on a barricade in December 1851 while protesting against the coup d'état, that a republican plan to erect a monument to him in 1868 had given rise to a court case in which Gambetta, as lawyer for the subscribers, had gained his renown.

tation, no doubt. Going beyond that, one cannot avoid a more general fact: Gambetta was what was not yet known as a 'charismatic' leader, and the most commonly held republican outlook would see in that charisma a predisposition for dictatorship. The image of the good republican was that of the old Roman drawn from Plutarch, or of a hero of virtuous America: Cincinnatus or Washington. If he shone too brilliantly or won too much applause, he would turn into Caesar or Bonaparte. Gambetta was the first victim of this type of political massacre based on puritanical anxiety. There would be others; it would be almost a tradition of the Republic, since it would take no lesser man than de Gaulle to reverse the trend.

There was therefore a return to the more classic type of government, led by Freycinet and then Jules Ferry. The work of the Republic continued: work on institutions, and colonial conquest, not yet touched on, which brought Jules Ferry down in March 1885. After his fall, Brisson's government, which tended more to the left, succeeded in voting through the list ballot that the Chamber had denied to Gambetta. By then Gambetta was dead, as the result of an accident on 31 December 1882. After eleven months of ostracism, that premature death conferred on him the status of national hero, to which the names of so many streets bear witness nowadays.

In the legislative elections of October 1885 the right, perhaps benefiting from those dissensions, was better represented (201 deputies, faced with 383 republicans). At the end of the year, Jules Grévy was re-elected by the National Assembly for a fresh seven-year term.

The opportunists still ruled, but the radicals (Rochefort, Clemenceau) who had headed the attacks on Gambetta and then Ferry, had some influence on the majority, and swung the government towards the left. The Freycinet government in 1886 continued the republican fight: a new series of secular laws on education, and the expulsion of the princes. It was in that government that the Ministry of War was entrusted to General Boulanger. He was not one who had recently rallied in support, but he was an indisputable republican – that is to say, by family tradition. His running of affairs was marked by some significant measures: vigilance with regard to royalist high-ranking officers (the Duc d'Aumale, son of Louis-Philippe, was struck from the ranks of army officers); improvement of the material lot of the common soldier; preparation of a law to reduce the length of service; moderation of the use of the army in social conflicts. They would have sufficed to make him legitimately popular with the left. Two traits could be added which were more facile and consequently created a greater effect: his imposing personal bearing and handsome appearance, and his assertion of patriotic firmness in the face of Germany. The General's popularity was revealed in the acclamations which greeted the 14 July review in Paris in 1886. But in the spring of 1887 his bellicose remarks in the Schnaebelé[11] affair overstepped what could be accepted by opportunist diplomacy, which

[11] A serious frontier incident in Lorraine, between French and German police.

opted for prudence and preferred to settle the incident. Isolated France did not possess the means of revenge. Goblet's government was overturned and Rouvier's, which followed on 30 May 1887, was formed without Boulanger. Our republican General would seem, therefore, to have been ousted because of his radicalism, and even more for his patriotism. Against all that was cautious, bourgeois and dull about opportunism in government, he made capital of all the feelings of intransigence, populism and dawning nationalism expressed by the radicals, and these feelings were particularly keen in a city which, less than twenty years earlier, had lived through the siege and the Commune.

In July 1887 Boulanger, being an embarrassment in Paris, was transferred to Clermont-Ferrand; crowds gathered into a mob at the Gare de Lyon to try to prevent his departure. At the 14 July review, the Parisian public cheered him in his absence and booed the government. Booing the government of the Republic, now there's a novelty! Until then, Boulanger had merely been a particularly eye-catching standard-bearer for radical republicanism. 'Boulangism' would surface when, in the wake of the General, other malcontents would form a coalition liable to call the Republic, or at least its current avatar, into question.

It all happened (or so the classic argument goes, nowadays qualified rather than dismissed) as if the various groups on the right had calculated, in the summer or autumn of 1887, that this very popular republican General could be used as a weapon to overthrow the regime, and as if Boulanger, also for tactical reasons, had accepted that prospect – each component of the coalition awaiting the chance to play its own game once that stage had been won. An episode, in which it must be admitted that coincidence played a part, helped to crystallize the situation.

The Wilson affair (a scandal over a traffic in honours in which the influential opportunist deputy Wilson, son-in-law of President Grévy, was involved) had absolutely no connection with the conflict in question. But it allowed the discrediting of politicians in government by the use of social and moral arguments which were as easy to orchestrate in radical terms (corruption of bourgeois who had risen to power) as in counter-revolutionary terms (inherent baseness of modern politics). The Republic's two adversaries, the right and the extreme left, found they were speaking very nearly the same language, and this shared language was consequently unifying.

The Wilson affair thus contributed to swelling the Boulangist tide. In November, the opportunists deemed it morally and politically impossible to defend Grévy. He was urged to resign. The way was thus opened for the presidential election on 3 December 1887 at Versailles.

The majority of republicans looked towards Jules Ferry who, since Gambetta's death, was the only eminent, forceful and prestigious leader. Because of his prestige, his past and his character, he obviously accumulated the grievances and hatreds of both oppositions against his person. To elect him would be to have a man of character as Head of State, with a programme which was the exact antithesis of that of the Boulangist coalition, clearly challenging its collective sensibilities. An uprising was in the offing in Paris, should an elected Ferry return from Versailles to the Élysée. Playing on that fear, Clemenceau torpedoed his candidacy, putting forward that of Sadi Carnot, also an opportunist but with a slightly lower profile.

For the second time, Ferry was defeated by Clemenceau. From another viewpoint, for the second time (after Gambetta), a strong man of the republican party was abandoned by his followers. There had even been some speculation as to whether Clemenceau might push his aggressiveness to the point of joining Boulanger's camp. He had known the General for a long time, and had strongly recommended him at the beginning of 1886; there had been contact between them (the 'historic nights'). In the end Clemenceau, a remarkable man, had remained in the government camp. The latter, in fact, defined itself as the camp of a Republic defending its existence and principle against a neo-Bonapartist adventurer. Such was the classic diagnosis made by Ferry, amongst others, when he had described Boulanger, in a shock-term, as a 'café-concert Saint-Arnaud'.[12] A soldier, wanting to become popular through a mixture of chauvinism and social demagogy, and whose supporters insulted members of parliament, had too many traits in common with 'Badinguet' not to be suspected of dictatorial aspirations.

Now, the recollection of the Republic's founding battles was still vivid enough for that mobilization of the spirit of the 1851 resistance to cause Clemenceau himself to tread warily.

The whole of 1888 was spent in this defence of the regime. The pensioned-off Boulanger at once became eligible for election. His campaign consisted of presenting himself as candidate at all the legislative by-elections that cropped up. By virtue of the list ballot, those elections, even for a single seat, brought the entire electorate of the *département* concerned to the polls, which heightened the stir caused by the ballot. Boulanger won nearly every time, resigned and started again. He had the popular, workers' votes – but that did not worry the republicans who knew from history that, between 1848 and 1870, great masses of the poor had remained over twenty years in the wake of one leader. For them it was not universal suffrage which decided what was good, it was the law. Popular suffrage could have its relapses. On the other hand, the political, electoral and even financial support brought by those on the right to the General's campaign could no longer be denied, and it gave the republicans' conscience a reassuring boost: basically, the right was opposing them, so everything was as it should be.

On 27 January 1889, Boulanger stood for election in Paris itself, confronting the entire electoral body of the Seine (nearly half a million voters). He crushed his rival, and there was amazement that he did not make his move when all Paris was buzzing beneath his windows. Perhaps, after all, he was not the right man for a coup d'état. But those of his supporters – and they were numerous – who hoped for a show of strength on that

---

[12] Minister of War in December 1851, the principal military executive of the coup d'état.

evening felt discouraged, and it is generally agreed that the Boulangist wave began to ebb at that point.

The year 1889, the centenary of the Revolution, was, coincidentally, also the year of the republican counterblast. Boulanger and his followers were treated like conspirators. The League of Patriots, which had strongly upheld him, was disbanded and its leaders hounded. Boulanger, warned by an organized 'leak' that plans were afoot to arrest him, fled to Brussels: the response was negligible. The list ballot was abolished by a suitable law, and multiple candidacies banned.

On the occasion of the centenary celebrations, among the batch of great men placed in the Panthéon – La Tour d'Auvergne, Marceau and Lazare Carnot – was the noteworthy inclusion of the representative Baudin, killed by Louis-Napoleon's soldiers on 4 December 1851. That choice solemnly signified that the Republic had adopted Ferry's judgement: Boulanger was an adventurer, an aspiring dictator, a neo-Bonapartist. That outline has long gone undisputed. It has not been without political importance: the following chapters will lead us to recall that, in 1958, the parties of the left would still be making use of the lively mistrust in which the figures of Bonaparte and Boulanger were held (sometimes even adding Pétain) in an attempt to oppose General de Gaulle's attaining power. Then the backlash: experience having shown that a popular, nationalist General, leader of a heterogeneous coalition, no friend of parliament (we are speaking of de Gaulle), could rule without harming either liberty or the Republic, the bogeyman version of Boulanger would lose its relevance, and his case would be reconsidered. A curious dialectic: as de Gaulle was decidedly neither a caricature Boulanger nor dangerous, one wonders, in return, whether Boulanger might not have been a modest, timid and distant prefiguration of de Gaulle.

The subject of institutions, basic to present-day reflections on the Fifth Republic, has given a new impetus to historical interest in the institutional problems of the Third, which were more complex than republican tradition would admit.

French politics in the years 1879–89, viewed overall, were typified by two fairly contradictory features: too complicated in parliament and the daily course of events, too simplistic in times of great crisis. An esoteric and muddled parliamentary government in the Chambers but, outside, a republican 'absolutism'[13] kept pretentiously in reserve.

Parliament, firstly, saw the emergence of a fairly numerous succession of governments, therefore each on average of short duration; so there were frequent government crises, outside the normal electoral replacements. That presupposes a far more intricate game of parties, factions and persons

---

[13] See Rudelle, *La République absolue*, to whom are due several of the following analyses, although I may not share her view in every case.

than would seem to be suggested by the large ensembles known as right-wingers, opportunists and radicals.

The deputies (or the senators) were not organized officially at that time. It would have seemed immoral for a representative of the people to depend on any authority other than his conscience and the will of his electorate; the idea of a party disciplined by a possibly imperious directorate was still far off. Unlike today, parliamentary groups did not play a precise role in the functioning of the work of the Chambers, which was still very little regulated.

About 1880, republican deputies officially formed four large groups, the most progressive being the radicals, the more moderate (of the former Thiers's hue, now that of the financier Léon Say), called 'centre-left', and the great mass – the opportunists – distributed between the groups known as the Republican Left (with Jules Ferry) and Republican Union (with Gambetta). Many ideas drew Jules Ferry and Gambetta together, and they were personally good friends, although rivals to some extent as well. The Gambettists were far more progressive and 'popular' than the Ferryists; some, like Brisson or Floquet, were forming a transition towards radicalism. All this went on, therefore, within very vague boundaries.

The deputies' true ties lay with even smaller groups: there could be solidarity among elected members from the same region, or those from comparable constituencies (with mining or wine-growing interests, etc.); among friends, comrades, old schoolmates and those who had served in the army under the same leader; among those who frequented the same political salon (in the evenings in Paris, once the Chamber's sitting was over, an active social life enabled deputies to get together for the freest interchange of ideas and opinions); or yet again, among the readership of the same newspaper. Why and how?

Republican or royalist commitment stemmed from profound cultural and historical allegiances which are quite easy to pinpoint, but what was the situation among republicans themselves? Why be a radical rather than a Ferryist or Gambettist? Obviously, there were more members of the upper middle class and businessmen in the centre-left seats, whereas those few elected members originating from the lower classes went more willingly to join the radicals or Gambettists, but the groups of deputies who were thus socially well defined remained as minorities. The great mass of deputies did not easily lend themselves to that kind of analysis.

A recent attempt[14] has been made, however, to throw rational light on political behaviours by examining the electoral circumstances. Such and such a deputy, well in with his constituency, very soon in the position of a notable, would be able to vote in the Chamber according to his convictions (for a moderate amendment, for instance) without fearing for his seat; another, with the same origins, the same culture, the same deep conviction, but elected in an unstable constituency, would not be able so comfortably to assume the same stance in the Chamber, for fear of laying himself wide

[14] Ibid.

open to being ousted by a competitor. Certain clues to parliamentary behaviour must be sought in a careful study of constituencies. But the more personal clues should not be eliminated: friendships, hatreds, ambitions. You did not become a politician (and successful, for it was a victory to be elected) without a certain psychological dynamism, and those aptitudes which helped you in the struggle to gain entry to the Chamber did not desert you once you were established. From time to time, however, that individualism must be disciplined in order to fly to the aid of the Republic, and that underlying prospect, sometimes exceedingly questionable, added to the prevailing tension in the atmosphere.

Was the 'Republic in danger' a real threat or a convenient myth? Before tackling that question, yet another general factor complicating political life must be mentioned – the problem of the Constitution. Opportunism had ensured the Republic's victory by accepting the laws of 1875, which were fairly conservative in tendency and tone. 'Chamber of Deputies' was used, in the vocabulary of old France, whereas 'National Assembly' would have been the republican term. In 1830, Louis-Philippe had been described as 'a king surrounded by republican institutions'. In 1875, that could have been transposed to 'a Republic surrounded by monarchic institutions', with a long-term presidency, and an oligarchic Upper Chamber, the Senate.

After the majority swing of the electorate towards the Republic, the temptation could therefore be strong for the republicans, masters of the three authorities, to revise the Constitution in order to bring it more into line with their principles. Indeed, the question was constantly aired. For want of an extensive revision, two minor ones were carried out, the first with a mainly symbolic content (the return of the Chambers to Paris, the suppression of public prayers), and the second political (alterations to the method of recruitment to the Senate). But the matter was continually discussed, each leader having his own ideas about revision. That is without counting the most important, the actual revision, due essentially to Jules Grévy, which consisted in the neutralization of presidential power. Ever since Mac-Mahon and his 16 May, it had been understood that the right of dissolution carried a whiff of coup d'état. Its use was therefore prohibited. Grévy, as President, kept himself very obviously at a distance from politics and left a minister to govern *primus inter pares*, known as president of the Council, but lacking any institutional existence and, moreover, dependent from one day to the next on the Palais-Bourbon majority. Apart from that, alterations to the text were contemplated. Changes would have been minimal for Jules Grévy, the most conservative of opportunists; maximal for Clemenceau, the radical, who would logically have got rid of the two items that were incompatible with pure democracy and government by the Assembly, that is, the President of the Republic and the Senate. But Jules Ferry, and Gambetta, also had their own ideas about revision. And even Boulanger. The famous list ballot desired by Gambetta should not, in his opinion, be a simple electoral law but should become a measure incorporated in the Constitution. Although that had come to nothing, one must bear in mind the persistent presence of the problem of the Constitution, from the origins of the Republic up till the Boulanger affair. It was only the Boulangist episode that would turn 'revision' into a watchword emphasized on the right, and would thus link republican orthodoxoy with attachment to the laws of 1875, which were revised in 1884. The constitutional conservatism of the republican camp, which would a priori render suspect any subsequent attempt to make alterations to the system, dated only from 1887–8.

Going beyond the strictly legal stipulations, reflection on the political system affected the actual relations of men and political groups in the country. Did certain leaders already have in mind what would one day be called 'republican appeasement'? What did that mean? Through the list ballot, which would obviously in itself lead to a better organization of the parties, Gambetta would have seen the prospect of a great majority republican party, all serene (since the essence of its militant programme had been accomplished). That party would be able to confront a large opposition party, composed of all those whom the Republic left dissatisfied, chiefly for religious reasons. In that way there could be an alternation – though within the Republic and in a state of tranquillity – of a great liberal party on the left and a great conservative party on the right, in the British style. That battle would have been more healthy than the over-heavy confrontation of issues, in the French manner, between a party of the Republic and a party that was inimical to the regime.

For that vision of a Republic which victory would render conciliatory and, later, unanimous, certain recent authors give credit to Gambetta, to Jules Ferry and even to Boulanger. For although the latter was not considered to be a thinker, and certain characteristics reveal him as a fairly colourless person, he nevertheless made some speeches in 1888 which went along those lines, and may well have been inspired by ideas drawn from Gambetta, who by then was dead. In the same direction, another such study[15] reminds us that, within the Boulangist coalition itself, the General constantly maintained his republican loyalty against representatives of the right-wingers or the Comte de Paris. In the end, Boulanger may be seen as the 'gravedigger of the monarchy', since it was he who, though providing the first example of a movement incorporating the right, yet nominally republican, dismissed *ipso facto* the idea of a monarchic restoration to the realm of dreams and utopias. Boulanger's dream, far more realistic, was that of the 'Constable', which was in keeping with the republican form of the state. In these historiographic reappraisals the twentieth century and de Gaulle are evidently on the horizon.

In fact, there was no appeasement in 1888–9, and the great majority of republicans formed a bloc against Boulanger; some saw him as a puppet, others as a Monk[16] in the service of the king, others as a would-be dictator, acting in his own interests – three fairly differing images, but all negative.

---

[15] Philippe Levillain, *Boulanger, fossoyeur de la monarchie.*
[16] The seventeenth-century English general who, after Cromwell, restored Charles II.

For those republicans it would have been inconceivable to regard the General as Gambetta's heir! In their view the Republic was in danger, since Boulanger was seeking to alter it, whereas they themselves refused to define it other than by its already traditional characteristics, its customs and, above all, its allergies.

With a brilliant stroke of verbal inspiration, the term 'absolute Republic' has recently been proposed for that republican attachment to a fundamental Republic outside which there could be no safety. It may be guessed that the epithet is pejorative, since it transposes to the Republic an 'absolutism' which good republicans had found reprehensible when it was applied (though in a rather different sense) to the monarchy. The supporters of this republican 'absolutism', which could just as well be termed particularity, intransigence or, quite simply, radicalism, were indeed radicals, and those of the opportunists on whom radical extremism could bring pressure to bear. Clemenceau-style radicals, having brusquely broken away from Rochefort-style radicals who had turned Boulangist, reconverted into the role of active element in the republican camp, would thus bar the route not only to the ambiguity of Boulanger but also to the noble objectives of the best part of moderate opportunism.

A useful challenge to French historiographic tradition. Is it totally convincing? For us, who know what happened afterwards, and who are aware that by means of various rallyings, or by one uniting, a republican right would actually make its appearance, it is easy to admit that the possibility had existed as early as the 1880s. But at the time, as men who base their arguments on precedent are always more numerous and more persuasive than those who argue from futurology (a precedent is a 'fact', futurology is hypothesis), negative interpretations of the Boulanger case inevitably gained more credit than optimistic ones. Jules Ferry, although neither a mediocrity nor a fanatic, showed himself as firmly anti-Boulangist as Clemenceau, and sooner. And the republicans could clearly see that, in the course of the 1888 by-election campaigns and the normal legislative elections in 1889, in the speeches of the Boulangists and their conservative allies, classic counter-revolutionary arguments considerably outdid those of republican revisionism. The right-wingers in 1889 had not all turned liberal, and the vision of Boulanger as a sort of Trojan horse of the reaction was therefore not a complete fantasy. At all events, such a vision did exist, and it was through that vision, or spectre, that Boulangism would serve to continue the tradition of a combative republicanism right up to the end of the century.

Speaking of combat, the Republic was waging other battles that were far from metaphorical. The 1880s, when the regime was finding its feet and establishing its rules, were also the years during which it decided to use its national forces overseas.

Hardly had the ghost of the Empire been exorcized when the Republic became an empire after its own fashion.

It was a decisive epoch. Its vocabulary speaks volumes. About 1870, 'imperialist' in France still meant a supporter of Napoleon III. Thirty years later, the word would be used in the British manner to mean a supporter of the domination of overseas countries by a great European state.

The Empire, around 1870, was an internal political regime; in the twentieth century 'the empire' would be that vast pink stain on the map, covering the north-west quarter of Africa, the Indochinese peninsula and several other territories where France had, as they say, planted its flag.

Glorified or held in contempt, that change was due in essence to the Republic. The opportunists, its founders, were great patriots. It would take an excess of personal animosity and partisan aggressiveness (and there would be plenty!) to cast doubt on the feelings of Gambetta about this matter – Gambetta, the man who always had National Defence on his mind – or those of Jules Ferry, whose last message left us that famous 'blue line of the Vosges', or to question their will to regain 'the lost provinces'! Certainly, they postponed revenge, but revenge postponed out of necessity is not revenge forgone!

Europe in the 1870s and 1880s was dominated by Germany or, to be more exact, it had been stabilized in a 'Bismarckian system', both menacing and skilful, which aimed at maintaining the status quo. In this sense, the overflowing French energy for expansion abroad could be taken for a relative decline in interest centred on the Rhine. As Boulanger had passed for a man of the Rhine and anti-Germanism, his eviction from power by the opportunists in the spring of 1887 could have seemed like an act of subservience towards Bismarck. But could anything else have been done?

Bismarck, who controlled Europe, had resigned himself to accepting a republican France, on condition that it was not too radical or too chauvinistic, which amounted to the same thing. The sovereigns of the other great powers, Tsar Alexander III, the Emperor-King of Austria-Hungary, Franz Josef, and even Queen Victoria, were scarcely more sympathetic towards the Republic. As for the other monarchs, they hardly counted. In that blocked diplomacy the only possible changes could come from the courts. Thence arose the interest shown by certain French statesmen in the supposedly liberal heirs of Vienna and London, the Archduke Rudolph and the Prince of Wales.[17] The only option was to take advantage of peace in order to prepare a strong army, and to make the most of the courses left open by Bismarck outside Europe.

The army was one of the principal beneficiaries of the attentions of the Republic, and even of the nation, for there tended to exist in people's minds virtual unanimity in favour of the military institution in the same way as there was virtual unanimity in favour of patriotism and the concept of nationhood.

No pains were spared. Its traditional internal organization (system of promotion, regulations of all kinds) survived, and was respected. Its great

[17] They could easily be seen about in informal fashion at the baths in Carlsbad or elsewhere. It was the era of 'spa diplomacy'.

leaders pursued their careers, even if they had shone under the Empire or against the Commune, provided only that they had not fallen from grace at the time of the National Defence. That, being a patriotic and not a partisan undertaking, remained the touchstone of accepted values. Bazaine who, by capitulating at Metz (that is, making one more enemy army available), had objectively given the advantage to the invader, remained the typical traitor, the bogeyman, whereas Chanzy or Denfert-Rochereau were model heroes.

Military service was still as laid down by Thiers's law of 1872, still fairly close to the old professional system, with many exemptions but a five-year period of service for those who enlisted. The republican policy of combining universal service with a shortening of the time spent with the colours continued under consideration until 1899. Only then did it result in the three-year law, which was heartily welcomed.

In the 1880s the opportunists quite logically even contemplated giving the army and national defence the backing of that other national institution, state education. That support, mainly moral, would be lasting: republican schools would cultivate patriotism, directly by moral and civic instruction, and indirectly by the teaching of national history and geography. But a still more tangible aid was envisaged, with 'school battalions', that is, groups of schoolboys in their last year of school (eleven to twelve years old) whom their teachers equipped with wooden guns and trained in parade-ground drill. There will be no surprise that this experiment failed: it required, on the part of families, a zeal that was not always present; setting up a fair-sized battalion also presupposed a density of habitation and transport facilities which were themselves uncommon; and above all, because superficial training acquired at about twelve or thirteen had every likelihood of evaporating during the seven or eight years separating the former schoolboy from the recruiting board. Despite their failure, the school battalions should be kept in mind, for their intention was typical of the thinking of people like Jules Ferry, Paul Bert or Freycinet.

The fourteenth of July, when the army is the star of the show, was a sign of the eminent place occupied by the military institution in the Republic. The national festival, borne along at that time by the attraction of its novelty and by the very real fervour of the republican camp, certainly had other aspects. First of all, the festival pure and simple, various entertainments and amusements, following the tried and tested programmes of local fêtes (in honour of local patron saints or votive and the political fêtes of yesteryear (1 May under Louis-Philippe, 15 August under Napoleon), together with the variety which municipalities and shopkeepers' committees could provide. From those traditions would emerge the popular 'local hops'. There was also the custom – well and truly vanished – of putting out flags: not just the decorating with bunting that we still know today, over public buildings, but a proliferation of flags at the windows of zealous private individuals, sometimes so numerous as to impart to certain favoured sites an air of unanimous enthusiasm, as if the entire street were dressed for a party. But above all, 14 July was the day for taking up arms, when the local garrison turned out and showed its strength; offered the spectacle of the fine precision of its drills and the dazzle of its uniforms; when it rejoiced (or at least overexcited) the spirit with its fanfares and, in short, poured out an enthusiasm at once political and sensory. Naturally, military celebrations reached their peak in Paris, and have already been mentioned in connection with Boulanger.

But what was to be done with those forces? On the Rhine, or rather, the Vosges, nothing before 1914, as we know. To the fury of the radicals, Boulangists and doubtless a good part of the right, the opportunists used the armies overseas.

First of all, following directly on the Congress of Berlin in 1878, came the war in Tunisia, on the pretext of pursuing the rebel tribes of the Algerian–Tunisian borders, the famous Khroumirs: in fact, to forestall the more active expansion and colonialism emanating from Italy and to settle the question of hegemony in North Africa to France's advantage. Tunisia's independence was fictitiously maintained by the protectorate established by the Treaty of Bardo. Strengthened in the Maghreb, by contrast the French presence fell back in the Near East, where the British imposed their protectorate on Egypt after buying a preponderant number of shares in the Suez Canal.

The other grandiose affair at the start of the 1880s was the development of business enterprises – until then partial and sporadic – carried on since Napoleon III in the Indochinese peninsula. These even involved, in passing, several months of war between France and China in 1885, in which the star role was played by Admiral Courbet, forgotten today but then a hundred times more famous than the homonymous painter of Ornans and his studio. They also unleashed the spectacular government crisis that saw Ferry overthrown by Clemenceau's interpellation on the news of a simple military setback at Lang Son. In the end, they resulted in the constitution of 'French Indochina', with five component parts: the colony of Cochin-China, the protectorates of Annam, Tonkin,[18] Laos and Cambodia. The former Minister of Public Education in the 'great cabinet', Paul Bert, had the task of presiding as governor general over the foundation of this Asiatic ensemble. It was remarked on that occasion that 'anticlericalism would not be an export item'. No one was more anticlerical than Paul Bert in France, but no one got on better with missionaries and nuns. In Asia, 'laymen' and 'clericals' shared an awareness of being French, of playing a humanitarian role (doctors, nurses) and, each in their own way, of feeling themselves to be 'civilizers'.

Elsewhere, through small explorations, limited expeditions, mini-wars, starting from the Algerian south, from Senegal (consolidated under Napoleon III

---

[18] Tonkin would later be completely detached, in stages, from Annam and treated as a colony.

by Faidherbe) and from posts on the Gulf of Guinea (where France had obtained a foothold under Louis-Philippe), began the first outlines of what would become French West Africa, extended into French Equatorial Africa. And already the way was being paved in the direction of Madagascar.

The Republic's imperialist commitment in the 1880s was obviously due to a variety of reasons, and it would be foolish to apportion relative import- ance or list their order of priority. Which were significant and which the trappings of propaganda? Let us set them out simply, for merely to list them will throw light on the spirit of the times.

Firstly, it must be remembered that, in part, those conquests developed under their own momentum. There were the initiatives taken by junior colonial officers, cut off from civilization but with a passion for their terrain, conflicts with natives, skirmishes that called for reprisals, so many *faits accomplis* which must afterwards be taken on 'for the honour of the flag'. All these were thus insidious processes of expansion relatively independent of metropolitan French politics. Indochina was rather part of Napoleon III's history bequeathed to Moral Order and then to the Republic by this kind of chain of events.

Secondly, there is the theory of the indirect preparation for revenge, already mentioned. Must the distant colonies be seen as a worrisome burden and an encumbrance, as Napoleon I, Bismarck and the adversaries of Jules Ferry seemed to view them? Or, as Napoleon III had sensed, was a modern power obliged to travel that path? Was not Prussian-style national greatness archaic, and did not British-style greatness point to that of the future? In geopolitical terms this analysis was then plausible, and can be attributed to the opportunists. Besides, Jules Ferry made a clear statement to that effect in a celebrated speech, by linking national greatness with economic power, and the latter with the possession of the sources of raw materials, markets, outlets and thus with diversified world positions.

This brings us back – the third set of reasons – to the Republic's encounter with the world of business. In so far as commercial interests, of Le Havre or Marseille for instance, were looking for profits from colonization, they now had the means to push state policies in that direction, since the Republic no longer appeared a priori hostile to large business undertakings or the acquisition of wealth. Furthermore, the opportunists, supporters of econo- mic liberalism, were developing an overall conception of progress in which resounded a sort of distant echo of Saint-Simonism: expansion, greater knowledge of one another's worlds, increased activity in trade, industry, overall wealth, the gradual spread of prosperity, 'openings' of all kinds – in their philosophy there was nothing in all that to conflict with political progress. Indeed, it was one of the prerequisites in a philosophy that could be described as very American. For – Bartholdi reminds us in passing – without a doubt, Jules Ferry's France and Cleveland's America, the donor and recipient of *Liberty Enlightening the World*, had never been so close.

Lastly – fourth reason – that happy consciousness of being a 'superior civilization' was not to be classed among secondary motives for the rulers of that period. There is a certain logic in discovering the same names in the imperialist operations of the 1880s as in works of pedagogy: Jules Ferry, Paul Bert . . . The concept of a liberal democratic Republic, inspired by the Declaration of the Rights of Man and the Citizen and, more widely, by the universalist philosophy of reason, seemed to them to be obvious progress compared to 'primitive mentalities', 'barbaric customs', persistent proslavery and the 'fanaticisms' of Mandarins or Marabouts. On the other hand, they certainly underestimated the portion of specific injustices and cruelties which Europe would bring with its gunboats. Nowadays we know only about the latter, but the history of France in the nineteenth century was created by the real impetus of all those motives, including the idealistic crusade.

At the start of republican colonization few critical voices were raised on behalf of the rights of natives. Ferry has been blamed chiefly for such things as authorizing a military initiative prior to debate in parliament, improper treatment of the mythical Khroumirs, the decimation of an expeditionary corps through fever due to ill-preparedness for climatic extremes, and lastly – even worse – the diversion of forces from the Rhine.

Later, the debate would take shape and become more commonplace. While the entire nation was experiencing its first taste of an 'imperial' type of pride, the Revolution would run into a whole new range of criticisms.

But in the years from 1879 to 1889 which we have just skimmed through, many undertakings that had been started did not reach full maturity.

2

The Conservative Republic
1889–1899

Once the republican regime had been defined and established, and after it had surmounted its first serious test in 1889 by containing the Boulangist upsurge, the final years of the century were ones of euphoria and triumphalism for the ruling powers. It was then that the Republic acquired the characteristics of a settled and thus, inevitably, a conservative government.

For if winning meant defeating their adversaries and affirming their own principles – those of the left, as it happened – it also meant, since they were in power, shouldering the permanent demands of public order and seeing the indifferent and neutral flock towards them. The last two circumstances almost unavoidably forced circumspection and moderation upon them.

Thus were formed the state and political society which, through the unforeseen occurrence of a simple judicial error, would be badly shaken by the Dreyfus Affair. The affair began, of course, with the arrest and sentencing of Dreyfus in December 1884. But nearly four years were to elapse before the scale of the movement in favour of reviewing the trial blew it up into a major political matter. It would take nothing less than this grave crisis (undeniably significant and dangerous) for the Republic to make a fresh start in 1899, bringing its message up to date. Then, for another period of time, it would once again become a key idea and not just an ordinary political regime. So, was the Republic conservative in the 1890s? For a good republican of that era, putting the two words together would have jarred. Only the intervening passage of time allows us nowadays to hazard the expression. Was it so new? Yes and no! From December 1848 to December 1852, then from May 1873 to March 1876, the Republic had certainly existed nominally, but under the direction of legislative majorities and governments formed of monarchists on the look-out for the chance of a restoration.

Those former examples of a conservative Republic therefore seem more like monarchies awaiting a monarch. At the end of the century, by contrast, we are speaking of a Republic governed by republicans who had stayed republican but become conservative – a new look, and one destined for a great future.

The year that saw victory over a fleeing Boulanger, 1889, was also the centenary of the French Revolution. The event of 1789 had been fittingly celebrated with all sorts of ceremonies and monuments, but with many precautions to avoid an apologia for popular dictatorship. The honour of having a public statue was extended as far as Danton, but was denied to Robespierre. As we have seen, the batch of those placed in the Panthéon in 1889 included, together with a legalist republican of 1851, three revolutionaries who were remembered rather as nationalists. Even more significant, the proposal – of radical origin – to build a great monument to the Revolution in the middle of Paris, on the site finally cleared of the ruins of the Tuileries, had been set aside in favour of simply enlarging the gardens. The year 1889 has left only the Eiffel Tower to the Parisian landscape, which is far from negligible but evokes the memory of the Universal Exhibition rather than the centenary.

In fact, Paris in 1889 renewed the splendours of 1878 in a spirit of festival, prosperity, artistic and technical progress and international cordiality, rather than one of republican defiance to the Europe of kings. What was most strongly symbolic about the Eiffel Tower was its proclamation of the radical modernity of the art of metalwork, and its gift to French national pride of a world height record. Two features not totally unconnected with the Revolution, but neither closely nor obviously. Public opinion would doubtless remember 1889 chiefly for the success of the vote on three-year military service, a popular measure in that it reduced the length of service (previously five years) and cancelled a certain number of exemption categories (clergy, teachers, etc.).

Meanwhile, at the summit of the state, there were some changes. Elected at the end of 1887, in the circumstances already mentioned, Sadi Carnot was about to complete his seven-year term of office when he was stabbed by an Italian anarchist in Lyon in June 1894. His successor, Casimir-Perier, lasted only a few months before resigning, overwhelmed by an extreme-left press campaign denouncing him as a socialite, linked with old bourgeois money and endowed with an authoritarian personal temperament.

What a lot of symbols all at once! However different they may have been, Caserio's dagger and Gérault-Richard's[1] pen shared the common feature that they expressed, each in its own way, the radicalization of the social struggles which loomed large during those years. To replace Casimir-Perier, the Congress elected Félix Faure, a more traditional figure. A minor industrialist from Le Havre, he was more a member of the 'new social strata' than of the ancient dynasties of notables. Moreover, he wanted to be seen as a disciple of Gambetta. Resolved to let current politics carry on independently of him, he devoted himself to his task of representation with a zeal and a taste for splendour which harmonized well with the contemporary climate. Like Sadi Carnot before him, he was a great traveller

---

[1] The most active polemicist in the campaign waged against Casimir-Perier in *La Petite République*.

through the *départements* and inaugurator of patriotic monuments. His presidential mandate almost entirely covered the legislature from 1893 to 1898 (extended by an exceptional prorogation), and saw the beginning of that from 1898 to 1902, when the Dreyfus Affair would upset the situation.

Numerous governments followed one another, separated by various crises with complex and sometimes minor causes, details of which hardly matter to us any more these days. Their leaders were moderate republicans, second-rate men of the opportunist generation, such as Jules Méline, or their epigones and younger colleagues, who were beginning to be known as 'progressives', Charles Dupuy for example. Jules Ferry left the stage prematurely in 1893, aged only sixty-one. His defeat at the hands of a Boulangist, in the legislative elections of 1889, was one of the republican camp's rare setbacks, going counter to the general trend. He was then elected a senator, and in 1892 the Senate elevated him to its presidency – a good waiting-room for the Élysée – when illness rudely snatched him from a destiny which he well deserved.

His end owed little to chance, however. At the time of the 'hate campaigns' unleashed against him personally after 1885, a fanatic had fired a revolver at him, piercing one of his lungs. It would seem that the wound, from which he had at first appeared to recover, had by insidious effects shortened his life. He himself, therefore, would not have the opportunity to symbolize the moderate Republic. By limiting his active career to the militant and founding years from 1870 to 1889, his premature death trapped him in an image of the left, that of the intransigent republican and secular educationalist. It was another man from Lorraine, his contemporary and companion in the struggles, Jules Méline (born in Remiremont in 1838, a barrister, deputy for the Vosges from 1876 to 1903, then senator from 1903 until his death in 1925), who would go down in history as the prototype of the man of the right to emerge from the 'republican party'. His press medium, moreover, was *La République française*, which had formerly served as a platform for Gambetta. As vigorously anti-Boulangist as his leader, Ferry, after 1889 Méline no longer had any adversaries except on the left. He was president of the Council from April 1896 to June 1898, the man for whom 'there *is* no Dreyfus Affair', and was an anti-Dreyfusard, and candidate for the Élysée against Émile Loubet in 1899. It is nowadays regarded as symbolic and more worthy of note that he concurrently held leadership of the government and the running of the humble Ministry of Agriculture. But that, too, was equally a sign of conservatism.

Of course, those republicans in the government called themselves 'progressives', since it went without saying that the Republic was marching towards progress, and the perhaps more suitable terms 'conservatives' or 'reactionaries' had remained traditionally bracketed with the monarchists. In fact, being a 'progressive' republican meant above all not being a 'radical'. For the fairly informal groups describing themselves as radical still constituted a left wing of the republican camp, and began to claim for themselves the role of custodians of republican principles and doctrinaires of the new tradition. They too were deprived of their top man when, in the legislative elections of 1893, Clemenceau lost his seat as deputy. He had to wait until 1902, when he in turn would benefit from the senatorial reshuffle.

Léon Bourgeois then became the principal leader of the parliamentary radicals in the 1890s. Born in Paris in 1851, the son of a watchmaker, a volunteer in 1870, then a barrister and finally an official in the central administration, after 1877 he was one of the first batch of republican prefects, before passing in 1888 into the parliamentary arena as the elected member for the Marne (deputy from 1888 to 1905, senator from 1905 until his death in 1925). A skilful politician, he is interesting chiefly as the theorist who tried to formulate, in *Le Solidarisme* (1895), what should be the ideal recipe for a humanitarian Republic: an economic liberalism amended by institutions and social intervention. Léon Bourgeois had but one chance to form a radical government, in 1895, which soon showed itself too daring to last. It would remain rather the model for those radicals who preferred to devote themselves more to great humanitarian causes than to the empiricism of everyday combat. Rarely a top-flight minister, more willingly president of the Chamber or the Senate, he was known mainly as president of the League of Education, a specialist in matters of public assistance and, in that capacity, as a pioneer in the great campaign against tuberculosis, and lastly as an adherent of the cause of international arbitration in conflicts – a fine aspiration that would win him the honour of the Nobel Peace Prize in 1920. By contrast, his 1895 cabinet, which nevertheless included such men as Combes, Doumer and Berthelot, is of less account historically.

Apart from that brief interlude, the Republic in the 1890s, although ruled by the so-called 'progressive' group, was therefore in reality rather conservative; in Marxist vocabulary it would be termed 'bourgeois', and that accusation began to be bandied about considerably. Bourgeois because it accepted the link with the dominant economic forces which were obviously not to be overturned. The overall link was that liberty was extended to the economic regime; capitalism was working and its laws must be allowed to have free play. But there were also more particular and closer links, when this or that group of businessmen, in need of this or that law, made approaches to legislators in order to persuade or cajole them. At that point, the acceptance of capitalism went so far astray as to become corruption by capital: that was the story of the Panama scandal.

Ferdinand de Lesseps, the creator of the Suez Canal in 1869, had undertaken at the head of a new company to cut a way through the central American isthmus. But natural geography made the enterprise much more difficult than expected, and the world economic situation had declined. Out of all this arose setbacks, the need to be bailed out and, for that, the necessity to obtain a parliamentary vote authorizing a last-chance loan. It was that vote that was partly bought. From the rather complicated details of the affair emerged at least the simple conclusion that the Republic's deputies could prove venal. Those newspapers which had remained sympathetic to Boulangism took a kind of revenge by broadcasting that discovery. In the end, the government, the parliamentary majority and the legislature acted as policemen by bringing some of the corrupt to justice, and universal suffrage finished setting the house in order in 1893 by eliminating certain deputies – including Clemenceau – who had, to say the least, kept unwise company.

As a whole, however, the 'bourgeois' Republic, having been taught a lesson by the trials of a difficult economic situation, or perhaps quite simply motivated by the profoundly money-conscious nature of French society, staked less on a 'law of the jungle' capitalism than on sound, straightforward capitalism. Jules Méline achieved his most enduring fame in this domain. As parliamentary leader, in 1892 he had managed to get customs laws passed in order to protect the textile industry and, above all, agriculture from international competition. Shortly afterwards, as a theorist, he published *Le Retour à la Terre* (Back to the Land) which, in precise terms, stated that France's vocation was to cultivate its agricultural and farming aptitudes rather than try desperately to compete industrially. Moreover, thanks to him, the panoply of French national honours was enriched by the agricultural Order of Merit . . . That ruralism constituted a considerable shift, even a contradiction, in relation to the Manchesterian spirit of Napoleon III, to which Gambetta and Jules Ferry were no strangers. There was a dual passage from a position of boldness to one of withdrawal, and from an ideology of true progress to one of defensiveness. Méline's policies strengthened the link which the founding fathers had already forged between the regime and the peasantry, but whereas, under Gambetta, republican ruralism had tended to take country people away from the conservatism of the notables in order to bind them fast to the Republic, under Méline it was rather the Republic which tended to attach its own political deceleration to a preserved rural immobility.

Conservative or bourgeois, Méline's Republic allowed what was social and humanitarian in its programme and its initial impetus to become bogged down. A law limiting the hours of industrial work for women and children, and another law encouraging mutual aid societies were doubtless a not inconsiderable achievement of social legislation, but neither were they exactly heavyweight. The government did not even take care to ensure that trade union freedom, legal since 1884, was observed in business undertakings. On the other hand, there was great vigilance when workers became even slightly restive or minimally disturbed public order: it is well known that the Republic which experienced Panama also witnessed Fourmies.

Fourmies, in the *département* of the Nord (*arrondissement* of Avesnes) but very close to that of the Aisne and Belgium, was a typical small industrial town. Three-quarters of its 15,000 inhabitants were manual workers. The dominant industry was textiles (weaving and chiefly spinning of wool), shared out among about twenty firms, the largest of which employed well over a hundred workers – men, women and children. The wages were low, the hours long. The law limited the length of the working day, because the workforce included women and children, but even that legal limit was twelve hours! Neither political consciousness nor union organization was yet established. Despite the vast majority of the working class in the elect-orate, the municipal council was not specially 'of the people', and the mayor was a shopkeeper who felt solidarity with the world of the employers. The only trade union in existence was the mixed union (employers and workers) of religious and paternalist inspiration. There was nostalgia for the good old days when, in each workshop or factory, the boss, the foreman and the workers would gather for a banquet . . . on the evening of 1 May. For the first day of the month of May was still recognized here, as in several other regions in the deep heartland of France, as a main date in the old (agrarian) cycle of seasonal festivals. For instance (a detail to be borne in mind), young people preserved the custom of going into the woods on that day and cutting a branch of may blossom to offer to their betrothed.

The proletariat had however been 'worked on' for some time by socialists coming from Lille or (chiefly) the nearer Saint-Quentin to announce the first general strike on 1 May, devoted to a claim for an eight-hour working day. How could that simple and fair idea fail to arouse echoes? Feeling anxious, the employers published a common manifesto on 30 April viol-ently denouncing the agitators as strangers to the area and, with regard to the eight hours, prophesying the certain ruin of the factories, employment prospects and the entire region. That was adding fuel to the fire. All the more so when, to lend a strong arm to the defiant stance of the industrial-ists, two companies of troops of the line were sent by the sub-prefect of Avesnes to reinforce the local gendarmerie in case trouble erupted.

The day of 1 May therefore dawned in a tense atmosphere. Many strikers were out on the streets, going through the town to call out workers still toiling in the factories to join them, and singing to a well-known tune: 'It's eight hours, it's eight hours, it's eight hours that we want.'

One of these gatherings, outside an open factory, was charged by mounted police. Some strikers defended themselves with stones and sticks. That first skirmish ended with some minor wounds, but also with the arrest of some demonstrators who were locked up in the police station on the ground floor of the town hall. Once the news was out, at the beginning of the afternoon, the processions of striking workers grew more numerous and were converging on the municipal building to demand that their comrades be set free. The refrain had changed to: 'It's our men, it's our men, it's our men that we want.'

The gendarmes could no longer cope and had fallen back behind the cordons of foot soldiers barring the way to the central square. The sub-prefect of Avesnes and the mayor were shut in the town hall as if in a besieged fortress. Outside, between the church and the town hall, the initiative belonged in theory to the commissaire of police, but in actual fact to one of the commanders of the 145th company of the line. Seeing his troops giving way before the thrust of the crowd, he gave the order to open fire. There were a few salvos lasting perhaps two or three minutes at most, causing terror, scattering, bewilderment. Nine dead and thirty-three wounded lay on the ground. Of those nine dead, only one was an adult (thirty years old, father of two children), the eight others being adolescent workers – between twelve and twenty years of age – four boys and four girls. History has preserved the name of one of them: Maria Blondeau, because under the hail of bullets she still kept hold of the sprig of may blossom that her sweetheart had given her in the morning.

The notoriety of that bloodstained spray of blossom is obviously connected with its dual symbolism: for the social historian, it has for a hundred years signified the contrast between the innocent, unarmed and inoffensive nature of the demonstrators and the irresistible brutality of the Lebel rifle; for the anthropologist, it illustrates and catches in real life the transition between the 1 May of folklore and the revolutionary 1 May.

There was a vast surge of emotion. The government (whose Minister of the Interior was Constans, Boulanger's conqueror) was violently attacked by both the right and the extreme left. The press, which had not long since been Boulangist, now nationalist and anti-Semitic, inveighed against the forces of order, especially calling into question the zealous sub-prefect, who was Jewish. Drumont came in person to Fourmies to hold an inquiry into the event, and the very detailed account of it which he left is still one of the sound sources of information. Furthermore, the entire right (anti-socialist and conservative) blew up out of all proportion the action of the curé, Margerin, who had rushed out from the presbytery to minister to the victims, not exactly, as was said at the time, under the hail of bullets, but immediately afterwards, for – a sign of the times – that mean-minded and appalling argument over the precise timing of the priest's appearance really did take place! Charity of religious forces against inhumanity of republican authorities on the one hand; on the other, the accusation by the republicans of clerical exploitation of the drama.

But those who 'made the most of it' were undoubtedly the anarchists and socialists, voicing throughout the country the protests that several radical deputies had also uttered in the Chamber. It was in the momentum and emotion of Fourmies that, on 8 November next, on the occasion of a legislative by-election in Lille, Paul Lafargue – Karl Marx's son-in-law and one of the leaders of the French Workers' Party (Guesdist) – was elected. His votes in the first round were more than three times the number of socialist votes in the same constituency in 1889 (5,000 instead of 1,400), and in the second ballot he received the decisive backing of the 1,500 radical votes in the first round.

Fourmies was a famous event because it was an example, and trebly so! Firstly, of the class struggle. Fourmies seemed made-to-measure to reinforce the hypercritical Marxist denunciation of the 'bourgeois' Republic. Secondly, of the first of May, that age-old and naturalistic festival which was then entering the social and political phase of its history, prior to retrogressing before our very eyes – the loop looped, the wheel gone full circle – to the rank of spring and plant festival (yet another public holiday and 'lily of the valley day').

The third example is too often forgotten: the institutional backwardness of the system of maintaining order. These days, Fourmies would not have become famous, because a couple of CRS companies, well equipped with tear gas, would have dispersed the crowd without bloodshed. But the Republic had not yet invented the relatively soft forms of repression employed by a civilized order. It was still at the stage, like Louis-Philippe and Napoleon III, of calling in the army when the gendarmes or local police were overstretched.

So the soldier, and above all the infantryman, was not trained to deal with jostling crushes or scuffles. His only weapons were bayonet or rifle – both lethal. As for the officers, the Republic had not been able in the space of a few years to inculcate in them the humanitarianism which its civil officials, for their own part, still practised so little. So Fourmies . . . Fourmies was just the most spectacular milestone in the reorientation of the course of republican politics.

Despite a certain mistrust with regard to popular movements, the regime during the 1880s had remained imprinted, on the left, with anticlericalism, the natural accompaniment to its great programme of secularization. But by now the educational laws had been put into place, their implementation in the provinces followed its course, with a rhythm that varied according to the local balance of power, but without major incident. On that particular front the regime could 'lower its guard', tone down its pugnacity, even assume what Spuller, Gambetta's friend and political heir, had termed in a noted speech 'the new spirit'.

The new spirit, that of moderate republican governments in the face of a Catholicism judged to be less dangerous, obviously strengthened the overall conservative tone of the times. To conjure it up, Anatole France created his quartet of novels, *l'Histoire contemporaine*,[2] in which are portrayed, in a small provincial town, right-thinking notables, republican civil servants headed by the prefect, who together with the clergy reconstruct a sort of small society of their own, while, distanced from that society, it is a peaceable teacher, a sound free-thinker with republican principles, who figures as the one who is out of things. The intrigues carried on by the ecclesiastics, with the help of appeasement and the Concordat, were effected

---

[2] *L'Orme du mail, L'Anneau d'améthyste, Le Mannequin d'osier, Monsieur Bergeret à Paris.*

within the framework of the official Republic. Retracing them, Anatole France's critical pen hit both targets at once.

That reorientation of republican politics in the 1890s was obviously possible (and justifiable for the rulers and defenders of the regime) only because new things were happening on the right. The Comte de Chambord had died in 1883, and the Comte de Paris, in exile since 1886, enjoyed infinitely less veneration and consideration. As for the Bonapartists, they were divided between the rival and contradictory tendencies of two princes of the family. In the main, monarchism seemed to hold very little danger because even in 1889 when it was taking advantage of its coalition with the Boulangists it had been defeated. How could it hope to win relying only on its own forces? The Republic, consolidated both by the continuing majority vote of the people, and by the passage of time which was transforming it into a custom, seemed well and truly settled.

Above all, were there not reassuring prospects of development in the opposing camp, where those faithful to the Roman Church formed the most convinced battalions? At this point the state of Catholicism at the end of the century must be considered, even if cursorily.

French Catholics, in that first great phase of the Third Republic from 1880 to 1914, were in a singular position, which has been the subject of the most contradictory opinions. For the first time since the French Revolution they found themselves under lasting subjection to a hostile state, either non- or anti-Catholic. In short, for them it was the recommencement of the Revolution – without the guillotine – and for them (or the vast majority) the Revolution was evil: a detestable philosophy that could result in nothing but disastrous policies and a corrupting moral influence. That pessimism, already a hundred years old, had been brought to its climax in 1870 and 1871 by three violent shocks – the defeat and isolation of France, a Catholic nation, under the blows of Lutheran Prussia; the loss of the Pope's temporal power; and the explosion of violence in the Commune, during which several ecclesiastics had perished, including the Archbishop of Paris. The France of Moral Order had made a good start on the work of expiation through piety and, for instance, had begun building the Sacré-Cœur on the red hill of Montmartre. But in 1879 the Revolution (Jules Grévy and Victor Hugo, Gambetta and Jules Ferry) had regained power. And it mattered little that the legal and methodical impiety of Jules Ferry was vastly different from the bloody impiety of Raoul Rigault. Satan could wear many faces. Under republican governments Catholics would come to describe themselves, in Tertullian's words, as *exsules in patria*, 'exiles in their own country'.

But the republicans were scarcely less worried. This Church that called itself exiled and persecuted remained, in their view, a power which was menacing because of its centuries-old hegemony. The great majority of the population resorted to it to solemnize the main private or collective acts of their lives: baptism, marriage, burial, blessing the fields and crops, adding the full weight of dignity to local saint's day celebrations. Half the electorate were open to its instructions.

High society, the 'social world', nearly all the ancient nobility and great bourgeois notables, and the higher officials and civil servants who came from among them, were Catholic at least in name and custom. In certain respects, the minorities – if not 'exiled', nevertheless ill-regarded – were formed by Protestants, Jews and (the largest group) resolute agnostics, those who refused all rites, even for the sake of propriety. The Church had deemed Gambetta's and Victor Hugo's civil funerals scandalous but, equally solemn, the national funeral of the assassinated Head of State, Sadi Carnot (June 1894), passed through Notre Dame, which was also greatly significant: the historic authority of the Roman Church over French society was very little shaken since so many undeniable republicans reconciled it with their political convictions. Was it not rather that radical anti-Catholicism was forming a counter-society growing like a cyst in society as a whole? And the internal exile – was he not the man who, for example, by having himself buried without benefit of clergy, 'like a dog', laid himself open to scorn? At all events, that was how things were in the heartlands of France.

Who was persecuting whom? Those reciprocal and incompatible accusations obviously stemmed from the many aspects of a complex situation that polemics improperly simplified.

The Republic in France, as numerical evidence shows, relied not only on Protestants, Jews and agnostics (rather summarily identified with Freemasons) – those three groups together would have formed only a slender majority – but also on a fourth component, with far larger numbers: Catholics who had wholeheartedly accepted 'the Revolution'.

Among them were the thinking men of liberal Catholicism (connected with the magazine *Le Correspondant*); and politicians who were sensitive to the tradition of state Gallicanism, for whom Rome and ultramontanism represented the danger of every impetus or every directive coming from beyond the frontiers. Above all, there existed the mass of middle- and lower-class Catholics – hardly theorists – who were content merely to be able to enjoy both the republican advantages of liberty and democracy and also the age-old practice of their faith; after all, the churches were open, priests numerous and paid by the state. It was because in many regions, even where the faith was practised, the Republic received the electoral support of those millions of Catholics who found modernity to their liking, that it remained in power. But occupying the forefront of the stage was a militant Church which combined a more demanding Catholicism with all the social and intellectual forces of rejection.

That Catholic 'party' – 'clerical party' in republican vocabulary – had waged and lost the defensive battle over primary schools, as we know. It had won others, which were less talked about: neither hospitals nor cemeteries had been completely secularized. Despite some adjustments, and sometimes skirmishes, the places of suffering and death were to stay surrounded by religion for a long while yet.

The Church was fully conscious of the extent of its social strengths and weaknesses. It was firmly entrenched in several rural zones of 'Christianity', the west in general, Flanders, the Basque country, the south of the Massif Central, to cite only the most prominent, but it deemed the remainder were 'mission areas', targeting especially the large towns and the working class. At that time 'good works' came into being, or, rather, became more generalized. The founding of the enterprise 'Catholic Workers' Clubs', by Albert de Mun, opened a path which would continually grow wider and branch out. It was then (between 1880 and 1900 or so) that – to quote the words of a fine scholar[3] – 'the traditional "good priest", drowsing in his rural presbytery, gave way to the big town pastor, an activist, his time consumed by a growing number of nonreligious activities – study circles, youth groups, unions, funds of all kinds; a factotum, he ran these enterprises, materially, by ceaselessly collecting money and, spiritually, by performing offices, retreats, specialized pilgrimages.' He was helped, whenever possible, by benevolent laymen. The typical good Catholic was not only a regular communicant and exemplary paterfamilias, but also henceforward a 'man of good works'.

Soon the Church would learn to make use of all the forces of the new sociability which the Republic had liberated and politicized at the same time – reading circles, singing societies, gymnastic clubs, brass bands, excursion clubs. Reds and whites would thus often form networks of social activities which were identical yet antagonistic. The Church proved itself capable of adapting, since sport, for example, was not taken for granted by an ethic which had for so long entertained a holy mistrust with regard to the body, its exercises and pleasures. But success demands adaptability. There were other instances. Industrial civilization had brought not only a further need for charitable work in its poor working-class suburbs, more plentifully endowed with bistros than with places of worship; it had also procured, with the coming of the railways, the means of a new triumphalism. Since the 1870s, the railways had allowed the new feature of mass pilgrimages to the great sanctuaries of La Salette, Paray-le-Monial, Pontmain, above all, Lourdes and even, on occasion, Rome itself.

In a living and revitalized Church, fired by an awareness both of its setbacks and of its strides forward, the paroxysms of devoutness that can give rise to 'saintliness' could not remain absent for long. The preceding era had seen the death of the curé of Ars, Jean-Marie Vianney (1859), an object of veneration before his canonization. The following era would be better symbolized by Charles de Foucauld, who would die in 1916 in the heart of the Sahara. Between the rustic apostle of yesteryear and the explorer apostle of the morrow, the moment evoked here belongs to a simple girl from Alençon, Thérèse Martin, who became a Carmelite at Lisieux, died in 1897 and was soon canonized as Saint Thérèse of the Infant Jesus.

[3] Michel Lagrée in chapter 6 of *L'Histoire des catholiques en France*, ed. F. Lebrun, Privat, 1980.

Catholic circles were ill at ease with the times and modernity, with which the Republic tended euphorically to identify itself. From that it was but a short step for the Church's secular struggles to turn antirepublican; and the man of good works, moreover, was often a royalist, as were the Mayenne peasants or the crowds who flocked on pilgrimages. But reflection on contemporary society could sometimes go beyond the question of the regime and the Constitution. Two political themes then emerged – one of conspiracy and the other of social renewal.

The former held that, to be so bad, the Republic must necessarily be something more than a mechanism, a regime or simply the absence of a king. It must be the instrument of a deeper force, the tool of a conspiracy. The republican label was really too prosaic for Satan. Satan was Freemasonry – this argument, which had appeared at the beginning of the nineteenth century, reached its height at that time, not without some apparent justification. Or else Satan was equated with 'Jewry', another theme that militant Catholicism borrowed from nationalism as much as from its own tradition. Such was the negative aspect of refusing to accept the world as it was.

On the other hand, the theme nowadays looked on as positive was that of social criticism. If France was faring badly, it was because not only politics but also social relations had gone astray. The liberal and parliamentary Republic was open to criticism, but so was its associate, liberal capitalism. Amid the distant origins of that Christian democracy which is today considered a Catholicism of the left, are to be found some solitary eminent men from the extreme right (legitimist) and its search for a Christian order: Albert de Mun, the founder of the Workers' Clubs; Henri Lorin, the creator of the Social Weeks; Léon Harmel, the prototype of the 'social' company head, associated with his workers, (rather like Godin, for instance, in the republican camp); and the Abbé Lemire, who would be elected deputy for Hazebrouck. That concern for the people, for the faith, and for the relations of the people with the faith, was in their eyes basically more important than concern about those who were at the head of the state. Their implicit reasoning can be seen to converge with that of Pope Leo XIII.

Indeed, Pius IX, the pope of the uncompromising counter-revolution, had been succeeded in Rome in 1878 by Leo XIII, a more politically minded pope, whose papacy was marked precisely at the start of the 1890s by two great innovations. On 15 May 1891, the encyclical *Rerum novarum* invited Catholics to consider that the existing social order was open to criticism; though socialism certainly did not embody the best solution, there were nevertheless Christian paths to be sought between socialism and capitalism. That was the first way of breaking with a certain established conservatism. On 16 February 1892, *Inter Sollicitudines* this time questioned the political confusion between Catholicism and monarchy. It must not be taken for granted that a Christian could be only a royalist. In itself the

Republic was not necessarily bad; only its secular legislation. But there was nothing to prevent one from recognizing the regime, so that its anti-Christian ploys, measures and practices might be all the more effectively and fairly challenged from within. This was how the 'rallying' (of Catholics to the Republic) was presented, a call made by Cardinal Lavigerie,[4] and accepted by Albert de Mun, which corresponded with the policy of appeasement mostly conceived, and in fact practised, by the republican heirs of the opportunists.

A bold avant-garde of the Church was thus 'rallied'. Very large numbers, perhaps the majority, of the clergy would take much longer to separate their age-old attachments to Rome and the monarchy, two branches of their overall traditionalism. At least French politics, including the parliamentary platform of the Republic, would now be able to count on several eminent actors from the Catholic right wing. Albert de Mun became the perfect example. Before him, of course, the parliamentary right, chiefly in the Chamber of Deputies, had not lacked orators. They were collectively known as 'the right-wingers', and were named more specifically after the possible dynasties (Bourbons, until the death of the Comte de Chambord in 1883; Orléans, Bonaparte), but shared opposition to the Republic had led them to co-ordinate their parliamentary activities and their votes, under the leadership of Baron de Mackau. When the great principles of the Republic were involved, their favourite orator was Mgr Freppel, Bishop of Angers and a deputy. But certain men who were already capable of eminence as much for their original thinking as for their oratorical talent were swept forward by the new situation.

Born in Lumigny (Seine-et-Marne) in 1841, Albert de Mun came from the ancient nobility, made a brilliant marriage, but was the younger son of the family and in the end had only a middling fortune. He had entered Saint-Cyr to become an infantry officer. Under the Empire, he had served in Algeria, and then been in the 1870 war. A conservative, royalist and patriot, quite naturally. A prisoner of the Prussians during the winter of 1870–1, he had renewed his relationship with the Marquis de la Tour du Pin, who had been a captive fellow officer with him in Germany. It was to him that he owed the strengthening of his Catholic faith, and the conviction that the most essential battle would be to restore to the Church the society that 'the Revolution', in its overall progress, had taken from it. More vital, in short, to re-Christianize the people than to bring back the monarchy. After all, if it took the form or tendencies of Orléanism, the monarchy itself could be tainted with liberal and secular modernity. In 1871 Albert de Mun devoted himself to the work of the Catholic Workers' Clubs, and their great expansion had characterized the period of intense struggle preceding the Republic's victory. A tireless organizer of societies and clubs, a lecturer who crisscrossed France and had many meetings with bishops, Albert de Mun at last let himself be persuaded to wage the fight in the Chamber of

---

[4] The toast of Algiers, November 1890.

Deputies as well. In 1875 he resigned from the army and sought a constituency, setting his heart on Brittany where, apart from a few exceptions, seats were safe for candidates from the right. It is true that there were also plenty of local notables to occupy them, whereas de Mun had no personal ties in the region and in his favour had only his reputation for national militancy. His elections at Pontivy (Morbihan) were therefore always difficult, if for that reason alone. But the other reason – latent though sometimes perceptible – lay in the fact that de Mun was more of an apostle than a conservative notable, and more Catholic than legitimist. Of course, he remained a hundred times closer to legitimism than to Orléanism or Bonapartism. But in his eyes, restoring society to Catholicism counted for far more than re-establishing a king, and that was what was noticeable about him, at least to those on the right. Viewed from the left, as is proper, those nuances normally escape notice, and the various groupings on the right are perceived as a single monarchist and clerical bloc, commonly called the reaction. But one can understand (after the event) that there was nothing paradoxical in seeing a man who was philosophically on the extreme right of the opposition become one of the first in his camp to accept the Republic. All in all, it was his lofty and all-embracing view of the counter-revolution which would help him to relativize the importance of the monarchic form itself.

That point had not been reached in 1880. Albert de Mun, while managing the sometimes difficult relations between his work with the Workers' Clubs and that with other Catholic works and committees, or with such and such an ecclesiastic, took part in all the right wing's defensive battles, as in all its complex negotiations and internal manoeuvrings. But above all, he clung to the idea of a specifically Catholic party, affirmed in 1885, then disowned by Rome and thus abandoned. Boulangism, which constituted a totally opposite strategy, had been merely an embarrassing nuisance to him, and he had played only a secondary role in it. On the other hand, he was on the alert for signs from Rome and ready to spot those likely to lead to a turning point.

The 'political landscape', to use a contemporary expression, was not immediately upset. The policy of 1892 – rallying and the 'new spirit' – aroused no enthusiasm, any more than did the policy of 'opening up' in 1988.

Just as many men on the right, more passionately antirepublican than loyal to the Pope, jibbed at his disruptive advice, so the vast majority of the left preferred to regard the '*ralliés*' as invaders sheltering in a disturbing Trojan horse. All the same, several were elected in the 1893 ballot. So, after 1893, the system of forces and denominations of the preceding decade was really transformed. The Republic and the left stopped identifying with each other, as they had in the 1880s, and consequently the right and hostility to the Republic were no longer confused. There was now, and would be for a long while, a republican right or, if you prefer, republicans on the right.

There were even two kinds. Old royalists (or conservatives) who had ultimately accepted the regime, either little by little, one by one and discreetly, tired of resisting, or after 1892, following the Pope's call, had become *ralliés* in the strictest sense. But also genuine republicans who had in fact passed from the left to the right, because their desire to defend the established order against a working-class movement that they considered worrying had led them to favour a defensive attitude towards attempts at social change and thus to follow a line which was closer to that of the clericals than of the radicals.

These political transformations, hallowed by history, were, however, not easily perceived in their time. On the left men refused – and would refuse for a long time – to consider that republicans worthy of that grand name 'Republic' could possibly exist in the camp of the right, because the left attributed such exacting demands to the Republic! The left continued to regard itself as the camp of the Republic, and the guiding principle in the alliance of those on the left was known as 'republican'. But that vocabulary was already passing from historical truth into legend or mythology.

The collection of words and concepts that political science borrows from history was fed until our own day on observations made at that period, so it would be impossible to refrain from briefly including their debates in this account. The most classic analysis[5] acknowledges the existence of bipolarization (right–left) in the political field, but adds that the right had only a negative character: the non-left. It was extremely varied, because formed of successive layers which had entered, one after the other, into opposition to democratic modernity, each with its own special shade of justification. Those various waves had matched the number of regimes in French nineteenth-century history, and it is the name of those regimes which the system quoted has, with a boldness sanctioned by recent custom, transformed into categories.

The only 'chemically pure' right, the first, and the only one prior to 1830, can be called 'legitimist' because it was a continuation of the political thinking of the ultra-royalists: the world after 1789 is bad, good existed before 1789, in the principles of tradition, authority and the Catholic Church.

Then came the Orléanists, the men of 1830, initially on the left, but whom the failure of their monarchy would throw into a right-wing opposition to the Republic, the people and progress. There, they remained modern because they stayed liberal (modern civil law, liberties, representative and parliamentary regime), but they used that legalism in a chiefly defensive

---

[5] Rene Rémond's, of course. *La Droite en France de 1815 à nos jours*, 1954. New edition entitled *Les Droites en France*, 1984.

way, against popular unrest and against any urge to change the social regime. Orléanism was liberal and conservative simultaneously.

Lastly would come the Bonapartists, who had also emerged from post-1789, and who had retained a sense of democracy, of the masses, with a feeling both patriotic and populist, but who preferred to act along paths of Caesarism (cult of the leader) rather than those, reputedly more bourgeois, of parliamentary government.

After the victory of the Republic, still according to the same analysis, Bonapartism as such was marginalized (the probability of restoring a third Empire was virtually nil), Orléanism and legitimism as such had also disappeared because dynastic merging had mingled them in a common royalism. There were therefore hardly any more Bonapartists, Orléanists or legitimists in the strict original sense. But 'Bonapartists', 'Orléanists' and 'legitimists' could be spoken of in inverted commas, abstract political categories which could describe respectively plebiscitary-authoritarians, conservative-liberals and complete counter-revolutionaries. There is nothing to stop us following their paths to bring us to the present day, when Messieurs Chirac, Giscard d'Estaing and Le Pen (or Mgr Lefebvre) would represent them.

A fine piece of work, perhaps a little too systematic (like every system, in short), but which has had the merit of stimulating historical research – too often prone to descriptive empiricism – by an example of well-thought-out conceptualization.

Orléanism undeniably remains the most robust of this triad of categories. There is nothing to prevent that name being applied, so strong is the analogy with the men of the July monarchy, to republicans like Méline, given that radicals and socialists alarmed them more than tamed royalists. Those republicans of the 1890s known as progressives, bound to the great principles of 1789, liberals, legalists, parliamentarians, but mistrustful with regard to the people because they were socially conservative, had everything of 'Orléanism' about them. As did the elected members who had come from the right, the *ralliés* for example, who gave up trying to overturn the Republic and, on the contrary, entered the parliamentary system thus accepting, at least implicitly, the principles of liberal modernity on which it was founded. In short, the 'Orléanist' category is well suited to all that part of the right during the 1890s who were republicans, whether they came from opportunism or from rallied monarcho-Catholicism.

The difficulty arises chiefly from the too clearly cut dividing line between 'Bonapartists' and 'legitimists'. The former are supposed to be identifiable by their Caesarism, plebiscitary demagogy, and possible solutions of authority and violence; the second by the total contrast in their ideology, and their absolute scorn for the principles and institutions of the era. Thus 'Bonapartism' is noticeable mainly in connection with means of action, and 'legitimism' in connection with principles and ends.

Could the two not combine? Therein lies the most important rider to be proposed to the current system of history and political studies. A young author[6] dared in 1978 to oppose the authorized ternary proposition with one that was simply binary. Basically, for him there were only two right-wing groups at the end of the nineteenth century. The republican right, which we have presented under this name and recognized in Rémond's 'Orléanist' right, Sternhell leaves outside his field of study to devote himself to the 'revolutionary right', that is to say, the one whose aim was extra-parliamentary disturbance and, eventually, the disruption or overthrow of the regime. Of course, 'revolutionary' here does not refer to the positive ideological content of the word 'Revolution' (principles of 1789, human progress, etc.) but is used in the somewhat rebarbative sense of the word, concerned with means (excesses in ideas and expressions, material acts of violence, illegalities, coups d'état).[7]

In fact, resorting to the unaccustomed category of 'revolutionary right' allows a realization of the still fairly violent nature of urban political life at the end of the nineteenth century. The Boulangist electoral campaigns had witnessed men and groups make their debuts in the field, before continuing their activities in the nationalist and anti-Semitic disturbances of the period of the Dreyfus Affair.

Such groups, indeed, bore closer resemblance to a 'league' than to a 'political party', because they were just as much in evidence outside as during electoral campaigns, and just as much against parliamentary representatives as in favour of one or other of them. The League of Patriots, having passed with Déroulède from Gambettism to Boulangism, had travelled that route. They demonstrated, marched in procession, booed and shouted and, on occasion, confronted the police. These were the activities of organized and convinced militants; sometimes, too, special paid men were brought in, some were recruited from among rough and tough neighbourhoods (many instances were quoted, for example, of workers from the slaughterhouses of La Villette); sometimes, also, members of the proletariat who were used to working-class struggles, since part of the working-class element of socialism, chiefly Blanquists, had turned Boulangist out of hatred for institutions; sometimes leisured bourgeois (there were still plenty of people of private means, property owners, offspring who did not need to work); or students, well-dressed young gentlemen whose cane – the obligatory symbolic attribute of the man of leisure taking a walk – could easily be transformed into a bludgeon or cosh in planned or impromptu scuffles. Leaders came forward: Paul Déroulède, the patriotic songwriter, or Jules Guérin, or the Marquis de Morès. One is forced to the conclusion that street violence, urban and Parisian, recruited from among the commons and, dare it be said, common in behaviour, was not necessarily confined to the radical, socialist or neo-

---

[6] Zeev Sternhell, *La Droite révolutionnaire*, Seuil, 1978.

[7] The revolutionary right exists, for Sternhell, because he makes no secret of seeing in it the ancestor of fascism, a category which for him is very real (whereas it is not, at least in France, in Rémond's system).

Jacobin extreme left; it could equally be used in the service of politics classified as right-wing. Or – another aspect of the same finding – the right's violence was not necessarily limited to having coups d'état carried out by soldiers, but while they awaited the coup d'état that would be called for at the decisive moment, they could put into operation a violence which would serve to stir things up beforehand.

In short, it would seem that the right in that period was not composed only of bourgeois, lords of the manor and ecclesiastics, who lamented passively in between elections or while waiting for a plot or putsch engineered in secret, but also contained an active fringe in a state of permanent effervescence. That effervescence was all the more lively because there was more hatred directed against the regime of the 'hideous' Republic which, since Paul de Cassagnac, had begun to be referred to as *la Gueuse* (the strumpet). And the more the philosophical distance from official principles increased, the more readily did that political hatred make its appearance.

Were the butcher lads of La Villette who jeered at the deputies and the corrupt, and would soon be jeering at the Jews, 'legitimists' or 'Bonapartists'? Both, to be sure, for there is a logical link between the philosophical extremism of a movement and the practical extremism of its methods: one is far less scrupulous about breaking a law or violating an institution if one sees less legitimacy in its existence.

What, therefore, was the ideology at that time behind this rejection of the Republic? Things were just beginning to take a new shape. At the beginning of the nineteenth century everything had been simple. It could still be considered that the liberal, then republican, forces – in short, the left – were fed by the rationalism of the Enlightenment, and conservative forces by a Christian traditionalism. In other words, that (for France) the Catholic Church was the sole provider of ideas and means of influence for the counter-revolution.

That was precisely what ceased to be true at the close of the nineteenth century. The slow movement of history which would consummate the divorce between the Roman Church and political and social reaction was beginning to take shape, as we have seen.

A liberal Catholicism, born about 1830, then condemned by the *Syllabus*, bravely persisted in thinking that a legal modernity which had emerged from 1789 could combine with the Christian faith – but it did not yet speak with the loudest voice or affect events. On the other hand and chiefly, the advances of science since the middle of the century (notably in biology, anthropology and sociology) had allowed agnostic bourgeois to seek rational bases for their conservatism. For, following the Revolution, the Church had lost a vast amount of ground in people's minds. Great masses of cultured men were not believers and were – as they were called – philosophers. They did not all draw the conclusion that it was necessary to be a liberal, a republican or a socialist, for they felt themselves first and foremost to be bourgeois. Then, when the social peril became stronger, their only defence was to become Christian, or at least to do battle in order that the people should become Christian (the agnostic Victor Cousin's naive admission in 1848; 'Let us run to embrace the bishops, they alone can save us', is still famous). It was a painful, even ridiculous, situation.

Now, the agnostic conservative of 1880–90 could save himself such recantations: greatly impressed by science, he would seek to give scientific (by which is meant nonreligious) foundations to political and social conservatism. In other words, the secularization of the right-wing's thinking was under way. That was principally the work of Auguste Comte's heirs. Hippolyte Taine,[8] who made the transition between Auguste Comte and Charles Maurras, could well be the most important man in this piece of history.

It would be useful at this point to tackle the idea of race. In an inextricable mixture of scientific gropings and searches for justifications, budding anthropology turned race into a method of rational classification to describe the diversity of the human species, which exploration and colonial conquests were then making known. It sometimes tried, in a materialist perspective, to put men's physical and biological characteristics into relationship with their spiritual characteristics, in order to further the explanation of our enigmatic totality. It had no hesitation in treating races as collective entities and placing them in hierarchies, whites being superior to blacks and yellows, Aryans to Semites, Anglo-Saxons to Latins, Gauls to Germans, Germans to Slavs, and so on, according to the contradictory necessities that may be surmised. To judge by the frequency of the word and speculations associated with it, masses of people in France (and elsewhere) were racist. They could hardly be reproached for it. The present-day rejection of racism and the very word 'race' is based on the horrific historic experience of Hitler, a racism in action, as well as on a century of scientific progress which has complicated the notion of race almost to vanishing point. But round about 1890 that stage had not yet been reached, and anyone with some education and some intellectual pretensions would talk about race. Yet for the great mass of the French, the perceptible and scientifically justified sense of belonging to the community, the supreme personification of collectivity, was the nation, the *Patrie*, France.

How did the idea of nation tie in with race? Most frequently, in confusion. To which race would the French belong, to the white race, the Latin race or a French race? And, if one existed, how was the French race to be defined? Was it the Celtic race, the 'old Gallic heart' which was its source

[8] A philosopher and literary critic. Rationalist and agnostic, the author of one of the most vigorous attempts at determinism in social sciences. The polemical range of his work before 1870 was chiefly directed against the Church system; after 1871, it would be mainly against that of the Revolution. Born in 1828, died in 1893.

and definition (and in that case, would Frenchmen from the Auvergne or from Brittany be more French than those from Alsace or the Midi)? Or should one imagine a recent French race, whose merit would lie in having been born of successive mergings and influxes? There were many of these vague ideas competing, but they were all current.

What was certain, apart from these variants, was that conservatives seeking simultaneously supreme and natural points of reference were now tending to latch on to France, French race, French nation or French spirit, whatever the precise expression might be. It was at this point that 'nationalism' could rightly be used, stressing by the '-ism' that the fact of nationhood had passed from the status of being acknowledged to that of being valued.

It has been said often enough that French patriotism already existed, with a warmth of which we have no conception today. But the republicans, or the left, justified love of France by linking it with humanist values and great principles, and it was those great principles (of the Enlightenment's morality) that were the real summit of their scale of values: which left open – at least in theory – the possibility of criticizing France should it ever stray from the true path.

On the traditional conservative, that is, Christian, side the situation was at heart rather similar. France was venerable, either because God made it a duty for the faithful believer to love his homeland, or because the 'Church's eldest daughter', despite recent painful misadventures, loyally served the divine plan for the world. Again there was something (or Someone) rising above the *Patrie*.

On the other hand, what appeared with nationalism *sensu stricto* – that is (if our analyses are accepted), with a secularized right wing – was the elevation of the entity, France, to the absolute peak of the scale of values. The supreme value because it was the highest manifestation of the principle of reality, because it was the greatest of the natural authorities that must be recognized, even above the law and every universal value. Although the French nationalist of that time had no liking for Britain (as we shall soon see), he willingly adopted as his own the cynical and laconic saying of his counterpart across the Channel: 'My country, right or wrong'. Of course, that nationalistic current, with its singularity and specific forms of expression, also exercised a certain power of attraction and contamination over pre-existing versions of patriotism.

Many Catholic conservatives and a number of republicans in that era pushed their patriotism until it verged on that national absolutism. But it was the latter that came to the fore at the time, imparting the dominant tone on the right and influencing part of the left.

Placing the *Patrie* at the highest point of reference had many consequences. In external politics, could it lead to policies of assertion and greatness?

Certainly, but it was not original in that, for the left and the clericals desired national grandeur as much as the next man. In internal politics also, nationalism aimed at strength through unity. Nationalism regarded as the enemy anything which carried the risk of breaking up the homeland, changing its nature or some day siding with foreigners against it. One could thus almost define nationalism less by its hostility to foreign nations – since that hostility was commonplace and shared by many – than by its hostility to the enemy within, the antinational, the international, the supranational.

And it was precisely during the 1890s that the enemy within arose in the form of the Jew, or rather the myth about the Jew. This is the period in the history of the Third Republic when anti-Semitism increased sharply, to emerge as one of the principal currents of ideas or feelings then circulating: it was reinforced by the existence of a specialist daily newspaper, *La Libre Parole* (Free Speech), and the considerable success of Édouard Drumont's book *La France juive* (Jewish France) (1886).

Of course, anti-Semitism went back a long way, but its resurgence in France in the last quarter of the nineteenth century is a historical fact with its own more immediate causes. They were complex, so let us try to marshal them.

At the end of the eighteenth century, Jewish communities in France were virtually confined to three small regions: part of Alsace, the Comtat Venaissin (which was papal, moreover) and the Bordeaux–Bayonne line. Emancipated by the Revolution, French citizens, they integrated and spread through the whole of France in the middle of the nineteenth century; the success, both in coming up in the world and being assimilated, of Adolphe Crémieux, Rachel, Michel and Calmann Lévy, Offenbach and the Pereire brothers, aroused sympathetic admiration rather than animosity. Only the Rothschilds were poorly regarded, but they were really very rich indeed and, above all perhaps, too European, since every state in western Europe possessed a branch of the family. However, it would be incorrect to speak of massive anti-Semitism prior to 1870. Even the Fourierist Toussenel's book (*Les Juifs rois de l'époque* – The Jews, Kings of the Era, 1845), the title of which is always quoted and never the content, criticized Protestant cosmopolitanism, Britain and Geneva far more insistently than Judaism.

Two new facts after 1870 explain this revival in anti-Semitism, giving the impression of a new and obtrusive Jewish presence.

Firstly, as patriots choosing France, many Alsatian Jews came to settle in the 'interior', at Belfort, Nancy and chiefly Paris. Then, fleeing the pogroms of tsarist Russia, many Jews from the East came to France, as others in the same era went to Great Britain or the United States. The Jewish community thus passed from the status of a minuscule minority undergoing rapid integration to that of a community which was rather more substantial and consequently more able to preserve a distinct cultural and religious identity.

The Jews would evoke several kinds of hostility in French society, and perhaps the new anti-Semitism would draw its strength only from the convergence of disparate hostilities. There was religious hostility: Catholics were brought up to hate the 'deicidal people' – but it should not be forgotten that Catholics of that time also hated Protestants. There was also xcnophobia: the Jews were seen as different, and some as of foreign origin – but it should not be overlooked that the French worker also hated the immigrant worker, Belgian in the north, Italian in the south. The difficulty was that Protestants, hated as heretics, were at least French (although they were freely accused of having too much fondness for Switzerland and Britain), and that Italians, attacked as foreigners, were at least Catholic. By contrast, the immigrant Jew, for his part, had already totted up two handicaps. He finally had to endure a third anti-Semitism of social origin ('the socialism of imbeciles', said Auguste Bebel). As the moneylenders and shady dealers in rural Alsace were often Jewish, and the great Jewish bank (Rothschild) had been the rival of the Catholic bank, *l'Union générale*, the victim of a notorious crash in 1882, there came into being the association of the Jew with the idea of a wealthy man with a flair for trade and banking, and getting rich at the expense of Christian circles. One could even speak in this connection of a anti-Semitism of semantic origin which, from the mid nineteenth centry, had built identity into the language: Jew equals capitalist, as Negro equals slave, Greek equals gambler, swindler, and there were other such metaphors, for this language had its own laws and effects, sometimes disastrous.

Around 1830 everyone knew, in theory, that many Negroes were not slaves (Africa) and that slaves could also be white (Antiquity). But as current events drew attention, with the slave trade and abolitionism, to those in the Americas who were both slaves *and* Negroes, the verbal identification Negro–slave had grown, (the poor writer, Parisian and white, forced to write the novel that will never bear his name, the ghost writer, began to be known as a 'Negro', and still is today).

In the same way and at the same time, let us note, although everyone knew in theory that many Jews were not bankers and many bankers not Jews, the rise of the Rothschilds and various others drew attention chiefly to those rare families who were both Jews *and* bankers. Consequently the word 'Jew', like 'Negro', took on its figurative sense. It is only too obvious that this semantic episode proved disastrous by its convergence with the other components of budding contemporary anti-Semitism.

Therefore, anti-Semitism was present, muddled, complex but none the less strong, for public success does not necessarily require rational thinking! But from the moment when that complex anti-Semitism turned the Jew into an entity, a being, it is easy to see by what logic nationalism took hold of it and gave it a central place in its system.

Nationalism had need of a bogeyman: the universal, always suspected of being able to damage the national. The Jews lent themselves well to that spectral role. On the one hand, defined by belonging to a religion whose faithful were scattered in various states and nations, they formed a supranational, transfrontier community. On the other, those among them who entered intellectual professions naturally embraced the ideas of the humanist and universalist left (which they found more attractive than those of conservatism, with their Catholic structuring), and sometimes brought to them an ardour more or less consciously inspired by the prophetism of their original religious culture. The meeting of those two features (possible cosmopolitan links, the leaning towards rationalist ethics) gave clear evidence, to anyone who needed it, of the idea that the Jew carried within him the virus of the universal, the natural antagonist of the national.

With hindsight, the conjunction of budding nationalism with this complex and renewed anti-Semitism is fairly easy to explain. It was decisive for French national history, as it led to the Dreyfus Affair.

There would never have been any 'affair', in fact, if Dreyfus had not been designated as suspect: (1) through the contingent circumstance of the similarity between his handwriting and that of the traitor; and (2) because he was a Jew, which, in the eyes of nationalism, meant that he must be guilty.

It will be noted, in passing, that a number of contradictions were implicit in this logic. For the nationalism of 1895 still held that Alsace was French and that Germany had been wrong to take possession of it. Alsatians (like Dreyfus) who had accepted leaving Alsace in order to stay French should have been regarded, for that alone, with respectful affection. Not a bit of it, for their Judaism had removed the benefit of their patriotism! That contradiction between anti-Germanism and anti-Semitism does not, however, seem to have done any disservice to the nationalists, since prejudices are seldom very bothered about reason. And so a formidable anti-establishment force came into being on the extreme right of the political spectrum.

It by no means eclipsed the threat of revolution, in the more usual sense of the word this time, which came from an extreme left with popular and socialist tendencies.

Since the Congress of Marseille in 1879, a workers' party claiming socialism had been in existence, but its unity had been short-lived, for ten years later there were up to four rival parties, each claiming to be socialist, and all four very small indeed. The workers' protest movement expressed itself in strikes that did not last, while the general feeling of malaise, social criticism and unsatisfied humanitarian demands resulted in radicals, and after 1887 sometimes Boulangists as well, being returned to parliament.

It was only after the wane of Boulangism, and the start of the radicals' slide towards the centre in the name of 'republican integration', that socialism found its place on the political chessboard. That element in the electoral realignment was given a further impetus in 1889. With the centenary of the French Revolution, the Workers' Congress which customarily accompanied the Universal Exhibitions had obviously been held in Paris. There had even been two, one gathering moderate parties and movements around the British trades unions, the other attracting the more progressive around the German social democrats. After many ups and downs, two great things had emerged: the reconstitution of a workers' Internationale (the second, 1889–1914), and the setting up of an international day of action, each 1 May, in order to achieve a restriction to an eight-hour working day everywhere. It was one of those early 'first of May' days (at that time considered scandalous, spoken of in terms of political strikes and revolt – a million miles from our present-day Labour Day celebrations) that we saw plunged into grief at Fourmies.

Socialism was now beginning to carry some weight numerically and to form a substantial force. It achieved the election of workers' councils in some very industrialized small towns (the first at Commentry, Allier) and even, occasioning some surprise, in a few big towns which would not always hold out, for example, Toulon, Marseille. It obtained some dazzling members, for example Jean Jaurès, who would never be out of the limelight.

Born in Castres (Tarn) in 1859, Jean Jaurès was the first outstanding socialist to owe nothing to working-class origins, or to the Paris Commune. He came from an average provincial middle-class family, with a few pieces of land and a taste for public service. Family tradition had a naval penchant. An Admiral Jaurès had been one of the naval officers switched to land combat who had taken part in the National Defence under Gambetta, well known in his day. In contrast, his cousin, Jean's father, had had to fall back on farming. That did not make the future popular orator a peasant's son; rather, the son of an impoverished country bourgeois. At all events, quite naturally, he was sent to college. He was able to forge further ahead thanks to a bursary, a reward for his outstanding intellectual gifts, which had been noticed early on (by a general inspector making his rounds). So there he was, first a *khâgneux* (arts student preparing his entrance exam for the *École normale supérieure*), then a *normalien* (student at the *École*) in the rue d'Ulm.

His younger brother, as was right and proper, would become an admiral. At the *École* from 1878 to 1881, Jean Jaurès, a fellow student of Henri Bergson, gained his *agrégation* in philosophy. He was a classical humanist, with a profound knowledge of ancient languages and retaining everything that mattered in literature within a prodigious memory; gifted, moreover, with a nimble, assimilative intelligence which would play a virtuoso part in metaphysical debates as well as in analyses of day-to-day politics. He was a good, affectionate, unselfish man, entirely devoted to great ideas and great causes; easily distracted, paying little heed to eventualities. His sartorial slovenliness soon became notorious, regrettably combined with the swiftly thickened outlines of the heavy eater. But the fascination of his wit and eloquence and, later, of his social standing, always let those superficial impressions be easily overlooked.

Meanwhile he married, early and conventionally, a young woman from the Midi, whom he did not try to convert into a militant. In fairly bourgeois fashion, he alone would throw himself into his profession and public life, leaving his wife to her home and her religion.

Public life in the 1880s, for a young *normalien* naturally meant a teaching post in a provincial *lycée*, and enthusiasm for the dawning Republic. The young schoolmaster at the *lycée* in Albi was soon noticed – the regime did not as yet have many notables installed. In 1885 Jean Jaurès quite naturally found himself on the republican – simply republican – list of the Tarn *département*, and was elected deputy thanks to the majority list ballot. He thus sat in the Palais-Bourbon from 1885 to 1889, in the most moderate section of the republican majority, nearer to Jules Ferry than to Clemenceau.

In the 1889 elections, when the single name ballot had been re-established, he had to choose a constituency, and was defeated. So he returned to teaching and involvement in local politics. It was as a member of the municipal council of Toulouse, which had radical leanings, that he discovered more precisely the extent of the social problems which the Republic 'pure and simple' and its very timid legislation had left unresolved. The struggles for public freedoms and progress in education – his sole passion up to that point – would be complemented by a belief in social interventionist policies. It was then, around 1890, that Jaurès crossed the threshold to the collectivist doctrine, a step to which Clemenceau would never reconcile himself.

Then, in 1892, an affair occurred which created a precedent. The mining commune of Carmaux (Tarn) was one of those who had elected a socialist town council composed entirely of workers, and one among them, a miner, was chosen as mayor. Now, the Marquis de Solages, the mine owner, refused the worker the right to absent himself in order to exercise his mandate. To protest against that refusal and defend the right of an elected worker to carry out the duties for which he was elected, the miners launched a strike which had national repercussions and from which they emerged victorious.

The episode is exemplary for its ambivalence: the struggle of the Carmaux miners stemmed from both the class struggle, since it defended a worker bullied by his employer, and the struggle for the Republic, since it defended the right of universal suffrage to be freely exercised in a local democracy. Though a little exceptional, almost too much of an example, the matter deserves to be quoted because that intimate union of republican and socialist combat was to remain at the core of Jaurès's politics. Solages, defeated, quit his seat, and it was none other than Jaurès who stood at the by-election in January 1893 and entered the Chamber as the elected representative of the Carmaux miners, and a declared socialist.

In the following August he was re-elected. Those legislative elections of 1893 witnessed the entry to the Chamber of Deputies[9] of about forty socialist members, who formed a single group at the extreme left, whether they were already organized socialists (Guesdists, Allemanists, Broussists

---

[9] Which then numbered 590 seats.

or Blanquists) or independent socialists, who had sometimes come from the radical ranks (like Alexandre Millerand).

The socialism making itself heard in parliament was very impassioned, full of vigour. The feeling that there was a universal and rapid upsurge of organized workers' forces (in Germany, Great Britain, Russia, the United States, Italy, Belgium) filled it with excitement; economic stagnation, which had emerged from the long depression dating from before 1880, seemed to presage the final crisis of capitalism; and then the breaking up and unpopularity of the regime (remember Panama) further opened up the possibility of change.

In short, the socialists fought hard; they occupied the front rank in the press and speeches campaign which forced, in the name of democracy, the resignation of Casimir-Perier. New municipal successes in 1896 gave them the chance, during a common celebration banquet at Saint-Mandé, to make resounding affirmations of their programme. These were moderate, in one sense, since in the declaration that was adopted they affirmed their attachment to the homeland, and their resolve to attain government only through the vote, which they then imagined to be progressing indefinitely towards the extreme left. But they were daring in their future perspectives, since they incorporated in their definition of socialism the concept of collective ownership, whereas many up till then had continued to profess a 'socialism' in the style of 1848 – reforming, humanitarian, social but respectful of the liberal framework.

That euphoric prospect, however, had not sufficed to channel all social anger. For the latter was not without cause. Salaries were low and poorly defended by the trades unions which, though certainly legal, were sometimes persecuted locally. There was an economic depression which, in the absence of any palliatives worthy of note, abandoned the unemployed to bourgeois charity, municipal soup kitchens or dire straits. Combined with that austerity, the siphoning of Panama wealth towards the 'influence pedlars' in the Palais-Bourbon, or the crack of the rifle-shots at Fourmies, and other similar dramas, found no difficulty in arousing an indignation that cried out for immediate vengeance.

Anarchy did not wait! From 1892 to 1894 there was a wave of bomb attacks, mainly in Paris, at first striking at the homes of repressive magistrates or police officers then, gradually, at symbolic targets: the semicircle in the Palais-Bourbon, or the dining room of a classy café-restaurant. The perpetrators were solitary fanatics, but fed on the doctrine of flourishing theorists. Since society is so unfair, they said, the law and institutions which uphold it are detestable and deserve nothing but hatred and, if possible, attack. Thieves and murderers, who take part in this assault on society, are fighting the good fight. Moreover, there were gangsters, like Ravachol, ready to assume this role and place their criminal career under the label of anarchy. Horrified public opinion allowed an inexorable repression to be put into effect. Bomb-throwers brought to court were sentenced to death and guillotined. And it was for having refused to make use of his power of reprieve on behalf of Émile Henry that Sadi Carnot was assassinated by the Italian anarchist Caserio who, in his turn . . . Charles Dupuy's government voted special repressive laws in 1894 which attempted to implicate socialist propaganda in responsibility for anarchist violence. The socialists then protested with all their might.

At last, brought to heel, the anarchist upsurge died down. Part of the educated and, as is said, 'aware' workers, whom anarchy had seduced for a time, renounced bombs but at least retained from the episode the idea that bourgeois society and its state were hateful and that there was nothing to be expected from them. Emancipatory progress would consist in turning one's back on them and building the future state around organized, co-operative and some day self-sufficient labour. The notion, hallowed by history, of 'anarcho-syndicalism' is a good expression of the idea that the themes of anarchy, with the exception of violence, were at that time shifted over to the trades unions.

Since the law of 1884 which had authorized them, a good number of unions had been formed, sometimes grouped in federations of types of employment, or federations of industries. Shortly before 1890, in Paris and several other large industrial towns and cities with a radical council, unions of differing occupations had grouped themselves into trades union centres set up for them. In that way it was possible to establish dialogues about solidarity and the battle to be waged, and organize common services (employment agencies, evening classes); thus also in principle it was possible to erect community buildings for the people, in contrast to the palaces and institutions of the bourgeoisie, in anticipation of their becoming the first edifices of the next state. All that was sketched out in 1894, with the founding of the Confédération générale du Travail (CGT, General Labour Confederation), the very first group of affiliated trades unions.

The beginning of the trades union history is just as complicated as that of the history of electoral, municipal and parliamentary socialism. Relations between the trades themselves, those of the trades federations with the trades union centres (federated in their turn) did not develop without conflict. Furthermore, by no means all trades union workers were anarchists; certain of them were quite simply socialists and would therefore have preferred to see co-ordination rather than potential rivalry between parties and unions. Thus, in the history of what is called 'the workers' movement' (parties claiming socialism, trades unions, co-operatives, mutual aid societies), and from its very origins, division was a constantly recurring theme. In ideological terms, how can that celebrated working-class division be characterized?

The traditional opposition between reformists and revolutionaries does not match up with the distinction between socialism and trades unionism, for although the democratic socialism defined at Saint-Mandé can pass for reformist, certain groups, such as the Guesdists, who accepted the vote if only for what it allowed in the way of propaganda, unrest and pedagogy, wanted to keep the prospect of revolution open. On the other hand, the anarcho-syndicalists, whose doctrine assumed a revolutionary radicalism, could hold a non-catastrophic view of the extinction of the state.

Bearing in mind the conditions peculiar to France in that period, one may doubtless more rightly consider that the clearest distinction has to do with what was understood by Republic. The republican part of the workers' movement, personified by a man like Jaurès, viewed the Republic as a minimum framework that was useful, even essential, to all future progress and therefore worth defending. If it was (all too obviously) bourgeois, that was because it was disloyal to its principles; its shortcomings could thus be combated in the name of those very principles by appealing to both the heart and the reason of genuine bourgeois republicans. The revolutionary sections of the workers' movement, on the other hand, considered any organized political system to be bad. Bad, like all bourgeois regimes, the Republic was harmful because of the illusions it had sown, and so must first be denounced, then rejected, in favour of a totally new working-class power.

In short, for the first, the bourgeois deviation of the existing Republic was accidental and reversible; for the second, it was disastrous. From that followed two strategies, which events would soon reveal. Two sets of feelings, as well. Once again, that point of vocabulary: it was on Jaurès's side, the republican side, that men would think of themselves as being on the left, and on the revolutionary side, quite logically, that they would want to challenge the right–left system, which was too tied up with the existing order, to replace it with an alternative, or else a division expressed in purely social terms. Of course, republican socialism remained more readily patriotic, whereas revolutionary socialism was more disposed to criticize the worth of Nation.

It was difficult to make that criticism, however, because the nation was to such a great extent the object of almost unanimous reverence! National feeling at that time was truly at the pinnacle of its pervasive strength. Republican patriotism, the traditional patriotism of the Christian conservatives and pure nationalism harked back to different philosophical beginnings but resulted in similar conclusions and common outcomes: France must be loved and served. All schools taught that sentiment to children, all official speeches and almost all publications repeated it to adults.

One of the principal authors and at the same time one of the main beneficiaries of that education was the army. The fact that the most stable and most visible element of the national festival on 14 July was a military parade, 'the review', is enough to show the eminent position it occupied in the nation.

In general politics, preparation for or the likelihood of war, on the Rhine or in the tropics, was ever present. And the people as a whole were associated with this through the dual channel of patriotic education and military service, which was gradually extended to include all male youths. The military institution thus became a very major national affair. Conscripts formed the troops of the line, from which a very specific selection process picked noncommissioned and junior officers; many of the latter, who were signed on again at the end of the legal term of duty, made it their career. Rarely did that early 'internal promotion' (more often termed 'quitting the ranks') lead to the *épaulette* (becoming an officer). Usually, officers came from a school which they entered by a competitive examination at least on a par with the *baccalauréat*, the Polytechnique or Saint-Cyr. Which is as much as to say that if the troops were by definition 'of the people', the officers were bourgeois. 'Bourgeois', however, towards the end of the nineteenth century described a somewhat blurred category, comprising many levels.

A good, hardworking student from the middle classes or the upper strata of 'the people' could certainly become an officer, just as he could become a minor civil servant. It was nevertheless fairly rare because of a contradiction that the rest of public office did not experience: remuneration was mediocre, while custom demanded a pretty extravagant lifestyle, especially after reaching the higher echelons (major, colonel and, even more so, general). The officer with only his pay to live on was at a disadvantage; normally an officer had some private means into which he could dig in order to cut a worthy figure, to shine in the festivities of the garrison town, to be seen in the salons and in company with the bigwigs.

That requirement was so important that it became a real constraint upon marriage. An officer had to marry a girl with an adequate dowry; he had to make a wealthy marriage, to consolidate his middle-classness, and not a poor marriage, which would lower his status.

This state of affairs obviously put the brake on the democratization of the body of officers; instead, it favoured the retention in its bosom of certain social strata and, consequently, of rather aristocratic traditions and behaviour. Without going back as far as the historic liaison between the armed services and the nobility, which the Revolution had certainly begun to break up – also without evoking the affinities which still exist between military life and the life of the great country landowner, sport, hunting, riding – it must be remembered that, since about the middle of the century, many royalist noble families who were resolutely hostile to the more or less progressive policies of the Orleans, the Bonapartes and the Republic, could find only one service tolerable – to serve the nation by means of arms.

Someone who would have scrupled about serving the modern state as a magistrate or prefect found it perfectly natural to command a regiment. Patriotism was the only element in modernity the counter-revolutionary would accept; or, to put it another way, patriotism was a value common to the two great opposing political philosophies.

In the army which the Republic inherited from earlier regimes, it is thus understandable that the aristocracy (socially) and royalism (politically) were over-represented.

This was only a limited drawback, in that the traditional military spirit, centred on the cult of 'the flag', combined with a scornful indifference with regard to 'politics', facilitated the acceptance of the Republic itself by the vast majority of officers.

The army of the 1880s thus comprised a minority of declared republicans, but the conservatism of the rest was contained or masked by the claim to be apolitical and by virtue of loyalty to the authority of the state. For the state was the *Patrie*'s means of existence. As for loyalty, its most obvious manifestation was discipline, 'the chief strength of armies', as we know. It would take fairly exceptional moments of crisis for officers to give vent to the contradiction between orders received and personal convictions; it happened sporadically, in the matter of article VII, as later in that of the inventories.

Certainly, opportunist governments watched the situation closely and did not forget to push republican officers to the fore, but, as regards the rest, placed far more reliance on the support to be expected of them in the name of a common awareness of the national interest. The links forged between Gambetta and General de Galliffet are a good example in this respect.

The army was still handled tactfully in that it remained the only institution which to some extent escaped political authority; in fact, in almost all the ministerial arrangements of that time, the portfolio of War was entrusted to a general and not a parliamentarian. When Senator Freycinet held the title (November 1898 to May 1899), it could almost be said that the exception proved the rule, so greatly was his renown associated with his role as organizer of the National Defence with Gambetta at Tours.

Apart from the army, other forms of education were necessary, typical of the end of the century and aiming at the same target. In social life, for a start, there was a profusion of those societies catering for the lesiure pursuits of young males. These did not yet include today's competitive sport (cycling, football), which would enjoy a boom a little later. The dominant societies in the 1890s were devoted to gymnastics, or shooting (sometimes gymnastics *and* shooting), choral singing or town bands. There were republican ones, sometimes linked with state education, and there were Catholic ones. But many, in both camps – by their regulations, their declared motives, their name, their repertoire – affirmed a wish for civic and nationalist education and even, for the first group, unpaid military training.

Furthermore, town councils, learned societies and all kinds of *ad hoc* committees accompanied the movement, enriching the town – sometimes village – scene with commemorative monuments raised by subscription, inaugurated with much pomp, and dedicated to the *Patrie*. Some were the statues of great men, others marked the site of a battle, or were devoted to the war dead of 1870–1. It was then that the 'monuments to the fallen', a network of which would cover France after 1918, were, if not invented, at least very widely known. It was characteristic of the spirit of the times that when these monuments to the dead of a recent war, 1870–1, were under way, France began the systematic erection of stone commemorations of more ancient battles which had not yet received that honour. In Saint-Quentin (Aisne), for instance, the monument celebrating the Defence of 1871 preceded one recalling the battle of 1557. Patriotic France 'turned to its past' for the first time on a large scale and conspicuously. All this was carried to the height of rapture by the Franco-Russian alliance. France was no longer in isolation. If a war of revenge should occur, the French would be alone no more, as they had been in 1870. The enthusiasm was fantastic. How did this come about?

Since 1891 Bismarck had maintained German hegemony on the basis of the European status quo (including the Treaty of Frankfurt) and the calming of regional conflicts, thanks to the good *entente* of the three emperors (Wilhelm of Germany, Alexander II then Alexander III of Russia, Franz-Josef of Austria-Hungary), thanks to the *Triplice* (in which Italy was linked with Germany and Austria because of its important dispute with France), and lastly thanks to a tacit complicity with Great Britain.

Certainly, the Russians found it hard to put up with a system in which the immobility desired by Bismarck thwarted their wishes to expand in the Balkans, an expansion that could take place only at the expense of the Ottomans, or of Austrian ambitions. But Bismarck was wily enough to contain his allies.

After the death of Wilhelm I and the very short reign of Frederick III (April–June 1888), Bismarck stayed on as Chancellor under the young Wilhelm II who, however, in a desire to stand on his own feet, ended by quarrelling with his old mentor.

On 20 March 1890, bringing the epoch to a close, Bismarck's resignation gave a freer hand and greater opportunities to diplomacy, and that unblocking of the system would profit the two great powers that had been kept in check, France and Russia. Powers which were geographically distant, obviously, but which were separated by no conflict (provided Poland was not mentioned too loudly, of course).

Combined with this purely geopolitical reason for *rapprochement* was at least one other, more secret. Russian governments, eager to modernize their country, were great borrowers of capital. At first in Berlin. Then, when they wanted to diversify their connections, Paris was seen to be an advantageous place. Since 1888 Russian borrowing had gone down well with the French public, which was stimulated by a press sometimes itself having interests in the enterprise. From that time, common interests were woven, and this must be borne in mind. Since 1890 secret discussions had been taking place. In July 1891 Admiral Gervais took a strong French squadron to Kronstadt, the great Russian war port in the bay of Saint Petersburg. The

Franco-Russian *entente* was thus made public. The obvious geopolitical need for it was of course challenged by ideological differences. 'The Republic', so touchy at home about liberty and democracy, overlooked its prejudices to visit the most blatant example of European autocracy. Optimists, it is true, could retort that the spectacle of the descendant of Catherine II, with his entire entourage of grand dukes and officers, standing to attention to listen to the 'Marseillaise', might well be taken for a sort of revenge of the spirit of the Revolution. But dominant French opinion was less subtle: it thought nation before ideology. That became evident when, starting on 13 October 1893, Admiral Avellane's Russian squadron sailed into Toulon's harbour to return the courtesy visit.

The official welcoming ceremony was grandiose. No expense spared in salvos of cannon fire, parades, flowers, flags. No expense spared as regards culture: Jean Aicard, from Toulon but already nationally famous, read an ode to Russia. No expense spared technologically: from the telephone station of the battleship *Emperor Nicholas I*, an officer was able to describe the unfolding splendours directly by wire to the Russian Embassy. Above all, the town reinforced the official welcome by its own enthusiasm. The municipal authorities, shopkeepers, a whole section of the people, in short, accustomed to making a living from the French fleet, its pomp and its activities, regarded the welcome given to the Russian squadron as a more solemn resumption of the dazzling naval reviews of 14 July. Thus one event followed another – the great ball for 5,000 guests in the arsenal, banquets on land and aboard the ships, evenings at the theatre, processions of floral floats.[10] Russian sailors who had been given shore leave were pampered, embraced, invited out, urged or accompanied into cafés, restaurants and other resorts which may be imagined.

This jubilation was then transferred to Paris, where Admiral Avellane and those of his crews not needed to guard the vessels went on a sightseeing trip. Though more diluted in the crowds and size of the capital, the welcome for the Tsar's sailors was no less striking. Various 'Franco-Russian' gastronomic specialities, as well as *la tournée des grands-ducs* (going on a spree or painting the town) remain in French culture and vocabulary as a legacy of that moment in time. Then they had to return to Toulon. President Sadi Carnot accompanied his guests, and they presided over a second wave of ceremonies, including the launching of the French battleship *Jaureguiberry*. When at last the Tsar's fleet made ready to sail, the Toulon crowds, massed on the port quayside, which had become the Kronstadt Quay,[11] sang the Russian national anthem. What foreign national anthem would a French crowd be able to sing today? The significance of the event may be judged from this detail.

Meanwhile, secret agreements were taking place, confirmed in an exchange of letters (1893–4) stipulating that the two powers would act in

[10] From Paul Gonnet in *L'Histoire de Toulon* (series), Privat.
[11] Changed to quai Stalingrad in 1945.

concert in any circumstance in which peace might be at risk, and that they would use their forces simultaneously should the *Triplice* attack either of them. The undertaking was therefore only defensive, but none the less considerable.

Politically it was not without contradiction. The Republic was being strengthened, but thanks to an alliance with a despot. The fleeting pleasure that might be experienced in seeing the Tsar stand to attention to hear the 'Marseillaise', which is after all a battle-cry against 'tyrants', was accompanied by the more enduring drawback of solidarity in baser and more concrete tasks. The French police would have to keep a close eye on Russian revolutionaries or foreign elements who had taken refuge in France.

The Republic's official diplomacy was therefore likely to be the object of criticism from the left, which was as yet only of feeble potential.

The Franco-Russian alliance, on the other hand, did not arouse as much anti-German feeling in France as might have been expected. At first doubtless ill-pleased, Germany had by no means felt itself ousted. The Russians knew how to keep their two 'irons in the fire'. Wilhelm II would be able to use means of pressure and seduction on the Tsars Alexander III and then Nicholas II; in short, it was a complex game. In 1895 there was even the outline of a sort of continental axis Petersburg–Berlin–Paris directed against the 'yellow peril' (China to be divided, Japan to be contained) and, potentially, against Great Britain which was then in 'splendid isolation'.

At this time, colonial expansion, which was galloping ahead (expansion in Africa, conquest of Madagascar), brought France into conflict with the British much more frequently than with any other power.

In 1898, in order to gain control over the Nile route, possession of the state of Fachoda became a stake in the game; it was a matter of determining who would establish a continuous trans-African link: the British cross-country route, north–south, from the Cape to Cairo; or the French, east–west, from Dakar to Djibouti. War was on the point of breaking out between Britain and France. France fell back, as is known, but the man who was defeated at Fachoda, Major Marchand, was hailed as a national hero in Paris. By contrast, on the Rhine (or rather, the Vosges) there was no longer a state of alert.

France in the 1890s realized then that, despite Rossbach, Leipzig, Waterloo and Sedan, despite Frederick II, Blücher and Bismarck, its principal 'hereditary enemy' was still Britain. The demigods proposed for the veneration of the French at that time – Joan of Arc and Napoleon – had they not been victims of 'perfidious Albion'?

The shepherdess from Lorraine had not yet been officially adopted by the Church, as either blessed or saint. But she had long been used by conservatives who were Catholic by allegiance or royalist by nostalgia to demonstrate that the Revolution, the Republic and the left did not enjoy a monopoly of French patriotism. We have now come to the era when this kind of pedagogy spread like wildfire. Staues of Joan of Arc dotted the country, rivalling statues of the Republic.

A little later,[12] when imperial Britain, entrenched in the Cape, waged war on the hitherto independent republics of Orange and Transvaal, patriotic and nationalistic France would simultaneously avenge Joan of Arc and Major Marchand by showing enthusiastic support for the cause of the Boers.

Several resigning or pensioned French officers even went to help them fight the British. One, Colonel de Villebois-Mareuil, met his death there. A hero going against the tide of history, his memory is today obscured by three-quarters of a century of *Entente Cordiale*, but his venture created a great stir at the time (1900–2).

This nationalist and military excitement naturally aroused some reaction. Antimilitarism, pacifism, anticolonialism, even antipatriotism, all with ancient themes long since formulated, had not disappeared, and the press was free to reproduce them. The heavy, gloomy, brutal, sometimes sordid nature of life in barracks, which all young men were now called upon to undergo, was depicted in *Sous-Offs* (Junior Officers) by Lucien Descaves with a potent bitterness. The stupidity of international hatreds, the ridiculous pomposity of official inaugurations, the derisory clamour of slippered old advocates of revenge, the deification of an unreal France, inspired Georges Darien, who had already written an anarchist novel, *Le Voleur* (The Thief), to pen a virulent pamphlet *La Belle France*. Rémy de Gourmont dared to write, in *Le Mercure de France* in 1891, that the Alsatians perhaps did not spend all their days 'weeping' under the 'jackboot' of the Teutons.

His reward was to be dismissed from his freelance post with the National Library, which would cause only a very minor scandal. For though all those criticisms could be published, they reached only a fringe readership. The antipatriotism, or antinationalism, of a few libertarian intellectuals had not yet (or only very slightly) begun to link up with the theoretical internationalism of the socialist movement, any more than it had with the workers' antimilitarism, fuelled by memories of the Commune or Fourmies. Those encounters would begin to take place through the Dreyfus Affair. Before that crucial episode, the great majority of the French in the 1890s were staunchly patriotic.

---

[12] Chronologically, I am slightly anticipating the next chapter.

3

The Radical Republic
1899–1906

Why, with the close of the century, should the 'opportunist Republic', with its inclination towards conservatism, have become 'radical', for such is the customary epithet given to that pre-war period? Was there something inevitable in its slide towards the left? Why, after the founding years, with their fighting spirit, would the conservative stabilization we have described not be continued? The turning point, which came in 1899, stemmed less from necessity than from a sequence of battles brought about by extraordinary events in which even chance played a part. It all began with the Dreyfus Affair, a singular drama from which a new Republic would emerge, as ardent as in the aftermath of Moral Order, warring with the Vatican, friendly with London and yet torn apart by class warfare which had also started up once more. The Republic of Waldeck-Rousseau and Combes and, after them, of Clemenceau, Caillaux and Briand, would no longer bear much resemblance to that of Méline.

The Dreyfus Affair must therefore be mentioned first. In principle it was simple, even though its detail and circumstances were striking in their complexity,[1] but the most important point is to understand by what logic a legal conflict could produce a veritable redistribution of political forces.

Captain Alfred Dreyfus, of a Jewish Alsatian family, a *polytechnicien* assigned to the army general staff, had been sentenced to prison in December 1894 by a court martial for having delivered confidential documents into the hands of a potential enemy – Germany. Wrongly, as we know. But a comparison of handwriting samples and the anti-Semitic presumption which turned a Jew into a likely traitor had gone against him. Hostile a priori, the military hierarchy had furthermore been far from scrupulous, since the first trial had included a procedural flaw: a piece of evidence, sent by the Ministry of War to the military judges, had been concealed from the defence. The family protest which Mathieu, the victim's brother, took it upon himself to organize, relayed at first by a solitary journalist, Bernard

---

[1] See the Chronological Survey of the Dreyfus Affair.

Captain Dreyfus, the innocent accused. (Photo: Agence d'Information photographique Harlinge)

Lazare, met very little reaction at the outset. One bridge was crossed when, after more than a year, through an ordinary changeover, Lieutenant-Colonel Picquart became head of the Intelligence Branch and, intrigued, reopened the file. Picquart was an Alsatian, but not Jewish. We will meet another

(Left) Lieutenant-Colonal Picquart – 'I shall not carry such a secret to the tomb.'
(Right) Émile Zola – 'Truth is on the march, nothing shall stop it!' (From a
leaflet published by Dreyfus's defenders, Paris, Bibliothèque historique de la ville
de Paris)

Alsatian very shortly. Although, at the start of this affair, there was something resembling a group, a circle, a network of influence, it was not a
Jewish network – despite the fact that B. Lazare was Jewish – but far more
an Alsatian network, and not denominational. Re-examined by Picquart,
the documents revealed another possible and much more likely culprit:
Major Esterhazy, whose handwriting also resembled that on the *bordereau*
(a covering itemized list) of the documents that had been handed over, and
who, what is more, had suspect motives – an indifferent morality, need for
money – which Dreyfus, an honest and fairly well-to-do man, did not
possess.

Picquart alerted the press (*Le Matin* of 10 November 1896) as well as his
superiors, but the latter, unwilling to reopen the trial, sent this embarrassment away from Paris by posting him to a command in Tunisia (6 January
1897). Nevertheless, Picquart had managed to alert another Alsatian, Auguste Scheurer-Kestner, the vice-president of the Senate, a very bourgeois,
moderate republican, related by marriage to Jules Ferry, and non-Jewish.
He would be the first politician to intervene in the affair. Broadly speaking,
he belonged to the government camp, then presided over by Méline. None
the less, after much consideration, he raised the question in the Chamber
in November 1897. Méline, adopting the stance of the military hierarchy,
rejected all opposition and declared: 'there *is* no Dreyfus Affair.' In reality,
it was just beginning.

From then on, the press could no longer ignore it. The name 'revisionists', before becoming 'Dreyfusists' or 'Dreyfusards', began to be applied to

those who, pleading the cause of justice, wanted the case reviewed because it had been badly conducted, was iniquitous or simply dubious. Their line of argument implied that justice, the scale of values recognized as sound by universal morality, in short, morality itself, had something to do with politics – which is without doubt the most enduring and basic of definitions of the left. If they were told – and they would be! – that this commotion was compromising France, they would reply – and they did – that France deserved to be loved precisely because (and inasmuch as) it proclaimed the law and set an example of the law.

On the opposite side, in the anti-revisionist, anti-Dreyfusard camp, that reasoning was refuted, either in the name of the nationalist conviction according to which the harmfulness and traitorous nature of Jews were self-evident, or by claiming the theory, less tainted with anti-Semitism but probably more widespread, that for its own security France needed to be above all doubt: if military justice and the army, that 'sacred ark' of the *Patrie*, were called into question, national cohesion in the face of the enemy would be weakened. But what about justice? An inadmissible objection; it had no business here; there were just the *Patrie*, the state and, politically, reasons of state. Anti-revisionist argument was therefore, in its turn, an example of right-wing thinking, through these two related and interdependent aspects: to accept a non-universal – France – as the pinnacle of the hierarchy of values; and to affirm the special nature of politics and its rules of action instead of subjecting political action to the rules of general morality.

One realizes that nationalism – such a powerful current prior to the affair, and already presented as such – blossomed out to some extent when it provided the spokesmen and large numbers of supporters for the anti-Dreyfusard camp.

For instance, it was at this time that Maurice Barrès became its intellectual leader. Born in Charmes (Vosges) in 1862, into a comfortably-off family which allowed him, after classical studies at the Nancy *lycée*, to set himself up in Paris in 1882 in the world of the press, literature and the salons, there was nothing conservative about him at the start; he was neither royalist nor religious, nor even – no matter what might be said – a man from Lorraine scarred by the recent defeat. The philosopher of the Nancy *lycée*, Burdeau (who would figure as Bouteiller in his autobiographical novels), had turned him into an innovator and a republican, and his personal taste was first and foremost individualistic. It was the era of egotism, of the 'cult of self'. In his first work, *Sous l'oeil des barbares* (Under the Eye of the Barbarians) (1888), the barbarians in question were not the Prussians, but the others, society, the social circle, the fashionable world. It brings to mind the young Flaubert of the Bovary era. Boulangism caused Barrès to enter politics. In the disparate coalition supporting the General, he was among those with an extreme leftist interpretation of the movement, criticizing the existing Republic as the new form donned by the official world, oppressive and unjust, a world or regime to which the soldier must bring a disruption that would be both salutary and exhilarating. In the elections of September 1889, this young Parisian writer of twenty-seven won a deputy's seat at Nancy, and sat during the 1889–93 legislature, priding himself on both his Boulangism and his socialism. In 1893 he was defeated in the elections and, in his novels about national spirit and vigour (*Les Déracinés, l'Appel au soldat, Leurs Figures* (The Uprooted, Call to the Soldier, Their Appearances), he became the historian of its youth and first struggles. It was then that his criticism of official liberalism, from being mostly social, turned more profound and philosophical. Evil stemmed from an excess of the universal which isolates the human being as much from its protections as from its natural resources. The remedy lay in putting down firm deep roots, in other words, in a conservatism rediscovered and transformed into an educating force. The homeland replaced the leader as the point of reference or, as has been said, Lorraine took over from Boulanger in the role of intercessor: 'the cult of the Land and the Dead', tradition, the truth about things not chosen but imposed. Logically, Barrès rediscovered in the Dreyfusards – enamoured of justice – the Kantian universalist morality of the republican teacher of 1880 who had 'uprooted' the students in the Nancy *lycée*. Since Dreyfusism was part of the logic of the established Republic, they must both be combated at the same time. But because socialism, after all, was also a universalism, the Republic could truly be fought only from the right. So Barrès turned himself into a conservative, and was soon rubbing shoulders with Action française, showing friendly feelings towards royalty and, principally, the Church, inasmuch as they were the most obvious of the forces maintaining tradition and order. It was on that footing, or in that persona, that he re-entered the Chamber in 1906 as deputy of the capital, and was elected in the same year to the Académie française, thenceforth becoming the outstanding spokesman for nationalism by virtue of his literary prestige and his articles in *L'Écho de Paris*.

The 1906 election that saw the definitive return of Barrès to parliament witnessed, in contrast, the failure of Paul Déroulède who, it is true, had taken more risks in direct action.

But the two men bear comparison. Certainly, Déroulède was a Parisian; he was of the generation before Barrès since, born in 1846, he had been in the 1870 war as a volunteer. His career had at first been different, too: a barrister before 1870, he had stayed on as an officer in the army after 1871, and only a serious accident in 1874 had forced him to return to civilian life and devote himself to literature. Not the same literature, nor the same talent, as Barrès. Déroulède was merely an orator and, chiefly, a poet and songwriter, the man who wrote the 'Chants du soldat' (Soldier's Songs):

> The air is pure, the road is wide
> The bugle sounds the charge
> And the zouave goes along singing

But up yonder on the hill
In the towering forest
The savage Prussian awaits him.

However, the path taken by the two men was much the same. A bourgeois patriotic Parisian in 1870, Déroulède had been a Gambettist republican and, under the most official patronage, had founded the League of Patriots in 1882. He went over to Boulangism, was elected deputy in 1889 and from that time onward became one of the big names in the parliamentary opposition. His arguments on the subject of Panama, which were outstanding, were marked notably by a duel with Clemenceau. Non-candidate in 1893, candidate and elected in 1898, still a songwriter and popular orator, still an organizer (League of Patriots), he retained the character of a man of action in which role we shall meet him again soon.

Was the left, therefore, to oppose this anti-Dreyfusard right? At all events, it was not seen to be in any great haste to become Dreyfusard! That in fact forms the other lesson, perhaps the most important in this story: the logic of the left was the one which had the greatest difficulty in emerging.

Such a serious and extraordinary event as a judicial error, confirmed and covered up by a veritable conspiracy of prestigious dignitaries, was already in itself difficult to swallow. Moreover, at that time the patriotic element in the republican message was so strong that, despite the theoretical difference in their premises, the broad mass of patriots on the left were but a step away from nationalism. Finally, even if convinced that justice demanded opposition to France and its authorities, it required courage to follow those principles to the bitter end. Natural inclination, social inertia, timidity, kept most left-wing citizens in conformist positions to which the culture of the right drew its adherents by conviction.

These general reflections permit an understanding of why the Dreyfusard party was at first, and for a long while, a minority, an avant-garde, perhaps an elite, before it was joined by all those on the left among the people.

What was the sequence of events that caused that union to take place? The following account tells the whole story. After the public accusation of Esterhazy, a court martial summoned that officer to appear and acquitted him in triumph on 11 January 1898. Filled with indignation, on 13 January Émile Zola published in *L'Aurore*, a daily newspaper edited by Clemenceau, an 'Open Letter to M. Félix Faure, President of the Republic', under the heading 'J'accuse'. This well-argued exposure of the initial judicial error and the collusion which went into covering it up was taken as an attack on institutions. Loyalty to the Republic's institutions at that time rather acted against the Dreyfusards, whom Zola's thunderbolt isolated in the first instance, before glorifying them afterwards, and for history. Zola and *L'Aurore*

The engraver Felix Vallatton (1865–1925) from the canton of Vaud, who became French, widely mentioned the Dreyfus Affair in *Le Cri de Paris*, taking the Dreyfusard viewpoint. In this great battle of opinion, the press played a fundamental role; to the point where Vallotton gave the title 'The Paper Age' to this cartoon showing the proliferation of newspapers. (Cover of *Le Cri de Paris* for 23 January 1898)

were charged, and tried in the assize court for criminal libel, and Zola was sentenced to the maximum penalty: one year in gaol. The trial took place 7–23 February in an atmosphere of bias in the court, and very hostile unrest in the streets.

In fact, people in the streets became mixed up in it. Nationalist troops demonstrated, booed Zola, the Dreyfusards and Jews in general. This climate, of the 'revolutionary right', began to provoke a defensive reaction on the left. On 20 February the League of the Rights of Man was founded, with many 'intellectuals' in its ranks. But what did that mean? It is known that at that period the term 'intellectuals' became popular as a way of designating – with ambiguities which no analysis would manage to dispel, but which current usage still accommodates – simultaneously a social stratum, a cultured elite and a certain public role. Its members included men of letters, artists and the more noteworthy members of liberal professions and the teaching field. They were thus well known, or should be (and would like to be), since they wrote and published, produced and performed. Many shared the belief that the portion of fame their calling brought them (savant, novelist, actor, etc.) should be placed at the service of the conviction – ethical, political or patriotic – that needed to be inculcated in the passive reading public.

The affair would show that, as in every epoch of French history, there were intellectuals on the right, others on the left and yet others who took no positive side – today we would call them 'uncommitted'. But the revelation of other significant nuances also dates back to the affair, such as the well-known fact that the right-wing intellectual did not willingly describe himself as an 'intellectual' because he did not attach a supreme value to that authority, which was only to be expected, since his overall conception of the state and society usually embraced, by contrast, a respect for institutional hierarchies, Church, army, government or nation. On the other hand, on the left, from which the first manifesto of the intellectuals had sprung, in support of Zola, worth was attributed to that role and title, to the point where sometimes the expression 'left-wing intellectuals' assumed the air of a pleonasm. In fact, as soon as it was thought – and the left did think so – that political affairs were to be judged by the same values as those of general morality, how could those men who prided themselves on being experts on Truth, Beauty and Good fail to teach the state a lesson when it strayed from the supreme values? This was the point taken up by a category of intellectuals whose appearance characterized the period of the Dreyfus Affair – the academics – upon their emergence from their ivory towers. A military clique had lied and committed a forgery. If falsification was a moral failing, universally recognized as such, without exemption for the state, the military clique had been culpable, and erudite historians and philologists who were expert at detecting forgeries, together with more generally learned men who were pledged to seek the truth, must contribute their expertise to a debate in which Truth was at stake.

They therefore did so, with conflicting pronouncements; the Collège de France, the Hautes Études, the Sorbonne, emerged from the shadows, and the *École normale* in the rue d'Ulm seethed, and for a time became subversive, as had the Polytechnique under Louis XVIII or the School of Medicine under Napoleon III. This division in the higher spheres of French thought involved such a large number of people that recent research has been undertaken into the correlation of categories, one might almost say its statistics.[2] To keep to the best-known symbols, the Académie française, the established types, classical aesthetes, were rather more inclined to be anti-Dreyfusard; the Goncourt academicians, naturalistic novelists, symbolists and innovators, more Dreyfusard. On the one hand, Barrès, already mentioned, Jules Lemaître, François Coppée, etc.; on the other, Émile Zola, Octave Mirbeau . . . But there were some noteworthy exceptions, like Anatole France, a man of classic talent, who had strongly criticized the Zola of the *Rougon-Macquart* novels but who, in the Dreyfus Affair, would reveal himself as one of the chief supporters of the Zola of 'J'accuse'.

The republican and free-thinking intellectual left gradually became completely Dreyfusard, fairly swiftly and fairly actively involved. Certainly, the Republic and the left had long claimed the moral patronage and support of top-ranking savants such as Marcelin Berthelot, one of the fathers of organic chemistry, lifelong secretary of the Academy of Sciences, senator, former minister. Born in 1827, he would see his scientific jubilee celebrated in the Sorbonne in 1901 with the Head of State presiding, and in 1907 a national funeral would convey him to the Panthéon. But the Dreyfusard battle was inspired mainly by intellectuals of an infinitely more modest station, whose ardour, capable of combining lecturing and writing with the militant tasks of propagandist or demonstration organizer, was truly characteristic of the epoch. After France and Berthelot, and still other illustrious men (Émile Duclaux, Ludovic Trarieux), after Jaurès and Clemenceau, who came from the world of politics, one must name as typical Lucien Herr – one of the best philosophers and German scholars of the era, a fundamental militant socialist, who spent his entire life in the modest post of librarian in the *École normale* – or Charles Péguy, a former *normalien* who had become an impecunious publicist, but the heart and soul of the movement in the Latin Quarter. Polemics and many forms of disturbance were continuous for nearly a year and a half.

The Zola trial was quashed in April for a procedural flaw, but the new trial confirmed the sentence, and Zola preferred exile in London (July) to serving time in prison.

Meanwhile, the elections of 8–22 May 1898 replenished the Chamber of Deputies. The clearly antirepublican right numbered about a hundred members (about 20 nationalists and 80 'conservatives', that is to say, royalists); opposite them, a left composed of about 180 radicals and 57 socialists. Between the two, a centre of 254 moderate republicans, the 'progressives'. This Chamber would swing or rearrange itself at the end of a year, as sometimes happens, without fresh elections and thus without any change in its composition.

The socialists had gained seats in comparison with 1893, but Jaurès had not managed to persuade them to adopt a pro-Dreyfus stance, and the

[2] C. Charle, *Naissance des intellectuels 1880–1900*, 1990.

Guesdist argument – the affair is a row between bourgeois, whereas *we* are concerned with the class struggle – had prevailed. Even worse: being too well known for his Dreyfusard involvement, Jaurès himself lost his seat for Carmaux.

That centre and, consequently, the Chamber overall inclined more to the right than the left: in the election of its president, the moderate Deschanel defeated the radical Henri Brisson. But the Méline government, worn out by over two years of difficult and challenged rule, resigned and made way for the Brisson government which seemed, from the personality of its leader, slightly more to the left. Thus in 1895 the government of the radical Léon Bourgeois had for a brief interlude taken over from that of the authoritarian Charles Dupuy, without any real change to the prevailing situation.

In that Brisson cabinet the Ministry of War was held by Cavaignac (the son of the general in 1848). On 7 July, challenged on the Dreyfus Affair, he displayed with sincere conviction a new document found by his department and damning for 'that scoundrel D—'. Alas! There were some officers in the rue Saint-Dominique who took their work seriously, and one of them, a Captain Cuignet, discovered that the document was a forgery (13 August). Major Henry, interrogated by his superior officers, confessed that he had lent himself to this deceit in order to wage the good political fight against traitors (the theory of the 'patriotic forgery'). A forger nevertheless, he was arrested, put into confinement and, on 31 August, committed suicide in his cell.

That was an argument of some weight in favour of Dreyfus's innocence for, if it was necessary to make forgeries to prop up an accusation of guilt, it was doubtless because that guilt lacked any solid evidence.

Henry's suicide encouraged the Dreyfusards (on 3 September the family made an official request for a revision of the trial), but also the anti-Dreyfusards, for whom Major Henry, the man who had placed the *Patrie* above truth, would become a hero.

Of course, Henry's superiors, including Cavaignac, had to resign. During the autumn ministers of war played 'musical chairs'; Brisson again yielded the government to the right (Charles Dupuy) and the affair was a permanent feature of parliamentary debates. But more than ever it occupied the man in the street, and it was here, at street level, that the nationalists were stirring. And, because they were on the move, the extreme left in its turn let itself be aroused. The various socialist groups, who had not had the stomach for getting involved in the Dreyfus cause (legal and ethical), found it for taking up the cudgels against anti-Dreyfusard activism, a more concrete political danger. They formed a common 'vigilance committee'. This was a significant event, which we shall see develop.

By now the battle was being waged everywhere; in the streets of Paris, where uproar, meetings and processions multiplied; in the press, where Jaurès, liberated from his parliamentary mandate, was now acting in the front ranks as journalist and publicist;[3] and lastly within the legal institution, since a revision had been requested.

On 29 October 1898 the Criminal Chamber of the Court of Appeal declared the request for a revision 'admissible in form'. That was the first legal victory and (after the Henry scandal) a second moral victory for the Dreyfusard camp. But it also galvanized anti-Dreyfusard reaction. Outside parliament, nationalist demonstrations, which went as far as threatening magistrates in their own homes, reached a paroxysm, and rumours of a coup d'état circulated. In the Chamber, a majority of right and centre united to pass the *loi de dessaisissement* (the removal of a case from a court), stipulating that the Court of Appeal would have to render a definitive decision on the revision 'with all Chambers combined', which would swamp the intractable members of the Criminal Chamber in a vaster and presumably better inspired whole. Despite their platonic victory, therefore, the situation appeared more menacing than ever for the revisionists.

The swing in the relations of the rival forces happened at that time, in the most unexpected and fortuitous way. On 16 February 1899 President Félix Faure died, in the scabrous circumstances which everyone knows. The dead President had been a former Gambettist, very patriotic, verging on nationalist, and he had clearly made known his hostility to revision proceedings. Of course, the Élysée had nothing at all to do directly with the affair, unless by the discreet and informal power of influence, which the President had . . . or had not used. His personality had counted, however, as all the evidence shows. On 18 February, by virtue of what was already almost a tradition, an unwritten law of the Republic, the president of the Senate, Émile Loubet, was easily elected to the position of Head of State.

The new President was hardly concerned with the affair. But the nationalist camp, already exasperated by the loss of the Élysée, was inclined to detest this man who, moreover, since Panama – when he had contributed to calming things down – had passed for the archetypal politician. They therefore treated Loubet's election as a defeat and vowed their unshakeable hatred for him.

At the time, the nationalists could not see that in this way they were preparing their own downfall! For from then on, the excessiveness of their attacks against the President, the institutions and the very dignity of the Republic would soon arouse against them the irritation of the majority of parliament and of the country at large, for whom the Republic was still something to be valued. In short, the Republic would replace the revision as the issue at stake.

On the evening of 18 February, in Paris, there were threatening demonstrations against Loubet's procession returning from Versailles. The Dupuy government took no action.

On 23 February, the occasion of Félix Faure's funeral, Paul Déroulède tried to get a regiment to march on the Élysée. He failed, but the impulse

---

[3] *Les Preuves* (The Proof) appeared in parts in *La Petite République* in 1898.

towards a coup d'état was clear. Déroulède was therefore arrested, but he was spared the High Court of Justice (which had been brought into service in 1889 against the Boulangists who had not attempted nearly as much) and was brought before the Assize Court, which acquitted him in May.

Legal proceedings were taken against the leagues, those of the right but also that of the left: the League of the Rights of Man. On 3 June, however, the Court of Appeal gave its decision which, contrary to the expectation of the preceding year's legislator, declared in favour of a revision. Exasperated by this piece of news, on 4 June at the Auteuil racecourse, the nationalists demonstrated and one of them managed to land a blow with his stick on the Head of State, who was inadequately protected by the police.

On 11 June at Longchamp, the left demonstrated in their turn to protest against the offence committed the preceding Sunday on the President of the Republic. This time the demonstration was energetically put down by the police.

That was the last straw! The growing partiality of Charles Dupuy's government in favour of the nationalists, who were themselves increasingly coming to resemble seditionaries, brought about the defection of part of its majority. On 12 June, the government was brought down, and over a matter that clearly concerned institutions, as can be seen.

Thenceforth the Dreyfus Affair followed its own course, and the Republic made a fresh start, since the glimpse (or supposition) of the threat to its existence had gone some way to rejuvenating the fervour of its followers.

Consciousness of the need for a change of men, in a situation which itself had been altered, had moved the President of the Republic to appeal to René Waldeck-Rousseau to form a government – after Poincaré had refused, it is true. Born in Nantes in 1846, he belonged to the 'republican nobility', his father having been an elected member of the Republic in 1848. Socially, he came of a good bourgeois family: the son of a barrister, he too was a barrister, made even wealthier by his marriage. He was the founder in Paris of the republican *Grand Cercle*, which would symmetrically balance on the left the great conservative social clubs. Elected deputy of Ille-et-Vilaine in 1879, he had taken an active part in setting up the regime, and was Minister of the Interior for the first time in the 'great cabinet' and twice afterwards in the same post in the Ferry governments. The important law of 1884 on trades unions may be recalled. He was a man of principle, a rigid legalist – one of the rare ministers of the interior, for instance, who had dared to remind people that Spanish-style bullfights came under the provision of Grammont's law.[4] He was a cold and not very sociable man, ill at ease in a parliament which he had left of his own free will in the elections of 1889 in order to devote himself to the Bar and to specialize in business and literary court cases, doubtless at that time with ambitions that were more worldly and academic than political. A friend had to entreat him

---

[4] A law passed in 1850 which treated as criminal cruel treatment inflicted upon domestic animals in public.

to agree to accept an easy senator's seat for the Loire in 1894. It was therefore to a man who was somewhat apart from the usual groups, and almost to a rescuer, that the Head of State turned, hoping for a daring and original solution. That hope was not disappointed.

Nationalist disturbances, the work of an active and 'revolutionary' minority, towards whom the republican right (Méline, Charles Dupuy) had shown indulgence, if nothing else, appeared to be a threat against the regime, in the same way as the recent Boulangism, Moral Order or, on another plane, Bonapartism. It was therefore the 'Republic' that was mobilized, that is to say, in effect, the left wing of opinion. Presenting itself before the Chamber, Waldeck-Rousseau's government had a narrow majority of 263 votes (all the radicals, half the socialists and only 61 progressives) to 238 (the extreme non-republican right and the majority of the progressives). This new majority which proposed to 'defend the Republic' to all intents and purposes mingled with the left and can be qualified as the Left-wing Bloc equally well as the 'great republican party'. The old connection between the concept of left and the concept of Republic, which the developments of the 1890s had rendered inadequate (and which it still was, in actual fact) was once again reaffirmed, and for a long while, in the polemical and electoral discourse of the new majority. The 'republican discipline' would conventionally designate those on the left, and republicans who chose the wrong side – the right – in 1899 were suspected of not being true republicans.

Defending the Republic, in the terms of the government declaration, meant firstly 'to ensure that legal decisions were respected and to defend the discipline necessary to the army'. That last point made the Ministry of War a fundamentally important post – Waldeck, president of the Council, having taken the Interior for himself. It was entrusted to General de Galliffet, an old soldier, an aristocrat, naturally royalist then Bonapartist, chiefly sceptical in point of fact, whom Gambetta (yet again) had been able to rally to the Republic in 1880–1 on the basis of their common and keen patriotism. He had also, it must be confessed, had Communards shot in 1871, but all generals of his age had done the same, and not all had had the merit of becoming Gambettists. Let us be bold enough to say so – Galliffet was a good choice. A young, radical and free-thinking general as Minister would not necessarily have succeeded in bringing into line officers who were often nationalist and anti-Semitic, had often remained royalist and sometimes been tempted to make a bid for power; an older man with prestige and the profile of a reactionary was more valuable, and he did indeed have success.

The only snag was that he was a bitter pill to swallow for the extreme socialist left, who formed part of the defensive republican majority and whom, for that reason, Waldeck had been resolved to associate with the government. There was a dearth of 'minister-material', especially if one remembers that Jaurès, beaten in 1898, was not a deputy – and at that time, except for the rue Saint-Dominique, a minister appointed from outside parliament was unthinkable. Waldeck therefore offered Alexandre Millerand the Ministry of Trade, Industry and Postal Services, which had least to do with the great functions of state but was closest to social matters. With the approval, notably, of Jaurès, Millerand accepted, despite his objection on principle to participating in a 'bourgeois' government, and his sentimental objection to becoming the colleague of an 'executioner of the Commune'. That resulted in only a bare half of the socialist deputies giving a vote of confidence, the rest abstaining. Thus materialized what we explained earlier: the 'workers' movement' was divided at every decisive occasion between those who were more republican than revolutionary, and those who were more revolutionary than republican. The first were Millerandists; the second, anti-Millerandists.

The essential point about Waldeck-Rousseau's government was the way in which it emerged, and its composition.

Its political task would consist in getting out of the crisis. Its social work would belong to Millerand, who tried to justify his presence in the government by obtaining appreciable, though reformist, results.

From the political angle first, therefore, the army was better run, thanks to the reorganization of the Senior Military Council, and the resumption by the Ministry of the right to appoint officers and assign posts, which had been taken over by a grading commission dominated by the caste mentality. In order to put down unrest among league members, Waldeck-Rousseau recalled to the Prefecture of Police the famous Louis Lépine, the first great republican police chief who had really succeeded in the post from 1893–6, and whom Méline had pushed aside; the 'Chabrol stronghold' of Jules Guérin,[5] patiently besieged, ended by surrendering, and the ringleaders were brought before the High Court.

As for the Dreyfus Affair, it was reaching its last legal episode. A revision having been decided upon, Dreyfus was brought back to France and retried before another military court, in Rennes (7–9 August 1899). The verdict of the new judges was tempered: 'guilty, but with extenuating circumstances', a pretty absurd phrase which only partly emended the initial verdict. Waldeck-Rousseau found the answer: at his suggestion, President Loubet pardoned Dreyfus.

To pardon is not officially to declare innocent, so justice had still not been done. The Dreyfusards, people of principle, debated much about it. Clemenceau, a hard man, advised the family to reject the pardon; Jaurès, more human, suggested that they accept, which they did. In the view of

---

[5] One of the leaders of nationalist street demonstrations. Under order of arrest, he barricaded himself for thirty-eight days in the premises of the Anti-Semitic League situated in the rue Chabrol.

general opinion, a free Dreyfus was still a victory. Galliffet, in a dispatch to the army, wrote baldly, 'the incident is closed.' His mission accomplished, he would seize the first opportunity to quit the government (May 1900).

The Dreyfusard camp was triumphant, and found an unexpected but significant occasion to celebrate its victory. A happy coincidence had just seen the completion of an old project, the erection of the sculpted group *The Triumph of the Republic* by Jules Dalou – that Marianne, both haughty and beautiful, treading on a globe, itself placed on a chariot drawn by two lions, with Labour and Justice pushing its wheels, and Peace completing the procession. Dalou, a republican and Communard, just returned from exile in 1880, had presented the work in the monument competition for the place de la République, but he had not won the prize. However, the Paris municipal council had bought the design; the model in plaster had been put up in the place de la Nation in 1889, the work in bronze to follow. Now it was completed.

The socialist newspaper *La Petite République* had the notion of inviting the friends of the Republic, the Dreyfusards, in short, Parisians who were in favour of the Waldeck-Rousseau government, to attend the inauguration on 19 November 1899, to turn it into a victory demonstration. For in the now common interpretation of the epilogue to the affair – a liberated Dreyfus, the nationalists in prison, the Mélines and Dupuys out of government – it all truly brought back former victorious outcomes, Gambetta over Moral Order, or the spirit of Victor Hugo over the spectre of Badinguet. Since tens of thousands of Parisians shared that view, the operation was a tremendous success; the corresponding accounts of the numerous witnesses of the event who have left their memoirs attest to that fact. The organizers had to allot access roads to the various *quartiers* for the processions converging in turn on the place de la Nation, their rather clumsy planning taking over from that of Prefect of Police Lépine, who took a benevolent view. The red flag was forbidden . . . if it was a flag, that is to say, all red and with no addition. But banners were tolerated, even if they were red, provided they bore the inscription of the name of the organization following them; they were therefore numerous, for popular demonstrators mostly connected with the workers' movement came in groups, and all that Paris possessed in the way of sections, study groups, employers' federations, members of co-operatives, were in attendance. The 'heavy troops' were supplied, quite naturally because that sector of the city was theirs, by Ivry and the 'Thirteenth'. The men marched abreast, sometimes trying to keep in step as in the processions of 1848. From the hawkers who were swift to appear on the scene people bought red eglantines, either real or made of paper, to adorn their buttonholes. Revolutionary songs were solemnly sung, freely permitted for the first time on the public streets, the old 'Carmagnole' and the young 'Internationale', the latter making a great impression with its grave beauty and enjoying its first Parisian success. Various slogans were shouted, vengeful cries against Déroulède and Rochefort; cries of goodwill, which were not much taken up, 'Long live Dreyfus!' 'Long live

Zola!' 'Long live Jaurès!'; shouts emphasizing demands and struggles, such as 'Hard labour for Mercier!'[6] a whole variety, both partisan and confused. But – according to Péguy's report,[7] which we are following in the main, and he is insistent on this – when the processions emerging into the place de la Nation finally caught sight of the statue, of which only the upright figure stood out above the throngs who hid the lower part of the monument, all the different clamours ceased spontaneously, to give way to 'Long live the Republic!'

It was repeated, a little farther on, before the official platform, which President Loubet and the government had left well before the end of the procession.

It is worth lingering over that peaceful festival day, because it contains a wealth of lessons. First, that a crowd could celebrate both politically and sentimentally the inauguration of a bronze allegorical group speaks volumes about the preserved vitality of that form of expression. Then, the tensions within the festival, that is to say, within the victorious republican camp itself, deserve consideration: from time to time Lépine's men had to use their fists to remove a black flag – a forbidden emblem, this. And then President Loubet had left early, rather displeased because he had nevertheless seen quite a lot of red on display, many banners, and many socialist slogans chanted. Did not the class dividing line between a proletariat slipping into socialism and a republican bourgeoisie, just as truly bourgeois as sincerely republican, pass through the very heart of the left-wing camp? And not between left and right? Perhaps all the complexity of the epoch is to be seen in that. Lastly and chiefly, one must remember the success and the size of the demonstration in a popular Paris which drew its warmth both from its hopes as a neophyte in socialism and from its already historic awareness of tradition. At all events, that is what Péguy would seem to suggest:

I shall never forget the best part of the day: coming down the faubourg Antoine (on the way back, to disperse the assembled crowds). Evening was drawing on and it was getting dark. Ignorant though we may be of the history of past revolutions, which are the beginning of the imminent social Revolution, we all know the legendary and historical glory of this old faubourg. We marched along the streets bathed in that glory. With careful tread, the bearers of *La Petite République* were walking at the head of this new procession. The people of the faubourg approached, spelled out, read 'The – Little – Socialist – Republic. – Neither – God – nor – master', applauded, cheered, followed. There was no longer any distinction between procession and spectators. The people came down into the crowd, and the one swelled the other. The old *Marseillaise* was sung again, after being recently discredited among revolutionary socialists by finding favour with nationalist crooks. The entire faubourg went along in the darkness, in a tremendous surge, without any hatred.

---

[6] General Mercier, Minister of War at the time of Dreyfus's sentence.

[7] *Cahiers de la Quinzaine*, of 25 December 1899, Bibliotheque de la Pleiade, *Œuvres en prose complètes*, vol. 1, pp. 299 ff.

The gardens of the Champ-de-Mars and the Palace of Electricity, Universal Exhibition of 1900. (Photo: L.L. (Levy))

How striking is that last detail, that final aporia: was the 'Marseillaise' reactionary because nationalism was tending to lay claim to it? Or revolutionary because it came from the Revolution? A conflict for a distant future. For the immediate future, let us rather keep in mind the involvement of the people with the Dreyfusard camp, without which it would be hard to understand the interweaving of republican defence and socialism, a major problem of the new political conjuncture.

There was another symbol, in 1900, on the occasion of a new Universal Exhibition. Among other festivities, the President of the Republic, surrounded by ministers, presided over a gigantic banquet to which *all* the mayors in France were invited (in 1889 they had dared to invite only the mayors of the main towns in each canton). Out of 36,000 invited, 20,777 attended; an appreciable majority when one thinks of what the journey to Paris could entail at that time for a villager from the Ariège or the Hautes Alpes. That rural majority acclaimed the Republic. Meanwhile Paris, loyal to the tendency it had already affirmed with Boulangism, gave itself a municipal council with a nationalist majority. Thus the capital would henceforward form a right-wing opposition to a government and state power whose reaffirmed anchorage in the left was upheld by the provinces. The situation became the exact reverse of what it had been for the greater part of the nineteenth century.

The political work of the Waldeck-Rousseau government included the celebrated law of 1901 on the right of association. It well and truly followed on from the Dreyfus Affair, inasmuch as certain religious houses (*congrégations*) had taken sides in it. In a general way, apart from one or two exceptions – among the rare Catholic Dreyfusards was the father of the future General de Gaulle – the Catholic clergy were strongly conservative, and sometimes with a proclivity for authoritarianism. The clergy, and those faithful on whom they had the most influence, were not confined to the republican right wing alone, they were also connected with the 'revolutionary right'. The Assumptionists, publishers of the paper *La Croix*, were the champions of anti-Semitism. On the left, the republican need to complete the array of fundamental freedoms by granting the right of association, and the no less republican mistrust with regard to possible subversive groups, provided a contradiction that had been a stumbling block for the past twenty years. Waldeck-Rousseau cut the Gordian knot by preparing a frankly discriminatory law.

In common law, freedom of association would be a legal right, subject to a simple declaration. That is the 'law of 1901' regime which the French still make use of every day. Religious orders would be the subject of a special statute, and would be dealt with separately. A law would be necessary to authorize new *congrégations*, and a decree for new establishments of existing *congrégations*. The law was passed by both Chambers after lively debate, but a start on its application was made fairly flexibly – the Council of State having simplified the procedure and the government having engaged in discreet negotiations with the clergy, who were still loyal to the Concordat. That was to change after Waldeck.

For the moment, the act allowed a new upsurge in the life of associations which had already been well under way since the 1880s under a tolerant regime. It also encouraged parties, which up till then (except for the socialists) had scarcely been organized, to give themselves a modern kind of status. Thus in 1901 the Radical Party came into being, and the one called 'Democratic Alliance', which regrouped the progressives who were members of the secular and republican majority, following the example of Waldeck.

Waldeck-Rousseau was really responsible for the social reforms of the period, inasmuch as the former opportunists of the better kind really saw it as the Republic's duty to reform and make conditions more humane. He had already taken action in that direction by his law of 1884.

But that work must remain linked also with the name of Millerand, for whom it was an imperative. In fact, for a republican socialist, being a minister in the government was already justified by the defence of the Republic, a regime reputed to be better for the working class than a dictatorship. But for those citizens unconvinced by that argument, it was important to have social results to turn to good account.

Prior to 1899, parliament had already passed several useful laws: one in 1884 on the trades unions; one in 1890 abolishing the workingman's hitherto compulsory identity papers; one in 1892 providing protective regulations concerning women and children working in industry; one in 1894 extending to state employees the right to belong to a union; and lastly, one in 1898 – in the development of which Millerand had taken a hand as a simple deputy – on responsibility (a priori of the employer, unless he could prove otherwise) for accidents at work. Outside the legislative field, unions and employers had come to some useful agreements on the coal-mines. And in 1891 the Ministry of Trade had been endowed with an Employment Office to collect documentation and social statistics.

Millerand developed the Employment Office and gave it responsibility for matters relating to labour in his own ministry – and it would form the nucleus of the future Ministry of Labour – in order to prepare fresh initiatives. Two projects reached a successful outcome: a law limiting the working day to twelve hours in factories employing only adult males, whereas until then it had been subject to no regulation, except in the mines, and another law limiting the time to ten hours in factories where both adults and children worked.

A decree laid down working conditions in undertakings contracted to the state (weekly rest day, reduced working hours) in the hope that the state would thereby provide a model to be imitated by ordinary employers.

Lastly, Millerand reorganized a consultative body, the Higher Labour Council, granting entry to workers' elected delegates, and made use of it to encourage arbitration in industrial disputes.

This appraisal certainly reveals notable progress in a social legislation the original timidity of which has been mentioned. However, that did not prevent rows from taking place here and there, bosses from being intransigent and sometimes the police from acting to maintain order. And every episode of that nature fuelled the arguments against Millerandism. A cruel caricature of the period shows the workers on a strike committee scanning the lists of supporting subscribers. The caption reads: 'And the Citizen-Minister (that is, Millerand – today we would say the Comrade-Minister), what has he sent? – He has sent the police!'

The 'Millerand case' was endlessly discussed in the working-class movement. It rapidly rendered untenable the first unification the socialists achieved, in the momentum of the Dreyfusian victory, in December 1899 at the congress in Japy Hall. Two years later, the split occurred.

In November 1901 at Ivry, uncompromising anti-Millerandists formed the Socialist Party of France, around Jules Guesde and Édouard Vaillant; it remained for the others to organize themselves (Tours, March 1902) into the French Socialist Party (Paul Brousse, Jean Jaurès, etc.)

In the general elections of 1902 it was the latter, the more government orientated, who collected the greater number of votes and elected members, one sign amongst others of the very popular character which republican defence had retained.

In the monument to Waldeck, which may still be seen in its place in the Tuileries Gardens in Paris, a worker figures prominently. And in the heartland of France, newborn babies received the forename Waldeck.

The enthusiasm aroused among the left-wing electorate by the victorious battles of the Waldeck-Rousseau government was to push politics beyond the wishes of its wise leader. That would soon become noticeable.

In the legislative elections of May 1902, republican defence was given a huge vote and won an overwhelming majority. There were very few abstentions. The left gathered together 366 elected members (99 Democratic Alliance, 219 radicals and radical socialists, 48 socialists) against 220 seats on the right. Waldeck, who was ill and did not feel he could go along with this radicalization, renounced his own succession, and the new government was formed by Émile Combes, a radical senator and provincial doctor. That government, one of the most disparaged in the Third Republic, was also one of its most popular. Historical reputations are not made by universal suffrage, and the collective memory, in the 'national' culture that was being formed, still leaned towards the conservative side. The image of 'little father Combes' ('little father' because he was old and looked it, and furthermore because he had rubbed shoulders with the Church as a former seminarist) was disastrous: a politico with a goatee beard, and 'square' (in today's parlance), an obsessive gobbler-up of curés, a Monsieur Homais in power, in short, 'an idiot coupled with a cop'. Yet the few years in which he was a representative of the people aroused a surge of popular approval, of confidence in the future, comparable before him to the founding years (1878, 1879, 1880, 1881) and after him to those of the Popular Front or the Liberation.

Another aspect of that paradox is the contrast between Combes's image, which was a disaster, and the rather respectable – even for non-socialists – image of Jaurès. Now, Jaurès, who had returned to the Chamber in 1902, backed this government to the hilt, as he had never supported and never would support any other. Elected vice-president of the Chamber, and *de facto* leader of the delegation of left-wingers (co-ordination of the parliamentary majority groups), Jaurès was truly very close to the government.

Over and above that problem of collective national memory, the Jaurès–Combes paradox raises another, namely, that of the relations between the ideal – reputed to be honourable, even if one did not share it – of socialism, and the ideal – today disparaged and deemed antiquated – of anticlericalism. Was there divergence or solidarity?

The government, despite socialist support, did not place the main emphasis on the social. Since the Millerand experiment had not been convincing it was not renewed, the cabinet contained no socialist, and Finances were in the keeping of Rouvier, who belonged to the moderate wing of the coalition. The combat – for they wanted to be a fighting government – was at first completely political, against clericalism of course, but also against the positions held by the old conservative and royalist world in the principal structures of the state, the danger of which was judged to have been revealed by the Dreyfus Affair. The attention given, notably, to republicanizing the army and navy – to cite the more outstanding examples – proceeded from that. Many instances are quoted – chiefly so that one may be scandalized by them – of ambitions of the 'jobs for the boys' type, and the declared intention of reserving appointments and posts for 'true friends of the Republic', that is, of the government. And it is true that not everything about that intention was pure, in 1902 any more than previously or afterwards. But it must be acknowledged that, although the politics of positions was connected, on the one hand, with the usual human frailty, the clique mentality and the 'spoils system', on the other hand it was also connected with a more reputable will to see that democracy was respected by civilian society. The work of General André in the Ministry of War and of Camille Pelletan in the navy would issue from the same spirit as that of the founding fathers, a quarter of a century earlier, in purging the magistrature or the Council of State. It was spectacular. Pelletan, purely civilian, a graduate of the École des chartes and never having exercised any career other than journalism, had the temerity to take on the navy, which was still known as 'the Royal Navy', and impose on it such significant transformations as giving republican names to its warships (*Danton, Marseillaise*), introducing a common wardroom for deck officers and engineering officers, and the abolition of the custom of flying flags at half-mast on Good Friday.

Much fun was poked at Pelletan. Public opinion, then history, which had seen nothing shocking in royal and religious survivals, regarded as ridiculous the first political man to try to take a hand in them. In addition, since he was also in charge of the arsenals, Pelletan instituted an eight-hour day there. As for General André, his activism, which would one day prove disastrous for the government, began from the premiss that the religious, conservative mentality, often nostalgic for authoritarianism, had been at a premium in the army and had browbeaten republican officers, and there was good cause to counterbalance it. He therefore wanted to offset or replace the old God-fearing, right-thinking networks of influence and information with those of Freemasonry, which were differently orientated – something that would create a shock, with good reason, under the name 'the affair of the dossiers'.[8] Perhaps it is only fair to say that, if plugging the state into a private network of influence was indefensible, neither was it admissible to regard as scandalous only the dossiers of the left, and not the procedures of the right. At all events, André was popular in other respects; he drew up the bill reducing military service from three years to two.

But the major battle was being enacted against the Roman Church, and first of all the *congrégations*. Contrary to what Waldeck-Rousseau had commenced and wished for, Combes and his majority applied the 1901 law

---

[8] A scandal arising from the revelation that promotions in the army were being affected by dossiers on the religious attitudes of officers, kept by the Freemasons with the connivance of General André.

rigorously and restrictively. New requests for authorization were almost systematically turned down, with the exception of the precious missionary bodies overseas. Schools run by unauthorized *congrégations* were closed, the right to teach (privately) of former members of dissolved *congrégations* came up against further obstacles, etc. There was in consequence a spectacular exodus of monks and certain of their colleagues to Belgium, Italy or Catholic Switzerland (Fribourg). Of course, between the bishops who protested and the government whose indignation was aroused by their protests, a contentious verbal warfare was unleashed. However, there was little in the way of public trouble, less than there would be some time later over the Church inventories, a cause more spiritual than material. In fact, many *congrégations* submitted to the rules, and the network of private schools was in the end little harmed.

The battle reached its height chiefly on the symbolic plane. On 13 September 1903 Combes presided personally over the inauguration of the statue to Renan, who had died eleven years earlier, a bourgeois academic as peaceable and moderate as could be, but whose *Life of Jesus* had been the shameful symbol of the scientific spirit invading the realm of the sacred. As the monument was in Brittany at Tréguier, his birthplace, and Minerva was to be seen standing behind the savant's chair, the impression was received that the Republic was imposing the statue of free-thinking on Christian soil (in a Christian region). The radicals, of whom Combes was the perfect embodiment, did not believe that it was possible to come to terms with the Church, and twenty years earlier had been shocked by the wiliness of the opportunists and progressives in maintaining the Concordat to carry on a permanent compromise with Rome.

Combes bluntly aggravated the split by demanding that papal bulls, canonically instituting bishops, should simply bear the words that the French government *eos nominavit* (has appointed them). Rome clung to the formula *eos nobis nominavit* (the government has nominated them *for us* – meaning, in order that *we* appoint them). Those five letters in Latin thus changed everything, as far as the principle was concerned! They opened up a conflict which would gradually become envenomed by the most diverse episodes, from minor rows regarding this or that bishop, to a trip by Loubet to Rome, where he visited the Quirinal to see the King before going to greet the Pope at the Vatican. To cut a long story short, on 30 July 1904 the Chamber of Deputies ratified by its vote the breaking off of diplomatic relations between France and the Holy See. All that remained was to set to work on the logical sequel, the separation of Church and state.

Until this affair, Jaurès had played the government game actively and even personally. The Pope's protest over Loubet's flouting of protocol had been registered only in confidence, in a note to the chancelleries of the Catholic sovereigns. But the Prince of Monaco, officially held to be a Catholic monarch, was nevertheless a free-thinker on a personal level, and he had the note passed to Jaurès, who made it public in *L'Humanité*, which then gave French diplomats grounds for protest.

For since spring 1904 Jaurès had had at his disposal a newspaper, *L'Humanité*, for which the bourgeois circles most engaged in Dreyfusism had raised the capital. The title chosen, moreover, evoked the abstract and overall idealism of the left rather than the strictly workingmen's and class-conscious aspirations, which socialism – with Jaurès's help, of course – would soon imprint upon it.

Here is an opportunity to take a wider view, going beyond the political and personal links between Jaurès and Combes, of the question of the relations between socialism and anticlericalism; a question that is posed throughout the history of this Republic.

According to a classic argument, anticlericalism formed an insidious barrier in the path of socialism. By provoking the alliance of secular workers with Freemason capitalists, and putting them in opposition to their class brethren who had remained Christian, the anticlerical battlefront would contradict and thwart the class struggle. The energy deployed by the people on the left against the curés would be drained from what they should be using against the bosses and the 'fat cats'. Anticlericalism would thus backfire or create a diversion from the class struggle. In reality, that argument seems very specious. It is not easy to see how such a manoeuvre could have shown itself effective for very long if it had resulted from such conscious cleverness alone. Furthermore, it is not easy to see how, as the argument implies, radicals (bourgeois) could have drawn with them into the battle against the priests reluctant socialist workers who were eager to fight elsewhere.

What is to be seen in the France of that era is that socialists, of every hue, showed at least as much ardour as radicals in inspiring free-thinking and engaging in all the forms of struggle against established religion. Having accepted that the tie between socialism and anticlericalism was strong and lasting, it only remains to consider why this revealed itself with such natural and spontaneous vigour.

Firstly, in many regions, it was not evident that large employers, bankers or big firms had become republicans and Freemasons. In the country at large, it still frequently happened that the Church ensured the electoral, social and even trade unionist support of the employers.

But above all, French society and culture in general remained impregnated with religion. Neither Jules Ferry nor even Émile Combes had changed anything in that respect. Religion continued to put its imprint on ordinary life; and anyone who wanted to display his rejection of the world as it was could do so first of all by refusing to accept that imprint. Getting married in church was to behave like everyone else; so anyone who desired to make himself conspicuous would have a civil marriage.

From that one can understand how class consciousness, class feeling, the intransigent doctrine of the class struggle, far from alleviating the anticlerical combat, on the contrary inflamed it. The overt irreligiousness and militancy of the free-thinker acted as distinguishing signs in relation to established society, and thus converged with that other absolute of distinctiveness, the doctrine of class. Nothing can demonstrate it more clearly than that second feature of socialist culture, the fact that they gave themselves and one another the title 'citizen'. The word, unlike the 'companion' of the anarchists or the future 'comrade' of the Communists, *in itself* had no working-class or popular connotation; it assumed that only *by distinction*, by contrast with ordinary folk who called one another 'monsieur'.

When bourgeois society was composed of people who said 'monsieur', the working-class party would be made up of those who said 'citizen'. And if that society called itself Christian, at least for propriety's sake, the working-class party would make its stand against it by *not* being so. This was most probably the logic at work.

Another observation may be added: many socialists were socialists only because they had first been anticlerical. The liberal, then republican, bourgeoisie had performed a formidable feat indeed by teaching the people for nearly two centuries to challenge the truths of religion and the Church. If the pope and the reverend curé could talk rubbish, who was to be trusted? After that first schism, everything became possible. The mayor, the employer, the republican deputy, the professional economist, could all be wrong in their turn. The impulse for criticism applied to metaphysics was easily followed by casting doubt on republican optimism and economic orthodoxy the moment they were slow to keep their promises. It was for that very reason that the secular educational system of Jules Ferry and Paul Bert, who were themselves anti-socialist, nevertheless produced so many socialist voters. They had desired education to be liberating, and it certainly was, even against their party and their good Republic.

One then understands why Jaurès and his followers had so thoroughly taken up the anticlerical fight. It represented part, and perhaps at first the 'foundation course', of their overall struggle. Why Combism aroused social expectations is also understandable. In 1902, 1903 and 1904, tens of thousands of motions of congratulation, coming from committees, lodges, municipalities, banquets, societies, were sent to the head of government, who religiously – if that word may be used – kept them in his archives, where they are becoming known today. There is a frequently recurring theme: let us have done with clericalism and reaction, let us clear the road, and then we can achieve social justice.

But Combes was to fall before even beginning on that stage! His government was in effect finished after getting into difficulties on both the left and the right. On the left, because Jaurès, his friends of the French Socialist Party and the gradualist theory we ascribe to them, which has been cursorily mentioned, did not achieve unanimity in the working-class movement; upholding a 'bourgeois' government, they laid themselves open to the same criticisms as Millerandism had provoked. The Socialist Party of France, a rival to the Jauressian party, took every opportunity to recall, on each sensitive occasion, that Combes still had bankers and gendarmes on his side.

Reformist, if not pro-government, socialism had not absorbed the entire capacity for mobilization and fervour on the part of the people. That was clearly to be seen one day in January 1905, when an enormous crowd assembled to accompany from the Gare de Lyon to the Levallois cemetery the coffin of Louise Michel, which had been brought back from Marseille where she had died in the course of a lecture tour. The tireless and modest propagandist of protest against social injustice was indeed a historic personage – symbolic and almost romantic. Born in 1830, her illegitimacy, her activity as a free-thinking primary teacher, thus a militant, in the Paris of the Second Empire, her participation in the Commune, her captivity in New Caledonia, her fresh plunge into the social movement in the 1880s and 1890s, interspersed with exile in London and time in prison, her rejection of every constituted organization combined with her readiness to fly to the side of anyone who groaned at fate or rebelled, her personal dignity and generosity, her gifts for defiance and compassion not blunted by age or experience – all that had made her, in the long run, the principal emblem of a lively humanitarian anarchism, and at the same time a figure who compelled respect. Her popularity uncovered forces of social protest which even the most left-wing of Republics could not completely channel.

That constant, though diffused, revolutionary pressure of the extreme left rendered the defence of Combism more difficult, like that of Millerandism a little earlier.

At the Amsterdam congress of the Workers' Internationale, to which the two rival parties were affiliated (August 1904), and where a motion was passed enjoining the French to unite, and to do so on a clear basis of principle, that is, over class, which meant a split with the bourgeoisie, even if progressive, it is understandable that Jaurès should have preferred to yield rather than give up belonging to organized socialism. It would be to risk at least weakening the Left-wing Bloc majority, and sapping its vigour.

That immediately encouraged defections or dissidence on the right. In the Democratic Alliance, Ribot and Georges Leygues, and in the radical camp, Doumer and Clemenceau, withdrew their support from Combes. For different reasons. Some were quite simply dissatisfied, disappointed or rivals on a personal basis; others were worried by the popular and daring element in the policies of a man like Pelletan, and socialist-orientated expectations; still others, from a strict liberal point of view, found aggressive and party politics, and notably the affair of the dossiers, quite shocking. That dignified argument was naturally the one most pushed to the fore, and Combes made concessions in November 1904 by replacing General André. But it was not enough, and on 18 January 1905 the cabinet resigned.

However dramatic the crisis of the Dreyfus Affair might have been, France had not been able totally to ignore the rest of the world. And the government had marked its passage with a considerable external achievement, the *Entente Cordiale*.

Émile Combes had hardly come into it. President of the Council and Minister of the Interior, he had busied himself mainly with internal and general politics, and left diplomatic matters to be dealt with, over his head, between the Head of State and the Minister of Foreign Affairs, Delcassé, who had occupied the post since 1898.

Can one see in the *rapprochement* with Great Britain an additional sign of the turn taken by the Republic in 1899? After all, Anglophobia in France was clearly marked on the right, and Anglophilia fairly clearly on the left. That would be a false piece of reasoning, however. Delcassé could just as well have been an epigone of the opportunists rather than a radical. His plan had less to do with ideology than with geopolitics: France could not be allowed to have two potential enemies as considerable as Britain and Germany, and since Germany, because of Alsace, was impossible as a friend, only Britain could become one. It still had to show willing. The situation was cleared on the British side by the death of Queen Victoria (January 1901) and the end of the Boer War (May 1902). Edward VII was more of an innovator, more liberal and Francophile than his mother; also more aware of the threat of competition posed to his country by the recent economic and naval expansion of the Germans. In short, the two men, Delcassé and Edward VII, were both disposed to contemplate a calculated *rapprochement* directed against Germany, their common rival. The Ambassador, Paul Cambon, was the architect of the operation.

In May and July the heads of state exchanged visits between Paris and London. The auditing of an immense and sometimes age-old colonial account was accomplished and resulted in the agreement of 8 April 1904. It concerned Siam and Cambodia, fishing in Newfoundland waters, frontiers between Niger and Nigeria, mostly accepted *faits accomplis*, the main bartering point being the recognition by the French of the British *de facto* protectorate of Egypt, in exchange for France's freedom to act in establishing a similar influence in Morocco, expanding from Algeria.

In the same spirit and with the same aim in mind, Delcassé's diplomacy mollified Spain (demarcated zones of influence in Morocco) and Italy (whom the French authorized in advance to conquer Tripolitania).

We have just seen one effect of the Franco-Italian *rapprochement* with the split between France and the Vatican; at all events, Italy broke away from the central empires.

The entry of the Franco-British duo into history was an event of considerable importance. The two nations had been enemies from time immemorial, apart from a few brief exceptions (the last chronologically being the Crimean affair under Napoleon III). And profound enemies, culturally: Anglo-Saxons against Latins; Protestants against Catholics; Marlborough, Nelson and Wellington against Louis XIV and Napoleon; the *Godons* (as the English were disparagingly called) against Joan of Arc, and so on. It was not certain that all this had been erased from people's minds, but it would be enduringly erased from politics. Despite colonial rivalries, or because of them? At such a decisive historic watershed, the explanation can come only from a general interpretation, that is to say, be linked with ideological presuppositions. For some, two sated imperialisms came to an agreement in 1904 in order to stabilize the division of the extra-European world to their advantage, creating together an obstacle to German imperialism, a new arrival on the seas and in big business. For others, they were two great nations which, well imbued with the ethic of liberty and striving come what may to have policies of principle, would find themselves on the right side in every decisive event. But was the Moroccan affair one of them? At all events, it was in that connection that the *Entente Cordiale* functioned for the first time.

Many of the consequences of the important choices made at the time of Combes would, in fact, appear after him, in the eventful months that separated the 'little father's' resignation from the coming to power of the 'Tiger' (January 1905 to October 1906).

A new government was formed under the presidency of Rouvier, the former Minister of Finances under Combes. It gave several tokens to the right (the nationalists sentenced by the High Court were pardoned), but chiefly it brought to a successful conclusion the two-year military service law, which was passed in March 1905, and brought up for debate the bill on the Separation of Churches and State, which was passed by the Chamber in July and the Senate in December. The Concordat was denounced, and the clergy (or rather, the clergies – pastors and rabbis just as much as Roman prelates and priests) ceased to receive a salary.

The fate of the heritage owned by the state and managed by the Churches constituted the most complex problem. The law provided that the state and communes should keep those possessions without usufruct, and that 'religious associations' formed by the faithful should have free enjoyment of them. But the Catholics, who looked on the Separation at that time as a disaster, a cruel blow that had been dealt to them, were unwilling to make its execution any easier by accepting the outline proposed by the Republic. The arrangement would have to be renegotiated and acts of worship brought into the same category as public meetings. The legislator proved accommodating, caring little that the conflict would be aggravated: the policy concerning religious cults was left to the communes, which meant that it was still liberal in practice; compensation and pensions were planned for old priests without any resources, etc. But, by law, an exact inventory had to be made of the material possessions for which the communes were taking responsibility. The inventory could and should be a quick formality, in itself insignificant; but it would border on profanation (from the religious viewpoint) if the investigation caused the tabernacles containing 'Christ's body'

Catholic demonstration in Paris. The row over the inventories did not overturn France, but once again brought to light its extreme diversity. The ability to present physical opposition to the republican state over such a Platonic matter (preventing secular officials from entering a sacred place in order to 'count the candlesticks') only occurred in exceptional places: Paris, where nationalism could lend strong backing to the clergy, and islands of Christianity of which the Haute-Loire is a good example. Even there few risks were taken in the fighting, no firearms being used. In both attack and defence the France of 1906 was far removed from that of 1793. (Photo: Agence d'Information photographique Harlingue)

to be opened. That kind of clumsiness or provocation could certainly be avoided, but in many rural areas the faithful had a wider sense of what was sacred; some statue of a saint carried in procession once a year was 'our saint', and should no more be touched than the holy ciborium. Moreover, the inventory, even carried out with some delicacy, was the first concrete symbol of the execution of a law which was deemed overall to be spoliatory and impious.

Thence arose the idea of turning resistance to the church inventories into an act of defiance and a counterattack against the hated law. The leagues of the extreme right, notably Action française, annexed it, overwhelming the bishops who had contented themselves with advising curés to issue solemn protests and offer passive resistance.

From that, starting in January 1906, there came a flurry of incidents; some provincial, mainly rural, in 'Christian' areas, others urban, where nationalist leagues could provide the faithful with guidance and training. For the Catholics, action took the form of assembling in a mass around and inside churches, and barricading the doors in such a way as to force the agents of the region's administration, and the police or gendarmes required to assist them, to smash down the obstacle; the obstacle would be smashed, but the assault on and breaking into the 'holy place', verging on sacrilege, would cause tension to rise. In Paris, on 1 and 2 February 1906, two churches, Sainte-Clotilde and Saint-Pierre-du-gros-caillou, had to be taken by force in this manner, under a hail of stones from the defenders. There was a skirmish, almost a riot. Similar scenes took place on a small scale in the west, the south of the Massif Central, the Basque country and the Haut Doubs, the familiar geography of 'Christian areas' which had turned into electoral bastions of the conservatives. It was nearly always in rural territory, where peasants armed with pitchforks and cudgels rediscovered, against officials and gendarmes, the traditional weapons and actions of a resistance uprising. These weapons were sometimes picturesque, as in the Ille-et-Vilaine village where the faithful carried beehives into the church.

Folklore? Doubtless. But sometimes fighting broke out and shotguns appeared. It was inevitable that a grave accident should happen. That occurred on 6 March at Boeschepe, a village in the Nord, in a very Catholic area of Flemish culture and, what was more, on the border and thus inspired with an inveterate animosity towards gendarmes. The crowd of rioters entered the church where the tax collector and his escort of soldiers were. There was a brawl. The taxman's son believed his father was in danger and fired at a demonstrator, who fell dead. Rouvier, roughly interrogated in the Chamber, resigned.

Incidentally, such an important matter as the Separation, both highly technical and arousing fierce passions, had opened the door to fame to the eloquent and clever spokesman for the project before the Chamber, Aristide Briand, deputy for Saint-Étienne. He was a son of the people, who had been educated thanks to the Republic and had entered public life via the extreme left. The son of innkeepers, born in Nantes in 1862, receiving a grant to attend the *lycée* in that town, then a law student in Paris, he first set himself up as a barrister in Saint-Nazaire, where he made himself the spokesman of the working class of that area. There he edited the leftist press, defended workers and trades unions before the courts, got on to the municipal council, espoused all social aspirations to the point where he became singled out in the workers' congresses as the apostle of the general strike. Then an incident of a personal nature prompted him to leave his native region and establish himself in Paris (1893). He was still the people's lawyer, contributor to the progressive newspapers (*La Lanterne*), an assiduous militant of the congresses. He was a candidate at general elections, on principle, and always defeated. However, at the turn of the century he opted for Jaurès's republican socialism in preference to the Marxist socialism of the Guesdists. And at long last, in 1902, he won his first election, at Saint-Etienne, a long way from Brittany but still in a working-class area. He was at that time in the Combist majority, and government was not far away. Then came a decisive turning point: after the Amsterdam congress he was among those who, like Viviani or Augagneur, but unlike Jaurès, rejected socialist unity with its condition, as may be recalled, of a strict ban on the 'collaboration of the classes'. Thenceforth he would be an 'independent socialist' deputy, as ministers were likely to be drawn from their ranks, whereas that did not apply, by definition, to the 'unified' socialists. So Briand was established as the archetype of socialists who had turned renegade through pushiness and opportunism. What followed would show, however, how much of his original humanitarianism he would manage to preserve. But in 1905–6 he had not yet reached the famous 'Away with the guns!' of 1927. All that could be seen was a brilliant forty-year-old bachelor, somewhat bohemian and indolent, with a casual hairstyle, cigarette in hand, but sure of having such superiority of eloquence, talent and charm over his colleagues that he would never lack a leading role.

The Rouvier government, ousted on the occasion of the inventories crisis, had also encountered another trial during the first weeks of its rule. A year earlier, on 31 March 1905, the German Emperor Wilhelm II had landed at Tangier to visit the independent sovereign of Morocco, the Sultan, and in a speech that attracted attention, had claimed to be the defender of that state, which France surrounded.

Wilhelm II proposed to call an international conference to debate on Morocco and, to his way of thinking, swamp French ambition by a ruling at the highest level. Curiously, Delcassé had been in favour of rejecting the conference, which Wilhelm could have taken for a *casus belli*. Rouvier, in the government, saw to it that acceptance, that is, peace, prevailed. It is a moot point whether Rouvier was in this instance the spokesman for prudence, or for large-scale capitalism which still preferred peacetime business to the profits of war industries. Whatever the reason, Delcassé resigned and left the Quai d'Orsay in June 1905 with the reputation of an uncompromising patriot who had been sacrificed to German demands.

In reality, the beaten Delcassé would quickly have his revenge: when the conference took place at Algeciras, from January to April 1906, the alliances which his diplomacy had procured enabled France to win the contest. Out of thirteen countries represented, Germany had only Austria-Hungary and Turkey on its side; France was upheld by Russia, Great Britain, Spain and Italy. The conference accepted the idea that the Moroccan state was incapable of assuming its obligations in the matter of international payments and policy and that an international association would take it under supervision. French presence was preponderant; in order to limit a predictable French takeover, they had just managed to stipulate freedom of international trade, known as the 'Open Door'. In fact, another door was opened: the one to French conquest of Morocco, but in rivalry with German. To sum up, a sort of second front, after that of the Rhine, was established between France and Germany. That is why there is often common agreement in saying that the 'pre-war' period dated from Algeciras or, if preferred, Tangier.

4

Belle Époque or Pre-war?
1906–1914

It is because the war began in 1914 that pre-1914 is termed 'pre-war'; that statement of the obvious is generally accepted, bearing in mind that, after the Tangier coup and with the increase in Balkan crises, there was a perceptible 'escalation of perils'.

That same war, with its own horrors and lastingly disruptive consequences, helps to impart a rosy hue, by contrast, to the era when it had not yet taken place. In this respect the cliché Belle Époque applied to the 1900s and the beginning of the 1910 decade has, relatively speaking, an undeniable value even if, as in every period, there were also the poor, the exploited and the victimized for whom the epoch was not really very beautiful.

The idea of Belle Époque, in short, transposes to the fatal date of 1914 what Talleyrand once said of 1789: 'He who did not live before 1789 can have no conception of the gentle way of life.'

Did the people of the era who, themselves, were unaware that they were living 'pre-war' experience such a feeling of euphoria at the time? A journalist who will be mentioned again later, Robert de Jouvenel, wrote in 1914:

This country no longer has institutions. However, it gets along admirably without them. France is a fortunate country, where the soil is generous, the craftsmen ingenious, wealth is divided up. Here, politics is according to individual taste; it is not the be-all and end-all of people's lives.

And this country lets itself be gently run by men who have no pretensions to provide it with an arrogant doctrine, a superior government, certain justice or brutal truth. It does not seek to borrow its prosperity from its institutions; it simply prospers.[1]

In short, the Republic was accepted philosophically, because it existed and the country felt at ease. True or false, tendentious perhaps, that page which we shall soon see in its precise context could certainly not have been

---

[1] *La République des camarades*, p. 5.

penned in 1900, or in 1925. Prosperity, to be sure, was badly apportioned and left many victims. But business was at last on the move. The long spell of economic depression which had begun around the third quarter of the nineteenth century had given way, at the approach of the twentieth, to a phase of expansion, a slow rise in prices, profits and salaries, better control over employment.

Above all, a not inconsiderable technical modernization was becoming apparent, likely to stimulate the economy and at the same time nurture a belief in progress and enrich daily life by rendering it more convenient and agreeable.

For that very reason, the period of President Fallières (1906–13) is noticeably more familiar to us than that of Sadi Carnot. At the risk of stating the obvious again, one might say that the nineteenth century was over and done with and the twentieth well under way.

Primarily, this was because of what has long been called the 'second industrial revolution'. People then were really beginning to live with the consequences of the scientific discoveries at the end of the previous century, notably electricity and the internal combustion engine. In the large towns and industrial cities, the worker no longer had to cover kilometres on foot in order to get to the factory; tramways were beginning to replace the horse-drawn omnibus and the bicycle became a functional everyday implement. Paris, copying London, though much later, was finally endowed with the métro. The car, albeit still rare and expensive, had nevertheless passed from the stage of curious prototype, or dangerous machine for the slightly deranged sportsman, to that of true means of transport. For the rich, of course, but it is well known that everything can become popular, given time. Aircraft were starting to take to the skies. About 1910, aeroplanes were still at the experimental and sporting stage at which the car had been twenty years earlier: Blériot crossed the Channel in 1909, Roland Garros the Mediterranean in 1912. His exhibitions (flying was even more astonishing than going overland without horses had been, around 1830) sent the crowds wild.

With these practical machines, glorified in the ideological climate of the time, when the spirit of enthusiasm for progress carried the day over nostalgia and pessimism, spectator sport took off. That alone would suffice to make us find 1910 more familiar than 1890. The first international Paris–Madrid car race took place in 1903, and so did the first cycling Tour de France.

Great exploits, sport, innovations, all the marvels of the new century, magnified the expansion of another big cultural phenomenon: the publication of popular magazines for leisure activities and entertainment, *Je sais tout*, *Lisez-moi*, *Nos Loisirs*, *Le Vélo*, which would be followed by *L'Auto*.

As for the mainstream press, formerly so political at the time of the battles and crusades, while preserving numerous and pugnacious opinion newspapers, it made way for not very politicized (at least in appearance) information sheets that allocated a great deal of space to sport and brief news items

Aeroplane race at Monte Carlo, 1909. These aeroplanes give the same impression of audacious and wanton fragility as today's ultra-light machines. They belong, however, to the generation that dared for the first time to cross a strip of sea (Bleriot, 1909). They all had propellors then, and monoplanes (with a single pair of wings) were distinct from biplanes (with two pairs of wings, one above the other, thus giving a doubled aerofoil surface). (Photo: Agence d'Information photographique Harlingue)

and consequently enjoyed mass success. The four Parisian titles, which people started to call the 'four greats' (*Le Petit Journal*, *Le Petit Parisien*, *Le Journal* and *Le Matin*), together made up 40 per cent of the national circulation of daily newspapers. Yet numerous and prosperous provincial papers also existed.

People could read serialized novels, and theatrical reviews, which were already well established. But – another victory for technology and another enrichment of leisure hours – there was the cinema, too. The invention of Louis Lumière dated from 1895, but the immense work of Méliès belongs to the 1900s; the big business undertakings arrived on the scene (foundation of the Pathé company in 1900, building of the Butte-Chaumont studios in 1906); and films with artistic ambitions, which were then little more than filmed theatre, began around 1908.

Some people have tried to extend the picture – or the argument – to the point of lumping all the intellectual life of the time under the dominant mood of the acceleration of innovation, and thus to contrast a dawning 'twentieth century' with a 'nineteenth century' laden with ancient conquests now merely boringly harped upon.

In fact, some observations lead in this direction. In 1907, the state authorities carried to the Panthéon the remains of the chemist Marcelin Berthelot, whose works had been materialist and whose influence had been in the service of free-thinking. Now, at that time Berthelot, who was hostile to the new atomic theories, was an outdated academic, and today's science was discreetly coming into being with Becquerel and the Curies, husband and wife.

The same antithesis was occurring in Art. In the streets, conventional sculpture was erecting an increasing number of statues of great men, about as lifelike as under Louis-Philippe, with an allegorical emphasis into the bargain, but Rodin had already audaciously made his Balzac burst forth from the block of rough marble.

In 1907, the revolution of cubism (Picasso, *Les Demoiselles d'Avignon*) provided an even more fantastic leap forward than that of impressionism in the 1870s. In the same way, the daring of Debussy seemed then a wider break with tradition than those with which Berlioz or Wagner had impressed the preceding century.

In short, 'beautiful' or not, the epoch was modern and relegated the century that had just ended to the category of the bygone, historic and dated.

Certain people could comment on this movement with provocative enthusiasm. The 'Manifesto of Futurism' (for the most part young Italian painters, but their article appeared in *Le Figaro* in 1909) dared to proclaim, among other imperious dicta, the aesthetic superiority of the 'roaring automobile over the Victory of Samothrace'. It may be objected that they formed merely a handful of fanatics. But more popular events reflected their mood.

For example, in 1913 the permanent Under-Secretary of State for Fine Arts, Dujardin-Beaumetz, a radical, former painter of battle scenes and great inaugurator of academico-civic statues, retired from the arena; he was old and weary, and had been ridiculed, to boot, because of the theft of the Mona Lisa, which some bold eccentric had stolen from the Louvre. His successor in the constituency of Limoux (Aude) had the same mentality and the same tendencies. Now, their opponents could think of nothing better than to present in opposition the candidacy of Jules Védrines, an aviation pioneer and hero of aerial acrobatics. What is more, the Védrinists, during this colourful campaign, overturned several statues presented by the radicals, and the man in the flying machine very nearly stole the seat from the specialist in allegory on a pedestal. Was that not a provincial echo of futurism, the symbolic struggle of modern dynamism against the antiquated Republic?[2]

---

[2] As for the question of knowing whether this overall dynamism would one day spill over into fascism, Bolshevism or a renewed republican democracy, it was obviously still only latent.

That dialectic of archaism and modernity applied perfectly to the question of the public role of women. Were they reduced to silence or could they have their say? Both are true. Political society was essentially masculine since women, not having the vote, were not encouraged to take part in its debates. Furthermore, the most widely held moral standards clearly advised them against it. But things were not that simple. As the Republic was a constant effervescence of struggles, disputes and liberations, there emerged from it a good number of feminine celebrities who did not all fit into the discreet roles which traditionally devolved upon women.

Let us begin with those who deliberately entered the field of social criticism and struggle. Louise Michel had died at the beginning of 1905, but Séverine (Caroline Rémy), who was also of modest origins and had had a difficult life, from the time of her liaison with Jules Vallès (1880–5) ceaselessly championed the cause of the wretched and libertarian aspirations in the publications of the extreme left. Boulangist for a while, then an uncommitted protester, Dreyfusard, always closer to anarchism than to socialism, but always hard at work.

The socialist, trades union and working-class movement had other obscure female militants, who were often equally preoccupied with women's rights. But in the bourgeois world itself, certain anti-establishment women attained celebrity, even influence. The first was Marguerite Durand, whose library of studies in feminism which she bequeathed to the city of Paris perpetuates her name. Born in Paris in 1864, and at first an actress, she left the theatre to marry the radical, then Boulangist, deputy Georges Laguerre, from whom she later separated. Free and rich, she made her mark by founding *La Fronde* in 1897, a newspaper edited entirely by women, which prospered until 1905, and which supported the general politics of the left and the advancement of women and their rights – *all* women's rights, from that of middle-class girls from the *lycée* to gain entry to the Bar to that of salesgirls in the big stores to sit down for a rest now and then. A radicalism and a feminism which, through that last item, rubbed shoulders with socialism and which, in short, completing a very significant blend, were combined with a free-thinking and libertarian spirit. Marguerite Durand's last claim to fame was for having founded the well-known dogs' cemetery at Asnières (Seine) in 1899, which at that time was not only a sign of sensitivity but also, to some extent, of antireligious provocation, if one thinks of what a cemetery meant to Christians.

If Marguerite Durand was bound to the left, another unconventional celebrity took her stance on the right. Marie Clémentine de Rochechouart-Mortemart, born in 1847, became by marriage the Duchesse de Crussol d'Uzès and belonged to the ancient nobility and the world of immense wealth. She is know to history chiefly for having been a militant royalist and in particular for having poured a great deal of money into General Boulanger's campaigns. She was renowned for her deer and fox hunts. Her son, an officer, would die in the Congo on a voyage of exploration. All that was logical and, one might say, to be expected. But the Duchesse d'Uzès, a woman blessed with many talents, also distinguished herself by boldly matching her life as a woman of the world with an artistic life. She published several works (novels, plays, books on local history and hunting) under the pseudonym Manuela, and made a name for herself as a sculptress (a Joan of Arc and a Saint-Hubert come as no surprise, but also an Émile Augier and a Gilbert). That personal dynamism could not help but lead her to the fringes of feminine demands. She had no hesitation in presiding over the Union of Female Painters; she prided herself on being the first woman to have obtained a driving licence (petrol engine vehicles), and even published a lecture on feminine suffrage.

Of course, other rich women, well known and talented and in greater numbers, contented themselves with taking part in politics through the age-old route of the influence bestowed by a salon. For there were salons under the Third Republic: literary salons, political salons or politico-literary salons. This form of sociability among the upper classes was no longer the only one imaginable, as in the seventeenth century, nor was it at its apogee, as in the eighteenth or beginning of the nineteenth, but it did better than merely survive – it still counted, notably in Paris. It would be tiresome and banal to make a list of them. Broadly speaking, the salons of the aristocracy supported right-wing politics, the more academic forms of artistic expression and anti-Dreyfusard meetings (Mme De Luynes and many others). But there were also salons and a society life on the left, scarcely less 'classy', because the Protestant, Jewish and free-thinking religious minorities, even in the highest spheres of wealth, preserved the nonconformist qualities on which the Republic relied. A typical example, in the early days of the regime, had been the salon of Mme Adam (Juliette Lambert, the widow of the prefect Édouard Adam), who inherited the brilliant liberal salon of the Comtesse d'Agout, the veritable general headquarters of the republican party in the great era of Gambetta. It is true that, after her break with Gambetta over the Republic's foreign policy, Juliette Adam had moved towards nationalism and, on the eve of 1914, her influence could be classified as right wing. But by then radicalism had found alternative society venues.

Mention must be made at least of the homes of Mme Arman de Caillavet and the Marquise Arconati-Visconti. The former, born in 1844, the daughter of an Austrian Jewish banker who had immigrated to Paris, married a French engineer, Arman, who was later vaguely ennobled, and had belonged to the Parisian society received at the Tuileries under the Empire. That was not so paradoxical as it may seem. An entire cultured society, liberal in the widest sense, that is to say, neither clerical nor revolutionary, had passed quite naturally and easily from the waning Empire to the reasonable Republic (one has only to think of Flaubert, Renan, the Goncourts, among many others). Thus, a young woman whose marriage had been celebrated at the Tuileries in 1867 was able, after 1878, to receive at her Wednesday dinners in the avenue Hoche a host of renowned writers (Heredia, for example) and well-read members of parliament (Poincaré was to be seen there, as well as Clemenceau). After 1888, at the start of a closer relationship between the lady of the house and Anatole France, Mme de Caillavet's salon would become the writer's real home and, later, one of the gathering-places of the Dreyfusard intelligentsia. Another was the home of the Marquise Arconati-Visconti, in the rue Barbet-de-Jouy. She had deeper republican roots, being the daughter of Napoléon Peyrat, the old militant who had whispered to Gambetta 'clericalism is the real enemy.' She had married a liberal Italian aristocrat from the elite of contemporary Italy, but was soon widowed and inherited his immense domains; she held her salon in Paris and, after the Dreyfus Affair, her Thursday dinners gathered together what really amounted to the combined headquarters of university Dreyfusism and the parliamentary Left-wing Bloc, the Gabriel Monods, the Émile Combes and many others, including Jaurès himself, at least while he seemed sufficiently attached to the Bloc and republican patriotism. The Marquise was far more than a society lady, being passionately involved in politics, and a rich collector of works of art. By keeping alive the optimism that had come from the Enlightenment, she linked the republican ideal to the progress of scientific knowledge and, as she had no offspring, made it manifest by presenting many gifts and bequests to university institutions (the Sorbonne library, Institute of Geography, Institute of Art and Archaeology, a Chair in the Collège de France, some items of furniture for the Museum of Decorative Arts). One might say that she combined the traditional, even archaic, role of the society woman who holds a salon and whose function in the world of politics is to act as hostess, with the very modern role of feminine intellectual.

Even more than by anti-establishment and society women, the pinnacles of female celebrity were scaled by the personal achievements of some women in the world of culture. On the eve of the Great War, among the ladies in the limelight Sarah Bernhardt and the Comtesse de Noailles were the chief stars. The first, born in Paris in 1844, came of a Jewish family, later converted to Catholicism, of modest social standing, and working in the entertainment business. She attended the Conservatoire, failed at the Comédie-Française in 1862, and had a hard time in the theatrical and bohemian world until she achieved success in 1869 in Francois Coppée's *Le Passant*. Thenceforward, she devoted herself solely to the theatre and became very much in the public eye. During the siege of Paris in 1870–1, a patriot, she set up and organized a first-aid post (an *ambulance*, as it was called) at the Odéon. In 1902, her triumph in the revival of *Ruy Blas* reopened the Comédie-Française to her. She met Victor Hugo, it could be said as one star meeting another, and won glory in France and on world tours, in the service of French and republican prestige, founding her Châtelet theatre in 1899 and enjoying her last and supreme triumph in Edmond Rostand's *L'Aiglon* in 1900. Her celebrity was complex, owing much to her art and theatrical successes, but also to what was known of her sumptuous and fantastic private life, and not least because of her true generosity in philanthropic works. From Hugo to Rostand she served with significant success an idealistic, high-minded, patriotic theatre, whose form of expression was the beautifully measured alexandrine.

The Comtesse de Noailles would provide the last illustration of that great nineteenth-century style of poesy, before the post-war period and surrealism relegated it to the museum during the 1920s. Anna Brancovan, born in 1876, was a rich Romanian princess, fascinating rather than beautiful, with – so it was said – a kind of 'strange genius' added to all her other dazzling advantages. Having settled in Paris through her marriage with Comte Mathieu de Noailles and because of her personal taste for French culture, she held her salon there, published poetry (*Le Cœur innombrable* (1901) and many other collections), travelled, engaged in politics on the Dreyfusard side, declaring herself now socialist, now Christian anarchist, now neo-pagan, but not insensitive to other, opposing beliefs and feelings provided they were elevated and harmonious. She would weep for Jaurès in 1914 and Maurice Barrès in 1923.

She was an admired and respected woman, and even by the innovative *Nouvelle Revue française* was held to be one of the great writers of the era.

Heirs to the aesthetics of the nineteenth century, Sarah Bernhardt and Anna de Noailles, those pre-1914 celebrities, are scarcely known today. By contrast, Marie Curie, whose name has been immortalized by radium, radiology, atoms and contemporary medicine, is far more famous now than she was at the time of her great work. Nevertheless, she belonged to the same generation as Marguerite Durand and the Comtesse de Noailles and, like the latter, was an immigrant who had become French by marriage. Born in Warsaw, then under Russian domination, in 1867, Marie Sklodowska was the daughter of a *lycée* teacher, a Polish patriot, with whom she shared intellectual gifts and a progressive tendency born of patriotic feelings about their country's oppression. In Poland she had a difficult youth as a rural primary school teacher and cultural militant, resolving in 1891 to exile herself to France. She was a brilliant student at the Sorbonne, and in 1895 married Pierre Curie, a teacher at the School of Physics and Chemistry in Paris. Then came the great discoveries, alternating with those of Henri Becquerel, of the phenomenon of radioactivity, and all that would follow: new elements (uranium, isolated and named by Becquerel, polonium and radium by Pierre and Marie Curie, in 1902), modern atomic theory, the first medical applications. Marie, a professor from 1896, taught at the Sèvres *École normale supérieure* from 1900 to 1906. Pierre, who had become professor of physics at the Sorbonne, died accidentally in 1906, and Marie was chosen to succeed him. In 1903 the Nobel prize for physics was shared between the couple and Henri Becquerel. She was only one woman, however, a *rara avis* in the learned world. Is it significant that in 1911 Marie Curie should receive her second triumph as a researcher (the Nobel prize for chemistry this time) and her first great social failure: defeated in election to the Académie des sciences? It is only fair to say that in 1922 the

Académie de médecine would summon her to its ranks, recognizing – apart from her laboratory work – the tireless activity she had carried on in the hospitals during the Great War.[3]

But we must return to the men, with the official universe of parliamentary, social and diplomatic battles.

Political history itself also presents that dual nature of tradition and originality, as the moment had come for Georges Clemenceau, an incomparable person as well as being a republican of the founding generation. Is it because of that double image that collective memory has difficulty in placing him correctly? Because he came to power in 1906, a quarter of a century after Jules Ferry and Léon Gambetta, it is hard to imagine his belonging to their generation; it is merely that *they* had governed at a younger age than is usual, and Clemenceau at an older. Because he governed again, from 1917 to 1920, in the limelight of war and victory, in an authoritarian and nearly nationalist fashion, he would be thought of as almost the prototype of a man of the right, whereas in 1906 he could pass for the purest of pure republicans and man of the left. Because he put down strikes, he is seen only as an example of the discrediting of democracy when it stays 'bourgeois'. The dead workers of Draveil would join those of Fourmies in the rather biased indictment continually levelled at republican idealism by the class struggle. Yet the Clemenceau of 1906 could pass for the paragon of that ideal Republic.

A survivor of the founding generation, and the first embodiment of opposition radicalism, he had 'brought down governments' without taking part in any; he had dazzled and caused a certain amount of disquiet. Besmirched by the Panama affair, in 1893 he had lost his seat as deputy for the Var, but his unwavering passion for justice had hurled him into the Dreyfus Affair, thereby 'rehabilitating him in the eyes of democracy'.[4] Having re-entered active politics in 1902 through his election to the Senate, where he managed to obtain the chair that Victor Hugo had occupied at the extreme left of the semicircle, he supported the Bloc, then fell out with Combes and became a dissident.

In March 1906, on the fall of Rouvier's government, the obscure Sarrien at last thought of entrusting him for the first time with a ministerial post. Clemenceau took the Interior – roughly, it was claimed, or through a misunderstanding. Picture a political gathering in Sarrien's drawing room:

---

[3] With the exception of Mme Arman de Caillavet, who died in 1910, all these famous women survived the Great War by some years until:

1923 (the Marquise Arconati-Visconti and Sarah Bernhardt)

1929 (Séverine)

1933 (the Duchesse d'Uzès, the Comtesse de Noailles)

1934 (Mme Curie)

1936 (Marguerite Durand and Juliette Adam).

[4] The expression comes from the socialist historian, Georges Bourgin.

The Pas-de-Calais miners' strike, 1906. The procession of strikers passing the miners' cottages. (Illustration from the *Petit-Journal*. Photo: Collection Viollet)

'What will you have?' asks the host, meaning port? orangeade? coffee? Answer: 'I'll have the Interior.' Real or imaginary, the anecdote is a good illustration of the man's categorical manner and his desire to go straight to the basic responsibilities without serving his apprenticeship first, like anyone else, in the Ministry of Agriculture or Public Education.

At that time the Interior was having to deal with two gigantic problems, different but simultaneous, and both dramatic: the resistance to the church inventories and the miners' strike. The latter had begun with an immense catastrophe at Courrières (Pas-de-Calais) on 10 March. A firedamp explosion, fire, a thousand dead! Rescue operations which the mining companies, in their haste to see work resume, had stopped too soon: survivors still proved able to get out from underground by themselves – could not others have been saved? The exasperated miners plunged into a resolute strike to demand better safety standards.

At first Clemenceau took the humanitarian course of action. As regards the inventories, he put a stop to the use of force: 'One does not have to kill men in order to count candlesticks.' For the miners, he went alone to Lens to the strike committee, showed clearly that he understood the workers and their fight, and asked them only to pursue it without violence or illegality. They would not listen to him; overexcited social protest rejected his optimistic humanism, and, without a doubt, at that moment and in that place, something inside him snapped.

Meanwhile, in May he had to preside over the legislative elections. The electorate, indifferent to parliamentary vicissitudes, again intensified its approval of the course that the Republic had followed for seven years. The right was reduced to 174 seats, the left exceeded 400: 90 republicans of the Democratic Alliance leaning, some 250 radicals and radical socialists, 20 independent socialists and 54 organized socialists. The latter were those who, since the unification of parties desired by Amsterdam, had been called the *unifiés*, or the SFIO (Section française de l'Internationale ouvrière, French Section of the Workers' Internationale). That seemed to impose a shift to the left in the government. Sarrien resigned and Clemenceau, still keeping the Interior, formed and presided over a new team (27 October 1906). It was a dazzling government, some of whose declarations of principle and symbolic measures form a kind of pinnacle of the pre-1914 Republic. In Public Education, which included responsibility for Religious Cults, was Aristide Briand, who had distinguished himself by his skilfulness in organizing the Separation. To Finance, Clemenceau recalled Waldeck-Rousseau's former minister, Joseph Caillaux, also a leftist choice.

Joseph Caillaux, born in Le Mans in 1863, came from the most conservative bourgeoisie. His father had been Minister of Finance in the Broglie government, the cabinet of 16 May (1877). Without falling out with his father, however, the young man had joined the republican camp. Was that the rejection of a very constricting Catholic upbringing? The scorn of a cultivated man for the prejudices of the God-fearing milieu? A desire to be able to serve the existing state and to win its acceptance of rational reforms? All these reasons have been put forward. At all events, he had opted for the most difficult studies, and had become an Inspector of Finance, in which post he had distinguished himself and acquired an exceptional knowledge of the fiscal system, with its imperfections and anachronisms. In 1898 he had won the constituency of Mamers (Sarthe) for the Republic and would remain its deputy until 1919. After having just turned thirty-six and been in parliament only a year, he had become Minister of Finance in the Waldeck-Rousseau government. At that time he had been able only to raise the question of income tax, but he made a name for himself by carrying out excellent technical reforms in fiscal administration and by managing to get the budget back on an even keel. Like Waldeck, in 1902 he rejected radicalism and kept himself aloof from Combes and Combist policies. But Clemenceau, who had himself become an opponent of Combes, could not hold that against him and, in 1906, recalled him to the Ministry of Finance, as an indispensable financial expert and a reformer whose name was linked with income tax. Clemenceau, who disliked the other great expert, Poincaré, could feel some affinity with Caillaux, like himself a positive, brilliant, dominating character, without prejudices, stimulated rather than worn down by battles and hatred, and too young (by twenty-two years) to be a rival. It would be foreign policy that would one day divide them. For the time being, in autum 1906 Caillaux, Clemenceau's Minister of Finance, arrived at a plan for taxing incomes. The idea of modernizing direct taxation in this way was then generally thought of as a panacea: a better-based tax, thus more fair, heavier for the well off and average taxpayers, would allow the state a more generous social policy; thus social justice through redistributive taxation would be initiated, satisfying humanitarian feelings while at the same time doing without socialism. Income tax at that time was nearly as clear a test between left and right as secularism or Dreyfusism.

For his Minister of War, Clemenceau chose none other than General Picquart – yes, the former Lieutenant-Colonel hero of the Dreyfus Affair, a significant endorsement if ever there was one! One last sign – a new ministry was created, the Ministry of Labour. As its first minister, for want of official socialists (SFIO), who were now hostile to any bourgeois commitment, Clemenceau appointed an independent socialist (a supporter of Jaurès who had not followed his leader into unification), René Viviani. Several other promises were added: an eight-hour working day, state purchase of the western railways, status for public servants.

Many of these projects would come to nothing. Nevertheless, from this triumphant start two lasting achievements would survive, obviously not connected but answering the same ideal of generous equity. In the social field, a law was finally passed on a weekly day of rest, usually fixed on a Sunday. And symbolically, as the Appeal Court had at last, after long-drawn-out proceedings, decided to quash Dreyfus's sentences, the unhappy Captain was solemnly readmitted to the army, decorated and promoted to a higher rank. Another of his great defenders, Émile Zola, who had died in 1902, received the honour of interment in the Panthéon in 1908.

Lastly, to succeed Émile Loubet, whose seven-year term ended in 1906, the combined republican groups made a choice even farther to the left by preferring the president of the Senate, Armand Fallières, a radical barrister and truly representative of that secular democracy, both bourgeois and progressive, that was so well represented in the Midi, to Paul Doumer who, since his opposition to Combes, had been fairly clearly stamped as belonging to the right.

Compared with all these signs of justice and progress, the almost routine event of having a strike in the Pas-de-Calais on one's hands was completely secondary, or so it appeared.

Nevertheless, those signs and that forward impetus would not prevent politics from becoming a very confused issue in contemporary minds.

With Clemenceau and, looking a little ahead, his successors, the Republic entered a muddled period, which no longer enjoyed the homogeneity that the Waldeck-Rousseau and Combes years had derived from the precision of their fields of combat and the clarity of inspiration of their majority. Under Clemenceau (1906–9) and with all the more reason after him, nothing would be as clear cut. Before seeing how events unfolded, we must weigh up several new factors: the parliamentary crisis, the intensity of social struggles, the matter of peace in international relations, all of which upset the usual pattern of conflict between the parties.

To tell the truth, parliament did not feel itself to be in crisis. It was even euphoric. It governed, in fact, by its constant capacity for gambling with the fate of ministries, and it passed laws, after a fashion. And it left deputies (and incidentally senators, who were more stable because less subjected to the spectre of re-election) the time to carry out the affairs and duties of their constituencies and their voters. For all those occupations, which were just as time-consuming as a job, deputies received a salary that had remained at the same level since 1848. This amounted to 9,000 francs per year (which matches, for 360 days a year, the '25 francs a day' which Baudin had made famous in December 1851). As the cost of living had risen, deputies quickly voted at the beginning of the 1906 legislature for an increase to 15,000 francs. That upward leap seemed quite considerable, and the *quinze mille* (the QM) found opinion against them.

Antiparliamentarism, to be sure, was as old as the Republic, but until then it had emanated chiefly from the regime's opponents, the most logical of whom disputed its very principle of election and representation. It was even the antiparliamentary element in Boulangism which had rendered it suspect in the eyes of many republicans. Then that antiparliamentarism had received the additional backing of a revolutionary and libertarian extreme left, desirous of shattering the illusions with which, according to their doctrine, liberal democracy lulled the poverty-stricken. But criticism of the parliamentary system had yet to gain followers in the camp of the Republic itself. In order to understand this chain of circumstances, we must first dispatch the Dreyfus Affair and its 'fallout'. In the heart of a young man like Charles Péguy, the crusading enthusiasm for justice which had launched his generation of young intellectuals into the affair was of the same nature and had the same moral aims as that of the volunteers of 1792 against the tyrants, or the republicans of 1848 against those responsible for the coup of 2 December. The word 'Republic' embraced all that in its almost religious resonance. What Péguy could not endure was that, once victory had been won, ordinary life should have resumed its course, simply with a majority on the left rather than the right, while the Republic became a sort of moral patrimony and political capital continually invoked by politicians who were not necessarily more likeable than their opponents. He summed up his views on the matter in this terse phrase, destined to be repeated *ad nauseam* after him: 'Everything begins in mysticism and ends in politics.' Translated: one starts with Bernard Lazare and Lucien Herr, pure apostles, and one ends up with Émile Combes.

It is known that Péguy never forgave his former friend Jaurès for having accepted the fellowship of the last-named after having known that of the other two.

But let us for the moment leave Péguy's destiny and the drama of his break with parliamentary socialism, and with Jaurès in particular.

It may be useful here to throw some light on how a Republic of the left, victorious, strong – perhaps too strong, since it no longer had the merit and the attraction of being threatened – which took responsibility for running the world as it was, should come down from its pedestal to suffer the harshest attacks from its own offspring.

The parliamentary regime, toppled from its pedestal at the same stroke, found itself on the carpet. In effect professionalizing the representatives of the electorate would create its own defects. Legislative work, technically badly organized, was slow and less efficient that it should have been. Divisions between deputies, which were clear when it came to setting the left against the right or the extreme left, became esoteric, blurred, easily suspect when they had to make their way through the enormous majority formed by the radicals and their allies. Personal connections? Social coteries? Regional interests? Affiliation to private business groups? The Palais-Bourbon, except for a few special occasions, became a world that was too enigmatic to be respectable.

In 1914 Robert de Jouvenel would methodically draw up a description of these observations under the title *La République des camarades* (comrades here meaning, of course, members of parliament among themselves, sticking together and on intimate terms).[5] Together with many a relevant analysis, some of its fierce declarations are memorable, for example: 'There are fewer differences between two deputies of whom one is revolutionary (let us say socialist) and the other is not, than between two revolutionaries of whom one is a deputy and the other is not.' And that remark at the end: 'France, whose forces are intact, is looking for institutions' – a statement that opens up historical perspectives, if one remembers that in 1914 Charles de Gaulle, then aged twenty-four, read a great deal and would make research into institutions one of his major projects. In short, in the very heart of the great party of the Republic, it was found that government demanded a specialized personnel, who did not always measure up to the loftiness of its noble mission, that too-frequent ministerial crises were prompted by ill-perceived causes and that legislative work was inadequate.

Despite the taboo that lay over revision (the 'Constitution of the Republic' was officially sacred, like everything else 'of the Republic'), remedies were sought, to avoid the disillusion that would otherwise be suffered.

It was not by chance that, during these very years, new political forces should come into being and be organized in propaganda and action associations, endowed with their own programme and a lasting life, rather than in radical-style parties, with activities that were electoral and consequently intermittent. Extra-parliamentary political associations? These were the leagues, which have already been mentioned. But the latter blazed forth at the time of the great crises and were rather forgotten afterwards. More enduring was Le Sillon founded in 1906 by Marc Sangnier, a 'movement'

---

[5] The socialists of that time called one another 'citizens' and the anarchists, 'companions'.

(and not a 'party') organized around a charismatic leader, with the aim of conquering opinion rather than parliament, to give life to a democracy which would be both modern and genuinely Catholic. In the France of 1906, apparently well divided between a bloc of irreligious republicans and a mass of Christians with authoritarian atavism, that smacked of attempting the impossible or wagering on the future. A year earlier, in 1905, another permanent and extra-parliamentary group had been born – Action fran-çaise. This was more traditional because, in the main, it continued the ideological tradition of the counter-revolution (monarchy, religion, tradi-tion, old France) while at the same time it embraced the activism and allergies of the 'revolutionary right' or members of the leagues. The origin-ality of Action française lay precisely in the merging of those two concepts. It was in the nature of the pugnacious and nationalist right wing (pre-fascist, Sternhell would say) to seek a leader. The logical genius of Charles Maurras consisted in persuading this sector of opinion that the leader was already found, his name 'the King', or at least the pretender to the throne. Thus royalism gained a fresh start. At the moment when it seemed ready to be relegated to the museum of utopias, it came back into actuality as the vanguard of an antirepublican combat redefined in modern terms, that is to say, nationalist and populist.

Yes, populist, for there was not one opposition force that did not dispute the official Republic's claim to have the support of 'the people', of which it was so proud and which, moreover, the elections confirmed. Action française, like Le Sillon, like the libertarians who were disappointed in electoral socialism, like every other group alive, would not fail to pay court to the workers' movement.

In contrast with the bipolar situation of 1899–1900, the cards were being dealt anew, and the power of a working-class movement with the wind in its sails made an important contribution.

All elements combined to intensify social struggles. Firstly, the state of economic expansion favoured the formulation of wage claims. Then, the working-class movement, which taken as a whole figured on the side of the victors in the post-1899 democratic revival, was able to consolidate its forces and enlarge its membership. The Socialist Party gained an advantage from its unification in 1905, despite the dissidence of some leading par-liamentarians (Briand, Viviani, Augagneur). The CGT gained a more solid structure at its congress in Montpellier in 1904.

Finally, if our general hypothesis is accepted, in that historical phase when the forces of the right are beaten, set aside, not in a state to threaten the Republic, it is usual for the left camp to be able to allow itself the luxury of being divided. Indeed, it needed no more than the defence of the Republic to cause so many socialists in 1899 to tone down their socialism and fly to the support of the liberal bourgeoisie. But when the Republic was no longer in danger, the bourgeoisie – if one dare say so – was once more qualified as bourgeoisie, and held to account for anything that was not going well in the social and economic machinery.

That was the situation that immediately confronted Clemenceau. Minister of the Interior, thus 'France's chief cop' (it is to him, with his scathing tongue and pen, a great producer of historic sayings, that we owe this energetic turn of phrase), he therefore went to Courrières to try, so he thought, to grant the miners a kind of acknowledgement of the legitimacy of their strike, on condition that they brought it within the framework of the law. An impossible attempt, perhaps. There were clashes, incidents and excesses. Everything happened as if the man whose goodwill had been unappreciated had received a kind of personal insult which he would not be able to forgive. Clemenceau who, towards the socialists was somewhat contemptuous ('a speech by Monsieur Jaurès is recognizable by the fact that all the the verbs are in the future tense'), exhibited a resolute hostility towards the CGT (that is, libertarian anarcho-syndicalist, pro-workers' power, even bordering on pro-illegality). And for three years strikes were put down with increasing harshness, and there were even a few deaths. No 'massacres' however, as extensive as at Fourmies. In Paris, the Prefect of Police Lépine, by deploying the cavalry, when the horses' breasts acted like tanks or bulldozers, thereby devised a method of dispersing processions without bloodshed. There were more accidents in the provinces (Fougères, Raon-l'Étape), before the great strike of the navvies in the Villeneuve-Saint-Georges region.

There, at Draveil in June 1908, three workers were killed by gendarmes. It is a fact that in this affair Clemenceau had wanted to make a show of intimidation and, for that, had used *agents provocateurs* who had infiltrated the trade union. That was squarely putting illegality, or at least a patent immorality, at the service of a lawful cause. Clemenceau even went as far as having the confederal committee of the CGT arrested. Logically (too logically?) he treated as an enemy the organization whose celebrated Charter of Amiens in 1906 had assigned to the proletariat the task of acting for and by itself, without parties or sects, to achieve social emancipation.

The accusation of 'anarchy', so commonplace in repressive vocabulary, was at that time not entirely inaccurate, because anarchy was far from being a marginal trend. It had its theorists, like the Russian Peter Kropotkin (1842–1921), who was settled in Paris, the brothers Reclus, Paul Robin; its travelling lecturers, who were very well known, like the tireless Sébastien Faure; its journalists, like Jean Grave, Séverine, Kibaltchine (Victor Serge); and its militants who had been redeployed in trades unions organization, such as Émile Pouget, who from 1902 to 1908 was one of the permanent confederal secretaries of the CGT, not to mention those whom the logic of total revolt and immediate action pushed into crime, like Bonnot and the 'tragic gangsters' of 1911–12. The police and the law would not refrain from lumping them all together, and Victor Serge, the future Bolshevik of 1917, would spend the war years in gaol in Paris accused of being an accomplice in Bonnot's gang.

It would certainly need far more to associate the CGT objectively with unlawfulness and subversion. Nevertheless, its class isolationism scarcely tallied with the republican view of things. Clemenceau interpreted it as a declaration of war. Jaurès, no less conscious of what was different between anarcho-syndicalist aims and those of the Republic, reached an opposite conclusion. From his two platforms, the Chamber of Deputies and the editorials of *L'Humanité*, he lashed out at the employers, the government and the police, defending trades unionists and workers even when he disapproved of their acts of anger, and put all his genius for reconciliation into holding together the two branches of the movement (unions and party) and similarly (on a different plane) the Republic and working-class society.

It is not an unfairly easy antithesis to contrast here the two protagonists of the Dreyfusard battle, who had now become two antagonistic voices of the left. Some celebrated, lively but high-level oratorical duels set the sparks flying in parliament, and public opinion recognized their symbolic roles.

By a stroke of ill-fortune, Clemenceau was to see the resurgence of a kind of battle one would have believed over and done with half a century before – that of the peasants. Agricultural society, which had had the pressure on it relieved by the rural exodus, enjoyed the advantages of the slow but general improvement in material benefits. Economically protected by Méline's tariffs, it had been pampered and gradually won over by the Republic, and it had seemed once again a source of tranquillity as well as of 'reliable' ballot papers. But the vine-growing Languedoc had staked too much on its vineyards. The prosperity of the Second Empire era and the trading facility provided by the railways had allowed the plains of the Bas-Languedoc, from the eastern Pyrenees to the Gard by way of the Aude and the Hérault regions, to be devoted exclusively to the cultivation of grapes. From that came several years of real wealth to which those substantial villages of the plain still bear witness, with their houses of fine hewn stone, their large 'squares' planted with plane trees modelled on urban esplanades, their monumental town halls, their gushing public fountains covered with allegorical sculptures. Then the phylloxera crisis struck; it was short-lived, followed by rapid reconstruction afterwards, but subsequently there was more than ever a monoculture. Regaining prosperity had united a whole section of society, simultaneously benefiting large landowners, their sharecroppers, agricultural workers and the numerous smallholders working their land as a family. But that constant overproduction soon brought about a fall in market prices. As with all economic phenomena, this had multiple and complex causes, but local opinion believed one above all others: if there was a surplus of wine, it was because in the big towns and Paris unscrupulous shopkeepers were stretching quantities by producing ersatz wines, by the addition of sugar. That was a dealers', capitalist fraud, and northern (talk of sugar meant sugar beet and its growers), tolerated by the government, by the state, by Paris. Thence arose a discontent which was at one and the same time that of the hard-working farmworker against speculation, of the Midi against the north, of the provinces against the state. The state was not unaware of these complaints (a deputy for the Aude, Albert Sarraut, was Under-Secretary of State for the Interior in the Clemenceau cabinet), so a commission of enquiry into wine-making fraud was set up in Narbonne. The movement began indeed by the dispatch of delegations of wine-growers formed in each commune to testify before the commission in Narbonne. What about fleshing out those delegations to the point where, in themselves, they became demonstrations bearing witness to the collective uneasiness? That idea was born in Argeliers (Aude) where the village café-owner, Marcelin Albert, founded the first action committee. He was a curious character, both hidebound and semi-cultured, always dressed strictly as a 'gentleman', a bit of a poseur but also one who stuck to his convictions. His fame and popularity spread rapidly. In the spring of 1907 the campaign against fraud, the slump and poverty took shape. Every Sunday, the wine-growers of all the villages would set off (in wagons or mostly by train – never had the network spread so far, with such ramifications of departmental lines, which have for the most part disappeared today) and converge on a town in the region, different each time, to hold a meeting there. And they were enormous and stirring gatherings; with women and children present; with banners, with placards bearing simple and expressive slogans, most often written in 'patois'. Today we would say in 'occitan' (Provençal French), and would suspect a certain amount of regionalism in that lament of an entire people against Paris, its wealth and its laws. Certainly regional feeling was not completely absent, for one Languedoc committee took the initiative of appealing to the patriarch of the Provençal renaissance, Frédéric Mistral, to join the campaign – to no avail, as it happened. It is more accurate to say that this regional sensibility was diffuse and implicit, and that people expressed themselves in 'occitan' simply because that was their natural way of talking in their working relationships and was, so to speak, the professional tongue of those peasants, who also spoke quite good French. They were the people, they marched together in villages, in columns, singing, with an ingenuous fervour which, at a distance, seems to us to bear a closer resemblance to the rural movements and single-mindedness of 1848–51 than to the agricultural battles of the twentieth century.

They were peaceable too, because the regime was reputed to be amicable. In fact, the region was almost entirely 'red', the majority of voters belonging to the left, of Combes and Clemenceau. Many had in their village a bronze bust of 'Marianne' bolted to the fountain. In any case, they were grateful to the government for its benevolence. No hindrance was put in the way of their travelling about or the demonstrations. The railway companies willingly hired out special trains. On 9 June 1907 it was Montpellier's turn to receive the assembled throng. It was said that there were half a million people, and a historian not suspected of southern exaggeration recognized it as the most gigantic demonstration the Third Republic had ever known. On that evening, to give shelter to the demonstrators who would not find a place on the packed trains and hence could not return to their villages until the following morning, the Cardinal-Archbishop of Montpellier, Mgr de Cabrières, gave them permission to camp in the cathedral. The Cardinal was a royalist, and it was a good move on his part to annoy the government by lending the opposition such spectacular support, coupled with a fine gesture of practical help. The other side managed to 'glean' even clearer benefits, however. Doctor Ferroul, the socialist deputy and mayor of Narbonne, gradually became the man in the public eye at meetings and rallies, rather than the outmoded Marcelin Albert.

Nevertheless, as the movement was marking time without achieving any result, the pressure was bound to rise. The committees decided to move on to administrative strikes: town councils would resign, all public activity would cease, even taxation. It was the crossing of this boundary of legality that Clemenceau had held against the miners of Courrières. He believed he had the authority to react: a legal investigation was opened, and summonses served on Marcelin Albert and Ferroul. Such threatening repression radicalized the movement which, in its turn, became classically violent: there were riots in front of public buildings, notably in Perpignan and Narbonne, fisticuffs, the death of a man. But the memorable aspect of this episode is not the rather commonplace one of violence and blood, as at Fourmies or Draveil, but the far more unusual 'mutiny' of the 17th regiment of the line. This regiment was in barracks in Béziers and made up of recruits who came from the area, obviously sympathetic towards the crowds of peasants. In the course of a move between Béziers and Agde, they thought they were being sent to put down the rural movement, and collectively refused to march. Their sole achievement would be to enrich the revolutionary repertoire with a particularly fiery song, the 'Hymn to the 17th', soon composed by Montehus of Montmartre, to the glorification of the thinking soldier who refuses 'to fire on his brothers / For the great men in power'. In fact, the movement was very quickly broken up at very little cost.

To start with, Clemenceau snatched the opportunity presented to him by the honest Marcelin Albert, who came all alone and in all innocence to Paris, in order to hold discussions. The president of the Council welcomed him with kindly words and, seeing that he was rather short of material needs, offered him 100 francs to pay for his return journey. The poor man accepted – and Clemenceau would take care to let it be known. From that time on, Marcelin Albert would be taken for a man who had let himself be bought. The parliamentary majority, however, hastily passed a law intended to curb fraud. Arrested rioters were speedily released. In short, things quietened down, because those radical voters, who were slipping gently towards social democracy, were so profoundly adapted to the culture of the Republic and France.

The social flare-up, which had died down in rural society (it would reappear in 1911 in the Marne and the Aube, also in wine-growing circles, over a matter of limiting the lands that could bear the Champagne designation), was to appear once again in urban and Parisian society in regard to extending trades unionism to state employees, and gave rise to strikes by post office workers and primary school teachers. Clemenceau held that civil servants should have a status (to protect them from the still common practices of recommendation and favouritism in recruitment, promotion and transfer) but he wanted no trades unionism or strikes from agents of the state, and he would not yield. Nevertheless, teachers began to be seen not only thinking and voting socialist, but also sometimes – to their grave risk and peril – belonging to the CGT and thus sharing the anarchistic aspirations it supported, of which we shall soon see a new expansion.

The social assessment of the Clemenceau years would thus in the end be reduced mainly to the emergence of those spectacular conflicts. And on the credit side there would be hardly anything other than the weekly day of rest. Income tax had failed before the Senate; the great law instituting workers' retirement pensions became bogged down and would surface painfully only in 1910 under Briand's ministry. However, parliament voted for the state purchase of the western railways, and passed two laws of an undeniably social nature, although they proceeded from Christian and bourgeois philanthropic circles rather than from 'working-class' inspiration: the creation of cheap living accommodation (*habitations à bon marché*, HBM, the forerunners of French *habitations à loyer modéré* or HLM), and the law on non-seizable family estates.

The class struggle by itself, as proclaimed and commented upon by revolutionary trades unionism, was enough to frighten many left-wing bourgeois whom Dreyfusism had united with the workers and their spokesmen. Jaurès, a man outstanding for the charm of his culture and his moral integrity, naturally found himself the key person in this configuration, for he was as fully representative of socialism as of Dreyfusism. And it was because he persisted in defending the CGT and expressing solidarity with the working-class movement in its totality that Jaurès, regretfully no doubt, saw many and the most brilliant of the intellectuals who had only recently been enthusiastic for the Bloc distance themselves from him.

There was an additional reason. The radical left, Combist and Clementist, remained patriotic, and was terrified to see that the revolutionary wing of the workers' movement was less and less so, that in the CGT the homeland and national defence were vilified as much as the Republic or universal suffrage were denigrated, that a similarly inspired trend was taking shape in the heart of the SFIO around Gustave Hervé, and that Jaurès, without sharing those ideas, refused to dissociate himself from them. Now, in this period when antipatriotism was on the increase, the danger of war seemed to be drawing closer. Conflicts and soon wars in the Balkans, where the protégés of Russia, France's ally, confronted the protégés of Austria-Hungary, linked with Germany, added to Franco-German tension in Morocco. In spite of Algeciras, in fact, Germany had not come to terms with France's gradual seizure of that country. At any moment the question might arise of whether, face to face with Germany, it would be wise to accept the chance of doing battle or negotiating some compromise. Jaurès and his friends declared themselves in favour of the latter course, but they were not alone. In the camp of diplomatic prudence, they were in the company of a man who attained the front rank of the Radical Party and gained a place in history. Joseph Caillaux, until now the 'income tax man', would soon (1911) be the man of the Agadir crisis, that is to say, the man who stood for a peace maintained in exchange for a certain diplomatic concession – a minor loss, but damaging to national self-esteem. With him, Jauressian socialism would be able to rediscover in the radical sphere of influence sympathies or solidarities that would compensate for those which social extremism had caused it to lose. Needless to say, in detail matters were infinitely more complex. Let us just remember that the question of foreign policy reappeared and contributed in its turn to splitting up old coalitions and reassembling them differently.

Such were the great problems and major confrontations forming the backdrop to the necessarily more complicated everyday politics from 1909 to 1914.

Overthrown on 20 July 1909 over a minor issue, Clemenceau withdrew, his scepticism intensified. The Briand government which succeeded him (July 1909 to February 1911), retained a certain kinship with his own, although the two men were as different as could be in age, profession and temperament. Like Clemenceau, Briand claimed to be strongly social – he passed the law on workers' retirement pensions – and again like him, took a vigorous stand in the defence of 'republican order' against strikes that were reputedly revolutionary. He presided over the 1910 elections, when the relationship of forces between the parties remained stable in terms of general politics, despite a considerable replacement of members (234 deputies were elected for the first time, the proportion of defeated outgoing men being very high). There is agreement in reading into that peaceable shake-up the reflection of the vague public dissatisfaction with the system, the possible causes of which have already been related. Briand believed he could find the remedy for the malaise of opinion in a purely institutional alteration. Without going to the extent of revising the Constitution, he tried to effect an improvement by the device of a new electoral system – revisionism in a minor key – a recurring tendency in French politics. There would thus be proportional representation, which would give each party – obliged to redefine itself more clearly – the exact number of elected representatives corresponding with that of its electorate and which, by doing away with the second round, would release candidates from having to negotiate with their nearest neighbours withdrawals that could harm the purity of principles. Briand aroused no enthusiasm among his own men. The majority of the radicals and the more moderate conservatives declared against, and proportional representation found support only among some of Briand's friends and mainly, as is logical, with the more sharply identified parties (the clerical right on one side, the SFIO on the other).

At the end of animated debates between *erpéistes* (from RP, *représentation proportionnelle*) and *arrondissementiers* (those in favour of voting by *arrondissement*), during which, in order to stigmatize parochial politics, Briand labelled sluggish constituencies 'stagnant ponds', proportional representation was passed by the Chamber but turned down by the Senate. It had added an extra dividing line to the traditional battlefronts: the social front, the ideological–religious front (which realigned itself at the least incident) and foreign policies.

After Briand and the brief interlude of the Monis ministry (March–June), the hour struck for Caillaux (June 1911 to January 1912), whose move to power was marked by the Agadir incident[6] and the peaceful solution he was able to achieve. Following him – peace having been rescued for the moment – everything seemed as if nationalism and the vague feeling of chauvinism, more sensitive to 'humiliation' than to being soothed, had been compensated by the return swing of the pendulum towards the right.

In January 1912 Raymond Poincaré formed his first government. Who was this man who would have to preside over the Republic in time of war? Born in Bar-le-Duc in 1860 into a very old bourgeois family – several generations of landed property and the exercise of liberal professions or public office – he no longer belonged to the cohorts of the regime's founders. Around 1880, after brilliant results in secondary education, then degrees in literature and law, he was a barrister at the Paris Bar and distinguished himself in the internal and informal rivalries within the profession by becoming *premier secrétaire de la Conférence*, a signal honour for promising orators. His personal character was already established as that of a very earnest, very gifted man, methodical and quick to learn in any field. It was the urging of family friends rather than a declared personal leaning which caused him to enter politics as principal private secretary to the Minister of Agriculture in 1886, then as the Meuse deputy in 1887, at the age of twenty-seven. Like all his family and quite naturally, he was republican through profound liberalism, therefore secular and socially moderate. The opportunist Republic as it had been formed and orientated suited him perfectly. He was thus a minister very early on and several times in 'progressive' governments, notably under Charles Dupuy. There he acquired the two major specialities which would single him out: on the one hand, public education, teaching, literary matters (as a barrister he was counsel for the literary society, Société des gens de lettres, and would enter the

---

[6] The dispatch of a German battleship to the Moroccan port of Agadir could be taken as an attempt at or the beginning of a sharp check on French expansion (1 July 1911).

Académie française in 1909), and on the other, finance. A great expert in this difficult field, he was also – and with good reason – reputed to be austere in his personal life and scrupulously honest and strict in business. That same moral rigour had made him, counter to the majority of the members of his group, a supporter of the revision of Dreyfus's trial. Though discreet and moderate and without taking part in the government, he had therefore numbered among the upholders of the left-wing majorities of 1899–1905. He had briefly returned to state affairs (Finance) in Sarrien's cabinet, but Clemenceau had not taken on to his team this man with the moderate profile, whose financial programme was less daring than Caillaux's, and whose strong and severe personality was ill-matched with his own. In any case, 1912 was no longer 1906, and people were thinking less about tax and more about the frontier. And they began to see in Poincaré the paragon of that patriotism to which he was dedicated by having been born in Lorraine. It was in this period that, from Joan of Arc to Jules Ferry, from the heroes of Erckmann-Chatrian's novels to the Marshals of the Empire, the sense of belonging, glorified and popularized by Maurice Barrès, almost managed to assume the guise of a political programme.

In 1912 the atmosphere started to change. Noteworthy are the fêtes and parades organized by the garrisons in the towns, which onlookers record as numerous. But most significantly, plans were afoot to prolong military service by returning to a term of three years, in order to increase the numbers in barracks of available Frenchmen who, it was common knowledge, were outnumbered by the German army, which was supplied by a larger population.

This matter of the three years – both a symptom of international anxiety and the abandonment of a popular part of the Dreyfus legacy (the two-year term, it will be remembered, dated from 1905) – was a major question in 1913 and 1914.

It was precisely at this juncture that the seven-year term of office ended for Armand Fallières, whose easy-going and likeable southern image and politically discreet presidency had turned him into a kind of archetype of the 'republican' Head of State, in the sense that left-wing tradition had begun to attribute to the word. Now, to succeed him, Poincaré presented himself as a candidate, something which had never been done before by a working president of the Council. Most of the radicals countered with a sort of new Fallières, named Pams, who obtained more votes than Poincaré in the internal preparatory ballots within the republican groups. But Poincaré, contrary to established custom, maintained his candidacy, and carried the day in the official vote thanks to the votes of right-wing members of parliament.

This double innovation led to the expectation of a presidency that would be both more political and more stamped with nationalism.

Presidency of the Council, after some complex ups and downs, landed with Briand (January-March 1913), Louis Barthou (March-December) and

Gaston Doumergue (December 1913 to June 1914). The three years' military service act was passed, but would be used as a principal stake in the
legislative elections of spring 1914. The left coalition, formed basically of
socialists and radicals with a Caillaux leaning, carried off the majority of
seats, thanks to complicated popular aspirations in which were mingled
nostalgia for the time of the Bloc, desire for peace (for which hostility to
the three years' service acted as a symbol) and the will for social progress
(embodied in income tax).

Already a Caillaux–Jaurès government was being mooted.[7] The one
formed by the independent socialist Viviani, just after the elections, was
attempting to evade the issue in this delicate situation, when the Sarajevo
assassination opened up new prospects that were singularly more dramatic.

In the face of imminent war, in what state was the nation's spirit? Firstly,
it was represented by the republican patriotism whose components were
analysed in the Introduction. Combes, Clemenceau, Poincaré might be
rivals or even loathe one another, but they were none the less all bound to
the great tradition of Jules Ferry and Gambetta or, more ancient and nobly
formulated, of Victor Hugo and Michelet. For them, to be a patriot went
without saying, it was natural to love one's country, France. The republican
ideal, it is true, lay in an ideal of justice which stemmed from universal
morality. Could there not be a contradiction between the general (ethics)
and the particular (France)? No, because France was the country of the
Revolution and the Rights of Man, and its most intimate national tradition,
one might almost say its personality, placed it at the head of progress. In
confrontation with Germany, it had right on its side (Alsace-Lorraine).
Faced with the vast colonized and colonizable world, it spread a superior
culture and the benefits of civilization – every kind of progress, moreover,
closely intermingled: 'In fifty years' time,' André Maurois makes one of his
characters say, 'no one will want to live in an apartment without a bathroom
or a country without a parliament.'[8] What optimism!

This concept of colonial mission is important, because it shows up the
nuance separating republican patriotism of 1910 from that of 1880. At the
time of Morocco, the fear that colonial imperialism might sidetrack French
forces from the Rhine, or weaken their strength, had disappeared from
republican circles, though Clemenceau for his part – a remarkable exception – still retained it. The recently awakened awareness of the worldwide
spread of power made it necessary to have extra-European backup, reserves
and storehouses. In any case, everyone was joining in (Germany, Japan, the

---

[7] Even though this prospect was soon set aside by a tragedy: Mme Caillaux shot the editor
of *Le Figaro* with a revolver following a violent polemic which had overstepped the boundaries
of private life. But the accident, which put Caillaux himself out of the game, did nothing to
change the political situation.

[8] In *Les Discours du Dr O'Grady* (a sequel to the more famous *Silences du Colonel Bramble*),
works of the 1920s.

United States, even Italy), so France must not be outdistanced in the race. The colonies existed, and there were colonial interests, specific and precise business interests, which were always close to the government. Quite simply, their defenders were now radicals (Albert Sarraut) rather than Gambettists (Étienne, Thomson).

That clear conscience with regard to imperialism was not as completely contemptible as it seems to us today, after the earthquake of decolonization. The republicans of the Belle Époque, to be sure, allowed trading companies or public works enterprises to exploit the 'natives' in conditions that were sometimes atrocious; and despite their universalism in principle, they grossly underestimated the aspiration of all those peoples to have an identity and possess their own flag. But they were not wrong in holding secularism to be superior to religious fanaticisms; they spread some concrete instances of progress, medical for example; and here and there they formed some nuclei of Gallicized elites (today we would say Westernized) from which would eventually emerge the only more or less liberal political men in the countries destined for emancipation.

In comparison with our era, the patriotism of the left (not extreme) in 1914 showed a fundamental difference: it accepted war. It was easily acknowledged that peace was preferable, but just as easily, that one should know how to make war when necessary. The notion that war is absolute evil and peace absolute good was yet to come – after 1914–18. Of course, the pre-war men were not unaware of the sufferings described and photographed by reporters dispatched to Mongolia or the Balkans, but they had no personal experience of them, except for the older ones among them, who would remember 1870–1, which had lasted but a short period. Their times and their spirit belonged to *before* Verdun, before Auschwitz, before Hiroshima. Their mentality was still that of after Valmy, after Austerlitz, after Bazeilles.

For the patriotic message was still nourished more by history than by abstract reasoning. And it spread massively because history occupied a large place in primary education, as in all the implicit pedagogy of public monuments and the cult of great men; it lived also through poetry, when the patriotic themes of Victor Hugo's *Châtiments* resounded like an accompaniment to the national anthem. The image of the 'French character' which literature at that time tended to make commonplace is morally one of rectitude and justice, and physically one of aggressive valour. And that jingoistic tone did not belong only to Déroulède, who was too nationalist to be named here, nor to the obscure writers of songs for schoolchildren; it emerged, for example – and with great success – from Edmond Rostand's trilogy, *Cyrano de Bergerac*, *L'Aiglon*, *Chantecler*.

Such was the dominant trend. What accompanied it, now convergent, now discordant? First of all, the potent inspiration of nationalism.

In nationalist sentiment, France, not universal morality, was paramount. Furthermore, to be exact, there were two versions of nationalism. The first, religious, through the intermediary of Saint-Louis and Joan of Arc, bound France to the system of Catholic values; the other, more recent, paganized or secularized, turned France itself into the supreme value, without any justification other than its mere existence, without any reason other than its reality, the 'nature of things' which compels and binds us. This nationalism was much stronger among the elite than the electoral results of the Catholics and conservatives would lead one to believe.

Crushed in the 1902 and 1906 elections, the right, which had seemed to rally in 1910, suffered a significant failure in 1914. But conservative ideas were always better represented in the upper social and cultural strata than in universal suffrage. The very conservative authors of the famous survey on youth, signed 'Agathon' and published in 1913, perceived that discrepancy perfectly, but it in no way dampened their optimism for the camp they represented, because they believed a priori that the elite always ended up by prevailing in influence, and because, among the young elite in 1913, nationalist ideas were gaining ground. At all events, that is what their survey intended to demonstrate.

Confined to educated young people, to the future executive layer of society, this work, though lacking any statistical pretensions, forms a historical document in itself for its qualitative indications. The 'young people' described have a taste for action rather than doctrinal speculation; they like energy, whether it is exerted in war (that of tomorrow or that of today, in the colonies), or simply in the risks of exploration, or in the healthy austerity of camp life in the Sahara, or, even more simply, in sport. They value the qualities of endurance, virility, self-control, ennobled by references to Stendhal or Nietzche.

Conversely, there is a scorn for the intellectual citizen or persistent student, bohemian, slovenly, unmarried. Young French people will want to marry early, have children and accept the conventional virtues. All the more so because, by another path, their sense of modernity has made them rediscover Catholicism. One of the work's arguments, in fact, holds that free-thinking is going out of fashion, because it had issued from the Sorbonne in 1890, whereas in 1910 the wind is blowing from another quarter.

The rejuvenation of nationalism and its influence on youth converged, indeed, with another cultural movement of those years – a certain renewal of Catholicism – without, however, becoming confused with it. The history of the Church, of doctrinal and religious beliefs, is too rich and complex to enter completely into political categories. Nevertheless, the situation in France was such that any revival of influence of the Catholic religion could be held to be useful to the right and dangerous for the dominant secular majorities. Not all the wretched, the desperate, or the compassionate people horrified by the misery of the world or the human condition became revolutionaries; there were those amongst them who sought a remedy in faith. Writers and artists, by definition in the public eye, provide handy examples; there had been well-known converts well before 1900 – Léon Bloy, Paul Verlaine, Joris Karl Huysmans, Paul Claudel. If the post-1900 generation, that of the 'Belle Époque converts' (Francis Jammes, Charles Péguy, the painter Georges Rouault, Ernest Psichari and others), drew far more attention and was more generally thought of as a social phenomenon, the reason was that it was contemporaneous, and in the main showed solidarity, with the Church's debates about modernism and philosophical criticism of scientism (Brunetière, Bergson); also because it often emanated from young people who had been brought up in the secular intelligentsia and whose conversation seemed to be a direct disavowal and rejection of the old nineteenth-century masters (Psichari was the grandson of Renan, and Jacques Maritain the grandson of Jules Favre). And lastly, it was because these new Catholics did not identify fully with the authoritarian and conformist religion of the polemicist Louis Veuillot or the God-fearing novelist Paul Bourget, but wanted to preserve even in religion something of the sensibility and spirit of their own time.

The most celebrated is Charles Péguy because, being a writer of genius, he has left a work that still speaks to us, and as he was killed in the first days of the 1914 war, his memory deserves to benefit from this posthumous praise. With good reason he is the most typical of the renegades: of them all, he had been the most involved in political combat, had travelled the furthest and, in spite of everything, would remain the most faithful to himself. The poor orphan of the suburbs of Orléans, elevated by student grants as far as the *École* in the rue d'Ulm, had originally been the best placed to experience not only the generous elements of the Republic but also the kinds of hardship endured by the people. Even before entering the *École* he had belonged to socialism, the crossroads of those two vital experiences. In character he was unyielding, fervent, uncompromising. No one worked harder than he to bring socialism into the *École normale* and, some years later, to inspire the Dreyfusard battle in the Latin Quarter, to organize it practically and – dare it be said – militarily. He was able to sacrifice the teaching profession to eke out a living from the more useful activities of writing, publishing and editing sound material. Right up to his death, his *Cahiers de la Quinzaine* would be the mainstay of militant literature. We have already seen how, having adapted to the elevated atmosphere of the crusade, he had been unable to breathe that of victory run on an everyday basis and permeated with the need for compromise. Start a fresh crusade then? Conscious of having saved the soul of the Republic in 1899 from Méline's 'Republic', he would want to save it again, after 1905, from Combes's 'Republic'. To go from there to seeking to redefine that soul, and eventually imbuing his ideal Republic with the colours of a traditional France, was but a natural step. But the impetus remained the same; Péguy had always felt himself to be of the people, always republican in the sense of 1848, always a patriot in the sense of Year II, always mystical. His style had not changed, nor had his themes: was it chance that Joan of Arc (Orléanais, in a way, like himself) was from start to finish the source of inspiration of his works?

Are we speaking too much of Péguy, who was a genius and therefore out of the ordinary? Should we turn to the representative young people of Massis and Tarde, the co-authors of Agathon?

Like Péguy, they despised both the left and the Sorbonne, that is to say, Kantism and positivism in its secular and scientist version; but in any case, it was outdated, we are told, because the (very successful) teaching of Henri Bergson demonstrated its philosophical naivety.

Of course, the young men of Agathon scorned parliament and parties; they paid more attention to 'movements' such as Le Sillon or Action française. Royalists themselves, the authors of the survey recognized in all honesty that not all the young people they had questioned shared their views, and that many of them would like to reconcile their nationalist and irrationalist code of ethics and potential activism with the existing republican structure.

In this work (in what one can accept, but at least it is valid as an indicator of trends and, judging by its success, as a reflection of opinion) there is something which stems also from the generation war. For our authors, the daring ways of bourgeois youngsters of the left in 1880 (bachelorhood and free and easy morals, a certain penchant for bohemianism, a taste for – even the writing of – naturalistic novels and poems in blank verse, free-thinking and faith in science) were now those of sober old gentlemen, with official status and immortalized in stone. In contrast with that cultural system of the left, paradoxically it was the return of Moral Order that was *young*, as if, to contradict their fathers, they felt a need to go back to the morality of their grandfathers.

In short, on the eve of 1914 nationalism felt itself to be young or rejuvenated, even if aware that it was less widespread than the more classic republican patriotism. At this point, it must not be forgotten that Charles de Gaulle, born in 1890, was the exact contemporary of these young educated people examined by Agathon. Some of his own traits are easily recognizable in that collective portrait of a young generation. A liking for energy and action – that explains the choice of a military career for a young man so gifted that he could have succeeded in any intellectual career. Unswerving Catholicism, beyond any shadow of doubt. A worship of France, confusedly mingled with the last.

He was a republican, however, and that was the generation gap between the de Gaulle brothers, young men of 1900–10, and their parents, who had remained royalist. The brothers were no longer so, either because they considered that the return of a king was reasonably unlikely or, more surely, because the Republic, notably through the military institution, had over-whelmingly proved that it had assumed responsibility for national continuity. But loyalty was to the Republic–state–nation, not to the system of government and even less to its leftist presuppositions or conditions. At the *lycée* or Saint-Cyr Charles de Gaulle, like everyone else in his circle, must have poked fun at the notables in the government. An unwarranted assertion? In 1962, when the septuagenarian Head of State set about the opposition politicians in a famous speech, he tried to ridicule them by labelling them 'Gustave, Hippolyte or Théodule groups'. Is it absurd to suppose that therein lay some faint recollection of the famous 1910 song mocking the provincial guests at the wedding of Mlle Fallières by playing on the comical nature of unusual forenames?[9]

And moving from the flippant to the serious, is there not a link between the choice of the cross of Lorraine in 1941 as the symbol of Free France,[10] and a youth spent in an era when Lorraine, together with Ferry, Erckmann-Chatrian, Joan of Arc and Poincaré, had assumed a symbolic value?

De Gaulle, then, was a republican in his own fashion. Not at all Maurrassian, consequently, although it has been said. He was doubtless more attracted by Le Sillon, as Jean Lacouture has established. It is interesting, in any case, to note that the strength of national feeling and the nationalistic education coming from republican patriots and nationalists resulted in some striking matching and reciprocal adaptations. In the same way that the most republican history textbooks found reason, in the name of the *Patrie*, to celebrate the names of Philippe Auguste, Dugesclin, Henri IV, Turenne and many others, so the manuals used in Catholic private schools, and the children of royalists, would manage to find merit and glory in the soldiers of Year II.

But there were also discords amid the harmony.

Antipatriotism formed a tiny but lively minority. Even before 1900 everything had been said about the absurdity and cruelty of war, the relative worth of the *Patrie* and the damaging effects of 'militarism' (the stultifying life in barracks, the use of the army against strikers, the harshness of military justice). But that nearly complete package of arguments gained only a derisory number of followers.

The early years of the twentieth century at first served to enrich and modernize the indictment. After the Dreyfus Affair, there was much more to say about and against the military hierarchy. The confrontation between strikers and soldiers was still illustrated by fresh instances, and Morocco offered a current colonial war. The garrisons in the Algerian or Tunisian south were sometimes atrocious disciplinary postings, and there was Biribi,

---

[9] In the refrain, these lines were intended to be comic: 'Y avait la tante Ursule / Et puis le cousin Jules / Et l'oncle Théodule / Et Timoléon.'

[10] The General, in his *Mémoires de guerre*, attributes the choice to his faithful follower, Admiral Thierry d'Argenlieu. It actually belonged to the other great Free French sailor, Admiral Muselier, a son of Lorraine, but it must not be forgotten that de Gaulle himself had commanded a regiment in Metz from 1937–9. From Pierre Barral, *L'Esprit lorrain*, Nancy, 1989, p. 134.

and the Aernoult scandal, which involved the death of a soldier during the harassment and ill-treatment that were part of punishments. Briefly, the criticisms levelled at the army, war – and sometimes at the *Patrie* which justified both – gathered an audience. It was almost institutionalized in the CGT, in the trades union centres. It had its echoes and trend with Gustave Hervé in the bosom of the SFIO. It had its specialized publicists, such as Paul Vigné d'Octon. It tried its hand at taking action and being combative: trades union campaigns for the 'Soldier's Sou', attempts at propaganda in the barracks; attempts to disseminate a counterhistory textbook that avoided the national gospel (by Hervé and Clemendot).

Now, not only were these criticisms being voiced, they also ceased to be marginal. A revolutionary extreme left, whose most significant feat of daring was to challenge the national taboo, had won a place in the French political picture. And it was the link that he tried to maintain with it which most compromised Jaurès's popularity with the left-wing republican bourgeoisie. For that antipatriotism was obviously just as inimical to the official patriotism of the left in power as it was to the nationalism of the right-wing opposition. This is a reminder to us that, if there was a three-party split in the French political setup, it was not between right, centre and left, but between right, left and something revolutionary which may at a pinch be called extreme left, but which for its own part challenges that conventional topography.

What was as yet unknown, before the trials of 1914, was the fragility of that revolutionary ideological culture, and how little it had succeeded in covering over the deepest layers of patriotic impregnation in the public consciousness.

Did Jaurès, whom we have met so frequently, belong to that third and revolutionary party? To tell the truth, in this respect it would be tempting to turn him into a party all on his own . . .

At all events, the survey would be incomplete without him, because he tried to define an original position. It is all the more necessary to seek to know what he was really like, as his assassination on 31 July 1914 was to translate him to the status of myth or symbol.

This photograph of Jaurès as popular orator is justly famous. His gesture, in particular, with the right arm giving rhythm to his argument, an extension of his body which leans towards the interlocutor as if the better to reach out to him, was captured a hundred times in photos, reproduced in the press and even fixed in sculpture. The immensity of the background of pale sky seems to have been centred round him to suit the orator's deliberately eschatological eloquence. Naturally, there are the (red) flags of the Workers' Internationale, accompanied by the (red) bonnets on poles, these a reference to a more French revolution. Like all the communes bordering Paris, the Pré Saint-Gervais possessed the open spaces of the former military fortification zone. On 25 May 1913 the fight against the three years' law was out in the open in every sense. (Photo: Agence photographique Harlingue)

A revolutionary humanist, Jaurès believed (like Victor Hugo, for instance) in a future of happiness and justice, but he also thought (more like Karl Marx in this) that the future would pass through complete transformations of political and social regimes. But that generous humanist – and generosity was perhaps his own personal contribution – could sacrifice nothing in history that had been an elevated thought or a respectable ideal. He wanted to grasp, to salvage, to align everything in a progressive historical destiny. Some would say, more simply and sometimes with a note of reproach, that he wanted to reconcile everything. Socialism, an ideal which he made his own, was not in his view contrary to a bourgeois Republic. He interpreted it more as the development, the extension, the 'beyond' of the Republic. And definitive peace – even farther distant – would come when socialism had been realized. In what is without doubt the most synthesizing text he wrote, the famous speech in Albi in 1902, Republic, socialism and peace (universal) follow one another in that order, respectively embodying yesterday's battle (now won), today's battle, and the subsequent programme. In 1902, it is true, Jaurès could not yet foresee that the defence of peace (at the moment) could rapidly become more urgent than social struggles. But he was already declaring – and on that point he would never change – that peace must also be just, and that the nation's right must if necessary be defended, even if it meant taking up arms. For the nation, too, was something of value and had a right to justice. Like the Republic, the nation was one of those great noble surges of spirit which must be transfigured and not destroyed. It was necessary to make this detour via the personal dialectic of Jaurès in order to place his national teaching, from *L'Armée nouvelle* (1908) to the fight against the three-year service law (1913–14), in context with the other positions held at the time.

His hostility was obviously directed in the first place against nationalism, finding its doctrine philosophically bad (Jaurès remained rationalist, secular, universalist) and politically dangerous (it could lead to war or, internally, to authoritarianism). Nationalism formed the proven and, in some way, classic adversary.

Jaurès was scarcely less distant from the antipatriots. Though he did not wish to cut himself off from the CGT or the Hervéists, his battle companions against social injustice, whom he regarded as desperate and enraged men who had good cause to be so and for that reason deserved understanding, he was at variance with them on the essentials. For him, indeed, the homeland would long remain a value; justice must exist between nations, a fact that legitimized national defence and, ultimately, the army itself. Certainly, it required reforms to cleanse it of the stains of militarism, but should not be abolished. On the contrary, if it were made republican and more popular, it would become more efficient. Even in 1914 Jaurès was putting the case, with the most carefully studied technical arguments, that the two years' service law was functionally preferable to the three years' law. It was therefore with republican patriotism, that is, with those in government, that the author of *L'Armée nouvelle* and *l'Histoire socialiste de la Révolution française* obviously shared most of his thinking. So in what way does he stand apart from them? Firstly, he criticized them for the conformity of their military policies, which still tended to follow the doctrines and traditions of the army general staff, as opposed to discussing them and being able to reform them.

He also reproached them over Morocco. Although as secular and as good a humanist as the next man, Jaurès could see no justification whatsoever in a civilizing mission effected by force of arms. Jaurès was anticolonial, and in his battle for universal peace he also included that struggle against an actual colonial war. Though he wanted France to be strong, he rejected that particular means.

But chiefly he blamed radical or moderate rulers for what might be called incautious diplomacy which, by accepting the idea of war too soon, proved incapable of making efforts that might have allowed them to avoid it. For Jaurès, war was not inconceivable, but could only be justified in a border-line dispute, as a last resort, when all else had failed. By contrast, how dangerous was French diplomacy, which was too closely bound up with Russian diplomacy, dubious in so many respects, not to be already enmeshed in events. That last point gives the impression that Jaurès's pacifism constantly found additional justifications in his socialism. Like all the Internationale, he held on to the idea that capitalism was one of the sources of that phenomenon, war (which liberal and even republican thinking did not consider as obvious). Furthermore, in solidarity with Russian socialists, he found the tsarist regime hateful and was indignant that official France should turn it into one of the props of its system.

That is why the last years of Jaurès's struggle for peace (from 1912, Basle Congress) had an international and revolutionary tone, and clung to a notion that a general strike crossing all frontiers could hold back armies.

Nevertheless, that does not efface the theoretical and technical debates we have mentioned, since in 1914 he was still tackling the military problem in national terms. In Jaurès's fight against the pre-1914 governments there was thus less prophetism, utopianism or total revolutionism than is sometimes said. And naturally there was not the slightest antipatriotism, whatever his enemies may have thought or some part of opinion may have believed. But there was far more in the way of concrete and carefully thought out policies.

That fight, which has been described so many times, was to come to nought with his death, one month after Sarajevo.

All France would therefore go to war, in the wake of Poincaré and Viviani, and also following the procession of the great efficacious spirits, Joan of Arc, Napoleon, Rude's *Marseillaise*, the armies of the great Carnot and Gambetta's *mobiles*[11] . . . Joyfully? No. Resolutely? Yes.

---

[11] The customary abbreviation at that time for the *gardes nationales mobiles* (young men available for national guard service) who had been called upon a great deal in 1870–1.

Part II

Years of Ordeal
1914–1944

5

The Great War
1914–1918

It was called the Great War as early as 1918. Then history, which changes everything, would transform even its title. Since we endured a Second World War, from 1939 to 1945, the 1914–18 war has become the First World War. The relativity, one might almost say the prediction, expressed by this term – why not a third, one of these days, since the list is open? – has rendered outmoded the Great War of our forefathers, who had no way of knowing what was to follow. However, let us accept this 1920s terminology in order to underline the importance of the French crisis of 1914–18.

The last war, from 1939 to 1945, was obviously decisive in the formation of the *world* we live in. At the conclusion of a conflict of almost global extent, political problems must be tackled on a world scale, and the planet experiences a definitive unity that no longer allows escape from economic solidarity, on which all crises have repercussions. The UN (United Nations Organization) plays a supervisory and watchdog role overall, as it is unable truly to legislate. Human consciousness believes it has discovered new horrors, and even the absolute horror, with genocide and the atomic bomb. Two superpowers[1] have emerged and politics is conducted by continental blocs. The whole world is entering the revolt against the supremacy of the Western and white nations, while the European states, if not Europe itself, are retrogressing. It is evident that 1914–18 did not bring the *world* anything quite so overwhelming.

On the other hand, if one considers *France*, one may wonder if what took place in 1914–18 was not the most important turning point. Once the war was won – but only just and at what cost! – it in fact left the country in a state of lasting enfeeblement. Materially, there was the loss of its financial supremacy and the heavy demographic depletion; morally, the challenging of the old scale of values, as henceforward the value of peace would balance

---

[1] At least until autumn 1989 (the fragmentation of the eastern Communist bloc).

the value of *Patrie* – this was to influence the nation's future for a long time. Before the Great War, France had been strong, or at any rate had felt confident that it was; afterwards, it was anxious. Before, it had lived; afterwards, it survived. In those circumstances, knowing who should bear responsibility for the tragedy was of the utmost importance.

For a long while, two simple replies conflicted with each other. The right maintained that the German Empire (jointly with the Austro-Hungarian Empire) was the guilty party, thus making France the one attacked and eliminating any French responsibility. The extreme left blamed the Russian Empire, and therefore France (or at least in so far as it showed solidarity with tsarist policies), therefore official France, chauvinistic and capitalistic, therefore Poincaré. Between the two, the position of the moderate left was undecided and vacillating. When Poincaré had taken over as Head of State, an atmosphere of national excitement and anxiety reigned, shared by parliament, seeing that it had passed the three-year law. Three years' military service was obviously not a law in direct preparation for war, but at least it was anticipating one, since its aim was to increase the numbers of soldiers in barracks. It may still be argued that, in matters of war, anticipation contributes quite substantially to preparation. But what would happen if nothing were anticipated or prepared? Hostile to the three-year law, the left (radicals and socialists united), notably through Jaurès's voice, did not say that preparation for defence must not be made, but that the three years' term was a bad preparation and that, for the sake of defence itself, it would be more worthwhile to keep the two years, plus a reliable organization of reservists.

The question of choice between war and peace, nationalism and idealism, figured only as a backdrop to the real debate. In the legislative elections of spring 1914, the left carried the day, mainly because a return to two years' service was at the top of its programme. Then Poincaré gave the independent socialist Viviani the task of forming a government sufficiently to the left to take account of the indications coming from universal suffrage, but one which would avoid changing the military law by confining itself to making a study of it, using the excuse of international difficulties. The left received at least one satisfaction: this selfsame situation bringing the prospect of new expenditure, parliament created new resources by at last voting for income tax, to which the right had until then been opposed.

On 28 June 1914, at Sarajevo, the assassination of Archduke Franz Ferdinand, heir to the Habsburg throne, by a Bosnian patriot from Serbia, lit the touchpaper: conflict between Austria-Hungary and Serbia. Now, Austria-Hungary was allied with Germany, and Serbia with Russia, which was allied with France. This game of alliances, which would end with France and Germany face to face, began five weeks of complex tension. From the French point of view it was a matter of knowing where and when action could be taken to break this fateful chain of events.

On 16 July Poincaré and Viviani left Paris (going from Dunkirk by sea) for an official visit to Saint Petersburg. Three days' voyage from Dunkirk

to Kronstadt, four days of Franco-Russian conversations, of which there is
no precise record. At all events, on 25 July Poincaré was so far from
believing a war imminent that he was making ready to leave again for
another state visit, also previously arranged, to Sweden. But a telegram
from Paris alerted him and caused him to cancel the Scandinavian tour.
On 28 July Austria-Hungary declared war on Serbia.

On the 29th, the President was back at Dunkirk. By that date mobilization measures were under way. The 29th was the day of partial mobilization
(southern region) of Russian armed forces, while Germany confirmed its
support for its Austro-Hungarian ally. On the 31st, Russia proceeded to a
general mobilization, to which Germany replied with an ultimatum, obviously rejected. On 1 August Germany and Russia were at war, and France
had to mobilize.

The commonly received opinion today can be expressed in general terms:
the ruling powers in every country, even if they did not want war, had to
accept its possibility. They considered it their duty to do everything in their
power to win, which meant keeping their forces at the ready. Now, how
much needs to be done to be in a state of readiness depends on the military
general staffs, whose job it is to bear in mind the technical requirements
and the time needed for mobilization. From that comes an almost auto-
matic sequence of measures wanted by the military and imposed on the
politicians. What statesman would risk putting his camp in a position of
weakness by delaying, for some chancy diplomatic ends, a defence measure
that is deemed essential? He would need to be an exceptionally daring
genius.

In France, during those feverish days, the man who claimed to be the
'apostle of peace', Jean Jaurès, did not blame the government for being
belligerent, but only for not being as completely active and bold as was
necessary in stepping up last-minute diplomatic attempts, and that is doubtless what he would have written in his latest article – if he had not been
assassinated on 31 July 1914, at the Café du Croissant.

Jaurès had become the moral leader and most prestigious spokesman of
the political left, as well as the best-beloved and most listened-to man in
the working-class movement. He was also the most hated by the nationalist
right which, merely because he had for years been advocating peace, negotiation and the primacy of legal solutions over solutions of force, and
because he did not turn a blind eye to Russian autocracy, regarded him as
a German agent. What we know to be a tremendous calumny proved then
to be a killer. One might have expected that Jaurès's unjust murder would
unleash in return the hatred and anger of the workers against the extreme
right – the government feared so for a while. That reaction would certainly
take place – but not till after 1918. An astounding deferred response!

At the time, that specific emotion ('They've killed Jaurès!') was swamped
by the greater emotion of war which, rather by coincidence, arrived on the
same day with the announcement of general mobilization. Everyone knows
the fine and grandiose simplification, which became legendary and has

since been repeated as if it were a proof: Jaurès was the defender of peace, 'it was necessary' that he should die for the war to take place. It would certainly have taken place, even had he been alive.

But nothing could prevent Jaurès's death and the onset of war, the disappearance of the man and the failure of his policies, from being linked symbolically and in people's emotions.

However, Jaurès's followers did not reject nation any more than he had. That is why, far from justifying the fears of the ruling powers, they choked back their grief and seemed to believe that, having lost the battle for peace, there was nothing for it but at least to win the battle for the nation.

The war, then. Jaurès's funeral, at which, among others, Viviani gave a speech, provided the Socialist Party and the CGT with the opportunity to accept that duty. The Minister of the Interior perceived the trend and had the wit not to start the legal proceedings which had been envisaged (in the famous B notebook)[2] against the more active revolutionaries. Viviani admitted two socialists into his government, Jules Guesde and Marcel Sembat. That was the National Union, which Poincaré would christen the 'sacred union'.

The 'sacred union' comes from both myth and reality, like many famous sayings. Myth in so far as it meets and strengthens a set of themes which were very marked on the right: union is good, disunion is bad; therefore the national defence that unites the French is good, whereas the politics dividing them is bad. Going beyond that, and to the very limit, systems of authority in which everyone obeys are good, but democratic systems are bad, when energies are dissipated in disputes. 'United as at the battlefront', the phrase would be much employed after 1918 to condemn, by contrast, the habitual disunion in the debates in the Chamber, or in those of the electoral fairground. The 'sacred union' of 1914 thus contributed quite substantially to updating the antipolitical ideology of the most inveterate conservatism.

The myth of the 'sacred union' was founded not only on the absence of trouble in the first days of August and on the very real national discipline, but also on the chauvinistic and bellicose enthusiasm which was unleashed. Flowers in rifle barrels, cries of 'To Berlin!' endless singing of the 'Marseillaise'. Those things did happen, a superficial aspect of memory. The serious history of that entry into war[3] definitively established two unrecognized features. On the one hand, political mistrust and conflicts would continue throughout the war, although discreetly. On the other hand, and chiefly, the general feeling in public opinion was one of resignation and of a duty accepted far more than of enthusiasm for war. In short, no 'sacred union' in the sense of absolute, simple and childlike union. But a true union for the defence of the nation. Those Frenchmen who could be called up

---

[2] A list, drawn up beforehand in police headquarters, of dangerous revolutionaries who were to be arrested should war break out.

[3] To which the name Jean-Jacques Becker is connected, *1914. Comment les Français sont entrés dans la guerre*, Presses FNSP, 1977.

left for the front, almost without incident or any desertions. And Jaurès? Would he too have left, physically or morally, for a war of defence? Nobody knows, but it may be put forward that such was the logic of his line of thought. Two years later, his only son Louis, who had barely reached the required age for joining up, would feel duty bound to leave for the front where he would meet his death, just one among millions.

France had a large army at its disposal, thanks to general call-up, well organized and well officered, and good armaments. Their equipment, however, suffered from some strange shortcomings; the foot soldiers wore red trousers, so noticeable, while the Germans were already wearing their drab uniform which blended with the neutral shades of the ground. It would take the military authorities several months before they clothed their soldiers in discreet sky blue. Similarly, the Germans entered the war wearing helmets, while the French infantrymen wore the *képi*; changing to helmets would also take months. One hardly dare think of the number of additional deaths attributable to those two failings. The army was solid, disciplined; the private soldier was tough, and it would always be easy to recruit officers from among the enlisted men with a little education – white-collar workers, shopkeepers, civil servants. The high command belonged to General Joffre.

Joseph Joffre, born in 1852 at Rivesaltes (eastern Pyrenees), in a modest and culturally secular milieu (a double contrast, let us say in anticipation, with his contemporary Ferdinand Foch), went through the Polytechnique. He experienced the war of 1870 (siege of Paris) as a young sub-lieutenant, then had a career as a specialist in the Engineers which entailed, logically enough, long periods in the colonies – Tonkin, Sudan and Madagascar. Like others he built barracks and forts but also schools and railways there, while completing their conquest, notably attracting attention by the taking of Timbuktu. After 1902, having been made a general, he alternated between commands in France and administrative office in the government (within his specialized engineering field). The summit of his advancement was reached in 1911. He benefited from the merging which was then decided upon between two hitherto separate positions, the vice-presidency of the Senior Military Council and the running of the army general staff. The new title, chief of the army general staff, qualified him to be the designated commander-in-chief if war should break out. This attainment of the heights was justified by a fine career and positive qualities of intellect, but several other great commanders of the same age could equal him in that. Working in Joffre's favour was his origin, which by definition made him a reliable republican. Responsible for the initial strategy (Plan XVII), he would also be responsible for its failure, since the famous plan anticipated an offensive on the Franco-German border, and neglected to take account of the simple eventuality that would nevertheless take place: German invasion through Belgium. Joffre was not disconcerted; he was able to adapt to the initial defeat with sang-froid, method and calm; master the problems of strategic retreat and reverse the situation on the Marne. By virtue of the latter he won a popularity which would rise above all previous setbacks and those yet to come. In 1915, in 1916, newborn baby boys would receive the forename Joffre.

Let us go back to the beginning: while the high command obtained a spectacular success by penetrating several kilometres into Alsace, the Germans fell on Belgium. That violation of Belgian neutrality, which had been hallowed by treaties since 1830, was to bring many consequences in its wake. Firstly, it directly provoked Britain's entry into the war, which surprised the Germans (what? for a 'piece of paper?'). Then, in French opinion it strengthened the idea that the Germans despised the law and the French side was, once again, its defender – quite a considerable argument to make a republican people accept war. A good conscience would undeniably prove one of its most essential resources when the going got tougher. But for the moment the easy crossing of a dumbfounded Belgium allowed the Germans to pass the frontiers and caused the army to fall back. The first well-known defeat of the 'frontier battle' at Dieuze, in Lorraine, at the end of August was at first admitted only as an exceptional incident, and an inspired Parisian newspaper, *Le Matin*, ascribed it to the 'Provençal' laziness of the regiments of the 15th Corps, recruited from the south-east. This was a scandalous slander, and in order to make amends, its memory is recalled in the 'avenues du 15e-Corps' still to be seen in towns in the Midi. Spoiling relations among Frenchmen themselves was not the least disastrous result of the officially encouraged chauvinistic upsurge! Then it became necessary to bow before the evidence; the inferiority was general and France had been invaded. On 2 September the Head of State, the government and parliament went off to install themselves in Bordeaux, leaving Joffre to supervise the defence.

This he did with sang-froid, managing a retreat in good order as far as the Marne. It was then that the right wing of the invasion armies, advancing in pursuit from the north-west to the south-east (roughly speaking from the course of the Oise to that of the Marne), presented its right flank to the north of Paris. General Gallieni, military governor of the capital, seized the opportunity of that vulnerability and hurled against the Germans all the forces at his disposal, some of which were transported by requisitioned Paris taxis, the famous 'Marne taxis'. That was the first sharp check to the German advance. Joffre followed it up by giving the celebrated order of the day to yield nothing more – to 'die on the spot rather than retreat' – then to counterattack. The German advance was halted and battle engaged, thenceforth to be known as the 'Battle of the Marne'. An immediate defeat, as in 1870, was thus avoided. It also marked the end of a rapid war and the inevitable start of a prolonged one. For a few more weeks yet the war of movement continued. The French and German troops, in contact from Lorraine to the Parisian region through the Champagne area, could no longer outflank one another except to the west. Between September and November they tried in vain, a real 'race to the sea', a term which described the continuous front line stretching from south of the Vosges to the Pas-de-Calais.

The outflanking manoeuvres therefore failed, and it was unthinkable to renew attempts to make a breakthrough after the losses suffered in the murderous first three months: all the armies could do now was to fortify their positions by digging themselves in. The 'war of positions' otherwise known as 'trench warfare' began; it was to last for over three years.

The authorities returned to the capital, while Joffre established his General Headquarters at Chantilly.

At the beginning of 1915 the front line followed a course from the Swiss border in a north–south direction along the crest of the Vosges, then turned towards the north-west as far as the north of Verdun, its sole enclave being the Saint-Mihiel salient on the Meuse; then, from Verdun to Noyon, from east to west, it followed the Aisne and finally became north–south once more from Noyon to Dixmude. Belfort, Nancy, Toul, Verdun, Reims, Arras, Dunkirk were on the French side, and Lille, Laon, Sedan on the German side of the front. In Flanders, a tiny part of Belgium remained free, linked with France; there the most popular of the allies of the *Entente*,[4] King Albert I of Belgium, the helmeted 'Knight-King', was holding out. Part of France (half of the *départements* of the Nord and Pas-de-Calais, most of the Aisne and Ardennes, part of the Marne, the Meuse and the Meurthe plus, of course, the Moselle and Alsatian *départements*) experienced life under an army of occupation. But this was less talked about than it would be during 1940–4, as public attention was concentrated mainly on the front.

The nation soon adapted itself to this war of unexpected duration. First, the economy, as a large proportion of the producers were at the front and many factories were situated in invaded areas. Therefore new ones had to be created to manufacture arms and munitions; specialists were recalled from the front, and women were taken on in metalworks and engineering factories. Female labour would, of course, dwindle after the war. Nevertheless, there were innovations prefiguring the future. The extensive industrialization of the Paris suburbs and the closely connected emergence of the metalworkers into the top ranks of the visible and aggressive working class both date from the war.

There remained a considerable deficit, to provide for civil needs, and there was no other solution than to purchase overseas. Despite a gradual mobilization of its foreign assets, France would not be spared a certain amount of hardship and even, sometimes, rationing. The vast scale of the charges imposed on the state by the war affected public finances. Taxation was inadequate to cover the shortfall; so borrowing was stepped up with

[4] To distinguish it from the Triple Alliance or *Triplice* (Germany, Austria-Hungary, Italy), the trio of France, Britain and Russia was called the *Triple Entente*.

the help of urgent patriotic propaganda; that did not prevent inflation: an enforced rate for paper money, then the issue of notes in excess of the customary receipts in metal coin. As the bulk of goods available on the market increased very little, while the means of payment grew, inevitably there was a tendency for prices to rise, leading to a high 'cost of living'.

At all events, the world of politics and administration, under duress, had its first taste of an economy partially managed or steered by the state. Here, Étienne Clémentel provides a good example. This radical deputy for Puy-de-Dôme, a great parliamentary worker, very able in most ministerial fields, entered the Briand government on 29 October 1915 as Minister of Trade and Industry. There he beat the records for longevity, as he kept the post through every government, including Clemenceau's, right up till January 1920, endlessly amassing further titles: Trade and Industry, Postal Services, sometimes Employment, then Agriculture, Transport, Merchant Navy. A veritable superministry of civil national economy – Armaments alone being managed separately – thus made its appearance, in everything but name. The worth of an eminent man, but also the necessity brought about by the times, caused the number of responsibilities recognized as belonging to the state to make great strides. But it was above all in the military field that the long war occasioned new adaptations. With the massive mobilization of the adult male population, the consequences of the conflict made themselves felt in every family, right down to the most remote villages – particularly in the villages, inasmuch as the peasant, who lacked any usable technical speciality and was only good as a solid infantryman or horse driver, never escaped going to the front, whereas the workman was sometimes kept in a war factory.

Two 'worlds' thus appeared very distinctly: the front and 'behind the lines'. The Second World War taught us to unlearn that division because, from 1942 to 1944, as the enemy was in occupation he was everywhere, and danger from aerial bombardment, or at least the possibility of it, also loomed in every area. In 1914–18, by contrast, 'behind the lines' (with the exception of the invaded fringe, to the north-north-east of the national territory) experienced the war only indirectly: women workers in the factories, the high cost of living, various upsets and, above all, that constant anxiety for the serving soldier, whose letters were so eagerly awaited. Apart from that, an apparently normal life went on, was adapted, reorganized, in work and trade, in schools, even in amusements, for mourning did not strike every family at the same time; the climate behind the lines was not always, nor for everyone, completely spartan.

As for the front . . . it was life under fire and life in the mud. That obsession with mud, with damp earth, because men dug themselves into the soil. What else were the trenches but a network of ditches deep enough to conceal a standing man, further protected by parapets of earth and, beyond, by rows of barbed wire; ditches connected by an intestinal labyrinth and extended by subterranean dugouts that served as lairs (the *cagnas*) where men lived and rested in between assaults, fatigues and guard duties, but where the cold was constant in winter and the damp in any season. The trenches: a universe of freezing mud, at best uncomfortable, at worst harrowing, even when there was relief from the danger of death. That danger came first from bombardment, not by planes (at the time aeroplanes were rare, light, with a short range of action, and were used chiefly for observation or hunting enemy planes), but by cannon. In that era artillery was at its apogee: heavy artillery, travelling on rails, with a range of several kilometres; field artillery, of the 75 type of cannon; or trench artillery, howitzers, mortars, *crapouillots* (trench mortars). From the beginning of 1915, poison gas shells were added to this arsenal. A bombardment, which could last several hours, generally formed the 'artillery softening-up' that preceded an attack. For both sides were given to making attacks, of varying importance, in order to win a few metres or a few hundred metres of enemy soil.

Attack therefore constituted the major danger, for men had to leave the relative shelter of the trenches, by means of makeshift wooden ladders, get through their own barbed wire entanglements, which had been snipped with wirecutters beforehand, and run towards the enemy trenches hoping that the cannons would have been effective enough to demolish the barbed wire and silence the machine guns facing them. If they had not, it meant death. If they had, if the enemy trench was reached and if it contained a few survivors, it was 'mopped up' by means of grenades, bayonets or knives. It was not until 1918 that wide use would be made of an invention dating from 1916, combat vehicles, then called more exactly assault vehicles ('tanks' in American slang) because they were capable of crossing barbed wire with impunity, facing bullets and to some extent clearing a way for the foot soldiers advancing in their wake. In between the fighting, and even under fire if the artillery duels went on for a long time, men had to live – that is, eat, drink and sleep. Here again, there was a kind of adaptation to this strange life in the countryside, which was both sedentary and action-packed.

The sky-blue clad soldier, who now had a helmet, protected himself from the cold as best he could. The officers tolerated his being swathed in woollies, extra items of clothing, even if not according to the regulations; it was accepted that he no longer shaved: thenceforth he would be the *poilu* (hairy one). There were front-line trenches, second-line trenches and, still farther back, less exposed areas housing the headquarters, various services and, most importantly, the kitchens (known as *roulantes* because out in the field the stoves were always on wheels). A daily or twice-daily traffic was organized through the communication trenches, 'fatigue parties' who went to fetch and distribute bread, 'grub', coffee (*le jus*), red wine (*le pinard*) and later bully beef (*le singe*); a to-ing and fro-ing of officers delivering mail, of messengers, of stretcher-bearers. A whole new mini-world came into being, which was no longer one of classical warfare or routine barrack life; it had its own laws, customs and language. It would soon become familiar through the novel, with Henri Barbusse's *Le Feu* in 1916, which enjoyed considerable success.

One of the rules was that units at the front should not spend too long a period in the perilous and inhuman atmosphere of tension in the front lines. Just behind the front, quite easily available in old, more or less deserted villages, soldiers could use quarters for rest and relaxation. Between the two sites there was a 'relief' operation, on which the soldiers kept a very careful check and which commanding officers had to organize efficiently and equitably. Fair treatment was one of the keys to troop morale.

At the rest quarters, men could at least wash themselves and their clothing, sleep at night and think about something else. In such places the 1914–18 war produced what would endure for a long time as the most famous piece of its folklore, the song entitled 'La Madelon'.

> For the soldier's rest and amusement
> Down yonder, a few steps from the forest,
> Lies an inn with ivy-covered walls,
> Its name is Au tourlourou.
> The serving-girl is young and pretty,
> As light as a butterfly,
> Her eyes sparkle like the wine she serves,
> And we call her Madelon.
> We dream of her at night, we think of her all day,
> She is only Madelon, but for us she is Love.
>
> *Refrain*
> Madelon comes and serves us wine,
> Beneath the arbour we lightly stroke her petticoats,
> And everyone tells her a story,
> After his own fashion, a story for Madelon.
> Madelon is not cross with us
> When we slip an arm round her waist or a finger under her chin,
> All she does is laugh,
> Madelon, Madelon, Madelon.

Into the facile verse and light style deriving from the café-concert songs of the turn of the century the author has been able to slip an allusion to sexual frustration, which was by no means the least of the *poilu*'s concerns. That frustration contributed in no small measure to concentrating the soldier's attention on the frequency and regularity of his leaves (periodic returns home for a few days, to be with his family behind the lines) as well as of his relief spells in the rest centres, and above all on the fairness with which they were allocated. As long as justice was shown to him, the 1914–18 *poilu* agreed to return from his leave and go back into the front line, knowing full well that he risked staying there for good. There was a tacit exchange of duty in return for justice.

Behind the front lines, however, the France of the noncombatants did not learn of the realities of war by reading *Le Feu* or listening to the accounts of soldiers on leave! Not everyone read novels, even those honoured with the Prix Goncourt, and not all soldiers on leave – even if they

'See the *Patrie* march past!' A popular patriotic song, words and music by Émile Trépard. (Poster 1915. Collection Viollet)

had wanted to – were capable of expressing themselves articulately and accurately on their life in the trenches and in combat. Many French people who had not been called up (women, children, old men, invalids and those exempt for various reasons) learned about the war through newspapers.

There it would remain for a long while something to be admired. Not only just, legitimate, heroic and certain of ultimate success, but embellished with exploits, shining examples of sacrifice, only made sombre by atrocities – which were always German in origin. In short, emphasis was ever on the virtues, rather than on the miseries, and on successes rather than setbacks. What would quickly come to be called – and is still a lasting creation of the language of those years – 'brain-washing'. With the articles in the press, which were its main prop, the speeches of notables and men in the public eye offered another, even more official, support. Thus the ground was laid, counter to the prevailing thinking, for many of the post-war antipathies.

National politics, however, was by no means effaced. The first reason was connected with the fact that the conversion of the left and the workers' movement to the nationalism of war had not been absolutely total. While Romain Rolland, the celebrated writer, musicologist and novelist (*Jean-Christophe*), friend of all the Dreyfusard and socialist-oriented intellectuals, had installed himself in Switzerland and there had published the significantly titled *Au-dessus de la mêlée* (On the Sidelines), in Paris obscure CGT militants who had remained attached to revolutionary tendencies maintained contact with one another. As the Internationale had not unanimously engaged itself in the war (although the German, French and British parties had rallied their respective national defences, the Russians – albeit citizens of a country at war – like socialists in the neutral countries, had remained pacifist and revolutionary), some international contacts were re-established in Switzerland.

France was represented there by the minority parties (at Zimmerwald in September 1915, they were the CGT members Merrheim and Bourderon, and at Kienthal in April 1916, the SFIO deputies Alexandre Blanc, Brizon and Raffin-Dugens). It was a small initial breach, destined to grow bigger, in the official unanimity.

There was a second, and decisive, reason for the political vitality: republican democracy continued. After the victory of the Marne – as we have seen – the government came back to Paris and, at the end of December 1914, the Senate and the Chamber resumed their sittings. Parliament therefore sat regularly, in secret committee when the nature of the debate demanded it. Its right to examine military matters was at first limited to arms manufacture, strategy and command still remaining outside its scrutiny and criticism. But that situation gradually changed. In 1916 parliamentary supervision of the armies began to operate, although the military did not always take a kindly view. Two years after the Marne, having checked the encroachments of the General Headquarters, the civil authority well and truly affirmed its pre-eminence in the management of the nation and the war.

That is the explanation for the existence of a fairly lively, though unobtrusive, political life, which did not spare the Ministry of War itself. At the end of August 1914, Viviani replaced its first incumbent, Messimy, with the energetic ex-socialist Alexandre Millerand. In October 1915, Viviani's team had to give way to a Briand government. The latter resumed the tradition of putting a soldier in charge of the Ministry of War, but would get through no fewer than three of them: the popular defender of Paris, Gallieni (October 1915 to March 1916), the obscure General Roques (March–December 1916), and finally Lyautey, recalled from Morocco, a haughty great leader who was soon put off by the hurly-burly of parliament (December 1916 to March 1917). In the winter of 1916–17, the last of the Briand government, the reshuffling affected even the direction of operations, as the conqueror of the Marne, Joffre, was replaced as commander-in-chief by General Nivelle. Those governments of the first years always included socialists, whose usefulness was obvious by virtue of their origins and affinities. One, Albert Thomas, who became Minister of Armaments, was very successful, thanks to his good relations with the organized workers' groups. More unobtrusively, other socialists were busy with international contacts. Indeed, to begin with, France had only four allies: Serbia, swiftly beaten in the Balkans; Russia, soon in great difficulties on the eastern front, but whose offensives had afforded decisive assistance in the Battle of the Marne; Belgium; and lastly Great Britain, whose land contingents on the main front were very light beside the French army. Britain, it is true, ensured the undeniable power of the *Entente* on the seas. Thanks to Britain, a Franco-British naval expedition first sought a direct strategic victory in the Near East (where Bulgaria and Turkey were the allies of the central empires). In February 1915, there was the attack on the Dardanelles, followed by the establishment of a bridgehead at Gallipoli (April 1915 to January 1916), afterwards transferred to a more durable base at Salonica.

But the great success had been to persuade Italy to enter the war on the French side. It had not been easy, as the Italian ruling class proved to be rather Germanophile, for various reasons, whereas only a minority, guardians of the anti-Austrian tradition of the Risorgimento, inclined towards France; the grandsons of Garibaldi, renewing the gesture of their ancestor in 1870, had come to fight in the French army in August 1914. As for the powerful Italian Socialist Party, it had remained revolutionary and on the side of maintaining neutrality. One body of opinion, however, had broken away to rejoin with belligerent and anti-Austrian patriotism – Austria still held unredeemed Italian territories south of the Tyrol – and that group possessed a dynamic leader: Benito Mussolini. It was he who had been encouraged by the Quai d'Orsay, through the channel of French socialist emissaries, to intensify the patriotic agitation which moved Italy to fight alongside France. That had been achieved in May 1915.

On the Franco-German front, 1915 experienced its share of battles – the term applied to combined series of assaults, attempts to pierce the enemy front, or at least nibble away at its defence lines and push the front farther back. It goes without saying that they were lethal, and without any strategic results: the battle of Champagne in February, of Artois in May and June, and again of Champagne in the autumn.

In 1916 the Germans took the initiative, with a large-scale objective: to capture Verdun. In the war of positions, 'Verdun' in 1916 was the equivalent of 'the Marne' in the war of movement in 1914: the defensive battle won by the French army, and immediately placed at the summit of national memory. But what, in fact, was 'Verdun'? Firstly, Verdun was a town, with a sub-prefecture, a bishop's palace and a large garrison which gave rise to an active commercial life, and was the focus of a spirit of patriotism and taste for military things even more pronounced than in the rest of France. And so it would remain throughout the war. The battle that bears its name certainly inflicted destructive bombardment in 1916, and caused the exodus of many inhabitants and various administrative services, but trade would not stop, as masses of troops would perforce still flock to the town. Verdun itself was therefore hurt by the great battle but was none the less always behind the front lines where the combat was taking place. It is not to be confused with Saragossa 1808 or Stalingrad 1942! 'Verdun' was, more precisely, the 'fortified region of Verdun', a network of forts built on the heights to the north-west of the town on the left bank of the Meuse, and to the north and north-east on the right bank, Douaumont, Vaux, Souville, Froideterre, etc., with, in between, small farming villages that were operations bases for the battles, those places fought for 'house by house', those buildings demolished by artillery fire to the point where one village, Fleury, was totally annihilated.

The entire fortified area of Verdun formed an essential operations base for the French defensive front established in 1914 and 1915. It was also symbolic. Without going as far back as the Verdun of the Treaty of 803, or the Verdun of the Three Bishoprics disputed between France and the Germanic Holy Roman Empire in the sixteenth and seventeenth centuries, people were aware (as much in Germany as in France) that the town had been the object of two decisive sieges in 1792 and 1870. For that reason, Verdun was just as famous as Lille, Strasbourg or Belfort – perhaps even more so.

The German commander-in-chief, Falkenhayn, wanted both to strike at that symbol – break that strategic deadlock or, at the very least, 'bleed the French army white' by compelling it to throw in maximum forces to defend it – and at the same time create a diversion to the offensive that Joffre was preparing on the Somme for the spring of 1916.

The battle is well known and its story has been recounted hundreds of times. On 21 February, the German attack consisted of nine hours of artillery 'softening-up' (from 7 a.m. to 4 p.m.), and a deluge of shells thicker and more devastating than ever, followed by the attack proper by well-prepared infantry equipped with flame-throwers. In three days, from 21 to 24 February, they advanced several kilometres into the hills and villages of the Hauts de Meuse on the right bank. On the 25th they entered the fort of Douaumont which, in the course of a reorganization of French defences that was taking place, was without a garrison. Nevertheless, that advance was slowed down as much as possible by the French units engaged. Despite the losses they had sustained in the initial bombardment, despite the disorganization of all their communications under fire, despite the absence not only of reinforcements but even of instructions, those troops taken by surprise held fast, and spontaneously applied the already classic formula, 'die where you stand rather than retreat'. An example may be recalled of the 1,300 *chasseurs* who for two days defended the Bois des Caures and who all perished there, including their leader, Colonel Driant, in civilian life the nationalist deputy for Nancy.

On 26 February, the day after the loss of Douaumont, Joffre appointed Pétain to the command of the Verdun sector.

Pétain, whose reputation for calm and method was already established, managed to restore order to the battlefield, and immediately concentrated on two urgent tasks. First, to bring artillery reinforcements to those positions on the left bank which had not been reached by the German attack on 21 February (by good fortune, one might say, or by a strategic error on Falkenhayn's part); this sub-sector would thus be better able to hold out and even, already, contribute to hitting the Germans on the other bank. Next, to organize as speedily as possible Verdun's communications with the south (along the Meuse valley, by road and rail, from Verdun to Bar-le-Duc) through which the wounded could be evacuated, munitions, supplies and reinforcements brought, and the 'noria' of relief troops set in motion. The reliefs were well organized, and on a very large scale; nearly all French units would pass through Verdun sooner or later, and that would contribute a great deal to the place the famous battle holds in the common memory. That umbilical cord, without which the long battle would not have been won, would remain in history under the title of 'sacred way'. Of course, German shells fell on it. The 'sacred way' carried an intense traffic, needed constant maintenance and repair by fatigue parties of soldiers who were scarcely less exposed than those in the front lines. Men went along it in order to die, but they also died in order to keep it passable.

From 26 February, the German advance on the right bank slowed down. On 6 March, when Falkenhayn widened his attacking front to the left bank, he found a reinforced resistance; he made some progress but never succeeded in going beyond the tenaciously held heights, the most famous of which were the Mort Homme and Hill 304.

From then on, German attacks and French resistance more or less balanced out, and positions on the ground varied little, though the fury of the combats and the loss of human life were undiminished. On 2 April, a general offensive as strong as the two preceding ones was halted within a few days, allowing Pétain on 9 March to issue an almost optimistic order of the day, one phrase of which has passed into legend: 'Courage, we'll get them!' It would still take months.

German pressure concentrated on resistance points now well equipped with artillery, which had to picked off one by one. At the western extremity of the front, the fort of Vaux thus underwent a veritable siege – a battle within a battle – from 2 April to 7 June. On that day, completely surrounded, its external structures demolished by shells, cut off from any reinforcements and any provisions, almost half the garrison wounded, groaning without medical care, and for want of water literally dying of thirst, its subterranean structures finally breached, the fort yielded.

Following this success, Falkenhayn made ready for two further assaults, still on the right bank, to make an end of it and at last enter the town of Verdun. On 23 June and 11 July, the attacks were as brutal as those that had gone before and, like them, gained a little more ground. At the Souville fort (south of Fleury) Verdun was in sight, 5 kilometres distant. But the Souville fort held firm, and the German offensive halted.

The Battle of Verdun was virtually won. There would still be a great deal of fighting, but thenceforward it would be more the French command that took the initiative.

July, August, September passed in battles without significant results. But on 24 October a carefully prepared offensive (General Mangin) regained Douaumont and forced the Germans to evacuate the fort at Vaux. In 1917 the ground lost on the left bank was also won back in its turn.

Verdun is, with good reason, the most famous high point of the Great War on the French front. The Germans had not managed to break through; they had not managed to weaken the French army, at least relatively, since they had fairly equally weakened their own (about 50,000 dead, even before the end of September, on both sides). It was a failure for Falkenhayn, who was in any case soon replaced by Ludendorff; a victory for Pétain, Joffre and the French side in general; and lastly, a turning point in the war. But that is not all. Verdun is still *par excellence* the highest pinnacle of vigour, stoicism and grief.

It may be seen in the Douaumont ossuary which, by its giant size alone, speaks of the extent of lives lost. It may be seen in the museums built since – sober, precise, realistic – their message perhaps more pacifist than their official creators would have wished. (Should one make an exemplar of patriotism of the event which allowed men to endure *that*? Or remember it as a unique lesson, 'never *that* again'?)

It may be seen also in the landscape where, for kilometre after kilometre, so much shell debris was incorporated into the ground that the very soil was denatured by it, fields could no longer be cultivated and forests struggled and were slow to grow again, like the grass after Attila's horse – little could he have imagined the truth of his words.

Lastly, it may be seen in the poignant literature of survivors' accounts, men such as Maurice Genevoix, Jacques Meyer, André Pézard and so many others. The horror of the missile that kills or mutilates, the gas that poisons or burns the mucous membranes, the suffering of the wounded who have to wait, sometimes for hours, lying anywhere, their wounds hastily dressed, jolted about on stretchers and then on lorries before being able to receive relief and treatment – all that is but a part of the wretchedness, the part that immediately springs to mind. Too often the rest is forgotten: the terrible weather; the perverse mess of the earth, razed and pulverized by shells, with the drenching rain, combining to create those lakes of mud which saturate and sometimes engulf men. The lack of sleep when, under the pressure of necessity, a man has to watch by his trench-slit, go on patrol, go on fatigue duty to carry out unexpected tasks, for the dead must constantly be replaced, snatching only rare moments of respite in which to have a doze. Hunger, when food supplies are interrupted. And even worse, thirst – with the temptation, or even necessity, to drink whatever water is available, whether it has flowed into a shell-hole after passing near putrefying corpses . . . Battle could thus force men to spend hours in cesspits where the danger of pestilence was added to that of explosion. Some men went mad. Others had the strength to survive, and some to write in order

Horses drowned in mud. Through their pictures, genuine photo-journalists present at the front gave a very realistic vision of the war. All the horror of the time is caught in this pool of mud with its dead horses and, in the background, a forest reduced to the trunks of decapitated trees. (Photo: N.D. (Neurdein))

to describe. They all bear the same witness: that they had scaled unimaginable heights of human suffering.

The martyr-heroes of 1916, turned narrator-witnesses in the 1920s, could not foresee that, in 1940, the battle would have another means of access to history: the attainment of power by the soldier glorified with the official title 'Victor of Verdun'.

Philippe Pétain had been born in 1856 in Cauchy-à-la-Tour (Pas-de-Calais), having emerged from rural France – peasantry rather than bourgeoisie. A family of small farmers, of Catholic tradition, with numerous offspring, and an ecclesiastical great-uncle who encouraged the studies of the most gifted of the boys. Philippe therefore went through the religious schools of Saint-Omer and then Arcueil, and entered Saint-Cyr in 1876, at a mediocre level. His intellectual qualities asserted themselves later, when he entered the War School. He himself would teach there from 1901 to 1907, before and after various posts in metropolitan French garrisons. At that time he was considered serious and cold rather than brilliant, and furthermore was Catholic and anti-Dreyfusard, which was commonplace. In 1914 he was still only a colonel. However, an original thesis of his was known, summed up in the famous aphorism, 'gunfire kills'. In other words, one does not launch troops into attack without having first neutralized the enemy's fire; modern combat had to take account of the effectiveness of machine guns and give preference to methodical preparations rather than élan. Method, caution, care for the fate of men, mistrust of the offensive – those principles or tendencies would be confirmed by the war and linked with his name. In August 1914 he attained the rank of brigadier, and various defensive successes in 1915 and 1916 attracted sufficient attention to carry him to the decisive responsibility of 1916. Pétain thus entered history at Verdun in that year.

Let it be added that Verdun is a well-known town, a place that is very precise and easy to locate (whereas the Marne battlefields are modest and scattered).

Let us look ahead for a moment: Verdun, the town and the site, the whole 'sector', would be the perfect place for monuments, ossuaries, museums, memorial pilgrimages – a battlefield with a geography as familiar as that of Valmy or Waterloo, in short a 'place of memories'.[5]

That victory, which today we regard as major, at the time passed as no more than a strategic coup, just like the Battle of the Somme, its contemporary.

Now, the Battle of the Somme in the summer of 1916 had been Joffre's great undertaking, at least as important as the defence of Verdun. And the

---

[5] As it is known since the publication of the series *Les Lieux de Mémoire* (Gallimard) edited by Pierre Nora. See, to be exact, in the part 'La Nation', III, 1986, the excellent 'Verdun' by Antoine Prost (pp. 111 ff).

Somme, in 1916, like the similar battles in 1915 in Artois and Champagne, had been very costly in human lives and shown little result in gaining ground. Moreover, as he was the supreme commander, Joffre could also be held to blame for the delays in works and lack of foresight which had cost dearly at the beginning of the Battle of Verdun. All that accumulated at the expense of the reputation of the victor of the Marne. In December 1916, the Ministry forced his resignation by appointing him to a less directly active office: technical adviser to the government. General Nivelle replaced him, but Joffre immediately received the most prestigious recompense: the baton of Marshal of France, re-established for him by the Republic. The Marshalship, title and dignity (it was not a rank, properly speaking) carried a whiff of the *Ancien régime*; the Revolution had ignored it, Napoleon had made it his own and rendered it illustrious, as we know (Ney, Davout, Masséna). The subsequent monarchies had continued it, but the 1870 Republic had again refused to create any: anyone who wanted a Marshal's baton, it was said, should go and win one 'on the Rhine'. That had almost been done. The baton therefore resumed its place in French history. Joffre would again be honoured in 1918 by an obviously triumphal election to the Académie française, and from then on any easy election would be termed precisely 'a Marshal's election'. More seriously, at the beginning of 1917, Marshal Joffre left for the United States at the head of a French mission, where he would give valuable service.

It was indeed from abroad that new and decisive events would arise, with the extraordinary and disquieting year 1917.

It began, however, with an event that was advantageous to France and her allies: the entry of the United States into the war. It was a rediscovery of international morality because, just as Britain had been drawn into the combat by the violation of Belgian neutrality, the American Republic entered into it to defend the freedom of the seas which had been compromised by German submarine attacks on neutral vessels. The torpedoing of the *Lusitania* on 7 May 1915 had caused the most outrage, and had given rise to the swing in American opinion. The break in diplomatic relations between the United States and Germany followed, and finally war, at the beginning of April 1917. American aid was slow to arrive (the country did not yet possess much in the way of military organization), but it represented an immense, inexhaustible potential, with the additional support of a good conscience. In order to defend what was right, here was the recommencement of the fraternal union of countries which had emerged from democratic revolutions: 'La Fayette, here we are!' General Pershing is reputed to have said when he landed in France as commander of the expeditionary force.

As for the eastern ally, the Russian Empire, it too fell prey to a revolution at precisely that time. In February the monarchy had been overthrown in Petrograd. Should France regret the loss of its great partner of 1914, in the person of Nicholas II? Or congratulate itself that his republican successors (Lvov, then Kerenski) who talked of continuing the war, offered the additional advantage of being politically more respectable friends? Paris sent emissaries, sometimes socialist, to support them in their good intentions. Nevertheless, it quite soon became apparent that the Russian Revolution had been effected at least as much for peace as for liberty and that neither the Bolsheviks, who formed an appreciable force in Petrograd, nor the masses of mobilized Russian peasants were disposed to fight to help 'French imperialism' win its duel with 'German imperialism'. It soon appeared also that the Russian army was no longer fighting, and that Russia was likely to quit the war, a defection which, *at that moment*, more than cancelled out the effect of the support expected from America.

In short, between the Russian exit from the war and the effective arrival of the Americans, in the face of German forces now concentrated on a single front, 1917 promised to be a difficult year.

Two strategies presented themselves: to hold out and wait ('I am waiting', Pétain would say later, 'for the Americans and tanks'[6]), or else attack in order to snatch a decisive success from the Germans before they could make the most of the Russian withdrawal. Commander-in-Chief Nivelle opted for the second strategy. He believed that a sufficiently intensive artillery preparation would allow a breakthrough, while refusing to take account of the reinforcement of the German defence, which had been obtained by its partial retreat to a slightly shorter line (the Hindenburg line). On 9 April 1917 the British in Artois, and on 16 April the French in Champagne, launched an attack. Failure. The Germans held their ground, the French infantry came up against their defences and sometimes suffered their own artillery's badly co-ordinated fire. On the 19th the offensive had to be halted. Strategically, the result was nil. In human resources, it involved heavy losses; for resources of morale, it was the equivalent of utter disaster.

In May several regiments demonstrated in a refusal to return to the front. Repudiated, Nivelle was dismissed, after less than six months in command. Quite naturally Pétain replaced him at the head of the French army.

Those mutinies of 1917 long remained a taboo subject for the dominant ideology and the conventional history associated with it. How could it be admitted that patriotic France, the France of the 'sacred union' and the war for right, had witnessed its soldiers disobey while in uniform and shirk the battle? In terms of heroic mythology it was unthinkable. On the other hand, this movement was praised without measure by an anti-conformist history which wished that France, too, had been capable of having its own 1917 revolution. With those 'echoes of the Russian Revolution', that breach of the sacredness of nation and army, and also with pressure from the class struggle in the background, did not France have its own potential Bolshevism?

---

[6] Tanks had already been invented – as was said – but not yet manufactured in quantity.

The fact is that sensitivity to pacifism and protest reached even as far as the front, an underground folklore in opposition to the acceptable folklore, expressed writings such as the 'Chanson de Craonne'[7] to parallel the inoffensive 'Madelon'.

We may read this song of complaint and revolt, by an unknown author, clandestinely circulated, and hunted out, since its existence was recognized. On condition, however, that we admit that its audience was necessarily a very small minority, and above all that the revolt it proclaimed did not put its threat into practice.

> When, at the end of our eight rest days,
> We return to the trenches,
> We are so useful
> That without us they'd be clobbered.
> But it's over, we've had our fill,
> And with hearts as heavy as lead
> We say goodbye to the civvies,
> Without even a drum or a trumpet
> We go off with lowered heads.
>
> *Refrain*
> Goodbye life, goodbye love,
> Goodbye all you girls,
> It's over, for always,
> In this vile war.
> It's at Craonne, on the plateau,
> That we'll leave our corpses,
> For we are condemned to die,
> We are the ones who are sacrificed.

Two other couplets follow, in which the complaint gradually slides into social protest against the profiteers and shirkers, and then comes the final refrain:

> The ones with the loot, they will come back
> Because they are the ones we are dying for,
> But that's over, for the squaddies
> Are all going to go on strike.
> It will be your turn, you fat cats,
> To go up to the plateau;
> If you want war,
> Pay for it with your own hides.

What was really going on? The troops must certainly have been aware of the serious events taking place in Petrograd, and of the social tensions

---

[7] Author unknown; printed for the first time in 1919. Quoted here from Robert Brécy, *Florilège de la chanson révolutionnaire*, Paris, Hier et Demain, 1978.

obtaining behind the lines (the cost of living was high, and the contrast between rich and poor had not been erased), and the weariness which had built up since 1914, and the wearing-thin of enthusiasm, and the breaches in unanimity. Beginning in 1916–17, a terrible winter, there was a succession of strikes, notably in Paris. However, the difference between the actions of groups of malcontent soldiers and 'revolutionary defeatism' is considerable. Mutinies were confined to a limited number of units. They were peaceable. They were not organized and had no connection with any headquarters, whether social or political. They were not defeatist: there was not a single desertion at the front, but only demonstrations behind the lines, without any immediate military effects. As citizens who were accustomed to debate, to the Republic, to trades unionism, they made use of demonstrations to make themselves heard by a high command too prodigal with human blood. It was democracy, not national nihilism.

In the same way that the extreme left tradition had improperly 'Bolshevized' the significance of the mutinies, it also, following the same logic, created the black legend of a Versailles-type repression. There was talk of thousands of shootings, decimation, executions without trial. History would record 3,427 sentences, including 554 death sentences, of which 49 were carried out, which in itself is a great deal and the sign of a serious situation, but is also very mild in comparison with that legend, wherein lies a refusal to acknowledge what the Republic had achieved in the way of national cohesion.[8]

General Pétain, as the new commander-in-chief, had to take charge of the affair. As he would be passionately argued over for his actions in 1940–5, his enemies would be able to add to his debit side the repression of the mutinies, and his friends to praise him for having done so at the least cost. In any case, it is certain that he tackled the causes of his troops' discontent: efforts to improve the soldiers' daily lot were redoubled (food, leave), and the blood-letting slowed down because, instead of attempting senseless breakthroughs, it was decided to wait for tanks and the Americans.

All that, however, made 1917 a more uncertain and unsettling year than the ones before. The workers' strikes, the mutinies (unheard-of events, however limited they were), the revolution in Russia, the duration of the conflict and the number of victims, could only accentuate and embolden socialist and trades unionist opposition to the war. This opposition, still minuscule in 1914, had since 1916 taken the form, in the Socialist Party SFIO, of a minority tendency – but self-aware and growing larger – which even had its own press organ, *Le Populaire du Centre*. Moreover, the prolongation of a war with an uncertain outcome caused the idea of a 'negotiated peace' to be contemplated in certain diplomatic circles. Pope Benedict XV showed himself in favour; the new Emperor of Austria-Hungary, Charles, successor to the old Franz-Josef since 1916, and his wife

---

[8] Guy Pedroncini, *Les Mutineries de 1917*, Paris, PUF, 1968; summarized in *Les Mutineries de l'armée française*, 'Archives' series, Julliard, 1968.

the Empress Zita (née Bourbon-Parma, and whose brothers were fighting in the French army) considered that Viennese diplomacy could keep at some distance with regard to Berlin. Such things were murmured, emissaries went to and fro, French politicians were approached.

In this less rigid atmosphere, official political life regained a certain animation (however dictated by expediency it might be). In March 1917, the Briand government was overthrown, replaced by Ribot, who held on until September. He was succeeded by Painlevé, who lasted no longer than November, after assuming responsibility, under Ribot and then in his own team, for the Ministry of War.

It was then that President Poincaré, who remained determined to pursue the war to victory, resolved to entrust the mission of forming the new government to Georges Clemenceau. Even if he did not like him very much, he at least knew that they shared the same objective. Like his predecessor Painlevé, he would combine the task of president of the Council with that of War Minister. But Clemenceau in power, the vigorous man of 1906 and, above all, 1908, was a kind of provocation for the socialists, who refused to take part in the new government. November 1917 therefore marked the official end of the 'sacred union' between the parties, and the start of a kind of dictatorship of public safety.

Public safety, dictatorship – the historic words come spontaneously when one recalls Clemenceau, the 'old Jacobin', the man of the Revolution-as-a-bloc, the man who in his youth had known and admired Blanqui, who venerated the Victor Hugo of *Les Châtiments* and *Quatre-vingt-treize*, the man who – at seventy-six years of age – presented the image, also like Hugo, of the grand old man still alive and kicking. In fact, this old republican was a dictator only in a vague and metaphorical sense. He had a majority in the Chamber, and nothing took place that was contrary to the Constitution. But he used his political power to the utmost, in a precise direction: to win the war, instead of interrupting it before victory, which meant that any vague impulses towards a negotiated peace were cut short and, consequently, that the contacts with the enemy – even indirect – which such plans implied were likened to treason.

He therefore had legal proceedings instituted against two radical members of parliament, Caillaux and Malvy. That was his nearest brush, so to speak, with Jacobinism. Clemenceau sending Caillaux before the High Court recalls Robespierre sending Danton before the Revolutionary Tribunal. With the same motive, basically: in war it is impossible for two diplomacies and two attitudes to coexist in the face of the enemy. The difference lay in the fact that Caillaux would save his neck, because in 1917 republican justice was independent of political authority. In Caillaux's circle, some dubious characters were more vulnerable, and there were indeed several condemnations for treason, followed by executions. The government suppressed the strikes and – a grave symbol – refused the French socialist delegation passports to go to Stockholm to take part in a new meeting of the Internationale.

But Clemenceau showed himself more similar to Carnot than to Robespierre in the way that he willingly went to the front to bring the soldiers direct testimony of his solicitude for them, and to give them encouragement. At that time he donned his helmet again, his greatcoat and laced boots, the apparel which his statue in the Champs Élysées would freeze for history. Finally, resembling the entire Convention, he held that the conduct of the war, in its most general sense, was the concern and responsibility of the government, thus of politics, and not the competence of specialists. We know his taste for incisive sayings: 'War is too serious a matter to be left to the army.' Really, the model who inspired him here, even more directly than Lazare Carnot, was the Gambetta of 1870, the minister of the Tours delegation, who simultaneously inspired patriotism, governed the country and organized strategy. The Gambetta who had been Clemenceau's contemporary, a personal friend, and whose death mask, together with a few antique reproductions, formed the sole ornamentation of his study.

As regards the war, Clemenceau threw his whole weight into obtaining a decision of major importance, the establishment of an inter-allied military command, which was entrusted to a Frenchman, General Foch (26 March 1918). Pétain remained at the head of the French army. Like him, the British, Belgians, Americans and Italians were answerable to the Generalissimo.

Ferdinand Foch, born in Tarbes (Hautes-Pyrénées) in 1851, came of a southern family who had been bourgeois for several generations and were very patriotic and very Catholic. His father, born in 1803, had proudly borne the forename Napoleon. He had been a high-ranking civil servant in the prefectural and then financial administration, under the Second Empire. One of the future Marshal's brothers became a solicitor, another a Jesuit. He was a very gifted child and shone in his studies, going through religious schools and entering the Polytechnique, taking up arms for the first time in the same year, 1870, as a volunteer against the Prussian invasion. Under the Third Republic, Foch rose easily through all the ranks; he was somewhat of an intellectual and theorist, teaching for many years in the War School. His marriage strengthened his bonds with the Catholic Church still further and made Brittany his adopted province. He served with various garrisons in various kinds of office, all in metropolitan France. He published two books. In 1914 he happened to be the general commanding the 20th Army Corps at Nancy. He was therefore in the front line of the frontier battles, but subordinate to Joffre, his junior by one year.

In the Battle of the Marne, he distinguished himself at the head of the 9th Army (victory in the Saint-Gond marshes); then he was appointed in 1915 to the command of the French Northern Armies. In 1916 and 1917, at the summit of the hierarchy, he carried out various functions in the army general staff and missions abroad. It was there that Clemenceau chose him for appointment to the supreme inter-allied command.

Not before time because, in spring 1918, with a desperate thrust the Germans in their turn attempted to make a breakthrough. On 21 March they penetrated the front held by the British on the Somme (it was the pure shock of this which allowed the single command to be imposed within the week!). In April and May they made further attacks and the Allies fell back in Flanders, Champagne and Picardy. After a respite in June, they made another thrust in July and advanced as far as the Marne, where they halted *in extremis*. Nearly four years after the first, the second 'Battle of the Marne' was waged, but this one marked the end of the exhausted German army's offensive. Foch, thenceforward master of his strategy, well provided with arms and men ('the Americans and tanks'), was able to launch ceaseless counteroffensives, from Villers-Cotterets (end of July) to Saint-Mihiel (mid September) and Sedan (beginning of November), to name only the principal battlefields.

In Germany, however, revolution was on the march. With the empire overthrown, the opposition parties – Centre (Christian democrat) and social democrat – which were its heirs, attended to the most urgent matter first: to get out of the war. They asked for an armistice on 9 November, before German soil was reached.

On 11 November at Rethondes (near Compiègne, in the Oise *département*), in a railway carriage fitted out as a mobile command post, the armistice was signed. The bugles at the front sounded the cease-fire. Clemenceau announced it in the Chamber in an emotional atmosphere which for a moment brought back the 'sacred union'. In towns and villages, peals of bells proclaimed the event. People came out into the streets, fraternizing with strangers, in a spirit of jubilation which those taking part would remember for the rest of their lives. It was victory, and it was peace. It would not take long before people were divided over which of those two ideals was the finer, the more outstanding and the more precious. But on 11 November 1918, it happened that their common accomplishment aroused the intense and short-lived unanimity of a great occasion. The French army still advanced, but henceforward peacefully. On 24 November it entered Strasbourg, the symbolic city. It is reported that on that day, overcoming their antipathy, Poincaré and Clemenceau embraced, weeping.

The crowds in Lorraine and Alsace cheered the restored French flags. 'That's the plebiscite for you!' said one of them. For the new ally, the President of the United States, Woodrow Wilson, concerned about justice and the law, had laid down the principle that any modification of the map of Europe would have to be made after consulting the population. And why not in Alsace too? But not for a moment did Clemenceau contemplate making the Alsatians vote in order to return them to France! A man of 1870, he was compensating for the wrong done by Bismarck. Would Wilson be able to understand that? The political and mental separation that would soon be revealed by the peace conference was already evident.

Schoolchildren in the place de la Concorde, 11 November 1918. A many-faceted and ambiguous explosion of joy. In Paris, one suspects that the crowding into the streets had undertones that differed from one *quartier* to another. This crocodile of schoolboys, kept well in line by gentlemen in hats, amply provided with flags, in good order, in the place de la Concorde, probably belongs to the nationalist leaning. (Photo: Branger)

In the final battle, Generalissimo Ferdinand Foch's methodical intelligence, his culture, his experience in international contacts, had been put to wonderful use, all in all making him – if one had to be singled out – the victor. Even before the armistice he had in his turn received the Marshal's baton, which put him on an equal footing with Joffre, by whose side he would ride, on 14 July 1919, at the head of a victory parade along the Champs Élysées.

Honours were then heaped upon Foch. Election to two academies (Académie des Sciences, Académie française), three Marshal's batons (of France, the British Empire, Poland), two statues inaugurated in his lifetime, before a national funeral on 26 March 1929, followed by interment in the Invalides, near Vauban, Turenne and Napoleon. In his person, post-war official France would have its emblematic hero.

To return to that moment in time, November 1918, France had won a war that it had come very close to losing. Knowing why and how is one of the most essential lessons of that cruel history.

As the 'morale of the troops' and the nation are no longer taboo subjects, we have learned to relativize national feelings, and to look the most radical subversions straight in the eye. And as we also know how to examine collective attitudes of mind, for over thirty years we have taken an unprejudiced look at the Great War, extending and bringing up to date an already abundant documentation. The innumerable accounts printed between 1918 and 1940 are ceaselessly supplemented by others, and hitherto unpublished ones still exist (such as that of the provincial gunner, Joseph V, shortly to be quoted).[9] Antoine Prost has still found survivors to question.[10] The 'Trench Diaries', the Postal Control archives, etc., have yielded their share of discoveries.

While it enriches the initial picture of the 'sacred union', this accumulation of new knowledge does not empower us to dismiss it as false. For the fact remains that the French were sufficiently patriotic and united to hold out, and to want to hold out, until they achieved victory. Of course – first rider – the 'sacred union' worked no miracle; it did not metamorphose the politicking and aggressive French of pre-July 1914 into a unanimous mass, quivering with chauvinism, overcome with docility and reconciliation. Neither the bitter mistrust that set anticlericals and clericals at loggerheads, nor that which created opposition between radical and socialist militants and the a priori reactionary body of regular army officers, disappeared from men's minds. The known memories of war reveal more than a trace of it.

The *Journal* of infantryman Barthas, a cooper in the Languedoc and an SFIO militant in civilian life, shows us a certain officer getting his men into line to lead them to Mass, while another had thought it a good idea to hand out a maximum number of fatigue duties for the appointed time, in order to thwart attendance at the service. As for Gunner V, he found the following incident very amusing, and recounts it joyfully. Behind the lines, somewhere in the Vosges, his bunch of pals, Provençal and far from God-fearing, noticed that the house of the civilian on whom they were billeted for the night was crammed with religious pictures. They therefore decided that one of their group who happened to be clean-shaven should pass himself off as a priest. There was an immediate change of attitude on the part of their host, who began to bow and scrape, and conducted the pseudo-curé to the most comfortable bed in the house; the other soldiers had to stay and sleep on the floor, deriding the bigot's naivety.

So anticlericalism was not dead. Nor was antimilitarism! The authors of the war diaries, all good disciplined soldiers who spent their time obeying their officers also spent their time judging them, less on their capabilities, however, than on their manner and behaviour; authoritarianism, arrogance and insensitivity were unforgivable.

Gunner Joseph V, already quoted, was a good soldier; he went through two years of war (before getting killed in 1916) with discipline and courage, while at the same time noting down, with sadness and precision, the sufferings and horrific sights. Only once does his notebook carry a criticism of a superior, and that is for an occurrence which was both mild and meaningful. Those men due to go on leave arrived from the front, late in

[9] Private document shown to me by his family.
[10] Antoine Prost, *Les Anciens combattants et la société française*, 3 vols, Paris, Presses de la FNSP, 1977.

the evening, at Belfort station; from there they were to go and sleep in a barracks in the town before catching another train south in the morning. The garrison officer who met them that evening at the station wanted them, worn out though they obviously were, to form fours and march behind him to the barracks, 'with no regard for the old territorials of forty-five years old'. And V refers to this brass hat who went by the rules as a 'whippersnapper'.

So the men kept their eyes open, were critical, moaners and groaners if you will, with an indiscipline just below the surface but always held in check; the indiscipline of a critical mind, of a democratic and trades unionist citizen, much more than of a 'hardhead' or 'primitive rebel'.[11] Those men had not scattered in 1914, they had endured at Verdun (among other places) the unheard-of sufferings we have so inadequately touched on, they had surmounted both the disaster of the Nivelle offensive and the last German thrust of spring 1918. The vast majority of them had simply had to be in accord, in order to hold out.

Of course, one would not be so simple as to forget the extent of constraint in military discipline. Every officer, equipped with his sidearm, was a priori the best prepared in case of physical rebellion by a soldier. And the slightest rebellion could lead to the harsh justice of the court martial. But those stern means of repression would obviously not have sufficed in the face of mass despondency. That was clearly to be seen in Russia in the same years.

To be precise, the French in 1917 were not poor moujiks. They felt themselves to be French, and with conviction. The ideology of the *Patrie*, a sacred value from the point of view of the religious ethic, and that of the missionary secular *Patrie* of the Law which converged with it, were doubt-less consciously recognized only by cultured minorities, but they had been so imbued in all citizens that residual traces remained subconsciously. France was *their* country. Being French was not then rivalled – as it is today – by being European or cosmopolitan, Breton or Provençal; whether it is seen as good or bad, the feeling of belonging to the nation had been absorbed and, on that account, as France was their country it must be defended as they would defend their own homes. A man who might have jibbed at leaving to win back Alsace-Lorraine or the Congo was willing to fight in order to prevent the invader from taking another province away from him.

Then the idea would be borne in on them that, since this war was a reality, and costing so dear – ever dearer as time went by – it became more and more necessary to win it to justify the sacrifices that had already been made.

Then came – or rather, was discovered simultaneously – another series of motives, drawn from a deep and widespread morality. National defence being men's duty and – for the time being – their job, the work to be done,

---

[11] Eric Hobsbawm, *Primitive Rebels*, New York, 1959. (French Translation *Les Primitifs de la révolte dans l'Europe moderne*, Paris, Fayard, 1966.)

it was better to do it well, following the rules and discipline, rather than drag their heels, make a mess of things or botch the job. For it also implied solidarity: to hold firm was to help the comrade alongside you, to let go was to make things worse for him. In effect the morale of the troops was shored up also by morals pure and simple, those of the seriousness of life, which were then almost unanimously taught and accepted.

More than one reader will have recognized these fairly recent but already classic analyses[12] which may be briefly summed up as follows.

No, the French had not wanted that war. Yes, they accepted it. Certainly they accepted it because they thought it would be brief, but it turned out to be long, and nevertheless they held out.

No, the 'sacred union' did not convert them into a nationalistic unanimity; it toned down rather than obliterated the conflicts.

Yes, something 'snapped' in that relative concord, at the time of the 1917 crisis, but even then no one thought that peace, so keenly desired, could be obtained by defeat.

Even better! Close study of the workers' strikes in Paris, which were numerous following the hard winter of 1916–17, constant in 1917, 1918, and certainly pretty varied, reveals that they quietened or slowed down during the weeks when Germany was on the offensive, and victory consequently threatened. So even those who were leading the class struggles had no wish to take responsibility for putting the nation in danger.[13] Why? It would be better to quote the words of J.-J. Becker:

In the last analysis, despite the weariness, the grumbling, even the anger, the national fabric was too tough, and had been woven for too long a time, to be torn apart. Even those who would have liked to create a revolution stopped, as if faced with sacrilege, at the idea that their action might jeopardize their homeland; or at the very least they sensed that they would not find – not yet anyway – masses to follow them . . .

. . . (the French) accepted the war because they formed one Nation, and they supported it for the same reason . . .

. . . France formed one of the oldest nations in Europe, one which over the centuries had slowly and steadily come together. This explains why, with part of its territory occupied or in ruins, its young men mown down when its demography was not in a position to undertake their replacement, more severely afflicted than the United Kingdom, less rich in resources and men than Germany, in spite of everything, it did not collapse.[14]

But the author goes on to wonder if such a historic trial could be undergone twice, and such exploits be repeated. The answer – in the negative – is only too well known. It remains for us to follow the paths of its progress.

---

[12] J.-J. Becker, *Les Français dans la Grande Guerre*, Paris, Laffont, 1980.

[13] Taken from the unpublished thesis of J.-L. Robert, *Ouvriers et mouvement ouvrier parisien pendant la Grande Guerre*, Univ. de Paris I. 1989.

[14] Becker, *Les Français dans la Grande Guerre*, conclusion.

6

Disillusion and Dissent
1918–1932

In the unanimous enthusiasm of 11 November 1918, how could those who were rejoicing because France had won be distinguished from those who were happy because the war was over? Victory and peace, together – so all people were happy together. It would not be long, however, before those who were content chiefly to have beaten 'the Boche' and those who rejoiced above all at the ending of the 'butchery' were to be found on different sides. The 'sacred union', far from complete during the war, was nonexistent afterwards. Although on somewhat different issues, the national division would reach depths comparable with those of the period of the Dreyfus Affair. And perhaps even more harmful. At least, such is our argument here.

France had won, that was the first piece of evidence: it had regained Alsace and Lorraine, enlarged its colonial empire, thanks to a share-out between the victors (under cover of administration by mandate of the League of Nations) of the colonies taken from the Germans and Turks (the French received Togo, which added to French West Africa, part of Cameroon, which increased French Equatorial Africa, and Syria-Lebanon, which reinstated them in the Near East). France would be able to impose reparations on Germany, whose army was annihilated, lastingly in an unfit state to do any harm. Out of the debris of Austria-Hungary and part of Russia, rose new powers which were a priori friends of France – notably Poland, Czechoslovakia, Yugoslavia – who could compensate for the estrangement of Russia, where the Tsar's empire had given way to the revolution. Emerging from the war, the French could at last believe themselves to be solidly linked, thanks to common sacrifices and an equally shared liberal, democratic and humanist inspiration, with the British Empire and the great American Republic.

To perceive the negative aspects of the balance sheet of those four years of battle, contemporaries needed a more abstract view and, today, the facility conferred by hindsight. With whole regions ravaged, France had to rebuild, whereas there was nowhere near such damage, by a long chalk, for the German foe. Worse still: to that must be added the immense losses of men, almost one and a half million dead and as many wounded, often mutilated for life; those losses were proportionately heavier than for any other country, and further aggravated the demographic handicap suffered by France in comparison with its neighbours and rivals. Lastly, the war had required such an economic and financial effort that it had exhausted its reserves as a rich country and world banker, and turned France into a debt-ridden country as well as enfeebling its productivity.

Another piece of evidence is borne in on us, when we take a second look: this material weakening caused by the war would be further aggravated by disappointments over the support it had banked on receiving from central Europe and its former allies.

Looking further still, is not the third evidence one of *moral* weakening? Let a word suffice here for what will be explained more fully later. The war had been won thanks to the virtues of patriotism. But as the war had inspired feelings of horror, patriotism, which had allowed it to take place and last so long, had become suspected of a sort of complicity. Those on the left, in particular, who by definition wanted to be more politically sensitive and humanistic, would no longer dare, would no longer be able, to be patriots like their elders of pre-1914. Overall, French patriotism must certainly be included among the most severely smitten casualties of 1914–18, though that is a finding which, from a revolutionary viewpoint, some regard as positive. But, to keep to a purely descriptive and explanatory history, it would have to be admitted that with the weakening of patriotic feeling, the national will to live, inseparable from it, also sustained wounds.

It was at this time, without a doubt, that the contemporary history of France, after the grandiose and sinister peak of Verdun, started to go downhill – lastingly or temporarily?

Hardly had the war been won, the cautiousness of patriotic union no longer necessary, when old scores would be settled, and social struggles resume until they bordered on a revolutionary crisis, at least in appearance.

A legal episode, more important as a symptom than *per se*, set the tone. Villain, the killer of Jaurès, had spent the war in prison awaiting trial, which no one had dared to deal with during the conflict. Now he was brought before the Assize Court of the Seine, where he was acquitted (29 March 1919). Feeling, with some justification, morally challenged by this verdict, socialists and trades unionists organized an enormous protest demonstration in Paris. Its atmosphere may be imagined.

Meanwhile, Clemenceau, president of the Council, governed the country where demobilization difficulties contributed to swell a wave of social movements, but that did not distract him from his principal concern: the negotiation of the peace treaty, signed at Versailles on 28 June 1919. Clemenceau got it approved by parliament and, in November 1919, won the legislative elections. In January 1920, at the close of Raymond Poincaré's seven years of office, he was replaced, in the circumstances which will be mentioned, by Paul Deschanel and then, in September 1920, by Alexandre Millerand. During this period the social, almost revolutionary, wave was swelling but, at the Congress of Tours in December 1920, it would receive a sharp check and its epilogue. Diplomacy, social unrest, political vicissitudes: problems crowded in on one another, even if accounts of them must be introduced separately.

Diplomacy was engaged first and foremost in the negotiations at Versailles, where the essentials were sorted out in the council of the four chief allies (Clemenceau, Wilson, Lloyd George and Orlando – or France, the United States, Great Britain and Italy). France obtained the retrocession of Alsace-Lorraine, but not the right, which had been vaguely contemplated, to create a reverse 'Alsace-Lorraine' by recovering a more extended Rhine frontier, or at least stimulating a Rhine separatism. It temporarily annexed the Sarre (where the coal would replace that of the ravaged Nord region); it had an army of occupation in the Rhineland as far as the Rhine; from the British and Americans it received the guarantee of their aid in case of German aggression. That was rendered improbable by the total demilitarization imposed on Germany. The latter would have to pay reparations, the legal foundation for which was in article 231 of the treaty, by which it acknowledged responsibility for the loss and damage due to the war which its aggression had unleashed. Germany also handed back territories to Belgium, Denmark and chiefly to a reconstituted Poland. All that was based on the respect of the right of peoples to self-determination (right of nationhood, plebiscites), a new right which the League of Nations would, in principle, make institutional and permanent. The total figure for reparations remained to be decided. Germany, like Turkey, lost its colonies. Other treaties ratified the splitting-up of the Austro-Hungarian Empire, in the name of nationhood, and reduced Austria to its Germanic part, without, however, giving it the right to be incorporated with Germany. Hungary obtained total independence, and other territories hitherto under Viennese rule became the components of the new Yugoslavian and Czechoslovakian republics.

Clemenceau, as has been said, had a hard job with his allies, who watered down French demands in respect of Germany, in exchange for a guarantee, which the American Senate's refusal to ratify the treaty soon invalidated as far as the United States were concerned. As for the British, who continued to give France their backing over the Rhine and took part in the League of Nations, they were its keen rivals in the Near East, in particular over the fate of the Arab countries emancipated from Turkish rule, which was a matter for the Treaty of Sèvres. Lastly, the Russian question had not been settled, as in 1919 the idea had still not been ruled out that the whites, loyal to the Tsar, might be able to overthrow the Bolshevik government. It was still uncertain whose weapons would prevail in that civil war, and conflicting hopes were aroused, some of which were revolutionary.

The social unrest can be adequately explained by post-war difficulties; demobilized soldiers came back to their workplaces to find wages ill-matched to the cost of living, and the over-timid legislation on labour of which we are aware. There was no longer anything to restrain men from expressing their demands, as had happened while the war was on. So there were numerous strikes. They were more easily excited on the workers' side, and feared on the government's, because of the climate and circumstances of the time. For the majority of the leaders and militants of the CGT, pacifism and hostility to the wartime rulers in effect reinforced and re-doubled social extremism. Moreover, for the first time since the fleeting episode of the 17th in 1907, there was the impression that the armed forces could be shaken: in the Black Sea had there not been, if not mutiny, at least demonstrations by sailors of the war fleet, demanding their repatria-tion and demobilization instead of going to act as gendarmes against the Russian Revolution? Echoes of those movements on the battleships even had repercussions in days of serious upsets in Toulon (30 May to 15 June 1919). If the business of the Black Sea had occurred, it was because there was revolution in Russia. It was known to be hatching in Germany as well. It was not yet known (and with reason) that all that would miscarry, would fall back within Russian frontiers and become encysted in a new socialist-dictatorial state. There was therefore every reason to think that world revolution was on the march.

To sum up, the development of social conflicts in France and the revolu-tionary aspirations in central and eastern Europe fed on one another. Lenin and his friends in the majority Russian social democratic workers' party (Bolshevik), soon rechristened Communist Party (Bolshevik) because they found the word 'socialist' to be discredited by the socio-patriotism of 1914, had quite naturally quit the Second Internationale of socio-patriotic parties and founded a Third Internationale. The question of which to choose thus arose for the French Socialist Party, SFIO. In this climate, pro-Soviet tendencies, the natural heirs to pacifism and hostility to national defence, had the wind in their sails. At its Strasbourg Congress (March 1919), the party broke with the Second Internationale. Would it go as far as to join the Third, that is to say, to commit the French workers' movement to the revolutionary path? That was the question debated throughout the whole of 1920, and its outcome would soon be apparent.

The government coped with the situation in various ways, sometimes by climbing down a peg or two. Hastily, at the end of April 1919, it got the vote through parliament on the law fixing an eight-hour working day for all em-ployees – a considerable gain, which had been sought for thirty years but was not enough to defuse the day of clashes on 1 May 1919, marked by some rough skirmishes, notably in Paris. The Black Sea fleet at last returned to the Mediterranean, and there was a flat refusal to intervene against the Russian Revolution, after the stabilization of the Polish front (September 1920). But the mutineers were brutally sentenced and supplied the French workers' movement with some martyrs (Badina, Tillon and, chiefly, André Marty).

By denouncing the revolutionary peril and broadly basing the struggle on that ground, Clemenceau and his so-called National Bloc majority easily won the November 1919 legislative elections.

During 1920, strikes sprang to life again. In the end they were contained, despite the tenacious and (by its nature) spectacular character of the railway workers' movement. After its failure there were thousands of penalty-dismissals, and even the dissolution of the CGT was contemplated.

Then the wave ebbed, but not without an enduring consequence.

The Congress of the Socialist Party, SFIO, held in Tours at the end of December 1920, was that of a party radicalized by the war. Had it not quit the Second Internationale, and was it not considering the 'rebuilding' of a united socialist movement, firm in its principles, in the bosom of the Third, Moscow's? It was led by a tendency known as the 'reconstructionists', former wartime pacifists, a minority that had recently become a majority in the party. Among them may be picked out the former schoolteacher, Ludovic Oscar Frossard, the son of a poor village shoemaker in the Franche-Comté, who had learned red politics in his father's workshop and made his debut at the age of sixteen by agitating in his teachers' training college. Or, more bourgeois in his upbringing, the journalist Jean Longuet, the son of a Communard and, through his mother, the grandson of Karl Marx. More recently won over to their tendency, Marcel Cachin, a philosophy teacher who had become a deputy and journalist, and who for a long time had belonged to the majority, that is to say, a socialist-patriot during the war. Others went further in adhering to the model proposed by the Bolsheviks, which seemed to them to extend certain aspirations and intransigences of revolutionary trades unionism. Among them were various workers, but also the teacher Loriot, the brilliant journalist and poet Raymond Lefebvre, and so on.

In Moscow, sent to observe at the congress of the Third Internationale, Cachin and Frossard made efforts to obtain the recognition and support of the Russian Bolsheviks (Lenin, Zinoviev), despite the outbidding tactics of the Loriot committee, openly in favour of a French Bolshevism. On their return, Cachin and Frossard would argue for the French party's joining the Internationale, without attaching too much importance to Russian demands for the exclusion of the moderates, that is, supporters of national defence and traditional democracy, and for the party to be restructured on the Bolshevik model (the 'twenty-one conditions'). Those demands were nevertheless formulated at Tours and adopted, in spite of their great severity. A considerable majority (3,247 mandates against 1,398) thus pronounced itself in favour of forging a party of revolutionary discipline, called 'Communist', incompatible with the tradition of democratic socialism, which was left with nothing in view but schism. It was for the latter (the departure of the minority to maintain a party called 'Socialist') that Léon Blum courageously argued. We shall shortly introduce this new leader of the 'old firm' when he reaches the summit of his historic role. His argument – to maintain the national and republican tradition of a democratic social-ism (social revolution is not achieved by short-circuiting the stage of liberty, there is no such thing as a good dictatorship, etc.) – would allow him to keep both Jean Longuet and even the old Jules Guesde on his side. But it was of no avail against the dominant current of sympathy for Bolshevism, which in people's feelings was fed by hatred for the recent war, the heat of the workers' struggles in 1918–19 and 1920, and the still plausible hope of world revolution (the Red Army had been able to reach the gates of Warsaw, and Germany was in turmoil). The Great War and its auxiliary, national defence, was the chief bogeyman used by the orators of the camp hence-forth known as Communist, for example, Paul Vaillant-Couturier, the young writer and artist. The debates were impassioned, first by the very gravity of what was at stake and of their principles, but also because the ghost of Jean Jaurès figured prominently in their arguments.

There was a redistribution of the cards in the workers' movement at that period which would last for a long time.

During this time national political life, too, defined its new course, an account of which must be given. Clemenceau governed at first with the Chamber that had resulted from the 1914 elections, whose majority was to the left. But conditions had greatly changed. Though a not inconsiderable minority of voters remained chiefly pacifist and tempted by new prospects, the overriding feeling arose that the painfully won victory was threatened, as much by the difficulties in the Versailles negotiations as by revolutionary agitation. Clemenceau knew how to gamble on that anxiety. The popular press and economic interests threw themselves wholeheartedly into the attack, for example financing against the socialists – likened in advance to the Bolsheviks – the famous poster of 'the man with the knife between his teeth' (the revolutionary in the guise of a hirsute moujik, armed with an assassin's dagger). The word 'National' was bracketed with the old repub-lican word 'Bloc' to group together everyone who felt the need for that defensive affirmation, that is, the entire right and most of the radicals. The remainder were crushed, and from the polls in November 1919 emerged a Chamber which Clemenceau, following Louis XVIII's example, might have described as *introuvable*, and which has stayed in history under the title 'Sky-blue Chamber'. Indeed, many of the deputies, new to parliament, were former combatants, and sometimes retained their uniform. And that 'sky blue' perhaps also recalled another symbolic blue, of the line of the Vosges, at last regained and taken back as far as the Rhine.

If we may play on the colour theme for another moment, it could be said that this blue Chamber, born – as we have seen – out of an anti-red reflex, also had some hint of white about it. For one of the major ideas of the right (and doubtless also part of left-wing opinion) was that pre-war anticlericalism was outmoded, since French patriots – both believers and unbelievers –

had met in the trenches, fraternized, learned to know one another better and lost some reciprocal prejudices. That was frequently true. Furthermore, official anticlericalism could, in terms of opportuneness, have political drawbacks. From that arose some far-reaching decisions, both practical and symbolic.

Diplomatic relations with the Vatican were restored. The old regime in churches and in schools as well as the Concordat were retained in the recovered *départements*; it was feared that Catholics of Alsace-Lorraine, offended by the Ferry laws and the Separation, might react by a desire for automony or regret the lost German regime. The festival of Joan of Arc, whom the Roman Church canonized in 1920 (after beatifying her in 1919), attained the rank of national festival. And the 1920 law fixed severe penalties for any propaganda or diffusion of birth control methods. That was a law which was truly typical of the moment since it combined two motivations: patriotic by its aim to increase the birth rate, and ideological by its convergence with the Catholic theory of conception.

Clemenceau did not join wholeheartedly in all these activities, maintaining his refusal on principle, as the head of a secular Republic, to be present *ex officio* at the Te Deum in Notre Dame. But that uncompromising attitude was beginning to seem rather outdated.

At that point, January 1920, the moment arrived for Poincaré to leave the Élysée. Clemenceau let himself be proposed as candidate, for an honour which it seemed would be his as a matter of course. Everyone (including himself?) was more than willing to forget that he had been against the institution of presidency ('a useless organ, like the prostate' – yet another of those medical students' jokes he could never give up). But, contrary to all expectations, the Congress rejected him. Was it the 'republican tradition' of getting rid of too pronounced personalities? The mistrust of Catholic conservatives for an old atheist who might well die in office and impose a civil funeral on the Head of State? The revenge of the innumerable members he had treated harshly, annoyed, scorned a little too obviously, even worried by his belligerence towards Caillaux and Malvy? A little of all that, plus the hostility of the leftist minority, certainly.

In short, the Congress carried Paul Deschanel to the Élysée in January. But as early as September the unfortunate man, afflicted by mental troubles, and after some glaring incidents, let himself be persuaded to resign. Alexandre Millerand, the former 'Millerandist' socialist, who had since become a sort of government radical, and in January had secured the presidency of the Council and confronted the railway workers' strikes, was elected President of the Republic. Georges Leygues formed the government.

From that point the post-war period entered a time of more stable political conditions, and it is easier to analyse their new configuration.

As before 1914, there were three camps: the right, the left and a revolutionary camp which challenged the principle of that distinction.

On the right, whether Catholic or not, men continued to espouse the cause of the Church (many of whose faithful still regarded the Republic as a bad thing), which had represented itself as persecuted since 1906 – even since 1880. But, as we have already glimpsed, that ploy was tending to lose importance in favour of the nationalism that was occupying the foreground. The right was the camp that gloried in having won the war and could be recognized, in 1918 and 1919, in the two great men united (despite their personal antipathy) at the head of the victorious nation, Poincaré and Clemenceau, not forgetting, of course, the marshals, in the front ranks of whom were Foch, the inter-allied supreme commander, and Pétain, head of the French army.

It was not by chance that Charles de Gaulle one day associated the two presidents in these portraits, expressed with a fine rhetoric, in reference to the 1914–18 war:

Poincaré, from the summit of the state, watched over the continuity of the homeland's plans. As firmly set on his target as in his position, familiar with every problem, every cog and spring in the mechanisms of state, he was predominant for his counsel. In the drama, which his prudence condemned but the arrival of which he could not view without some secret hopes, he continually pushed back up the slope, right to the summit, the boulder of traditional plans that was forever tumbling down again. Poincaré was France's reason.

Clemenceau was its passion. If matters were to be left to this unrestrained fighter, the crisis would need to have reached the stage where all tactful handling was ruled out. He could squarely face the worst of happenings. 'Nothing but war.' That suited him perfectly. He hurled himself on traitors, in fact or in intention, on Germany, on the House of Austria, in order to tear them to pieces. Of course, his passion struck out blindly at times. France would pay the price for his excessiveness. But, for the moment, it received from this fiercely impulsive man the fierce impulsion demanded by a fight to the death.[1]

Both of them came from the left. Poincaré, the epigone of the opportunists, Clemenceau of radicalism, both Dreyfusards (although unequally committed), both secular and agnostic. In theory, their patriotism stemmed from republican patriotism, but their present line of thinking attributed such great worth to the component 'France', at the expense of the component 'great principles', that it merged with the 'pure' nationalist reasoning, in which France was enthroned at the summit of the scale of values. Clemenceau who, of the two, had the more developed feeling for a turn of phrase, had coined the following, on 11 November 1918, in the moving speech announcing the armistice to the Chamber: 'France, yesterday God's soldier, today Humanity's soldier, is always the soldier of the ideal.' In that sentence, France, destined to play leading roles of some sort by nature,

---

[1] Charles de Gaulle, *La France et son armée*, Paris, 1938, pp. 273–4.

became an object of affection much more real than a vague 'ideal' or a relativized 'humanity'.

That had been seen materially at the peace conference, when Clemenceau's chief antagonist had been the President of the United States, Woodrow Wilson, whose message to Congress in January 1918 had sketched out the principles and the 'fourteen points' of a peace in conformity with the law. There was nothing more typical of the ethics of the left than the Wilsonian idea of making politics subject to the law, in this instance to the right of peoples to self-determination, if necessary at the expense of national egoisms; demanding, in short, that states (even French, British, Italian and Russian) should have morally respectable war aims. In opposition to him Clemenceau, who had turned sceptic and, in 1919, no more believing in Wilson's talk of law than he had believed ten years earlier in Jaurès's talk of the future, held that it was worth more to ensure France's safety by reputedly reliable classic methods than by a formal law for which there was no assurance that it would be respected. That was to mark himself as right wing, without a shadow of doubt. Of course, he further did so, one might almost say instinctively, when he assumed his 1917 character, of firm-handed, quasi-military leader, full of scorn for politicians. And even more, his 1919 persona, declaring war on the subversiveness of socialists and strikers.

Poincaré, having travelled less distance, took on the same tendencies, with less fuss. Since it had become the majority in parliament – a new historic event – the republican right was equally recognizable in both of these two men. For history, however, they did not represent it in the same way, as their paths diverged.

Clemenceau, defeated, as has been described, in the January 1920 presidential election, retired for good from political life (also renouncing the renewal of his mandate as senator). He was to live a further nine years, between Paris and the Vendée, in a retreat adorned with flowers, cultured leisure activities and pessimistic meditations, deliberately isolated, but drawn in spite of himself to the role of a military-cum-patriotic symbol. His statue (together with Joan of Arc's) is one of the few in Paris whose existence and location are known to the ordinary French person. Standing on a rock, wearing a soldier's greatcoat and helmet, at the edge of the Champs Élysées where, on 14 July 1919, the unforgettable victory procession took place, he completes in the west of Paris what might be called the perimeter of the military–national cult: Invalides, Arc de Triomphe, Napoleon (place Vendôme), Joan of Arc (Pyramides),[2] and on occasion official processions halt before him when returning from the Étoile.

While Clemenceau thus took off towards the symbolic, Poincaré, who was younger and still in full vigour, got back into harness. Having regained

---

[2] It is significant that the Joan of Arc by place de la Concorde is the most famous. Those in the place Saint-Augustin and boulevard Saint-Marcel are less well known, as if they were lacking a meaningful environment.

his seat in the Senate, he took on ministerial tasks, then those of president of the Council, more modest than the supreme post.

He, too, was a conservative symbol, but his place is in political typology whereas that of the Tiger lies more in national 'make-believe'.

Philosophically, therefore, the right was in opposition to the left on the by now crucial question of peace and French security. In the Treaty of Versailles, it would lay emphasis on what guaranteed that security, defined as the supreme value. The left, on the other hand, would chiefly have liked to see the prospect of a world regulated by the law, with the League of Nations as the first attempt to realize that hope. Of course, the left also cared about French safety, but insisted on seeking it in the paths of justice and general pacification: the left was Wilsonian and Genevan; the right was for classic diplomacy.

It must not be thought that we are making matters overly rigid. We are merely setting out here a theme so familiar to contemporaries that it was transferred into literature at that time by a then very successful novel, Jean Giraudoux's *Bella*. An idyll set in the society world of Paris in the 1920s presents Montagus and Capulets under the names of the Dubardeaus and Rebendarts. The Dubardeaus, a great secular and republican family of savants and diplomats, have all the characteristics of the Berthelots, one of whom, Philippe, did a great deal at the Quai d'Orsay to try to build a republicanized Europe along Versailles lines. As for Rebendart, with a name that almost speaks for itself, a gloomy politician, holding forth on monuments to the dead to keep alive the military flame – this is Poincaré. It is obvious to which camp the novelist himself belongs. Naturally, the right gladly revealed itself as clerical, much concerned with order, and conservative in social matters. Its camp, which the polemicists of the left called 'the right' or 'the reaction', had for its part given up calling itself 'conservative'. The right's usual terms for self-designation were thenceforward 'the moderates' or 'the nationals'.

'Moderates' was a term that had value as an implicit contrast: it suggested that adversaries were fanatical or 'over the top', people who would take the risk of disturbances, chiefly social.

Even more significant, 'nationals' implied that the left was not national, that it attached itself either to an Internationale (of Moscow or Amsterdam), or to a supranational utopia (League of Nations, Geneva, Europe), or that it was becoming edgy about the absolutely essential concord with the British. Against that collection of national deficiencies of all kinds, the 'nationals' boasted that they had French interests as their sole point of reference.

This explains how a man like Charles Maurras came to be at the peak of his influence at that time. Born in 1868 in Martigues (Bouches-du-Rhône), he was proud of his Provençal origin, which seemed to him to be supremely French, since for him the spirit of France was composed of light, sunshine and clear-cut horizons, of Latinity and classicism. In 1918, at the age of fifty, for young people he possessed the authority of age, the prestige of an already lengthy past (he had been crossing swords in politics since the time of the Dreyfus Affair), but also without doubt the attraction deriving from his dual role of politician and writer; he theorized and debated on the state, history and the government, as he did on literature and art, with equal authority and vigour. Maurras was not a statesman dabbling in literature as a hobby, nor was he an artist who from time to time might engage in a political spat: he possessed and kept well balanced a mastery in both fields. He even arranged them in a unique system with a logical coherence which, offering the appearance of a complete and rigorous truth, exercises an attraction on intellectuals of which history provides other examples. Also impressive was the man's purely cerebral aspect. Short, austerely dressed, faithful to the goatee of the 1920s, stern in manner, he lived entirely for his newspaper, *L'Action française*, which had been a daily since 1908, and for his books of political debate and art criticism, without ever abandoning his pen; in any case, he had never followed any other profession than the press and writing. He saw few people, being afflicted by total deafness. It would be easy to ramble on about the symbolic analogy between his deafness to outside noises and his imperviousness to objections, and it would be hard to refrain from doing so. But, for the time being, his handicap merely adds a touch of harsh singularity to his portrait.

He was an 'integral nationalist', the most rigorous (we know he was not the first or the only one) of those who placed France at the summit of the scale of values. France was such because it existed, and because the French belonged to it: that was a datum, an acknowledged fact, by which Maurras linked himself with the empiricism of conservative thinkers of the preceding century. But he added considerations of a more literary nature: France is Latin, and great classical literature and language form a part of its 'genius'. By contrast, the modernity claimed by the spirit of progress is romantic, therefore intellectually foggy and geographically foreign. The evil came from the north with the spirit of criticism, subversion and disorder: Reformation (Protestant), revolution, romanticism. And Republic, naturally; the Republic is thus twice evil, both because it partakes of that false inspiration and because it enfeebles France by allowing the authority of those foreigners and rebels – Protestants, Jews and Freemasons – to grow at the expense of the authority of the state. To replace the Republic with a system that renders the state more powerful and its tradition more French, is to return to the monarchy. This is the justification for Maurras's royalism. The young thinker, who had not even been a royalist in his early days in 1896, reinvented the monarchy as the logical complement to his system, justifying by a complex mechanism what for nineteenth-century royalists had been a naturally present and primordial tradition.

Lastly, religion (Catholic, it goes without saying) was for Maurras quite as instrumental as the monarchy. It completed the system, supporting and strengthening the cult of order, the *Patrie* and the national past. Personally,

Maurras did not disguise that he was at bottom agnostic and professed to be Catholic for simple doctrinal reasons.

His was a powerful and brilliant system of thought, which enchanted the royalists by dusting off their ideal, and attracted yet more Catholics who had been accustomed for a century to march alongside anyone who fought against the Republic. When the Church of Rome denounced the intrinsic 'paganism' of that mental construct, the faithful would be obliged to choose between Catholicism and Action française, resulting in a drama that began in 1926, the whole impact of which we shall have to evaluate.

Meanwhile, by gathering together in an original and, in literary terms, prestigious synthesis the elements of right-wing thought, not all of which he had invented, Maurras had given them considerable momentum. That system, royalist because it was nationalist, and in essence more nationalist than royalist, met the needs of a post-war situation where the dominant theme was national drama far more than institutional combat. Furthermore, it provided an overall criticism of the optimistic, humanitarian, modern and triumphant republicanism which had blossomed in the Belle Époque. To attack the radical establishment of the beginning of the century, the dissatisfied intellectual youth of the 1920s could, of course, become Communist – but that alternative was very theoretical, and as yet very little to be seen. Stronger and closer was the attraction of Maurrassian negation. During the 1920s the young students drawn by Action française were far from being entirely the sons of local squires or academicians; more than one *normalien* from a university family joined it in order to repudiate a Dreyfusard father.

Action française therefore projected its influence far beyond royalist circles, partly because it had at its disposal a well-written, keenly aggressive newspaper, but chiefly because the theme of France, uniquely France, which it constantly orchestrated, was shared by the whole conservative side.

The right loved the army, and its great leaders, notably Pétain, who would soon be the sole surviving victorious marshal and whose name, above all, had both the merit and the advantage of evoking Verdun, that most symbolic of victories.

People were proud of the empire, which had stood firm, and which had contributed to victory. Men were proud of being 'old soldiers' and decorated; those who had served were honoured, pushed to the fore, glorified – sometimes more than they themselves would have wished. In right-thinking society circles, an expression was current which summed up the story of such-and-such, a twenty-year-old conscript, returned from the war at the age of twenty-five with his captain's gold braid, covered with medals and minus one leg: 'He had a very fine war.' Pretty well unrepeatable today, the expression depicts the epoch, and one aspect of its collective ways of thinking.

What was happening to the left? Just after 1918, it was disorientated. Certain radicals, outraged by the way in which Clemenceau had come down on Malvy and Caillaux, were anti-Clemenceau, and among them was the rising star, Édouard Herriot. But others, such as Jules Jeanneney, retained their loyalty to the old leader. Above all, in 1919, through republican patriotism, the majority had been swept into the National Bloc, terrified as they were, besides, by the wave of strikes and the attraction exercised on the socialists before the Congress of Tours by the Russian Revolution. Those among the socialists who were nearest to them because they had supported national defence, kept on the defensive in the face of the pacifist and pro-Soviet wave of 1918–20, and had to await the aftermath of Tours in order to find themselves once more in a position which was both clearer and classic. The policies of post-1920 right-wing governments would in the end thrust radicals back into the opposition and create the conditions for reconstituting the Left-wing Bloc. That political outcome would easily blossom on their common ground of ideas and sensibilities.

Of course, the left, radical and socialist, and the great mass of the electorate without any precise commitment who voted within their common sphere of influence, remained patriots. Pride in victory, respect for war veterans, even respect for the army and the empire – none of that was unacknowledged, far less repudiated. Even in the SFIO, anticolonialism was regarded as an idea held by specialists (Jean Longuet, Charles-André Julien), members of a tiny minority whose voices cried out in the wilderness. But the left's patriotism was a shade less emphasized in comparison with that of the right, because thenceforward the main concern would be to reconcile it with a human ideal known as law and, even more, peace. France must be made as safe as possible, but above all peace must be preserved because war was definitively recognized to be the absolute evil.

That was why the men whom the left-wing citizen revered beyond all others were now the men of peace. First was President Wilson, who seemed to bring back from America the echo of the great idealism of the nineteenth century; and shortly after, Aristide Briand, who – having seen it all as far as international politics was concerned – would commit himself to one battle alone, that of the League of Nations, of disarmament and Franco-German reconciliation. As he sometimes succeeded in making that policy prevail even in moderate governments, the left, to which he hardly belonged any more, still kept its respect for him. But, since Wilson was a foreigner and distant, and Briand active though rather a 'politico', the veneration of the left was directed chiefly towards the memory of Jaurès.

When the left-wing coalition was in power for several months in 1924 and 1925, the most enduring of the decisions it bequeathed to history would be the completely symbolic one of transferring Jaurès's remains to the Panthéon. As Poincaré appeared to be resuming the classic political path of military force and action, the left, to counter this revival of nationalism, could find no better way than to exalt Jaurès, perceived as the man who had fallen while trying to hold back the war. This deserves to be pinpointed, because it tends to be overlooked.

In 1981, when President Mitterrand inaugurated his term of office by laying flowers on that tomb, there was talk (either to complain or rejoice) of paying homage to socialism. That was – let us confess – a sort of anachronism. Socialism had nothing at all to do with the 'Panthéonization' of Jaurès! In 1924 there was no majority to decide to honour the socialist idea! The SFIO did not even take part in the government, and the leader of the government, the radical Herriot, did not share socialist doctrines. Jaurès quite simply represented the common feeling of the left-wing coalition: peace, antinationalism, antimilitarism and, secondarily of course, the memory of the humanist fight for Dreyfus. In short, he had been placed in the Panthéon in spite of being, and not because he was, a socialist. Moreover, during the 1920s he was not merely Panthéonized; about thirty monuments to him were erected throughout France, just as often in radical as in socialist or Communist communes, and more frequently under the title 'Apostle of Peace' than the label of working-class leader. That distinction aside, he had in effect achieved symbolic status.

The symbol of peace, therefore, in the major key. A symbol also, in the minor key, of the noble times of Dreyfusism, which Herriot and Blum could not have forgotten. For not everything was new and post-war in the spirit of the left during the 1920s.

It had preserved its pre-1914 values: secularism, mistrust – mollified or not – with regard to the Catholic clergy, attachment to the parliamentary republic and its traditions.

'Republic' was still a key word, which set the left a-quiver, and which the right had not yet fully learned to claim.

For radicals and socialists alike, the crucial matter was still the consideration of the war and its consequences. Happy to have regained Alsace-Lorraine, they rejoiced still more at the creation of the League of Nations, in which shone the hope of a world without war and a reconciled and republican Germany. And as two safeguards are better than one, they clung to the idea that a British alliance was essential. In the diplomatic conflicts, the right would easily rediscover the Anglophobe tendency in French nationalism, while the left would become the guardian of the *Entente Cordiale*. After all, even under Conservative governments, Great Britain belonged fundamentally to the democratic camp.

By contrast, as regards the dictatorships, of Russia on the one hand and Italy on the other (Mussolini and fascism had gained control in 1922), the channels of traditional diplomacy would be impeded for some time by objections raised by politics of principle.

To sum up, radicals, socialists and other good 'republicans' remained patriots but, enamoured of peace, they insisted on being distinct from nationalism, and that distinction was expressed at that time chiefly by casting a critical eye on the war.

Without that, it would be hard to understand why retrospective controversies on 1914–18 should have occupied such a prominent place in the 1920s in the press, in books, in constant polemics, going far beyond the rubric of specialized cultural history. The war had been conducted, to some extent, by 'brain-washing' (the falsification of facts, defeats concealed, victories exaggerated, hatred and scorn for the Germans, incredible tales of prisoners' ill-treatment, and so on); the publicity-mongers of the left were therefore insistent in their condemnation.

Masses of accounts of the war were published, frequently conformist, sometimes courageously truthful. Some were praised, others attacked and criticism of their testimony (the then famous writings of J. Norton Cru) thus became a great public debate.

The right glorified the great leaders; the left subjected them to criticism. The right minimized the extent of the mutinies; so the left concentrated on exposing them and, in turn, exaggerated their scale. There were countless debates, but none so crucial as that on the origin of the war. The right held to the official argument, hallowed by the Treaty of Versailles; the left dared to echo (and with reason) the German, British and American argument that the responsibility must be shared. Pierre Renouvin on the one hand, Jules Isaac on the other.

In all those discussions, people began to feel that nationalism, which was more or less in power, and doubtless corresponding to the most spontaneously received opinion, had prolonged the frequently naive, simplistic, France-centred and noncritical elements in pre-1914 republican teaching of history and civics. However republican it might be, the post-1918 left had to learn not to copy its elders completely, and post-war school textbooks contained a more toned-down, more remote patriotism than those of the founding years of the Republic. The Republic, or the left, after the testing time of war, was watering its wine; adding the clear water of pacifism and a critical spirit to the red wine of exaltation.

Others, the impatient ones, wanted to break the glass and spill the wine. They were the revolutionaries.

Those intellectual exercises with which we have just credited the left were indeed difficult, and too subtle to hold everybody! Certain people, in the surge of their loathing for war and the nationalistic ideology that underlay and justified it, went as far as rejecting the nation. Of course, that was nothing new; everything had been said before 1914, but marginally or in very fragile declarations of principle. With the shock of 1914–18, anti-patriotism changed its scale.

Briefly, the war had certainly brought about two effects on French left-wing opinion: one tempered existing republican patriotism with a combination of doubt, critical reappraisal and a demand for peace, and the other imparted to revolutionary antipatriotism a noticeably increased strength of conviction and potential for expansion.

That was initially the action of the French Communists. The Socialist Party SFIC (which soon became officially the Communist Party SFIC) emerged from Tours with a majority, allowing it to keep the newspaper

L'Humanité, which Marcel Cachin took over while L. O. Frossard became general secretary of the party. But most of the deputies, municipal councillors and old urban executives, deeply imbued with republican socialism, stayed with Blum and the SFIO and, under the effect of their social influence, the SFIO would rapidly grow stronger by far, one or two years after the break, than the rival Communist Party. Moreover, two years after Tours, the split had consequences for trades union organization. In 1922 it was the Communists, together with a few former anarchists, who left to found the CGTU (U as in Unitarian, paradoxically), while the reformists, who were generally close to the socialists, kept the majority, the old initials, CGT, and the best-known leader, Léon Jouhaux.

This was a new configuration for the working-class division in France. Prior to 1914, roughly speaking, the reformist (or republican) tendency had been represented by the then single party (SFIO), while the similarly single union (CGT) had represented the revolutionary tendency. After 1922, the system was established which would last for over half a century, with a party–union coupling in each of the two camps. From 1922 to 1935, the moderate pairing was thus composed of the SFIO and the CGT, the revolutionary couple of the PC and the CGTU. It is the latter which concerns us here.

It was revolutionary, that is to say, closely linked with the new Communist Internationale, and consequently with Moscow, the Soviet government and the Bolshevik Party. Without hang-ups (we would say today), in accord with an era when Moscow regarded itself as the centre of a revolution on the march, a 'country of soviets' vowed to spread quickly and indefinitely to any nation that would abolish capitalist government, a country which had not yet made up its mind to solitary survival within former frontiers and the rebuilding of a nation (or a multinational entity) in the midst of others.

At the start of the 1920s, the French Communists (like those in other countries) loudly declared themselves strict Sovietophiles, 'Bolsheviks' and also, following the same line of thought, no less strict in their denial of French patriotism, the nation, its policies, the Republic. Of course, they rejected the ideas of both left and right as out of date and designed to deceive, recognizing one struggle alone as legitimate – that of the workers against the bourgeoisie, which is as much as to say their own against all others.

It reached a point where, in certain *départments* with a longstanding republican tradition where the idea of conflict between reds and whites still survived (reds designating the 'seculars' and whites the 'clericals'), reds thus designating, in fact, the powerful, easy-going and classic coalition of radicals and socialists, a number of Communists refused to admit that they were in the red camp! Nevertheless, red was the colour of the flag they brandished, that of the Paris Commune and the October Revolution in Petrograd, but there was more than one shade of red, and the flag of the proletariat should not be confused with that of a French folklore dating from 1848!

Such was the tone of the 1920s. Not until the dawn of the Popular Front would the PC begin to make use of the confusion between national red traditions and those of the revolutionary culture.

The PC thus pressed on in every struggle, even where it was at its weakest, with a courage more millenarian than desperate, but it turned the denunciation of war, militarism and the national taboo into an essential part of its propaganda, which led it to receive all the more knocks, the barracks being as yet better defended than the factory. Lawbreaking became an accepted fact, and men took for granted the risk of prison and other repressive forms of violence, ranging from the loss of a job to a beating-up. And storehouses of hatred were accumulated.

Against the right, of course, and against Poincaré, 'the man who laughs in cemeteries'! He inaugurated many of them, indeed, with a train of journalists and photographers, one of whom captured him on one occasion with a rictus on his face that might be taken for a smile. The sun, apparently dazzling him for an instant, could alone have caused him instinctively to screw up his eyes. The PC did not for a moment doubt their spiteful interpretation, and the photo would feature for a long time in their propaganda arsenal, in which violence was more sought after than sincerity.

But the PCF had no less loathing for the left, middle class to the hilt, social-patriot, twin sister to those German social democrats who had shot the Spartacists. It even hated the official pacifism of Wilson, as the League of Nations was then held to be a hypocritical tool of the imperialist Franco-British pair's domination over Europe.

The sole symbol of the left that the Communists could not resign themselves to abandon to the republican left was the great Jaurès, of hallowed memory, and founder of that very *Humanité* which the party had inherited after Tours, as we have said. They argued over him and made counter-claims to him, and the PC even managed to slip in a revolutionary procession at the tail end of the official procession to the Panthéon.

But the Communists were not alone in representing revolutionary opposition to the post-war political system and outlook. They exercised a certain power of attraction, by their courage and romantic refusal to compromise, but they were not without their repellent aspects: Moscow, dictatorship and violence; Moscow, legal squabbles among the Bolsheviks, then the USSR resigning itself to assume little by little the form of a new state; and the PC itself, organized and disciplined to the point of authoritarianism.

Certain splinter groups, while rejecting those last aspects of Communism, and even fighting them, proved as violent as the PC itself against the state, war, the *Patrie*, the republican establishment, the bourgeoisie and social proprieties.

They formed a whole little world, complex and shifting: anarchists, dissident Communists, soon known under the generic title of Trotskyists, young intellectuals attracted by surrealist artists and poets, or gathered around the magazine *Clarté*. In the interim before the generation of Aragon and André Malraux reached its height, other very famous writers took their place on the frontiers of the organized PC and the independent revolutionary nebula – Henri Barbusse, the author of *Le Feu*; Romain Rolland, the author of *Au-dessus de la mêlée*; Anatole France, who had produced the shock phrase, 'They think they are dying for the *Patrie*, but they are dying for the industrialists.' Three names that perfectly demonstrate by how much hostility to war, rather than the classic hostility towards the rich and the employers, contributed more to arousing revolutionary vocations. Even if theory was deemed to show the link between war and capital – the most oft-quoted saying of the Jaurès to whom they laid claim was precisely the celebrated 'Capitalism contains the seeds of war as dormant clouds contain the storm to come' – above and beyond all theory lay sensibility; now, revolutionary sensibility in that era had been born at least as frequently in the trenches as in the factories.

The spirit of the extreme left, which was far more libertarian than republican, as anticlerical as in the good old days but mainly antimilitarist, somewhat antiparliamentary and, above all, pacifist, profoundly rebellious to conventional expression, belonged – as will have been recognized – to the *Canard enchaîné*. Having emerged from the war, it carried on afterwards without a break, and its very vitality provides the proof that the third stream had a strong enough life not to fear any future eclipse.

The violent hatred experienced by young people who had come out of the war and who detested official France, in that it had acquiesced in being patriotic and bellicose, could now express its indignation in the new art form of free verse, humour and derision. Jacques Prévert provides some measure of it in a famous poem, 'Attempt to describe a dinner party (where the fare is less important than *who* is to be seen there) in Paris, France':

Those who piously . . .
Those who copiously (stuff themselves)
Those who 'fly the flag' ('over the top' patriots, nationalists)
Those who inaugurate (all the monuments, etc.)
Those who believe . . .
Those who believe they believe (but with no true spirituality)
Those who caw like crows (spreading malicious rumours, backbiters)

Those who bless packs of hounds (giving moral backing to a cruel activity)
Those who kick out (bosses to workers, masters to servants)
Those who shout 'Up guards!' (even to the dead)
Those who cry 'Bayonet!' 'Charge!'
Those who give guns to children (the generals)
Those who give children to guns (the politicians)

Those who are proud just because Mont Blanc is 1,810 metres high and the Eiffel Tower 300 metres high, and their own chest measurement a mere 25 centimetres

Those who suck France (a reference to Sully's famous saying: 'Labourage et pâturage sont les deux mammelles de la France')
Those who run, fly and avenge us (a reference to Corneille's *Le Cid*, when Don Diègue says to Don Rodrige, Le Cid, 'Va, cours, vole et nous venge!'), all those and many others proudly entered the Élysée, crunching the gravel, all jostling one another, scurrying, because there was a great dinner party and everyone had donned an expression to suit the occasion.

Neither Victor Hugo nor Racine escapes his sarcasm. Perhaps because Jules Ferry's educational system had, in some sort, so frequently called upon them . . . Prévert struck a little too hard, however. 'Those who inaugurated' were not all war-happy, as we know better today.

At that time, the typical inauguration was of monuments to the dead, not always Poincarist. Many people were not politically minded, and could not see themselves belonging to any party. What was the public outlook, in general? Well – another sign of the times, more fallout from the war – it discovered a specific form of framework and expression in war veterans' associations.[3] But before coming down to groups and men, the entire measure of the phenomenon must be assessed: France itself was a 'war veteran', which gave 1918 almost as much importance in French national symbolism as 1789, 1830 or 1880.

In fact, a new national festival entered the calendar, and would be truly honoured: 11 November, the anniversary of the 1918 armistice and a day devoted to remembering the dead. Perhaps this festival of unanimity and patriotism, thus especially worthy of respect for those who resented 14 July, prevented Joan of Arc's saint's day from becoming really entrenched, with its partisan and conflicting undertones.

On the other hand, a new place for national worship appeared with the burial, under the Arc de Triomphe of the Étoile in Paris, of an unknown soldier, chosen at random from among the thousands of unidentified corpses, and thereby destined to receive the homage due to all those whose graves were unknown. In short, the war's collective dead. The Arc de Triomphe, already more than a century old, was morally renewed and enhanced by this act, and became the chief place for official civic events, the obligatory centre of every public ceremony. There is no doubt that this also contributed to pushing other pre-1914 Parisian sites into the background, for example the Invalides (where Marshal Foch would nevertheless be interred in 1929), and above all the Panthéon, which began to sink into oblivion with its Republic of yesteryear, despite the efforts to dust it off that the left would make spasmodically.

---

[3] Their importance was sensed, and is now well known, thanks to the thesis of Antoine Prost, from which part of the following analyses is borrowed, *Les Anciens Combattants et la société française*, 3 vols, Paris, Presses de la FNSP, 1977.

Douaumont, 1919 – the chief battle centre then place of remembrance. From the Verdun sector, eight coffins of unidentified soldiers have been chosen. They will be lined up, and one, picked at random, will leave for Paris to be buried under the Arc de Triomphe. This is the start of the most observed and most official of French national cults. (Photo: Albert Harlingue)

The movement developed equally strongly in the provinces. The three major functions of the veterans' associations are familiar: first, to defend the claims and rights of survivors, the wounded, widows and orphans of the victims, in short, to look after the wellbeing and material interests of a huge new category of state pensioners. Over and above that, in most rural areas and small towns (the matter being naturally less clear cut in the large ones), to give a new context to masculine socializing (reunions, ceremonies and festivals, excursions – a fraternization that crossed the barriers of membership of other organizations), an unwritten social and cultural function which was given new life by these activities. Lastly, to maintain the new place of local veneration, the monument to the fallen. That was the fresh element in French local landscapes (either urban or rural) during the 1920s, omnipresent and familiar to the point where to say, in France, 'the monument' thenceforward obviously implied . . . 'to the dead of 1914–18'.

French towns and even villages had, of course, enjoyed a growing propensity during the Belle Époque for erecting decorative, commemorative or meaningful edifices: decorated fountains, crosses and Calvaries, but also 'great men', busts of the Republic sometimes, more frequently of Joan of Arc or the Holy Virgin, but the monument to the war dead extended this movement of symbolically setting a mark on municipal ground; it spread everywhere (reaching even the most rustic hamlets), it absorbed, effaced and sometimes replaced all the rest, and in the end provided the heartland of France with a sort of common sign of remembrance.

The monument nearly always bears an engraved list of the dead; very moving at the time, because they were the names of men whom the living had known, mixed with, loved, and it remains so today because – in the country – the length of these lists is often in marked contrast with the small number of inhabited houses, thereby giving the impression that the war really and truly emptied the countryside.

The monument was visited in a group (veterans, town council, school-children) at least once a year on 11 November, and often on other occasions (local festival, 14 July, etc.). Then, 'wreath laying', 'minute's silence', and a salute to the dead if there was a bugle available. And this happened every-where. Of course, beneath the uniformity of this great French ritual various conflicts arose, even within this established institution. There was a tug-of-war between monuments of parish origin and municipal monuments, diffi-culties about choosing a site . . . They have been forgotten today.

What really catches the eye, on the other hand, is the variety of ornamen-tation. Rich towns treated themselves to ambitious monuments, original works by well-known sculptors, while industrial cast-iron monuments, mass produced and sold at a reasonable price, finished up in the small places.

There were *Patries*, soldiers, cockerels, singly or in various combinations. Sometimes, simple pyramids. The cockerel was always the emblem of French fighting spirit. In contrast, the *poilu* might be standing firm, vigilant, or leaning forward into the attack, or perhaps have fallen, wounded. As for the allegorical woman, if there was one, she could be a goddess-*Patrie* in classical draperies (sometimes with a Phrygian cap), solemn and triumph-ant, or a woman of the people in regional costume, and weeping. Between them there was more than a nuance of meaning! The general diffusion of the cult of the dead, therefore, did not efface all discordances of feelings and ideas. Explicitly pacifist monuments to the dead were very rare ('Down with war' may be read on the one in Gentioux, Creuse, where a schoolboy in a smock extends his fist, indignantly, towards the plaque). Some reveal a tone of national glory, others one of mourning with, between the two, a mass of symbols that are hard to decipher. Which brings us back to the role of the veterans in French politics and ideology between the wars.

According to the most widely held idea, the veterans formed a force on the right, because they conveyed, through their natural vocation, respect for the flag, the *Patrie* and official national culture. History has recently refuted that simplism by showing that the spirit which most often inspired these associations (they were in any case very varied, but we will not go into details here) did not stem from a chauvinistic and bellicose nationalism but rather from a republican-style patriotism. With regard to the war dead, the feeling of solidarity and the care to honour them was accompanied by an equally firm resolve never to repeat such a terrible experience, which encouraged a favourable view of Franco-German reconciliation. There was therefore doubtless a certain ideological conformity (in so far as France, *Patrie*, honour, Republic and sacrifice were still respected), but serving future aspirations that were fundamentally peaceful, and probably closer to Briand's thinking than that of Poincaré or Clemenceau.

Within the argument that likens attitudes of mind on the right to the 'veteran spirit', another theme remains true, however, as stirring and as widespread as the desire for peace – that of the brotherhood of the trenches and the wish to stay 'united, as at the front'. Thence arose the undeniable possibility of a slide towards antipolitical argument, since politics, by definition, is divisive.

It is also true that a man engaged in and committed to politics (an occurrence then more common on the left than on the right) normally reacted more politically. A veteran who was a member of the SFIO would identify himself first as a 'socialist', and not as a 'veteran'. Whereas an uncommitted veteran, thus without a conscious political ideology, thought of himself as a 'veteran', since he had no other clear point of reference available. The label 'veteran', therefore, had perforce slightly more worth and power to attract on the side of a right wing that was willingly anti-politician, than on the left where there was more readiness to take on political partisanship. But that observation is not enough to put the veteran spirit on a par with nationalism.

Truly, to come to a conclusion on this new panorama of the moral forces of the time, it is still the concept of peace that is most imperative. Was it new? No, of course not. Everything had been said before 1914 about the benefits of peace and the evils of war, but in unapplied theories or on the fringes of politics. But 1914–18 had demarginalized pacifism and turned it into a major aspiration. In different forms, however. Absolute, intransigent, violent pacifism, going as far as social anarchism and antipatriotism, because the *Patrie* helps to make soldiers (the libertarian, intellectual and artistic extreme left). Pacifism linked (tactically perhaps) to social revolution, for the Communists. A watered-down pacifism, vaguely reconcilable with the old patriotism, among the Wilsonian and Briandist republican left. And then, less obvious but just as deep, a latent, below-the-surface pacifism, to which many men of the right were sensitive despite an adherence to traditional national thinking; Pierre Laval is a representative of this form of pacifism.

Each in its own way, all these trends of opinion reflected, by what they held in common, the profound reality of a country drained by its ordeal and which never wanted to go through it again.

Against that background of feelings, practical politics continued to unfold, with the traditional problems of international relations, and others more in keeping with the era.

Briefly, the sky-blue Chamber elected in 1919 had returned to power a right wing that had been excluded from it, broadly speaking, since 1899. Viewed from the left, the measures pertaining to the clergy mentioned earlier in this chapter were bound to seem like the emanation of a spirit of revenge, which in its turn would have to be bridled. That was the first matter for anxiety.

The second was common to diplomacy as a whole. Despite the brotherhood of arms that was deemed to have welded the *Entente Cordiale* together, and in spite of the great principles of Geneva, it soon became clear that state interests had to be taken into account and that those of the French clashed almost everywhere with those of the British: in the Near East (oil, relations with the Arabs, Graeco-Turkish relations); with regard to the Russian question (the British were urging the resumption of some kind of contact with the Soviets – the Genoa conference in April–May 1922 – while France made the prerequisite of the settlement of debts owed to it); in the matter of naval armaments (the Washington conference fixed a quota for France much lower than that of the British, Americans and Japanese); finally, in the matter of reparations. In the end, the French share had been fixed at 52 per cent of the total, but as Germany was unable or unwilling to put it into effect, at the end of 1922 Poincaré, who had become president of the Council, resolved, with the sole support of Belgium, to bring pressure to bear. In January 1923 he took the drastic course of sending regiments to occupy the mining basin of the Ruhr.

Intimidation, the taking of forfeits – that might be regarded as an attitude of force and militarism, nationalistic in inspiration, and according ill with the spirit of Geneva. When the electoral campaign opened for the legislative elections in 1924, the Head of State, Millerand, in a speech at Évreux abandoned the traditional neutrality of the Élysée to support Poincaré's vigorous national policy. That was a third matter of anxiety for the left, which had elevated to doctrinal status the political neutrality of the highest office in the land, and saw in Millerand the reappearance of the presidentialist impulses of Mac-Mahon or Casimir-Perier.

Those three causes for concern, by galvanizing 'republican' forces, led the radicals and socialists to rebuild, under the name 'Left-wing Cartel', the old alliance of the Left-wing Bloc type that had enjoyed such success from 1902 to 1904. In May 1924, the Cartel won the elections with all the more credit because it did not have the advantage of all the popular forces, since the strictly class-conscious politics of the PCF kept a share of its electorate separate from the coalition, under the name 'Working-class and Peasant Bloc'.

Édouard Herriot, the undisputed leader of the Radical Party, formed a government which the SFIO would support with its votes, but without any ministerial participation.

The 'republican tradition' part of the programme was accomplished first, albeit at the price of a crisis in the regime. All those suitable to become ministers among the newly elected left majority, approached one after the other by Millerand to form a cabinet, refused, in a veritable strike which forced the Head of State to resign. There was thus a presidential election: the victor was Gaston Doumergue, a senator, a fairly moderate radical, of Protestant family although from the south, and a former minister under Combes, defeating Paul Painlevé, whom the Cartel would have preferred. But Millerand's dispatch signified that a certain republican orthodoxy was jealously preserved.

In power, Herriot tackled the anticlerical target: he announced the introduction of secular legislation in Alsace-Lorraine. There was a general outcry. From the right came a hue and cry and even disturbances in the streets, and stormy meetings. The idea was abandoned. The Concordat in Alsace and the embassy to the Vatican were maintained. Herriot had better success, at least to start with, in his German policies, as he decided on the evacuation of the Ruhr, which was a step in the direction of a return to the spirit of peace and the League of Nations. Negotiations began which would lead to the pact of Locarno while, in the same spirit of peaceful diplomacy and rejection of any new warlike venture, the government officially recognized the existence of the USSR, virtually giving up support for the white counter-revolution and demand for the repayment of Russian loans.

Lastly, there were the great symbolic measures. The principal one has already been mentioned – Jaurès taken to the Panthéon – while another, minor, victim of the nationalism of war, Caillaux, received an amnesty and resumed his place in parliament.

All this created much enthusiasm on the left, where Herriot, acknowledged as the supreme republican, enjoyed huge popularity. That sentimental upsurge in 1924 forms, in this history, a sort of relay stage between the spirit of the Left-wing Bloc, of which it is a last echo, and that of the Popular Front, which it somewhat prefigures. However, there was growing uneasiness in the face of unprecedented, and pressing, difficulties.

The outstanding novelty was the place occupied by the economic, financial and monetary situation, thenceforward in the forefront of French political problems, something which had not really been the case before 1914.

It was partly the consequence of a war which had profoundly impoverished France and which, besides, established a close link between financial and foreign policies: France, in debt to its former allies, chiefly the Americans, was the creditor of vanquished Germany by way of reparations. Now, although it would seem logical to the French to combine the two transfers (getting paid by the losers in order to reimburse the fellow-victors), the Americans would not accept that logic, as they were anxious not to put too much pressure on Germany.

Well before 1924, Poincaré's government had already had to face up to difficulties. The solid franc of Germinal (Year XI), convertible into gold and on stable parity with the pound (25 francs) and the dollar (5 francs), artificially maintained at its rate during the war, had begun to drop on the exchange market as early as 1919. Its fall had been accentuated at the beginning of 1924 to the point where an appeal had to be made to the American Morgan Bank to support it. Meanwhile the policy of occupying the Ruhr had failed, with Germany not making payment and its own mark collapsing in spectacular inflation, and this state of affairs had forced Poincaré, just before the elections that were to overthrow him, to accept the plan of international experts – called the Dawes plan – which reorganized German finances and fixed a new, reduced schedule for reparation payments. With the arrival of Herriot, the evacuation of the Ruhr had settled the political aspect of the problem in France, but that was not enough to rally the British, who had had their fingers burnt, to the French argument on the connection between payment of debts and payment of reparations, and all the less because the latter was beginning to be put into effect, thanks to the coming into force of the Dawes plan.

Above all, during the course of 1924, the fall of the franc continued and even – taking into account the suspicions aroused by a markedly left-wing government – grew worse. Capital fled abroad, Treasury bills were renewed with difficulty, it was hard to get loans, and the government had to 'go through the ceiling' (that is, exceed the lawful total) of advances requested from the Banque de France for the Treasury. The time was April 1925. Failure and resignations. Despite a complex spate of ministries and expedients, the fall of the franc worsened, with the pound going well beyond 100 francs.

In July 1926 a Briand–Caillaux government was formed, very centre oriented, but was overturned through having the right wing and the socialists against it simultaneously. Herriot then made a last attempt to form a government from the Cartel, but the Treasury was empty, the pound quoted at 240 francs, and the atmosphere turned almost to one of riot.

On 23 July, replacing the resigning Herriot, Poincaré, who had suffered such a defeat in 1924, formed a government and obtained a centre-right majority. The pound immediately fell back, 'confidence' (it is easy to see whose) having returned. Poincaré rapidly consolidated the situation by various fiscal and technical measures (a self-governing fund for paying off the public debt), and by purchasing foreign currencies the Banque de France secured the stabilization that had occurred.

The failure of the Cartel government in the face of economic difficulties aggravated by the mistrust evinced towards it by the major financial forces (what Herriot bitterly termed banging one's head against a 'wall of money') provided the first instance of a situation destined to recur in the future, when a left majority, carried to power by a clear choice of universal suffrage, comes to grief through a sort of force of circumstance, and passes power to the right without any new elections.

That swing would often take the form of a simple change of alliance on the part of the radicals, who might as easily form a left majority with the SFIO on the ideological basis we have seen, as a centre-right majority (of National Union, so-called) with the moderates, on the basis of economic orthodoxy.

In 1926 the one who benefited from this return swing of the pendulum was Raymond Poincaré, who came back to head the government, Gaston Doumergue, let us remember, being President of the Republic from 1924 to 1931.

After the vicissitudes of 1923 4, France's German policy adopted the path of diplomacy to consolidate the Treaty of Versailles through international harmony. In October 1925, with the Locarno agreements, Great Britain, Italy, Belgium, France and Germany gave their common guarantee to the security of the Rhine frontier. Reparations, as we have said, began to be paid.

The conclusion of Locarno at the time of the Cartel thus modified the European climate, and the second Poincaré government altered nothing. Briand, who stayed in charge of Foreign Affairs, began the great diplomatic undertaking of Franco-German reconciliation (with Stresemann as his opposite number): confidence in the League of Nations, the setting up of disarmament negotiations, the 'outlawing of war' (Briand–Kellogg pact) – subjects which, unlike internal policies, would gain him great popularity, notably in left-wing opinion.

Meanwhile, the rebuilding of the country was taking place. Around 1930, war damage in the former areas of the front was repaired. That task was stimulated by a good economic situation, which it stimulated in return. The 'national income at constant prices from 1920 to 1931', which in 1923 had regained the reference level of 1913, and wavered between 1924 and 1928, realized a marked rise between 1928 and 1930, at that time exceeding the 1913 level[4] by 33 per cent.

France, as an economic entity, slowly resumed its growth. There were 39,600,000 people within its 1914 boundaries, but only 37,500,000 in the same area in 1921, the losses being due to the war; those were compensated

---

[4] See A. Sauvy in *Histoire économique de la France entre les deux guerres*, vol. 1, Fayard, 1967.

for by the reintegration of the regained *départements*, and there were 39,200,000 inhabitants *in toto* in 1921. Ten years later, they would number 41,300,000. Those 2 million gained were the difference between a stagnant national demography (birth and death rates, both down, more or less balanced out), and heavy foreign immigration. There were 1 million foreigners living in France before 1914, but almost 3 million in 1931. Some North Africans (chiefly Kabyles from Algeria), but above all Polish (in the north), Spanish and Italian (in the south).

Can another external force be added – from overseas?

France was at the height of its extra-European power. The word 'empire', plain and simple, no longer evoked thoughts of Napoleon; it immediately brought to mind the colonial empire, that global wealth of possessions which in its extent yielded only to the British Empire.

Its population was estimated at 100 million, including metropolitan France. The theme 'a France with 100 million inhabitants' aimed to reassure, even to uplift, those who might be worried by France's poor demography. Official nomenclature made the distinction between colonies, properly speaking; protectorates, which in principle were states that had abdicated only part of their sovereignty and had kept their 'native' dynasty (Tunisia, Morocco, Annam, Laos and Cambodia); and territories under mandate (of the League of Nations) awarded by the Treaty of Versailles.

The colonies did not all enjoy the same status; that of Algeria and the old colonies, with a substantial French population and which sent deputies to the French parliament, being the most favoured. But in French imagination all that melted on the map into a single pink stain, to be marvelled at for its amplitude and far-flung extent. This overseas France was principally African. By and large, it was the whole north-west quarter of the continent. Uninterruptedly continuing into one another were Arab-Muslim North Africa (Algeria, Tunisia, Morocco), French West Africa, an ensemble of seven colonies forming a bloc, from Dakar to Lake Chad and from the Sahara to the Gulf of Guinea, and French Equatorial Africa, another group of four colonies extending as far as the Congo. In East Africa, France held only the French Somalian coast, with Djibouti, but it was the key to the Red Sea and the only railway outlet for Ethiopia (independent). Lastly, off the coast of South Africa, lay Madagascar (the 'big island') and Reunion Island.

In Asia, France had a presence in the Near East through its mandates over Syria and Lebanon, and above all in the Indochinese peninsula, where the name French Indochina was given to the culturally heterogeneous area formed by Laos, Cambodia and Vietnam. The latter name was as yet unknown, the French at that time knowing Vietnam only under the three names of Tonkin (in the north, colony), Annam (in the centre, protectorate) and Cochin-China (in the south, colony). To designate the populations, the term 'Annamite' was the most usual. Familiar to the French were the names of the two large towns, Saigon and Hanoi; they had heard of an extraordinary temple, Angkor-Vat, in Cambodia; and knew of the rich resources – rice, rubber and anthracite.

Lastly, still in Asia, strung out on the coasts of the Indian subcontinent, which was almost totally a British possession, a vestige of the times of Dupleix, were the five Indian trading posts. These slender survivors were nevertheless names familiar to the French, because the litany learned in geography lessons – Pondicherry, Chandernagor, Yanaon, Karikal and Mahé – had the pure-poetry charm of a nursery rhyme.

In America, France owned Saint-Pierre-et-Miquelon, off the coast of Canada; in the waters of Central America, the French Antilles (the name Caribbean was not yet in use); and, in a little corner in the north of vast Brazil, French Guiana, with Cayenne and the dubious renown of the penal colony. Finally, in Oceania, a few islands, of which only New Caledonia and Tahiti are noteworthy. Average Frenchmen were proud of that imperial power; those who were more politically educated gave honour and merit to the Republic for having rebuilt a domain equal to the one conquered and then lost by the Bourbons; they believed that such power was legitimate and deserved, because it spread civilization to overseas subjects; and they saw the proof of that virtue in the additional backup which black troops had provided for the armies during 1914–18. That is why the discordant voices, which did exist, were rare, far from widespread and, when they did sound, were apt to scandalize rather than convince.

What a scandal created by the Communist Jacques Doriot's attention-grabbing telegram of support for the Moroccan rebel Abd el-Karim in 1925! And another scandal over the denunciation of the murderous forced labour demanded by the big colonial companies in Africa, in André Gide's *Voyage au Congo*, in 1927. Only specialists and civil servants knew what was stirring, *being* stirred and organized in Algerian Islam, in Vietnamese Communism or North African emigration to the Parisian region, around Messali Hadj. Incidents or revolts, when they occurred, appeared sporadic; almost no one spotted the signs that were the forerunners of an inevitable decolonization.

One event shows to what extent the wrong ideas were held about the sensitivity of the colonized peoples. In May 1930, at Carthage in Tunisia, a huge eucharistic congress took place, a monument of Catholic and French colonial triumphalism, in which even the distant memory of Saint Louis's crusade was evoked. To represent this as a scene in the spectacle, hundreds of schoolchildren took part, mostly Muslim of course, wearing crusaders' costumes. It would seem that budding Tunisian nationalism received some fuel from this tactless blunder.

In France, however, the ordinary citizen was more of an armchair colonizer than a pioneer or emigrant. The French population of North Africa – the colonials properly speaking – was stable, prosperous and scarcely increased. Those French who were linked personally and materially with the empire as traders, administrators and soldiers, were in the end but a slender proportion of the nation. The ruling powers wanted more.

In order to develop France's imperial vocation, initially by making what had already been accomplished more widely known, a colonial exhibition of great prestige was organized in 1931. Rather by chance, it almost exactly coincided with the centenary of the conquest of Algiers. In fact, the idea had been conceived just after the war, but held up by a certain amount of trial and error.[5] At first, the plan had been to extend the international exhibitions in the nineteenth-century tradition, by placing more emphasis on overseas; therefore to conceive an international colonial exhibition, as much universalist as French. It was the lack of enthusiasm of the other imperial powers, notably Britain, that 'Frenchified' the undertaking more than had been foreseen.

Poincaré had entrusted its planning to Marshal Lyautey, an expert if ever there was one, owing to his great success in Morocco. Ultimately, the chosen aim was to demonstrate to the French public 'the work achieved by France in its empire and the contribution of the colonies to the home country'. It was a matter of informing and educating visitors, in a spirit favourable to official doctrine – in other words, propaganda – as was underlined by several demonstrations and polemics on the extreme left. As it happened, at that date in 1931 the exhibition found itself following close on the heels of the first Indochinese anticolonial riots of any magnitude, in Yen Bai. In short, the first cracks were appearing in the empire at the very hour of its apotheosis.

From April to November 1931, the exhibition occupied the bois de Vincennes, at the gates of Paris, and received an estimated 8 million visitors (4 million Parisians, which implies several visits by many of them, 3 million provincials and 1 million foreigners). The visit was coupled with one to the zoological park, a natural complement of information on the vast world.

There were as many different pavilions as there were colonies, each seeking through its architecture and decor to give an authentic flavour of local culture: a Moroccan palace, a Sudanese village street, a Tunisian mosque, a Khmer temple, Cameroonian tribal huts in the equatorial forest, and so on. Other pavilions exalted the French presence: Catholic missions, Protestant missions, colonial army. Everywhere there were objets d'art, charts giving statistics, maps, all the typical educational materials. But there were also men, craftsmen and tradesmen in the reconstructed souks, or costumed performers to bring to life processions or festivals representative of native cultures – that was the spectacle and action part. The desire for authenticity and beauty was undeniable but, as is always the way in such cases, selection was made, in the name of beauty, of what was oldest and most elitist: the sumptuous trains of Annamite mandarins of yesteryear, rather than the daily life of today's poor peasant. As in every exhibition, in short, Paris came for the spectacle, such as has been described, plus the African, Malagasy and Moorish orchestras, the Asian dancing, not forget-

[5] For further details, see Ageron, 'L'Exposition coloniale' in P. Nora, *Les lieux de mémoire*, II: *La Nation*, Gallimard, 1984.

ting (on a more trivial level) the camel races or trips in dugout canoes on Lake Daumesnil. When the event was over, some museums and lasting monuments would remain, a new wealth to be added to the patrimony of Paris, but without any notable effect on the then unforeseeable fate of the empire. The key to French vitality continued to lie in the home country.

Agriculture remained a sector characterized by the large number of people it employed and its economic backwardness. Not until 1931 did the so-called urban population (communes of more than 2,000 inhabitants) numerically exceed the rural population. This agriculture, which still employed a great deal of labour, was routine, protected, not very productive and rarely exported. But, for the time being, those handicaps were scarcely noticed. Much more emphasis was laid on the 'balance', 'harmony' and 'tradition' it would bring to the French nation and its culture.

Towns grew slowly therefore. To the big industrial regions of pre-1914 (Parisian region, large Atlantic and Mediterranean ports, Nord-Pas-de-Calais, Alsace and Lorraine) were added several more scattered developments (Alpine *départements* with hydro-electricity, Provence with bauxite).

Oil refineries were the principal addition to traditional production (textiles, metallurgy, mining). However, the most outstanding, which best gave the impression of progress and modernity between the wars, was the development of two French pre-war specialities: automobile and aircraft construction. They were to be seen to the south of Paris and its nearby suburbs. A typical captain of industry was André Citroën; a typical industrial zone was the 'red belt' from Ivry to Aubervilliers, from Saint-Denis to Puteaux; a typical worker was the *métallo*, or metalworker, soon to supply Communism with its big battalions. But before 1931 that was no longer, or not yet, an obvious 'peril'.

On these broadly favourable national and international foundations, Poincaré succeeded in his management. His position strengthened by the 1928 legislative elections, won by the right, he abandoned a revaluation of the franc and went for 'legal stabilization'. The law of 25 June redefined the franc as equivalent to 65.5 mg of gold with a purity of 900 per thousand, which corresponded to about 125 francs to the pound and 25 francs to the dollar. That was the 'Poincaré franc'.

In 1929, Poincaré also had parliament ratify the Mellon–Berenger agreement which had been concluded with the United States by his predecessors in 1926 on the total sum and schedule for the repayment of French debts. As reparations were coming in, all was at last going well. In 1930 the Finance Minister, Henri Chéron, would reputedly be the custodian of a 'treasure'.

All that must have had some vague connection with the new euphoria in social, cultural and intellectual life, summed up by the hallowed name

'Wild Years'. The nightmare of 1914–18 was receding, what was to come was unpredictable, as Weimar Germany had become Goethean again, while the USSR was bogged down in its own internal difficulties. It goes without saying that not all France was having a picnic. But the expression 'Wild Years' evokes the sparkle of society life in Paris and at the seaside, the joyfully welcomed innovations of the cinema, by now widespread, radio – called the TSF (*téléphonie sans fil*) – and the car. Or the discovery – not of America itself, as it was still very exceptional to go there – but of its art, and chiefly jazz music. Perhaps those years were 'wild' quite simply because people danced then with an additional touch of frenzy. They were the setting from which emerged Marc Chagall and Fernand Léger, Maurice Ravel and Erik Satie, Chaplin and René Clair, the Exhibition of Decorative Arts (1925), the apogee of the NRF (Nouvelle Revue Française) and a host of other successes and stars who would shine until the great world crisis of 1939.

The close of the 1920s thus saw the last pre-1914 generation of politicians approach the end of their careers accompanied by plaudits, Poincaré as the paragon of 'wisdom' in domestic politics, and Briand the herald of noble hope in diplomacy. It was in 1929 that Poincaré withdrew, stricken by illness. In 1931, when Doumergue's seven years were up, Aristide Briand, like Clemenceau in 1920, would let himself be tempted by the supreme ambition and make a bid for the presidency of the Republic. But he was elderly, ill, and did not have the unanimity of the right, and the Congress opted for Paul Doumer, who had become a nationalist symbol through the sad circumstance of having lost his three sons in the war. We know that he would be assassinated by the madman (or suspectedly so) Gorgoulov in 1932, to be replaced by a moderate originally from Lorraine, Albert Lebrun.

In the meantime, the world economic crisis had broken out. The Black Thursday of the Wall Street crash (24 October 1929) did not have immediate repercussions in France, which had enjoyed some slight advantage in its trading because of the recent devaluation, and the relative slowness of its industrialization tended to cushion the effects of international capitalism's upheaval. In 1930 and the beginning of 1931, the man who rose to the head of the conservative camp, André Tardieu, was still able to rely on the soundness of public finances to launch an innovative programme relating to the economy (massive public works – Tardieu was conscious of France's relative backwardness) and also to introduce legislation on social issues (24 April 1930, a law giving the final form to the social insurance that had been established since 1928). It was during the course of 1931 that the effects of the world slump were reflected in France by the drop in various economic indices, the appearance of unemployment, and several spectacular 'affairs' (the Oustric affair).

At first, the crisis struck from another quarter – international payments. In 1929 the Dawes plan had been replaced by the Young plan (fixing a definitive schedule for reparations, and agreement on French troops leaving the Rhineland), and reparations had continued to flow in. But almost immediately Germany, bearing the full brunt of the crisis, had no longer been able to pay. In June 1931, the Hoover moratorium suspended all international settlements for one year. When that year had passed, Germany was not back on its feet and it was clear that France would get nothing. Would it then have to resume its own payments to the Americans?

Neither the moderate government of Laval nor the radical government of Herriot, who had returned to power after the 1932 legislative elections, which were favourable to the Left-wing Cartel, could persuade the Americans to accept the principle of linking the two settlements. Herriot, with his back against the wall, decided to pay (to keep France's word, even if national sensibility was shocked by the separation of the two flows of money). The Chamber did not follow his lead, and overthrew him on 14 December 1932.

The country then definitely entered a new era, directly or indirectly dominated by the crisis, the repercussions of which in domestic, social and diplomatic politics would soon be added to financial consequences.

The conservative side could have been brought up to date and rejuvenated by André Tardieu, a brilliant man, very capable in economics, a Parisian, somewhat authoritarian, quite different from a Third Republic notable and nearer to our own times in various respects. But illness soon cut short his career. In 1932, the Cartellist left (still lacking Communist support) thus won back the legislative elections, but Herriot soon lost power, as in 1925, though for rather different reasons. His second failure begins to give substance to the 'law' that was mentioned regarding non-electoral alternations.

With Poincaré and Briand gone, after the meteoric passage of Tardieu, the most conspicuous man in the right-wing majorities was thenceforward Pierre Laval. Seen from a distance, the antagonistic duo that he formed with Herriot is a good illustration of the politicians typical of the waning Third Republic. This new stage must be looked on as the 'comrades' Republic'.

On the whole, it functioned normally, if one excepts the 1924 presidential crisis – even then, it could be interpreted as a defence of the spirit of the regime – and the 1932 assassination. Elections of deputies and senators took place amid calm and at regular intervals. However, there were frequent governmental crises – too many to quote them all. The public would begin to wonder why the political battle appeared so simple when it was a matter of rousing the electorate, and why it became so complicated when the deputies were romping about in the Palais-Bourbon. Part of the difficulty stemmed from the fact that the various political questions at stake did not necessarily engender the same types of alliance. But that complication itself is still too simple to take account of everything. Institutions were thus blamed for not exactly stimulating the clarity of procedures, chiefly because of the system of parties, or because of their absence. Indeed, parties as such hardly existed. On the right, the URD (Union républicaine et démocratique), the Republican Federation, the Democratic Alliance, etc., were parliamentary groups extended by uneven networks of electoral committees far more than bodies organized in real associations.

Most of the elected members on the right were still notables who were well and truly entrenched in their constituencies and their area of social influence, and therefore easily recalcitrant towards central structures; in Paris, they had their true groupings in coteries, friendships, various networks of private interests; and they were liable to become divided amongst themselves over such-and-such a measure demanded in one place and unpopular in another.

The partisan phenomenon was more marked on the left. Moreover, André Siegfried's teaching reached its apogee at that time, and the diagram: 'notables' parties, on the right – militants' parties, on the left' became a 'pons asinorum' of political science.

But one must not exaggerate. Between the Radical Party and the right was a whole cohort of deputies, belonging to the left as far as their basic convictions were concerned, but remaining organized in small bodies where they were less constrained and thus more easily able to manoeuvre and more likely to be offered a ministerial appointment. And the Radical Party itself was not very homogeneous, or very simple, or very disciplined.

The Socialist Party was more so, despite its division into tendencies. Furthermore, it wanted to put only one foot in the parliamentary game, the other being, so to speak, in the revolution. Constrained by its doctrine (officially Marxist) and, perhaps even more, by the fierce vigilance of the PCF which kept it under a running fire of accusations, the Socialist Party had no desire to enter into bourgeois governments. 'The exercise of power' on which Léon Blum sincerely tried to build a doctrine in keeping with this attitude must be regarded as an exception.

Everybody made do with these old habits and sometimes Byzantine solutions. But the members of parliament, who were almost all decent men, were nevertheless unable to render encouraging or even clear, for public opinion, the complicated system in which they themselves were circling about like fish in water.

On the whole, the men who emerged from the politics of between the wars still resembled the pre-1914 members of parliament, like them being very liberal, very adaptable, very clever. Fairly good symbols of the political personages of between the two wars are to be found in Édouard Herriot and Pierre Laval.[6]

[6] To whom two great recent biographies have drawn attention, *Édouard Herriot ou la République en personne*, by S. Berstein, Presses de la FNSP, 1985, and *Pierre Laval*, by Fred Kupferman, Balland, 1987.

Born in Troyes in 1872, the son of an officer, with little money, helped in his early studies by an uncle who was a curé, Édouard Herriot 'climbed' through the meritocratic network of secondary education and the *École normale supérieure* to attain a teaching post in a *lycée* and then a university faculty. A doctor of literature, with a learned thesis on Juliette Récamier ('a thumping great tome on a rosebud', mockers would say), he would also leave some good work on the dramatic fate of Lyon during the Revolution. At the same time, a free-thinker and Dreyfusard, he was quite naturally a radical militant. Highly gifted, charming, eloquent, he also succeeded as a militant and became the mayor of Lyon (1907), then senator for the Rhône, a minister (of Food) for the first time in 1916. We know what followed. Of his origins he had preserved a characteristic not yet mentioned: an interest in education, teaching and the democratization of entry to *lycées*. Lyon would remember him as a great mayor, of exceptional longevity to boot (1907–53). And in fact he would leave his mark on it very noticeably: the creation of the Bron Airport, one of the first in France; of the Lyon Fair; the strengthening of the school network and the whole series of large modern hospitals on the eastern boundaries of the town.

For all those reasons together, the town of Lyon looked on him as a veritable father-figure, and the secular left as an idol; or even, according to Serge Berstein's words, as 'the Republic in person'. Popular both for his worthiness and achievements and for the more personal admiration inspired by his culture, brilliance and charm, success – social and other – would be heaped upon him.

But the opponents of the Republic would accuse him of being a different archetype – that of the member of parliament who sacrifices too much to professional cordiality and to an eloquence cut off from reality. As for the caricaturists, they latched onto his liking for the good things of life, and popularized the image of the pipe from which he was inseparable, and the embonpoint denoting the gluttonous eater. Contemporary sycophants marvelled at the admirable speeches which he himself wrote when he had to inaugurate this school or that monument. A sterner judge might think he could have better served the state if, like everyone else, he had left a secretary to write his ceremonial speeches and devoted the time saved to tackling some daunting dossier or other.[7]

In fact, in order to be able to give him a sympathetic final judgement, his biographer[8] cannot find anything better to say than that he was the best product that the pre-1914 Republic could provide (honest, distinguished, deeply attached to the great founding principles), it being understood that subsequently he did not develop, while France was changing all around him. One of the changes, among others, was the economy, which Herriot never quite succeeded in mastering.

---

[7] J.-N. Jeanneney, in *Leçon d'histoire pour une gauche au pouvoir*, Paris, Seuil, 1978.
[8] Berstein, *Édouard Herriot.*

In 1903, in the Lyon *lycée*, Herriot the brilliant *agrégé* had made the acquaintance of Pierre Laval, then aged twenty, who was working for his law degree, the son of a café proprietor in Châteldon (Puy-de-Dôme), and who was acting as a tutor to finance his studies. As logically as the *agrégé* was radical, so the tutor was socialist, and even progressive. But the former was to remain all his life within his party and his ideological mainstream, whereas Laval, going from the extreme left to conservative dictatorship, and from poverty to opulence and power, would traverse the entire political and social gamut. The temptation is therefore strong to impute to this outcast, shot in 1945, all the failings of opportunism and social climbing. A courageous biographer has recently preferred to air his own line of thinking.[9] From this it would appear that the man who would be condemned as Hitler's principal French accomplice was neither a blackguard, nor a cynic, nor corrupt.

He was a lowly man, which gave him the energy to make his fortune in the 1920s, but honestly, in local press and radio undertakings (the TSF, still in its early days, did not amount to much), then in mineral water springs, which gradually prospered, by dint of perseverance and respectable shrewdness. His lowly beginnings also, and most importantly, imbued him with compassion for the humble, and more sympathy for feelings than for abstract ideas. Before 1914 he had set himself up as a lawyer in Paris, taking many cases for workers and unions, as had Briand in his early days. As a socialist, he had been a candidate in the poorest and at the time most sordid suburb: Aubervilliers. He was elected deputy for the sector in 1914, and would be its mayor from 1923. One might extend the contrast sketched earlier between Laval and Herriot, and find the same symbolic separation between Aubervilliers and Lyon as between the hard-up tutor and the brilliant university don. Naturally, however different and opposite they were, the two men were on informal terms in the Palais-Bourbon. During the war, Laval had been a pacifist and had busied himself looking after his wretched suburban flock. Poverty and war were the two spectres that always haunted him, and it was with the intention of being effective in battling them that he would be utterly opportunistic in his choice of means. Defeated in the 1919 legislative elections, he did not desert Aubervilliers; on the contrary, he devoted himself to it, became its mayor – as we have said – in 1923, and occupied himself with social matters, tacking adroitly between socialists, Communists and 'reactionaries'. In fact he established his political base there, at the same time keeping his country business and the centre of his modest wealth. Elected deputy for the Seine in 1924 on a Cartel, thus left-wing, list, he supported Herriot, then became a minister in a short-lived Painlevé cabinet, still as a Cartellist, and remained so in a Briand cabinet which had already moved back more towards the centre. It was then (in 1926) that he could be said to have made the transition, in Briand's sphere of influence, from left to right. From then on, he emerged

9 Kupferman, *Pierre Laval.*

as a well-known parliamentary figure – the more easily, besides, since his physical appearance singled him out. On the short side, with a matt, sallowish complexion, thick, straight, very black hair, with a lock across his forehead,[10] he invariably dressed in black, with a white shirt and tie, as if clinging to the finally attained sign of bourgeois ceremonial. The last trait he shared with Briand was an interest in foreign politics, in a spirit of peace. He would remain faithful to it after Briand's death until the advent of the dictatorships. When, in the name of the principles of law, the men of the left – mainly the socialists but also to some extent the radicals – found themselves unable to associate with Mussolini, Laval would talk to him. That was the difference, and it was also the start of a chain of events, or so it seems to us with the benefit of hindsight.

[10] Male hairstyles with a side parting, like Laval's, were not very common then. Men tended to wear their hair cut *en brosse*, as before 1914 (Herriot did so), or they had long hair completely swept back, known jokingly as the 'shirker' (because a good way from the front).

7

Confronting 'Fascism'
1932–1940

'Fascism' rather than fascism? Indeed, the word was argued about then, and still is.

Since 1920, in Italy, 'fascism' has been the name given to the simultaneously nationalist and populist dictatorship, with its single party and cult of the leader, established by Benito Mussolini. That specific designation poses no problem; controversy begins with the extension of the word outside Italy, which implies the generalization of the concept. It was, indeed, extended to other more or less comparable dictatorships (Hitlerian national socialism in 1933), to the movements, sometimes violent and of authoritarian inspiration, which rumbled in France (1934), to the Spanish *pronunciamento* (1936), and lastly to the Vichy regime after the defeat in 1940. That tendency to turn fascism into a category, and above all to make it large enough to embrace all that, belonged distinctly to the left in the 1930s, or anyway was common to the simply liberal left (radicals, for example) and the more or less Marxist left (SFIO, PC).[1] By contrast, on the right, there was a dislike for elevating fascism into a category, and a preference for seeing phenomena *sui generis*, and national particularities as more significant than similarities.

Judgement may be reserved on this debate while at the same time using the problem as a leading strand in the history of the regime's last years. The French left, rightly or wrongly, believed in the 'fascist' entity and the threat it represented; it was therefore galvanized by a surge of 'antifascism', and it is really the appearance, rise, peak and ultimate rupture of that surge which forms the graph of these eight years, at the end of which the Franco-German war was resumed, ending in French defeat.

In 1932, fascism was still confined to Mussolini. The left hated him because, being sincerely attached to liberty, it hated dictators and, more

---

[1] A tendency still present, apart from some minor shifts, and chiefly revived recently by the work of Zeev Sternhell. It will be remembered (chapter 2) that he saw in what he called the 'revolutionary right' the beginning or embryo of fascism.

precisely, because blood had already flowed. In 1924, in fact, the Italian socialist deputy Matteoti had been assassinated by the fascists; for Léon Blum and his followers, Mussolini was thus the murderer of one of their brothers, and not just of democracy. The right did not share this repugnance to the same degree. The less liberal among the moderates had no decided objection to a strong power which would put an end to parliamentary chaos and trades union disturbances; as for the more liberal, without liking dictatorship, they considered that morals and politics had nothing to do with each other and that national interest should come before blame. Of course, the Italians were in direct rivalry with the French in Tunisia, where they had a lively immigration, but on the other hand, Mussolini had a Francophile past (he had argued in favour of Italian intervention alongside France in 1915) and, as an Italian, would be just as worried as France about the possible rebirth of a German hegemony in central Europe. He therefore had to be kept in the French camp. In fact, Italy signed the Locarno agreements. In June 1933, after Hitler's advent, it would still be associated, in order to 'keep the peace', with a sort of confirmation of Locarno, called the pact of four (France, Great Britain, Italy, Germany). The following year, Mussolini, by vigorous mobilization, would check a first German attempt to annex Austria. The Italian position was therefore still reassuring from the French point of view. But already Hitlerian activism had moved into the foreground.

In Germany, the so-called Weimar Republic had been shaken, notably by the economic crisis which had existed in the capitalist world since 1929, its ravages particularly prominent in that heavily industrialized country, where the number of unemployed soon ran into millions. A rapidly growing party, the National Socialist Party of German Workers (Nazi, when abbreviated) was challenging the Social Democrat Party and the Communist Party for their members. Not unsuccessfully.

As its name indicates, Hitler's party professed itself very popular, very socialist, with the word 'national' besides denoting a patriotic rejection of foreign ideologies. In a nation humiliated by Versailles, that could strike a strong chord, directing anger against the foreigners who had imposed the 'diktat', against capitalism and wealth (in which the Jews were held to be the masters), against the republican state, its impotence, its ups and downs, etc. The party was organized in paramilitary groups and on occasion fought in the streets. Therein lies a family resemblance to Italian fascism in 1920. Hitler attained power in January 1933, first as Chancellor (head of government) under the presidency of the old Marshal Hindenburg, then as sole master of the state and the party.

His anti-liberal, anti-Marxist, anti-Semitic dictatorship did not seek to disguise its aims. One was rather mythological: the primacy of the Aryan 'race'. Others were more concrete: the destruction of the Treaty of Versailles and the humiliation of France. The latter was the designated enemy, both detested for traditional geopolitical reasons and despised for some specifically Nazi reasons: 'Jewified' and 'Negrified', the French in particular would be far from 'Aryan'. Scorning the Versailles stipulations, Hitler gradually rearmed (military service, the creation or revival of war industries), and that rearmament, which should have made Europe anxious, offered the advantage of helping to re-establish industrial employment, thereby consolidating, and even conferring some prestige upon, the regime.

Meanwhile, France was absorbed in its own crisis. It was not so much the economic crisis, in the spectacular style of the United States or Germany, for its slow development afforded it some slight protection. A country where farmers and the middle classes constituted a substantial proportion of the population, it had its unemployed, of course, and they had a very hard time, but their number and obviousness were less than beyond the Rhine. Because the crisis was more diffuse, it was all the easier to discern which aspects of it were political and which due to force of circumstance. Latent antiparliamentarianism had always resurfaced when politico-financial scandals erupted – those affairs involving the classic types of swindler, the second-rate deputy trafficking in his influence, and the truly Parisian adventurer.

The Airmail Service, Mme Hanau, Oustric . . . In 1933, the one known as the Stavisky affair was current. His swindle concerned forged bonds of the Bayonne Crédit municipal, issued with the complicity of a local deputy; his enterprises carried on thanks to an incredible series of delays in inquiries and legal proceedings, the postponement of which was obviously due to some secret protection. That could only have been mixed up with politics, and politics in power, from which the radicals never kept away for long.

The affair reached dramatic proportions when it became bloody. On 9 January 1934, Stavisky was found dead in his Alpine chalet, on the day when the police finally came to arrest him. Officially, he had committed suicide, but it might be that 'they' had prevented him from being able to give too many details . . .

The indignation of opinion in the face of this excess of enigmas was obviously exploited by the antirepublican press, by the 'revolutionary right' and by all those who were league oriented. But it also awakened echoes in 'veteran' circles, who preserved the legitimate taste for moral strictness, and also a certain propensity for welcoming anti-politician talk.

Now it was thought – quite wrongly – that all the radicals and, going to extremes, the Republic itself, were becoming corrupt and blameworthy.

During January, summoned chiefly by Action française, unrest directed against the regime was incessant, with the cry of 'Down with the thieves!' The favourite sites were naturally more bourgeois than popular; the big boulevards, Champs Élysées and place de la Concorde on the right bank, and boulevard Saint-Germain on the left. There was also the area around the symbolic target of the Palais-Bourbon. Those taking part in these street

demonstrations were numerous; Action française militants, calling themselves by the expressive and picturesque name 'Camelots du roi' (the king's
pedlars), were but one of the organized bodies. There were others: Patriotic
Youth, French Solidarity, and so on. There were also demonstrations by
certain groups of veterans of politically right-wing tendency, connected
with the UNC (L'Union nationale des combattants, National Union of
Veterans). Colonel de la Rocque's Fiery Crosses had a bastard character,
stemming from both the veterans' movement and the activists' league. That
'revolutionary right' was thus divided into groups, leagues or movements
whose ideological differences were scant, but who were separated by competition and rivalry. This is probably one of the major differences between
the French-style 'fascism', polymorphous and with many factions, and the
single parties of Mussolini or Hitler, and one of the reasons why it was less
efficient.

Nevertheless, they were out on the streets every evening, weakly contained by forces under the command of the Prefect of Police, Jean Chiappe,
a moderate.

When, with Daladier, a left-wing head of government arrived, worried
about possible connivance between the Parisian police and the trouble-
rousers, and consequently resolved to entrust the maintenance of order to
a dependable official, the crisis erupted. At the end of January, Daladier
and his Minister of the Interior, Eugène Frot (an independent socialist –
therefore minister material) removed Chiappe and replaced him in the
Prefecture of Police with Bonnefoy-Sibour. The right protested violently in
the Palais-Bourbon, notably through the voice of André Tardieu, its current
strong man. But Daladier managed to obtain confidence, with the support
of the socialists.

Protests against the government, and to have Chiappe's dismissal
revoked, then reached a point of paroxysm on the streets. On the evening
of 6 February, there occurred the most extensive of this almost chronic
series of demonstrations. Responding to united appeals came all the groups
and leagues of the extreme right, (moderate) municipal councillors of Paris,
obscure men, sometimes racketeers – it was for them, so it is said, that
Marcel Pagnol had created the character of Topaze, whose name would
soon become generic – but popular in their *quartiers*. The National Union
of Veterans was also present, and even the ARAC (Association républicaine
des anciens combattants, Republican Veterans' Association) directed and
supervised by Communists. The latter certainly had no wish to see the
reappointment of Chiappe, their *bête noire*, going one better than Daladier
and demanding his arrest! But they also called for an end to the 'regime of
profit and scandal', in other words, the bourgeois Republic. In the centre
of Paris, however, their troops would be less numerous than those of
the nationalists or moderate antiparliamentarians, or those with fascist
leanings.

So there were long processions, along all the great arteries of the right bank, converging on place de la Concorde, and on the left bank going westward along the boulevard Saint-Germain. As on the preceding evenings, there were scuffles and paving stones were hurled. On that particular evening, things went much further: buses were overturned, newspaper kiosks set on fire, the grilles round trees torn up to be used as missiles; there were even sporadic bursts of gunfire. The rioters resisted the Republican Guards, who charged on horseback to break up the groups, by wounding their mounts' legs with razors attached to sticks. The Prefect of Police had had the pont de la Concorde barred in order to prevent the enormous crowd, who filled the place de la Concorde and were trying to cross the Seine, from reaching the Palais-Bourbon right at the exit from the bridge. Around midnight, on the point of being overwhelmed and scattered, the barrier of *gardes mobiles* (anti-riot police) extricated themselves by opening fire. The dead would number thirteen, with countless wounded. What is surprising is that the other barrier of police, who covered the Chamber of Deputies facing the line of the boulevard Saint-Germain, did not have to take similar action. Colonel Rocque's Fiery Crosses, who formed the bulk of the uprising on the left bank, fell back without attacking. It was to that as much as to the fusillade on the bridge that the material, physical victory of public order was due. Above all, it would be used later as a basis for denying that 6 February had really been an attempt at a putsch. The right would resume power, but through the indirect effect of that violent evening.

Daladier, an honest man, a total stranger to any Staviskyan contacts, thus found himself promoted to the title of 'gunman'. In a sitting of the Chamber, the right thundered against the government, which was accused of having shed blood to defend 'thieves' against indignant worthy citizens. The left, and chiefly the SFIO leader, Léon Blum, on the contrary supported it for having defended, together with the seat of national representation, the integrity of the Republic in the face of rioters and perhaps seditionaries. Such, in principle, was the argument of Daladier himself. However, he did not dare to assert it and resigned as if he were to blame, thus providing the demonstration with an unhoped-for success.

The place left empty by the radical cabinet was immediately filled, in the name of the necessary 'national union', by a government clearly slanted to the right – with the backing of the radicals, of course; Herriot had his place in it – and to give it due solemnity, its president was the former Head of State, Gaston Doumergue, who had returned from his retirement.

So here was a very conservative right back in the saddle, indirectly but in fact, through the strength of 'the streets'. That was enough, on the left, to reinforce their analysis of the 'Republic-in-danger'. The CGT, in accord with the SFIO, therefore called for a general strike to take place on 12 February.

The PC and the CGTU, still playing their own game, were aware chiefly of the overall dramatic, possibly revolutionary, aspect of the situation, and decided to demonstrate on the streets on the 9th, against 'the class enemy' in all its forms, fascist or governmental. On the evening of 9 February, the east side of Paris was virtually in a state of siege, and there was some rough fighting around the place de la République between workers and police – the latter getting the best of it, naturally. After that demonstration, the PC decided to take the other path open to them and, in the night between 10 and 11 February, promised to obey the strike order for the 12th issued by the reformists. The day of action on 12 February was thus transformed into a unitarian political strike and, as such, met with clear success. Thus, in the reaction to 6 February, what was to become the antifascist group got under way one week after the drama.

The liveliness of this reaction throws some light on the spirit of the times. For left-wing citizens, the Republic (liberal – which is almost tautologous – and parliamentary – liberty could not be conceived otherwise) was the supreme political value. By comparison, scandals were minor matters. In 1888, for instance, it had been of relatively little import that Wilson should have been a trafficker; on a completely different plane, Boulanger had put himself in the wrong by stirring things up dangerously for the Republic *in situ*. Similarly, in 1934, the irritating detail of the Stavisky affair mattered little; the really serious point was that an antirepublican bid for power could be conceivable.

The antiparliamentary agitators of February 1934 passed for 'fascists' because the word was current, and because there was a vague similarity between their actions and protests and the pre-dictatorship turmoils in Italy and Germany.

These analogies may appear incomplete, and there is no lack of good arguments – as has been said – for not imputing the character of fascists to the Parisian league members of 1934; but for the understanding of history, the importance lies less in the truth of later analysis than in the convictions that were held at the time. For it was conviction which launched the movement leading to 1936.

In short, the antifascism of 1934 reveals a defensive impetus which vividly recalls the sudden bursts of the left in 1924, or 1899, or 1889, or even further back. And at the same time, one can see to what definition of fascism 'antifascism' refers. Let us throw light on that definition, which the entire left of that time claimed as its own, by means of a simple outline.

The left-wing citizen of the time believed that, with regard to ideals or *ends*, one was either on the left, the side of good, progress and the march towards justice, or else on the right, the side of evil, attachment to the past, conservatism. Furthermore, as regards *means*, good lay in liberal procedures – here, our citizen, curiously did not use the word 'liberal', but rather 'democratic' – and evil in authoritarian and dictatorial procedures. That crossing of the two options logically created four quarters.

The first (ours, the good one, said the man on the left) belonged to good 'republicans' (Herriot, Blum), uniting the merits of being progressive as regards ends and democratic as regards means. If absolutely necessary, the two quarters which were only partly bad could be forgiven: the Communists, dictators as regards means, but well-intentioned as regards the ultimate ideal, and the parliamentary conservatives, poorly inspired in their philosophy, but at least accepting republican methods. But the absolute evil lay in the fourth quarter, where both a bad ideal and bad ways were to be found. It was called 'fascism', the word of the times, but obviously it held shades of the eternal white, the counter-revolution, the Badinguet of 2 December, etc. And one may well think that antifascism became such a popular cause in France through the very strength of that recollection.

However, there was a vast difference between what was then being made ready for 1936 and what had taken place in 1924: the Communists had returned to the 'republican' fold.

From the tentative encounter of 12 February to the solemn affirmation of the pact of popular assembly of 14 July 1935, by way of the pact of Socialist–Communist unity of action of 27 July 1934, and the *rapprochement* with the Radical Party in spring 1935, the path of the PC towards readmission into the left-wing family was slow and sometimes bumpy. Its ups and downs are less important to us than its driving forces. The essential point is that, while 'fascism' was becoming a danger in France, Hitler was becoming a danger in Europe. He was doing so fairly obviously, but Stalin still had to be convinced of it. He became convinced, but with a certain slowness which must be understood by reference to Soviet Communism's own particular line of reasoning.

Since the October Revolution, for Marxism–Leninism, socialism (the name given over there to the first phase in the realization of a just society, Communism being only a later stage) had not been a theoretical, abstract or diffuse ideal, or to be capitalized on in instalments (as in the thinking of socialists and social democrats), socialism was 'real': it existed in the USSR. The safeguarding and advancement of the latter thus decided what was politically good. But if the good could be embodied so concretely, so also could evil. Evil, therefore, was not (as it was for socialists) capitalism in general, or poverty, exploitation, war, barbarism . . . generally and just about everywhere. Evil was identified with real power which might annihiliate the USSR; so not capitalism, but imperialism and, even more precisely, the most dominant and aggressive imperialism. In short, the enemy was politico-military even more than economic, and each era recognized its own.

With hindsight, one can observe three avatars of evil at the time, as viewed by the Communist universe. First of all, the Franco-British pair of Great War victors, the people of the cordon sanitaire and intervention in favour of the White Russians, the powers which hypocritically dominated Europe through the League of Nations. Then Hitler. And after him, the United States of America. We shall look at the change of attitude toward the second of these in due course; for the moment we will stay with the first.

Continuing its initial hate-filled mistrust of France and Great Britain, the USSR had kept itself apart from the League of Nations, had loathed the Treaty of Versailles, but had looked kindly, in a turbulent Germany, not only on the potency of the workers' movement but also on nationalist aspirations tending to revise the 'diktat'. So the German PC, while fighting Nazism, which was in direct competition with it for influence over the working class, had been slow to turn it into the chief enemy; the evil was the Republic, which had resulted from Versailles, and was judged to be pledged to the French and British. It had been necessary for Hitler to achieve power, for his dictatorship to take shape – brutally anti-working-class and likely to relaunch a fearsome German imperialism – to cause Stalin to do him the honour of elevating him to the rank of enemy number one. That seems to have been in May 1934. *The* turning point!

As a result, the French Republic, deprived of its diabolical primacy, became on the contrary a possible ally.

But what a lot of things were changing then (from the Communist point of view)! The Treaty of Versailles was no longer open to criticism; the League of Nations and 'collective security' were no longer mystifying (the USSR gained admittance to it); France had the right and even a duty to show its patriotism and keep a watch on the Rhine; the tricolour flag was the associate, and no longer the shameful antagonist, of the red flag. Fascism? The Communist Internationale would officially define it, in order to connect it in some way with the materialist doctrine, as 'overt terrorist dictatorship by the most reactionary, chauvinist and imperialist elements of financial capitalism'. From then on, liberal democracy (class dictatorship, doubtless, but neither 'terrorist' nor 'overt', and made up probably of more anodyne 'elements') retrieved at least some defensive virtues. And it would be the turn of the French worker to regain the right to be a patriot and a Republican.

That apparently suited him very well.

The French Communist Party was indeed to develop far more during this phase of reintroduction into the left, into customary republican culture and into French society than during the previous phase of class isolation and denial of the old values. The man who had guided it since 1931, Maurice Thorez, had faithfully assumed the revolutionary line, but he seemed to direct and orchestrate the new one with a sincere jubilation. In rediscovering the Republic, one rediscovered France, its patrimony and traditions of progress, and above all the French Revolution. That gave rise to some very interesting reflections. France did not only play the role, for the USSR, of Germany's natural enemy, it also represented a fine heritage. The great Revolution of 1789 was not confined to a mere model battle which, via 1793, had to some extent prefigured 1871 and 1917, but also in itself formed an exhilarating heritage. For Maurice Thorez, inspired either by the Czech, Clément Fried (the tutor left with him by the Internationale), or by the historian Jean Bruhat, or perhaps by both, drew from the history of the French Revolution a very simple outline: in each era, the 'rising class' is the guardian of patriotism, the 'declining class' is pledged to betray the nation. Yesterday, the bourgeoise of 1789 embodied France, and the aristocracy were Koblenz. Today, the working class is preparing to become France, and it is the bourgeoisie (fascist, or with fascist leanings) who are preparing to betray it. In any case, the proletariat can affirm their Frenchness, since history itself makes France their heritage. How simplistic all that was is borne out by the evidence! But the fact is that after 1934 the PCF placed this scheme at the heart of its convictions, and that the more intelligent of its members became patriots again not only out of obedience to the strategic reasons which suited Stalin, but also by virtue of a specifically French hope; not to mention what they might possess in the way of atavisms which were the product of former education and were now revived.

The first difficulty about this new policy arose from the fact that often the Communists trumpeted it immoderately from the rooftops. Incapable of doing anything by halves, because of that generosity in their collective temperament which gives them their charm, and ultimately their strength, they – yesterday's antipatriots – would soon be handing out lessons in patriotism to everyone!

The speech of Jacques Duclos at the Buffalo Stadium, on 14 July 1935, in which Communist adherence to the red, white and blue and to the 'Marseillaise' became obvious, created much annoyance on the left. Certain socialists, in particular, who had hardly changed, found themselves from then on farther to the left than the PC on patriotic–military ground, and laughed self-consciously. In any case, the disputes over conflicts of every nature which existed between the two close and competing parties were not going to be settled without a few clashes. But at last the signal had been given, the first steps taken, for a new start on the left for the 'Republic', and that recalled 1899 even more than 1924.

The left, then, undertook to shift opinion. In 1932, two celebrated writers, Henri Barbusse and Romain Rolland, had contributed to setting up a World Congress against War, held in Amsterdam, still very revolutionarily 'anti-imperialist', thus fairly pro-Communist. In 1933, after a new congress in Paris at the Salle Pleyel, it decided upon the title Congress against War and Fascism (called the Amsterdam Pleyel movement) and through that re-orientation gained the beginnings of an audience among other intellectuals, and even among a small fringe of SFIO socialists. After 1934, antifascism moved into the foreground. A Watch Committee of antifascist intellectuals, precisely directed towards French internal problems, was created under the triple leadership of the philosopher Émile Chartier (Alain), the ethnologist Paul Rivet and the physicist Paul Langevin, regarded as close respectively to the Radical Party, the SFIO and the PC – a three-way split which would become classic and which we shall meet again. The question of whether antifascism was ready for a new aggressiveness had not yet been formulated.

Official France also reacted. In the moderate governments following Herriot's failure, that is, from the end of 1932 to 1934, now that Briand was no longer there, French diplomacy had been steered by Louis Barthou, an old friend of Poincaré and the last veteran of the pre-1914 government teams. Rediscovering the familiar situation of danger from Germany, he had undertaken to use every opportunity of forming counter-alliances. To that end, he had renewed contacts with the USSR and, besides, sought to tighten the links with France's natural allies in central Europe, the states which had emerged from Versailles.

Those contacts had caused hope to be reborn on the Soviet side, and disappointment on the part of the Poles, for whom the old anti-Russian hostility opened the way for a favourable response to fascism, but had also raised hope among the Czechs, Romanians and Yugoslavs. All that was shattered on 9 October 1934 in Marseille, when, while welcoming King Alexander of Yugoslavia on an official visit, Barthou was fatally wounded at the side of the assassinated monarch. Since the Croats were oppressed by the Serbs in the Yugoslavia of that time, which was anything but federative, the attack was in response to a specific inter-ethnic conflict. But it was also a blow, on the part of a movement which would be revealed as pro-Hitler, delivered to the objectively antifascist policy pursued by Barthou.

At all events, the tragic death of Barthou had opened the way for Pierre Laval's diplomacy. At the end of 1934 and in 1935, Laval continued Barthou's policy on one point: to persevere with the *rapprochement* with the USSR, but he went against him on another.

The contact with the USSR took a spectacular turn, not so much in respect of the content of the Franco-Soviet pact – which merely talked of dialogue and help in case of aggression, without any very practical stipulations about putting it in concrete form – as for the public declaration of Stalin, who gave his explicit approval of France's policy of military defence. It was, of course, within the logic of the 1934 turning point but this explicit statement underlined the new patriotism of the PCF, which for thirteen years had been characterized by violent antimilitarism.

Unlike Barthou, Laval had almost no faith in any backing to come from central Europe, where France's potential supporters were letting themselves become involved, through active Hitlerian diplomacy, in an entire political setup of commercial and economic agreements. He judged it more realistic to bet on Italy once again.

In January 1935, he came to an important agreement with Mussolini in Rome, settling the whole Franco-Italian dispute favourably (the status of Italians in Tunisia, frontier problems between Tunisia and Tripolitania, Italian and French Somalilands), and recalling the shared commitment of the two countries to Austria's independence. On 14 April, at the Stresa meeting, Great Britain associated herself with these Franco-Italian pledges to maintain the European status quo.

Laval, however, was by no means unaware of another aspect of Italian politics – the plan to form a colonial empire in Africa at the expense of Ethiopia. Between October 1935 and May 1936, in fact, Italy would attack, defeat and annex Ethiopia, which was the only independent state in Africa, and even a member of the League of Nations. Geneva should have declared sanctions – economic to start with – against the Italian aggressor, as provided for by the basic pact. But Laval, obviously, was not keen, and the British Conservatives hardly more so. Months of tension and debate altered nothing: Italy won its prey and the League of Nations lost its credibility.

The important point is that in France, just at the moment when left-wing opinion was discovering yet another grievance – and a very serious one – against Mussolini, Laval appeared to be the man whose diplomatic opportunism had sacrificed international law and morality. That could only further strengthen the spirit of antifascist resistance among radical voters, for whom adherence to the principles and spirit of Geneva still counted. The socialist and Communist electorate were affected even more strongly.

Since Hitler meanwhile was scoring points (the Sarre plebiscite favouring a return to the Reich in January 1935, and, primarily, the reoccupation of the Rhineland in March 1936 without meeting any French resistance), it is easy to understand how combined anxiety for the law and French safety contributed to the make-up of what would be the spirit of the Popular Front.

Other factors, of a purely internal kind, added further fuel. Laval, who was president of the Council at the same time as Minister of Foreign Affairs, had undertaken to curb the economic difficulties by means of a rigorous deflationary policy. The 10 per cent reduction in civil servants' salaries, which provoked serious disturbances in the streets in Toulon in August 1935, alienated a section of opinion from him.

In March 1936 – as a direct consequence of the improvement in relations between socialists and Communists – the groups of affiliated trades unions were reunified at the Toulouse Congress, resulting in a single CGT with Léon Jouhaux staying as general secretary.

The 'popular union', more frequently called the Popular Front, launched its campaign under a triple watchword, both striking and appealing: 'Bread, Peace and Liberty.'

'Liberty' was in the grand tradition, the major theme of the French Revolution, the first ideal of the Republic, hostility towards dictators. 'Peace' was the mark of the era, the inevitable call since 1918, which also included antifascism, since foreign fascism was reputed to be 'warmongering'. 'Bread', lastly, metaphorically signified the right to a living for the lowly; it denoted the social dimension, inherent in every left-wing surge, but emphasized in the current situation.

In comparison with this renewal, the splits which affected the two big workers' parties – in November 1933, Marcel Déat, Pierre Renaudel and Adrien Marquet had left the SFIO in order to found a Socialist Party of France (called 'neosocialist') and in June 1934, Jacques Doriot had been exluded from the PCF – seem of far less consequence.

Moderate governments would thus again lose elections, but this time in the face of a coalition of the left much extended and galvanized by anxiety. In 1936, on 26 April and 3 May, there was an ordinary election, to replenish the Chamber of Deputies.

The surprise did not stem so much from the fact that the left-wing coalition had a majority, since it had achieved majorities in 1924 and 1932. It arose from two striking novelties, exciting for some, but disquieting for others. On the one hand, the PC formed part of the coalition, and benefited from the 'republican discipline'. On the other hand, a development in the relationship of forces within the left caused enough voters to slip from the radical to the socialist sphere of influence for the latter to become the stronger of the two. In this case, it was more of a tradition than a novelty: the radicals, who had been too involved in power since the beginning of the century, too often in alliance with the moderates, had found others who had advanced more than they; the socialists were doing to them what they themselves had done to the opportunists less than forty years earlier. Out of a total of 615 deputies, the Popular Front coalition numbered 376: 72 Communists, 147 SFIO, 106 radicals and 51 members of minor left-wing groups. The majority of the majority, therefore, was made up of elected members claiming socialism (*sensu lato*) and the working-class movement.

From that it was but a step to thinking that collectivism was at France's gates . . . We shall see that the social effect of the election indeed constituted the second novelty, since a socialist was attaining power while the working class was getting under way . . . That socialist was called Léon Blum.

Born in Paris in 1872, Blum was a well-to-do Parisian intellectual. He was thereby rendered equally vulnerable to demagogic heckling from the extreme left and every sort of sarcasm from the extreme right. But the working class and its movement have always drawn some of their combatants from converts coming from more favoured social circles. A typical representative of that type, Léon Blum never passed himself off as a man of the people, and never abandoned a bourgeois appearance, slightly modified by an artistic touch. His wide-brimmcd black felt hat, together with the bar of his spectacle frame, the parallel line of his long moustache, and his large straight nose descending from one to the other, were his distinguishing features for caricature. The child of a family of Alsatian Jewish traders who had settled in Paris after 1870, he had done well in secondary school studies and succeeded in the competition for the *École normale supérieure*. In the rue d'Ulm, he could have emulated his fellow students,

Édouard Herriot or Charles Péguy, and chosen a university career. Instead, he chose to resign and follow other paths, both more liberal and more ambitious. After some years, he in fact became a high-level civil servant, a member of the Council of State, while, as an amateur, he wrote critiques which were noticed in innovative literary and artistic magazines, such as *La revue blanche*. His first piece of writing to attract attention was an *Essay on Marriage*, of libertarian, thus feminist, inspiration, since it extended to young women the right to pre-conjugal experience which the right-thinking world reserved for young men. His theory on trial marriage created something of a scandal. He could hardly *not* be Dreyfusard, and drawn into the socialist orbit. His originality was in staying there. After the Dreyfus Affair, he followed neither Charles Péguy into a nationalist conversion, nor those numerous other intellectuals who remained on the left but with the distance of dilettantism and the comfortable status of sympathizer. Following Jaurès from afar, Léon Blum stayed as a militant of the SFIO. His dual attributes of member of the party and extremely able civil servant made him the perfectly natural choice, in 1914, for principal private secretary in Marcel Sembat's ministry. Thus began his life in active politics.

Elected deputy of the Seine by list ballot in 1919, he swiftly became the indispensable man of the SFIO parliamentary group. Well prepared by his legal education to take matters in hand, he impressed his colleagues with his evident intellectual superiority. For the party, he was *par excellence* the parliamentary strategist and theorist, which theoretically is less elevated in dignity than the general secretaryship, but in actual fact counts for a great deal more. It was that kind of supremacy which Jaurès had exercised before 1914. Blum's, however, would be slightly more challenged by the official leader, Paul Faure. But it is to Blum that democratic socialism, in the 1920s, owes the three great initiatives already mentioned: the schism of the minority at the Congress of Tours, that is to say, maintaining the 'old firm' (the word 'socialist', the second Internationale, the title SFIO, scrupulous respect for Republican democracy, a firm anchorage in the camp of the secular left); support, though without ministerial participation, for the governments of the Left-wing Cartel; the theory of the distinction between the 'exercise of power' and the 'conquest of power', the first, permissible in certain circumstances, not being used to slide improperly and disloyally towards the second.

An intellectual, Blum wrote a great deal. *Le Populaire*, of which he was editor and frequently leader writer, served as his platform. A man of principle, he detested dictatorships – of fascism just as much as of Bolshevism. The economic successes of the USSR would not cause him to change his views and, in the era when the *Piatiletka*[2] and the great barrages on the river Don started to stir imaginations, he would clip the wings of Stalinist neoromanticism with his shock statement: 'When you have slaves, it is easy to build pyramids.'

[2] A Russian word, familiar at the time, for the 'Five-Year Plan'.

Strike in the Delahaye factory, 1936. The 'sit-down' strike, that is, with a permanent presence in the occupied factory; a euphoric presence, as the accordions remind us. (Photographer unknown)

Quite simply, there must be no slaves.

In 1928, Blum lost his deputy's seat for Paris, beaten by a Communist. This was a catastrophe for the parliamentary group, which made haste, in order to see him back in the Palais-Bourbon, to find him a safe constituency. A generous deputy from the Aude made the sacrifice, creating a by-election, and thenceforward Léon Blum was the official representative of the left-wing wine-growers in the distant *arrondissement* of Narbonne.

Such was his standing in May 1936. Circumstances and the very machinery of the Republic obviously provided the necessary conditions for 'the exercise of power', and the man who had put forward the theory could not this time avoid taking on the responsibility. He scrupulously took his time about forming a coalition government (SFIO and radicals – it was the PCF's turn at 'support without participation'), while awaiting the setting up of the Chamber and the official departure of his predecessor. Blum did not want to create the impression of rushing towards the Hôtel Matignon. It was the workers who rushed into action.

After the elections, in the euphoria of victory and thanks to this brief interregnum, a wave of strikes broke out, with factories being occupied – 'sit-down' strikes, as we say today.

The Popular Front, as may be seen, was therefore not a 'working-class' government, swept to power by a social movement, rather, the social movement was unleashed by the facility given to it by a political swing. It all happened as if the working class, by demonstrating its strength, had wanted to make sure that it would not be thwarted in what it might expect from a favourable situation; as if it wanted to present the entire gamut of its demands to a friendly government, and in an exceptional circumstance. That objective, in the end almost plaintive (you, whom we have elected, this time don't forget us), appeared to the right to be triumphalist and almost subversive: after all, occupying factories was an attack on the authority of the employers, and almost on their property.

The new government was formed. A classic coalition? Blum, as president of the Council, without portfolio, placed his socialist friends in the posts of major social responsibility: Roger Salengro in the Interior, Vincent Auriol in Finance, and entrusted the great affairs of state to the radicals: War for Daladier, Foreign Affairs for Yvon Delbos.

But in a symbolic innovation, he set the tone in brilliant fashion by appointing three women as under-secretaries of state,[3] although women did not have the vote at that time. Léon Blum was well aware that no majority in the Chamber of Deputies (and even less in the Senate) would approve a law giving women the right to vote (as the great majority of radicals and right-wing representatives were against), but by appointing women to the government he gave an indication of the ultimate target and nudged opinion in the right direction. There was something revolutionary about the innovation. At all events, it would be a government 'unlike the others'.

The first priority was to deal with the social problem. The strikes were extensive, solid, and peaceful through their very powerfulness. They were also effective, since for a time they even threatened Paris food supplies.

On 5 June, the head of the government invited delegations from the CGT and the CGPF (Confédération générale de la Production française) to meet under his presidency at the Hôtel Matignon, and by 8 June the famous agreements had been concluded: increases in pay (between 7 and 15 per cent), collective work contracts, election of workers' delegates in firms, no sanctions for striking, trade union freedom would be respected; the factories were cleared.

The government would hasten to deal with everything in the legislative area and, in fact, in the following weeks a whole series of laws was presented to the Chamber and swiftly passed (even in the Senate, whose unaltered composition was dominated by moderates and radicals, thus without a majority for the left-wing coalition). The working week was limited to forty hours; two weeks' paid holiday, to be funded by the employers, for all wage earners; nationalization of the manufacture of war weapons; reform of the status of the Banque de France. For the peasants, there was the creation of the Corn Office (which

---

[3] Cecile Brunschwig, Suzanne Lacorre, Irène Joliot-Curie, respectively connected with radicalism, socialism and Communism, and appointed – respectively – to National Education (the Minister being Jean Zay), the Protection of Children and Scientific Research.

fixed prices and monopolized external trade). As regards progress in general: extension of compulsory schooling to the age of fourteen.

This work was noteworthy for its enduring humane and civilized nature, which deserves a little additional reflection. Paid holidays allowed the worker, who was poor and urban, to rediscover the countryside, perhaps his native region, and in any case some fresh air; to come across some remains of châteaux along the Loire, or a strip of Mediterranean beach; in other words, they let a little oxygen into the stifling conditions of the proletariat, and half-opened the door of national heritage to those who had been shut out. It is understandable that those who benefited were – let us put all its meaning into the word – happy about it, and the left-wing intellectuals vastly elated. It is less easy to understand why there should have been so much hostility and scorn in the opposing camp. Who today would want to do away with the right to holidays? This comment is not intended to award the Popular Front an additional piece of praise, but looking at it dispassionately, to situate it by analogy in the series of stages in the French collective conscience.

In the same way that government without a king, the abolition of privilege and universal suffrage had started by being ideas and victories of the left, before achieving the rank of basic principles and institutions which would be accepted by the grandsons of those who had opposed them, so a certain advance in social progress was deemed to be partisan in 1936 before becoming commonplace today.

For the left, in any case, that euphoric situation of political, social and moral victory provoked much reflection. Even within the victorious coalition, not everyone interpreted 1936 in the same way.

The most modest interpretation belonged to the radicals: for them, 1936 was the happiest repetition of 1924, or of 1899, the good old Left-wing Bloc, with a complete republican, but not revolutionary, programme. By contrast, that of the advanced wing of the SFIO and a nebulous libertarian extreme left was maximalist: the bourgeoisie was shattered, the masses had shown their capacity for a general strike, thus 'anything was possible!' (Marceau Pivert). In-between views inclined more to making the Popular Front a reality *sui generis*, slightly more than the radical Republic, but far, far less than the Revolution. So thought Léon Blum, who was conscious of 'exercising' power and not of having 'taken' it. So thought the Communists as well, for whom the Popular Front and the movement of June 1936 constituted a legitimate and unprecedented form of class action, but strategically limited because revolution did not feature on the agenda. Push, therefore, and push hard, but not as far as breaking point. In this frame of mind, three days after the conclusion of the Matignon agreements, as work here and there was slow to resume, Maurice Thorez had had the courage

If everything seems to have been said on the subject of the cultural and human progress afforded by paid holidays, numerous documents bear further fitness. (Top) The great era of the tandom, that auxiliary of camping and roving. It was not uncommon for a pair of cyclists (married of course) to wear matching outfits. (Photo: Henri Roger-Viollet) (Bottom) What is memorable about this beach scene is, first, the very fact that someone captured on film a social practice that at the time was quite an event (and no longer is), and also the clothing: almost chaste bathing costume in the foreground, and in the background (even more astonishing to our eyes to see on a beach) men in dark suits and hats. (Photo: Albert Harlingue)

to say (in words which have remained famous): 'We have to know how to bring a strike to an end!' That was the first obvious sign, on the part of the PCF, of an anti-leftism inherent in its international conception of the movement. Many others were to follow.

The main disagreements among the men of the Popular Front, however, were not over interpreting and labelling what they were doing, but over two much more concrete problems, the economy and Spain.

According to Blum, the economy in crisis needed a fresh boost by increasing purchasing power, thus stimulating internal demand, rather in the style of F. D. Roosevelt's New Deal, to which he paid a great deal of attention. But 'the fundamental obstacle to recovery was the excess of French prices over foreign prices. It is useless to swell demand if it must be met by imports; one wouldn't inflate a punctured tyre . . . There are two ways of overcoming that obstacle: the liberal method of monetary align-ment, that is to say devaluation, and the socialist method, exchange con-trol, or closing up the gaps.'[4]

Léon Blum rejected the second solution as too authoritarian, but delayed for a long while in opting for the first, which was unpopular and would be an admission of failure, as the 'defence of the franc' had such a strong symbolic connotation. In the autumn, when price rises showed a growing imbalance with world prices, when capital made itself scarce, he had to resign himself to it; on 26 September the gold value of the franc was lowered.

Psychologically, thus politically, the measure seemed disappointing, even though it had good economic effects. At the end of the year, movements of gold at the frontiers tended to slow down, industrial production got going again and unemployment dropped. Then 'on this economy making a brilliant comeback which, like a horse finally freed from its harness, was striding towards full employment, at the end of the year the law (on a forty-hour week) passed in June came into effect, strictly limiting the production of wealth'. At the end of spring 'the rapid upsurge which had begun after devaluation was halted in an unwonted manner, and gave place to a recession.' Let Sauvy himself comment on this contradiction: '(There is) an almost perpetual agonizing conflict between the economic and the social, in a capitalist regime.'[5]

As for escaping from the difficulty by abolishing capitalism, that was out of the question.

Léon Blum had to cobble together the classic remedies: taxation, bor-rowing and recognition of a 'pause' (the word would create a shock) in the plans for the social programme. As if the drama of economic foundering

---

[4] Alfred Sauvy, *Histoire économique de la France entre les deux guerres*, Paris, Fayard, 1967, Book II. p. 198.

[5] Ibid., p. 192.

were not enough, a second drama, as spectacularly evident as the first was hidden beneath the surface, was developing on the Pyrenean frontier.

Spain, a Republic since 1931, was stricken on 17 July 1936 by civil war, following a revolt against the government by the majority of the armed forces, under the command of General Franco. It would be impossible to underestimate the importance of that event, in a country so close, firstly for relations between right and left, and then even for relations within each camp. Fairly naturally in France, on both the left and the right, political parties shared points of doctrine, experienced affinities and solidarities, with their Spanish 'opposite numbers'. But Spain brought an additional bitterness to the conflict. At that time, it had several features of what was not yet called an underdeveloped country. That is, the social divisions were enormous, social tensions very sharp, and collective mental attitudes brutally archaic, all conditions which combined to unleash violence . . . as it had been unleashed in France one or two centuries earlier. Civil war in Spain was not metaphorical, it existed in the true sense, that is to say that people were cutting one another's throats. The *French* had long since developed sufficiently not to cut one another's throats any more, but their respective friendships for the Spanish of the two enemy sides had tiresome effects on sensibilities. For a right-wing Frenchman, in solidarity with traditional Spain, a red Spaniard was a murderer, and the left-wing Frenchman, siding with the red, was an accomplice to murder. And vice versa, of course! This was looking at the other side with a different eye from that of the customary polemics!

There is no doubt that, from 1936 onwards, Spain thus raised the level of hostilities between Frenchmen a notch, as if blood and fury had started to rage between them through interposed Spaniards.

Meanwhile, what was to be done? It was up to Blum's government to decide.

The Spanish Republic appealed for aid, and there were two good reasons for coming to its assistance by sending armaments: one, because the appeal came from the legal government; the other, because the government was friendly, whereas Franco was finding support, approval and aid from among France's potential enemies – the Italian and German dictators. Letting Franco win would amount to allowing pressure to be placed on the frontier of the Pyrenees by a power showing solidarity with those already menacing the Rhine and the Alps. In short, it was the situation of François I at the time of the empire of Charles V of Spain.

In contrast, opposition to sending aid, to 'intervention', as it was termed, arose from the reluctance of most French radicals and the British Conservative government (all in principle the friends of legality, but who nevertheless found the Spanish republicans far too red); from the danger of a general war for which Hitler and Mussolini were cynically preparing; and from fear of provoking within France itself an excess of internal tension. Blum

The Spanish Civil War. (CGT poster on behalf of Spanish children. Collection Viollet)

therefore resigned himself to accepting, under the aegis of the League of Nations, a policy of 'nonintervention' which scarcely bothered the Italians and Germans (or, very shortly, the Soviets, for the opposing side), and to discreetly covering up a small, clandestine and unofficial supply of arms for the republicans. But it would cause an upset among his electorate, who were passionately attached to the Spanish Republic, and more sentimental than realistic.

The PCF, for its part, did not hesitate, not only to throw all its weight into giving concrete aid – some of its best officers joined the republican camp to fight in the International Brigade – but also to reproach Blum's government pretty bluntly for its nonintervention, though well aware of the facts. Subsequently, serious dissensions in the very heart of the Spanish Republican camp would give rise to acrimonious repercussions in France between the Communists and their partners.

Other effects of opinion emerging from the Spanish War would involve the right wing also, and those we must look at later. Let us stay with this plain fact: for Léon Blum's government, the Spanish War, right from the start, was at least as stern a test as that of its economic semi-failure.

The Popular Front at first governed for a year (4 June 1936 to 22 June 1937) marked by the 'pause', the Paris International Exhibition and by two dramatic events: the suicide of Roger Salengro and the Clichy shooting.

Blum ended up by being placed in a minority in the Senate, where the moderates felt the moment had come to raise their heads again, and where the radicals themselves, less bound than the radicals in the Chamber by an electoral alliance with the socialists, often showed suspicion with regard to economic policy. It was Joseph Caillaux, whose reappearance in 1924 and centrist position in 1926 we have seen, who 'toppled' Blum before the Upper Assembly. Léon Blum was then succeeded by the radical Camille Chautemps, at the head of a fairly similar government.

He made his mark by a new devaluation of the franc on 30 June 1937, and by the disquieting discovery of a conspiracy against the government, and perhaps the regime (arms dumps). A mysterious Secret Revolutionary Action Committee (CSAR) had organized it. Amongst the seditionaries' supplies were hoods (*cagoules*) to cover their faces. From then on, for people on the left, *cagoulard* became the familiar equivalent of 'fascist'. As the economic situation did not improve, strikes returned in the autumn and, with them, the tensions between socialists and radicals which broke up the government (January 1938). After a painful ministerial crisis, Chautemps formed a homogeneous radical government, which the socialists did not tolerate for long. There was another resignation by Chautemps in March, at the precise moment when Hitler's army entered Austria and obtained the *Anschluss*. To this new and staggering act of defiance towards the Europe of Versailles, France – without a government – was unable to react.

The SFIO, a sizeable group in a pivotal position in the Chamber, seemed indispensable, and President Lebrun recalled Léon Blum. The latter, who had realized the gravity, and by now prime importance, of the international crisis, wanted to form a government of national union, including Communists and the moderate right. By their refusal, the second group forced him to set up a government of socialists and radicals very little different from his former team.

One month later, the financial situation obliged Léon Blum to propose exchange control. Once more he came up against the Senate's refusal, and had to resign (April). Should battle be waged against the Upper Assembly, which had emerged from restricted suffrage, and which once again thwarted the government that had come from universal suffrage? Some socialist demonstrators thought so, and went to file past the Palais du Luxembourg. Their anger was pathetic; there was no longer any popular enthusiasm to support it and give it wider expression. But the Senate of 1936 would be remembered when, in 1945, it was time to rebuild a Constitution.

For the time being, to succeed Blum, the President turned to the radical Édouard Daladier, to whom the SFIO refused its support. All he had to do was to replace the socialist defection by reinstating moderates in his majority. Yet again, the ambivalence of the radicals allowed a majority swing from the left to the right without fresh elections. At that time, however, the 'rules' governing the functioning of the parliamentary regime counted for less than the external perils. We now need to take a closer look at the reaction of opinion to these new circumstances. In those critical years, it was not lacking in sustenance. Never perhaps had politics enjoyed debates so rich, so varied and inspired by such deeply held convictions.

The tradition of political involvement of the intellectuals (savants, university men, theorists, but also artists and literary figures), seemed at first to follow familiar trends. The humanist and republican left, Dreyfusard in 1900 and pro-Cartel in 1924, was still in opposition to a conservative, religious and patriotic right, which upheld the opposite choices. On the one hand, the *École normale supérieure* and the Sorbonne, on the other, the Académie française and the Law Faculty, to simplify matters and speak in symbols. These two camps were still clearly identifiable in the years of the Popular Front, each being both flanked and stimulated by a more demanding wing. On the far right, there was the extremist tendency, purely nationalist, of Action française and some similar and rival groups (fascists, quasi-fascists, 'revolutionary right', a label applied retrospectively is of little importance). On the far left: the most progressive socialists and the Communists. But that bi- (or quadri-) polarization seems and is too simple. An entire generation of young men (and a few young women, already, if we think of Simone Weil) born in the 1900s, children or adolescents during the war and matured in the 1920s, partly eluded this pattern and attempted to think and act on fresh foundations. It is in order to characterize that climate of research and innovation that it is possible to speak of a 'spirit of the thirties'.[6]

The fact that war had constituted an extraordinary drama did not necessarily only bring about a will to create peace, but could also suggest that pre-war themes were outdated. The episode of the Left-wing Cartel as a

[6] J. Touchard, 'The Spirit of the Thirties', *Tendances politiques dans la vie française depuis 1789*, Hachette, 1960.

resumption – and a failed one – of what the Bloc of the same name had been, had only reinforced that judgement for many young people. Thence arose the extensive spread of challenges, the desire for philosophical depth, the daring in tone and thinking, which were the common features of a galaxy of austere and intense magazines, not conformist because they were innovatory, *Réaction* (Jean de Fabrègues), *Esprit* (Emmanuel Mounier, Georges Izard), *Ordre nouveau* (Arnaud Dandieu, Robert Aron, Denis de Rougemont), *Plans* (Philippe Lamour), etc. Here, the desire was to rejuvenate the nation, there, to rejuvenate and modernize Christian expression; elsewhere, republican expression, or economic thinking (was the idea of a Plan, for instance, necessarily to be suspected of collectivism or corporatism? or could it be a useful source of inspiration?).

The political parties themselves were being offered the chance – not always taken – to replenish their stock of ideas; that was the hope of, for example, the Constructive Revolution group, inspired by Georges Lefranc, in the service of the SFIO. Did that turmoil of excitement ideologically and morally reanimate traditional politics? The 'Young Turks' of the Radical Party (Pierre Mendès France, Pierre Cot) and Paul Reynaud's entourage (Alfred Sauvy, Michel Debré, Dominique Leca) are rare examples. Above all, it formed the intellectual and militant sustenance of the great new waves which would launch themselves towards the future from the 1930s onwards: Communism, Christian democracy and Pétainism. All this intellectual activity was soon overtaken and fed by the stimuli of events.

The crisis of 6 February 1934, the victory of the Popular Front, the social movement in France and, externally, Hitler's dictatorship and soon the Spanish War, then placed French society in one of those extraordinary situations in which politics ceases to be a routine engaged in by specialists, and somewhat despised by the rest, and becomes the constant preoccupation and heartfelt concern of the majority.

It was then that literature and art were seen to open the door of their ivory tower. A student of the École des Chartes, curator of a museum and an already noticed young novelist, André Chamson became Daladier's principal private secretary, before representing radicalism in the antifascist coalition, as co-editor of *Vendredi*. His fellow editor in the socialist tendency was the professor and essayist Jean Guéhenno, while the Communists were more modestly represented in the triumvirate by the journalist André Viollis. Communist intellectuals, however, were on the increase, their leader then being Paul Vaillant-Couturier, who was also a member of the party management committee and deputy and mayor of Villejuif.

Louis Aragon, the only – or almost – surrealist turned Communist to remain in the PC, took a hand in the work of the Association of Revolutionary Writers and Artists, and made ready to add another string to his bow: a lifelong poet, he would become, with *Les Beaux Quartiers*, the novelist of the 'real world' genre. Among the savants, it was a militant

Communist and declared Marxist, Marcel Prenant, who obtained a Chair
at the Sorbonne. At least two other savants belong to the political history
of antifascism, the physicist Paul Langevin, a Communist sympathizer, and
the ethnologist Paul Rivet, a socialist, whose election in 1935 to the post
of municipal councillor of Paris for the Latin Quarter as the sole candidate
of the left provided a portent of the electoral spring of 1936. In his wake,
a young savant and militant-to-be, a *normalien* and antifascist, Jacques
Soustelle. And, to stay in the field of ethnology, a discipline itself stimulated by the spirit of 1936, one Georges-Henri Rivière.

The most vital area, however, was literature, especially the literature of
those great writers who commit themselves in the name of principle while
refraining from a partisan engagement. The Zola and the Péguy of the era
were André Gide and André Malraux. The former was already a grand old
man, having been born in 1869; he had experienced the Dreyfusard battle,
he had been radicalized by his personal nonconformity which he had
courageously shouldered, and had placed himself in the role of revolutionary critic of society with his *Voyage au Congo*. With antifascism, he became
an ally of the extreme left, even the type of renowned 'fellow traveller' who
is urged to chair meetings and put his signature to manifestos. Plus his
celebrated journey to Soviet Communism and back again, which would
shatter his role at the time, while ensuring his genuineness and dignity for
history. André Malraux was his junior, having been born in 1901, a young
writer with an adventurous life, whose exotic tastes gave an anticipatory
glimpse of Third Worldism until Spain brought revolution to France's
gates. That would result in his best-known novel and the most genuinely
military of his wanderings. Though less in the limelight, great intellectuals
would be the advisers listened to by the leaders, and shortly the ministers,
of the left, for example, Julien Benda, Jean Cassou.

Naturally the left, even revitalized by antifascism, would not manage to
keep all the personalities attracted by social protest. When social democracy was discovered to be a sort of moderatism, and Communism to be
Stalinism, although there were purists who clung to the libertarian spirit
(Jacques Prévert), others would go looking elsewhere for rebellious causes,
at the risk of losing their way; thus Pierre Drieu La Rochelle or Roman
Fernandez would join with Doriot, a dissident national Communist, who
would drift into a genuine French fascism.

On the conservative side of opinion, supporters were just as renowned,
even if not so much was made of them. Henry Bordeaux, one of the great
novelists of the era, a pillar of the Académie française, was also well known
to be a pillar of the everlasting party of order. So was Henri Massis.
Genuine historians upheld the right and nationalism in their analyses
(Jacques Bainville), unafraid of carrying on the production of a historical
work at the same time as waging a press battle (Pierre Gaxotte). Weekly
papers like *Gringoire* and *Candide*, on the right, enjoyed just as good a

cultural level – and a higher circulation – as their rivals on the left, *Marianne* (Emmanuel Berl) or *La Lumière* (Georges Boris). Lastly, and most importantly, the right was not confined to a conformist and defensive conservatism. It had – as has been said – its 'revolutionary' wing. For a novelist like Louis-Ferdinand Céline, the revolution of language and the revolt of the gaze cast on raw poverty did not bring about support for political revolution, because the ideological filter of anti-Semitism pointed anger in another direction. In short, the polemic to be conducted against the antifascist and 'republican' coalition, which had become the Popular Front government, offered young people whose intellectual sustenance was Action française the opportunity to display their talents. Thierry Maulnier, Robert Brasillach, Lucien Rebatet, like their master, Maurras, managed to produce brilliant works of criticism or fiction together with a virulent journalism. In the implicit rivalry for fame setting the two halves of France at odds, the only thing that tended to weaken the conservative side was the fracture which had occurred in Catholic society. If François Mauriac is to be singled out from the bourgeois ranks of novelists of psychological realism (Paul Bourget, Henry Bordeaux) to become a complex figure, a questing conscience, a source of inspiration or an unexpected polemicist, it is certainly from that angle.

The fracture had even been twofold.

Firstly, as has already been noted, in 1926 a papal condemnation had put Catholics on their guard against the solely political content ('politics first') of Action française – politics that were completely secular were therefore too secular. Then, two years later, in quite a different connection, the Halluin strike had occurred. In this Flemish industrial town, entirely given over to textiles, class struggles had preserved their nineteenth-century bitterness. An ultra-red trades unionism dominated among the proletariat, with Christian trades unionism painfully trying to gain a footing alongside it. Now, here were the Christian trades unionists also launching appeals for solidarity against the poverty caused by the employers' intransigence. A former curé from Tourcoing, just recently appointed Bishop of Lille, Achille Liénart, gave them his support and thus entered into open conflict with the employers of the Nord. It was a historic event in Flemish Christendom. Even more historic, because Pope Pius XI publicly took the Bishop of Lille's side against the God-fearing bourgeois.

So good Catholics could (and even, in principle, should) dissociate themselves from a purely conservative order. That double rift in the heart of the religious bloc paved the way to a future crisis. François Mauriac, who wrote in *L'Echo de Paris*, the daily which had been edited by Barrès, would contribute articles to *Sept*, the Catholic magazine founded by the Dominicans, supporting the new spirit encouraged by Rome. From then on, there were Catholic intellectuals who would no longer be *ipso facto* identifiable as right-wing intellectuals.

Is there any need to say that not everyone could be classified? Famous 'committed' figures of the morrow, or the day after, like Jean-Paul Sartre or Simone de Beauvoir, have admitted in their published memoirs that they observed the universe of the 1930s with a distant gaze, and a critical eye more attentive to the matter of personal behaviours than of social and political forces, and that they neither voted nor demonstrated. It would be up to the 1940s to provide fresh experiences and bring about new vocations. The effect of the 1930s, or the Popular Front effect, did not move the whole of French society and thinking, but an appreciable part.

Similar observations could be made from an overview of artistic creativity. Whether committed to right or left, a libertarian or fascist attitude, or even impervious to any socio-political perception at all, creative artists could be fitted into the various categories within the overall picture. As their public influence was less than that of the writers, we will not attempt the task. One exception must be made, however, for one work and one art.

The work was *Guernica*, painted by Pablo Picasso for the Spanish (republican, legal, governmental) pavilion of the 1937 Exhibition. Its subject: the grief and destruction of the small Basque town of Guernica under aerial bombardment by Hitler–Franco forces. Message: feelings of love for Spain and revulsion for war. Revelation: how horror and suffering could be expressed in the tortured style of an artist in whose work the public at large had until then perceived only its wantonness or its formalism.

Art meant the cinema, by then the 'talkies'; the usual popular entertainment, with a vast and varied production. It belonged to the era, however, or, one might say, it was in harmony with the France of the Popular Front, indirectly through the populist inspiration exploited by directors like Carné, Duvivier, René Clair; and directly through two works with a commitment, but which had great success and have remained in the film buffs' lists – *La Grande Illusion*, pacifist, and *La Marseillaise*, 'republican'.

In this general climate, with partially renewed intellectual leadership, current opinion combined the old and the new. Even before the Spanish War, right-wing opinion had hated Léon Blum and openly expressed its anti-Semitism. Those very men who denounced anticlericalism as outdated because Catholics and unbelievers had fraternized in the trenches, saw nothing outmoded in their own anti-Semitism, even though there had also been Jews in the trenches. It must be said that the Catholic Church, with a few exceptions, had not yet as a whole condemned anti-Semitism, as would happen later. Even the overall condemnation of Nazism by Pius XI (encyclical *Mit Brennender Sorge*) would not appear until 1937, and then coupled with 'atheistic Communism'. The ordinary conservative Frenchman had spontaneous prejudices against the French government being run by a Jew. The extreme right-wing press really 'laid it on thick'; it portrayed as fabulously wealthy a Léon Blum who was only moderately so, and claimed that his family had come from eastern Europe, whereas in truth they were Alsatian and had patriotically moved to Paris after 1870.

However, the right did not always boast of its 'social' attitude. Part of its hostility towards the Popular Front stemmed from the role played in it and the advantages derived from it by the workers, those Parisians in their peaked caps emerging from the factories, their lunchbags slung over their shoulders, pushing their bikes, as they are so often to be seen in the populist films of Réne Clair or Marcel Carné. For many men of the right, the proletariat was still perceived as brutal, drunken and gullible, indoctrinated by Communist 'agitators' in the pay of Moscow, agitators who themselves, in that mythology, smacked partly of hoodlum and partly of secret agent. They were currently known as the *salopards* (bastards or sods). To be fair, it must be admitted that the representation of the employers, industrialists and bankers, members of the '200 families' by the workers and militant Communists and socialists was just as simplistic and caricatured. Let us remember that in 1936 'class hatreds' existed which, from a distance, appear to us closer to what they had been in 1848 than in 1900.

And Spain – as we have seen – had merely exacerbated those aversions.

It must be recognized that hatred manifested itself in its most outrageous form on the right wing of opinion. The slanderous campaign waged against the Minister of the Interior, Roger Salengro, by extreme right-wing publications provides the perfect example. Salengro had been falsely accused of having deserted from the front in 1914–18, and then cleared of that accusation. The theme was nevertheless taken up again with such savagery that the wretched man, in any case worn out by overwork and depressed by the death of his wife, had a nervous breakdown and committed suicide. Slain by slander, indisputably. Regarded as a kind of first victim of 'fascism' in France, his memory is perpetuated for that by the hundreds of streets bearing his name.

None of this was entirely new; here was something more so: the logic of antifascism, that is to say the Popular Front, led to opposing Hitler, resisting his activities and, should he resist that resistance too much, to war. By a complete inversion of what had been the moral situation in 1923–4, it was now the right that could accuse the left of warmongering. In any case, were not the more dynamic elements of the left demanding that the French should 'intervene' in Spain, alongside the reds and Moscow?

The replies of the left, according to which firmness with regard to Hitler, Mussolini and Franco would not necessarily bring about war because the German war machine was not yet ready, and would withdraw or collapse, constituted a pretty complex line of argument. They had little weight in the face of new evidence: the right plumped for appeasement, the left for firmness. Now, middle-of-the-road opinion, neutral and massive, was for peace. It has to be said that the penchant of the right (not unanimous, but dominant) for not resisting Hitler was in keeping with the collective weariness of a people who had still not recovered from 1914–18, and that would seem also to have been the deep motivation of Pierre Laval.

In November 1935, thus two and a half years after the advent of Hitler, the French and German governments had agreed to the creation of a France–Germany Committee in France and an equivalent body in Germany to encourage the idea of peace between the two states. One may judge it harshly, read into it a camouflage for Hitlerian imperialism, the breeding ground for future 'collaboration', the infiltration of the pacifist tendency by the Hitlerophile 'fifth column' – but without any doubt it also included unimpeachable intellectuals and nobly motivated veterans. The circumstances were such that appeasement by pro-fascism and appeasement by pure pacifism could hardly fail to have a common recruiting ground. This was not the only possible explanation, however. The matter could be interpreted in simpler terms, as was done, chiefly, by the Communists. Hitler, fascism, equalled capitalism. The French right wing meant capitalism, as well. They therefore shared the solidarity of the propertied and a common hatred of the democratic and working-class movement rising in France. Frightened, the French bourgeoisie would be happy to have a firm-handed regime in the land, even to accept Hitler as policeman. Repeating *ad nauseam* the scandalous statement uttered by a provincial journalist, 'Better Hitler than the Popular Front', the Communists outdid one another in declaring that this was the line of the French bourgeoisie. What was more, they added, it was only to be expected, judging on past performance: a condemned class, the bourgeoisie were taking the Koblenz route.

The Marxist analysis was erroneous only in its rigidity and generalization. For testimony to the mortal hatred of politicians for the Popular Front, and French accommodating attitudes towards foreign brands of fascism, was not in the least imaginary. The fault lay in putting the bourgeoisie in the singular, so to speak, or rather, regarding the pro-fascist and virtually antinational section of the ruling classes as the only important and significant one, while relegating their other factions to second or residual place. The latter, however, were emerging, albeit discreetly. With hindsight, we can better appreciate their importance today. Who were they?

Firstly, there was the emergence of a Christian democrat current. For more than a century, links of solidarity had been woven between French Catholicism and the counter-revolution. We know how isolated the distant avant-gardes of a liberal Catholicism had been. Even after the majority of Catholics had in fact accepted the Revolution, whether as a result of the Pope's appeal for a rallying, or by force of circumstances, they remained deeply embedded in the conservative camp (to which in any case the ruling anticlericalism incited them). Between their attachment to the Church and the nationalist cult of the French *Patrie*, links of proximity, habit and contamination had been established. That led many Catholics to sympathize with the carefully considered traditionalism, sociological rather than evangelical, which had taken shape shortly before 1900, and in which we have seen a secularized version of right-wing thinking. Such was the doctrine of Charles Maurras, who openly extolled Catholicism above all for its role as the backbone of society. In short, from the Christian point of view, there was an indisputable drift in that direction.

Pope Pius XI had wanted to put an end to it by his great decisions in 1926 and 1928, which have been mentioned. In this way he gave his backing to that Catholicism – at the same time (and indissolubly) more religious and more democratic – which had been searching for an identity for over half a century. That now expanded rapidly, with the appearance of the Popular Democrats group, which included one or two deputies, with some intellectual magazines (*Esprit*, *Sept*), and even a daily political newspaper, *L'Aube*, in which Georges Bidault, a history teacher in a Lyon *lycée*, made his debut as a political writer; and with the Young Republic, directly inspired by Marc Sangnier, a more limited group, but more clearly inclined to the left since it supported the Popular Union.

From then on, a Christian democrat trend existed in France, usually destined to grow, even if the left, by tradition, mistrusted it and the right, ever conservative, detested it.

And that hatred increased with the Spanish War. In the civil war, Franco's rebels, who claimed to be 'nationalist', supported the Spanish – or perhaps Castilian – tradition of a single centralized state, which threw into the republican camp all the peripheral groups of people who wanted to retain their cultures and autonomous institutions, notably the Catalans and the Basques. Now, if Catalonia, the developed region of the peninsula, was, like southern France, mostly democratic and secular, the Basque country was, like the traditional west of France, and perhaps even more strongly, a land whose moral and social structure reposed on the Catholic Church.

To put it briefly, with the Basques, an entire people who were undeniably Christian found themselves in the camp of the reds. That helped the French Christian democrats, who were well informed about it, to perceive how much harshness – often not at all Christian – there was on Franco's side, and to class him as a fascist, despite the support he received from nearly all the non-Basque clergy.

Thus spoke *Sept*, or *L'Aube*, or *Esprit*. Or François Mauriac and Georges Bernanos. Naturally, the right (Action française, and most of the organs of the classic right) furiously attacked those left-wing Christians, who had gone over to the side of evil. A lasting division was thus formed for the present and the near future.

It was not the only one. On the right, there were men who, without necessarily having anything to do with the Christian democrat tendency, held the idea that German revisionism in central Europe was placing European equilibrium and French security in danger; and who, furthermore, if only through reading *Mein Kampf*, could see the inhuman aspects of Hitlerism as a political regime. Without any liking for the Popular Front, they were not exclusively obsessed by the notion of bringing the workers back to heel. After the assassination of Louis Barthou, his place was taken by the man who, on the right of the Chamber of Deputies, seemed the best embodiment of that state of mind, Paul Reynaud.

The representative for the Basses-Alpes, he was an atypical 'moderate', with a more open mind than his colleagues to a global vision of affairs – he had family business interests in Mexico – and was better informed about economic realities, since as early as 1931 he had advocated the devaluation of the franc.

And it was in the wake of Paul Reynaud that Charles de Gaulle, another atypical character, made his appearance on the public scene.

Charles de Gaulle, born in Lille on 22 November 1890, was the third child in a large family which had come from old traditional France, with noble and bourgeois connections, provincial roots, and a deep-seated Catholicism.[7] His father, Henri de Gaulle, taught history in a private Catholic establishment and was of course a royalist. A somewhat atypical royalist, however. In 1870, when the war was lost, far from sharing in the scepticism, sometimes approaching defeatism, of many conservatives, he had fought as a volunteer in the defence of Paris. And thirty years later, in the Dreyfus Affair, he would be – like very few in his social sphere – convinced of the Captain's innocence.

Royalists nevertheless, the parents of the future General would not easily see their sons become republicans – which, for them, around 1910, by no means meant going over to the left, but simply accepting the state for what it was, and considering the restoration of a king highly unlikely. The important thing was not so much fighting for a regime as serving the *Patrie* in existing institutions, one of the soundest of which was the army of the Republic.

Like his brothers, the young Charles was brought up on a mixture of history, patriotism, religion, and the moral and family sentiments which are inseparable from them. The family was very united. Loyal to the Church, the boys attended a school run by Jesuits and, when the latter were expelled by Combes, accompanied them to Belgium to pursue their studies there. Then, for Charles, it was the choice of a military career and entry to Saint-Cyr.

The future statesman seems, from his childhood, to have stood out among his brothers and sisters as the most gifted intellectually and the most unusual by nature. Very self-confident, assuming the role of king in his childhood games and, barely in his teens, convinced that he would one day be commander-in-chief of the French army.

The young officer Charles de Gaulle was obviously interested in politics, and in a very critical way. It goes without saying that what he had to say

---

[7] The monumental three-volume biography of Jean Lacouture will be recalled, Seuil, 1984.

and write was clearly hostile to the left, and no less to the parliamentary regime. However, he reveals no trace of attraction towards the royalist Action française, but rather for Le Sillon, founded by Marc Sangnier, a liberal Catholic and republican. Must Charles de Gaulle's ultimate philosophical message be sought in the two inscriptions which, since 1970, have adorned the gigantic cross of Lorraine at Colombey-les-Deux-Églises? One states that 'there is only one cause which matters, that of Mankind', the other that there is an age-old pact 'between the Greatness of France and the Liberty of the World'. Herein is expressed the tone and the ideal of a humanist patriotism, not those of a narrow nationalism. In his letters written during the 1914–18 war, Charles de Gaulle is a stern critic of successive governments and the political world from which they emanate, until Clemenceau's management of affairs wins his praise and his adherence. For he took part in the 1914–18 war and even, as people dared to say then in conformist circles, 'had a fine war'. A captain, wounded in the first fighting, recovered, sent back to the front, wounded again at Verdun and left for dead, picked up and taken prisoner by the Germans; an escape attempt, recapture; he ended the war in a special surveillance camp. While in captivity, as he did always and everywhere, he read, wrote, reflected and, whenever he could, gave lectures to his companions.

His post-war period was marked by his appointment to the army sent to Poland in 1920 against the Bolsheviks; his marriage (to Yvonne Vendroux,[8] in Calais in 1921); and by his achieving the unofficial status of theorist, writer and soldier with ideas. Between 1918 and 1940 he would pass from captain to colonel, and would alternate between garrison commands, teaching in the War School, and various posts at staff headquarters, and his path would then cross that of Marshal Pétain. The contrast between the choices those two soldiers would make in 1940 naturally adds piquancy to the complicated history of their relations in the years leading up to it.

It is not at all surprising that they should have known each other: Pétain was the real chief of the army and the military institution in which de Gaulle was emerging as a brilliant officer with a future; it was perfectly normal that the former should have wanted to have the latter on his staff. If de Gaulle ended by opposing his leader, quite apart from any anecdotes about disagreements or ups and downs, it was because in all conscience (national and professional conscience) he believed that the Marshal was taking the wrong road and that the true path of their profession would lie in innovation. At that point, their antagonism becomes of interest to national history. In de Gaulle's view, the top military authorities, including the Marshal, were preparing badly for the probable conflict to come. (How horrible, it will be said, to contemplate another conflict, when the whole of France firmly believed in the 'war to end all wars' – but, after all, it was their professional task.) They were preparing for it routinely and from the lessons

---

[8] By whom he had three children, Philippe, Élizabeth (Mme de Boissieu) and Anne (died in 1948).

of the past. The defensive system of trenches was improved and consolidated in a continuous line of buried fortifications built to withstand fire: the
Maginot line. That system answered both the atmosphere of pacifism and
a strategy of pure passiveness; but another of its results was to absorb much
in the way of resources chiefly at the expense of those needed for more
modern armaments. All that was cloaked by the authority and popularity
of Marshal Pétain who, under various titles, for almost twenty years held
the topmost responsibility for national defence.[9]

When de Gaulle came to write his *War Memoirs*, he would interpret that
routine as an effect of French gerontocracy. The equivalent in the high
command of the lassitude prevailing in society as a whole. De Gaulle
himself was one of those who, doing their job well, were seeking modernization and efficiency in the military art. Thence developed the theory of
mobility, speed, motorization and armour-plating, and new forms to give
the organization and use of that new weapon – the mechanized infantry.
Not forgetting the wonderfully common-sense idea of working out strategy
and diplomacy together: if France based its security on alliances in central
Europe, it could not logically tie the French army to a policy of simply
waiting on the defensive, which would prevent it from ever going to its
allies' aid.

As these ideas did not manage to filter up the military hierarchy, de
Gaulle, first a major, then lieutenant-colonel, tried to get them circulated
among the more open-minded and innovative of the civil authorities. Some
years before 1940, he was therefore already on the side of Paul Reynaud,
and not of Marshal Pétain. In 1936, he even had an opportunity of presenting his ideas to Léon Blum, who invited him to come and see him at the
Hôtel Matignon.

Recounting that interview led de Gaulle to write in his *Mémoires de guerre*,
concerning Spain, in autumn 1936: 'It was not inconceivable that, in the
presence of national socialism triumphant in Berlin, fascism reigning in
Rome, phalangism approaching Madrid, the French Republic should want
simultaneously to transform its social structure and reform its military
strength.'

By lumping Hitler, Mussolini and Franco together in the same camp, one
that threatened France, he was in effect delivering the same judgement on
the situation as the left. De Gaulle merely regretted, in the continuation
of the account, that Léon Blum did not come to the same conclusion on
the military policy that he had proposed, which is another matter altogether.
But his judgement on the essentials, that is to say the negative assessment
he accords to Francoism, is striking. And it helps us to understand the future
and spectacular association between Charles de Gaulle and André Malraux;
it had its logic, even before that of the Resistance properly speaking.

---

[9] In *La Décadence* (*1932–1939*), J.-B Duroselle has devoted an entire volume, decisive and
absolutely essential, to this combined weakness of thought and will. Ed. Imprimerie nationale,
1979.

On the left, too, regrouping was taking place. Firstly, if the Communists had turned swiftly, others were turning slowly, and yet others not at all. We have already remarked on how the PCF made itself the champion of antifascist firmness, and how it had justified that. It was not alone in using this way of rediscovering a republican national tradition – or Jacobin, one might say. The French Revolution remained popular among the people on the left, among many intellectuals and academics. By evoking the struggles of yesteryear for democracy, the progressive social side of the government and of the movement of June 1936 at the same time revived the old republican patriotism. If June 1936 brought to mind the abolition of privilege, the struggle against Hitler would recall the struggle against 'Pitt and Coburg'. The Spanish War, its progress passionately followed, and bloody as it was, reinstated the idea of a just war, which 1914–18 had harmed. People's emotions were stirred for the defenders of the university buildings in Madrid, for the tank-drivers in Teruel, the airmen . . . André Malraux, indeed, had gone beyond lectures and meetings of revolutionary writers to the organizing of military flights for the Republic. In short, the left was able once more to see both the usefulness and the romantic quality of fighters. That remobilization was making headway in the socialist, radical and comparable tendencies.

Without complete unanimity, however. For others, pacifist intransigence held firm. Some radicals (more to the right of the party), some socialists (here, more to the left of the party), some Trotskyites, some libertarians found the neo-Jacobinism all the less appealing because its chief spokesman was the PCF. For the Communists, who had so violently changed course in 1934, who had praised the USSR of the great Moscow trials and who, moreover, were being compromised by Stalinist acts of repression being perpetrated at that time in the very heart of the dying Spanish Republic – the Communists, then, could arouse as much revulsion in some as they could exercise attraction for others. Thus there existed on the extreme left a camp that was very different but resolute in its mingled intransigent anti-war and anti-Communist attitudes, and would not be shaken by the fact of its effective convergence with the position of the pro-fascist right.

Other developments were taking place on the left. If one reads the recollections (admittedly, written much later) of the teacher Robert Debré,[10] and the impressions (these written at the time) of Marc Bloch in *L'Étrange Défaite*, one is struck by the amount of sympathy, mitigated by many reservations and even some disquiet, evinced for 1936 by those two great citizens, typical left-wing intellectuals of the turn of the century, Dreyfusards, secular, imbued with republican patriotism and sensitive to social injustice.

A horror of Nazism, and dictatorships in general, did not prevent people from thinking that the governmental instability of the parliamentary Republic handicapped France in the face of the energy and continuity that

---

[10] Robert Debré, *L'Honneur de vivre*, Paris, Hermann et Stock, 1974.

characterized authoritarian regimes. Taking that viewpoint, many sound minds formed in the republican tradition began to become receptive to the old conservative line on the weakness of institutions.

The undertakings of 1936 were hailed as acceptable, socially necessary, noble by reason of their humanism and cultural effects, the Popular Front was defended against the excess of slander by which it had been overwhelmed – but it was not absolved from every fault, the chief one being its introverted nature: in short, France had enjoyed too euphoric a period, there had been too much dancing and too little work, while Hitler . . . Let us also recall Sauvy's recently quoted economic criticisms of Blum's work. These reservations on the part of an old republican bourgeoisie with regard to the left in 1936 are important, because they pave the way for a historic swing. Despite several striking instances of continuity (Langevin, Alain, already mentioned, or Victor Basch, president of the League of the Rights of Man), not by a long chalk did *all* the Dreyfusard bourgeoisie (or its sons) gather alongside Léon Blum. It may be said without paradox that the left in 1936 was fewer in number than the left in 1902.

Of course, one will not reach the blunt conclusion that a fringe of the republican bourgeoisie 'veered right' and joined the conservative camp, and certainly not from a 'spirit of class'! The mass of right-thinking bourgeois are sharply taken to task by our two witnesses, quoted above, for their indulgence towards fascism or their tendency towards appeasement. From 1936 on, they inclined more towards the section of the republican right that had remained patriotic (Paul Reynaud), before joining it under the banner of Gaullism. So, even before 1940, it was noticeable that confidence in the traditional conception of the Republic (parliamentary orthodoxy and social humanitarianism, no enemies on the left, etc.) was shaken within its own camp. In other words, the crisis of national survival was accompanied on the quiet by a crisis in the institutions and a debate on the Republic which already foreshadowed post-1944. Munich would be the first visible sign of those regroupings. For from then on, external politics dominated.

Hitler's Germany had left the League of Nations, recovered the Sarre, reoccupied the Rhineland, rearmed; in short, it had invalidated the Treaty of Versailles, in its specifically German clauses. Secondly, it had obtained an alliance with Italy, which even in 1934 and despite the similarity between the regimes, could not necessarily be taken for granted. But Mussolini, Ethiopia's aggressor, was not acceptable to republican France, above all after 1936. Furthermore, Hitler and Mussolini had joined together, during the summer of 1936, in supporting Franco's nationalist rebellion in Spain. The link seemed decisive: the 'Rome–Berlin axis', hostile to France, extended its influence south of the Pyrenees. Thirdly, Hitler was able to revise the European clauses of the Versailles Treaty. The *Anschluss* merely marked the first stage. The second would come with the destruction of the francophile Republic of Czechoslovakia, by way of the support given to its

On their way from Munich, Édouard Daladier and Georges Bonnet have just landed or Orly. Conscious, particularly Daladier, of having yielded to Hitler and registered a defeat, they are acclaimed for having 'saved the peace'. It was not customary for travelling statesmen to be awaited at the airport, a distant venue, by any sizeable crowd. This scene of welcome is therefore usually cited as a sign of the strength of the desire for peace at that time. (Photographer unknown)

inhabitants of German origin and language, who were established in the Sudeten mountains.

The pressure on Prague lasted throughout the summer of 1938, combining internal disturbances among the Sudetens and external threats formulated by Berlin.

The epilogue is known only too well. A last-ditch meeting took place in Munich on 30 September 1938 between the heads of government of Germany, Italy, Great Britain and France (Hitler, Mussolini, Chamberlain and Daladier). The British and French subscribed to the detachment of the Sudetenland from Czechoslovakia, which rendered the latter militarily indefensible, industrially weakened and morally humiliated, thus ultimately condemned. In return for which, Hitler agreed not to send in his troops – which 'saved the peace'. When he came back to Paris, Daladier was acclaimed by the crowd for that precise reason.

Pro-Munich France, in fact, gave expression to its feelings and shouted aloud its relief. Anti-Munich France kept a low profile, though it was without doubt stronger than it would seem in informed circles, the press, the political class, but – as we have said – it was difficult to put across a position reputed to be 'warmongering'. That was clearly to be seen when, in the Chamber of Deputies at the debate on ratification of the agreement, the pro-Munich majority proved overwhelming; there were only seventy-five against, seventy-three of whom were Communists, the nationalist journalist-deputy Henri de Kérillis, and a socialist, who would subsequently repudiate his vote.

Thenceforward France would be split along this new line of division.

For Munich, a *de facto* coalition united the overall and diffuse pacifism of the majority of opinion, the determined and doctrinal pacifism of various left wing, extreme left wing or apolitical groups, and the more accommodating pacifism of those who preferred fascist regimes to democracies.

Against Munich, there was an even more heterogeneous spread, in which at that time the PCF formed the only organized force. In all the other political forces, upsets and dissensions had the upper hand. The polarization between those who would push the Munich logic to the point of collaboration, and those who would pass from a deep-rooted anti-Munichism to the Resistance was as yet only potential.

But already 'Munich' was entering political vocabulary as a symbol of non-resistance to evil and refusal to fight for what was right, a symbol and a refusal made worse by an error of judgement, because experience would show that there would still have to be fighting, and in more difficult conditions.

At all events, that was the definition of 'Munich' that the Second World War would make almost official. Meanwhile, since the possibility of war had been touched upon, it was logical to make ready for it – which would bring the history of the Popular Front to its epilogue.

The moderate Paul Reynaud, one of the leaders of the group beaten in 1936, had returned in April 1938 to the Daladier cabinet as Minister of Justice. On 1 November, thanks to a reshuffle, he transferred to Finance, thus to the head of the economy. In order to improve armaments output, he maintained that it was necessary to increase the working week, in other words, to abandon one of the greatest conquests of the Popular Front. There was no longer any need to scruple with regard to the Communists or to worry about handling them tactfully; since Munich, the PC, whose audience had grown considerably in 1936, 1937 and 1938, both in the number of its adherents and its influence in the reunified CGT, had been going tooth and nail for the 'Munichois' Daladier. And in October, at its Marseille Congress, the Radical Party had taken up the challenge, ostentatiously remarking on the break-up of the Popular Front. The Communists incited the workers to stick to their forty hours. Was that really logical, when in principle they declared themselves supporters of firmness in the face of Hitler? Their reply was that national defence seemed far less threatened by the workers' Saturday off than by the betrayal or defeatism of the 'bourgeoisie'.

Moreover, certain bourgeois did not disguise the fact that, with a return to longer working hours, they were seeking revenge on the social spirit of 1936. 'The two-Sunday week is over', Paul Reynaud had dared to say, rather provocatively. However, the PC was not alone in clinging to the forty hours, the symbolic legacy of the grand summer of 1936. As early as August 1938, two ministers, including Paul Ramadier, had resigned from the government for that precise reason. And on 30 November, it was the entire CGT, headed by the reformist Léon Jouhaux, that gave the word for a 24-hour general strike for the defence of social gains.

It was a failure. The strike was only partly supported, and the government was able to exercise sanctions of dismissal in state establishments.

The reasons for this failure were probably complex: had the official line of argument on the demands imposed by the international crisis been tacitly accepted by the workers? Or had they been paralysed by the patent dissensions between the political forces claiming their allegiance? Or disheartened by the overall impression that the euphoric era of 1936 had really come to an end?

Whatever the reason, a victorious government received a new lease of life. It would engage in intense activity, from which would emerge notably the series of measures supporting the family and a rising birth rate, known as the Family Code (29 July 1939), thanks to which the demographic balance would be restored on a fairly lasting basis.

From Munich until the war, that is, from October 1938 to August 1939, we see the first eleven months of a Daladier government with its very own 'personality', if for nothing other than the high profile and popularity of the president of the Council.

Under the influence of the extreme left, he has long been regarded as a link in the chain leading from Munich to the collapse in 1940, indicated by his complaisance towards fascism, a complaisance fed by his political and social hostility to the PC, in other words, to the most determined antifascists. It is true that the government which came down hard on the CGT after 30 November was also the one whose Minister of Foreign Affairs, Georges Bonnet, welcomed his German colleague, von Ribbentrop, to Paris in December 1938; the one which, in March 1939, formally recorded the entry of German troops into Czechoslovakia, and at the same time recognized the new government established in Spain by the victorious Franco, appointing Marshal Pétain as its French ambassador; the one which received refugee Spanish republican fighters in France only to treat them as suspects and intern them in concentration camps (the government of the Spanish Republic would have to seek asylum in Mexico). Abandoning the spirit of the Popular Front would thus seem to have brought about the abandonment of the antifascist spirit, and thereby a sagging in national energy in the face of what were by now obvious potential enemies. But certain signs which are more willingly stressed these days contradict that argument. Daladier busied himself, made reforms, pushed for improvement in the military forces, spoke firmly to Mussolini, who was starting to demand Tunisia, Corsica, Savoy, Nice ('No, we will not yield an inch of our territory'), and was acclaimed in those selfsame disputed regions. There he gained a certain popularity as a patriotic leader. Was he acting the Poincaré of 1913–14? He seemed to be wagering on a new 'sacred union'. At a pinch, that interpretation can be given to the appointment of Pétain to an official mission and, more precisely, to the refusal of the chief parties to enter into competition for renewal of the presidency. Contrary to the tradition of the single seven-year term, agreement was reached to re-elect Albert Lebrun to the presidency of the Republic, which post he had held since 1932.

In the country at large, a certain firming of opinion was taking place. Hitler's activism which, in the summer of 1939, with Czechoslovakia absorbed, was now demanding the north-east part of Poland, with the corridor which separated eastern Prussia from Germany, and the partly German city of Danzig, rendered war a probability. We know that the logic of Munich would lead to other retreats – as Marcel Déat dared to write in the famous article 'We don't want to die for Danzig'. In the SFIO, divided as usual, the friends of Paul Faure upheld that line, while Léon Blum, on the other hand, tried to tone down his 'Munichism', showed himself in favour of strengthening national defence and felt closer to both Communists and patriotic moderates.

That logic, which gradually led to the formation of a collaborationist coalition and a resistance coalition well before the event, was to be rudely interrupted by an external incident.

War, which was by now likely, in order to check Hitler's imperialism by helping Poland to defend itself, could not be managed without allies. The only possible alliance, apart from that with Poland itself, was with the Soviets. During the summer of 1939, the French and British governments therefore dispatched a mission to Moscow to work out the possible methods. The difficulty lay in the fact that the Poles were just as much afraid of help from the USSR (for them, an enemy both historical and ideological) as of German aggression, and refused to contemplate allowing Russian troops to set foot on their territory.

While the Moscow negotiations were thus foundering, German diplomacy managed a startling coup: following secret approaches, it persuaded the Soviets to give up these disappointing western contacts and sign a pact of nonaggression with Germany. Stalin and Molotov accepted. The news broke on 23 August. So here was the USSR in the German camp, and Hitler with a free hand in the west.

The opportunism of Stalinist diplomacy was not without some justification. On the one hand, the hostile attitude of the Poles they were being asked to help was scarcely encouraging; on the other, the attitude of the

French and British who, at Munich, less than a year earlier, had given in to Hitler without envisaging the slightest recourse to Russian aid, left room to doubt the antifascist determination of London and Paris. Those good reasons for Moscow would be endlessly recalled, right up to the present day, by advocates of the Germano-Soviet pact.

For the moment, however, Communist propaganda, which had since Moscow been channelled via the Internationale, was not content merely to plead opportunism, tactical withdrawal and 'playing for time'. Very swiftly, it constructed a strategical justification. Going back on all it had said since 1934 about 'fascism' and Hitler, it rejoined the tradition of the time, in which the capitalists of London and Paris represented the chief enemy and in which 'their' war was consequently an 'imperialist war', thus unjustifiable, even guilty of being anti-revolutionary.

The French Communist Party, in solidarity with Moscow, would thus be obliged, in morally and intellectually difficult conditions, to defend the pact firstly as a peace initiative that would alter nothing in the antifascist legitimacy of the likely war, then as an acknowledgement of the illegitimacy of that war.

For the war broke out very quickly. Sure of Russian neutrality, Hitler attacked Poland on 1 September. Then, doing for Poland what they had not dared to do for Czechoslovakia, the French and British entered the war on 3 September.

'Funny sort of war', people said about the period from 3 September 1939 to 10 May 1940. 'Funny' firstly because it was hardly waged at all. The French army, whose strategy was defensive, did nothing to relieve its Polish ally, which the 'lighting war' of the Wehrmacht crushed in a few days. The French contented themselves with expressing indignation when, in the spirit of the pact of 23 August, the Soviets sent forward troops to recover the territories on the Polish–Russian borders that they had lost in 1920, which had all the appearance of a rerun of the old 'share-out of Poland'. France waited passively to endure the assault, only sending an expeditionary force by sea, in mid April 1940, to try to help Norway which, like Denmark, had in its turn been invaded by Hitler.

Then a 'funny sort of war' because it was not engaged in unanimously, even on the surface, as a considerable group crossed over to the enemy side and went underground. Neither the Daladier government nor public opinion bothered much about the successive nuances of Communist propaganda. Immediately the PC approved the pact, and the pact united Hitler and Stalin, the PC found itself in solidarity with France's enemy, therefore itself an enemy and a traitor. Within a few days its press was banned, the party itself dissolved, Communist mayors dismissed, Communist trades union officials barred from the CGT (by the reformist majority), and the militants who tried to maintain the links of a thenceforward clandestine organization were hunted by the police. The repression would be extended, after a little hesitation, to the forty-five loyal deputies (out of sixty-three, the others having repudiated the pact and therefore broken with the party) who had re-formed the parliamentary group, banned as 'Communist', under the name 'workers and peasants'. In January 1940 they were declared stripped of their mandate and sent before a military tribunal which sentenced them to prison terms. Twenty-seven would undergo those, in France and then in Algeria, the rest going underground.

But it was as early as October 1939 that the chief among them, Maurice Thorez, having been called up, had quit his regiment at the order of the Internationale, and crossed the Belgian frontier to join what Stalin considered his revolutionary battle station in Moscow. In ordinary language, that was called desertion. The effect on opinion was considerable. It may be said, with hindsight, that Thorez's departure did not deprive the French army of one fighter, but only the French political prisons of one inmate, but nothing could gainsay the fact that 'Thorez's desertion', reinforcing the effect of the approval given to the Hitler–Stalin pact, placed the PC beyond the pale of the national community.

It was a moral ghetto, akin to the one which had surrounded the pacifists in 1914, but doubtless containing more people. How many exactly? Certainly not the whole of the powerful PC which, at the apogee of the Popular Front, had 'weighed' over a million and a half voters (male) and perhaps two or three hundred thousand followers. For many had quit, members who had become numerous in the surge of antifascist and neopatriotic politics, faithful to that line (which was also a feeling), and who had repudiated the leadership that had disowned it. Others remained attached to the party during that difficult time, either because they had been glad to rediscover the pre-1934 revolutionary line; or because they had accepted that Stalin knew what he was doing, that all would be revealed later, and Hitler would once more become the enemy; or because they had reached the higher level of conviction which cared only about the survival of the USSR and the PC, the supreme end in relation to which all strategies took second place. As for knowing in what proportions the Communists, active militants or sympathizers, were divided among these theoretical options, we have scarcely any means of judging.

Lastly, a 'funny sort of war' because, quite apart from the Communist exception, the French themselves were disoriented. It would have been logical to admit that, since the two archetypal dictators, Hitler the 'fascist' and Stalin the 'Bolshevik', were marching hand in hand, the war France was waging at least against one of them was a war for liberty. But it is not apparent that this purely intellectual logic numbered many followers or had much effect. Common opinion in that 'funny sort of war', so it would seem, experienced more of a revival of anti-Communism: Stalin, with the pact, had deserted France and allowed the outbreak of war, he was directing on French national soil a 'fifth column' of traitorous Communists, he was retreading the paths of Russian imperialism by taking back his piece of Poland and by attacking Finland.

In fact, the Red Army, in order to push back a frontier dangerously close to Leningrad, had undertaken the conquest of Karelia. As a result, Finland, which had managed to defend itself well for a few weeks in the winter before succumbing, earned far more ardent and (platonically) belligerent sympathies in French opinion than had ever been aroused by Czechoslovakia or Poland. The predominant tone in France between 1939 and 1940 was undeniably anti-Communist, and that did not stimulate the antifascist crusading spirit which is deemed to have inspired the war.

The war was thus carried on, behind the lines, with rather an effort to recapture the spirit of 1914. There were demonstrations, good works, speeches. A songwriter launched a 'popular' song which was intended to be for the soldiers of 1940 what 'La Madelon' had been for the 1914–18 *poilus*. That 'daughter of Madelon' he thought it natural to call . . . 'Victoire'. It was not sung very much! Because there was no brainwashing as such, it was decided to set up an acceptable war propaganda. But its most elaborate messages, the work of the very official Commissioner for Information, Jean Giraudoux, a highly talented novelist, went completely above people's heads. As for the more intelligible slogans – 'We shall win because we are the strongest', 'The iron ore route (from Norway) is and will remain cut off' – they were received with a sort of weary irony.

Meanwhile, political life went on in parliament, unobtrusive and complex, even derisory by comparison with the gravity of the times. On one of those days, 20 March 1940, the worn-out Daladier was forced to resign. Paul Reynaud assumed the presidency of the Council and, in political circles, this was seen as a sign of increased determination. Léon Blum allowed six of his socialist friends to enter the government, as if he had confidence in Paul Reynaud (more than in Daladier) to achieve the National Union he had himself desired two years earlier. It is true that Daladier kept the Ministry of War, which would undergo a terrible strain.

On 10 May 1940, Hitler attacked. Columns of very fast armoured vehicles thrust boldly along the roads of Holland, Belgium and Luxemburg, their advance covered by light bombers employing 'dive bombing' tactics. The cream of the French army went to encounter them in Belgium in an attempt to halt them along the line of the Dyle. Then, on 14 May, a new German thrust broke through the front at Sedan, at the pivotal point of the Maginot line and the Belgian frontier, through the Ardennes, a natural obstacle whose reliability had been incautiously overestimated. So France was invaded, and the French troops in Belgium, in any case beaten, were caught from the rear. On 18 May, the Germans gained control of nearly all Belgium, and in France reached Saint-Quentin. On 18 May, Paul Reynaud, in the face of imminent disaster, changed those in the highest posts.

Daladier left the government and handed the Ministry of War to Marshal Pétain, who was regarded as being accustomed to victory and capable of galvanizing opinion. In the same spirit, Generalissimo Gamelin yielded supreme command to Weygand, Foch's former right-hand man in 1914–18. Lastly, Colonel de Gaulle, promoted to general for the occasion, became Under-Secretary of State for War (5 June).

De Gaulle, several days earlier, had in fact managed to pass from theory to practice. At the head of a special formation, completely motorized and armoured, he had for three days victoriously held out against the German advance in the Laon region. Twenty years later, that battle of Montcornet would provoke the derision of the anti-Gaullist polemicists. Montcornet, the back of beyond with a name like something out of an operetta! That is an unseemly and unfair sarcasm, however. If all the regiments had been similarly equipped, if all the colonels had had *his* energy and talent, the French campaign could have taken quite another direction. But at Montcornet Colonel de Gaulle could obtain no more than an exceptional, almost experimental, success.

In his role as General and junior minister, he could not do anything more, seeing that operations on the ground depended on Weygand. Reynaud, in fact, appointed de Gaulle to liaise with the British government in which, by a curious parallelism, Winston Churchill had replaced Chamberlain around the time when Reynaud himself had succeeded Daladier.

On 21 May, Amiens and Arras were taken. Announcing this, Paul Reynaud declared with pathos: 'And if I were told that only a miracle can save France, I would say, "I believe in miracles, because I believe in France." '

The author, at that time just emerging from childhood, listened to those words coming 'live' over a radio loudspeaker which the patriotic headmaster had set up in the *lycée* refectory, and can bear witness to that national pathos, probably quite sincere, but which was more worrying than inspiring. Was not saying 'Only a miracle can save us' in fact merely a way of saying 'We are sunk'? Unless the miracle was that of 18 June, which would indeed take place, but with a long-term result.

For the time being, the east–west drive of the principal German armies reached the Channel on 28 May, while the Belgian army capitulated. From then on, the French and British forces were trapped in a rapidly shrinking pocket around Dunkirk, with their backs to the sea. They escaped total annihilation only by embarking for England, under constant bombardment (28 May to 3 June).

There was then nothing to prevent the Germans from pushing towards the south, reaching the Seine; Paris, whence the government had departed for the valley of the Loire, was occupied on the 14th; then the Loire in its turn was reached, and the authorities finished up in Bordeaux. The military disaster of May–June 1940 was far more than a war of movement which was finally lost, like that of Napoleon in the spring of 1814, or that of Napoleon III, prolonged by Gambetta, in 1870. From certain aspects, it

German parade, 6 July 1940. The Germans on the Champs Élysées – the place for all symbolic parades. It had seen the victory parade of 14 July 1914, but here one thinks also of the one on 1 March 1871 which, on the same route, had marked a much earlier defeat. (Photo: Les Actualités photographiques Internationales)

was accompanied by a total collapse which makes it one of the most sinister and enigmatic moments in French history.

A large part of the civilian population of the invaded countries, first Belgium, then France between the Belgian border, the Paris region and Burgundy, had left their homes to travel south, panic-stricken, fleeing both the spectre of Hitler and the unaccustomed fury of the screaming, thundering, terrifying and murderous aerial bombardments. This was the 'exodus', with its pitiable processions, so many times described in all their harrowing detail. And in all their social inequality as well. Some had cars and petrol coupons at their disposal, and were going to stay with friends; others went on foot, or in some vehicle which soon broke down, and journeyed aimlessly. Some had a bit of money put aside; others carried their bare essentials on the roof of their old 'banger'. More troubles and more worries were caused by the congestion on the roads, the hindrance to troop movements, the overburdening of the local authorities in the towns and villages along the route or where people finally stopped. With the exodus, national panic did more than accompany defeat, it made it worse.

Exact proportions are unknown – there are played down or exaggerated according to the overall idea one has of that period – but acts of panic or desertion took place even among those in uniform. Officers were seen really making a beeline for the south.

To that were added the effects of administrative lack of preparation and general ossification. A bureaucracy which had badly planned and badly prepared for this war, disconcerted by the way things were going, often revealed itself incapable even of organizing an improvised parade. Above all when its men were, for ideological reasons, little motivated a priori for a crusade on behalf of democracies. All those who wanted to fight, or simply act with dignity, encountered administrative obstacles about which there are swarms of the most distressing anecdotes. Marc Bloch's *L'Étrange Défaite* – a testimony above any suspicion of partisanship – provides an exemplary illustration.

In the face of the collapse and swiftly insurmountable disorder, there arose an antagonism between those who wanted to resist and those who wanted to limit the damage. That antagonism produced cruelly absurd effects. On the very same river, some kilometres away from a bridge where soldiers were getting themselves killed trying to prevent the enemy from crossing, there were other bridges which the enemy crossed easily because the town had been declared an 'open town'. That choice, which cropped up everywhere, finally split the government itself. It withdrew to deliberate. Soon the division appeared between those who sought the means to fight, keeping contact with Britain, hoping to set up a 'Breton hideout', considering falling back on the 'Empire' (Algiers, Casablanca, Dakar), forming the camp with Paul Reynaud as its leader, and those who, knowing the game was up in France and not thinking it playable beyond, were resigned to throwing in the towel. That was the camp of Marshal Pétain, supported from outside by Generalissimo Weygand.

On 16 June, in Bordeaux, realizing that he was in a minority in his team, Paul Reynaud resigned from the government. President Lebrun at once entrusted Marshal Pétain, the leader of the other tendency, with the task of governing.

De Gaulle, on a mission to London on 15 and 16 June, learned the news on his return to Bordeaux on the 16th, at 9.30 p.m., and comments: 'It meant certain capitulation. My decision was taken immediately. I would leave in the morning.'

De Gaulle, on his own evidence, would not succeed in persuading Reynaud himself to perform the act of transporting the government to Africa, for example. He at least received his encouragement and approval, made more concrete by the handing over of secret funds worth 100,000 francs. On the morning of 17 June, de Gaulle took off for London, where he would hear what had happened that day. Marshal Pétain asked the Germans for their armistice conditions. Then, on 18 June, he wrote and broadcast the appeal which would indicate the alternative choice and the alternative prospect.

Appeal to the French, 18 June 1940

The leaders who for many years have been at the head of the French forces have formed a government.

This government, using the pretext of the defeat of our armies, has contacted the enemy with a view to halting the combat.

Certainly, we have been, we are, submerged by the enemy's mechanized forces, both on land and in the air.

Infinitely more than their numbers, it is the tanks, the aircraft, the tactics of the Germans, which have made us fall back. It is the tanks, the aircraft, the tactics of the Germans which have taken our leaders by surprise and brought them to the pass they are in today.

But has the last word been spoken? Must all hope vanish? Is defeat final? No!

Believe me, and I know whereof I speak, when I tell you that nothing is lost for France. The very means which have conquered us may well bring victory one day.

For France is not alone! She is not alone! She has a vast empire behind her. She can join with the British Empire, which holds the seas and is continuing the struggle. Like Britain, she can make limitless use of the immense industries of the United States.

This war is not confined to the unhappy territory of our country. This war is not ended by the battle of France. This is a world war. All the errors, delays and sufferings cannot prevent there being, in the universe, all the means for us one day to crush our enemies. Struck down today by mechanized force, we shall be able in the future to conquer by means of a superior mechanized force. That is where the world's destiny lies.

I, general de Gaulle, now present in London, invite French officers and soldiers who are on British territory, or who may manage to get there, with or without their weapons; I invite engineers and workers who are specialists in the arms industry, who are on British territory, or who may manage to get there, to make contact with me.

Whatever may happen, the flame of French resistance must not and will not be extinguished.

Tomorrow, as today, I shall speak on the radio from London.

Such was the historic text, and rarely has that adjective been more appropriate to a man's action, even if at first it was no more than words.

It indissolubly mingles two acts of faith which later texts would clarify: the first, truly national, is that France cannot perish, 'Providence' always finds a way out in the end; the other, humanistic and moral, is that liberty will get the better of Nazism. For, without that second wager, that second necessity, it might be accepted, with Vichy, that France was awaiting its moment by adapting itself to a Hitlerian Europe. For de Gaulle, by contrast, since liberty not only *must* win the war but also had a *duty* to do so, France's future should be prepared for with that prospect in view, that is, ensuring a French presence as early as possible in the camp of the future victors.

The wager on the victory of liberty could itself be reduced to two hopes: a bet that Britain would hold firm, and a bet that America would lend its aid. We know that both bets were won, but it not easy to judge today how difficult it was to take them. Hitler had nothing to fear in the east, as Russia had been neutralized, and the rest, the Balkan countries, were almost negligible. He had conquered France with ease. All he had to do to crush the little army on British soil, and thus to be complete victor, was to cross the Channel. We must confess that there was every likelihood that he would do so.

Nevertheless, Britain would win, thanks to the technical abilities and courage of its men of the Royal Air Force, coupled with the civilian stoicism of its citizens, despite the hail of bombs; supported by a government led by a kind of British Clemenceau named Winston Churchill, borne along by the virtually intact partiotism of a people who felt themselves in mortal danger each time a single master tried to rule the European continent (Louis XIV and Napoleon in former days, Hitler now).

To wager on this British capacity, de Gaulle had needed a good knowledge of history, and to have overcome the tradition of Anglophobia which was so powerful in French tradition.

He used the same breadth and depth of view in placing his second winning bet – on America. In spite of distance, selfishness and isolationism, it would commit itself, because the North American continent was fundamentally a land of liberty and because it was, moreover, a land of British culture. This fact, which seems obvious to us today, was known to the General, but the average Frenchman, and quite a few politicians, fed on childish clichés about the United States, were unaware of it. In that respect, the appeal stemmed from the vision of a statesman and the vision of a free man.

The deed, however, was that of a rebel. The government presided over by Marshal Pétain, on 17 June 1940, in no way smacked of a team of seditionaries. The outcome of an internal reshuffle, with the backing of the President of the Republic, of the last government properly vested by the deputies, it was quite legal.

For de Gaulle to be justified, he had to be allowed to infringe *legality*. Then he invented *legitimacy*. The theory may be put thus: the chief task of the state is to guarantee the independence and life of the nation, and to do everything with that aim in view. Hitler threatened France, which had to defend itself and could still do so because to the south of the Mediterranean an immense area of Africa was then – French. By abandoning a still possible combat, Pétain failed in his major mission, and *therefore* became illegitimate from the point of view of the national criterion, so there were grounds for replacing him. By transferring the combat to London, de Gaulle – whose movement would be known as Free France – was transferring *ipso facto* a national legitimacy in comparison with which the criterion of legality was reduced to second place.

In this way legitimacy re-entered the theoretical trappings of French politics. Not the legitimacy of 1830, which distinguished Charles X from the usurper Louis-Philippe, and which would produce legitimism, or ultra-ism, in the broader sense proposed by René Rémond (a right ideologically hostile to the principles of 1789). Not legitimacy or legitimism in the sense which has more recently become trivialized in the press, and which flatly indicates an attachment to existing institutions, or even a tendency to vote the same way as the government! No. On 18 June, it was a matter of a legitimacy *sui generis*, a value linked to national existence, and a supreme value because it could (in exceptional circumstances?) dispense with fol-lowing legality.

For the moment, de Gaulle was better armed theoretically than patriots who had been brought up in classic republicanism since, for them, respect for the law constituted the highest value. Old republicans would have to wait – not long, at all events – until 10 July to be called upon to disobey Pétain and Laval, who would then appear as authors of a coup d'état.

On 18 June 1940, the left could not put forward any theory to justify an '18 June' – in any case, nobody paid it much heed.

From where did de Gaulle derive his theory of a national legitimacy opposable to legality? The question must be asked because, subsequently, that legitimacy would be used again. How can one fail to see in it – whether consciously borrowed or vaguely recollected – an echo of Bonapartism? The Bonaparte of 18 Brumaire had doubtless been little bothered by scruples. But his emulator of 2 December had been more worried by them, and knew that violation of the Constitution posed a problem: 'Six million votes have just *absolved* me' – the choice of that word was an admission of guilt. He then produced this statement: 'I left the path of legality only to return to the law.' Badly chosen words, because it is hard to see 'legality' in opposi-tion to 'law'. But it would have been easy to put: 'I left the path of legality only to return to . . .' – and here insert the name of a supreme value that may be placed in opposition to the law on special occasions.

It is in this sense, and this sense alone, that we might seem to find something Bonapartist in Gaullism. By contrast, for the republicans, the 'purer-than-pure' republicans, of the resistance to 2 December, and their last disciples in the twentieth-century left, anyone who abandoned legality was doing wrong. Although it could not be foreseen, this was a foretaste of a great debate which could take place in another violent spring – of 1958.

But on 18 June 1940, French patriots had more to worry about than such casuistry. The effects on political philosophy were only potential and today it is the hindsight of history alone that allows us to work out its origins. At the time, the evidence of June 1940 pointed first and foremost to a major national crisis.

On that crucial date in French history, 18 June 1940, de Gaulle thus planted in London the standard to which all the patriots who were left in

France could rally. For the moment, there were hardly any, and the great majority of the French (the parents, grandparents and great-grandparents of those living in the 1990s) were generally resigned to being the vanquished.

Regarding the drama itself, several divergent trends of explanation were being formed – the causes of such a complex event as the French collapse in the summer of 1940 in any case crisscrossing and running side by side – but three simple arguments emerged.

One came from the extreme right, and could appropriately by termed that of moral flabbiness. A people who had been badly raised since 1789, subsequently ruined by a century of politicking Republic and corrupting modernity, and finally finished off by the paroxysm of popularity-seeking that the Popular Front would seem to have been could not fail to be brought to their knees. But that theme, which Gobineau had already used to explain the defeat of 1870, could have explained even better a defeat in 1914 . . . had one taken place! Nevertheless, one must keep that 'explanation' in mind because, under Vichy, it would become almost official.

The other simple thesis belongs to the extreme left, and is the Communist one of betrayal by the bourgeois elites because of class hatred ('Better Hitler than the Popular Front'). Although it accounts for many disturbing deeds and attitudes, it is nevertheless revealed as inadequate, rather than false, for the elites were not alone in providing examples of discouragement and desertion.

We feel more drawn to the third argument, which has recently emerged in the work of great specialists[11] and which, to tell the truth, our own account has disclosed: France was still drained by the victory so dearly bought in 1918. Could that ill, born of one war, be put right by another? That would be one of the things at stake, a truly national gamble, in the struggles of Free France and the Resistance.

[11] Duroselle, *La Décadence*, already quoted, followed by *L'Abîme (1939–1944)*, Imprimerie nationale, 1982, and J.-J. Becker, *Les Français dans la Grande Guerre*, Lafont, 1980.

8

Torn Apart
1940–1944

France had known nothing like this since the Hundred Years' War: its national territory divided on a long-term basis into two zones, each with its own capital. By contrast, when it came to the existence of a government installed in a foreign country and disputing the legitimacy of the one ruling in France itself, it had a more recent precedent of the 'king' in exile, Louis XVIII, before 1814. But that two such heart-rending events should coincide was simply unheard of. From 1940 until 1944 France suffered a real four-way split, between Vichy, Paris, London and the invisible fourth pole which would soon be formed by the underground movement. Needless to say, that material, territorial dispersal of the centres of authority reflected the even more dramatic explosion of wills and minds. Changing the metaphor, and taking up the title of a great and fine work, it was *The Abyss*.[1] The 'free zone' governed from Vichy, the occupied zone (Paris), Free France (in London), and the internal Resistance (in underground networks) carried on a parallel existence. For clarification they must, however, be presented separately, in each case taking November 1942 as the crucial date, as it saw the invasion of the 'free' zone by the occupiers.

As for the actors, they will be described in order of their entrance on the scene, therefore starting with de Gaulle, who was in London on 18 June.

General de Gaulle may be said to have felt fairly at home in London because, in Paul Reynaud's ministry, he looked after the liaison between the French and British governments, and because he had already shuttled several times by air between the two countries, even carrying over Churchill's plan for a Franco-British merger. There are many reasons to justify his establishment there, without the need to recall London's ancient tradition of providing a refuge-haven for French dissidents or exiles of all shades since at least the seventeeth century. First, London, at the height of the air

---

[1] J.-B. Duroselle, *L'Abîme (1939–1944)*, Imprimerie nationale, 1982.

De Gaulle in his London office, 1942, reminds us that from the start Free France was an embryonic state, entailing a collection of papers to be drawn up or signed, not to mention the speeches, which now belong to history.

battle over the Channel, was virtually the main war front. Because of its relative proximity, London would also prove to be the most appropriate place for the transmission of radio messages to France, for the reception or dispatch of emissaries, those courageous clandestine users of the fishing boat or parachute. Most of all, London was the place where Churchill governed, and on him everything depended. De Gaulle, and the France he represented, would receive from him a mixture of hospitality and supervision that he would have to shoulder and manage as best he could.

But what did this 'Free France' want? De Gaulle deliberately allocated it a dual aim.

De Gaulle wanted France and, to begin with, the greatest possible number of Frenchmen, to stay in or come back into the war, *not only in order that the war might be won more quickly, but even more so that France should have a right to have its say after victory.* The first and most obvious objective was to win the war as soon as possible, because Hitler was the enemy. But after all, as we have seen, de Gaulle himself had wagered that Hitler would be beaten. Would it then be enough to wait for the victory of the British, soon helped by the Americans (foreseeable) and the Russians (rather less so)? No, for deliverance received as a gift would obligate the French after the war, thus placing them in a diminished position. That would simply be another way of losing national independence. There, now the vital word was out! They had to fight, therefore, to safeguard French independence against Hitler in the first instance, and later, indirectly, against possible supervision by France's Anglo-American allies. And, according to the General's strategy, it would be all the easier to take a tough line with the Allies after the war, the more the French could prove their usefulness alongside them in combat.

For the moment, de Gaulle had to ask Churchill for the wherewithal to rebuild an army and a French state, while at the same time proclaiming that this army and this state would not always be docile auxiliaries. A difficult problem!

The importance of this double-barrelled strategy enables us to understand an aspect which sometimes astonishes the reader of the *War Memoirs*, namely the number of pages devoted to recounting de Gaulle's disputes with Churchill or Roosevelt, in comparison with those attacking Hitler. The reason is clear. Fighting Hitler went without saying, it was pointless to keep going over it, whereas negotiating with friends, though doubtless less dramatic, was far more complicated and, in the long run, more decisive. To start with, there had to be negotiations over de Gaulle's stopping in London, together with those who would join him, and the financing of the embryo state and its embryo army; therefore the diplomatic, legal and logistic procedures of this unprecedented symbiosis needed to be established. By the end of June de Gaulle was very glad to have with him a lawyer of great worth and resolute patriotism, in the person of René Cassin. The professor took charge of that essential civilian task, while de Gaulle took on the roles of supreme chief, head of the armed forces and symbol in the eyes of the world. For his service, notably, René Cassin was to attain the exceptional honour of interment in the Panthéon, awarded to him in 1987.

For quite a long while de Gaulle remained the only political man, and indeed the only well-known man, at the head of Free France. His repeated appeals chiefly to Weygand and to Noguès, then Resident General in Morocco, having brought no response, he resolved to burn his boats, placing himself at the head of an independent movement, on 28 June, thereby earning himself, in France on 2 August, the death sentence *in absentia*.

His first civilian assistants, besides René Cassin, were men at that time without fame or prestigious office, such as René Pleven. Among the military, many held a modest rank, for example Philippe de Hautecloque (Leclerc) and Pierre Koenig, then captains. However, some generals, higher in the military hierarchy than de Gaulle himself, such as General Catroux, came to put themselves under his command, thereby indicating that they regarded him as the representative and head of a budding state authority, and not just of the remnant of an army.

With its single, self-appointed chief – and military, to boot – was this improvised state 'republican'? In the summer of 1940 its head hardly dreamed of proclaiming it as such, with the result that French civilian refugees, antifascist and for the most part left-wing, were to be found in London, gathered around the newspaper *France*, keeping themselves apart from the General and even somewhat mistrusting him. In fact, in order to oppose Vichy, de Gaulle referred not only to the value of national legitimacy but also to the continuity of the state, which Vichy had broken by its 'revolution'. And that state was none other than the Republic. The proof was to be seen in 1941 when having gained control of a few pieces of Africa where French public buildings still bore engraved on their façades the watchword 'Liberty, Equality, Fraternity', de Gaulle, in opposition to Larminat, insisted on its being retained. France and the Republic certainly kept their continuity with him.

Nevertheless, these political and constitutional matters were not in the forefront of national anxieties in the summer of 1940.

As early as the beginning of July, British acceptance of Free France underwent a severe test in the Mers el-Kebir episode. In that war port near to Oran, and thus under Vichy authority, the main part of the French fleet was assembled and, in principle, neutralized. But Churchill did not believe Vichy capable of maintaining that neutrality, and was unwilling to run the – deadly – risk of that naval force one day passing into the hands of the Germans. He therefore had an ultimatum sent to Admiral Gensoul, ordering him to hand over his ships. As the Admiral refused, the British fleet undertook to put them out of action with gunfire. The operation was achieved with the loss of hundreds of French sailors' lives. De Gaulle reacted with a politic and subtle speech, in which grief and anger against British aggression did not prevent the conclusion that there must be no mistaking the real enemy, and that the French war must be conducted against Hitler. There would be other setbacks . . .

At first the colonial empire rallied only in dribs and drabs (New Caledonia, Cameroon, Saint Pierre and Miquelon, Chad, the latter in August

1940, thanks to its governor, the West Indian Félix Éboué, who for that reason would one day become the first coloured man to be interred in the Panthéon), successes effaced by the failure, at the end of September 1940, of a big Anglo-Gaullist naval operation trying to occupy Dakar. The main part of the African possessions thus remained obedient to Vichy.

There were diplomatic upsets as well. Britain alone broke with Vichy and supported de Gaulle, whereas the USSR and the United States in 1940 maintained their embassy with Pétain. And when those two countries entered the war with Germany (respectively in June and December 1941) and their diplomats left France, they would in no way recognize Free France as a diplomatic partner. To obtain that would take a long while yet. Nevertheless, on 23 September 1941, de Gaulle would have fleshed out his team sufficiently to christen it French National Committee and organize it into a sort of government.

A third series of setbacks arose from the constant tensions with the British host, friend and ally. As has already been said, the *War Memoirs* overflow with accounts of them. The Syrian affair: the war having spread to the Middle East because of German support for the Iraqis' anti-British revolt, the British, in reaction, were forced to get a footing in Syria, a former French domain. De Gaulle insisted on sending a part of his scanty troops there, at the risk of their clashing with garrisons loyal to Vichy – the first direct confrontation between Frenchmen, in June 1941. The Madagascar affair: the British occupied the 'big island', and took six months to return it to Gaullist authority. But success eventually materialized for the Free France enterprise. In 1942 an important battle front appeared in the deserts of Libya. The Germans, who in spring 1941 had conquered the Balkan peninsula, arrived in force in this Italian colonial territory and threatened British positions in Egypt. Suez, the crossroads of the world, formed a decisive stake in the game. After various military vicissitudes, a great battle was enagaged in June 1942 which broke the assault of the Afrikakorps. Because the Allies had at all costs to cover Egypt, Free French elements took part in this decisive battle, under the command of General Koenig, winning fame at Bir Hakeim. Two years after the call, with a classic armed force, France well and truly resumed an effective part in the fight against Hitler. Free France had attained its first goal.

That prospect had been rejected, however, by a whole section of the nation, which was represented by Vichy.

'Vichy' was first situated in Bordeaux. From there the new president of the council, Marshal Pétain, launched a demand for armistice conditions on 17 June, and from there also, on the 21st, the liner *Massilia* left for Morocco. It had been chartered some days beforehand with the prospect of a general transfer of the state authorities to continue the struggle for the territories of the empire. So several republican and patriotic former ministers and deputies embarked – Édouard Daladier, Georges Mandel, Jean

Zay, Pierre Mendès France – and were picked up and arrested on their arrival in Casablanca, and were very improperly represented as runaways or rebels by Vichy, which had meanwhile accepted the armistice. The armistice had been well and truly negotiated in a matter of days and signed on 22 June at Rethondes, the Germans' symbolic revenge for the one of 1918. Its clauses were harsh: France was divided in two principal zones, one *occupied* by the Germans (all the northern half of the country, extended towards the south-west by a coastal strip as far as the Pyrenees), the other called *free*, under the administration of the French government, which also kept the colonial empire. Moreover, France lost Alsace and Lorraine, which were reincorporated in the Reich; the Nord and Pas-de-Calais, associated with occupied Belgium and similarly under military rule, and the Ost Land of the Lorraine–Champagne borders. With the exception of a few categories, French prisoners of war remained in captivity (about one and a half million), the war fleet was to be disarmed and neutralized. The government of the free zone kept a small army of 100,000 men ('the armistice army') and paid a heavy charge for the occupation.

As we have seen, the clause on the fleet had worried the British government enough to provoke the attack at Mers el-Kebir on 3 July; a moral test for Free France, the episode also represented an increased disarray in public opinion, and perhaps a boost for the propaganda of the new government, whose new policy already smacked of a large dose of Anglophobia.

This government, however, did far more than change camp and change alliance. On 23 June Pétain brought Pierre Laval into it, with the rank of vice-president of the Council and in supreme control of an internal policy determined to adapt institutions to the new state of affairs.

However, they had to leave Bordeaux, which would be in the occupied zone. The government and public authorities went first to Clermont-Ferrand, chosen for its central position, then on 2 July were finally installed in Vichy, a town for taking the waters and enjoying leisure activities, crammed with empty hotels which were busily converted into ministries. Moreover, it was only a few kilometres from Châteldon, where Laval had his home. The name of Vichy thus entered French history, symbolism and almost political science.

It was there on 5 July that deputies and senators were summoned, gathered together in a common session under the (constitutional) title of National Assembly, in order to debate a revision of the Constitution proposed by the government. There was an idea in the air that imperfect institutions, whose shortcomings might have had a certain part in the defeat which France had just suffered, needed to be reviewed. But how far should such a review be carried? Laval wanted it to be complete and expeditious, and was able to get what he wanted by a complex game of cunning and menaces (the Germans were not far off, threatening mobs were booing former leaders of the Popular Front in the streets, and so on) against a general background of confusion.

On 10 July the Assembly voted for what had been asked of it: suspension of the constitutional laws, and the granting of plenary powers to the

Marshal Pétain reviewing officers from the Youth Camps in front of the Hotel du Parc in Vichy. June 1944. (Photo: Collection Viollet)

Marshal's government for the establishment of new ones. The suicide of the Third Republic was achieved by 569 votes, against 80 'noes' and 18 declared abstentions. 'The 80' (people would say 'the 80', as they had 'the 221' in 1830, or 'the 363' in 1877, other historic groups of friends of liberty, but *they* had been in the majority, winners . . .) who defended the existing Republic to the very last would afterwards be honoured for having played, as far as the law and political morality were concerned, a similar role to that of de Gaulle in the national sphere: saving its honour.

Twenty-seven of them were senators and fifty-seven deputies. Politically, there were three former Communists (who had broken from the party since August 1939), thirty-six SFIO (including Léon Blum, Vincent Auriol, Jules

Moch, Félix Gouin), twenty-six radicals, seven members of other left-wing groups and eight coming from the right.

In relation to the parliamentary strength which had been represented by the Popular Front, that number of eighty is minuscule. Even if one fictitiously adds a few dozen non-voters such as the Communists in prison or gone underground, or the twenty-seven passengers on the *Massilia*, or even the abstainers (among whom was Herriot), one still obtains only a small minority of the parliament.

That arithmetical decline, better than anything, reveals the measure of the chaos into which France had been plunged by the disaster. Seeing its effects on the political class, one gets a taste of what things were like in the country at large. On 12 July, however, Pétain transformed the episode into a veritable coup d'état since, by his first constitutional Act, he accorded himself in addition and without further ado the title of Head of State. Vichy then really took shape as a new regime. But what was Vichy?

It has remained in history as the 'collaboration government'. Collaboration with the occupying enemy. And when that enemy bore the name Hitler, such collaboration was laden with shame, or so it is usually considered. Perhaps the word should be relieved of that sulphurous notoriety, and the principal opprobrium defined in another way.

For de Gaulle, who, thanks to the success of his extraordinary gamble, has had his argument accepted by France and by history, the wrong lay first and foremost in the *armistice* and cessation of fighting. Very well. But starting from there, that is to say, starting from the point where a French government decided to remain on the soil of France in contact with the German army, collaboration with it became unavoidable and technically necessary (if for nothing else, for example, than to regulate the traffic, on the same railway lines, of German and French trains). Thus for some years now certain historians have proposed making a distinction between that necessary 'collaboration', imposed by force of circumstance, and admissible, from 'collaborationism', which is culpable. For there were actions (Montoire) and men who presented their collaboration as support for Hitler, acceptance of his victory and his future. There were therefore to be found in Vichy collaborators of the first kind, resigned, dedicated, who were none the less concerned, and collaborationists, who were the real accomplices of the Nazis. This story involved not only cruel necessities but also ideology in action. Perhaps emphasis should be placed on another aspect of Vichy, without any direct connection with the armistice and maybe more insidiously harmful: it was a real *change of regime, imposed on the people by virtue of defeat, invasion and the temporarily irresistible presence of a foreign army*. Is not that where the supreme immorality lies?

Have not the vast majority of the French, including those nostalgic for Vichy, from 1945 to 1989 daily blamed the Polish, Czech or Bulgarian Communists for having imposed their system on their nation thanks to the might of Stalin's army? Nevertheless, that was the essence of the 10 July operation, and the days that followed. French citizens, all of whose pre-1940 and post-1944 votes fully demonstrate a clear majority support for the republican form of government and the principles which underlie it, found themselves swung by surprise into an unprecedented regime, non- (or anti-) republican, and into a total ideological counter-revolution. From that bid for power two ineffaceable drawbacks would ensue – at all events, which the Liberation in 1944 would not manage to efface – two drawbacks with effects that are still perceptible fifty years later. On the one hand, a new deepening of the moral civil war between French people; on the other, the discredit cast even on the few good ideas which Vichy was able to include in its batch of plans or endeavours.

From then on France was known as the French State, and no longer as the French Republic, mirroring what had happened in Portugal in 1926 when the Republic gave way to the *Estato novo*. It therefore no longer had an allegorical face, but a real one, the head of Marshal Pétain replacing that of Marianne on the postage stamps as, in 1852, Louis-Napoleon Bonaparte's had replaced Ceres. The motto 'Liberty, Equality, Fraternity' was abolished. The Vichy politicians did not, however, dare to replace it with the triad of philosophical values which would have been its exact antithesis (authority? hierarchy? order?) and which represented their true thoughts. They preferred to advocate a trio of trite social values, which all Republics had tacitly respected and which had figured in the preamble to the Constitution of 1848: 'Work, Family, Homeland'. Thus the most elementary social morality found itself compromised with this famous trio. Even today, as everyone knows, any attempt to 'moralize', however timid it may be, is immediately accompanied by a suspicion of 'Pétainism'. Of course the French Revolution was held in contempt officially, in favour of the ancient France of paternalisms, corporations and provinces. The representative regime disappeared, replaced by appointment at all levels (provisionally, it is true; more complex systems were and would remain at the planning stage). A National Council, composed of several dozen appointed notables, was set up to take the place of the legislative authority to some extent. It would be installed but would never play any effective role. Lastly, with the rejection of state secularism, too marked by the spirit of the two centuries which were being repudiated, Catholicism was restored to an honoured position, grants to private schools were re-established, and the disputes over the difficult education issue were thus aggravated for a long time to come.

Last but not least of the significant acts, in October 1940 the statute relating to the Jews created discriminatory conditions affecting citizens of Jewish faith or family origin. That 'statute', further modified and worsened on 2 June 1941, and applicable to 'Jews of French nationality' defined them by a combination of criteria based on religion and origin (Jewish meant every person with three grandparents 'of the Jewish race', or only two

Exhibition: 'The Jews and France', Paris, 1941. (Photo: Collection Viollet)

grandparents if one's spouse also had at least two Jewish grandparents; or any person practising the Jewish faith even if he or she had only two Jewish grandparents). They were excluded from all public and elective office, their access to the university and certain liberal professions limited by *numerus clausus*. That would lead to the creation of a general commissariat for Jewish questions, and to the subsequent events which everyone knows, roundups, deportations – in short, the whole of France's contribution to Hitler's genocide.

At that time the armistice imposed nothing of the kind, and moreover the Vichy legislation was not an exact copy of that of the Reich. That is why the imitation of Hitlerian racism was doubtless held to be of less account than the old French nationalist ideology whose upholders had just attained power.

In the same spirit, and with the same odious consequences, anti-Nazi Germans who had taken refuge in France before 1939 as anti-Nazis, and were then interned in 1939–40 as . . . Germans, would be handed over to Hitler. Among them were many Jews. Their fate may be imagined.

How did such considerable volte-faces manage to gain acceptance? The explanation is that it happened by degrees.

The first stage to be accepted was the armistice, and that acceptance was massive and effective. A minuscule number of Frenchmen, and no ministers whatsoever, left to join de Gaulle in London. The French had laid down their arms and were making their way homewards, without protest. Carrying on the war, in unusual and adventurous conditions, plainly had no attraction for ordinary people, for whom the immense weariness of 1918 was once more having its full effect. Furthermore, that acceptance was not dissociated from confidence in Pétain, a man who was known to be rather conservative but who gave absolutely no indication of being a standard-bearer of the counter-revolution. Had not the Republic supported and honoured him, even making him a minister? And how could there be any doubt of the patriotism of a soldier?

Let it be added that Pétain's popularity was widespread because so many views converged in it. In the most chauvinistic version, confidence went to the 'victor of Verdun'; in the humanitarian version, to the commander-in-chief who was 'sparing of the blood of his troops'. Petain thus benefited *at one and the same time* from the attachment felt by the conservative-minded (the right, broadly speaking) for military leaders, and from the gratitude which the pacifist left, even if antimilitary, owed him for having minimized the cost. Praised by some as the author of peace, and by others as the *ex officio* Marshal of France, for many Pétain simultaneously enjoyed those two heterogeneous qualities, though in rather vague proportions.

The second acceptance lay in the agreement of the majority of deputies to revision of the institutions, an acceptance evinced in the vote of 10 July 1940. Besides the preference for armistice and confidence in the Marshal, for the political elite the idea of constitutional revision more precisely included a criticism of the functioning, or even the spirit, of the Third Republic, either as a result of the disaffection referred to in the preceding chapter or, more vaguely, because of the overall feeling of rejection of a 'regime responsible for the defeat'. Far too general to be fair, that feeling drew its strength from its simplicity. After all, in 1870 the budding Republic had benefited from it against Napoleon III. Must fear pure and simple be added to the reasons for the passivity of the deputies facing Laval? Fear of additional troubles if they tarried over the solution offered? Or fear of a very uncertain future? What alternative did they have? De Gaulle, of whose dissidence they were vaguely aware, still had the appearance – suspect in the eyes of 'good republicans' – of a career soldier who had appointed himself leader! And he was the protégé of the British, who had deserted the French at Dunkirk and caused their blood to be shed at Mers el-Kebir. There were therefore many elements which combined to influence what remained of parliament to turn over the page of the Third Republic and entrust to Pétain the task of writing a new one.

It was not the image of an amended Republic that was inscribed on this page but, by an immensely wide return swing of the pendulum, one of a sort of monarchy without a king, traditionalist and religious, somewhat evocative of Mac-Mahon's seven-year term, or of the pre-imperial year of the Prince-President, against a background of the mythical old France of pre-1789. For a time it too met with a certain public approbation, a fact which calls for a third set of explanations, or at least reflections.

To begin with, it must be said that the radically reactionary nature of the regime took several weeks to become apparent, whereas the grand declarations of intent likely to make it popular had been perceived at once. Stopping the fighting, first, then the announcement of the change in the regime, and lastly the intention of a 'moral recovery', all under the leadership of a nice old man willing to sacrifice himself despite his advanced years: 'I make France the gift of my person in order to alleviate her woes.' That could, and in fact did, find a favourable response even in that section of opinion usually influenced by the left. For the idea of 'moral recovery' itself was not new. After all, Victor Hugo and Jules Ferry had been great teachers of morality. It would take a while for these well-intentioned citizens to grasp that, in Vichy, it was not a matter of reactivating the exclusively social and civic morality of the Republic, but going right back to the overall Moral Order, with its religious foundation, of the time of Mac-Mahon. When it dawned on them, and they weighed up the official anti-Semitism and clericalism, when civil servants and mayors were dismissed simply for holding the wrong opinion, it would be too late; confronting them they would have an authoritarian and repressive regime, firmly in place, and there would be nothing left to do but hold their peace and wait. Thus, to take a classic example, the young men who were members of the officer training school founded at the Château d'Uriage (Isère) in the spirit of the regime by Dunoyer de Segonzac, a Catholic officer, would pass from the most official Pétainism to a voluntary dispersal, and thence to the Resistance, when they became aware of the certainty of the factual immoralities which were being perpetrated behind the proclaimed morality. But the tacit condemnation that came into being around the end of 1940 could not entirely efface the effect of the more explicit and almost unanimous support (or illusions) of the first months.

On the right, however, a number of citizens remained Pétainist for longer, because they were less shocked – or not shocked at all – by those antirepublican, or even simply antiliberal, reactionary aspects. The regime had no trouble in recruiting notables to replace dismissed republican mayors, to fill the ranks of the French Veterans' Legion, to sing its praises in the press. Crowds thronged to acclaim the Marshal on his travels without in the least being forced to do so. There was a whole area of France that Vichy did not shock, even after the statute on the Jews, or even after the meeting at Montoire. Its size had been rather overlooked because, under the Republic, many strongly conservative electors had voted for moderate deputies who were integrated into the system, to which they had adapted very well. But that republican right, in certain circles or certain regions, had apparently rested on an electorate which was less republican than its representatives, and to which Vichy gave the opportunity to reaffirm and recognize itself afresh.

In the absence of opinion polls and electoral consultations it is difficult to say more about the scope of those phenomena of public opinion. Lacking statistics, we have at least sketched out a rough typology.

Behind these trends were people. Who governed at Vichy?

Officially, Marshal Pétain, the Head of State: 'Marshal, Saviour of France, Behold us before you / We, your children, swear to help you and follow in your footsteps.' So began a hymn which was widely broadcast and sung, and which rapidly became a kind of unofficial national anthem. Propaganda did not invent any French equivalent of 'Führer' or 'Duce' for Pétain; he was sometimes referred to as 'the Chief', but more often 'the Marshal', plain and simple.

Was he really the chief? It has been questioned. Some have tried to lighten his responsibility by saying that he was senile; despite his appearance of fine bearing and good physical health, he is said to have had limited periods of clear-mindedness, only a few hours each day, and too little to have everything under control. Others, with the same purpose in view, have credited him with a Machiavellian, wait-and-see policy, patriotic at heart, bending before the storm and putting up with the Nazis and their French accomplices rather than associating with them. Several signs and hints bear witness to that, but it must be admitted that nothing of that kind ever went far enough to bend the system, much less to break it.

Marshal Pétain broadcasting at Christmas 1943. Radio communication played a decisive role in the war.

Pétain was not the prisoner or hostage of Laval or any of the 'vice-presidents of the Council and their designated successors'.[2] But whatever the degree of his actual capacities (very difficult to evaluate), he let them govern more than he himself governed. Chiefly, he supported them and clothed them with his prestige and popularity. Viewed from that angle, he certainly was a key figure in the regime with which his name would remain associated. Bearing in mind the judgements of French opinion on the politicians of pre-1940, it is indeed difficult to imagine the populace allowing itself to be bewitched and led by a man like Pierre Laval, a man who had come straight out of the 'harem'.

Furthermore, the appointment of ministers from parliamentary assemblies was exceedingly rare and, as it happened, Laval was the exception rather than the rule. For its successive governments Vichy recruited in two main categories – higher civil servants and intellectuals. Top grade civil servants, civilian or military, no longer surprise us, after 1958. With the Fifth Republic the French resumed their custom of seeing directors of education, councillors of state, judges and ambassadors become ministers

[2] Flandin and Darlan, whom we shall meet shortly.

in the administrative branch to which they belonged. But de Gaulle in 1958 would merely be resuming a Vichy innovation which, in 1940, went against nearly three-quarters of a century of republican parliamentary tradition. Thus great university men such as Joseph Barthélemy and Jérôme Carcopino would pass into the government, together with *polytechnicien* Treasury inspectors such as Lehideux, Bichelonne, Barnaud, and generals, admirals, judges and councillors of state, like Raphaël Alibert, the main theoretician.

Other ministers, neither civil servants nor deputies, came from various intellectual circles; journalists, writers and ideologists such as Paul Marion.

Vichy's personnel were as varied in their political shadings as in their professional origins. What was there in common, for example, between a French admirer and imitator of Nazism, a wealthy Catholic bourgeois from deepest France and a trades unionist like René Belin, who had emerged from the working-class movement via the route of pacifism and anti-Bolshevism? Very little indeed. It was therefore a complex world, split into coteries and crisscrossed with conflicts. A world which would know its own variation of government instability, the 'ministerial crises' of parliamentary origin simply being replaced by rebellions in the palais and intrigues in the antechambers, not to mention the defections of those who would eventually wake up to the system and its impasses.

How can Vichy be characterized, apart from its most glaring singularity, the person and the renown of the Marshal?

Can it be seen as a fascist regime? Once again, it all depends on the definition of the term. For the left, a regime at once reactionary in its aim and anti-liberal in its practice was obviously fascist. By contrast, for the right and the majority of political scientists, too many ingredients were missing in Vichy to allow it into the same category as the dictatorships of Rome and Berlin: no single party; no modernist populist doctrine; militarism and nationalism limited by circumstances; not even a true dictator because, although there was a leader and a cult of leadership, it is not certain that his power was entirely his alone; in short, it is impossible to claim a total likeness.

The absence of a single party deserves comment: a party, the voluntary association of men who choose to devote themselves to politics, is in itself a modern democratic phenomenon. And when a party wishes to seem popular, whether it belongs to Hitler or Mussolini, it cannot do without a touch of democracy in its style and a touch of populism in its programme. For those two reasons together, the real fascist party which Doriot or Déat could have provided for France was repugnant to the deep attachment to the past held by the ideologists and notables of Vichy. In contrast, their whole logic lay in staking all on the pre-partisan structures of traditional social influence, churches, notabilities, wealth, the employers. To them, however, was added a new elite, more natural than voluntary, composed of Frenchmen who had shed their blood: Vichy wanted to be seen as the regime of veterans. They were strongly invited to regroup their various associations into a single organization known as the French Veterans' Legion (LFC, Legion française des combattants), very soon to become 'the Legion'. Its official unanimity at first met with some success, to the point where, in the early days, militant veterans of the left sometimes accepted a local presidency.

There was the same ambiguity regarding the young people. Vichy no more created a single youth group than a single party. The Companions of France certainly formed a new movement, with a Pétainist slant, but scouting, or rather scouts' and guides' movements, survived. The regime regarded them as worth keeping or tolerable because they cherished aims which were often religious, or at the very least 'healthy' and educational. Thus a certain pluralism went on in that sector, thanks to a moralistic inspiration which was taken to be common. It was a far cry – as can be seen – from Hitler Youth or the battalions of Mussolini's young *balillas*.

Should Vichy be seen as a right-wing regime? If a positive reply arises more easily in this instance, it nevertheless requires us to make certain qualifications.

To the extent that Vichy clearly and explicitly takes its place against the characteristic values of the left – the principles of 1789, a democratic Republic, secular humanism, and so on – there is scarcely any ambiguity. However, that will not allow the establishment of equations: Vichy equals right and Resistance equals left. For a part of the left joined Vichy, sometimes as far as the government (René Belin), or allowed it to be set up (the

1939–45 war. Youth Camps. Group no. 37 at Gap-Charance (Hautes-Alpes). 'Bayard the fearless, beyond reproach.' April 1941. (Photo: Collection Viollet)

vote of 10 July). Conversely, part of the republican right which stayed patriotic did more than contribute to the national Resistance: with de Gaulle, it founded it, as it would later found more than one network of the internal Resistance.

There remains the undeniable fact that Vichy would compromise the right more than the left, because it would borrow the majority of its ideas and characteristics from the general system of right-wing values. Vichy was the extension of a 'revolutionary right' which circumstances had allowed to demarginalize itself, as well as the revelation of that portion of deepest France whose old counter-revolutionary culture had survived, covered over rather than destroyed by the liberal acclimatization and official humanism of pre-1940.

Many were the prelates who, delighted with taking revenge on official secularism, spoke loud and clear in favour of the Marshal (Cardinal Gerlier, Mgr Feltin and plenty of others). Rarer and less heard were those who helped the persecuted and condemned the repressive laws (Mgr Salièges, Mgr Théas, Mgr Rémond). Under Vichy, the old, frankly conservative, sometimes royalist, clergy would give voice to what would be their swan song, while the new Christian democrat clergy were still in the shadows, when they were not in the clandestine opposition, like P. Chaillet, editor of the *Cahiers du Témoignage chrétien*.

It was therefore the French right wing that Vichy divided most bitterly and most lastingly. When the day came, in 1944, the left would easily dissociate itself from those of its adherents who had been collaborators, presenting them as traitors to their principles and exceptions, whereas the patriotic right could not so easily treat the Vichy right as a misguided minority. The strength of numerical evidence contradicted it. It was rather the case that Vichy, for four years, and with some appearance of reason, was able to label the right-wingers who had gone across to London or gone underground as gullible fools who had strayed into the camp of the 'Communist', 'secular', 'Jewish' or 'Anglo-Saxon' enemy.

Lastly, there is the most pertinent question: was Vichy antinational? Again the answer is yes, but with essential reservations.

It is perfectly certain that in Vichy (and Paris) there were people for whom France was finished, negligible, and for whom the only prospect was that it should merge into Hitlerian Europe in order to wage the planetary war against 'Bolshevism' and 'Anglo-Saxon Jewry'. They could not be elsewhere than in that camp.

Pierre Laval, with his pessimism and scepticism, did not distance himself much from that line of thought. Patriotic at bottom, but convinced of Germany's victory, he concluded that the only worthwhile struggle consisted of being adaptable and using every possible means of limiting the damage.

For other Vichy men, or those supporting Vichy with voice or pen, like the influential Charles Maurras, the principle of nationalism was not defunct; if, for him, France remained something of value, Europe an illusion and Germany a worrying power, his systematically and comprehensively counter-revolutionary doctrine had given him such a low idea of the France of post-1789, and still more of post-1848, that he saw no possible future for it outside the counter-revolution. Thence arose the concept of seizing the opportunity (the 'divine surprise') which presented itself to apply the remedy, with the 'national revolution'. For want of a monarchy, at least the lifetime chief, Pétain, would restore the principle of authority, deemed to be superior to the disastrous principle of holding voting rights. Governing with civil servants and officers, he restored to a place of honour the principles of order, state, discipline, therefore unity (the antithesis of the parliamentary system of parties and the dispersal of power). By restoring traditional morality, Pétain was putting France back on the right track, that of the only conceivable recovery. But that boiled down to making the future of France subject to a return to Charles X or Louis XIV. The most argued about and the most logical of the justifications for Vichy was finally revealed as the most utopian.

To that it was easy for de Gaulle and his followers to reply that this was merely a dream cut off from the real world, while France was actually part of the Europe of Hitler, who at the moment was crushing it and would soon drag it with him in his downfall. The only effective French nationalism would therefore be the one that would set France back in the camp of liberty.

Among men from the right, among nationalists, what was chiefly at stake in the argument could be clearly expressed in terms of a gamble on the future. And when it became evident that Vichy had made the wrong bet, that was when disaffection set in.

For the essence of the history of Vichy perhaps lies less in its own actions than in its relations with opinion. That requires a word or two on its vicissitudes.

Pétain and Laval governed to begin with, and their first six-month term (July–December 1940) was their apogee. The regime was set up, got its institutions in place and affirmed its authority; on 23 September it inflicted a real setback on de Gaulle and the British by holding on to Dakar.

It openly declared itself a 'collaborator' with Germany. The word was launched at Montoire, where Laval, on 23 October and then the Marshal, on the 24th, met Hitler in person. The handshake they exchanged was symbolic; for history, after the armistice and the vote of 10 July, it gave the regime a sort of third seal. However, the Marshal's entourage was divided: Laval had enemies and rivals, who persuaded the Head of State that he was negotiating on his own account, that he had contacts with extremist collaborators in Paris, and that he might be tempted to seize sole control. On 13 December Pétain therefore dismissed Laval, and even had him arrested. The Germans demanded and immediately obtained his release.

Nevertheless, Pétain entrusted the vice-presidency to another former deputy, Pierre-Étienne Flandin. The latter seems to have tried to carry out a more moderate and less pro-German policy. He rapidly became convinced that it was hopeless, and resigned on 9 February 1941.

Pétain at once appointed as vice-president of the Council, Minister of Foreign Affairs and his designated successor Admiral Darlan, who would last fifteen months (9 February 1941 to 18 April 1942).

This clever, energetic naval officer, very hostile to the British, completely upheld the Montoire undertaking. Economic collaboration went ahead in full (payments of money, commitment of labour). Even a form of military collaboration, at least symbolic, was sketched out.

The war became global. On 22 June 1941 the German army invaded the USSR, then on 7 December the Japanese attack on Pearl Harbor caused the Americans to enter the fray. In France, on 11 July 1941, the Legion of French Volunteers against Bolshevism (LVF) was formed, destined to fight alongside the Germans on the eastern front. On 5 November those Frenchmen wearing Nazi uniforms were honoured by a message from Pétain. In France itself, where we shall soon see the Resistance begin its struggle, the Vichy regime accordingly took action. On 14 August 1941, it created special courts of justice causing the reappearance in French history, in defiance of the famous separation of powers, of the actual subordination of justice to politics, and of general law to the exception of the moment. A regression which would not be without a future . . . In the same period, the government instituted the selection, from the core of the French Veterans' Legion, of groups of men who were more strongly committed in favour of the regime. These groups were organized for action, armed and called the Service d'ordre légionnaire (SOL) – a significant step, the outcome of which we shall see.

Finally, Vichy took steps to strengthen its moral authority by confirming the discredit of the republican regime it was replacing.

On 19 February 1942 in Riom, there began the first hearing of the proceedings instigated against those 'responsible for the defeat', that is to say, the leaders of the Popular Front governments, Léon Blum and Édouard Daladier in the front rank, and with them some top civil servants. But those two statesmen, together with their fellow accused and their barristers, defended themselves with courage and precision and won the battle: they demonstrated convincingly that their governments had taken the German threat seriously, increased military funding and rearmed, and that the weakness of the French battle corps had its origins far more in the passive and routine governments (most frequently conservative) which had preceded them, and in the untouchable military hierarchs, whose chief was Pétain. The trial rebounded so well against the accusers that on 10 April 1942 it was suspended without a verdict, and the defendants were sent back to their place of custody.

Some days later, on 18 April 1942, Darlan was dismissed from favour. Apparently he was over-fond of manoeuvring and had in his turn become suspected of playing a double game. Pierre Laval made his comeback, with the new title of head of government, Pétain remaining Head of State. Had Darlan begun to envisage that the war might take a different turn and tried to obtain other forms of insurance? As for Laval, he had faith in German strength and undertook to adapt France to it. He negotiated, bargained, and encouraged the departure of the French workforce for factories in the Reich in exchange for the release of certain prisoners of war: the 'relief exercise'. In the radio broadcast announcing it he made the famous statement, 'I hope for Germany's victory', because without it Bolshevism would invade Europe. Laval was doubtless not mistaken in thinking that the majority of the French feared Bolshevism. Nevertheless, that 'I hope for Germany's victory', declared with some solemnity by a French head of government, sent a shock of surprise and disapproval through French opinion that he had not expected. It was precisely against Hitler that 'France' – however vague its collective expression might now be – felt itself to be at war. That war would constantly affirm its presence and consequently reinforce the evidence of hostility.

On 8 November 1942 the Allies, whose main force in the West had become American, succeeded in landing in Morocco and Algeria and holding on there. With northern Africa, the Americans and British now held the southern Mediterranean. The German army had no option but to go itself to control the northern shores. So, on 11 November, it invaded the free zone. A few days later the armistice army, some of whose members (General de Lattre de Tassigny in Montpellier) had shown an attempt at resistance, was dissolved. On 27 November, however, the Germans suffered a setback. That part of the French war fleet moored at Toulon, which they could have seized, was scuttled.

The war's presence was now visible across the whole extent of French national territory. It was a further step.

In spite of distance, another large portion of France must figure in Vichy's institutional extension – the prisoners of war. The 1940 blitzkrieg had not been very lethal (100,000 dead all the same, a small number only when compared with 1914–18), but it had surrounded many units netted from the rear in huge hauls, notably those of the Maginot line. With the exception of a few releases by category in insignificant numbers, one and a half million men went to spend nearly five years in Germany, in stalags (camps for other ranks) or offlags (camps for officers). It was a massive phenomenon, and far more noticeable than captivity had been in 1914–18, when the front gained all the attention. The prisoners' living conditions were very varied. Some men made them almost tolerable by taking charge of the internal management of their collective life, or adapting well to the outside rural work on which they were employed. Others escaped. Yet

Collaboration in its most brutally unbearable guise. (Top) On the practical side, discrimination measures of a racial kind: one of the children's play areas set up in Paris in November 1942. The notice reads 'Banned to Jews'. (Bottom) On the symbolic side, shaking hands with Hitler, here much magnified, on the occasion of the anti-Bolshevik exhibition at the Salle Wagram in Paris, March 1942. Under the mural, among the personalities at the opening, is Fernand de Brion (in uniform, flanked by two German officers). (Photos: Les Actualités photographiques Internationales)

others, who had been recaptured after previous escape attempts, were harshly treated in punishment camps. There were moral differences too: some were susceptible to propaganda from Vichy, which kept an ambassador (Scapini) whose special task was this liaison; others spontaneously organized within the camps forms of propaganda and education in the spirit of resistance. The important choice lay before everyone.

The third quarter of the disjointed nation was the occupied zone, with Paris in the forefront. Civilian administrations were dependent on the ministries established in Vichy, but from Paris the Germans, with their occupation forces, controlled the centre of communications and had their own forces of repression and policing. To their high command, Vichy was represented by a sort of ambassador, given the title of 'general delegate', an office whose longest-lasting holder was Fernand de Brinon. Political activities between Paris and Vichy were rarely revealed in broad daylight. On one solitary occasion, 15 December 1940, there was a spectacular gesture of conciliation, arising from the obscure bargainings going on at the time of Laval's departure: the Germans returned to France the remains of the Duc de Reichstadt ('l'Aiglon' – the Eaglet – son of Napoleon), exactly one hundred years after the return of his father's ashes.

The occupied zone had its own political situation, by all the evidence more sensitive to the war and therefore less vulnerable to the illusions of that free and almost normal France which Vichy would give over to its renewal treatment. Above all, Paris was a pole of influence over which Vichy had hardly any hold. This was the place where that extremist collaboration made its presence felt – the collaboration which found Vichy too lukewarm and which Vichy, for its part, found compromising. Here appeared *Je suis partout* (I am everywhere), whose radicalism was to *L'Action française*, from which its editors had come, what Parisian politics were to those of Vichy. Here Jacques Doriot ran his French Popular Party (PPF) while his rival Marcel Déat created his Popular National Assembly (RNP). These were the two principal strands of a French fascism, in the minority but strongly resolved on both collaboration with Nazism and reproducing several of its examples. They were different from the traditional, personalized and archaistic conservatism of Pétain, whom they despised in the main, and against him they constituted the goad of adverse criticism and the threat of a policy of replacement which the Germans might be able to implement. They were of course at the forefront of the LVF.

It was in Paris that the Jews caught the full force, and with the least chance of flight or protection, of the lash of Nazi anti-Semitism, marching towards the 'final solution'. From May 1942, they were compelled to wear a yellow star sewn visibly on their clothing. And on 16 and 17 June 1942, with the assistance of the French police, the enormous roundup took place of over 12,000 people – men, women and children – destined for concentration camps.

Paris, finally, is the special place in which to recall the cultural world.

Intellectual and artistic life was as much upset as any other kind by the war and occupation. A certain number of writers and artists, either by happenstance or deliberate choice, lived through those difficult years outside France, generally in America. Jules Romains, Saint-John Perse (Alexis Léger), Jules Supervielle, Louis Jouvet, and Antoine de Saint-Exupéry, who would return in 1944 to take part in the Free French air force and meet his death, are only the best known.

Division into zones favoured a certain decentralization, because many Jews, well-known left-wing intellectuals and antifascist foreign refugees thought they would be less threatened in a free zone than in an occupied zone, which was true for a while. As Vichy was a very small town and filled with political and administrative offices, the role of intellectual capital of the free zone was played by Lyon.

There, René Tavernier launched a fine and free literary magazine, *Confluences*. Charles Maurras had transferred the editorial offices of *L'Action française* there. Other university towns must not be forgotten, such as Clermont-Ferrand, which housed the teaching profession of Strasbourg, or pleasure resorts and traditional places of retirement, like Nice, not to mention the more modest centres formed by chance because they contained the home of a brilliant, influential or active man, for instance, Carcassonne, around Joe Bousquet, or Villeneuve-les-Avignon, around Pierre Seghers. And not forgetting Algiers, even before November 1942, where Max-Pol Fouchet brought out a poetry review, *Fontaine*, and which soon became a focal point of independent thought. Regardless of all of them, Paris remained the centre.

In spite of departures, persecutions and having to go into hiding, which in the end affected only outstanding but not very numerous groups, there remained in the capital a whole population, a whole clientele, a whole range of trade associations, for whom the university, the theatres, bookshops and museums had to continue with their activities. Furthermore, the Germans wanted 'Paris' to go on as before. They did not want to create the impression that, because of what they had done, Paris would lead the lacklustre life of Warsaw, but rather the normal life of Vienna or Rome. For intellectual and artistic France, Nazi policies thus had two complementary aspects: the repressive aspect symbolized by the famous Otto list (a list of works or authors banned for having 'poisoned French public opinion'), but also the attractive aspect. To the latter, Otto Abetz, a cultivated and high society Nazi diplomat, longtime French speaker and Francophile, devoted his abilities. At the invitation of the Reich, writers and artists made study trips to Germany; German diplomats and officers assiduously patronized the big restaurants, theatres and all cultural events. The peak was reached in May 1942, when Paris, to the accompaniment of much propaganda and celebrations, played host to an exhibition of the works of the Nazi sculptor Arno

Breker, the disciple and friend of Aristide Maillol. Paris, therefore, went on – and went on shining brightly. As its brightness, on which the Germans set such store, smacked for that very reason of collaboration, the spirit of resistance might in principle have advocated a boycott. Sheer utopia! The world of literature, art and the theatre, the publishing and leisure activities trades could not afford to practise asceticism without committing suicide. People had to live, or survive. That was what made it so extremely difficult to 'purify' those areas. Between the collaborationist intellectual, pro-Nazi by conviction, and the young music hall artiste who, earning his crust by plying his trade, played a tiny role in German festivities, by way of society people whom politeness to this or that friend constrained to attend a party where there might also be the friend of a friend who might be Abetz – every degree of compromise existed.

There were contradictions everywhere. Sacha Guitry, for example, could continue in 'Germanized' Paris to exercise the role of society royalty that he had acquired, but also showed himself capable of making use of it to obtain the release of Tristan Bernard, who had been arrested as a Jew. There were therefore courses, concerts, paintings and published works; the prestigious NRF (*Nouvelle Revue française*) reappeared, Jean Paulhan only handing over the editorship to Drieu La Rochelle. The Comédie-Française performed, and it was even during this period that Montherlant's *La Reine morte*, Cocteau's *Renaud et Armide* and Claudel's *Le Soulier de satin* were created. Sartre also made his debut in the theatre with *Les Mouches*, a tragedy in the classical style, unobtrusively libertarian, but slated by the press and a flop. It was staged at the Théâtre de la Cité, the new compulsory, 'de-Jewified' name given to the Sarah-Bernhardt Theatre.

The cinema, amid a thousand difficulties and contradictions, managed to produce some brilliant and unforgettable masterpieces: *Goupi-mains-rouges* and *Les Visiteurs du soir*. The geography of art and culture, which over the past century had seen its main focus leave the Latin Quarter and the big boulevards for Montmartre and then Montparnasse, experienced its last great migration, towards Saint-Germain-des-Prés. That was partly the result of the misfortunes of the times, with their economic hardships. Apartments were difficult to keep warm, so many budding or future authors came to write, from morning till night, their drink in front of them, at the tables of the Café de Flore or the Deux-Magots, which had good stoves. Born out of shortages, that sociability would last.

This new intelligentsia, amongst whom J.-P. Sartre, Albert Camus, Simone de Beauvoir and Boris Vian were beginning to stand out, was both 'Parisian' in its behaviour and nonconformist (therefore resistant) in spirit. That was one of the dominant tones in this circle, where the most widespread was without a doubt a policy of 'wait-and-see'.

Though in a minority, there were more marked commitments. As early as December 1940, at the Museum of Mankind, an active resistance group had been formed, which was soon hit by arrests but which had provided French science with its first martyr for patriotism (Boris Vildé). Founded and run in complete secrecy, with the difficulties that may be imagined, there was also the resistance of the 'Éditions de Minuit' enterprise, through which the writer and artist Jean Bruller, borrowing his pen name of Vercors from the most celebrated of all the maquis, produced his *Le Silence de la mer* in February 1942. 'Minuit' went on to publish, under pen names, work by Aragon, Chamson and Mauriac.

The left-wing intellectuals of the 1920s and 1930s were scattered between Paris, the southern provinces and overseas, also split morally between the two by now irreconcilable values of antifascism and peace. They were, moreover, obviously deprived of the classic collective forms of expression afforded by the free press and fly-posting. When they at last regrouped, their press was clandestine: 'Éditions de Minuit', already mentioned, and *Les Lettres françaises*.

By contrast, the part of the right and extreme right that had become collaborationist could speak freely. Its press took pride of place (*Je suis partout, La Gerbe*). Its members even gathered together in large numbers on 9 March 1942, the day after a murderous aerial bombardment of Parisian suburbs by British planes, for a demonstration of anti-British fury which turned into an apologia for pro-German politics. There the most impassioned extremists – Robert Brasillach, Phillippe Henriot, Abel Bonnard, Céline, etc. – rubbed shoulders with right-thinking conservatives such as Maurice Donnay or Jean de la Varende, who were more famous at the time but more moderate. But it would be pointless to multiply the lists of names. In the world of literature, science and the arts, as in every other circle, any classification or picture made at one moment would be false the next day. Positions would change with time and awareness. André Malraux, who in the spring of 1942 thought that all one could do was wait, was to take part in armed action in 1944 in a south-western maquis group.

Finally, the picture is completed by one last section of the population, invisible, underground and at first tiny in number but whose importance the future would reveal – the Resistance, already called to mind a little by an inevitable anticipation.

Resist – the word speaks for itself. But in its precisely accepted form 'Resistance' entered history through the appeal of 18 June ('the flame of French resistance will not be extinguished'). For de Gaulle, the Resistance was originally organized in London; so mention is sometimes made of 'external Resistance' and 'internal Resistance' to distinguish between those who respectively fought outside and inside France. In fact, it was more usual to say 'Free France' for the fighters in London and overseas, and plain 'Resistance' for people and groups acting clandestinely in French territory. That is what we shall do here. The Resistance and its members would in any case be so called only after they had achieved a certain renown, and chiefly by themselves before history adopted the name. They were also happy to be known as 'patriots'. The official world of Vichy described them more in vague and would-be offensive terms, 'Gaullists', 'Communists' and (after they had become active), 'terrorists'.

Its members were few. It was in the nature of things, and it would be ridiculously unfair to compare the tiny minority of fighters in the 1940s with the mass of soldiers of 1914–18. During the First World War, an official, supervised and organized war, the norm for an adult male was to go to the front, and it was desertion which constituted the exceptional, and in some respects courageous, act.

By contrast, in the Second World War, going to war (whether by leaving for London or plotting) was something out of the ordinary and blameworthy, and thus was a voluntary act, nonconformist and dangerous. Dangerous for oneself and perhaps for one's family. It was therefore the act of an elite or someone outside the mainstream of society, especially before 1943 (for a reason we shall see). Not everyone is capable of transforming himself into a rebel, especially in that society brought up in the Third Republic, in which a truly civic respect for legality and official matters was far more widespread than in our day.

Perhaps there was another reason for the meagre numbers who made the choice. To become involved it was necessary to reverse the initial currents of opinion which found Vichy acceptable, and also to re-examine the slightly older tendency which found war unacceptable. Chiefly on the left, where pacifist influence had been deep. One Christian militant,[3] who had been antifascist and pacifist before 1940 but would be convinced in 1943 that his duty lay in taking part in the physical fight against Hitler, would be conscious of making a veritable renunciation of his nonviolent convictions. He did so, and died for it, without managing to persuade all his former fellow-believers of the rightness of that reconversion. For them, and they were many, the Resistance was the *Patrie* again, rifles again, sacrifice again – a kind of return to 1914. Many of those who had been traumatized by 1918 could not bring themselves to do it. To overcome that last conditioning required a physical, moral and also intellectual courage of which not all potential antifascists were capable. The weakness of the Resistance thus resulted in part from the delayed effects of the great wound of 1914–18.

Members of the Resistance were of a special kind. They were doubtless prepared – though here we are in a realm which has eluded history – by having a certain psychological aptitude, a certain type of temperament. Of two men holding the same opinion, all else being equal, who can say why one should be content merely to approve of militant action while the other goes as far as engaging in it? They would also often have been prepared – and this view is supported by certain former Resistance members themselves – by rather atypical situations of life, training or career, and consequently more drawn to the unusual. After all, in the pre-1940 army, de Gaulle himself, because of his relentless attempts to persuade the

---

[3] Jacques Monod, *normalien* of the rue d'Ulm, *lycée* teacher, confirmed Protestant.

politicians about his system, had been a 'black sheep' rather than a representative officer.

Although not everyone was made of the stuff of heroes, at least the heroes had friends. Alongside the militants engaged in the active networks and the major risks they ran, mention must be made of the sympathizers who, fairly vaguely informed, created a circle to which the activists could sometimes have recourse: for shelter, or more usually as a 'post-box', or for concealing documents.

Resistance fighters came from all walks of life, bringing with them very different motivations. For some, the fight was mainly a matter of patriotism: the German enemy had invaded France, as in 1914, and once again it was necessary to try to get rid of it. For others, the fight took on an essentially moral definition, the enemy being Hitlerian 'fascism', whose inhumanity was the absolute evil. For others, the evil they perceived originated in France, being identified with Vichy reaction and counter-revolution, whether or not it was called 'fascist'. If some Resistance members felt themselves to be fundamentally republican and blamed Vichy for 10 July 1940, others, in contrast, whose political thinking was not so far removed from that of Pétain, principally blamed Vichy for having built itself on the back of the German foe. Among the civilians, in the general left-wing sphere of influence, those who were particularly motivated were the radicals and socialists who had best preserved the old republican culture, following the example of 'the 80' (anti-2 December, anti-Badinguet, anti-Moral Order, anti-whites, etc.). And on the conservative side, precisely those who had begun to detach themselves from the conservative bloc, that is to say, the Christian democrats. The classic historical accounts of the 1930s are too often dominated by the cycle of the Popular Front, and there is a tendency to overlook the bitterness of the polemical struggle which set the old right against the new trend of Catholic democracy, whereas it was really one of the deepest lines of cleavage in recent French history. Thus, when Vichy had given the impression that Action française would become the inspiring force of the regime, *L'Aube* and its circle threw themselves into the Resistance in great numbers, with François de Menthon, the numerous Teitgen family, Georges Bidault, and a whole group of lawyers and university men, chiefly around Lyon and Montpellier.

Where did they meet, those men and women who had come from every kind of political persuasion and inspiration? And what were they going to do? Certain deeds in the summer of 1940 seem to be not so much precursors of the Resistance as the last desperate bursts of the June campaign. For example, the action of the solitary Achavanne in Rouen (sabotage, for which he was shot by the Germans on 6 July).

Others swiftly embarked on intelligence work, to the benefit of the British military command which was able to set up its own networks.

The majority, however, those who felt the need to do something, had to begin by establishing contact with possible associates, for one cannot conspire on one's own! It was a difficult quest, first because France, following the war and exodus, was profoundly disorganized: homes and jobs had changed, and so on. Secondly, because under conditions of dictatorship, one cannot ask someone to contemplate a forbidden act without sounding out his feelings beforehand, and with some cautiousness. It was for that rather special kind of getting in touch that the verb 'to contact' was coined and entered into common parlance. Having 'contacted' friends, the first thing to do was get out propaganda leaflets, to take the place of an opposition press, reminding people of the evils of Hitlerism, denouncing those of the occupation, giving true news about the war, talking about London, etc. At first, Resistance would for a long while be a matter of buying paper and using a roneo hidden in some alcove or 'borrowed' from some administrative office.

For immediate direct action was swiftly revealed as costing too high a price. On 11 November 1940, in occupied Paris, patriotic students of all political creeds managed to gather at the Arc de Triomphe (the tomb of the unknown soldier) and begin a procession down the Champs Élysées. They were greeted by rifle shots, imprisoned and deported, and proved, involuntarily and heroically, that some other form of action would have to be taken.

Thus networks were formed, first and foremost clandestine, the main ones being in occupied zones: 'Ceux de la Résistance', 'Libération Nord', the 'Organisation civile et militaire', the 'Armée secrète'; and in the southern zone, 'Combat', 'Franc-Tireur' and 'Libération Sud'. Names began to emerge: those of the Christian democrats, already mentioned; those of Henri Frenay, Emmanuel d'Astier de la Vigerie, both former soldiers, and Pierre Brossolette.

What did they do? In the first place they got themselves organized, and learned to cover their tracks, inventing or reinventing 'rules of secrecy': assumed names, making false identity papers, putting strict limits on the number of personal relationships and acquaintances by the compartmentalization of base groups, changeable and mobile meeting places, how to detect if one was being 'tailed', carrying no compromising papers, keeping everything in one's memory, training in covering long distances on foot, in endurance, disguise, cunning. For what action? Putting out propaganda material, certainly, but also seeking and maintaining contact with kindred networks and chiefly with those of Free France; the Resistance could in fact help allied military action by collecting and passing on observations on German forces of occupation and their military installations. Part of its initial activities thus involved the stuff of classic espionage.

Another part consisted in moving and helping to move those who wanted to leave for London, whether from Brittany by boat, or later from northern Africa via the Pyrenees and Spain (hostile), or from anywhere at all in France by means of a small plane from London, making a secret landing on an improvised runway; this was how anonymous people who wanted to fight were helped to leave, and then later this method was used by political notables who had decided to get to London where their abilities and, above all, their former renown would help Free France by giving it their backing. But help was also given to threatened noncombatants, Jews or foreign refugees, to depart for overseas or rural hiding places.

Yet another part consisted in physical battle against the enemy military forces by sabotaging this or that installation, electricity cable, vehicle depot. Having learnt how to work a roneo and make a false rubber stamp, Resistance members learned to use explosives. Little more was done before the end of 1942 . . . apart from a final apprenticeship, in enduring barbarity. For Resistance activity was repressed immediately it was located, by Vichy or the Germans, according to the time and the place. Repression was not merely a matter of putting an end to the activities of such and such a person and inflicting such and such a punishment on him; efforts were always made to find out from the arrested man or woman about the activities of his associates and network. The one interrogated naturally refused, denied or lied; the enemy (for he was one, far more than a judge) therefore made every effort to wrest the truth from him or her, and in this way and at that period systematic torture – to its most atrocious and sometimes lethal degree – made its reappearance in French history, after a century and a half of almost total exclusion. Its rebirth would not, alas, be confined to the summer of 1944.

The Germans adapted to 'underground' fighting, and not just by investigation, interrogation and torture; they had their specialists in the battle against the networks, their infiltrated agents, their spies, their traitors who had been 'turned'. Thus, in the underground war, unscrupulous adventurers rubbed shoulders with heroes, and situations worthy of a crime novel were elevated to the level of great history.

Resistance fighters came from every kind of background. There were those with no political past or clear political awareness but who instinctively maintained their patriotism; right-wingers in the nationalist tradition, for whom anti-German nationalism had ranked before conservatism; republicans in the liberal, radical or socialist tradition; Catholic republicans (the Christian democrats). Communists too – but they must be considered separately, without any preconceptions, since their politics obeyed its own laws and had its own particular nature.

They are all the more deserving of special consideration because they had the longest experience of clandestinity, dating back to the banning of their party in September 1939.

In June 1940, the party was thus extremely weakened, first of all because, dumbfounded by the glaring contradiction that the Germano-Soviet pact of nonaggression had inflicted on the antifascist line which had filled them with enthusiasm, a very large number of militants and even deputies (nearly twenty) had abandoned it; then because mobilization and the war had deprived it of many male militants and officers in the prime of life; and lastly because the ban, surveillance and repression, one after the other, had made it difficult for those officials who had escaped arrest and gone underground to keep it functioning. In addition, there is the fact that management maintained uneasy communications with Moscow, where Stalin had demanded that Maurice Thorez should settle, for which he had been branded a deserter – for he too had been in the army – which had cost the PC dear in terms of unpopularity. Would the PCF resist? And whom?

Stalin appeared to have drawn the conclusion from Munich that the antifascism of the British and French was very timid, or nonexistent, that the USSR could not by itself take on resistance to Hitler and that some sort of accommodation must be reached. Hence, the pact of 23 August 1939. Coming to an arrangement with Hitler for just as long as it would take to prepare for war was in fact one possible interpretation of that event. But Stalin and the Internationale (the same thing, in effect) had given the impression that this turning point was more far-reaching, and a return to the pre-1934 phase, when Germany appeared tolerable while French and British imperialism constituted the main enemy. In France that had not bothered the old party leaders; on the contrary, it had revitalized them.

During the war and the collapse the PCF had thus appeared to be in a state of total chaos which, even today, makes any generalization questionable. Militants serving with the colours had fought at their posts against the invaders with above-average keenness (from ancestral and instinctive patriotism or continued antifascism?); some were quick, after the armistice, to circulate anti-German agitation publications (Tillon in the Bordeaux region as early as June 1940); in contrast, other highly placed members, just after the occupation of Paris, went to the Nazi occupiers to ask for the right to publish *L'Humanité* again (Duclos, Tréand, also in mid June 1940). That overture met with failure, because of the Germans and because of Vichy. The PCF then resolved to remain underground, to try to regroup its officers and launch propaganda denouncing both Vichy, as the new embodiment of capitalist power in France, and London as foreign imperialism.

It was only gradually, as it re-established its contacts with the people, that the party realized how far the aspirations of its rank and file were moving in an anti-German direction. In particular, the working class of the Nord and Pas-de-Calais lived in conditions that were specially difficult in all respects: they were badly provisioned, when a miner's life is so hard; German oppression was particularly noticeable (the region was detached from France – bad memories were revived of the harsh occupation which had been endured in 1914–18). Clandestine trades unions and the party readily embraced the political trend and in the spring of 1941 organized a protest strike by the miners which might well be considered implicitly patriotic, and which gave the PCF a claim to resistance prior to 22 June 1941.

For on 22 June 1941, Hitler's aggression against the USSR rudely brought Stalin back to what was once more the number one enemy. Henceforth, now that the period August 1939 to June 1941 was put in parenthesis, the PCF could resume the thread of its antifascist patriotic line. The majority of its young officers would blossom once more. A small nucleus of loyal members had managed to get through those three years of dramas and enigmas by pinning their faith on the Revolution, above and beyond the ups and downs; on the leaders, who knew what they were doing; and on the party spirit, a powerful successor to the class spirit.

From then on the PCF was well and truly in unison with the other currents of French Resistance. It was distinct from them, however, because of this late entry, which immediately, and for thirty years to come, would give birth to many polemics. It also distinguished itself from them by a singular activism. On 21 August 1941, in the heart of Paris (at the Barbès-Rochechouart métro), a small group led by a young worker called Pierre Georges (later known under the name of Colonel Fabien) attacked a German officer and shot him to death with a revolver. The loss thus inflicted on the army of occupation was obviously derisory. It was therefore either symbolic (but symbols count!), or else intended to widen the general fight by setting in motion the cycle of repression–indignation–combat. That was what would in fact happen, but at what a price! The Germans retaliated by executing hostages: fifty for one. The mass shootings of political prisoners in Châteaubriant, Nantes and Bordeaux (end of October 1941) figure among the events of that war. But in one sense they also added to the difficulties of the Resistance, for hardly had it become substantial, diversified and active when it experienced internal tensions with regard to methods and strategies.

The PC was 'radical' in the methods it advocated, for which its very nature gave it the means: it had at its disposal activists who were often 'international', immigrants from eastern Europe and therefore trained in clandestine work, inured to tough battles with the dictatorships and police of their former countries, strongly motivated, frequently further trained for physical fighting in the International Brigade of the Spanish War. But tactically it was moderate, in the sense that henceforth its propaganda would push patriotic defence rather than the class struggle; in May 1941, at the time of the miners' strike, it launched an appeal to the 'national front', thus rediscovering the existence of potential patriotism among the bourgeoisie and Christian circles.

> The man who believes in Heaven
> The man who does not believe
> Both adore the Beautiful Prisoner of the soldiers.

The first two lines of this verse by Louis Aragon would really catch on. It went far beyond the famous 'hand outstretched to the Catholic worker', which dated from 1936 and was part of a simple class struggle logic (all workers share the same interests). Here, the logic was meant to be national – all French patriots shared the same values. As in 1935 Communist discourse had brought back Valmy and republican patriotism, so here it opened the way to rallying Joan of Arc. But that goodwill on the part of the Communists affected or softened only a fraction of their partners. It annoyed quite a few others. It is a fact that the PC was just as worrying when it was being peaceable as when it was extremist. Already the polemics of post-1944 were looming on the horizon, and not just those of 1939–40.

The course of the Second World War began to change.

In November 1942, with the Allies holding northern Africa and the Germans occupying the former free zone, the war had moved close and oppression was omnipresent. A new period began which would alter the history of each of the four parts of the country.

Vichy carried on, run by Pierre Laval under the continued backing of the Marshal. There was still great instability among executives, ministers and top civil servants, but henceforth Laval would choose some from the 'reservoir' of extremist collaborationism in Paris; for example, Philippe Henriot, a former extreme right deputy before 1940, whose daily propaganda speeches on Radio Paris had a brilliance and ardour which for a time made them very effective. Vichy was becoming weaker, however, for want of any important international links; the USSR and American ambassadors had now left. Above all, Vichy was gradually losing its most important link, that which it had established with many French people at the time when they had felt relieved by the armistice and protected by an old leader who would take care of them. It seems that, little by little, from the middle of 1941 opinion began to swing. As the war became general, it was impossible to believe that Germany would win. In the summer of 1941, an almost triumphal German advance into Russian territory had been halted before Moscow. In the summer of 1942 Hitler's troops had carried their offensive farther south and obtained more spectacular successes, reaching the Caucasus and the Volga. But in October 1942 it seemed that they were marking time and that the town of Stalingrad, in the bend of the Volga, might well prove to be the Red Army's Verdun. And lo and behold, one month later the Americans were in Algiers! It was impossible not to realize that Vichy had wagered on the wrong horse.

Furthermore, Vichy could no longer boast that it protected the French population from the conflict. The Germans were now physically present everywhere. Economic impositions aggravated the hardships. Everything was rationed, everything was in short supply, there were food ration cards, monthly allocations of 'coupons', 'points' to authorize the purchase of small quantities of goods of all kinds; official provisions, which were often mediocre, were sometimes lacking because the available stocks had vanished from the legal circuits to resurface on the black market.

Women queuing for lipstick. (Drawing by Pem, Salon des Humoristes. Paris, February 1944. Photo: Lapi-Viollet)

This is an important point: during the occupation, Frenchmen who were neither members of the proletariat nor unemployed experienced food shortages. During the occupation, two sorts of underground existed – of patriotism and trafficking. During the occupation some of the simplest forms of the class struggle were rediscovered, there were the former or newly rich who bought and sold on the black market, and there were the ordinary folk, on fixed incomes, or with certain scruples, who suffered shortage and want.

Vichy had not even been able to keep France separate from the war, because the latter sometimes . . . fell from the skies. The British and Americans had in fact developed their air forces tremendously, and an essential part of their operations consisted in hitting the German war machine in its factories and communication lines. Some of these were situated in France. In 1943 it was no longer out of the ordinary to see French towns being bombed. Of course, when they killed French civilians those 'blind' American bombs were exploited by Vichy propaganda, but these efforts at moral counteroffensive by the official government could not offset the overwhelming evidence: the French knew that they were held and pressured by an enemy army which was going to lose the war and a government which was losing face. Those who fought against the Germans and Vichy were by now slightly more numerous, and increasingly cruelly treated when they fell into Nazi hands.

If the vast majority of French people, who had remained passive with a wait-and-see attitude, did not have to suffer direct experience of Gestapo barbarity, they certainly heard about it! Having in fact become distrustful of the Vichy regime and the newspapers that served it, the population listened on a massive scale, despite jamming and interference, to the broadcasts in French from the BBC, Free France or Radio Geneva (neutral and impartial, but fairly anti-Nazi). The French wanted true news about the way things were going; they obtained it, and into the bargain learned about the executions, deportations and tortures of which they had no personal knowledge and which the collaborationist press concealed or denied.

The regime thus grew weaker, lost its audience and, conscious of the increasing hostility it was arousing, grew more rigidly defensive. On 30 January 1943 the Service d'ordre légionnaire was renamed the French Militia, strengthened its paramilitary organization, its armaments and mobility to become an instrument of war against a Resistance whose reality could no longer be refuted. The Militia which, by its origins, brought together the toughest and most convinced of the regime's political partisans, who had therefore most often come from the extreme right, was reinforced by new recruits tempted by sheer adventurism. Under the direction of Joseph Darnand, a small-time contractor in civilian life, it rapidly acquired a pretty sinister reputation for efficiency and cruelty. From the institutional point of view it was a bastard entity, being something of a complementary police force, and something of a single party. The existence and practices of the Militia would admit the proposition that, if Vichy had not been initially fascist, it was at least tending to become so.

Laval, however, pursued his logical line of helping Germany. On 16 February 1943 his government set up a Compulsory Labour Service (Service du Travail obligatoire, or STO) applicable to three groups of youngsters who had not done military service: the classes of 1940, 1941 and 1942 could be made to 'serve' in German war factories. It was a decisive measure: in effect it imposed on several thousands of young people the clear choice between active collaboration by leaving for the STO, and active resistance, by refusing. It offered the maquis an unexpected and substantial recruitment pool.

During the last two years of the occupation and the Vichy regime, the Resistance thus changed in its turn, because it drew new forces from the growing disaffection of the public and the reaction of a section of French youth anxious to flee 'labour deportation'.

That is what gained it new militant, or even military, resources. But new problems as well: it had to get itself organized, improve connections with London, debate strategies and future programmes, and prepare for the liberation that was by now sure to come. The Resistance could no longer confine itself to a romantic 'shadow army', it had to develop a real 'internal policy'.

Since the beginning of these activities, the militants pinpointed by the police and therefore obliged to 'disappear' had been living from hiding place to hiding place, in the homes of friends or in rooms rented under a false name, helped by the anonymity of the big towns; experiences evoked by the French word 'clandestinité' or the English word 'underground'. But as their numbers grew, it was necessary to find another sort of refuge, completely different, which would allow them to live in bands, off the beaten track, where they could camp or hide if the need arose, where the police hardly ever came and where the local population – scattered but not totally absent – would accept or tolerate them; in short, mountains, forests and peasants who would help. In other words, the sort of countryside for Robin Hood, Mandrin or Jean Chouan. The terms used did not, however, refer to any of these precedents, and the metaphor that prevailed was borrowed, goodness knows through what route or on what intitiative, from the folklore of the 'Corsican bandit': 'prendre le maquis' or 'to take to the bush'.

It was in this way that the name 'maquis', borrowed from the vocabulary of geography and botany, entered the vocabulary of history. There had been 'maquis' in Savoy (the Maurienne valley) as early as 1942, and they had made an appearance in Limousin at the beginning of 1943, but their expansion dates from the spring of 1943 and the flight from the STO. The phenomenon chiefly concerns the Massif Central and the Alps, regions which, fifty years ago, were much less provided with good roads and less abandoned by the farming population than they are today. If the worst came to the worst, the maquisards could share the crude life of the peasants there, and receive arms by parachute drops which passed unnoticed in well-chosen isolated spots.

But what could they do in those refuges? Wait around doing arms drill and making use of these areas of scrub as training grounds, and then, when the time was right, rise up for a national rebellion? At first the Communists

thought the establishment of such large camps somewhat premature because, situated in out-of-the-way places, they hardly made any immediate
impact on the German war machine and could therefore only play a waiting
game. Furthermore, they would be very vulnerable when the Germans
came in force to encircle and attack them. Their preference lay in having
groups of fighters hidden and dispersed among a dense population, gathered
together for an efficient strike and then hidden once again while they waited
for another opportunity for harassment, a tactic that was better adapted to
the urban lower classes.

In fact the Communists too had rural maquis because they were not
without influence in certain of the appropriate regions: Limousin, Cév-
ennes, Haute-Provence. Tensions between Resistance members with regard
to the maquis did not stem only from problems over their composition and
use, but also their weapons. The Communists complained because the
maquis under their control (known as FTPF, Francs-Tireurs et Partisans
français, Irregulars and French Partisans) were less favoured in the parachute drops of arms than the secret army of maquis, whose officers were
often bourgeois and military.

But that brings us to another major problem of the Resistance – the
ulterior motives they attributed to one another over the liberation struggle
and the political effects of that disunity. The internal politics of the Resistance cannot be reduced to a conflict, only too evident a priori, between,
on one side, a bourgeois section which identified with de Gaulle and
traditional patriotism and, on the other, a popular section inspired by the
PC. The majority of the movements, whether composed of more or less
apolitical patriots, republicans from the secular, radical or socialist left, or
Christian democrats, were capable just as much of opposition to the Communists, when they seemed too influential, as to the London men when
they seemed too imperious. They were a veritable third force before it
properly existed.

All those elements met in the great concern of 1943: unification. Real
communications, precarious and dangerous though they were, had finally
been established between London and the underground (secret routes,
improvised runways for departures, parachute drops for the return). General
de Gaulle had gradually learnt that there were resistance fighters, passionately dedicated, not very numerous but spread through every region and of
all beliefs and persuasions, and formed into various networks and movements. At the end of 1941 he had made Jean Moulin his general delegate
in occupied France, with the mission of unifying the Resistance.

Jean Moulin, born in Béziers in 1899, was a prefect, a secular republican
of radical socialist tendency, like the majority of the members of that body
before 1940. He was, moreover, a man of refinement and taste, keen on
painting. There was something else in his heritage which, from a distance,
might be taken as symbolic: his father, a teacher in Béziers in the 1900s, a

Dreyfusard and keen republican, had been the initiator of the monument erected to the local victims of the coup d'état of 2 December in his small town. From one Resistance to another, in a manner of speaking; that kind of connection would be claimed more than once in the 'red Midi'.

Meanwhile, during the 1940 campaign, Jean Moulin, prefect of the Eure-et-Loir, had already made his mark. A man with a sense of duty, he had done his best to ensure the material wellbeing of his town of Chartres, from which the exodus had drained most of the public services, while refugees in confusion had flocked in from Paris and the north. On 17 June the Nazi invaders, who had come up against some resistance on the part of a French military unit made up of black soldiers, tried to foist responsibility on the latter for oppressive acts against civilians, and get their accusation confirmed by an official proclamation signed by the prefect. Jean Moulin, convinced of the falsity of the imputation (the corpses that were shown to him were riddled with shrapnel, the obvious and commonplace victims of bombings), refused to sign, despite pressure of a violent nature which went as far as blows and solitary confinement. It was then that he tried to commit suicide in order to be sure of not yielding should the pressure be resumed still more violently. His throat cut by slivers of glass, he nevertheless survived and on the morning of 18 June was brought back to consciousness and released. The fanatical Nazi officers who, even in the eyes of their commanders, had gone too far in this affair did not press the matter. The Pétain government, which was set up at that juncture, could do no less than acknowledge the professional conscience, courage and dignity of this prefect, and kept him in his post for several months before dismissing him for 'offences of opinion' (too many Masonic and republican connections). Jean Moulin then joined the underground, went over to London and, eventually, engaged in another and final encounter with the Nazis and death.

In the meantime, his name would be attached to the unification of the Resistance; it was even a dual unification: between the movements themselves, and the whole of their clandestine organization with the man in London. That successful undertaking officially created the renown of Jean Moulin; unity was a good thing in itself and moreover 'unity means strength'; it was, however, to inflict on his memory a slight which has still not been cleared. A certain survivor of the Resistance[4] would one day point out that the transformation of the amorphous masses of the Resistance into at least a vaguely unified apparatus had made it easier for the best-organized of its components, the Communist Party, to work its way into the posts created, and thus into several key positions, and to gain too much influence. It made it seem as if Jean Moulin had acted as an accomplice of Communism. Such a thing is not believable, let us admit, if only because it rests on an error of reasoning: the fact that a decision has produced a certain result (among others) does not mean that it was conceived *in order*

---

[4] Henri Frenay, in *La Nuit finira*, R. Laffont, 1974.

to produce that result. Nevertheless, that controversy still carries on in French history, together with other more directly dramatic ones that we shall meet later.

The unifying enterprise had in fact succeeded, after months of slow and complex progress, meetings and partial consultations, rare and perilous discussions, such as were imposed by clandestine conditions. In 1943, 15 May witnessed the birth of a National Resistance Council (Conseil national de la Résistance, or CNR), in which all the organized Resistance movements acknowledged one another, and which linked them with London. Jean Moulin combined the function of de Gaulle's general delegate with that of president of the new clandestine body. A unified institution was similarly planned for combat: the French Forces of the Interior (FFI), whose initials marked their parallel status with de Gaulle's army, known as Free French Forces (Forces françaises libres, or FFL). In fact, although an FFI staff was set up at the summit, there was no system in place to facilitate an amalgamation in concrete terms of the basic elements or effect any changes at all. The Communists, for example, in the maquis under their control, contented themselves with sporting a complicated set of initials – FFI(FTPF).

Another problem reared its head, that of the political parties. They were banned by Vichy, and there was no election to nurture their existence. Discouragement and sometimes conversion to Pétainism took many men away from them. In contrast, certain of their militants, of patriotic spirit, rallied Resistance movements. Others, however, dreamed of renewing the links between their scattered friends in order to reconstitute or maintain a specific partisan organization. Did there have to be parties in this clandestine France which prefigured liberated France? Two answers could be offered. For some, yes, it was necessary because the future France would be democratic, and there can be no democracy without debates, voting, organized competition and consequently parties to frame and express each of the currents of opinion. For others, on the contrary, liberated France would be pure and pristine, rid of the discredited regime of before 1940, and thus of their politicians, rituals and methods. Only the elites and structures picked out by the Resistance would have the authority to run the country, as any other form of government would carry the risk of re-establishing its old bad habits together with itself. The question was decided in favour of parties, and was the solution most in harmony with national traditions and also with the spirit of this war. After all, the war was really a crusade of liberal democracies (thus more or less parliamentary and multi-party) against 'fascist' regimes (with parties banned or just a single party). Liberated France could hardly go against it. The CNR thus officially comprised representatives of Resistance movements, affiliated trades union groups (the CGT united underground, the CFTC) and lastly parties: Communist, socialist, popular democrat and – without a precise

name but represented by former patriotic deputies – the forces who had
come from the old parliamentary right.

It set itself a broad and progressive programme. Though the restoration
of classic politics, with its consequent partisan organization, could pass for
traditional, other points revealed an innovative and bold ambition. Great
political reforms would be accomplished, more pressing concern would be
shown for social justice, yesterday's victims or forgotten ones, women or
colonial peoples, would be treated more fairly, stern action would be taken
against the powerful rich who had put their own interests before those of
the nation; of course, traitors would be severely punished and Germany
would be 'de-Nazified'. It was a very advanced programme but, in the
enthusiasm of the times, unanimous. *The programme of the CNR* would be
a dazzling banner, and we shall see how it was used.

Its application depended on circumstances and the balance of power. In
principle, the CNR had overall responsibility for study committees, which
also maintained direct relations with London and made concrete preparations for the replacement of the existing authorities when the liberation
came, ranging from the filling of ministries to providing for regional, departmental and local authorities.

The composition in terms of personnel of these new structures was
influenced by two factors, one classic, striking a balance between the rival
collective forces (movements and parties), bearing in mind their representativeness and abilities; the other, accidental – but the accident often
happened – the capture of a leader by the Germans or the police, necessit-
ating his replacement. 'The Song of the Partisans', composed in London
by Joseph Kessel and Maurice Druon, was to become a sort of second
French national anthem:

> Friend, do you hear
> The low cry of the country in chains?
> Friend, do you hear
> The black flight of the crows over the plains?

'The Song of the Partisans' expressed it well, in moving terms:

> Friend, if you fall
> A friend will emerge from the shadows to take your place.

But the friend who emerged from the shadows was not always of the same
hue as the one for whom he was the improvised replacement. Amid the
grief of disappearances and deaths, the internal life of the Resistance,
increasingly political in step with the approach of victory, thus assumed the
air of an ever more complex network of schemes, risks and sometimes
rivalries.

The most dramatic of those disappearances took place at the very top.
On 21 June 1943, during a meeting at Caluire (a suburb of Lyon), Jean

Moulin and several other leaders with him were captured by the Germans, who had obviously been tipped off. By whom? By what traitor? Or as a result of some indiscretion? It is argued about to this day.

Jean Moulin died under torture shortly afterwards, without revealing anything to his torturers. In 1964 national gratitude would confer on him the honour of interment in the Panthéon.

The CNR had to meet to replace him and provide itself with a new president. He was the leader of the Christian democrats, Georges Bidault.

His qualifications were genuine and the trend he represented important. Why should it not also be recognized that the choice was already explicable in terms of the political spectrum? Between the forces which were heirs to the Popular Front, socialists, various *laïques* (committed to secularism), Communists, on the one hand, and, on the other, Resistance members who had come from conservatism and were inspired by traditional patriotism, the Christian democrat group was well and truly placed, and before its time, in the centre of the spectrum. Georges Bidault would still be in office at the time of the Liberation.

From London, General de Gaulle followed these events, movements of opinion and adjustments in the balance of power. Free France gradually filled out with new arrivals. Henceforth there appeared on the scene people with a past, who were well known, and even given a mandate by an entire political trend: SFIO socialists (André Philip), moderates (Louis Marin), radicals (Henri Queuille). In January 1943 the PC itself sent its representative (Fernand Grenier). These tendencies and people gave London the same problem as the constitution of the CNR: would not those men wearing the labels of Third Republic parties distort the image of Free France and commit the Liberation to being a kind of restoration of before the war? In 1942 voices were raised also in London to say that parties should disappear. But de Gaulle did not heed them. He was well aware that in the United States President Roosevelt, as a good democrat, was very suspicious of the leader of Free France, a soldier by profession and self-designated political head. What would happen if, in addition, a single party were recommended in this Free France? What de Gaulle needed was that the part of the old republican 'establishment' which had remained patriotic should be seen by the Allies to give him its backing. An old radical notable like the president, Queuille, might not please some romantic young Resistance fighter in France, but in London he was of great use to Free France by confirming that he embodied the continuity and future of a republican France.

All this combined wisdom did not produce an immediate result, however, because it took Free France six months to obtain the means to transfer from London to Algiers, or in other words, to pass from the state of a group of exiles to that of a government in its own capital. On 8 November 1942 the Allies, under orders from the American General Eisenhower, had managed to get a foothold on the coasts of Morocco and Algeria (Operation Torch). A minute number of secret Gaullist Resistance members in Algiers had tried to help them. But their patriotic action was far less noticeable and far less important than the three days of military resistance which the armed forces put up against the landings, under orders from Vichy (General Noguès and General Juin). Then they had ceased fire. In fact, Admiral Darlan happened to be in Algiers, for private reasons. A former collaborator of the first water, but now in disgrace, he had apparently wanted to put himself completely in the clear by taking the lead in what was becoming inevitable: the swing of northern Africa to the allied camp. This recantation was given a warm welcome by the Americans (locally, General Clark) who came to an understanding with him (22 November). The patriots of long-standing, the Gaullists, were indignant. On 24 December Darlan was assassinated by the young Bonnier de la Chapelle (a Gaullist patriot from a very small group which is suspected of encouraging him and being directed from a distance by a more substantial body. Which one exactly? That is still being disputed).[5]

The Americans, however, did not give up their search for a French soldier to take on the role mapped out by Darlan, so mistrustful were they of de Gaulle, who seemed to them to be too awkward and too much surrounded by revolutionaries. The role sketched out by the Admiral fell to General Giraud. He had a patriotic past, having escaped from captivity in Germany and then deliberately left occupied France. He was a high-ranking soldier, theoretically apolitical, that is to say somewhat conservative but, by the same token, well placed to gain the sympathy of professional army men and the majority of the French in Algeria. His rather right-wing image stood him in equally good stead, on the whole, with the politico-social forces dominating in Algiers and with the American authorities. For de Gaulle, on the other hand, Giraud was a quasi-Pétainist coupled with an usurper; the man in London had on his side the precedence of his combat and the links he had forged with those fighting in France, plus the support of Churchill (even though the latter was discreet, in order not to jeopardize the indispensable *entente* with American allies). The politics of Free France would thus, for several months, take on the aspect of a conflict between the two generals, Giraud and de Gaulle, supported respectively by Washington and London, and each by a group of French personalities.

In January 1943 a first contact at the interview in Anfa (a residential suburb of Casablanca) between the four protagonists, Roosevelt, Churchill, de Gaulle and Giraud, still did no more than commence a compromise. There was a new meeting in Casablanca at the end of March. Free France was to be two-headed. At the end of May, in fact, de Gaulle and the French National Committee installed themselves in Algiers. The two generals were co-presidents of the Committee and Giraud, in addition, was commander-in-chief of the FFL. The silent struggle to gain influence continued worse

[5] Free French secret service? The Comte de Paris's clique? British secret service?

than ever, reaching a climax in November 1943 when Giraud resigned, leaving de Gaulle as sole president. In contrast with a Giraud too tainted with Pétainism and American allegiance, de Gaulle was more representative of the specific spirit and the independence of the national struggle, could pride himself on the support of the internal Resistance, and compelled recognition of the superiority of his talent as much as of his worthiness.

The Communist Party alone, very conscious of the strength and independence of de Gaulle, seems to have had an inclination for a while to back Giraud as a sort of counterweight, but had quickly abandoned it. The PC, in Algiers, represented a not inconsiderable force, despite having an influence that was very weak among the colonials (or Europeans), and only just dawning among the natives. There was certainly no lack of officers or militants, because the successive governments of Daladier and Pétain had made use of prisons and army camps in southern Algeria for the internment of numerous Communists arrested in France in 1939 and 1940. After the American landing, Giraud had had to make up his mind – not without some hesitation – to release them, as victims of pro-German oppression, and they had stayed there.

In Algiers, from the autumn of 1943 to the spring of 1944, a unified Free France, under the undivided presidency of General de Gaulle, assumed increasingly complex structures: not only did the French Committee of National Liberation (Comité français de Libération nationale, CFLN, its new title) function as a real government, whose ministers simply bore the name 'commissaires' (commissioners), but it also had in opposition to it a representative and deliberative instrument known as the Consultative Assembly, to which representatives of all forces (movements, parties, trades unions) engaged in the Resistance had appointed their own representatives. A sort of broader equivalent of what the CNR had been in the underground in France. Many of the underground leaders, moreover, with the consent of their members and the backing of Algiers, left France to come and take their seats.

This political system intended to be unitarian, with none debarred: there was a Communist group in the Consultative Assembly, and two Communist commissaires in the CFLN (Billoux for Health and Grenier for Aviation). Thus, the policy of national union had brought the Communists farther than the Popular Front had been able to: they were sitting in a non-revolutionary government. The Allies recognized this French system as legitimate. From the British point of view, it was a matter of course, through continuity with London; then the USSR followed suit; and finally the United States at the end of August.

Algiers worked. In its various bodies, appointments of future officials were studied, in preparation for the Liberation – in liaison with the work of the underground committees. General legal decisions were also carefully worked out. Ordinances specified the abolition of laws and decrees emanating from Vichy, looked on as a *de facto* government, without legitimacy; another ordinance announced the extension of voting rights to women (April 1944).

It seemed accepted that future French politics would be both republican and renewed; the expression 'Fourth Republic', revealing that double objective, appeared on 14 July 1943. It was still no more than an indication of intent, the constitutional problem remaining in its entirety.

Algiers waged war. The FFL was by now recruiting widely among the youth, both European and native, of northern Africa. Thus was formed the army which, on the orders of General Juin, fought in Tunisia before the dazzling campaign in Italy. In September 1943 the commando force of the future General Gambiez landed in Corsica and liberated the island by supporting the rebellion of the maquis: it was the first liberation of a non-colonial French territory, foreshadowing the hoped-for joint operations of the FFL and FFI.

Lastly, Algiers was preparing for the future in another sense, by anticipating what was taken for granted by Resistance members and patriots alike: the punishment of treason. Chance provided an outstanding example. Pierre Pucheu, former Secretary of State for the Interior in Vichy, having fallen from grace, had left France and via Spain reached Morocco to try to join the Free French Army. An act of volte-face and rehabilitation for which he had the backing of General Giraud, but not of General de Gaulle. When de Gaulle won, Pucheu found himself not in a barracks but in prison, accused of collaboration. As he had been a minister at the time of the first executions of hostages by the Germans, he was supposed to have designated by name those prisoners to be shot; he defended himself against the charge, but unconvincingly, and many Resistance members, chiefly Communist, demanded his head. He was sentenced to death, de Gaulle refused a pardon and he went to the firing squad in March 1944. It was the beginning of the purge and all its dramas. The stormy chapter of the Liberation was already opening.

Part III

The Transformation of France
1944–1992

9

Liberation
Summer 1944 to Spring 1947

Liberation – the word is hallowed, and today filled with popular, euphoric and noble connotations. In its first sense, 'Liberation' means the end of enslavement, in this case the end of the German occupation. It thus designates the series of combined operations of war and revolt, from the allied landing of 6 June 1944 to the symbolic march of the head of Free France through Paris on 26 August. But the term was broadened to encompass the whole period, lasting two or three years, that it opened and determined; in short, to the point where it signified the initial phase of the Fourth Republic.

For the Republic was replaced, with the refusal to resuscitate the Third which had been abolished on 10 July 1940. Since Algiers, had not a better and different Republic been promised? At the end of August 1944, with the disappearance of Vichy and the Third Republic not re-established, the provisional system transferred from Algiers to Paris might well be considered as the Fourth Republic in its temporary (and pre-constitutional) phase, exactly as earlier Republics had had their provisional phase: the Third, from 4 September 1870 to December 1875, the Second, from 24 February to 4 November 1848, and the First, from 21 September 1792 to Fructidor Year III. The Fourth, not without some trouble, would have its Constitution in November 1946. It would not assume its lasting political features until a little later, with entry into the cold war, at which point this chapter will find a natural close.

The years 1944–7 were also obviously the start of a post-war period, and one which was on the whole victorious. But did people really feel, in those troubled years, as if they were in the afterglow of victory? They would scarcely dare to say it, so distant did it seem from the atmosphere of 1918.

The fact was that the present war had ended twice: once with the Liberation, on varying local dates (most often summer of 1944, sometimes later), depending on the place; the second time, officially and as a whole, in May 1945, when Germany finally capitulated. As a result, this war had lost out on its symbolic outcome: it had not aroused the equivalent of 11 November 1918, simultaneous, unanimous and explosive. Commemorative ceremonies – the French realize every year – are divided between local liberation celebrations, which are staggered according to place from mid August to mid September, and celebration of the German capitulation, the official 'victory', on 8 May. Because of that division, if for no other reason, neither 25 August nor 8 May is a serious rival, either in the official calendar or the collective consciousness, to 11 November. The latter lives on, like an autumnal 14 July or a secular double for All Souls' Day. The Second World War did not really replace the First in the depths of French consciousness, which is why it has made less of an imprint on French folklore.

It must be added – a second point of difference – that because the 1939–45 war, unlike that of 1914–18, had not brought about the commitment of the entire population, neither had it plunged every family into anguish and mourning. Those mobilized for the campaign of 1939–40 were either overshadowed in the collective memory by the extraordinary nature of the Vichy/occupation episode, or reduced to the passive role of prisoners of war. As for the participants in 1944, Free French soldiers (a minority of volunteers), fighters in the Resistance or the maquis (another minority of volunteers), those engaged in the campaign of winter 1944–5 (yet again volunteers, and thus again a minority), plus two small categories of mobilized troops, the men of northern Africa and the 1945 contingent on mainland France – all of these put together did not form a batch of combatants involving the whole population, as had the immense army of 1918.

Less involvement, then. Less euphoria also, for the single-mindedness of the joy of 11 November 1918, however brief and illusory it may have been, could not happen again. There was in fact a third difference: the war that ended in 1944 or 1945 was something of a civil war victory. Certainly, 1914–18 had not completely abolished the class struggle, or created total unanimity with regard to the national war effort, but at least the enemy had not had whole sectors of French society as its collaborators. The occupying forces in 1940 had found them in plenty, and the victory of 1944 had been achieved against them as well, so that national rejoicing was darkened and hardened by the accompaniment of an experience from the distant past: purges. A not inconsiderable part of post-1945 France would be made up of those who felt vanquished, and the vanquishers whose victory tasted bitter.

One final difference: the victory of 1945 was tinged with anxiety. The vast majority of the French in 1918 had believed themselves to be not only citizens of the strongest military nation in the world, but also inhabitants of a universe which had suffered too much from war to dare to begin it again. Only a few clear-sighted minds had swiftly gone beyond those two illusions – the illusion of military might and the illusion of the 'war to end all wars'. By contrast, in 1944, with victory on the horizon, even the least informed French person had already had the opportunity to hear distant rumbles about Stalin's vast 'Russia', and feel close at hand the generous but invasive United States. So how could they go on believing, as they had in the time of Poincaré, Foch and Clemenceau, that France still held the controls of world machinery at its fingertips? Such was the general state of morale on emerging from the conditions of war.

Between June and December 1944 one of the most chaotic and dramatic periods in the history of France unfolded; six months of battles, sudden new developments and crises, in which a spectacular peak was reached with the swing of central political power at the end of August (Pétain and Laval left Vichy on the 20th, de Gaulle arrived in Paris on the 25th).

It all began on 6 June with the success of Operation Overlord. Coming from England, on the orders of the American General Eisenhower, the allied forces (chiefly American, but also British, Canadian and Free French) gained a foothold in Normandy, to be more precise on the Calvados beaches which they reached by sea and by parachute. They managed to establish a bridgehead and thus to receive reinforcements, but the Germans put up such very stiff opposition that, for more than a month and a half, a land front established itself around a pocket of a few square kilometres, going from Troarn to Sainte-Mère-Église by way of Caumont. This zone, which was fought over with land and air bombardments, would in a matter of weeks become one of the most ravaged corners of France. De Gaulle, who had hastily gone back from Algiers to London after 6 June in order to be nearer the front, was able on 14 June to pay a symbolic visit to Bayeux, the first liberated sub-prefecture in mainland France.

The sixth of June naturally gave the signal for the uprising and entry on the scene of the maquis, with a clearly defined strategic objective: to attack the occupying forces, pin them down and above all hinder their progress along the roads, causing them to make detours or preventing them from getting to the Normandy front, thus assisting the Allies who had gained a foothold there. A good number of ambushes and encounters, chiefly in the south-west of France, contributed to this diffused battle, and General Eisenhower would acknowledge that by this means he had received help equivalent to that of several divisions.

It sometimes happened, however, that the news of the landing on 6 June unleashed hopes of a rapid victory and, on the part of the maquis, a premature attempt to liberate the small town in their area. Swiftly forced to evacuate by the arrival of a German force, they left the population a prey to reprisals (the ninety-nine who were hanged in Tulle, for example). During those two months of warfare (June–July) which was bitter but split up into distinct episodes, the occupying troops were still capable of holding the Normandy front, getting reinforcements to it, although with difficulty, confronting the maquis and even launching attacks to wipe out those who seemed the most substantial and most dangerous. And all that with a brutal resolve, unsparing of the civilian population. Out of those two cruel months

The ruins of Caen, March 1945. Caen was liberated by the Allies on 9 July 1944, after five weeks' fighting.

emerge two episodes which have become symbols: Oradour (Oradour-sur-Glane, Haute-Vienne, 642 inhabitants of both sexes, including children, shot or burnt alive in the church which was set alight) and Vercors (a maquis of 4,000 men, besieged, conquered and obliterated, together with the civilian population of a village which had helped them). Oradour was inscribed on the already long list of Nazi atrocities; Vercors, in addition, was a kind of large-scale war operation, a pitched battle with a strategic role, and on that account posed a problem to the Algiers Committee. The Commissaire for Air, Fernand Grenier, a Communist, claimed that Vercors should be helped by aerial intervention which could be – and then, which could have been – employed; General de Gaulle thought otherwise, and compelled Grenier to submit to the humiliation of a retraction, which caused the first political crisis in the government of Free France.

Then the allied force won the day, in two new strikes which came very close to each other. On 30 July, an American land offensive (General Patton) broke through the German front in Normandy at Avranches and began a rapid advance in the direction of the south-east and east, as far as the loop of the Loire and the town of Orléans. And on 15 August, another air–sea landing operation allowed the Allies to penetrate into Provence in the sector of Saint-Tropez, Saint-Raphaël, Fréjus, and the Maures and Estérel shores. After surrounding (and quickly taking) Toulon and Marseille (28 August), this force, which included the First French Army of General de Lattre de Tassigny, reached the valley of the Rhône and followed it in the direction of Lyon. To avoid being trapped between the arms of these two converging thrusts, the German forces in all the western, central and southern regions of France hastily evacuated towards the regions to the north of the Seine in order to rebuild a front, leaving behind only troops who were well entrenched in the 'Atlantic pockets' (notably the peninsula of the Verdon with Royan and Saint-Nazaire). For the greater part of France, the last fortnight in August and the first few days of September would therefore be the period of liberation, this time definitive.

It was a simultaneously cruel and euphoric period. It was war, with the Germans savagely on the defensive and still on occasion meting out harsh treatment with or without their accomplices: the killings of imprisoned former ministers Jean Zay and Georges Mandel, the latter in reprisal for the execution by the Resistance of Philippe Henriot, the killing of Victor Basch, etc. But it was accompanied by the total disorganization of daily life caused by the cutting of means of communication as railways and bridges were shattered by aerial bombardment or by acts of sabotage. These impediments to transport aggravated still more the shortages of essential goods, from flour to fuel. Fear, of present dangers and sometimes also of the future; tension, linked with malnutrition, the heat of the season and the extraordinary nature of the period people were living through, all combined to produce very extreme feelings and very unusual behaviour.

It was by then certain that the Germans had lost the fight in France, and consequently – no one doubted it – so had Vichy. But who was going to pick up the abandoned power?

Free France? The Resistance? Both of them, because for some time already they had planned and organized their co-operation. It was understood that each liberated region would be headed by a commissaire of the Republic, armed with full powers, delegated by the provisional government which had appointed him in advance. In fact, it was expected that France would be liberated piece by piece, and the commissaires of the Republic thus unable for some while to establish their lines of communication with the de Gaulle government. Thence arose the need to temporarily vest its authority in these trustworthy and meritorious commissaires (about twenty in number), who had been given almost dictatorial powers. In short, they were regional prefects with strengthened authority. But as the superprefectoral office, which has become familiar to us, was then known as a Vichy innovation, it was better not to use the title. 'Commissaire of the Republic' – a term which came from 1848 – was a good indication of the temporary nature of the mission, and its left-wing connotation. These commissaires had to rule in contact and in agreement with Comités départementaux de Libération (CDL, Departmental Liberation Committees) which had emanated from the internal Resistance, were collegial and composed of an equitable balance of opposing forces (Resistance movements, and reconstituted parties and trades unions).

This new authority, born of the Resistance, 'Gaullist' in the broad sense of the word, confident that Vichy would be rapidly swept out, had cause to fear competition from two other sources, the Communists and the Americans. It was known that the allied command had in readiness a military administration department to manage the liberated European countries: the AMGOT (Allied Military Government for Occupied Territories). That would be the equivalent of being placed under supervision, which was not necessarily essential and was contrary to French sovereignty and dignity alike. On the other hand, there was room to fear a priori that, in the somewhat revolutionary nature of this situation, the Communist Party, whose official doctrine was after all revolutionary too, would try to seize power. Those were the facts.

The battle to brush AMGOT aside was easily won. The commissaires of the Republic took up their posts hard on the heels of the liberating armies; the CDL emerged from underground; provisional sub-prefects and mayors, designated beforehand, quickly took control. In any case, General Eisenhower does not appear to have shared the excessive distrust felt by Roosevelt towards de Gaulle and, broadly speaking, the popular Resistance. And since he maintained closer contacts with de Gaulle, it happened that he yielded to his reasoning. Thus, in another connection, de Gaulle persuaded the inter-allied general-in-chief to allow a French unit to be placed in the vanguard so that it could be the first to enter Paris. General Leclerc was to be the bearer of that symbolic role.

As for the possible Communist subversion, the answer had been planned theoretically in the very organization of the replacement of powers. Although Algiers had admitted two Communists among the ministers, no member of the party figured among the commissaires of the Republic, and the necessarily pluralist structure of the CDLs was bound in the ordinary way to leave them in a minority everywhere. But people were afraid of an excessive presence of Communists who could not be identified as such in this or that Resistance movement (the 'submarines' would be one of the obsessive fears – and thus a typical word – of the time); or they were afraid of *de facto* power being seized through popular commotion, or thanks to rapid enlistments of last-minute combatants.

Did the Communists justify these fears? It is well known today that they did not! In August 1944 Hitler was far from being written off, and one of his last chances (together with the V2 rockets brought into use against Britain under the fearsome name of 'pilotless aircraft') would have lain in including Germany in an alliance of the Western powers, uniting in a front to 'save Europe from Bolshevism'. If the Italian or French Communists had tried to take power, a frightened America could have been strongly tempted to play that card. It was therefore in the interests of worldwide Communism not to upset the strategic situation as long as Hitler was holding on. If only for that reason, the PCF had to remain loyal to Free France and the united Resistance. That is what it proclaimed, at all events, although many people did not believe it, so commonly held was the idea that 'Communist' equalled 'revolutionary', and that a revolutionary seeks to create a revolution.[1]

Of course the Communists were not disinterested, and they tried (like many others) to extract from the Liberation advantages that are always ripe for the picking, positions of strength and influence which could be useful in any future eventuality, but without running the risk of scandals which might isolate them.

Taking others' places, obtaining influential posts, that could be achieved still more swiftly if the people to be supplanted were physically eliminated. This was where the problem of 'wildcat' purging arose.

Free France, the Resistance and, doubtless, at the end of four years of suffering, many ordinary Frenchmen held it to be self-evident that 'traitors must be punished' and administrations purged of any elements of collaboration. But – and this went without saying – in forms that were consistent with a legal state or, if exceptional procedures were called for, they should be regulated, known, and afford some guarantee of being held in public and of fairness. Obviously, all that could be set up only when the fighting was over, but as everyone knows, many 'dispensers of justice' did not wait, and there were numerous executions of presumed traitors and 'collabos' during the dramatic months of turmoil, battles and, in effect, interregnum – June, July, August and sometimes even September.

Today it is referred to as 'wildcat' purging to convey the idea of spontaneous and non-regulated purges (the adjective comes from Britain, where a spontaneous strike, that is, not controlled by the trade union, is known as a 'wildcat strike'). But at the time of which we are speaking the more usual term was borrowed not from British political science, but from ordinary crime: the purges were usually described as 'settling old scores'.

Common opinion almost systematically attributed those acts to the Communists – an assumption which on the whole was fairly logical, as in the France of that era the PC was the only flourishing party whose theories legitimized violence. This argument needs several corrections. The existence cannot be denied of ordinary criminals, fishers in muddy waters, opportunely converted into patriots in order to 'settle old scores', in the

---

[1] Forty years of earnest study of Communism have ultimately rendered commonplace for the French of today the carefully thought out, subtle and complex nature of Leninist strategy. But in 1944 that point had not yet been reached.

commonplace sense of the term, with old personal enemies. Or of groups of Resistance fighters who, though genuine, were badly led and badly controlled, but no more Communist than anything else, and who may have 'executed' some genuine informer in the heat of a no less genuine thirst for vengeance. As for armed groups under Communist direction, under the cover of FTPF maquis, or 'patriotic militias', they also took a part in these affairs. It does not appear that they committed 'class' murders, aiming to destroy this or that notable in order to obtain this or that social gain, but rather 'settlements' of an internal nature, targeting dissidents ('renegades'), 'Trotskyists' and other popular militants likely to rock their hegemony in the 'working-class movement'.

This type of act, with its system of settling accounts as macabre as it was uncertain, would play a considerable role in the life of the new Republic.

Thus, in the provinces which were not yet called 'the depths of France', the Liberation also contained some hidden depths. Governmental power was being achieved, however, first of all in Paris.

Well before mid August, clandestinely, the Resistance and emissaries of Free France, the designated authorities, were in their places. It happened that the Communists held a large share. Promotions on the heels of arrests had given them a majority in the COMAC (Comité d'action de la Résistance, Resistance Action Committee) and, in addition, one of their men, the workman Rol, known as Tanguy, was commander-in-chief of the FFI in the Île-de-France region.

Today, those anxieties seem very remote. From a distance, it is surprising to learn from history to what extent all those ardent, pure and courageous patriots, whose last survivors fraternize today when they meet at commemorative ceremonies, mistrusted one another in those days.

Paris was naturally at the heart of those tensions. In the German plans the city and its suburbs formed a fortress armed with 17,000 men and about a hundred tanks, under the command of General von Choltitz. Eisenhower had planned to go round it rather than attack it frontally. But the Resistance unanimously insisted, for symbolic and fairly de Gaullian reasons, that the capital and its inhabitants should play an active and not a passive role in the Liberation. The Resistance had all its chief officers in Paris, the CNR, its military branch (COMAC), its local authority, the Parisian Liberation Committee, the FFI command for the Île-de-France, which had established its headquarters in place Denfert-Rochereau down in the catacombs. The Resistance had been joined by de Gaulle's new representative in France, Alexandre Parodi, who bore the title 'ministerial delegate for territories not yet liberated'. It had men available by the thousand, but very few weapons (2,000 rifles for 20,000 FFI). It is true that they knew how to improvise, with bottles and a few chemicals, makeshift bombs that were useful in anti-tank battles – 'Molotov cocktails'.

The popular and patriotic unrest which had swelled during the summer acted as an encouragement and a basis: conspicuous demonstrations, although forbidden, had taken place in various *quartiers* and suburbs on

14 July. In August strikes had begun (railway workers on the 10th, then the postal workers and, lastly, the policemen on the 15th). That allowed the FFI command, the former Communist deputies and underground trades union leaders, on 18 August, to put up posters summoning the population to a general mobilization, ratified by the office of the CNR some hours later. On 19 August, Parodi gave it a legal form by a mobilization decree affecting all men between the ages of eighteen and fifty-five.

On the 19th, insurgent Parisians occupied the Hôtel-de-Ville, the Prefecture of Police and the *arrondissement* town halls, gleaning a number of valuable firearms as they went. Because of the element of surprise, German reaction was feeble. However, the occupying forces hung on to several solid operations bases: the stations, the Palais du Luxembourg, etc., that the rioters did not have the means to attack, deprived as they were of any kind of artillery. But news of that budding insurrection had been communicated to Eisenhower by emissaries dispatched through the German lines. On the 22nd the General-issimo decided to alter his plans and send a unit towards Paris, General Leclerc's second armoured division: 15,000 men and 200 tanks.

Since 19 August, the battle had been scattered and sporadic; here, roads were cut by barricades formed mainly of felled trees; there, ambush attacks were made on German soldiers going from place to place. Was it dangerous and premature, in those days when the Allies' decision had not yet been made? Some thought so and accepted that Nordling, the Consul-general of Sweden, a neutral country, should act as intermediary between the German command and certain elements of COMAC and the CNR to negotiate a truce (with the obvious prospect that eventually von Choltitz would evacuate Paris without a fight and thus without major destruction). Between 20 and 22 August the question of the truce therefore divided all the underground authorities, in bitter and enduring debates, some (chiefly the Communists) denouncing the truce as a manoeuvre intended to halt the surge of the people and deprive them of their victory, others arguing the case of damage limitation. There was a majority in favour of the truce on the 20th – though it was scarcely observed – then a majority on the 22nd confirmed that it should be rejected.

On 22, 23 and 24 August urban guerrilla warfare was thus resumed, but still without any decisive successes. Success came at last with, at the close of the 24th, the emergence of the Second Armoured Division from the southern suburbs. At the Porte d'Orléans, the monument since erected to General Leclerc fixes this point of military topography in the memory. An advance platoon of three tanks even pushed as far as the Hôtel-de-Ville.

But it was during the day of the 25th that Leclerc's soldiers delivered the decisive attacks against the German strongholds, this time with evenly matched arms. They were brief but real fights: the Second Armoured Division numbered 130 dead and 319 wounded, German losses being estimated at 2,800 dead, and those of the Parisians, civilians as well as enlisted members of the FFI, at 3,000. Those few hours of combat were enough to persuade von Choltitz not to persist.

In the afternoon of the 25th, captured after the taking of his HQ in the Hôtel Meurice, in front of Leclerc at the Prefecture of Police he signed a 'pact of surrender', and renewed it a little later at Montparnasse station, this time with two symbolically associated French signatures, of General Leclerc and Colonel Rol-Tanguy.

Lastly, during the course of that same historic afternoon General de Gaulle arrived, accompanied by his 'minister for liberated territories', André Le Troquer. He had come from Brittany, which had just been liberated, and followed the armies' advance, eager to reach Paris. He too arrived from the south, and went hotfoot to the French HQ in Montparnasse station, where he met Leclerc and immediately reproved him for having accepted the co-signature of an FFI leader: under wartime regulations, in any post there is only one chief; furthermore, was it not risky to let a Communist push himself forward in this way to the status of co-liberator in chief? Thus, even amid the euphoria of victory, de Gaulle established himself as a stickler for abiding by the rules and maintaining state vigilance.

Next, as if first to renew a connection with former political legality, he went to the Ministry of War, in the rue Saint-Dominique, where he had had his offices in June 1940. Finally, in the evening, he agreed to go without further delay to meet the CNR at the Hôtel-de-Ville. This was a famous scene, with the emotions of reunion and joy, and an impassioned speech about Paris 'ravaged . . . broken . . . martyred . . . but liberated, liberated by its own action'. A historic encounter, whose moving and imposing memory must not be allowed to be overshadowed by the episode of the controversy with Georges Bidault, although that was not without significance. For they were at the Hôtel-de-Ville, the supremely important place to which was attached the custom of 'proclaiming the Republic' in those heroic bygone days when a throne was overturned every twenty years. Georges Bidault had suggested renewing the rite. But de Gaulle refused, alleging that as Vichy had been an illegitimate regime, null and void, the Republic was doing no more than continuing. Having taken refuge in London on 18 June 1940, it was at last making its return and therefore had no need to be reinvented by a proclamation. So principles still came first and foremost, together with vigilance, this time in the face of revolutionary romanticism. As for the problem of the continuity of the Republic, it would not take long to reappear.

Thus the day of 25 August drew to a close.

It only remained to add the finishing touch by a sort of festival of consecration. In the afternoon of the 26th General de Gaulle and his entourage, by now numerous and varied, crossed Paris, in the midst of an immense crowd, from the Arc de Triomphe to Notre Dame, by way of the Champs Élysées and the rue de Rivoli. That passage through Paris was also a symbol, though less frequently recalled, cutting across the city and linking the smart districts of the west with those which, in the east, were both more working class and more laden with history.

At the finish, in Notre Dame, there had to be a Te Deum. The ceremony proved doubly unusual, first because the Cardinal-Archbishop (Mgr Suhard) was absent, excluded for collaboration, and then because the organ had the constant accompaniment of rifle fire, caused by fanatical militiamen waging a rearguard battle from the rooftops of nearby buildings.[2]

In the days that followed, all the ministers rejoined the General in Paris.

On 2 September de Gaulle reshuffled the government to admit representatives of the internal Resistance. The president of the CNR, Georges Bidault, became Minister of Foreign Affairs; François de Menthon, one of the fighters' leaders, Minister of Justice; Charles Tillon, commander-in-chief of the FTPF, Arms Minister. The latter was a Communist, and his entry into the ministry made up for the departure of Fernand Grenier, a victim of the battle of Vercors.

In that autumn of 1944, the rebuilding of the country made a slow start. Little by little, postal and rail communications were re-established, and offices, factories and schools reopened their doors. But life had not yet resumed its normal course by a long chalk. Prisoners of war and those who had been deported were still missing. The continuing war was absorbing resources, food and other shortages were showing little improvement, and ration coupons were still in use.

There were even two combat zones. From the Ardennes to the Vosges, on a reduced front, the Germans were stubbornly defending themselves, and sometimes went over to a counteroffensive. Strasbourg, liberated on 23 November, was still threatened in January 1945, to the point where the American command was talking of evacuating Alsace, and France had to intervene vigorously so that this symbolic town was not abandoned. The Rhine was crossed only during the course of March. As for the Atlantic pockets, the siege was maintained chiefly by the badly equipped forces which had come from the FFI. In this dual and brutal winter campaign, the French army increased its participation in the allied fighting, units from Africa and Italy being reinforced in September by the engagement of volunteers, then gradually by the formation into regular units of groups which had come from the FFI. Between them and the army a sort of 'amalgamation' sometimes took place, in the style of 1793. The FFI were very keen on it, despite the reluctance of certain generals. De Lattre, for his part, showed himself in favour and thereby gained some popularity.

The war went on, therefore, and life's difficulties, and shortages; and trouble, too, for it was time to proceed with the purging, that is, to arrest those presumed guilty of treason, the informers, torturers, traffickers, and so on. Someone had to see to it that this was carried out according to the

---

[2] For the details of the liberation of Paris, I have followed the account of Jean-Pierre Azéma, *De Munich à la Libération*, Paris, Seuil, 'Points-Histoire' series, 1979, itself frequently indebted to the exhaustive *Libération de Paris* of Adrien Dansette.

rules, to regularize what had been done in an improvised way, and even to redress wrongful arrests and illegal confinements. An unobtrusive, but none the less real and painful part of the activities of the commissaires of the Republic consisted, in that pathetic autumn, in trying to put right, sometimes with difficulty, the errors or deviations of the summer's wildcat purges.

To a large extent, rebuilding the legal system amounted to reconstituting the state, a task which de Gaulle considered paramount and made his own. In September, he devoted a whole week to a tour of the seething principal regional towns – Lyon, Marseille, Toulouse – where, amid revolutionary excitement, collegial authorities who had emerged from hiding, combined with the initiatives of Resistance members who had remained armed, gave the appearance of anarchy or of 'duality of power'. From a distance, those symptoms appear to stem more from the inevitable muddle than from any leanings towards red republics in the furtherance of some improbable plan.

Nevertheless, a closer look needed to be taken. De Gaulle went everywhere, letting himself be seen supporting and strengthening the authority of those who held it legally: commissaires of the Republic, generals commanding the military regions, prefects, sub-prefects, and so on. His extraordinary popularity as head of Free France and living symbol of the Liberation and victory easily outweighed the austere part of the undertaking: the restoration of a regular and centralized authority; and the occasional disagreeable parts: ordering to attention (sometimes in the actual sense of the word) this or that hero who had excelled more through courage than through a sense of hierarchy.

The problem did not present itself only in psychological terms, however. Certain armed Resistance fighters (FFI) who had enlisted individually or in groups in the regular army were still fighting at the front; others had gone home; but a third category remained armed, organized and on the

Military images of the liberation of Paris. (Top) De Gaulle on the Champs Élysées. The victors grouped behind General de Gaulle on the occasion of a military parade at the end of August 1944. Three of the four future marshals can be seen: on de Gaulle's left, Koenig (Bir Hakeim), and on his right, walking-stick in hand, Leclerc (Koufra, the entry into Paris) and, on his right, wearing riding breeches, Juin (the Garigliano, Monte Cassino). Missing is de Lattre, who was on the Alsatian front (Rhine-and-Danube) at the time. (Photographer unknown) (Bottom) The vanquished. German prisoners on the place de l'Opéra after the capture of the Kommandantur. The relative correctness of their uniform contrasts with that of the FFI surrounding and guarding them – civilian clothes and an armband ... and a weapon. The fighting in Paris in August 1944 was murderous but, compared with what had been feared, short-lived and not very destructive. The words 'And Paris was not destroyed' would remain famous. (Photo: Les Actualités photographiques Internationales) spot, under the name of 'patriotic militiamen'. Even while underground, the Communists had persuaded the CNR to accept the principle of creating a popular force emerging from the Resistance, and intended to help in the pursuit of traitors and black market dealers, and in the defence of the population against the 'fifth column'. Just after the Liberation, it appeared to be chiefly the Communists who urged the creation of these patriotic militias, who insisted on them, and placed their men in them (FTPF were transformed *en bloc* into MP). To what end? It cannot be ruled out that the intentions put forward were sincere: after all, the Communists were obsessed by the precedent of the Spanish Civil War, they believed in the 'fascism' of Franco and the 'fascism' of Vichy; as the 'fascists' of the 'fifth column' had effectively waged civil war in Spain, why should not the 'fascists' in France form a sort of white maquis whom it would be necessary to confront?

But opinion, from de Gaulle down to the ordinary grass-roots Frenchman, did not believe in that theory, and in any case experience revealed its foolishness (the 'collabos' had no thought of prolonging the civil war; they fled or went into hiding). It was believed, therefore, that if the PC set so much store by having armed civilians at its fingertips, it was for party reasons. On 28 October 1944, the government (with the Minister of the Interior, Adrien Tixier, an SFIO socialist, in the front line) crossed swords with the PC and declared the dissolution of the patriotic militias. The Communist ministers had to accept the measure but, from outside, the party voiced strong protest, chiefly through Jacques Duclos, claiming that the government was insulting the Resistance and trampling on its rights and, on that sensitive topic, even obtained the support of the CNR. The protest, however, remained at the level of speeches, and no serious pressure was planned to sustain it. The situation stayed like that, undecided and tense, for several weeks.

The matter was resolved when Maurice Thorez returned from Moscow. In order to re-enter France he needed the backing of the government, for he was still under a sentence for desertion pronounced in 1939 (thus under a legitimate republican regime). Having obtained that backing, he landed in Paris on 27 November 1944 and, amid the enthusiasm of his reunion with the militants and crowds of popular Paris, he supported and won acceptance for the legalist line which the party would formally adopt at the central committee of January 1945: 'A single police force, a single army'. The dissolution of the MPs was accepted, the party joined the game of constitutional legality, elections, co-operation with the classic political parties and integration into the normal apparatus of state.

It was with complete serenity, at least on that score, that de Gaulle was able to leave for Moscow, just as Thorez returned, to meet Stalin and conclude the necessary alliance with him, 'the fine and good alliance', simultaneously in the tradition of the Republic of Sadi Carnot and Poincaré, a guarantee against the rebirth of German militarism and a counterweight to 'Anglo-Saxon' supervision.

From January 1945 to January 1946, the most critical period of the Liberation being over, the Republic, in its provisional phase, retained Charles de Gaulle as president of the Council of Ministers, also filling the office of Head of State. The year 1945, with the General presiding, was in many respects one of extreme importance.

First of all, the Resistance fell back into line. The restoration of the state, followed as we shall see by that of electoral democracy, necessarily brought back with it political parties, old and new. The institutions which had specifically emerged from the underground, the CNR, CDL and CLL (Comités locaux de libération, Local Liberation Committees) therefore no longer had any power, apart from moral, and were ineffectual or at most consultative, before they were reduced to a part of history. The movements would turn into an association of former combatants; their institutional role would consist only of issuing their members with certificates of action in the Resistance qualifying them for pensions and medals. From the personal angle, former Resistance fighters found themselves with the alternative of re-entering (or entering, for many were young) private life, or becoming (perhaps once more becoming) militants in the political parties. The impression was quickly received that republican political life of pre-1940 was returning to normal. The PC itself stopped counting on the National Front (which, even underground, had never managed fully to achieve its desired character of broad patriotic union)[3] and wanted to renew its links with history on the level of the Popular Front. A PC–SFIO committee of unity was re-established.

De Gaulle's government comprised four categories of members: some rare Communists, as we know, slightly more SFIO (we have already named Adrien Tixier, for the Interior), some MRP (a new party, of Christian democrat inspiration), and lastly a sort of fourth component made up of various personalities who were independent and, for that reason, regarded as being closer to the General (Louis Jacquinot, Jacques Soustelle, André Diethelm, René Pleven . . .). At the end of April 1945, without waiting for the end of the war or the return of prisoners, the French were called to vote in municipal elections. They took place calmly but with enthusiasm and, by reinstating legitimate authorities through universal suffrage, they contributed even further to ousting temporary teams and Local Liberation Committees from the stage.

A republican rule, therefore – but one renewed and improved because, for the first time in France, women had the vote. This was the easiest, most unanimous and least disputed gain of the Resistance. Not that it was a present to women from the General, as later unscrupulous propaganda would sometimes claim. Nor was it even a reward for the roles played in

---

[3] And even less in the spring of 1945, when the MLN Congress, by a politically very clear vote, would refuse to engage in a process of merging with the FN.

clandestine combat by so many heroic women; it was far more the corollary of the overall change in forces which had come about as a result of the war. The pre-war parliament had been dominated by two political groups inimical to votes for women: on the one hand, the right-wingers, almost to a man, through conservatism or overall traditionalism; on the other, the Radical Party, progressive in theory, but convinced that the feminine vote would harm the left. Each group had in mind the stereotyped image of those very French peasant or petit-bourgeois couples, where Monsieur was anticlerical while Madame attended Mass – a stereotype which has persisted from Michelet to *Clochemerle*, and which still persists quite frequently. But the old conservative right-wingers and the old 'rad-soc' left had had few representatives in the Resistance, and were discredited, sometimes excessively, by recollections of the state of politics before the collapse.

By contrast, the Liberation brought to the fore a progressive left (socialist and Communist) on the one hand, and on the other a new Catholic party (the MRP), which paid more heed to the particular interests of its religion than to the sweeping prejudices of old society; thus, two camps who were equally at pains, even if for partly opposite reasons, to let female citizens have their say.

At the beginning of May the war came to an end. The armistice was signed near Berlin. Opposite the German signatory were four allied representatives, British, American, Russian . . . and French. That last presence symbolically hallowed the Gaullist and national success which had been launched, like a utopian dream, on 18 June 1940: France had rejoined the victors' camp, and was officially numbered among the four great powers.

The popular jubilation that swept through the country between 5 and 8 May was obviously concerned more with the end of suffering and combat than with the diplomatic victory. For many families the rejoicing was accompanied by personal joy: the return of prisoners of war. But for others there was tragic grief: the return of deportees had brought back only a very limited number of victims, and in what state! Into those places which the public learned to describe randomly as 'concentration', 'deportation', 'extermination' and 'death' camps, Büchenwald, Dachau, Ravensbrück, Auschwitz . . . the Nazis had crammed Resistance members and political prisoners as well as members of those populations they had pledged to exterminate (Jews, gypsies). Over 150,000 French men and women, of whom some 30,000 returned![4] It was then that the public came to learn the truth about the extent of the massacre (almost nine-tenths) as well as details of their sufferings (ill-treatment at the time of arrest, transport in

---

[4] Here we follow Azéma's rich and reliable work *De Munich à la Libération*. This supports the approximate figures of 63,000 nonracial deportees, of whom about 25,000 returned, and 83,000 racial deportees, of whom 2,500 returned (see pp. 184 and 189).

cattle wagons, lack of food, heat and medical attention, to which were added exhausting physical labour during detention, and finally sometimes extermination in the gas chambers). People were above all shaken by the swiftly omnipresent image of the surviving deportee just after his liberation: a creature with huge staring eyes, his head shaven, thin as a skeleton, his body engulfed in his striped pyjama uniform. Those images were more important than the cruelties of the occupation and oppression, which not everyone had experienced, because no one could escape them: they were to be seen in the press, in photograph exhibitions, in the windows of party and Resistance movement offices, on cinema newsreels. The horror they inspired rebounded on the Hitlerian ideology that was responsible, and vaccinated the next generation and most ordinary people with a strong dose of antifascism. At least, for twenty years or so . . .

After these various jolts, to emotions and institutions alike, political life during 1945 revolved around three major problems, or three choices of direction: purging, economic orientation and the Constitution.

The purification, or purging, was by now regularized. There was an administrative cleanup, the work of commissions specially created in the ministries for that purpose, and a legal cleanup, by the High Court and the regional courts of justice. The most important trial was that of Marshal Pétain who, having left Vichy on 20 August 1944 with his ministers and entourage to set up a kind of exiled and phantom government in Sigmarigen in southern Germany, had returned to give himself up.

The situation was an exceptional one, and so was the court of law! For crimes committed by ministers against the state, the Third Republic had possessed a High Court of Justice which was nothing other than the Senate. But it was not clear that the Third Republic was still legitimate, and even less its Senate, the majority of whose members had put Pétain in power in July 1940. It was therefore necessary to constitute a High Court of Justice for this special circumstance (decree of 18 November 1944). It comprised twenty-seven members: three magistrates and twenty-four jurors, the latter designated by lot out of a list of one hundred chosen by the Consultative Assembly. Of the hundred, fifty were former deputies from before 1940, and fifty were not. The jury of twenty-four members had to contain the same balance, twelve and twelve. Selected by the Consultative Assembly, those hundred (and the twenty-four) were estimable men and women, of honourably varied opinion but obviously closer to the Resistance than to the collaboration. The High Court began its work at the beginning of 1945 by sentencing to life imprisonment Admiral Esteva, former Resident General in Tunis, and by imposing the death sentence on General Dentz, former commander of the Vichy troops in Syria (the punishment was commuted). Marshal Pétain was expected to be tried in his absence when he gave himself up, reaching France via Switzerland on 25 April, and was imprisoned in the fort of Montrouge.

Investigations were lengthy, aiming to link his acts in Vichy with his political action of hostility (conspiracy?) against the Third Republic. The trial took place in Paris, on the premises of the Palais de Justice (easier to protect against untimely demonstrations than palaces such as the Luxembourg or Palais-Bourbon).

It opened on 23 July 1945. For the prosecution: Mornet, the public prosecutor; and leading the defence: Maître Jacques Isorni – two names which immediately became famous. The atmosphere was overheated, in every sense of the word, with an enormous throng, chiefly of journalists, in a hall that was too small. But the defendant refused to make a spectacle of the affair. At the outset he announced that he rejected the court, would not recognize the validity of the trial and would abstain from taking part in it. In fact he would maintain a silent presence – on principle, and perhaps also because his waning strength (he was eighty-nine years old) no longer enabled him to play an active role. There then followed an immense procession of witnesses in which all the leading lights in French politics over the recent years made their appearance, and where all possible arguments were put forward about responsibility for the disaster of 1940 and what motivation there had been for the armistice or collaboration. Even so authoritative a participant as Pierre Laval, brought from the prison where he was awaiting his own trial, was called to appear as a witness. He was no less ready to put up a fight. After some days the prosecution abandoned the accusations for events prior to 1940 (Pétain the conspirator, Pétain and the *cagoulards*) and decided to concentrate on the grievances linked with the armistice and afterwards. Closing speech for the prosecution, speech for the defence, seven hours of deliberations.

On 15 August the jury declared Pétain guilty of dealings with the enemy, a crime which carried the death sentence. Condemned to death, but his sentence accompanied by a request for non-execution because of his advanced age, Pétain was indeed spared and put into detention in a fortified place, the last being the Île d'Yeu, where he died on 16 July 1951.

In October it was Pierre Laval's turn. He had been active to the very end; even on 12 August 1944 he had tried to persuade Herriot, hastily removed from his house arrest, to help him formulate some plan of transition between Vichy and what was to follow. Herriot, having refused, had been sent back to Germany, and Laval had returned empty-handed to Vichy, which he had left on the 20th for Sigmaringen, like the Marshal. In the end he, too, had given himself up. At his trial, which was short, violent and turbulent, he defended himself as best he could but, predictably, received the death sentence. Refusing on principle to think of himself as a classic traitor, he tried to escape the classic firing squad by swallowing poison at the moment he was about to go before it. He did not die immediately, however; his defenders then begged for a reprieve; the Head of State denied it and, as a matter of principle, the dying man was dragged to the place of execution where, tottering, he suffered the ritual rifle fire. That scabrous epilogue caused – and still causes – a sensation. That capacity for intransigence, already revealed in the Pucheu trial, adds an important touch to the moral portrait of de Gaulle.

To the service of France, liberty and even humanity, the inspired patriot of 18 June brought a hard and vigorous sense of state, a Roman (or in other words, anachronistic) coldness which would always prevent him from achieving unanimity in the very camp of which he was leader. The same accusation of inflexibility had been made against him the same year after the execution of the writer and journalist Robert Brasillach, who had been condemned to death and executed on 6 February 1945. A substantial part of the intellectual world, including men who had chosen the Resistance, like François Mauriac, after pleading for mercy in this affair, took every opportunity to point out, in more general terms, that writers, who were often very blameworthy but above all very conspicuous, were more easily punishable than the anonymous crooks of the economic collaboration or sordid double-dealing. Paul Chack, Jean Luchaire, Georges Suarez and other less well-known journalists like Paul Ferdonnet, the once famous 'Stuttgart traitor', were also shot. Sentenced to death but reprieved: Henri Béraud, Charles Maurras, Lucien Rebatet and Jacques Benoist-Méchin. That is without counting lighter punishments, trials avoided by suicide (Drieu La Rochelle) or exile (Alphonse de Châteaubriant, Louis-Ferdinand Céline and Paul Morand). Or legal proceedings which were taken, though with judicial results that were minor or nil, but at the time were considered defamatory in themselves. Such high-flying stars or notables as Pierre Benoit or Jérôme Carcopino, Jean Giono or Sacha Guitry, were thus to be found in gaol.

The main injustice, however, was to appear afterwards: the trials of 1944, 1945 and 1946 gave rise to relatively harsh sentences; those of later years to verdicts softened by the erosion of memories and passions over time. The guilty who had been imprisoned at the Liberation and thus rapidly tried, were, all else being equal, treated more harshly than those who came before the courts after managing to hide for a sufficient number of years in Spain, Switzerland or America.

Is too much being made of injustice and severity when speaking of a procedure – the punishment of traitors – the intrinsic legitimacy of which is admitted by the majority of opinion? The fact is that this debate belongs to history because it filled people's minds; it notably formed the sole preoccupation of a large but bridled sector of opinion.

Part of the classic right wing had in fact upheld Vichy to the very end, and scarcely had the means or the audacity to offer a full defence for Vichy or its principles, and still less for fascism or collaboration with the Nazis. Its only way to counterattack was therefore to challenge de Gaulle, the Resistance and the new political personnel, catching them in their turn *in flagrante delicto* for harshness, repression and arbitrariness. Of course, in these arguments the 'settling of old scores' of summer and autumn 1944 was laid on the table as much as, if not more than, the consequences of regular courts of justice. Concerning the 'blood baths' of the Liberation, the counteroffensive of the extreme right would circulate numbers of victims, soon exaggerated to fantastic amounts, 50,000, 100,000 . . . After the most painstaking inquiries, the work of the Historical Committee of the Second World War would come up with the figure of slightly below 10,000, which is still a good many. As for the official 'purification' through the courts, according to an assessment made at 31 December 1948, it would result in 45,017 cases not proceeded with and 50,095 cases brought to trial, the latter including 8,603 acquittals, 4,397 sentences to death in the absence of the defendant and 2,640 pronounced after due hearing of the parties – and of that last number, 791 executed; let us leave the list of other punishments there![5]

The subject of the purges cannot be closed without reference to two important special instances: the clergy and the press. Archbishops and bishops had greeted the advent of Vichy as a victory and had openly supported the new Pétainist order. Then, as time went on, the tone became more restrained, and a handful of bishops had even courageously raised their voices against the anti-Semitic persecutions. Another minority, on the other hand, had continued to praise the Marshal's government and compromised themselves to the very end. Was there not a risk that they might compromise the entire Church as well? In order to avoid such a situation, those prelates who were most deeply committed would have to be publicly punished. De Gaulle and the more Catholic of his ministers were well aware of this and succeeded, not without difficulty, in tactfully getting the Vatican to accept the necessity for it. The purge was finally reduced to dismissing three bishops and changing the holder of the nunciature, which was not much but at least significant.

Regarding the press, an order from Algiers had stipulated that all newspapers that had come out under the occupation could no longer appear. All the titles of the 1940s thus vanished, except for a few which had wound up in time in 1942. So a new press, that had 'sprung from the Resistance', made its appearance, before being gradually brought back by commercial and financial necessity into the classic circuits of economic power. In 1945 that point had not yet been reached; this press was poor, largely reliant on the government for the allocation of sequestrated premises and rationed stocks of paper. It was patriotic, and represented, in intellectual debates of high standard, the very wide range of social, moral and political forces which had emerged from the dark years. A place apart must be reserved for an initiative boosted by the government: in December 1944, patriotic journalists who had come from the former *Temps*, with Hubert Beuve-Méry as their leader, created *Le Monde*, a dry, unofficial newspaper striving for impartiality.

---

[5] Statistics from the *Cahiers français d'Information* of 15 March 1949, quoted from the book by the American historian Peter Novick, *L'Épuration française 1944–1949*, Paris, Balland, 1985.

Economic orientation was also nationally inspired. In Gaullist and Resistance circles it was generally admitted that 'the people' were more patriotic than 'the bourgeoisie', that the new Republic should show itself more generous towards ordinary people and more equitable towards the working class than the preceding Republic, that 'cartels' should be punished and 'the forces of money' better controlled and kept under better surveillance by public authority. Those declarations of intent figured for the most part in the programme of the CNR, which the Communists in particular referred to frequently and insistently. In fact, the balance of power between the opposing forces obviously did not allow the development of everything that was virtually socialist in that famous programme. General de Gaulle in particular, at the heart of the government, put his authority at the service of the most moderate thesis – the one placing an upper limit on the extent of nationalizations. The Renault factories were therefore nationalized, but making it quite clear that it was a matter of punishing the collaborator Louis Renault, and not creating the first nucleus of collectivist industry, also the coal mines, the companies producing and distributing energy (giving birth to EDF and GDF), some war equipment and aviation factories (SNECMA, etc.) and a small number of deposit banks and insurance companies. The country thus turned towards a system of capitalist economy, partly limited by an interventionist state with a public sector at its disposal. The idea of directing or steering the economy by means of a Plan made its appearance, thanks to Jean Monnet; it could easily be justified by the extent of the urgent tasks demanded by the reconstruction of the country.

But the current administration itself imposed still more urgent choices. Significantly, in Algiers the government had provided itself with a commissaire, then Minister, of National Economy (Pierre Mendès France) alongside a Minister of Finance (Lepercq, then Pleven). Their realms were very closely linked, a fact which soon brought in its wake conflict between the two ministers and the overall policies they recommended. Mendès France proposed severity: the blocking of bank accounts; the changing of bank notes in order to reduce the stock of money in circulation and bring it down to the level (very low) of available goods; and putting the brake on wage and price increases – all of which tended to restrain consumption (and also corresponded with a care for social justice, for there were shortages in general and only the black market enjoyed abundance). For the moment, it was to be austerity and equity, and then the resumption of progress on healthy foundations, in step with the recovery in production. The Lepercq–Pleven tendency found this austerity excessive and not very realistic and wanted to replace it with gentler and more classic remedies, such as borrowing. In a minority, Mendès France tendered his resignation in January 1945; de Gaulle refused to accept it, but after much hesitation ended by agreeing to his minister's departure on 5 April. The General seems not to have wanted to take the risk of imposing too hard a medicine on a country that had already been through so much. The economic machine would have to get started again as best it could, even at the risk of inflation.

De Gaulle was not wrong in believing the nation exhausted by its ordeals and problems. For a choice as important as those concerning justice and material needs still remained to be made: the choice of institutions.

It carried with it a dilemma and a contradiction before which de Gaulle himself really seems to have hesitated. His logic, of 18 June, holding Vichy to be illegitimate and the acts of July 1940 null and void for that reason, implied that the Republic had been transported to London and then brought back again, just as it was, with its Constitution having already grown old in sixty-five years of continuous functioning. By refusing to proclaim some new Republic or other on 25 August, de Gaulle had implicitly just picked up the threads of the old. Moreover, that logic could be based on good republican doctrine: the idea that a constitutional system is worth less for its intrinsic perfection than for the respect it engenders; that the best constitutions are thus the oldest because people are used to them and regard them as untouchable (the positive example of the United States of America); that on the contrary a nation accustomed to changing its Constitution every twenty years can feel no respect for outmoded entities (negative example of nineteenth-century France); that the Third Republic had begun to inculcate the virtues of long life into French democracy and that there might be a danger, therefore, in relaunching France into its national sport (changing institutions after every serious crisis) and its national failing (perpetual fighting over the rules of the game being added to the fighting over the basic matters at stake). In this way one can just about reconstitute the doctrine of the old moderate and radical deputies, at least one of whom (the great radical lawyer, Paul Bastid, who had been active in the Resistance) had the General's ear.

But on the opposite side, what a yearning for change! What a rejection of pre-1940! What a will to modify a Republic that some found too chaotic and others too 'bourgeois'! The socialists in particular who, like their radical allies, were generally attached to republican tradition and culture and might have appreciated their value, swung over to the other side, clearly because the Senate, that slanted reflection of popular suffrage, had less than ten years earlier put an end to Blum's government. Hence the great temptation to create a new Constitution which would be rid of the conservative brake of the Upper Assembly.

The government decided to put the choice to the popular vote, which in itself represented a change and almost a revolution. The tradition of the Third Republic, in fact, fed on hostility towards Bonapartism, considered the 'plebiscite' disastrous, and had forgotten that the Great Revolution had known consultations of that kind. The referendum thus made its reappearance in French history. On 21 October 1945 the now complete electorate (men, women and prisoners returned from Germany) was called on to answer two questions. Should a new Constitution be made? Yes or no. Should the powers of the constituent Assembly be confined to that constitutional mission? Yes or no.

De Gaulle and the principal parties to emerge from the Resistance (notably the SFIO and the MRP) declared themselves for a double 'yes', the

Communists for 'yes' to the first question and 'no' to the second, the radicals for a double 'no' and a few isolated right-wingers for a 'no–yes'. The votes were 96 per cent for 'yes' to the first question and 66 per cent for 'yes' to the second.

There would therefore be a new Constitution; France thus linked up with a tradition that was not republican but far more revolutionary, that of constitutional perfectionism. The search for the ideal Constitution was about to be recommenced.

On the same day, the electorate also voted to choose, by proportional representation, the constituent National Assembly that would have to develop the project, which the people would afterwards ratify by referendum.

That vote of 21 October 1945 gave for the first time an exact measure of political opinions in a France that had emerged from the drama of war. The Communists obtained 26 per cent of the votes cast, the SFIO, sometimes in alliance with a few groups of similarly inspired Resistance members, 25 per cent, the MRP, 24 per cent, the radicals, 9 per cent and the classic right wing, 16 per cent. Two new forces thus joined the political scene, by an impressive leap forwards: the PC and the MRP.

The fact that the most revolutionary of the parties had become the most numerous, the 'first party in France', elated the Communists but it frightened the more bourgeois and conservative elements of society. Of course, calmer minds could find reassurance in noting that, after all, if the PC had forged ahead of the SFIO in 1945 it was merely imitating the process by which the SFIO had itself overtaken the Radical Party in 1936. A shift to the extreme that was already classic, thus reassuring, in the heart of 'red' France. Looking at the new electoral geography of 1945–6 and the subsequent years, it in fact becomes evident that the PC of the time found it easier to win the votes of the peasants in Provence and Limousin than those of the iron ore miners and workers in the iron and steel industry in Lorraine, as if the red tradition of 1848 provided it with an even better hunting ground than the proletariat! It was a traditional and almost archaic pattern. Nevertheless, objected the worriers, the party was revolutionary, organized and disciplined, perhaps armed (no one believed that all demobilized Resistance fighters had surrendered all their guns); it recruited *en masse*, and would soon announce that it had a million members, it transformed factories into fortresses, etc. This was the party which was conspicuously linked with Stalin, which had joined in the Resistance only when it felt the time was right and in its own fashion, and which in 1944 had perhaps contemplated seizing power.

The fact that, despite these strong prejudices, the PC at that time attracted the vote of one out of four of the electorate and welcomed tens and hundreds of thousands of enthusiastic new members, poses one of the real problems of the history of the period.

Its position on the extreme left goes some way to offering a partial explanation. Like the radicals of former days, it was now the turn of the socialists to become the men of the centre-left, of moderation, of management, of contact and sometimes alliance with more moderate partners, in short, to give the appearance of opportunism naturally presented by a centre position, whereas the Communists could flourish the opposite impression of non-compromise and thus of purity.

The position of the Communist Party among the working class, notably Parisian, adds another useful touch to the picture. Socially, the France of 1945 still belonged to the 1930s and the Popular Front, with a still numerous industrial proletariat (there were no robots) which was still completely French, thus entitled to vote (there were scarcely any immigrants either); and still poor. French towns, and Paris itself in the east, had a very substantial working class, much in evidence, with no tendency to become middle class; on Sunday mornings they jostled to buy *L'Huma* sold in the markets, and on Sunday afternoons they went to the stadium or the cinema, not on car outings to the countryside.

This working class belonged to the CGT, a group of affiliated trades unions which almost held a monopoly, and in which the Communists reigned supreme. In fact, if many reformists, Jouhaux to the fore, had been patriots and Resistance members, others, such as Belin, through pacificism and anti-Communism had rallied to Vichy via Munich. The path they had travelled was somewhat compromising to reformism, and without too many scruples, the Communists had used that assumption to thrust their militants, who had come from the Resistance, into key posts within the unions. They were thus by far in the best position to represent and espouse the strength that the working class drew from its numbers, its coherence, the difficulties of its life, and from its pride. For – and this is the essential point – the PC of that era played immoderately on the memory and popular enthusiasm for the national struggle. The idea that the collaboration had been bourgeois and the Resistance linked with the people – however simplistic it may have been – then enjoyed a vast amount of support. 'Only the working class in its masses was loyal to a desecrated France' – the sentence dates from the era and was uttered by . . . François Mauriac. For years the Communists would make it the purple passage of their speeches. The miners' strike in May 1944 and the role of the railway workers in the 'battle of the railways', on the one hand, the conspicuous presence behind Pétain of troops of local squires, socialities and 'right-thinking' people, on the other, gave some appearance of evidence to that official amalgam of the class conflict with the national conflict.

To this argument the Communists gave the additional advantage of elevating it into a theory. As in 1935–6, there was then a greater than ever reappearance of the 'scientific' theme of treason, which was inherent in the erstwhile ruling classes, and patriotism, which was consubstantial with the class (working) making ready to step into their shoes. In short, to that idea of a working class which resisted as a whole and by nature, the Communists added, as if by way of confirmation, the resistant role that had been played in actual fact, individually or in groups, by 'working-class militants', that is to say, themselves. Following the Liberation, the PC issued propaganda only secondarily on the theme of pure class struggle, but chiefly on the theme of patriotism. Many Communists had indeed been heroes; many, more simply, remarkable militants whose Resistance companions from other walks of life had often envied and admired their specific qualities of vigour, earnestness and sense of organization. As quite a few of them became martyrs, it is rather a delicate matter to appear to play down their merits by making critical reservations.

Nevertheless, it must be said that, heroism being equal, Communist martyrs were made use of ten, a hundred, times more than the rest! No party in 1945 came anywhere near the Communist Party for issuing so much propaganda, and so massive, so insistent, so simple, so impassioned and so overwhelmingly dominated by the theme of patriotism. No other party had arrived in 1945 holding its list of heroes ready to be imprinted

Speech by Charles Tillon, June 1946. Pierre Georges, known as Frédo, Fabien and finally Colonal Fabien, was the best known of the Communist underground fighters (the attack at the Barbès-Rochechouart métro). Having escaped every danger, after the liberation of Paris he brought his FTPF group into the French army, absorbed into a regiment, and died in the Alsace campaign of the winter of 1944–5. The cult in his memory began very early. Here, a plaque is being placed on a building where he had lived. The speech is being made by Charles Tillon, former commander-in-cheif of the FTPF, member of the PCF's political bureau and minister at the time. It will be noted that Fabien is not represented as a young worker, a romantic civil war fighter, but as a classic French army colonel. In Communist scenography, as in all propaganda in general, the image of integration (of popular forces with the nation) carried the day over the image of subversion. (Photo: Les Actualites photographiques Internationales)

on urban place names thanks to the enthusiasms of the Liberation. Gabriel Péri, Danielle Casanova, Pierre Sémard, Colonel Fabien . . . at that time became familiar street names because of their ubiquity. Everything was national then! The enemy? The capitalists? Of course they were treated as exploiters, but above all as 'cartels without a homeland'. Are we fighting for justice and wellbeing? Without a doubt, but above all 'we are ensuring that France carries on.' Did Stalin run 'the country of socialism'? Yes, but he was above all the man whose name, through Stalingrad, made him Hitler's most outstanding antagonist.

The Communists went as far as attributing a symbolic title to themselves, the 'party of those who were shot', and some flattering statistics: according to them, the party had given '75,000 of its members so that France might live'. That was the origin of a series of polemics, both annoying and complicated, which must be mentioned because they drag on to this very day. The expression 'party of the 75,000 shot', for which the Communists are so often reproached with derision or anger, because of its falseness and emphasis, is nothing more than the usual mixing together – subsequent to the event and incorrect, but no doubt inevitable – of two separate expressions originally issued by the PC, the symbolic phrase *to which no figure was given* 'the party of those who were shot', and the suggested figure of 75,000 who died 'so that France might live'. But under the occupation people died in many other ways than in front of a firing squad. If the PC had claimed 75,000 shot *sensu stricto*, its *total* number of martyrs would have been well in excess of 75,000, and it would have prided itself on that higher figure. One must therefore compare the famous 75,000 with the total number of French victims (over 300,000) and not merely with the 30,000 Frenchmen who were shot, as is sometimes too easily done. That being said, even for a total number 75,000 is very likely exaggerated. Moreover, it seems that this figure resulted from an assessment rather than from an inquiry, and it is hard to see what data an inquiry could have found in the PC archives of those troubled times.

Be that as it may, the combination of the contemporary atmosphere and all that spreading of an ardent and unscrupulous propaganda proved to be highly effective. The weight acquired at that time by the PCF in politics and in public opinion was to leave its mark very heavily on the next fifteen years or so of history that were just beginning, and justifies the extent of the analysis devoted to it here.

The other revelation of post-war politics, the Popular Republican Movement (MRP), was quite a bit different. Founded clandestinely at the end of the occupation, it crystallized into a political party the trend of Christian democracy that we saw establishing itself in 1926 and running through the 1930s, a courageous minority clearly marked as left-wing by the logic of its 'personalist' humanism and its hate-filled belligerence towards the old conservative right. It has already been said, at the cost of a deliberate but convenient simplification, that as the old conservative right, clerical in the old style, often Maurrassien, could be recognized in Vichy, its Christian democrat antagonist had become *ipso facto* part of the Resistance. The MRP perhaps more than any other party could present such a list of first-rank veterans among its leaders: Georges Bidault, Pierre-Henri Teitgen, François de Menthon and others; a fine blend of Catholic militants, ranging from Christian trades unionists to professors of law faculties; they had a strong common inspiration, with distant origins in Lamennais, aiming to wed French Catholicism once and for all to liberal and democratic modernity by emphasizing what Christian humanism could share with the liberal humanism of the republican tradition.

The fact that, following the occupation, it was *that* Catholicism which was henceforth stronger in the Catholic part of France, and the old cryptoroyalist conservatism weaker, was a historic turn around.

It could also provide just as historic an opportunity to strengthen the left by integrating into the coalition it represented, and whose principles we have already defined, the Catholic component from which past struggles had inevitably severed it. Why was that opportunity not grasped? In other words, why was the dividing line between right and left to reappear, under the Fourth Republic, somewhere between the MRP and the socialists and not between the MRP and the old right? It is a complex problem, but the facts and consequences which appeared at the time of the Liberation still continue to the present day.

Within the MRP, as within the SFIO, not everyone could see matters as clearly as we can with hindsight. Inside each of the two parties innovatory elements were pushing for a *rapprochement*, and thus the emergence of a new tendency, sometimes described as belonging to a French-style Labour philosophy (the British Labour Party in fact being a type of socialist party inspired more by religious philanthropy than by materialism and Marxism), but each was also subject to the strength of its traditional elements, that is to say, faithful to secular intransigence and anticlericalism on the SFIO side, and sensitive to the immediate interests of the Church on the MRP side. Naturally, the Communists urged the socialists to stand firm for secularism and vigorously denounced those socialists who were too keen to hang on to the MRP. One of the great slogans of the PC's electoral propaganda was: 'The MRP means reaction'. On the whole, the PC normally preferred a narrow left (PC–SFIO) to a broader left in which it would be weaker.

All the same, there was a certain amount of truth in that biased slogan identifying the MRP with 'reaction', and what followed was to demonstrate it. The MRP of 1945–6 was certainly electorally inflated by an influx of moderate Catholic voters who might perhaps have voted more willingly for candidates from the old right – but after Vichy, which had compromised that old right as a whole, it had few candidates in the arena, and those that did venture into it lacked both means and authority. In other words, the MRP electorate was certainly far more conservative than its group of leaders, its parliamentary group or its executive officers. To put it yet another way, the MRP might have been a possible left, but was brought back or held to the right by a somewhat circumstantial electoral sociology. In any case, its emergence, even if the size of it needs to be re-evaluated, was an important occurrence that raised a series of problems of political strategy, and it is not certain even today (1990) if they are over and done with.

At all events, viewing the result of the elections, General de Gaulle, whom everyone wanted to see kept in power, had to reshuffle the government in order to increase the share of the three victorious parties. We are now in November 1945. The Communist problem presented itself then in all its clarity. Maurice Thorez asserted that his party, representing as it did roughly one third of the forces of the tripartite majority about to take up government, ought to have not only roughly one out of three ministers, quantitatively, but also qualitatively one of the three decisive ministries: Interior, Foreign Affairs or National Defence. De Gaulle refused, arguing that a party which, whatever its merits, none the less enjoyed privileged connections with a foreign power, should not be able to manage any essential state organization: neither the police, nor the armed forces, nor diplomatic affairs. The PC solemnly protested that it was thus being turned into a party which was officially less French than the others, and that was an insult to the sacrifice of those 75,000 who had died for France. 'The party of France' or 'the foreign party' – those were the two violently antagonistic and absolutely irreconcilable images of the PC that would loom up at every decisive moment.

It had no chance of winning, for at heart all the other parties thought like the General. He, however, did not want a split, and everyone accepted a poor compromise, which consisted in giving the Ministry of Armaments to a Communist (Charles Tillon). It was of course a piece of the National Defence, but a limited piece and not the most prestigious: the arsenals, not the administrative headquarters.

After this affair, would de Gaulle appear to be the head of a coalition of resistance to Communist power? No, because for him, apparently, there was something even more serious than Communism – something that he would soon refer to as 'the system'.

As soon as the government had been formed, the Constituent Assembly which, following French tradition, simultaneously fulfilled the function of National Assembly and control of the executive, discussed the budget. Strife erupted over the military budget, one which the left always found extravagant and symbolically heavy, and the socialists, although represented in the government, were unwilling to allow the Communists the monopoly of demanding cuts. They even took the lead in quibbling over this budget to which the General, of course, was giving special attention.

In de Gaulle's view, it was a resurfacing of the parliamentary tradition of putting obstacles in the way of the executive, therefore of the state. On

20 January 1946, brusquely summoning a meeting of his ministers, he informed them that the 'party regime' was making its comeback and he intended to dissociate himself from it. He resigned, leaving the government without being constitutionally obliged to do so.

From January 1946 to January 1947 the Fourth Republic, from the constitutional point of view, was still in a provisional phase. It was from the political point of view that the General's resignation changed things. For a little over a year it made way for coalition governments of the MRP, SFIO and PC, whence the name 'tripartism' for that year in French history, and also the first few months of 1947. Like de Gaulle, the presidents of the Council in 1946, Félix Gouin, then Georges Bidault and lastly Léon Blum, simultaneously acted as provisional Head of State.

During 1946 the general directions mapped out in 1944–5 were adhered to: morally, the spirit of the Resistance still breathed, being celebrated at every occasion, and the series of purge trials continued; legally, the framework was republican (electoral, parliamentary, legalist); socially, the atmosphere was progressive and generous – that was the period when, after the nationalizations, social security, works councils, the status of public office, and so on were set up.

The urgent and pressing problem of the Constitution would find its solution, not without difficulty. Two more problems would arise and remain in the foreground for a long time: the fate of the colonies, and of Germany.

On 20 January 1946, though the General's resignation created a stir it provoked neither disturbances nor any apparent desire for a demonstration to enforce his recall or implore him to return. It brought about the retreat of most of the ministers without a party and left the three major ones face to face.

The Communists would willingly have tried to rule together with the socialists in a united 'working class' bloc, but the latter were very wary of accepting a tête-à-tête and insisted on the tripartite coalition, in which the MRP and PC cancelled each other out. In its central position, the SFIO was able, thanks to the PC, to impose secular policies on the MRP (nationalization of private schools dependent on coal-mining) and, thanks to the MRP, to prevent the PC from being imperious or interfering. That central position naturally attributed the presidency of the Council to the socialists, in the person of Félix Gouin, an idealistic and good-natured Provençal barrister, who had been one of 'the 80' in 1940. This government – like the not very different one of Bidault which would follow it – worked hard. Special areas began to be mapped out: the MRP in Foreign Affairs and Justice, socialists in the Interior and Finance, Communists in the technical and social tasks. It presided with great enthusiasm over the reconstruction of the most glaring results of war damage and the development of economic production. The Communists, who felt quite at ease and almost euphoric, tackled the task unstintingly. Maurice Thorez, in an outstanding approach and speech would, in the north, call on the miners to 'win the production battle' (the Waziers speech). Inclinations to strike or partial strikes, justified by the way in which price rises outstripped pay rises, were poorly regarded and sometimes opposed by the CGT. The PC conducted itself like a 'government party'.

In the Assembly's Constitution commission, meanwhile, draft texts were being carefully worked out. Here, socialists and Communists got on well together to win acceptance for very democratic views, that is, giving maximum power to those elected by universal suffrage, without being held in check by a Senate or too confined by the executive. The MRP, in the commission and then in plenary session, voted against the project, which was nevertheless adopted by a small PC–SFIO majority. It was logical for the MRP to call on the people to vote 'no' in the ratification referendum. So, with even stronger reason, did General de Gaulle who, in his famous speech made at Bayeux on 16 June 1946, explained his own ideas on the Constitution, which were in complete opposition as they were based on the primacy of the executive. In the electoral campaign, it sometimes even happened that in order to fight the plan for a single-chamber constitution, to fight the spectre of an 'Assembly regime', supporters of the 'no' vote conjured up the bogeyman of the Convention!

In the referendum of 5 May 1946, the Constitution was rejected, which was a setback for the PC and SFIO and a victory for the MRP, de Gaulle and the right-wing forces. It was therefore necessary to elect another Constituent Assembly.

Elections were held on 2 June. The PC's position remained stable, the MRP, close on the heels of its recent success, moved slightly ahead of it and became the 'first party' in votes and seats, while the SFIO fell back a little. Taken as a whole, the balance of the forces had been only faintly shifted, so the tripartite coalition was re-formed to govern, the only change being that presidency of the Council went to Georges Bidault, the leader of the MRP.

Work on the Constitution resumed, and the new one would be more moderate, because an Upper Chamber was reintroduced into it (under the title of Council of the Republic). This time the MRP could vote for the plan, as did also the PC and SFIO, and call on the people to vote 'yes', while de Gaulle and the entire right again declared themselves for the 'no' vote.

In the referendum of 13 October 1946, 'yes' carried the day, but not by much (the MRP had been able to get the result, but had evidently not managed to persuade all its electorate to vote 'yes'). The Constitution of the Fourth Republic was thus in position. On 10 November, the voters by proportional representation elected a National Assembly, for a five-year term, and a Council of the Republic. The PC remained stable and found itself back in the lead, for the MRP had fallen slightly behind, and the SFIO yet a little more. In the Council of the Republic, right and left balanced each other.

According to the terms of the new Constitution, as in the time of the Third Republic, the entire body of deputies and councillors of the Republic were called upon to elect the Head of State. The vote took place on 16 January 1947. In the first round an absolute majority was reached (only just) by the common vote of Communists, socialists and overseas representatives, and the socialist Vincent Auriol, their common candidate, became the first President of the Fourth Republic.

Once the Constitution was formed, pure politics resumed its rightful place, inextricably mingled with the need for decisive choices in external problems (Indochina and Germany) which had developed in the meantime and called for political handling in terms that were sometimes new. Let us say a word or two about the politics before explaining the facts about the external problems.

Following the election of 10 November 1946, it had been necessary, according to custom, to rearrange the government. Having once more become 'France's first party', the PC had claimed the presidency for Thorez. The SFIO had agreed in principle but, at the investiture vote before the Assembly, some socialists had defected and prevented Thorez from obtaining a majority. Bidault then offered himself as candidate, but the Communists, feeling frustrated, stood in his way. Impasse. It had then been decided to call back the veteran Léon Blum to form a transitional government, which was entirely socialist (December 1946). After the presidential election (16 January 1947), Blum handed over his powers quite normally and the governmental problem cropped up again. After some debates, the solution of tripartism was returned to, under a socialist presidency, and that was the Ramadier government, which would last in that form until the crisis of May 1947. On the occasion of its formation, the PC put forward a demand, as it had in October 1945 and using the same arguments, that one of its members should be given a 'great' ministry. But Ramadier was as unwilling to take that leap as his friends and mentors, Auriol and Blum, had been, or de Gaulle a short time before. Hence once more a ridiculous compromise: the Communist François Billoux became Minister of National Defence, but he was flanked by three under-ministers (all non-Communist) who, each in charge of one of the armed services, formed a screen between him and important files. It can be seen that two years of working together had not really filled in the chasm of mistrust between the PC and its closest partners. But that situation, which helps us to understand the imminent rupture in May 1947, had undoubtedly been aggravated by external problems: those of overseas and beyond the Rhine.

France had colonies. It was determined to treat them better, but not to part with them. Neither the already outdated speech of General de Gaulle at Brazzaville (30 November 1944) nor the preamble to the Constitution of 1946 legitimized or gave any indication of a near and total 'decolonization'.

In Algeria, the victory parade of 8 May 1945 had given rise in the Constantinois, notably in Setif, to a nationalist demonstration that had

turned into a riot. The surprise which the event had aroused, the extreme
brutality of the repression and military reprisals and, even more perhaps,
the indifference of the French public to this remote happening, reminds us
that, in affairs of that kind, the France of 1945–6 was closer to the 1930s
than to our times.

In black Africa, in Madagascar, a certain political life was awakening, and
some reforms had increased the number of Africans voting for a few deputies' seats (we saw them appear at the presidential election), but it was
still only a broadening of what Senegal had already been under the Third
Republic.

But none of all that was as immediate or pressing as Vietnam.

Vietnam: the French were barely beginning to discover its name. In days
gone by, school and *lycée* had taught that 'French Indochina' comprised
two colonies properly speaking, Tonkin (Hanoi) and Cochin-China (Saigon), and three protectorates, the empire of Annam (Huê), the kingdoms
of Laos (Vientiane) and Cambodia (Phnom Penh). It was left unremarked
that there were three peoples: the Khmer in Cambodia, the Lao in Laos
and the Vietnamese in Vietnam, Vietnam having been arbitrarily sliced up
by the vicissitudes of colonial conquest into Tonkin, Annam and Cochin-
China. Now, for the Vietnamese, the last three countries were nothing but
the three parts (the three *ky*) of their homeland.

At the time of Vichy, isolated Indochina had been governed, in the name
of Marshal Pétain, by Admiral Decoux. But the Japanese had quickly
appeared on the scene, and though they were theoretically Vichy's allies
because Japan was waging war on the same side as Hitler, in fact they were
quite hostile to the white colonizers who were the French.

It even happened that Vietnamese patriots (gathered together in the
Viet-minh front whose main component was the 'Indochinese' Communist
party of Ho Chi Minh) and the Japanese were playing a subtle game
between them at the expense of the French. Vichy had vanished in August
1944, but its administration had remained in place because liberated France
did not have the means to go over and replace it as long as the war in Asia
continued . . . In March 1945 the Japanese had put an end to that piece of
French make-believe and had seized all the power for themselves. French
soldiers and colonials, for all that they were Pétainists, were dismissed,
bullied and imprisoned very harshly. The Vietnamese patriots then began
to play the Chinese card – the nationalist China of Chang Kai-Chek, allied
to the Americans, British and French. But in August the bombing of
Hiroshima and Nagasaki forced Japan to make peace, and its troops evacuated Indochina. They were replaced by the allied forces who were most in
range to do so, the Chinese entering in the north through the land frontier,
the British coming by sea from Malaysia to Saigon. Then, on 2 September
1945, the Viet-minh emerged from underground and proclaimed the independence of the democratic Republic of Vietnam.

Liberated France had persuaded its allies to recognize its rights to re-occupy this former portion of its empire. De Gaulle's government appointed a High Commissioner for Indochina, Admiral Thierry d'Argenlieu, and entrusted to General Leclerc the command of a small expeditionary corps which was to replace the British in Saigon. In the autumn of 1945, the relief of the British by the French was effected without difficulty or any major incident on the part of the Vietnamese. France now had a presence in a former colony which had proclaimed its independence. But there was no clash, for all that. At that time, Ho Chi Minh seems to have much preferred a French presence to that of the Chinese, who had shown themselves to be domineering and thievish occupiers, undesirable neighbours, and had not yet gone over to Communism (it was not until 1949–50 that Mao would oust Chang). In Hanoi, in particular, the Commissioner for Tonkin, Jean Sainteny, maintained good relations with the Viet-minh. Everything was going well, the Chinese agreed to return to China (in exchange, France gave up the former concessions it had held in their ports), Leclerc was thus able to re-establish French garrisons all over the country, even in the north, without meeting any obstacles. In February 1946 negotiations took place which resulted in a sort of agreement, in Hanoi on 6 March (under Félix Gouin's government). The Viet-minh recognized the French presence, Vietnam would regain its unity (the union of the three *ky*) and would have its own administration within the framework of French Union, after ratification of these arrangements by referendum.

In France, to all those with a liking for colonization (and there were many, in that period), to those with business interests in that country, and to the traditional nationalism of most of the military, including Thierry d'Argenlieu, this looked like a very extreme climb-down. The latter, on 1 June 1946, provoked or authorized the proclamation in Saigon of an autonomous Republic of Cochin-China, which amounted to tearing up the agreement of 6 March and challenging the adversary. That did not, however, prevent Ho Chi Minh from agreeing to come to France to renegotiate at governmental level. The summer passed in talks at Fontainebleau, which had to be concluded on 14 September 1946 by a provisional agreement of *modus vivendi*, accompanied by a recognition of dissension on the crux of the matter (notably the question of the three *ky*). Nevertheless there was no formal break. By now the Bidault government was in power. With this disappointing and difficult to control status quo the situation on the ground could only get worse. In France, the right, the Gaullists and even, in government, the MRP and certain socialists were talking about a reconquest. In the country itself, Ho Chi Minh vainly maintained contact with France, the maquis were formed anew and incidents between patriots and French soldiers began to occur. Apparently the compromise had its enemies on the Vietnamese side as well. In reprisal for one of those encounters (a staggeringly disproportionate response), the French fleet severely bombarded Haiphong. Reaction set in on 19 December, with an anti-French revolt which erupted in Hanoi and killed soldiers and civilians.

In Paris, Léon Blum's short-lived government, whose leader was peaceable and well-intentioned, was unable to do anything, all the more so because General Leclerc, on whom it was relying to have moderate policies put into effect, allowed himself to be dissuaded by General de Gaulle, whom he had believed it was necessary to consult.

It must be admitted that in this affair the de Gaulle who would figure in the need for decolonization and the view of the colonies as a burden had not yet revealed himself. He was still at the stage of the warrior of 1940, clashing swords in order to preserve, against Churchill, against Hitler, against anybody at all, every morsel of 'empire'. In short, it was war.

While the Fourth Republic, in 1946, was tackling the management of that imperial heritage in so risky a fashion, it also had some crucial decisions to make on economic policy and the German policy – two distinct problems, yet connected by . . . coal.

France in 1946–7 still had many ruins to rebuild. Housing was scarce. Food shortages persisted and there would be a need for ration tickets for some goods up till 1949. Industrial plant was worn out. Currency was weakened by an increased fiduciary circulation, inflation set in and became chronic. A change of notes in June 1945, devaluation in December of the same year, were only effective for a few months and had to be repeated in 1948. In the long term, it is true, France had some trump cards: a demographic renewal, the post-war 'baby boom', which was doubtless also the result of the 1939 legislation to encourage a rise in the birth rate; the increased authority of a state with a Plan, a public sector and a scientific policy – the Atomic Energy Commission of Frédéric Joliot-Curie emerged in 1948, with the putting into service of the Zoé reactor, the first controlled production of nuclear energy with the prospect of use for civilian purposes. But these trump cards were to be played later. For the moment, among the urgent needs, beating inflation and obtaining cheap energy for the nation took priority. As a nuclear source was as yet little more than a hope, reliance was placed on hydroelectric power, and it was then that EDF (French Electricity Board) won renown by continuing and extending its array of great dams (Génissiat, Serre-Ponçon, Donzère-Mondragon, etc.), but above all the immense hunger for coal went on. The national coalfields attained their maximum extent and output, from Lens or Faulquemont to Alès or Decazeville. In Communist mythology certainly, but also to a certain extent in national mythology, miners would henceforth rank as glorious and exemplary workers *par excellence*. And lastly, the French were firmly counting on German coal.

Taking it from the Saar was based on the precedent of Versailles. But the main stock was in the Ruhr, which came under the British sector.

France had signed the surrender of Hitler's forces, as has been said. Although it had not been represented at the great conferences between the Allies at the end of the war, at Yalta in February or Potsdam in August

1945, it had obtained an occupation zone (Pfalz and Baden, plus the Saar) like the three other great powers. All the victors were in agreement that Germany should be demilitarized and 'de-Nazified'; the question of whether, in addition, it needed to be 'deindustrialized', because Nazism could have derived some help from big money or because large-scale industry is in any case a source of power, achieved less unanimity. It was a theme dearer to the hearts of the Soviets than the Anglo-Saxons.

France's greatest fear was of the rebirth of a German force; it demanded coal most insistently, from both the Saar and the Ruhr, although the latter was in the British zone of occupation; since the de Gaulle–Stalin treaty in Moscow, moreover, it had hoped to enjoy Soviet backing should the western allies put up a refusal. That was the initial state of affairs.

On the Saar, France was at first able to act unilaterally without too much difficulty (customs annexation in December 1946). As for the Ruhr, in 1946, the Franco-Soviet tendency to claim a great deal of goods by way of reparations was still balanced by the Anglo-American tendency to spare the Germans economically. The French government, from the MRP to the Communists, could therefore be almost unanimous in defining the national interest. But it was not only a matter of the economy. The Russians soon began to behave like complete masters in their own occupation zone, helping the German Communists to monopolize power. Even if Thorez's friends could see nothing wrong with that, the MRP and socialists, faced with this 'iron curtain' which was beginning to come down, had reactions that were similar to those of the British and Americans – hostile. It was at that point, in March 1947, that the conference between the four foreign ministers opened (Bidault, Molotov, Bevin and Byrnes). Soviet diplomacy, changing course, decided to set out to win over German opinion, and present itself in the guise of the best defender of the conquered country's interests: Molotov spoke of reunification. Worried, the British and Americans opposed it, and Bidault obviously shared their rejection. Did Bidault then claim confirmed rights over the Saar? It was Molotov's turn to refuse – which allowed the two others to uphold the French claim this time. But the Moscow–Paris line of common interest was well and truly snapped, and if the conference broke up without deciding anything, it was clearly on a three to one front (the three western nations facing the Russians).

That was the real point of entry into the 'cold war'. It had been several months since Winston Churchill had coined the expression 'iron curtain' (which was descending in the middle of Europe) in order to condemn the policy of Sovietization and Communization of eastern Europe. But a more important signal had come from the speech made on 10 March 1947 by the President of the United States, Harry Truman, stating that there was a world which remained free, and that his country would come to its aid. Such was the background to the conference of the four and its failure. It is superfluous to point out that this moral antagonism over the way the world was going divided the French government between the pro-Soviet option of the Communists and the 'western' option of their partners. But that overall moral and diplomatic conflict weighed down even more heavily dispute and disagreement concerning two other items.

As a desperate measure against inflation, the Blum government had decided in December in an authoritarian way to freeze wages and prices. Also it had started the war in Indochina, or at least allowed it to start. In both those matters, the Ramadier government merely continued the line taken by Blum, whatever the views of his Communist ministers, whose ministerial departments were not directly concerned.

The PC had been enduring all this since January 1947: the wages policy, the colonial policy, the German policy; yet it had apparently not given up the analysis according to which the best strategy was still, despite disagreements, to cling on to the government in order to defend the positions it had recently acquired in the state and society.

The end of this historic period soon came about spontaneously. On 25 April 1947 a strike broke out at the Renault factories against the wage freeze. It was an independent, reputedly Trotskyist strike. It was by its nature an anti-government strike, with real social motivation, however, but of the kind that in 1945 and 1946 the PC and the CGT would rather have tended to hold in check. This one proved to have a large following, spread quickly, and the CGT had to take account of it in order not to be outdone and rebuked by its wide working-class membership. Consequently, the PC found itself involved and, at the end of the month, in a debate on wages in the National Assembly the Communist group voted against the government. That was breaking ministerial solidarity.[6] Logically, Ramadier punished that split by withdrawing their governmental offices from Thorez and his friends. Thus, for the first time since the Algerian spring of 1944, the PC returned to the opposition.

And the Fourth Republic, which had gradually broken with Gaullism during 1946, found that it was now breaking with the most popular of the forces which had arisen from the Resistance. The regime thus inaugurated the long years of struggle on two fronts that were to characterize it for history.

France henceforth would be run without de Gaulle and without the PC, or even against them. This is a good point to mark the end of an epoch, known as the Liberation period, in which the two actors who had played such great roles now exited from the scene.

---

[6] At that time, unlike what has happened since 1958, ministers in office retained their deputy's mandate and voted in the Assemblies.

10

The Ill-loved Republic
1947–1958

Together with national independence, and to wide, frequently enthusiastic approval, August 1944 thus brought back the Republic, pure and simple, the Republic in the singular, permanent and without a number. For the successive and numbered forms, things went differently. We know that it took some while to confirm the official abolition of Republic number Three (October 1945), and even longer to endow number Four with a Constitution, only just adopted in November 1946. Too new to be venerable, that Constitution would be constantly criticized, and the idea would gain ground that the 'weakness of institutions' was the chief cause of the difficulties of the era. That analysis would inspire the overthrow of the Fourth Republic and allow the emergence of a Fifth, based at last on institutions reputed to be good. The Fifth (still in force since 1958) was thus founded on an insistent criticism of the Fourth, rather as the Third had lived for a long time on the hideous memory of the Bonapartist regime. That argument, Gaullist in origin, and supported by the moral authority – during his lifetime, then posthumous but still growing – of General de Gaulle, is difficult to gainsay. It must be remembered, however, that even with the best institutions in the world no regime could have enjoyed plain sailing through two immense waves of difficulties – unavoidable because they came from outside France – the cold war and decolonization. The former dominated the horizon until 1953–4, and the second formed the major problem from 1954 to 1958.

The cold war period, then. We have seen how, in the spring of 1947, the diplomatic difficulties between the Allies had found an echo in the very heart of the French tripartite government. That first important sign of conflict between 'East' and 'West' was a part of the complex bundle of causes explaining the rupture, in France itself, between the Communists and the other parties. But that tension did not immediately assume the

The expression 'the ill-loved Republic' is borrowed from J. Barsalou, *La Malaimée, histoire de la Quatrième République*, Plon, 1964.

air of a 'war', which would be total although metaphorical, in other words, what came to be called the 'cold war'. It would have to wait till autumn.

Between spring and autumn 1947, France experienced only a series of protest strikes that were persistent but without major incident. A still untamed inflation, leaving prices always ahead of wages, sufficed to explain them. Let us add that the PC no longer had any reason to discourage them, to say the very least. Perhaps it even encouraged them. It was to give vent to this suspicion that Ramadier coined a popular expression: was it not possible that there might be a 'secret conductor' orchestrating these strikes? Maybe, but they could do just as well without one.

In any case, the PC did not yet regard itself as outlawed from the nation, and was not yet exposing its former partners to public scorn. At its Strasbourg Congress in June 1947, it did not think its return to government entirely ruled out. The great event of the spring, the offer by the American Secretary of State, Marshall, of a plan for financial aid to help rebuild the nations of Europe, was not yet deemed to be a dark conspiracy.

Everything changed at the end of September, when the Russian Communist Party invited delegates from the leadership of the principal European Communist parties to a meeting in Poland lasting several days. Two major decisions resulted from it; one, which concerned organization, consisted of the rebuilding of an Information Bureau of Communist and working-class parties, soon to be known under the abbreviated Russian name of Kominform – a reconstitution, on a lesser scale, of the Internationale, which Stalin had officially dissolved in 1943 in order to reassure his western allies.

The second decision had to do with doctrine: the constitutive meeting of the Kominform ratified and adopted the report which Andrej Jdanov had presented to it on behalf of the Soviet Communist Party. It was the theory of the cold war. The world was divided into two camps: the good one was the 'peace camp', that of the USSR and popular democracies, some rare already decolonized countries (India), and colonial peoples yet to be liberated; the bad one was the 'war camp', in other words, all the rest, under the direction of 'American imperialism'. 'Peace camp', in Stalin's language, thus corresponded with what political science would call the 'East' or the 'Communist world', and 'war camp' to what was known as the 'West', the Occidental countries or the 'free world'. The 'war camp' was held to be desirous of war to crush the USSR (a capitalist crusade against the 'country of socialism'), and it was in order to make war that it sought its material and practical unification. The Communists' task, therefore, under the title of the 'struggle for peace', was to frustrate the entire western plan.

The United States was considered to be acting exclusively in the pursuit of war; every supranational world organization, Atlantic or European, which it inspired or would inspire, was or would be reputed bad, and the jealous defence of national independence reputed good. There was no more important task for the Communist parties of Europe than to 'raise the flag of national independence'.

The PCF enthusiastically adopted that analysis, which both extended and modified that of the preceding period: extended, in that it regarded patriotism, and even a sort of French neonationalism, as something of value, as had been the case since 1934–5 (with the exception of the parenthesis of 1939–41); modified, by endorsing the attribution of the role of enemy number one, which Hitler had held for ten or twelve years, to the United States. The fight of the French Communists against the ruling class of their country still consisted of denouncing the 'national desertion' of the 'bourgeoisie'; the day before yesterday, it had betrayed by pacifism and Munichism, yesterday by defeatism and collaboration, and henceforth by grovelling before the 'new American masters'. Thus began a long period, as yet unfinished it would seem,[1] when the national theme formed the heart of Communist doctrine and – in the long run – feelings, and a veritable phobia developed, on their part, towards everything that was or would be American, western, Atlantic, European or German (Europe and Germany were supposed to be inspired and used by the United States). Obviously, that analysis engendered especially bitter feelings and actions in the few years that we shall be retracing, when the cold war began and then reached its height.

Retrospectively, the French Communists were invited to get a better appreciation of the gravity, precocity and systematic nature of the events they had lived through in the spring: their break with Ramadier became their 'eviction from the government', 'on Truman's orders', by an SFIO statesman, thus by a member of the 'active wing of the American party'. The offer of the Marshall Plan was nothing but a tool – some sort of bait – in the undertaking of subordinating Europe to America, and those that accepted it were making themselves accomplices in 'Marshallization', or in other words 'vassalization', etc. The Communists' self-criticism for their under-dramatized initial interpretation was compensated for by a fierce resolution for the future. In October 1947, the PC literally went to war, alone against the world. That 'alone against the world' is open, as always, to two superimposable interpretations, one social and the other political: the Communist solo was just as much that of the working class against the forces of the bourgeoisie as that of the 'party of peace and national independence' against the 'American party', going from Blum to de Gaulle.

Autumn 1947 thus brought with it violent strikes, because it was a bad time of year, the life of the people was hard, prices soared, and also because the PC wanted at least to intimidate and if possible hinder the activities of

[1] At the beginning of March 1990, when these lines were revised, a certain amount of prudence was necessary because the autumn of 1989 had witnessed so many upheavals, and so many more were to be expected.

a henceforth detested government. When that government defended itself and the blood flowed, loathing gave place to a hatred expressed in ways that leave us flabbergasted today. Strikes went on, therefore, from the first days of October to the first days of December. They were protest strikes, fairly widely supported, thus social at bottom, but also political and almost revolutionary, due to the hard line imparted to them by numerous officers and militants of the CGT belonging to the PC and reinforced by their dramatic interpretation of the situation. Factories, warehouses, coalyards and stations immobilized by strikes were occupied, and when the government tried to clear strategic points such as the stations, the men fortified them, defended them and even got themselves killed there (three dead at Valence on 7 December), which allowed an exasperated working-class France to claim that, for the first time since the Liberation, it had a government of 'murderers'.

Exasperated in its turn, and perhaps frightened, the government was not to be outdone. On 12 November, because in Marseille two companies of CRS (whose officers, having emerged from the Liberation, had stayed Communist) had wavered, left without orders, in the face of demonstrating crowds, it denounced the 'treason' of the Communist officers and made use of that excuse to purge the entire institution. Moreover, the government was developing some muscle. On 19 November Ramadier resigned, Robert Schuman (MRP) formed a new team and, at the Ministry of the Interior, the amiable and hesitant Édouard Depreux had to give way to the vigorous Jules Moch. At the start of December, near Arras, some mysterious activists even derailed a train that was supposed to be carrying police reinforcements; it was nothing more than a train carrying ordinary passengers, and there were some deaths. The government reacted by announcing exceptional laws. From then on, the two sides reached the point of accusing each other, quite seriously, of preparing for a coup d'état, and incidents repercussed right up to the Palais-Bourbon, where a Communist orator occupied the rostrum and clung on there for hours before being forcibly expelled. That episode, minor in itself, gives some measure of the climate of civil war which, in the space of six weeks, the cold war had managed to re-establish.

Nevertheless, government and police held firm, and the movement had difficulty in becoming general despite the formation of a central Strike Committee. This, entirely in the hands of the Communists, in point of fact organized and co-ordinated the majority of the CGT.

Now, for some weeks, the confederal minority, grouped under the name of the 'workers' force tendency' – taken from the title of the weekly newspaper in which it found expression – had been worried by this pressure, disowning its political inspiration. In the end it openly opposed it. Mid December thus witnessed both the ending of the strikes and schism within the CGT, the consequence of the drama which proved ultimately to be the most enduring.

The Communists, led by Benoît Frachon, retained the majority, and thus most of the Confederation's assets, as well as the prestigious initials CGT (plain and simple). The minority kept their historic leader, Léon Jouhaux, but had to take the complicated initials CGT-FO (Confédération générale du travail – Force ouvrière). Furious at having lost plain CGT, over the years they would stubbornly work away to lumber the majority confederation with the disagreeable CGTK (K as in Kominform). This habit, which gradually disappeared, leaves us with a striking testimony to the angers and fears of the era.

In the rolling programme of strikes, there was one on 12 November in Marseille. The day of action in the great port had been exceptionally lively and impassioned, because the Communist mayor had just had to hand over the town hall to an RPF deputy.

Why RPF? Because a newcomer had entered the scene, in fact, another creation of that extraordinary year 1947, the 'Rassemblement du peuple français' (Union of the French People), the fruit of an initiative by General de Gaulle.

The man of the Bayeux speech, the theorist of good institutions, had suffered a setback, because although the Constitution of 1946 had been voted, he could only regard it as fragile, since barely half of those who voted were in favour, and scarcely more than a third of the registered electors. Rightly or wrongly, therefore, he considered France to be badly constituted at the time when danger was growing. Like the parties in power, he thought that the danger came from the East. It was de Gaulle who created a sensation one day by saying that, by its presence at the borders of Saxony and Bavaria, the Soviet army was merely 'two laps of the Tour de France' away from French soil; and a further sensation by affecting to call the Communists 'separatists'. At the start of the cold war, the General was thus as western as could be, and the PC would not refrain from saying that in fact his troops formed one of the components of the great 'American party'.

If de Gaulle wanted to replace those in power, it was not in order to have a policy more indulgent towards Communism, but to fight it more effectively. On 7 April 1947 in Strasbourg, believing the idea had ripened sufficiently, he thus announced the creation of an organization named 'Rassemblement du peuple français', to gather together patriots and people of good sense around the one and only patriotic end: France, a France that would be fortified by the best institutions, and the proven leadership of the historic head of its national Resistance. That assembly was naturally to grow at the expense of parties, even better, to attract to itself, outside the parties, their generous and disinterested elements, to marginalize the others, and come naturally to power at the summons of the people and the electorate.

The RPF was both a success and a failure. A success because it had an existence: the General established it by getting enthusiastic crowds together at a series of meetings; by gathering brilliant staff around him (André Malraux, Jacques Soustelle, Gaston Palewski); by collecting at his first electoral trial – the municipal elections of October 1947 – a sufficient number of popular votes to achieve the election of RPF mayors in Marseille, as we have seen, Lille, Toulon, etc. and in many suburban areas. Even in Paris, a Gaullist majority allowed the General's own brother, Pierre de Gaulle, to become president of the municipal council.

The RPF was a failure, however, inasmuch as, while aiming to sound the knell of the party regime, or even of the parties themselves, it only succeeded in creating – an additional party! That last statement would doubtless have scandalized the General and would today shock many of his loyal followers for, in Gaullist vocabulary, the word 'party' was so pejorative they refused to apply it to themselves. What else was it, however? It was because there was this diplomatic difficulty in calling the RPF (and its succeeding avatars) a 'party', that political science and good journalism resolved the problem by introducing the overall concept and the neutral term of 'political formation' or, quite simply, 'formation'. Parties, therefore, were not emptied of their members, and hardly even dwindled; it was only the MRP that was slightly 'nibbled' by the RPF, losing to it some historic militants and a few deputies: Edmond Michelet, Louis Terrenoire and Maurice Schumann.

Among the people, the RPF attracted many, voters and militants, thanks to two mainsprings, or two characters. First of all, it lured and incorporated many former Resistance members (from within France or from Free France) who until then had been politically uncommitted. As we have said concerning the veterans of post-1918, the man whose mind has already adopted a political culture generally tends to keep it; the former Communist, socialist or Christian democrat Resistance member thought of himself more as a Communist, socialist or Christian democrat than as a former Resistance member, however proud of it he may have been. But many Resistance men did not have a consciously assumed political upbringing, did not want to be (or did not know they were) tributaries of a political 'family', had not had the opportunity to have contact with, or information about, politics; they thus had a tendency to think of themselves, first and foremost, as former Resistance fighters pure and simple. One can understand how these patriots were particularly receptive to the appeal of a de Gaulle, who was engaged in politics apparently without ever having served any other ends than the fight – supra- or extra-political – for the *Patrie*.

The RPF's other recruiting ground was the 'strong-arm' right. Former Resistance members or not (even in certain cases, discreet former Pétainists), there were plenty of people in France who were sufficiently worried about the 'red peril' to feel themselves attracted by a movement which was explicitly anti-Communist, clearly antiparliamentary and which spoke with a popular and strong voice. It was because this conservative, or plebiscitary –populist, tendency would always be fairly marked that the RPF and the formations which would follow it would often be flanked by a little dissident group of 'left-wing Gaullists' – that too in various successive forms – made up of men whose attachment was not only to an overall loyalty to the General but also to a refusal to commit themselves to the right.

The PC, of course, but also a good number of the SFIO were not long in applying the diagnosis of 'fascism' to the RPF – a recurring quarrel, as we know.

As for the RPF, it obviously refused to recognize itself as 'fascist', or even right wing. It declared itself more progressive than the classic right because, in order to resolve the social question, it announced a panacea: an association of capital and labour, which would reject capitalism just as much as socialism.

Here, then, towards the end of 1947 were the parties and men who were pillars of the Fourth Republic engaged in what, between the multiform activism of the PC and the scornful challenging of the RPF, must be termed a battle on two fronts.

In order to designate the whole formed by the SFIO, the MRP and a few others of lesser importance, the expression 'third force' made its appearance at that time. Third, because the Communists and Gaullists formed the other two. Third, because like the third-parties in the language of the nineteenth century, its vocation was to steer a middle course between extremes, and to govern.

We have glimpsed that socialists and MRP in 1945 and 1946 could hold in common certain positive (democratic, humanist, social) aspirations; they now had an additional link, but negative and entirely defensive. That defensiveness would sometimes take on the air and the language of the 'Republic in danger', for neither the PC of the Stalinist era nor the Gaullism of the RPF epoch yet gave much thought to claiming the republican idea for its own.

But this centrist and ruling Republic would be chaotic for a certain number of reasons, the chief of which was already virtually in position: it would constantly have to deal with two oppositions, capable of acting effectively and overturning governments but not of aligning themselves in such a way as to form new ones. That was the cause of painstaking appointments, fragile ministries and frequent crises. Before making an assessment of it, it would be useful to recall the moral climate of the era. Because the current situation was tense and impassioned, the intellectual world did not turn aside as much as one might think from the problems of the state; on the contrary, it was going through one of its phases of strong politicization.

The literary and artistic life of France at that time was of a richness that defies description, let alone a simple résumé. Only its relations with political life can be mentioned here, for they existed, as in every era, and – let it be repeated – perhaps to a greater extent than usual.

The Liberation brought serious tensions into the small circle of literary and artistic celebrities – that has been seen in regard to the problem of the purges – but it also brought new, or renewed, inspiration.

For example, the desire to democratize culture, to bring art to the people, without which one could not understand the creation of such things as the Avignon festival or the Théâtre national populaire (TNP, popular national theatre; Jean Vilar, Gérard Philipe), pioneering enterprises, today reproduced everywhere and rendered almost commonplace, but at that time borne along by an enthusiasm equal to that of 1936.

Another instance was the discovery of the United States of America. A gradual discovery, certainly, because people rarely went there (the journey was expensive, and also long, for until about 1950 crossings were generally made by ship), but they were more widely and deeply fascinated and inspired than in the period of the Wild Years by jazz, Hollywood's films and the great naturalist novelists of the south. Before it was resented as 'cultural imperialism', American influence would long be perceived as a window that opened on to innovation.

On the opposite side, Soviet influence was of another order. It was less that of a culture – although some fine novels and musical works were coming from the East – than of a political system which flattered itself both on having made the largest contribution to the defeat of Hitler and on pointing the surest way to the building of a just society. Those affirmations were relayed in France by the Communist Party, then at the apogee of its organizational power and its electoral influence. Its influence was perhaps slightly wider in intellectual circles than in general society. In the enthusiasm of the Liberation, 'the Party' had recruited many young people, fresh from the barricades . . . or a little ashamed at not having been there. Its oldest militants, good underground fighters, had retained bonds of brotherhood of arms that the cold war would not always be able to sever. Its cultural policy ('labour amid the intellectuals') was in no way empirical but, on the contrary, wisely and discreetly organized in clubs, commissions, committees or movements that were well controlled. The prestige of several great names was widely displayed and used; Joliot-Curie, Picasso, Aragon . . . who better? Picasso painted, Joliot-Curie discovered and invented, but Aragon did not confine himself to writing. The author of *Aurélien* and *Le Nouveau Crève-coeur* was also the man who ruled the roost (through the pages of the weekly *Les Lettres françaises*) and the man who exercised great fascination. Complex, exceptional, a bit of a genius? There was something about him of both guru and apparatchik. Of course, that was the era when, the cold war and its brutal oversimplification coinciding with the end of Stalin's paranoic rule, the PCF reached unparalleled heights of dogmatism: the 'socialist realist' art of Fougeron being preferred even to Picasso's revolutionary art – 'proletarian science' (of the charlatan Lyssenko) opposed to 'bourgeois science' – Aragon rediscovering now Barrès, now the art of composing sonnets in the name of the sacrosanct national tradition (to reinforce the independence of that national tradition) – and that was not all. But like all quasi- or pseudo-religious ravings, these excesses, declaimed in chorus by a young, ardent and disciplined party, could exert as great fascination and attraction on some as it aroused revulsion in others.

The strength of the PCF in the intellectual sphere around 1950 was so much in evidence that – from a distance – there is a greater danger of exaggerating it, as may be seen in many present-day works and many polemical texts. Nowhere was Communism in the majority, not even – despite the myth – in the *Écoles normales supérieures*. But it occupied the foreground.

The classic right was, if not reduced to silence, at least hampered in expressing itself because, although it had provided its fair share of patriots, its conservative, religious and nationalist values were compromised by their undeniable kinship with those flaunted by Vichy. It was for reasons of this kind that the Catholic philosopher Jean Guitton, for example, would have difficulty in 1954–5 in attaining a Chair at the Sorbonne.

As for the republican left, radical, socialist, even Christian democrat, it was certainly in the majority in the university, powerful in the world of letters, science and law, but it demonstrated and petitioned less: first, because the reformists were less militant by nature than the revolutionaries, and then because it was more or less in solidarity with the ruling members of the 'third force'. Should a socialist minister direct or approve a colonial war, the socialist intellectual who disapproved would often prefer to hold his peace rather than sign a protest petition alongside a Communist intellectual dragging his party in the mud. Dissidence would be the exception rather than the rule.

Similarly, although for other reasons, the intellectual sphere of influence of Gaullism and the RPF, which was substantial, has been greatly underestimated; it was far from being reduced only to the dazzling names of André Malraux, Jacques Soustelle, Raymond Aron and the Mauriac family.

The dominating politico-cultural upheaval did not arise entirely from the Communist side. Another made its appearance, around Jean-Paul Sartre and Simone de Beauvoir, out of the Parisian microcosm of Saint-Germain-des-Prés, and the magazine *Les Temps modernes*, founded in 1947. As the manifesto-editorial of its first issue pointed out forcefully, the political 'commitment' of the intellectual was not episodic or occasional, but formed the natural extension of awareness of his situation. We cannot go any further here in expounding this 'existentialist' foundation for public action. Suffice it to say that in its philosophical premises it differed from both civic commitment based on traditional humanitarianism and the revolutionary commitment of the Marxists 'in the service of the working class'. There were as many competing ideas (in principle) as there were possible meeting-points (in practice), and material for some fine controversies.

But many intellectuals who believed themselves to be apolitical, or felt more in sympathy with the right, kept out of the battles, which might today lead us to underestimate their number. Or from time to time they would participate in a roundabout way, through some article or other, to inform people that it was ridiculous to intervene or petition, indeed to claim the title 'intellectual', which in itself was to pontificate and show a left-wing bias. It was very nearly the state of mind of the young right-wing 'hussars', who shone no less brightly in the fields of literature, the press, the theatre and the cinema: Roger Nimier, Jacques Laurent . . .

Jean-Paul Sartre and Simone de Beauvoir were in that period (and the one that followed, where we shall meet them again) the undisputed champions of the manifesto and petition.[2] Their line of thinking, which was on the whole very political since it was open to the idea of overall choice, was to bring them, from the time when they labelled capitalism, colonialism and 'American imperialism' as evil, closer to the working class (metaphorically: Billancourt) and the 'peace camp' (or to put it plainly, Communism), whose avowed allies they were between 1952 and 1956. They would, however, have to withstand bitter controversies with men who were philosophically close to them but had remained resolved not to involve themselves in politics, but to apply intellectual criticism to the Communist system itself: Camus of *L'Homme révolté*, and Raymond Aron of *L'Opium des intellectuels*. As for the basis of these controversies, the crises of the petitioners can be easily classified in chronological order.

First of all, there was the aftermath of the war, the wide rejection of former collaborators, a theme very much to the fore on the left, timidly countered on the right by speeches in opposition on the need to forget and the excesses of the purges. The possibility of extensive rallyings of intellectuals against the Vichyssois persisted for quite some time, for instance even in 1958 managing to create an obstacle to the election of Paul Morand to the Académie française. Nevertheless, such rallying had very soon ceased to be institutionalized by the National Committee of Writers, which had emerged from the Resistance and was kept well in hand by Aragon and the PC. In 1951 Jean Paulhan denounced it with great to-do in a veritable lampoon: 'Lettre aux directeurs de la Résistance'. Sartre and Mauriac had detached themselves more gradually.

The anti-Communism of indisputable and seasoned left-wingers (such as André Chamson, Jean Cassou, Claude Aveline) based at first on whatever weight was carried by the party's authority in the antifascist and patriotic sphere of influence, was obviously strengthened by the development of the cold war. The East–West conflict little by little superseded the Vichy–Resistance conflict in the foreground, without in any way being confused with it, of course. The great era was around 1950; the Communists and their fellow travellers (Vercors, Louis Martin-Chauffier, etc.) denounced the peril of the atom bomb, the wars in Indochina and Korea, all the authoritarian or antisocial acts that the French government had been led to commit, not to mention MacCarthyism in the United States – while the opposing side attacked Stalinist dictatorship, his 'labour camps' which, though officially rehabilitation penitentiaries, were virtually 'concentration

---

[2] The topic is amply dealt with in *Intellectuels et passions françaises*, by Jean Sirinelli (Fayard, 1990), from which I have borrowed several points.

camps' – in short, the entire system. The publication in French translation of the Russian émigré Kravchenko (*I Chose Freedom*), and of the *roman à clef* by the Hungarian former revolutionary Arthur Koestler (*Zero and Infinity*), were far more than intellectual events. Political, definitely. Moreover, in this confrontation anti-Stalinism had as many champions from the Trotskyist extreme left as from the right or social democracy. For instance, David Rousset, who has left the French language the adjective *concentrationnaire* (in or of concentration camps), and Koestler, to whom our political jargon is indebted for the expression 'Number One'.[3]

Then, little by little, times changed. The battle of the CED (Communauté européenne de défense, or European Defence Committee, 1952–4), which will be mentioned later, had its share of remarkable interventions and unprecedented divisions. A certain independent pacifism made its appearance, seeking to create a balance between anti-Sovietism and anti-Americanism in order to advocate democracy, in internal politics of course, and in foreign politics a disengagement from the cold war. That 'neutralism' was a matter for intellectuals, before one day becoming an option for diplomacy.

Lastly, the Algerian war opened a long and final phase in the war of the manifestos. In a sense, as we shall see, it was the one that most nearly resembled the Dreyfusard prototype, setting those who revealed truths that were uncomfortable for the army and reasons of state against those who placed greater importance on the value of the nation. However, it was not a complete analogy, and the left was not wholly on the side of resistance to the Algerian war and solidarity with the rebels. A not inconsiderable part of the intellectual left was for 'French Algeria' through a firm belief in the idea – certainly Molletist, but just as much Ferryist – that the Republic's flag was worth more to liberty and the law than that of Islam. An enormous problem, which is still with us. But before taking a closer look at its terms, let us return to parliament and the official polls.

The parties which joined forces, combined with or sometimes challenged the government were those of the 'third force'. The two main ones were still the socialists (Jules Moch, André Philip, Daniel Mayer, Christian Pineau, Gaston Defferre, etc. as ministers, with Guy Mollet at the head of the party) and the MRP (Georges Bidault, P.-H. Teitgen, Jean Letourneau, André Colin, Robert Schuman, and so on), but their influence tended to wane after their common apogee in 1945–6. Increasingly often, they had to give way, either to some new little centrist party like the UDSR (Union démocratique et socialiste de la Résistance, Democratic and Socialist Resistance Union – a group of fairly diverse personalities: René Pleven, Eugène Claudius-Petit, François Mitterand), or to parties that were gradually

---

[3] In *Le Zéro et l'infini, roman à clef* about the Moscow trials, Stalin is never referred to other than as 'Number One'.

overcoming the handicap of their initial unpopularity; for example, the radicals (Henri Queuille and André Marie as ministers, Édouard Herriot as a respectable patriarch, Édouard Daladier, who was rather kept aside), or the heirs of the old right wing, known as Independents (Paul Reynaud, Antoine Pinay).

The Assembly elected in 1946 reached the end of its normal term in 1951. The legislative elections of June 1951 slightly altered the balance of the forces, as much because of the slow erosion of the socialists' and Christian democrats' influence as because of the emergence of a new partner, the RPF, showing a presence for the first time at the legislative elections. During the campaign, it had marked itself as right wing by putting itself forward as the defender of independent Catholic schools, effectively challenging the MRP for the votes of traditional Catholicism. At the beginning of the term of office, the superabundance of those votes would bring about the first law to dent secular legislation by allocating public funds, through some expedient, to independent Catholic schools (Barangé's law). That renewal of the schools argument would cause a rift between partners in the 'third force' and complicate still further the basis of its existence. Taken as a whole, the Assembly elected in 1951 was somewhat further to the right than that of 1946–51, and certainly right and left would be spoken of more than before. On essential matters, however, the 'third force' remained unanimous at first. For essential matters concerned foreign policy.

All the successive rulers from 1947 to 1951 showed solidarity with the western allies. The American funds of the Marshall Plan arrived, the system worked and was complemented by an outline of European organization to distribute them (OECE, Office européen de coopération économique, Organization for European Economic Co-operation). France was firmly joined to its allies by the Atlantic Treaty (signed in 1948), complemented in 1949 by a military organization under a single command, OTAN (Organisation du traité de l'Atlantique nord, or NATO). France gave its support to the stiff resistance put up in 1948 to the Russian blockade of Berlin; to the unification in 1949 of the three western occupation zones in Germany into a Federal Republic; to the sending of a United Nations international expeditionary force to Korea in 1950 to help the South Koreans face attack from the North Koreans, who were backed by the Russians and Chinese.

Principally, France made its contribution to the defence of the 'free world' by waging war in Indochina . . . and reinterpreting it. For it was no longer, as in 1946, a matter of imposing itself on the Vietnamese in order to re-establish a more or less colonial French presence. Since the Vietnamese national movement was led by a Communist party, and since, from 1950 onwards, it was backed by the Chinese Communists (victorious in Peking in October 1949, masters of all continental China in the following year, and not yet on bad terms with the USSR), it is easy to see the Indochinese peninsula as a volatile front in the East–West war, in the same way that there were fronts along the demarcation lines in Germany and Korea.

What kind of a front? Intermittent. The French expeditionary force held towns, roads, ports and plantations, but the Vietnamese patriots were impregnable in the 'maquis' (or rather, the jungles and forests), and after 1950, thanks to Chinese aid which could be more conveniently received across their northern frontier, and despite the military talents of General de Lattre de Tassigny, they were able to gain control of a whole series of posts along that frontier, and hold on to them.

One thing gives a good illustration of the new, global as opposed to the old, colonial nature of the French fight in Vietnam: at the same time as fighting Ho Chi Minh, France was negotiating the granting of independence to the former emperor of Annam, Bao Dai, an astute politician whose loyalty to France was not even reliable! (June 1948: the Bay of Along agreement). The political stance as a whole formed by the American alliance, the Atlantic military organization and France's war in Indochina was combated by French Communists with exceptional vigour, sometimes reaching the violence of commando actions (against this or that transportation of war materials), or attempts at propaganda among the armed forces (the Henri Martin affair).[4]

The war in Indochina was not without consequences in internal politics. At the most prosaic level, it provoked scandals because of the speculation that flourished on its fringes: one could get rich by transporting piastres and playing on the difference in their rate of exchange between Saigon and Paris. Thus, one fine day there was the 'piastres affair', which contributed not a little to justifying the slogan 'dirty war'. On a higher level, during the winter of 1949–50 it produced the 'affair . . . of the generals'. That name was given to the imbroglio caused, this time, by the divulging of a report drawn up by General Revers, giving a pessimistic (that is, realistic) view of the situation on the ground, and recommending a complete change in the high command. Conflicts of strategic ideas and conflicts of personalities were mingled, in an inextricable muddle, with intrigues involving South Vietnamese politicians, rivalries between the parties in power and even to some extent between police (DST) and secret services. The Revers report and subsequent commissions of inquiry came to nothing, and only in France did the affair have any effects, one being to exacerbate the secret conflicts in the bosom of the political class, another to aggravate a demoralization of opinion to the advantage of the Communists, who obviously derived an additional argument from it.

---

[4] A young Communist who came from the Resistance, a volunteer in the navy, prosecuted and sentenced for circulating pamphlets (proven) and sabotage (false accusation). The campaign to free him provided a persistent and impassioned accompaniment to the struggle to bring the war to an end.

Never, perhaps, had the conflicts of internal politics and foreign affairs been in such close and impassioned agreement. All the same (except for internal use) the Communists did not push their revolutionary solidarity with Stalin, Mao Tse Tung and Ho Chi Minh; the public propaganda which they organized, through all sorts of committees from which the Peace Movement would emerge, made use of the classic motivators of the horror of war, anticolonialism and fear of the atom bomb (the bomb that the Americans had made such a show of possessing since Hiroshima, while the Soviets were then (August 1949) only reaching the experimental stage). They thus managed to go a little outside their usual sphere of influence, notably in intellectual circles (a petition campaign known as the Stockholm Appeal for the outlawing of atomic weapons, launched in the summer of 1950 at the start of the Korean War).

One act emerged from French diplomacy of that time that was not entirely to do with those arguments of war, and which today seems avant-garde, and that was Robert Schuman's proposal, on 9 May 1950, aiming to create between France and its neighbours (notably the German Federal Republic and Luxembourg) a European Community for Coal and Steel: CECA. This would form the economic nucleus of the Europe of the Six (France, Germany, Italy and the three Benelux countries), and the beginning of rational industrial co-operation over coal-mining and the iron and steel industry; it also represented a desire to consolidate renascent German democracy, with help being given, obviously, by the common political and religious thinking, both conservative and liberal, of the Christian democrats – led by the Frenchman, R. Schuman, the Italian, Alcide de Gasperi, and the German, Konrad Adenauer.

Viewed from a distance, Robert Schuman, who was not at first the most noticeable of the MRP leaders, is certainly the one who has left the most enduring traces in history. Besides, he was a singular man in many respects. He had a strong personality, although unassuming. Competent, hardworking, sensible, he had a monastic side to his character, being very pious, a bachelor and, it seems, a member of a religious third order.[5] But he was a cultured monk, a well-informed bibliophile. He was a Frenchman from the outer edges, so to speak, having been born in German-speaking Lorraine in 1886 and, from a legal point of view, German until the Treaty of Versailles, a fact which one day allowed an orator of the PC in a paroxysm of neonationalist fury provoked by the CED, to call him a 'Boche'. He is among those to whom we owe Europe, even if today's continent on the route to federation has gone far beyond the bounds of the 'little Vatican Europe' conceived somewhere between Metz, Luxembourg and Bonn. That was obviously denounced on the extreme left as yet another American-imperialist machination.

---

[5] At the time of going to press, it was made known that his beatification was being considered by the Catholic Church.

For Robert Schuman the economic goal was no less vital. For the other great matter for the rulers of the 'third force', after maintaining their position in the defence of the West, was very much the material rebuilding of the country.

It had taken place to start with, thanks to a unanimous national effort, in the two initial years when the class war had been rather put into parenthesis or transferred to other planes. In 1946 coal production and railway transport were very nearly re-established. The rest followed gradually, thanks to various favourable conditions. There was plenty of work (they did not revert to the 'forty hours'; its principle was maintained, but served only as a qualification for 'overtime' and, as such, extra payment for excess hours, and the working week in fact often reached fifty hours in industry). There was plenty of public investment by the device of the nationalized industries already mentioned: mines, EDF (French Electricity Board). It was the apprenticeship of a policy, if not of an interventionist planned economy at least voluntarist (there were 'plans', the first launched in January 1947 for five years; a second would follow; rulers, deputies, civil servants, even the public at large would become familiar with the concept of national and regional development, the idea of liaison between research and industry, the notion of increases in productivity, etc.).

In the autumn of 1947, the state-owned Renault Company, a national enterprise but endowed with ample autonomy of management and brilliantly run by Pierre Lefaucheux, began to put on to the market the little 4CV, whose moderate price and originality of design would quickly win immense success and make a first-rate contribution to putting France back in the leading ranks of car producers.

The consumer market, given a fresh boost by the demographic boom and the increase in family and social income (social security, family allowances), was proving very buoyant. Marshall Aid was also a boost for the economy, as well as private investment, of course (chiefly by the big oil companies). Between 1950 and 1960, economists recorded, in total, a growth in the value of the gross domestic product at the very respectable rate of 4.4 per cent per annum. In material form, that meant that housing was built; modern industries such as metallurgy and mechanical engineering would for the first time offer more employment than textiles; agriculture would be equipped with tractors, beginning to free labour to work in industry; and shortages would diminish. In 1949 the Ministry of Food vanished, together with the last traces of rationing. The end of shortages was a contributory factor in the disappearance of one of the inflationary tensions that had been so worrying since 1944, to the point of bringing about the social and even political consequences already mentioned. The franc, which had to undergo yet another devaluation in 1948, was stabilized around 1950 at the rate of 350 francs to the dollar (still in old francs). Certainly, there were weaknesses: growth proved less strong than in Germany or Japan, the home and colonial market (franc zone) absorbed nearly all production, so exports were low and the external deficit always threatening.

But an undeniable recovery was becoming noticeable, even before the end of the first term of office (1951), even though in 1950 a worldwide rise in the cost of raw materials, linked to the war in Korea, set inflation going again for a time.

In the Assembly elected in 1951, with a left–right split tending to re-establish itself and a certain superiority of the right within the 'third force', two governments emerged from the chronic instability; one was Antoine Pinay's and the other that of Pierre Mendès France. As for historical evolution, it was making its way, in broad outline, towards economic prosperity, but also towards defeat in Indochina, the general breaking-up of the colonial empire, and lastly towards the national crisis of conscience of the CED. What a complex bundle! After two short-lived governments, of Pleven and then Edgar Faure, it was a moderate, Pinay, who came to power in 1952.

Antoine Pinay was born in a small town in the Loire *département* in 1891, the son of a manufacturer in the hat industry, whom he was preparing to follow in the business. In fact, it was his father-in-law, similarly the boss of a medium-sized firm (about one hundred workers), but in the tannery trade, at Saint-Chamond, that he was called upon to replace after 1920. In the meantime, he took part in the 1914–18 war, briefly but courageously, surviving with a serious wound in the arm and a flattering decoration. His family and Catholic upbringing stamped him with a rigorous provincial conservatism, with that strong culture of social and civic duty which the centre-right and the centre-left held more and more consciously in common. A competent employer, with an effective paternalism, he very quickly became the most popular and honoured of the notables in his small town and, despite his unfeigned modesty, ended by receiving all the honours it could shower on him: mayor in 1929, regional councillor in 1934, deputy in 1936, senator in 1938. In 1936 his election as deputy had impeded the Popular Front's candidate, a Communist. Pinay, although officially 'clerical', had in fact been sought out and pushed forward by the Minister of the Interior, Albert Sarraut, officially a radical, but above all anti-Communist. Even Édouard Herriot, in theory more left-wing than Sarraut, would always regard Pinay as one of his close associates.

In 1940 Pinay had voted for Pétain to have full powers, and Vichy had kept him in his town hall in Saint-Chamond. The official religious and conservative ideology of the national revolution was naturally dear to him, and his character led him to believe that his social duty lay in staying among his own people in order to assist them from the heights of his customary positions of mayor and business head. That appearance of collaboration earned him a place in 1941 on the first list of proposed members of the Vichy National Council. He did not figure on any of the following lists, however, having kept at a distance from the government, and in the end rendering real services to the persecuted and members of the Resistance. So the Liberation saw him, like many others, punished at first (he lost his position as mayor), then promptly rehabilitated and restored to eligibility. He easily regained his seats and his mandates. Nevertheless, under the Fourth Republic, a man who was a Catholic notable, an employer and former Vichyssois could only be classed as utterly right wing. The Communists saw in him the doubly detestable symbol of Pétainism and capitalism. It is not certain whether their imprecations, out of all proportion as they were, did a disservice to the Loire deputy whom President Auriol, for instance, took seriously and even esteemed.

In March 1952, however, Antoine Pinay was not yet a top-ranking leader; he had only just made his ministerial debut in 1951 in the fleeting formations of Pleven and then Edgar Faure, but had never been sounded out for a place in the Hôtel Matignon. Now he obtained a majority, on the promise of a technical programme for fighting inflation by means of liberal orthodoxy: budgetary and fiscal severity, borrowing and an appeal to the confidence of savers. What is chiefly important is that this policy succeeded because its appeal to a sort of Poincarist tradition had, if it may be so expressed, got across to his audience. Its success was partly due to the effect of the measures themselves, happily coinciding with a drop in world prices of raw materials. But also by virtue of what would today be called Pinay's 'image' – of a politician, but one who was not like the rest. Of medium height, with a pleasant though rather serious face with an old-fashioned short moustache, austere clothing with no particular feature other than a small, round, felt hat from which he was inseparable; and, ethically, all the assumptions of sound and sensible realism implied by success in local economy and municipal management, as well as a preference for dossiers rather than speeches.

The socialists refused to be associated with this too classically liberal – that is to say, in principle, non-social – way of running things. Pinay, however, managed to overcome the financial crisis by avoiding any devaluation or new taxation, thanks to budgetary economies and thanks to the confidence of the wealthy, who were attracted by a tax amnesty and borrowing that was index-linked to gold value and tax-free. The crisis, which was in part due to current economic conditions, came to an end and the economy (worldwide) would take off towards expansion. Those were the first of the 'thirty glorious' years, baptized thus in retrospect by Jean Fourastié. The economic euphoria and the 'image' of traditional, reassuring, provincial notable gained Pinay a popularity above that of all his predecessors. Against the PC, whose revolutionary activism bordered on rioting in the huge *journée* (day of action) of tough demonstrations on 28 May 1952 ('Ridgway the Plague'),[6] his government brought vigorous repression

---

[6] The pretext was a protest against the arrival in France, to head NATO, of the American General Ridgway, whom Soviet propaganda accused of having employed bacteriological warfare during his previous command in Korea. It was untrue, of course. The real purpose of this violence is not clear. The close of Stalin's reign is full of such convulsions.

to bear and had legal proceedings started on charges of conspiracy (Jacques Duclos was even put in prison for a few days, over an affair known as that of 'the pigeons').[7] Against the RPF he used a subtler method. The conservative spirit of the president of the Council attracted a certain number of deputies who had been elected on the RPF lists but who were right-wingers more than Gaullists; one fine day they voted for Pinay and entered his majority ('into the system', said a bitter de Gaulle, accusing them also of 'climbing on the bandwagon'). The hardliners remained in a much-reduced and less important RPF group. For them, as for the General, this setback marked the beginning of 'the wilderness period'.

Pinay, however, was not working miracles everywhere. He could not prevent the army from marking time in Indochina without being able to beat the 'maquisards', and even losing the initiative. It was Vietnam that made progress towards Laos, which soon gave the French command the idea of going to fortify Diên Biên Phu – we shall speak of it later. And the nationalist movements, still barely perceptible in Algeria, were raising their heads in Morocco and Tunisia – in Morocco, around the Sultan, and in Tunisia, in the maquis.

Pinay's successor, after the ephemeral René Mayer, was another moderate, Joseph Laniel. He governed throughout nearly all 1953, and his chief team-mate was Georges Bidault, who had returned from the Quai d'Orsay. Both were grappling with the war in Indochina, which, as had by now become obvious, France could not win on its own. Should it then seek American aid? But that would be to run contrary to the new wind which seemed to be signifying the end of the cold war, or at least 'détente', to use a current term that was more finely shaded and more accurate.

On 5 March 1953 Stalin died. With a slowness at first imperceptible, his successors, among whom Nikita Khrushchev had not yet gained elbow room, relaxed the harshness of internal dictatorship (or, rather, to begin with brought its most glaring excesses to an end) and softened the severity of the international confrontation; in July 1953 the armistice which took place in Korea gave some sign of it. It was in this climate that, a few months later still, other negotiations would become possible. No one believed, however, in a complete and immediate peace process, and the West did not lower its guard.

At this point it is necessary to backtrack a little in order to recall the European facts in the military problem.

Whoever wanted to ensure the security of western Europe in the face of the Soviet army had perforce to deal with the question of Germany's rearmament. It was a thorny problem! NATO had need of it, but was it

---

[7] The Communist leader was arrested, having obviously had some connection with the riot. However, the police made themselves look ridiculous by trying to pass off two edible pigeons, found in his car, as carrier pigeons with mysterious origins.

safe to rearm this nation which less than ten years earlier had fought behind Hitler? Hence arose the idea, conceived in 1951, of creating a European Defence Committee (CED) in which the rearmed Germans would be kept well in check by an integrated supranational high command. But that control system would also control . . . the French army. Would not France thus be forearmed against the danger of German militarism only at the expense of a diminution of its own military independence, in other words, its independence plain and simple?

It was a difficult intellectual problem, but also and chiefly one that aroused very strong passions. German rearmament – the emotional impact of the mere idea in 1951 may be guessed, only six years after the armistice of 1945, thirty-three years after that of 1918. There was an enormous national debate.

Two homogeneous forces declared themselves against the CED – the Communist Party (whose motives we know), and that of General de Gaulle and the RPF, no more surprising when one considers the importance of the theme of independence in the history of Free France. In contrast, the MRP declared itself *en bloc* as pro-CED, being more prepared for the supranational idea because of its attachment to the Church and the Christian democratic European premisses already established by Robert Schuman. All the other political 'families', classic right (Independents), radicals, SFIO, uncommitted former Resistance members, were divided. Two camps were created, between which men who might otherwise have every reason for coming together would separate according to whether, in the face of this unprecedented problem, the fine edge of their sensibility favoured French patriotism or a desire for supranational authority.

That dividing line did not correspond, as may be seen, with a line of right against left, or Vichy against the Resistance, or bourgeoisie against the people. It was without precedent, let it be said again. And very disruptive. It brought together, for example, Communists and Gaullists, who were at one another's throats in matters of domestic or colonial politics. For the moment, it muddled the cards in the political game even further. Lastly, how can one fail to see, with hindsight, that it posed a problem which is still with us in 1990: how to reconcile without too brutal a contradiction the necessary rebuilding of the nation's morale with the no less necessary construction of a strong Europe? It is understandable that the debate on the CED should have dragged on, from 1951 to 1954, before politicians dared to place it on the actual agenda of an Assembly. The year 1953 passed, under Laniel, with a conservative government which had to face up to a money-dealing scandal (piastres) on the fringes of the Indochinese war, a powerful wave of strikes in August (in the state service, over the question of retirement age) and nationalist agitation in Maghreb (to which it reacted brutally, with the deposition by force of Sultan Mohammed V and his replacement by the Pasha of Marrakesh).

At the end of the year, in December, the seven-year term of Vincent Auriol expired. For the presidential election, the political confusion reached its height with the interweaving of the multiplicity of dividing lines and personal ambitions. It took no fewer than thirteen ballots before a majority, more inclined to the right, elected a senator from Le Havre, René Coty, beating the principal left-wing candidate, the socialist Marcel-Edmond Naegelen. From the second ballot onwards, to general stupefaction, the Communists gave their votes to this candidate who, despite his very anti-Communist and (as we shall soon see) colonialist sentiments, nevertheless had the strategically decisive merit, in their view, of being known as anti-CED.

Laniel's government continued beyond the election into the first months of 1954, and allowed matters to get bogged down. The CED was discussed without being voted on. And above all, the war was being lost in Indochina. What was happening?

The French army held the delta of the Red River, the heart of Tonkin, with Hanoi and Haiphong, but since the Vietnamese had been able to obtain arms more easily across their northern frontier, it had lost the posts guarding it, near to China (the latest, Sam Neua, on 13 April 1953). The Viet-minh had then undertaken to slip part of its forces in the direction of Laos.

It was then, towards the end of 1953, that the French command (General Navarre) had the idea of fortifying the post of Diên Biên Phu, situated in a basin, the obligatory route, at least for heavy equipment, of any army marching south. Something was constructed at Diên Biên Phu, therefore, which might become the Verdun, or the Maginot line, of the defence of Laos and, farther on, of the rest of the peninsula. There, amid a circle of mountains covered in dense vegetation, lay a depression some 10 kilometres in diameter, easy to equip, but which would be dependent, first for its construction materials and thereafter for all its provisioning, on convoys coming by air from Hanoi. But the conviction remained that French material and logistic superiority would carry the day, and that any army trying to take Diên Biên Phu by force would obviously be repulsed and beaten.

During the winter, elaborate preparations were made to fortify Diên Biên Phu: an airfield, camps, a ring of entrenchments, an inner ring and advanced operations bases, a good radio transmission network, and the necessary personnel, some 10,000 men, under the orders of Colonel de Castries. All that had been underestimated, or denied, was the capacity of the Vietnamese to win a battle as classic and as technical as a siege operation. In fact, making use of both the cover of the tropical forest, which concealed their movements from aerial observation, and the incredible human potential of soldiers transformed into porters, marking out paths for foot soldiers and bicycles (bicycles that were pushed, and actually used as wheelbarrows) and getting dismantled artillery pieces transported on foot over dozens and dozens of kilometres, General Giap managed to install secretly around Diên Biên Phu forces that no one imagined could have got there other than by road.

On 15 March 1954, when Giap launched his attack, his artillery quickly achieved some decisive successes, for example putting landing fields out of service. Then his infantry attacked, in large numbers, eager, galvanized by the importance of what was at stake, and shortly knocked out two bases of operations. The French army defended itself every inch of the way, so vigorously that it continued its resistance for nearly two months, in spite of the precarious nature of its supplies (which could be effected only by parachute), and in spite of its undoubted numerical inferiority.

France followed these events from afar, certainly the only military engagement in the history of its colonization that bore any resemblance to a classic battle. The public learned about the collapse of the positions 'Beatrice' and 'Gabrielle', the feats of arms, the exceptional devotion of the chief nurse, Geneviève de Galard, the last parachute drop in which Hanoi sent Castries his general's stars and the bottle of champagne to 'wash them down' – all the picturesque symbolism that had formerly been the usual accompaniment to 'real' wars. But the downfall of the last defences became inevitable when the United States refused to use their aircraft to relieve the besieged camp. It fell on 7 May 1954.

The French army lost thousands of dead, thousands of prisoners who would go into a cruel captivity, and strategic control of central Indochina. The name Diên Biên Phu would become a symbol, and we shall soon see it in that form. Meanwhile, there was no other solution than to go to Geneva and accept the international negotiation that détente now permitted.

Laniel and Bidault had to resign themselves to it, but not for long because it would soon be the task of Pierre Mendès France to take their place there.

Indeed in every parliamentary debate the lucid and imperious voice of Pierre Mendès France had been raised against Pinay and against Laniel: there is a need to govern, there is a need for drastic action . . . Very shortly, he was asked to do so. When Laniel was overthrown on 12 June, Mendès's investiture was on the 17th. Pierre Mendès France was Jewish, it has to be stated because a persistent anti-Semitism among certain of his enemies will not let it be forgotten. His family had distant connections with Portuguese Jewry, having been driven out of the Iberian peninsula in the seventeenth century and then settling in the Bordeaux region. It is rather unfair, however, to put this aspect of his identity first. He had no ostensible religion, and his deep-rooted and declared attachment was to modern, liberal, all-absorbing and secular France or, to put it in one word, the Republic. Mendès France would be the last of the politicians of any stature for whom the Republic was a reference point, because he loaded the name with the same assortment of combined values that had been vested in it by Victor Hugo, Jules Ferry, Waldeck-Rousseau, Jean Jaurès and Édouard Herriot. The Republic features everywhere in his writings, and the magazine which his close connections would publish between 1956 and 1961 was entitled *Cahiers de la République* (Notebooks of the Republic). For that reason, his friends would designate him a man of continuity; his adversaries and those who were indifferent would condemn it rather as an attachment to the past. Let us call it a tradition. For in all other respects, there was nothing archaic about Mendès France. Unlike the radicals of the preceding generation, such as Herriot, with whom his political culture obviously gave him some affinity, he took a serious view of the weight and complexity of economic questions and the worldwide nature of diplomatic problems, and he did not have too many illusions about the actual functioning of the parliamentary regime. Without doubt, that tension between so many 'old-world' principles and so much modern awareness was the basis of some of his attraction for intellectual young people of a left-wing background. He also fascinated them by the level of his intelligence, his great capacity for hard work and his austerity. And by a life that was rich and irreproachable.

Born in Paris in January 1907, into a family of cloth merchants, he had studied law and his debut as a militant had consisted, at the head of the LAURS (Ligue d'action universitaire républicaine et socialiste, University republican and socialist league of action), in fighting the nationalist, Maurrassien and fascist-sympathizing leagues for the streets of the Latin Quarter. A barrister, he soon entered political life as a radical, but a 'Young Turk', and in 1932 became the deputy for Louviers (Eure). Léon Blum, who had noticed him and held him in some esteem although he was not a socialist, opened a ministerial career to him by appointing him Under-Secretary of State for the Budget in his second government (March 1938). Then came the end of the Popular Front and a return to his deputy's seat; after that came the war and mobilization. In 1940, as we have seen, having come back to Bordeaux, Mendès France took part in the voyage of the *Massilia*, at the end of which the Vichy authorities apprehended him in Morocco and imprisoned him, to sentence him at the close of an iniquitous trial. He escaped from the prison in Clermont-Ferrand in 1941, lived in hiding, managed to get to London and joined the Free French air force until General de Gaulle, finding that he was more irreplaceable as an expert in public finance than as an airman, summoned him to sit on the Algiers Committee. We know what followed. Mendès France was as proud of that Resistance activity, of fighting for Free France and working close to the General as he was of his republican battles in calmer times. Gaullist after his own fashion, his first gesture on getting into government in 1954 was to send a deferential message to the General.[8] Not the least fascinating of the stresses exerted on this man – after 1958 – was the coexistence of his genuine attachment for the hero of 18 June and his profound political difference of opinion with the man of 13 May.

The most obvious aspect of the contradictions – or dramas – of Mendèsism is that this left-wing man, invested as president of the Council, would have to recruit his team and his majority from the right. The MRP wanted

[8] It is true that, by a curious chance, it was on 18 June . . .

nothing to do with him, suspecting that he was anti-CED; the SFIO supported him, but did not wish to participate. The Communists voted for him, in order to hasten the peace in Vietnam, but Mendès refused to take their vote into account when calculating his majority (explaining that being about to negotiate an armistice with the Viet-minh, still at war with France, he could not in all decency compromise his government with a party that had so long and so clearly chosen the side of that enemy). He obtained an ample initial majority because he profited from the weariness of an Assembly abandoning itself to a last-ditch remedy. But he built up his team from men with whom he felt an affinity, without taking account of its proportions of parliamentary groups.

Edgar Faure had Finance; Mitterand, the Interior; General Koenig, National Defence; Chaban-Delmas, Public Works – their names are the best known today – with Robert Buron the only MRP member despite the hostility of his party, Christian Fouchet and Jean Berthoin (radical, in National Education). The president of the Council reserved Foreign Affairs for himself, in a duality of position formerly quite usual but tending to become the exception rather than the rule.

Mendès governed with his style, strict and courageous, of 'telling it like it is' before that term existed: an appeal to a wider public opinion by regular talks on the radio, after the fashion of Roosevelt's 'fireside chats', a public resolve to deal with problems in order and to fix precise times for their results; to avoid pretence; to face up to unpopularity (of his government's domestic policy, which was not the most important work, the war declared on the home distillers and alcoholism in general will be recalled, together with its dietetic and symbolic counterpart, the glass of milk distributed to schoolchildren).

With Vietnam, the first important date awaited him. The 'big four', plus Communist China, took part in Geneva in negotiations to settle the conflict in the Far East. The Viet-minh was present; Mendès France had to replace Laniel there.

Diên Biên Phu having fallen a month and a half before he came to power, all that remained for him to do was negotiate the best possible conditions for a cease-fire. That was the choice of the seventeenth parallel as the demarcation line, the French armed forces having to regroup to the south of that line in the southern half of Vietnam administered by Bao Dai, the Viet-minh regrouping its own forces in the north, which was abandoned to their control. The definitive status of Vietnam (in theory to reunite it) would emerge from free elections which would be organized on each of the two sides. As we know, they never took place. The war, at least, was over, and it was the end of June.

The Tunisian matter took over in July. Mendès France resolved to apply to Tunisia, which it may be recalled was officially a protected state and not a colony, a wise strategy of negotiated progress directed towards independence. Flanked by Marshal Juin, who brought him the backing of military and 'pied-noir' nationalism, Mendès went to Carthage to inform the Bey of his decisions, and it was regarded as a success.

In August, a fresh act of courage consisted in finally bringing before the Assembly the debate on the CED. It was a short one, the 'preliminary question' immediately posed by two anti-CED members having received a majority vote, which was the equivalent of a rejection without further ado. The symbolic duo who toppled the CED was composed of a deputy from Algeria, General Aumeran, very conservative and colonial, and the old Herriot, a radical and patriot as in 1917. Mendès and his ministers appear to have accepted this elimination quite easily. In any case, one boil had been lanced.

The problem of the German contribution to European defence now remained to be resolved. It was the subject of the London and Paris agreements, negotiated in the autumn. There was no longer any question of CED; Germany would have its army, but with specific limitations (no atomic weapons). So it would be, and in May 1955 it joined NATO. The restitution of the Saar to the German Federal Republic completed the normalization of its status. Allied troops stationed on its soil would henceforth be there as allies, not occupation forces.

Together with that concern (renegotiating the German affair) another arrived, and a sizeable one to boot! On 1 November 1954 rebellion erupted in Algeria! Mendès France's government confronted it with resistance. This was beginning to be standard procedure.

As the wonder doctor had treated the two former maladies for which he had been summoned, Vietnam and the CED, he ceased to be indispensable, and the deputies could punish him for his bothersome nature. On 6 February 1955 he would be overthrown, in the course of a fairly stormy sitting, which would in no way affect his popularity among the extra-parliamentary left – far from it.

Meanwhile, with Algeria, a new (and final) phase opened in the history of the Republic.

Since the end of the world war, the cold war had set East against West in a direct confrontation that left the greater part of the colonized mainlands passive. By contrast, after 1953–4 while East–West détente was beginning, the upsurge in decolonization was accentuated and tended to introduce a sort of third partner into world history, looked at overall. The two colonial wars of the Fourth Republic were thus placed in two fairly different perspectives. Whereas the war in Vietnam could easily be seen as an element of the cold war, if for nothing else than the fact that, on the Vietnamese side, it came under Communist direction, the Algerian war, on the contrary, would be defined by both the ideological woolliness and the specific nationalism that characterized in general the revolt of colonial peoples, with of course some other specifically French-Algerian features.

What in fact was Algeria in 1954? Three French *départements*, but with a singularly original population: eight and a half million natives, Muslim Arabs and Kabyles, and slightly fewer than one million inhabitants of European extraction, for the most part born in Algeria: chiefly French but also Spanish, in addition to natives of the Jewish persuasion, who were French by virtue of Crémieux's decree in 1870. There was a political life, organized in outline around three types of party: elements of metropolitan French parties (radicals, socialists, Gaullists, etc.) which recruited almost entirely from among the European and Jewish population; nationalist parties which recruited solely among indigenous circles; and the Algerian Communist Party, which was proud to be the only one to include militants, and to enjoy a certain audience from both sides of the ethnic barrier.

Old and different, the Algerian nationalist movement prided itself on a rather religious component (Islamic) in Algeria itself (several notables, ulemas) and a less religious, more social, sometimes vaguely Communist component in the working classes, whose migration to France had started in the 1920s. It was from there that Messali Hadj had emerged, with the North-African Star, then the PPA (Algerian People's Party). The effervescence of 1942–4 had acted rather as a stimulus to the movement. The Algerian Communist Party (PCA), with the help of numerous French Communist officers then present in Algiers, had made progress. The PPA, banned under this old title, had re-formed under the name of Movement for the Triumph of Democratic Freedoms (MTLD), and was to remain the largest numerically and the most popular. Lastly, some moderate notables had shown signs of rebellion and, regarding the status quo as humiliating and national independence as a utopian dream, had made demands on behalf of the natives for liberal reforms and assimilation to France. That had been the line of the manifesto presented to the authorities in 1943 by the pharmacist Fehrat Abbas. It was continued by the creation of a moderate indigenous party, the Democratic Union of the Algerian Manifesto (UDMA).

Let us return to 8 May 1945, which had seen the outbreak of revolt in the Constantine, on a large scale mainly in Setif. Was it spontaneous or provoked? At all events, it was popular, violent and anti-French. All the political men repudiated it, but it was a matter of some moment because the extremely brutal repression carried out by the army must have driven many an Algerian to anger, and thence to nationalism.

In the aftermath of a world war that was officially emancipatory, and in the framework of the progressive constitutions of 1946, it was impossible to leave in their current state three French *départments* in which only a minority enjoyed full citizenship and the right to vote. In 1947, parliament had therefore granted Algeria a status that was fairly innovative because it envisaged everyone having the right to vote. The only reservation was that, in order to avoid European colonials being swamped by the native majority, two series of deputies were planned, emanating from two distinct electoral colleges. The first elections took place in 1948. Normal in the European college, they were anything but in the second college, where the administration exerted every possible pressure to ensure that 'yes-men' obtained preference over nationalists. The chance was perhaps lost there to integrate representative nationalists into a system of deliberation and negotiation. However, a rigged ballot could do nothing but push Arab Algeria into the violent forms of political protest. The governor general presiding over that disaster was M.-E. Naegelen, who has already been mentioned.

Between 1948 and 1954 nationalism had thus ripened in the shade. Despite the secrecy to which the MTLD had once more been reduced, its militants mounted raids, obtained money by revolutionary hold-ups, grew toughened in confrontations with the police, and recruited new members. The PCA and UDMA were free, but carried out a propaganda of moderate criticism not uninfluenced by the theme of independence.

The MTLD led a complicated internal existence, since its leader Messali Hadj was under house arrest in France. Conflicts arose between him and the clandestine central committee. It was the 'centralists' who made ready for the armed struggle (OS: Secret Organization). From these ups and downs a third group finally emerged, the Revolutionary Committee of Unity and Action, or CRUA, made up of the 'nine historic chiefs' who would give the order for the uprising on 1 November 1954.

At first there were some isolated attacks, against Europeans, chiefly in the distant massif of the Aurès. Revolt would spread only slowly. But rather than recounting its military history, emphasis will be given here to its political significance in the life of France.

The rebellion followed a principal trend, almost the only one in fact. The CRUA which had launched it was henceforward called the FLN (National Liberation Front). It directed three sorts of militant forces: maquis in the numerous mountainous, wooded and less accessible zones of Algerian territory; underground networks in the towns; and representatives close to foreign nations sympathetic to its cause, first of all Arab states, and chiefly Egypt, ruled since 1954 by Colonel Nasser.

The FLN was soon in a position to hold general meetings in Algeria itself, in various out-of-the-way valleys as, for example in September 1956, the Soummam Congress. That is worth mentioning because it was there that the aim of the revolt was quite clearly set out: independence, that is to say, the setting up of a democratic and social sovereign Algerian state based on Islam, certainly, but respecting fundamental liberties and rejecting racial and religious discrimination. Of course, the future would show that these principles so sympathetically lumped together would not be apportioned in the same way by everyone: would it be more Arab or more multiethnic? Muslim or modern, revolutionary, even secular and with Marxist sympathies? At the height of its international audience, and on the eve of its success, the FLN had in its ranks one of the principal theorists of revolutionary

'Third Worldism', the West Indian Frantz Fanon, a doctor whom French colonial administration had made 'Algerian' by appointing him to the hospital in Biskra. But Fanon died prematurely in 1961 and Fanonism retreated rapidly before Islam. Nevertheless, for several years he contributed to imparting appeal and prestige to the 'Algerian revolution' in the view of the European left. In fact, opinion to the north of the Mediterranean was – and would be – decisive, and we must pick it up where it began.

At the end of 1954 French opinion was divided between several positions. The nationalist argument of the Algerian rebels at first found only the tiniest support – a few isolated intellectuals, generally 'Trotskyists' (the vague generic title then applied to the nebulous revolutionaries who wished to be independent of the PC and even further to the left).

At the other end of the spectrum was the vast majority of Algerian Europeans, together with the vast majority of opinion in France (virtually all the right and part of the left): 'Algeria is France.' The natives belonged to an inferior civilization. That judgement of them could sometimes stem from a simply cultural estimation, sometimes quite clearly from a racist point of view. The problem of knowing whether to keep them as inhabitants subordinate to France, or to assimilate and integrate them, remained vague. The vital thing was to beat them, and conquer the rebellion.

The official French position, of Mendès France's government and part of the left, was situated midway between the two. If, like the preceding groups, it recognized that Algeria was France, and that the rebellion had to be put down, it brought a specific addition. Algeria was France, the war must be won, but the rebellion was the result of objective causes which must be addressed without delay: Algeria was in revolt because it had not been assimilated, and that had not been done because it had been neglected. First of all, it was 'under-administered' (people suddenly became aware that the three 'French *départements*' were immense, and they were divided into twelve with a ramification of the network of officials so as finally to cover or reach distant communes). Next, it was 'underdeveloped' (therefore there was a need to equip, instruct, carry out agrarian reform, and to this end 'special administrative sections' were created, harking back to the old military tradition of the impartial educational officer). Such was the line of the governor, General Soustelle, a brilliant university man, who had come from the Popular Front and the Resistance, then became a Gaullist, and was appointed to Algiers by the Mendès government; he committed himself sufficiently to this path to be initially frowned upon by conservative colonials, that is, almost everybody.

As always, the PC developed its own doctrine. Distinct from both the nationalism of the FLN (Algeria as an Arab country to be restored) and from the French Algerian argument, it still held to the interesting theory formulated by Maurice Thorez in 1938: Algeria was a 'nation in the process of formation' in the act of being created by 'combining twenty races'.

All these positions were to evolve during the course of the war. Evolve because of the vicissitudes of the war, but also because of its conditions and nature. For the singularity of this tragedy in French history is that, more than in many other cases, the form somehow outweighed the content. So important were the controversies over the methods of combat that arguments about the means made more impact than considerations of the ends, and were even able to modify them.

The FLN organized the maquis, which soon became real military units capable of waging a kind of moving war against the French army in regions that were not easily accessible, particularly in Great Kabylia and the south of the Constantine. But it also had available a clandestine apparatus, which had, or would have, its hidden agents in every 'douar', every town and every quarter of the towns in mainland France where émigré Algerians were living; it needed them to get its propaganda circulated, to recruit fighters, organize raids and, above all, obtain contributions – a veritable tax imposed by the Algerian state before such a thing existed – secretly but imperiously demanded. It was all very well for this apparatus to be 'in its element' among a theoretically sympathetic population, it had to make itself known and obeyed, to strike at informers, traitors and the recalcitrant. In short, it soon acquired a sometimes bloody reputation for harshness. Besides, it stepped up raids in Algiers and other towns, and had few scruples about making spectacular bomb attacks in public places, striking sometimes peaceable groups of Europeans. For this combination of reasons, in the great bulk of French opinion, the FLN rapidly gained an image of terrorism and cruelty.

The opposing camp, of France, did not prove any more angelic. It was made up of the army, the police and, after a while, territorial units formed from colonial volunteers. The French army dealt with the war on the ground, with some tactical handicaps which it made up for by the superiority of its weaponry. The air force therefore bombed and sometimes burned suspect villages or forests.

The police arrested rebel militants, who were brought to trial. As France was not at war, for want of a state to oppose, rebels were tried as common law criminals and, if they had caused death or even only attempted to do so, they were frequently sentenced to capital punishment and guillotined.

The army and the police, in short, systematically sought out the underground fighters, which suggests those operations of total investigation that have brought into the French language those sinister metaphors, commonplace today, 'tight control', 'combing' and 'going through something with a fine-tooth comb'. The underground member, or the individual presumed to be familiar with him, had to talk and was made to talk. The horror of the crime he was preparing to commit – a blind murderous attack – justified in advance the means used to obtain the information in time: torture. Thus that practice was established, and would gradually develop, starting from rough ill-treatment still close to the classic 'beating-up' and reaching a mechanical refinement more evocative of the occupation period.

This escalation of violence gave rise to a certain number of consequences. The cruelty of the rebels reinforced the argument of the supporters of French Algeria: those people were savages, and it was right to reduce them to obedience in order to conquer them; all methods were justified.

The cruelty of the repression, on the other hand, shocked those sectors of opinion whose doctrine and culture denied that 'all methods' could be used, or that politics could be separated from morality. On the extreme left, in certain left-wing circles and certain Christian circles, denunciation of the torture led to fixing attention on the Algerian problem, an increasing awareness of it and then sympathy towards finding a new solution: those individuals, at first defended as victims, ultimately aroused interest in the cause which they represented. Apart from the problems of violation of the law, was there an overall problem in Algeria of the fate meted out to these people? Some progress was made along those lines.

In order to reconstruct and render understandable the political conditions of those appalling years, one must take account of the contradiction contained in the argument of upholders of French Algeria: if one turns moralist by accusing the FLN enemy of barbarism, how can one be completely absolved of acting barbarously against it? So, for the time being, the use of torture by the forces of repression was far less often justified than . . . denied. Consequently, the propaganda of the Algerophile camp, which would appear and gradually increase on the left (and which was sometimes hindered by the recognized brutality of the FLN), was at first used to establish the fact of torture in the face of official denials. Thus polemics made their reappearance; of the type which searches for the truth (revelations of documents, analyses, production and criticism of testimony) and the type which argues for the right of truth against reasons of state. In this way the Algerian war made the history of France regress, well short of the occupation period, to the time of the Dreyfus Affair.

During 1955 the governments of Mendès France (until February) and Edgar Faure (February–December), both represented in Algiers by Soustelle, initiated the reforms already mentioned and, on the other hand, waged war. Army and police fought. A 'state of emergency' was declared in Algeria, which brought in its wake censorship of the press and the dissolving of the Algerian PC, although it had straightaway kept its distance with regard to the rebellion and was trying to conduct an original and more finely shaded policy of action.

From spring onwards, the call-up of national service conscripts swelled the ranks of the army, while the rebellion began to receive visible moral support from the outside world: in April 1955 the Bandung Conference, a powerful common demonstration by peoples who had become independent, Third World, or nonaligned countries (Nehru's Indians, Nasser's Egyptians, Tito's Yugoslavia, with the Chinese of Mao and Chou En-lai forming a link between nonalignment and the Communist universe), received and acclaimed an FLN delegation. In September friendly countries put the Algerian question before the United Nations' Assembly. French diplomats violently rejected this initiative, since France held the conflict to be an internal matter. Meanwhile in Algeria a political development was being outlined: the deputies of the second college of the Algerian Assembly, originally fairly docile towards the official government, while repudiating the terrorism of the rebels, condemned the excesses of the repression. They would soon come to demand more rights for their electorate and raise the 'idea of Algerian nationalism'. As the administration would not listen to them, they retaliated by boycotting the institution. The process of a slide towards the FLN by the more moderate Arab notables – a process which would be long but decisive – was already perceptible in these first rifts.

In France, meanwhile, the year 1955 belonged almost entirely to the government of Edgar Faure, to which Antoine Pinay had returned, curiously enough, as Minister of Foreign Affairs. Edgar Faure had other than Algerian difficulties to confront. With economic growth now in evidence, new tensions made their appearance, setting the social struggle off again in complex and sometimes unprecedented conflicts. It was the year when violent strikes in the metal industry in the west of France (Saint-Nazaire) revealed a young and fresh proletariat whose Catholic trades union, CFTC, was in a position to challenge the leadership of the CGT. Chiefly, it was the year that saw the development, against inland revenue officials, of protests, demonstrations and sometimes violent resistance organized by the Union for the Defence of Shopkeepers and Artisans, known as the Poujade Movement after the name of its leader.

Poujadism, moreover, was not merely a corporatist movement of economic resistance to the state; muddled but vehement speeches caused anger to slip from hostility to taxation to hostility towards officials, the state and the privileged, distant, intellectual world of Paris; this Poujadism revealed the feelings of the people and the provinces, sometimes on the verge of anti-Semitism (Mendès France was hated for drinking milk, like an American, and for criticizing the wine of his own country), at all events Gallic and chauvinistic, which made it easier for them to converge with the defence of French Algeria.

For the topic was on everyone's lips! In 1955, Algeria having forced its way on to the front pages with reports and polemics, there was a vast increase in studies on the subject, making it the year in which the great mass of public opinion discovered not only the problem in all its complexity but first of all, quite simply, the existence of a colonial situation. Between the 'repress' of the right and the 'repress but also reform' of the left, it might be that the second option would gain ground.

On another important point Edgar Faure continued the work of Mendès France: he astutely solved the Moroccan problem by bringing back Sultan Mohammed V to Rabat, amid the cheers of his people. It was to accord victory to Moroccan nationalism. But it could also be hoped that Morocco and Tunisia, two very nearly independent Arab nations, under moderate leadership, and on good terms with France, could one day in the near future help in some way to resolve the Algerian affair which affected them so closely.

What else was to be done? Opinion seemed inscrutable and the National Assembly uncertain. Edgar Faure took the step – unusual in France, and therefore courageous – of precipitating early elections by asking President Coty to allow the dissolution of the National Assembly.

The year 1956 thus opened with general elections on 2 January. A critical year, like 1946 and 1947, it must be followed closely, because it is so densely packed with events and turning points cheek by jowl.

One major fact had marked the electoral campaign of December 1956: the formation of a coalition of centre-left known as the Republican Front. It regrouped the SFIO, Mendèsist radicals (Mendès France and all his young recruits, Servan-Schreiber, the team of *L'Express*), the UDSR of François Mitterand and a few Gaullists of liberal and secular tradition, those who had been part of the Mendès majority in 1954, Chaban-Delmas, Christian Fouchet, for example. For the Algerian question they recommended war, but also the solution of the underlying problem by making bold reforms. Opposite them, the right-wing candidates, on the same question, put the emphasis more exclusively on repression.

Keeping themselves separate were the Communists who, though not supporting the Republican Front, were obviously closer to it than to the conservative camp; and the Poujadists, who by contrast made their entry into politics appealing to French nationalism. The vote of 2 January 1956, under a system of proportional representation, was chiefly favourable to those in opposition. The Communists, with five and a half million votes had 146 elected members, the Poujadists, with almost two and a half million votes, 51. The right (17 Gaullists, 100 independents, 71 MRP) had clearly more numerical strength than the left (89 socialists and 70 radicals). Paradoxically, the Republican Front declared itself the winner, and so it was, all in all; certain Gaullists wore its label; the MRP was open to a liberal and social language; and, above all, the Communists – though without any stated alliance – were prepared to support it as the lesser evil or comparative progress. From the outset, that solidarity would act to oust a good number of Poujadists from the Assembly, by means of some fairly questionable removals from office. Was there a tendency towards revenge and the return of Mendès France to the Hôtel Matignon? Some part of opinion no doubt expected that, but the MRP would not have accepted it because of the disagreement over Europe. The MRP, on the other hand, did not have such strong prejudices against the socialists. Well aware of those subtle affinities, President Coty designated the SFIO leader to form a government, since his parliamentary group was after all more numerous than the radical group. Guy Mollet's government thus came into being, with Mendès France as vice-president of the Council (an elegant way to keep him away from the Quai d'Orsay, to the advantage of a good European, Christian Pineau). François Mitterand was Keeper of the Seals, Gaston Defferre, Minister for Overseas France, and General Catroux was appointed resident Minister in Algiers, as a replacement for Soustelle with the rank of minister in addition. By changing the governor general, the new government announced a clear reorientation of the Algerian policy, war but also a negotiated active search for a liberal solution to the problem. Moreover, during this time socialist emissaries secretly left for Yugoslavia to make contact with FLN representatives.

But, before describing how that intention fell foul of 6 February, some other by no means negligible aspects of Guy Mollet's government must be mentioned.

The man himself, as a deeply convinced socialist, wanted to interrupt the conservative slide of French politics that had been started, basically, by the crises in 1947, and even to link up with the great tradition of the Léon Blum of 1936. Getting a law passed that added a third week to the amount of paid holidays had a social, but also slightly symbolic, note. It was then, too, that the famous road tax disc made its appearance, the revenue from which was to be specially allocated to aid for the old. But the views of the government and its leader went beyond the social.

It had two long-term successes, the blueprint law developed by Defferre for black Africa, which allowed a peaceful decolonization to the south of the Sahara, and the negotiation with France's partners in the CECA of what was to become the Common Market, the little Europe of the 1957 Treaty of Rome.

It also had an unfortunate failure, but one which had started out with a great goal: the commencement of talks with the aim of finally resolving by straightforward negotiation, free from passion because held in secret, what remained of the age-old dispute setting the Republic and the Roman Church in opposition. The former MRP minister Robert Lecourt, together with the socialist Maurice Deixonne, Guy Mollet's right-hand man, began discussions that were eventually to go right to the Vatican. But nothing would be achieved by the time when, in 1958, the secular left would lose power again for a long while. All that, therefore, was for the mid-term future, or for history. The near future, and opinion, awaited Guy Mollet in Algiers.

Soustelle, in contact with the realities of the war, had reached a stage where his feelings were resolutely anti-Arab, which had put him at one with the colonists. They cheered him when, recalled to Paris, the time came for him to leave them. In contrast, General Catroux was awaited with hostility.

Guy Mollet decided to go himself to install him in Algiers on 6 February. He was met by a hostile crowd who jeered at the ministers and snubbed them severely (legend has it that tomatoes were thrown at them). Guy Mollet gave in. Impressed by the popular character of the resistance by the pieds-noirs to the proposed change of status? Had he believed beforehand that the colonists were reduced to an aristocracy of planters or local squires? Did he only then discover that Algiers contained a large share of ordinary people, just like the French ordinary people in metropolitan France? The fact remains that he reshuffled the government, and appointed Robert Lacoste (SFIO) as resident Minister to replace General Catroux. By a mischievous twist of history, the date was 6 February, as in 1934 . . .

The year 1956 really began then, running from 6 February to 6 November, ten months marked by four major developments followed by two thunderbolts. The first development was the responsibility of Guy Mollet (and Robert Lacoste). He waged a hard war (calling up reserve officers, sending national service conscripts to Algeria, exerting harsh repression, with torture tolerated or covert), dissolved the Algerian Assembly and convinced himself in addition that, far from being just, on the contrary the FLN cause was part of an Arab expansionism of external origins. Now in Cairo, in July 1956, Nasser nationalized the Suez company and canal and that unilateral decision created a crisis between the Egyptian state and French and British interests. Guy Mollet had the idea of seizing the opportunity of this conflict to strike at Nasser and, in his person, at what he thought to be the source or the mainstay of the Algerian rebellion. He made his preparations in great secrecy with the help of the British and Israeli governments (A. Eden and Ben Gurion). Finally, in October, he covered and approved the initiative of the military command in Algiers, which intercepted a Moroccan aircraft heading for Tunis, where the leaders of the Algerian rebellion had found a place for themselves. The satisfaction of having Ben Bella under lock and key was dearly paid for by the offence given to the King of Morocco, whose aircraft had been stopped in defiance of the law.

The second development was that of the PC. There were many reasons why one would naturally have expected it to oppose the actively colonial orientation of the government. However, it did not do so. First of all, it still regarded as decisive the policy being pursued in metropolitan France, in which the left-wing union which seemed to have been outlined since 2 January appeared to hold the only prospect of success. From that came the idea of remaining linked in overall terms with Guy Mollet even though, on the particular point of Algeria, he was in the wrong. Thus, on 12 March 1956, the Communist parliamentary group accorded its votes to the government for the granting of special powers (it was sacrificing 'the part' – Algeria – for 'the whole' – left-wing union – so argued Thorez before an astounded Communist rank and file). It must be added besides that the PC found it all the easier to support Mollet because it still nurtured an extreme mistrust with regard to the FLN, which it considered now bourgeois, now reactionary and Islamist, now irresponsible, nay, liable to be influenced by ... the United States. Another matter had been causing the PC some discomfort since February 1956, namely remarks that had been made at the Twentieth Congress of the PCUS, where Stalin, yesterday's god, had begun to be the object of criticism. The PC was therefore emerging from the era of unanimous certainties, which had been its strength in the cold war, to enter that of problems, difficulties and doubts, where it is still struggling.

The third development cut across the preceding one: the main anticolonialist criticism opposed to the government originated henceforward from the non-Communist left, and almost from within the government itself. On 23 May 1956 Mendès France resigned. In October it was the turn of Alain Savary, whose own responsibility as official in relations with Morocco and Tunisia had been directly made a laughing stock by the affair of 'Ben Bella's aeroplane'. It is said that Mitterrand and Defferre stayed on as ministers only with reluctance. In short, the opinion of the new left learned to dissociate Mendèsism from Molletism, blaming the latter and praising the former.

Yet – fourth development – overall public opinion seemed to be drawing closer to Molletism than to Mendèsism or Communism. It was maintained at the time that Guy Mollet recovered as much popularity on the right as he lost on the left, and that there was a 'national Molletism'. A cruel and perhaps extreme term, but the fact remains that French nationalism was getting organized; the argument that Algeria was French and that the war must be won at all costs seems to have regained in 1956 the ground lost in 1955. Now, indeed, national service conscripts were in the combat, and for the few soldiers who courageously denounced the colonial situation and the brutalities inflicted by the side of order (of France), there were ten times as many who saw the rebel as an uncivilized and cruel enemy, and spread that image about.

At the beginning of November, in so changed a political landscape, the two thunderbolts burst, their completely accidental simultaneity serving only to multiply their stupefying effect. Budapest and Suez! Budapest? The de-Stalinization initiated by the Twentieth Congress of the PCUS in February had started a crisis for the regime in Communist Hungary and Poland. In Poland, Gomulka managed to take the leadership of the party while remaining acceptable to Moscow. In Hungary, Imre Nagy did not succeed and, on 23 October, Budapest revolted and formed a free popular government. On 1 November, the Soviet army entered Hungary to crush Budapest.

The French PC gave loud, spectacular, triumphal approbation to the entry of the Soviet tanks into the Hungarian capital. That immediately unleashed two things: a remarkable series of resignations, notably of intellectuals, and a powerful wave of anti-Communism, rather comparable to that of summer 1939 after 'the pact'. The PC, weakened by its peripheral dissidences, returned to a state of moral isolation that was perhaps more serious than that of 1947–53.

Furthermore, the emotion aroused, in favour of rebellious Budapest, against the Soviet tanks and the French PC, was not confined to the abstract. In some places, notably Paris, around the besieged premises of the PCF, then situated at 44 rue Le Peletier, there was fighting and several men died. It was at this time that, to commemorate these critical days by saluting the father of the first liberation of the Magyars (in 1848), the Paris municipal council decided to rechristen the Châteaudun crossroad, where number 44 was on the corner, as Kossuth crossroad.

Now, during those very same days, the combined military operations of Israeli, British and French forces on the Suez Canal erupted. Leaving Cyprus, then a British possession, allied airborne troops took control of the disputed zone. France and its allies were on the point of crushing Nasser. But a Soviet ultimatum put a stop to it. Would war break out? Paris and London would not be able to go ahead, and defy Moscow, without American backing. The Americans refused: Eisenhower preferred to favour détente. From then on, Mollet, Eden and Ben Gurion could do nothing but beat a retreat, and Nasser was saved.

Suez was thus a failure. But French opinion, on the whole, did not hold it against Guy Mollet. The villains were the 'Russians', doubly detestable because they were seen simultaneously to crush the likeable rebels in Budapest and rescue Nasser, the friend of the wicked rebels in Algeria! The Russians were to blame and, in second place, the Americans, who had 'abandoned the French' for the sake of keeping good relations between the two superpowers.

Towards the end of 1956, after Budapest and Suez, a certain French nationalist feeling reached its peak, hostile to both the great powers and the Arabs, possibly Molletist for some months, but why not virtually Gaullist? In any case, Mollet's fall was brought about neither by the blow of Suez nor by the war in Algeria, but because, in May 1957, the more moderate elements of his majority, emboldened, refused to tolerate any longer the left-wing fiscal and social policies he maintained.

A Bourgès-Maunoury government was thus formed, lasting from June to September 1957, in principle still harking back to the Republican Front (Bourgès himself belonged to the Radical Party), but the liberal elements of Mollet's team (Mitterrand, Defferre) no longer figured in it. Lacoste, on the other hand, remained in Algiers. It was war, and more bitter than ever. 'The battle of Algiers' was won by General Massu against FLN terrorism and its underground networks; but in mainland France the fight was against the spreading antiwar campaign, which concentrated on the question of torture. The two best-known cases, however, were not Arab and FLN, but Communist and 'European'. First, Henri Alleg, a journalist, who had survived cruel interrogation, found a way to get his long and poignant description of it, under the title *La Question*, through to the outside world. Copies of the pamphlet appeared in February 1958, and were immediately

Massu speaking in Algiers, June 1958. (Photo: Roger-Viollet)

seized and hunted out, but circulated actively. Maurice Audin, an assistant lecturer in the Algiers science faculty, died under 'interrogation', and his disappearance was passed off as an escape by the military authority. But after an unofficial inquiry carried out by some courageous young university men, allying the humanitarian passion of their aims with professional exactness in the discussion of proof, the truth of the matter also circulated, although obstacles were put in its way.[9] Newspapers and bulletins writing about it were seized, but they circulated, mainly in the scientific and teaching world, thanks to complicity which went beyond the circles of the extreme left and Mendèsist left; thanks notably to the Christians. As early as 1956, in their hunt for banned literature, the police had searched the home of a Sorbonne professor, a very well-known Catholic personalist and a member of the Institut de France.[10] Of course this police visit raised an outcry among his disciples and friends, but the Minister of National Defence, Bourgès-Maunoury, is said to have contemptuously replied that it was a lot of fuss to make just because 'the dear professor's papers have been slightly disarranged'.

Such was the atmosphere. The humanitarian camp was of some account because of the diversity and eminent nature of its recruits, for the university, the press, literature and all the young intellectuals who had been attracted by Mendès for three or four years were broadly represented in it. *Le Monde* for the daily press, François Mauriac for literature, were not to be sneezed at! From those names, it will be seen that it was quite a different matter

---

[9] The name of Pierre Vidal-Naquet comes into our story on this account.
[10] Henri Marrou.

from 'the left' in the usual sense of the word. That is doubtless the reason for the reappearance in everyday political language of the word 'liberal' – an elastic word, but here usefully rediscovered and brought up to date. It signified a double opposition to the war in Algeria: by the defence of the rights of man against reasons of state in matters of repression, and basically, by the wish to open negotiations in preference to the military solution.

On the opposite side, the upholders of French Algeria would soon be termed 'ultras' (ultra-colonialists?). The antagonistic pairing of liberals and ultras had already existed . . . under Louis XVIII and Charles X. French politics, gorged with reminiscence, as we know, curiously rediscovered here one of its most ancient semantic duels.

In November 1957, Bourgès-Maunoury yielded his place to another president of the Council, also a radical, Félix Gaillard. But the fiction of the Republican Front was over, because this time the MRP and the right entered in force into the majority and the government. Félix Gaillard painstakingly sought a solution. Presenting a blueprint law for Algeria in January 1958, he spoke of an 'Algerian personality', which seemed daring, and also of an 'integral part of the French Republic', which seemed in contrast to block any changes. But chiefly, he too made war. Now, French troops, who were numerous and increasingly seasoned to battle, were gaining success, and the FLN had to resign itself more and more often to withdrawing its own forces, for rest or in reserve, to the other side of its frontiers, that is, into Moroccan or Tunisian territory, with the uncomfortable toleration of the governments in Rabat and Tunis. Should France respect those 'sanctuaries'? Or violate them, pleading the 'right to pursue' that went back to the era of uncertain frontiers and tribes which wandered nomadically on the fringes of the Sahara? On 8 February, in an attempt to destroy one of these Algerian rebel border camps, the air force dropped bombs that killed some of the civilian population in the Tunisian village of Sakhiet-Sidi-Youssef. Conflict then erupted with Tunisia; it would remain at diplomatic level, but very acute. At the end of some weeks of great tension, the British and Americans jointly proposed that they should use their 'good offices' to reconcile France and Tunisia. Was there a fear that, after discussing the dispute created by the bombing of Sakhiet, the conversation might slip towards an Anglo-Saxon mediation between France and the rebels, a mediation which would of necessity be to the advantage of the latter? The majority of French opinion and, with even greater reason, the ultras appeared to fear so. Robert Lacoste himself warned that the good offices would turn out to be a 'diplomatic Diên Biên Phu'. In short, the moment Félix Gaillard announced that his government accepted the offer of the good offices, he was overthrown.

It was 15 April. The government crisis was to last until . . . 13 May. In fact, the unfolding of the movement of unrest leading to suggest an appeal to de Gaulle started from 15 April.

The process of overturning the Fourth Republic thus began on 13 May 1958. The Fifth would not be formally established until 28 September, the day of the ratification of its Constitution. But the principle of that change of system would be acquired on 1 June, that is, the day of General de Gaulle's investiture as president of the Council. This is therefore a suitable point at which to relate the rapid swing that occurred between 13 May and 1 June 1958. When the moment arrived, de Gaulle would be in power.

De Gaulle in power? Under the Fifth, he would be so as President of the Republic. All the same, he would twice have been president of the Council during the Fourth: from the Liberation until January 1946,[11] and then from June to December 1958, the beginning and the end . . .

Wherefore this final crisis for a regime established fewer than three *lustra* ago? Certainly, the crisis in the colonial system made a large contribution. Yet it must be noted that Britain, Belgium and the Netherlands decolonized without internal upheavals. It would be more worthwhile to talk of the singularity of French decolonization, hesitant, alternating concessions (Bao Dai, Tunisia and Morocco) and repression, exasperating at one and the same time convinced colonialists and convinced anticolonialists.

Crisis in the institutions? Certainly, the Constitution was only recent (1946), too young to be sacred, or hallowed. But how were majorities to be found among two implacable oppositions (PC and RPF) who, as has been said, involved themselves in the game of overturning governments and remained on the outside when it came to constituting them? Those two tough hostile forces without doubt contributed more to the collapse of the regime than any congenital weakness.

In any case, Algeria provided the immediate cause. The war was increasingly hard; at the beginning of May, in the midst of the government crisis, it was learnt that three French soldiers, prisoners of the FLN, had been shot in reprisal for the death of FLN fighters executed for terrorism. It seemed very difficult to win this war against a resolute people who were gaining increasingly powerful support from outside: Nasser, who had surmounted the 1956 crisis; the Third World, which was gradually gaining some weight in the bosom of the United Nations. Even moderate men, silent up till then, were starting to say that, perhaps, the day would come for negotiation (Pierre Pflimlin, MRP, in an Alsatian newspaper). Meanwhile, the long-drawn-out government crisis contrasted with the gravity of the problem and the weight of the tragedies. The time was ripe to launch the idea that the Algerian affair required France to have a government capable of measuring up to it. While small posters and stickers appeared on walls on the theme 'Let us call for de Gaulle', other preparations were being started more discreetly. Let us leave what was happening behind the scenes for what was going on in the open, and the major movements of opinion.

---

[11] We consider that the Fourth Republic began in August 1944, which Gaullists will not allow. But this point has been discussed in the preceding chapter.

The day of 13 May unfolded in stages, with those prompt messages from Paris to Algiers and Algiers to Paris that radio by now allowed and even made commonplace. Pflimlin, then, after the failure of several other deputies and after a month of crisis, presented himself for investiture in the Assembly, announcing a very wide government (MRP, radicals, socialists). That simple announcement triggered the first stage: Pflimlin being taken to hold 'liberal' views (perhaps considering negotiation, as has been said), that is, views that were unacceptable to the ultras, the news of his possible advent unleashed in Algiers the revolt that took control of the general government, without any opposition from the military. Several people, civilians as well as soliders, formed a Committee of Public Safety headed by General Salan.

This item of news – Algiers in a state of riot (putsch? dissidence?) alarmed Paris and facilitated the investiture of Pflimlin, who received very wide support; even the Communists, from hostility to colonialism and the Algerian putschism, saw him as the lesser evil.

But, the final stage, Pflimlin's success radicalized Algiers in return, and General Salan, urged on by the Gaullist emissary Delbecque, brought the day to an end with the cry 'Vive de Gaulle'.

From that moment, the Algerian question was temporarily overshadowed by another – that of de Gaulle's return to power. On 15 May de Gaulle announced publicly that he was prepared to take on the government of the country should the need arise. On 17 May Soustelle, one of his followers, eluding police surveillance, managed to get to Algiers.

There was, and still is, much argument about de Gaulle's role in this matter. The Algerian affair, the Algerian 13 May, brought him to power. Did he seize the opportunity, or did he provoke it? At all events, it is certain that he accepted that his accession to the rank of Head of State came about by an act of rebellion by the army and the Algerian people – the putsch, or coup d'état, as his adversaries would say, rather exaggeratedly.[12] Let us say that he accepted it without scruple, by virtue of the theory of legitimacy. When a regime gets enmeshed in a difficulty to the point where it is weakened, discredited, where it perhaps brings discredit on the nation, or risks being placed under external supervision, then it is no longer sufficiently *national* to be *legitimate*, and *legality* may for the instant be set aside in order to replace the regime with a better one. His aim seems to have been to strengthen the nation, and Algiers provided the opportunity or the means.

On the other hand, for metropolitan France and chiefly for the political classes, Algeria appeared to be a difficult and dangerous problem; for the

---

[12] According to a well-informed witness, the longtime confidant of the General (Alain Peyrefitte), de Gaulle was unaware of the 13 May conspiracy, taking it in his stride, to a certain extent, in order to gain the advantage, and prevent it from taking on a violent and military aspect. The bid for power was toned down, or even replaced, by a 'coup' based on authority, prestige and arbitration.

left and the liberals it was, moreover, a threat. The General's advantage lay in having played on the ambiguity of his relations with Algiers which, let us not forget, appealed to him. He did not present himself as pro the Committee of Public Safety, but neither did he repudiate or condemn it. He preferred to appear as popular leader, relatively more liberal than the extremists, the man who could both solve the problem and avoid resorting to the violence of the paratroops.

In short, everything happened as if de Gaulle had made use both of the pressure of the army in Africa and of his ability to contain it, in such a way that he was summoned by some as a soldier, and by others as a barrier set up against the soliders! That ambiguity about the form (was de Gaulle an accomplice of the putsch? or the last rampart against the putsch?) was clearly matched by an ambiguity of content. There is no more precise information on the extent of the links or connivance of the General with the men in Algiers than there is on what he then thought of the Algerian problem: was he the man to inspire and win this war? Or the man to wipe out the problem, in one fashion or another, even a liberal one? Opinion speculated passionately on all this.[13]

In Colombey-les-Deux-Églises, de Gaulle built up his contacts. Some discreet, some obvious; he established them with Algiers, the army, his networks of henchmen; with Paris and politicians, even those in government. For the latter were utterly bewildered.

The Pflimlin government officially showed great hostility towards Salan's putschists, and consequently towards de Gaulle who, by his declaration of the 15th, revealed some appearance of complicity with them. It therefore defended itself and was conscious, as the legal government, of defending 'republican legality'. Besides, in his team, Pflimlin entrusted the Interior to the socialist Jules Moch. The choice was doubly significant; first, because his energy and *savoir-faire* were technically well proven; then because, morally, he claimed to be republican. Jules Moch, who believed he had 'defended the Republic' in 1947 and 1948 against the worrisome Communist thrust, was the man who was to defend it again, on another front, against tough opponents.

Left-wing opinion, or at least its conscious militants, whether they were liberals, socialists, Mendèsists or Communists, stuck to this point of view and thus supported the Pflimlin–Moch government. There was a feeling of being mobilized for the Republic and the law, against 'personal power' or (and) 'the paras'. That strategy failed. In general opinion, the expected republican reflex did not really work. The majority of the French, perhaps already rather weary of the war, thought that de Gaulle would put an end

---

[13] This will still be argued for a long while to come, because there are contradictory writings and testimonies. Nevertheless, today it seems established that on the eve of 1958 the General was already convinced of the impossibility of preserving the status quo in Algeria, and that at the very least more flexible links would be necessary. Jean Lacouture, *De Gaulle*, vol. 2, *Le Politique*, Seuil, pp. 510–11.

to it somehow, and the danger of 'personal power' apparently seemed no more threatening to them than that of foundering.

Just as easily, even in top political offices, certain men who had come to terms with the General's arrival, accepted the contact and handled the transition. The greater part of the SFIO behind Guy Mollet showed resignation rather than fight. As for the PC, which had at its disposal troops who were motivated and more eager, whether it was also more resigned to the change in power, without admitting it, or whether it was locked into the strategy consisting of letting everything pass through the union of the left, it restrained its faithful from demonstrating and waited for the SFIO to agree to common action. It would have to wait a long time for that agreement . . .

Above all, the republican reflex was missing in the state. Jules Moch and the most resolute ministers met with no zeal, as if each civil servant, certain of the General's victory, either desired or awaited it. Police, army, transports, none of them 'responded'. The government thus practised a complex and incoherent mixture of decisions that were firm but badly applied, and secret procedures.

Such was the general climate.

On 17 May, having come from Algiers, the paratroops arrived in Corsica and there set up authorities favourable to dissidence. This seizure of power took place easily in Ajaccio, slightly less so in Bastia, where a socialist deputy mayor put up a symbolic resistance, which at once gained him the honour of Chevalier of the *Légion d'honneur* bestowed by 'the government of the Republic'. That was enough! Could there have been possibilities of or leanings towards popular resistance, maquis against the paras? Were they encouraged or discouraged? There were all kinds of contradictory rumours on this point.

All the same, Corsica was an ordinary French *département* where a coup d'état operation had just taken place. Psychologically, that made 13 May even worse. In mainland France the event redoubled the indignation of the minority, but also the fear of civil war and, consequently, for most people, the desire to have done with it. Corsica could be a precedent and a staging post for a new leap towards the north. De Gaulle, informed about it, would remember it, or keep it in reserve.

For the fruit was ripening. President Coty soon mentioned publicly the possibility that France might appeal to 'its most illustrious son'. Contacts and approaches increased. On 27 May, the last stroke was psychological. De Gaulle made public that he had 'begun the process' of accession to investiture. It was untrue, but very quickly became true when Pflimlin, on the 28th, not daring to deny it formally and thus confront the General directly, preferred to resign.

This upheaval of the left, on that same 28 May, was therefore in principle forced upon it. There was a day of general strike, summoned by the FEN alone, and a great protest procession in the streets of Paris; at its head, Pierre Mendès France and all the chief personnel of the regime's last battle. It was at once dubbed a 'funeral procession–demonstration'. De Gaulle meanwhile agreed to save appearances; since there was no longer a government, he agreed to come to the rostrum of the Palais-Bourbon to ask for appointment in order to form one. He obtained it by 329 votes (the right, the MRP, most of the radicals and about half the socialists, including Guy Mollet). Two hundred and twenty-four deputies voted against (the minority of the radical group with Mendès France, various men of the centre-left, including Mitterrand, 49 SFIO, including Gaston Defferre, and the 147 Communists). On 3 June, the same majority decided that there was reason to change the Constitution.

The Fourth Republic was therefore dead, that was certain. But was the Republic plain and simple in a bad position or threatened? That is what the General's adversaries thought at the time. What is interesting, for history, is to note that they did not manage to convince opinion, not that of the left wing. Was it the result of the defection of certain leaders of that left? Or the wearing-out of a form of republican culture which had known great influence under the Third Republic but which, badly maintained since then, had also undergone a great deal of competition? Or – the last hypothesis – did the French know the General well enough to be unable to imagine him as a dictator?

11

The General
1958–1969

General de Gaulle was in power from 1 June 1958. Formally, he at first carried out the function of president of the Council, René Coty remaining as Head of State.

The change in the Constitution that would allow him to attain the supreme office would take six months – six months of formalities. But the reality of his presence made itself felt immediately. At that point the man became a familiar figure to the French.

His name, to start with, had been known to them for a long while; was not 18 June 1940 already a part of history, and a history that was officially exemplary, honoured, recounted, taught? It is no small achievement, for a political figure, to come back on the scene when he has already made an excursion into legend. It brings to mind La Fayette, who was a hero of the already mythical year 1789 when he made a triumphant 'comeback' between 1820 and 1834. There the analogy must stop, mainly because La Fayette . . . did not appear on television!

For the General's second piece of luck was that his attainment of power coincided, broadly speaking, with the spread of television sets into the majority of French homes. From then on the General was in their presence, either because television news reporters were filming his comings and goings, or because he himself arranged to give an address or a press conference. Fully aware of this advantage, he made much use of it. Everyone thus came to know that tall, erect figure, his great height compensating for and almost rendering unnoticeable the portliness that had come with age; his alternating civilian and military clothing, according to whether he wanted to appear as the chief dignitary of normal times or an extension of the national hero; that long, heavy, severe face, with the large nose that caricaturists delighted in exaggerating still further, straight hair, the direct and insistent gaze, the studied play with his large spectacles; above all, that voice, low-pitched, sometimes to the point of huskiness, with a slow and heavy delivery – a rare quality which provoked a

desire to smile, was easy to imitate and 'send up', but which more often impressed. And then, his eloquence. Here, too, it was as if de Gaulle knew how to play on his peculiarities, and turn to his own advantage characteristics which, in other people, might have seemed bizarre and consequently irritating. A cultured man, the former brilliant student at the beginning of the century, de Gaulle spoke as people no longer can, or want to, speak today; for every ten who smiled, another hundred or more were enthralled; his memory and his vocabulary provided him with verbal strokes of inspiration, many of which would remain in the folklore of the period, while others – as we shall soon see – would be veritable political weapons.

His working week was spent in Paris, for a few months at the Hôtel Matignon and then in the Élysée Palace. As often as he could, he went back to La Boisserie, his family home in Colombey-les-Deux-Églises (Haute-Marne), for what he would *not* have liked to hear called *le week-end*. He, or rather they, would go there, for the General and his wife liked to be together as much as possible.

Madame de Gaulle, née Yvonne Vendroux (1900–79), existed with him in a natural yet remarkable balance of presence and absence. She was tactful enough not to lay herself open to accusations of political meddling, present enough to make it clear that the General was the head of a united and Christian family.

It has been claimed that 'Aunt Yvonne', widely known to be pious, austere and conventional as in the good old days, reinforced the General's tendencies to traditional bourgeois conformism. But he was quite capable of appreciating others. Among his entourage, André Malraux, closest of the close to him, with a revolutionary and agnostic past, modern tastes and a sulphurous talent, brilliantly held the centre stage for modernity. Like Napoleon III between the devout empress and the agnostic Victor Duruy, it must be admitted that General de Gaulle thought and did as he pleased. But he held fast to old and natural attachments, Free France, with its old companionships, and the family. His only son, Philippe de Gaulle, a naval officer, made his career at sea. His son-in-law, General de Boissieu, the husband of one of his daughters, was to serve him more closely as aide-de-camp. As for the memory of the other daughter, who died in 1948, it will be found in the cemetery where the present chapter closes.

For the moment, de Gaulle's second passage through French history began brightly. The General very quickly formed a government of National

Press conference on 31 January 1964. The General's words and writings aroused much comment. But in the age of television the image was just as important, and thus expressions, mannerisms, gestures. Press photographers, who indulged to their hearts' content, show that de Gaulle had also mastered this aspect of his art. (Photo: Keystone)

Union, in which were gathered representatives of all the parties (or pieces of parties) that had supported him. Symmetrically backing him, therefore, were Antoine Pinay and Guy Mollet, Félix Houphouet-Boigny representing black Africa, and Nefissa Sid-Cara representing both Muslim and progressive Algeria. Chief among the ministers appeared to be Michel Debré, the Keeper of the Seals. Only the Communists and Mendèsists remained on the outside.

Two interlaced problems were left: Algeria, and the institutions. In the view of the general public, there was no doubt that the tragedy of the war was the prime concern, and the remaking of the political machine of only secondary importance.

For de Gaulle, these priorities were certainly the other way round: Algeria was *one* of the problems that France had to deal with, but in order to deal with that and others it must be strong; now (a postulate) it would not become strong other than by means of institutions which allowed it to 'govern'.

Should we recall here the General's political line of thought? Its essence has already been set out at various points. It was a nationalism, since France, the object of a veritable cult, occupied the peak of his scale of values and the centre of his preoccupations. France must not be brought down, therefore must not be subordinated, must have its independence and, if possible, a standing worthy of it (that is, elevated) in the world. As France could expect nothing from others, it was up to the French to ensure its major status by being strong. From that basic desire for strength issued a concern for modernity (on the economic plane) and, chiefly, a concern for efficiency (on the political plane); in other words, a concern to have stable and well-managed political institutions. That nationalism was not confined to itself alone; it accepted, if not submission to, at least association with, other equally demanding values, and ends that were not specifically French.

Firstly, liberalism. De Gaulle, like all republicans of old or new origin, accepted the programme of the law-based state, the sovereignty of the people, and all civil and political liberties. Next, humanism, which led to combating Nazi-style barbarity as well as the brutality of social exploitation (hence the importance attached to capital–labour association). Whether those liberal and humanist components of Gaullist thinking had been borrowed, as it were, by permeation from the victorious republican trend or from that of social Christianity, or whether both those paths of influence had acted together, is of little moment here, since the aim is to sketch the general history of France rather than to penetrate the life of each of its heroes. De Gaulle's policies were sufficiently faithful to liberal principles for him not to be denied the label 'republican', should he claim it. But that republicanism was undeniably closer to the right than the left, as may be seen from his worship of nation, from his display of deference for religion, from a few old antiparliamentary reflexes and, lastly, his strange theory on legitimacy.

After 13 May, and perhaps because of it, de Gaulle believed he must take power in order to remake the state. The drama lived through by Algeria had provided the opportunity at least as much as it had created a problem. But the General could no longer fail to recognize the objective urgency that it presented or the importance that anxious public opinion attached to it.

That is why, on 4 June, he went by plane to Algiers. Did he already have in mind the solution for which he must win acceptance? It is probable, but it was certainly confidential. Relations between the colonial empire, the ruling powers in France and French opinion have formed the subject of a synthesizing examination which carries conviction.[1]

From 1880 to 1930, the colonies appear to have been wanted and exploited by French capitalism amid a certain indifference of public opinion. After about 1930, in a remarkable changeover of attitudes, it was by contrast opinion, gradually trained by the Republic, that seems for the most part to have accepted the colonial mission, become attached to it, deemed it a good thing, while French capitalism more accurately measured its poor profitability, its cost, nay, its nuisance value. Decolonization accepted as a relief would appear to have been the normal outcome of a realization of the situation in which capitalist circles were well ahead of the public at large.

From that to making de Gaulle the spokesman, or the product, of that inclination was but a step. However, no matter how modern in outlook the General may have been in other respects, he had not been seen, in 1945 for instance, to be in any hurry to decolonize Vietnam. The question of when he personally yielded to the analysis of colonialism as a burden thus remains completely unresolved.

The only certainty is that in Algeria he found himself acclaimed by large throngs of people, the races commingling, with Europeans and Muslims exchanging fraternal embraces that were not all part of an act. After all, are not the most successful enthusiasms and unanimities always those to which everyone contributes his wishes, where convergence with those of one's neighbour is sometimes the product of a misunderstanding? Another certainty, the most famous and most acclaimed of the phrases in his great speech delivered in Algiers was 'I have understood you', which singularly lends itself to equivocal interpretation. It was much observed, at the end of this trip, that the perfectly clear expression 'Long live French Algeria' was uttered only once (at Mostaganem). For the moment, the war continued in the mountains, while dissident Algiers came back under the authority

---

[1] Jacques Marseille, *Empire colonial et capitalisme français: histoire d'un divorce*, Albin Michel, 1984.

of the Paris government, which had come to make its presence known (rather – relatively speaking – like Toulouse in September 1944). Metropolitan France continued to be divided, but in an atmosphere of calm, between those who relied on the General to bring the rebels to heel, those (much more rare) who pinned their hopes for decolonization on him, and those who merely wanted the whole affair to be over, no matter how.

During the summer, the government, assisted by several lawyers, prepared a new Constitution. Michel Debré was in supreme charge of all this work. Out of it emerged the system which still governs France, but with two sets of measures that would soon be obsolete: those pertaining to the French Union, that is to say, dealing with the relations of France with erstwhile colonial states still associated with it; and those touching the election of the President. As the opposition and part of opinion were currently likening 13 May to 2 December (1851), and as men such as Mollet and perhaps Debré were, by tradition, sensitive to that argument, resort was not made to universal suffrage to elect the President, but to a bastard joint electoral body of a more or less senatorial type (deputies, including municipal councillors, plus an addition of supplementary delegates to the urban councils to take some account of the mass of their population). There were about 80,000 electors in all.

The new Constitution made its mark by two features which still characterize it: restrictions on parliamentary power (limited sessions, a not entirely free agenda, conditions for overthrowing the government made difficult by the motion of censure procedure, etc.); and the granting of an effective political role to the President of the Republic. As a Prime Minister was retained, at the head of the other ministers, the problem of the exact sharing of executive responsibilities between him and the Head of State was undeniably badly defined, and still is, as we know.

Outside the Constitution, but in a way just as significant, an electoral law stipulated the abandonment of the departmental list ballot with proportional representation (a system deemed too favourable to the 'parties'), and a return to the single name ballot, in two rounds, in limited constituencies (as in the majority of the years and regimes prior to 1940). In order to escape 'parties', there would thus be a return to notables, including moreover party notables and Gaullist notables.

The Constitution was completed at the end of August. On 4 September, the anniversary of the Third Republic (4 September 1870), de Gaulle and Malraux presented it at a great meeting in the place de la République in Paris. A rather laboured but none the less significant symbolism: the new team had no wish to leave the opposition with the monopoly of the power to attract that the Republic was deemed to possess.

More effectively, the General had brought Guy Mollet into his game, and the clever secretary general influenced his party to come down in favour of a 'yes' in the referendum planned for 28 September. Guy Mollet's arguments were not to be scorned. His rallying to de Gaulle, in the second half of May 1958, had the 'double aim of avoiding a civil war that would be lost in advance and putting an end to the bloodshed in Algeria'.[2] While the first goal was attained, the second would not be, for reasons that we shall see. All the SFIO would thus vote 'yes', including certain members who had voted on 1 June against de Gaulle's investiture, the best known of these later supporters being the mayor of Marseille, Gaston Defferre. The implacably anti-Gaullist (or, if preferred, anti-13 May) left wing of the SFIO then broke away, around Daniel Mayer and Édouard Depreux, to found the PSA (Parti socialiste autonome, Autonomous Socialist Party).[3] These anti-Gaullist socialists formed a coalition with the friends of Mendès France and François Mitterrand to create the UFD (Union des forces démocratiques, Union of Democratic Forces). Only the UFD and the Communist Party called for a 'no' vote. Needless to say, all the parties of the centre and right were in favour of the 'yes'.

On 28 September, the triumphal acceptance of the Constitution (about 80 per cent 'yes' votes registered in a turnout of 85 per cent) inaugurated the setting up of the Fifth Republic and, as Louis Napoleon would have said, 'absolved' 13 May. In total round figures, the 19 per cent 'no' vote represented 4,600,000 electors, an extremely low number if one considers that, until then, the PC alone never 'weighed' fewer than 5,000,000 votes. For the traditional Republic, it was the low-water mark.

Gaullism, however, as has been said, had no desire to crush the idea of the Republic in itself: the RPF, arisen from its ashes with the victory of the man who inspired it, reconstituted itself for the elections under the name 'Union pour la nouvelle République' (Union for the New Republic, or UNR). In the elections of 23 and 30 November 1958, the advent of political Gaullism was consecrated by a new triumph. The PC found itself with just ten deputies; the UFD had none at all (Mendès and Mitterrand were beaten); the left that had said 'yes' received scarcely any recognition from the electorate, with only about forty representatives (including Guy Mollet, but Gaston Defferre was beaten). Opposite, the Gaullists of the UNR obtained 198 seats, and the moderates, conservative notables of various political shades, favourable towards 13 May while refusing the Gaullist tag, achieved 133.

On 21 December, the finishing touch to the Constitution remained to be put in place: the President of the Republic. The restricted electoral body already defined caused no surprise when it elected General de Gaulle by a 77 per cent vote. The Communist candidate, Georges Marrane, an old and seasoned militant, a working-class man, senator and mayor of Ivry,

---

[2] The expression comes from his closest companion at that time, Maurice Deixonne (autobiographical note quoted by Georges Canguilhem in his Obituary, *Bulletin de la Société des anciens élèves de l'ENS*, 1989).

[3] The PSA would soon merge with several other, sometimes ex-Communist, little groups to become the PSU (Parti socialist unifié) of Michel Rocard, Gilles Martinet, Jean Poperen, etc.

collected 14 per cent, and the UFD candidate, Albert Chatelet, a *normalien*, teacher, former Dean of Faculties, a mathematician, in the great tradition of left-wing intellectuals . . . 9 per cent. On 8 January 1959, de Gaulle installed himself in the Élysée, in place of René Coty, and appointed Michel Debré to succeed him at the Hôtel Matignon, with the new title of Prime Minister.[4] His government was immediately sent off towards the right by the withdrawal of participation by the socialists, in disagreement with Antoine Pinay's economic policy.

So began the Fifth Republic *sensu stricto*, bearing the full imprint of de Gaulle, with the institutions that he wanted and the office of President that he filled. It was still the Republic, reaffirmed with insistence, but it was not at all the same! According to custom, the new President had a medal struck to commemorate his accession to the highest office of the state. On the front his own image, and on the reverse a symbol. From Jules Grévy to René Coty, all his legitimate predecessors (excluding Pétain, obviously) had chosen a woman's head as a symbol of the state. De Gaulle, however, opted for a cross of Lorraine inscribed in the letter V. Exit Marianne, to some extent . . . She would never again appear in that discreet but noble position.

In the Élysée Palace, de Gaulle worked, received people, consulted and assembled, under his presidency, the weekly Council of Ministers. The Élysée Palace was to become the real centre of power, and it was then that it began to be referred to customarily as 'le Château'. Thus there came back into use – and not by chance – an ancient but forgotten feature of French political vocabulary, evocative of the time when, from 1815 to 1848 under the constitutional monarchy, the French had done their apprenticeship in modern and free politics. The king (Louis XVIII, Charles X, Louis-Philippe) then reigned and, more or less, governed, although he also had a principal or prime minister. There could therefore sometimes be some hesitation about supreme responsibility and, even when the government exercised its specific prerogatives (or when the deputies were preparing to vote), one could not completely avoid taking account of what views on the matter were held at 'le Château'. A timid liberalism had invented that euphemism to mean the intentions of the king, the court or the entourage, because those monarchs then lived in the Tuileries, which Paris had always called 'le Château' (and not 'le Palais') because, in the era of its construction in the sixteenth century, that royal residence had been outside the city walls (and people said 'Palais' when the residence was in the town, and 'Château' when it was in the country). We must therefore go right back to the time of Catherine de Médicis to give a true explanation

---

[4] To succeed him, at least formally. De Gaulle, and the Gaullists after him, considered that power had been transferred from Matignon to the Élysée, and that the General therefore had no 'successor'. Similarly, power was transferred to Matignon between Pompidou, who headed the General's office, and Debré. (A detail of which A. Peyrefitte reminded me.)

of this term in modern political jargon – but the important point is its resurgence, because that is enough to tell us that the Constitution of the Fifth, with its badly shared executive power, could not fail to confer on the Head of State an additional, elastic and unofficial authority.

Besides, as is well known, the opposition would constantly trot out the monarchic metaphor to attack the Head of State, even when it was no longer de Gaulle. *Le Canard enchaîné* ran a weekly chronicle, which lasted for years, featuring de Gaulle as Louis XIV, and worth mentioning chiefly because it enriched French jargon. As André Ribaud, in this chronicle, was doing a pastiche of the *Mémoires* of Saint-Simon, in order to avoid anachronisms he had to speak of daily happenings using only the words that were current in the seventeenth century. Thus, an aeroplane became a 'flying coach', and the television 'strange windows'. The nickname has remained.

The Algerian war was then entering its second era. If de Gaulle had sought power in order to bring that conflict to an end, the enterprise was not very successful, since the war lasted under his authority slightly longer than under the Fourth Republic (three years and seven months, from 1 November 1954 to 1 June 1958, and three years and nearly ten months, from 1 June 1958 to 19 March 1962)!

But Algeria was not – let us repeat – the aim of the operation. As for its final settlement, that could not be achieved in the short term because it would have to go through two contradictory phases between which a change in policy would take place.

The war, in fact, appeared at first to forge ahead on the French Algerian option. How is it possible to explain otherwise the 96 per cent 'yes' vote obtained in Algeria by the referendum of 28 September (in theory on the Constitution, but actually *carte blanche* for the General)? The Europeans who mostly wanted French Algeria had thus interpreted the 'I have understood you.' As for the Arabs . . . it has frequently been said that, in the villages, the army had forced the vote. But that would not explain everything. Some may have hoped that the change taking place in France would improve their lot; others perhaps believed in the fraternization. Why refuse to be French if they were to become, as the General had also said, 'French with full citizenship'? 'French with full citizenship' undoubtedly implied giving up being Algerian, but that was better than being the subordinate and despised 'French' they had been up till then. *Carte blanche*, therefore, even if misunderstanding reigned, as we have already seen in connection with the ovations of 4 June.

For its part, the rebellion had so surely perceived 13 May and what followed as a Gaullist success, and as danger for the Algerian cause, that it decided to radicalize the combat. The FLN created a provisional Government of the Algerian Republic (GPRA), and the formerly moderate leader Fehrat Abbas, a disillusioned assimilationist converted to nationalism, agreed to accept its presidency. The GPRA set up its headquarters in

Tunis. Secondly, in that same autumn of 1958, the FLN brought the war to mainland France: to start with, its commandos blew up the petrol storage tanks in the port of Marseille.

De Gaulle thus continued and intensified the policies of his predecessors. In the field, drastic military measures were taken, drastic methods of repression, too (the policy of resiting the fellahs in controllable villages or camps, to cut off their contacts with the maquis).

The army was brought to heel and restored to its hierarchical order (the officers had to leave the committees of public safety). Attempts were continued to defuse national demands through social justice (providing schools, entry to public office, the beginnings of industrialization and job creation – this was the 'Constantine plan' – some redistribution of land). In return for which, combatants were to give up fighting, being offered a way out that would preserve their self-respect, 'peace with honour'.

As all that came to nothing, since the armed rebels were often beaten but never wiped out and their links with the population were far from being entirely severed, General de Gaulle arrived at a quite different policy.

On 16 September 1959, he announced that he could envisage three possibilities for the future of Algeria. One was 'secession', otherwise known as independence. The second, 'total Gallicization'. The third, 'self-determination', which de Gaulle explained as follows: 'The government of Algerians by Algerians, based on aid from France, and in close union with it for its economy, education, defence and foreign relations' – adding that only the third appeared viable.

That was a completely different matter from French Algeria, which would have corresponded more with the second option. A split was to follow between the government and those, whether European inhabitants of Algeria or army officers, who had acclaimed the General fifteen months earlier after contributing so much to affording him access to power. It would take time to try to get this new policy and these new prospects accepted by an army and a population whose disappointment and despair were aggravated by anger at having been duped.

De Gaulle first explained his policy to the military, on the spot: that was the 'canteen tour'. But he failed to convince them all. In reality, what began, and went on for over two years, against a background of general war with the FLN rebellion, was a second war between de Gaulle and French Algeria. From then on, the majority of the European population of Algeria and a large proportion of army officers saw the Head of State as an enemy, and treated him as such. The various stages and episodes of that battle are well known.

The first act, from 24 January to 1 February 1960, in Algiers, was the eruption of the week of barricades, urban revolt, both civilian and military, quickly contained and ending in surrender. Next, in April 1961, this time more serious, what was more or less an attempt to repeat 13 May, the entry into the rebellion of the four generals, Challe, Jouhaud, Salan and Zeller: they held Algiers for only a few days and, for want of all the support on which they had relied, gave it up, surrendered or went underground. Finally, the OAS (Secret Army Organization), without wanting to seize power, engaged in the struggle by the use of violence.

To counter it, in addition to the state force kept well under control in France itself, de Gaulle could count on two other sources of support. First, the Gaullist army officers: in contrast with the most widespread type of professional army officer, patriotic and colonial in the traditional spirit, who had often preferred Pétain to de Gaulle in 1940 and mistrusted politics, the typically Gaullist soldier was either a former pioneer of Free France or the Resistance, attached to the General since the great choice of 1940, or an officer with political leanings (there were some – whether of left-wing or Christian democrat culture) and, consequently, more receptive to decolonization or humanitarian arguments. Before, and above all after, the putsch of the four generals, a skilful game of transfers diminished the posts of the first group to the advantage of the second.

The other Gaullist force was that of popular opinion in mainland France which, consulted by referendum on 8 January 1961, amply ratified the policy of self-determination. As in 1958, the average Frenchman preferred a prospect of settlement to one of war, and liked de Gaulle better than the rebel generals.

Although de Gaulle managed in this way to contain the upheavals in the French Algerian camp, by no means did he have it easy on the other front. For the FLN put up a resistance in the military field of operations, in spite of setbacks. The international forces that it felt were backing it continued to gain influence: the Arab world first – the Third World in the process of decolonization more broadly – and the forum of the United Nations in consequence; soon the great powers would be on the scene, feeling the need to organize or seduce the Third World. Tightening its links with India, and re-establishing them with Yugoslavia, Khrushchev's USSR took that route. And in 1960 a certain Senator John F. Kennedy declared that, after all, the American liberal tradition should show more sympathy to the rebel colonial than to the colonizer . . . The FLN therefore had the wind in its favour. If one adds that its leaders could clearly see the difficulties de Gaulle was having with the pieds-noirs, and the support being gained by the anticolonial cause in important sectors of French opinion, it is understandable that they should make him pay dearly in negotiations. For negotiations were taking place. Secretly, because in theory there was no war, only 'pacification'. But very soon, openly.

The first overt attempt at talks with an emissary of the FLN in France (Melun, June 1960) failed, however. In December 1960 de Gaulle toured

Algeria again; the FLN wanted to show its strength by large demonstrations in the towns, but they were repressed.

Then came the referendum of January 1961, already mentioned, following which negotiations were resumed (May 1961, in Évian, then in Lugrin). It ended in a fresh failure, for France then claimed to keep the Sahara: with a very sparse population, it formed a good practice ground for French atomic bombs, and possessed a substratum rich in the oil that France had discovered and exploited. A Sahara Gallicized by some kind of military and economic influence. But for the FLN the Sahara could be nothing other than a continuation of Algeria. In September 1961, de Gaulle yielded,[5] abandoning the idea of dissociating the Sahara from Algeria, and definitive negotiations took place, still slowly and with difficulty, in the winter of 1961–2, in Les Rousses then Évian.

Before revealing their conclusion, emphasis must be placed on the extent to which the Algerian war occupied the heart of French national debate during those years, 1960, 1961 and 1962, contributing in no small measure to the redealing of the cards in the political game.

At the end of 1958, de Gaulle's adversaries were to be found only on the left, even the extreme left, because besides the PC, that opposition comprised only the UFD, which formed a brilliant political elite – Mendès France, Daniel Mayer, Mitterrand, Rocard, Poperen – but had a very slender electorate.

The centre-left next rallied opposition to the General, without excessive virulence and without really challenging the new institutions that he had approved; but several other reasons added to its discontent. Mention has already been made of the SFIO socialists' opposition to the Debré–Pinay government's economic and social policies, and we shall shortly see that of the MRP to the General's European policy.

But the main cause lay elsewhere: the Gaullist option of 'self-determination' for Algeria saw the appearance, at the end of 1959, of a new, right-wing opposition, faithful to the idea of French Algeria, thus hostile to de Gaulle, with an added shade of anger imparted by disappointed hopes. It was around that stake in the game that the enormous Gaullist parliamentary majority elected in November 1958 would split and regroup, the fracture passing through the very heart of the UNR itself.

That criticism of the right and extreme right against the policies and even the person of the General affirmed itself first and foremost nationalist and colonial (Algeria was French; the empire must not be 'sold off' or 'the flag struck'), but for some people it also rearoused other grievances: those who had remained faithful in heart and mind to Vichy and Pétain, and who bore

---

[5] The same about-turn, or rearguard battle, took place with Tunisia. It wanted to force France to evacuate Bizerta (July 1961). France responded with a bloody military operation. After this, several months later, Bizerta would nevertheless be evacuated.

a grudge against the General for having beaten their old white party with the help of blues and even the accursed reds; those who, on the other hand, precisely because of their hatred of the reds, reproached de Gaulle for having stood aloof with regard to the Atlantic coalition and kept the door ajar towards Moscow. When that ensemble of grievances coincided and combined, it is understandable that real hatred should be felt towards de Gaulle, who was looked on as a revolutionary and a traitor to the France which had made him.

That right-wing opposition to Gaullism, a major component of French politics at the beginning of the 1960s, took two forms: one, terrorist, and the other . . . liberal.

The terrorist form was the OAS which, in 1962, had its ramifications in mainland France where they grafted themselves, by a very comprehensible logic, on to the circles or networks which had always constituted the extreme right of the political spectrum.

The liberal form found expression in the press, as well as in the ranks of deputies and senators, now discovering that de Gaulle exercised 'personal power', and governed with firm-handedness! Those who had not noticed on 13 May or 28 September, when the person and the firm hand had been going in a direction that suited them, dreamed of raising the flag of liberalism again as soon as the *content* of Gaullist policies displeased them. Judgement on content, judgement on form, the eternal dialectic . . .

The left also appeared varied and complex, with a discontent that fed on such diverse difficulties as social policies, Europe and diplomacy, and showed itself sensitive to the deadlocks and harshness of the Algerian war, a fact which did not always prevent it from sharing the liberal grievances of the parliamentary right.

For its part, the Communist Party, anti-Gaullist but isolated, demonstrated hostility or at least extreme distrust against anything other than itself. However, it never chorused its agreement with the ensemble of opponents in launching a total indictment against de Gaulle, for the regime's foreign policy contained some 'positive aspects'. In spite of a real opposition to the Algerian war and the OAS, its actions remained prudent and restrained. Never, in deed or word, did the PCF show as much solidarity with the FLN as with the Viet-minh.

The FLN appeared – not without reason – to be completely foreign to what inspired the PC and, moreover, likely one day to come under the American thumb (and, in order to shore up that very excessive grievance, to make use of the speech by Kennedy, already quoted). The PCF in the 1960s was certainly less far ahead in Third Worldism than its Soviet leader. No doubt it also weighed up the unpopularity that a bold policy of active support for the Arab rebellion would encounter among the working class, whose patriotism it had itself so keenly rekindled.

That policy was being sketched out, however, on the extreme left. There, intellectuals, whether or not friends of Jean-Paul Sartre, who was merely the most famous of them, some supporting the Mendèsist UFD, others

Trotskyism or the libertarian tradition, atheistic or Christian pacifists, student youth beginning to be aware of a romanticism of liberty brought up to date by Third Worldism – a whole group, therefore, limited in number but brilliant and fervent, who as the years went by and the war was prolonged became increasingly revolutionary. They were against colonial domination in general, against the methods of war in particular, against torture, and on that basis of analyses and feelings the idea of taking more resolute action could germinate. Propaganda committees, calls for street demonstrations (here the students' union, the UNEF, having gone over to the left, was in the vanguard), in short, incitement to rebelliousness.

On 5 September 1960 there appeared in the press a manifesto, followed by a long series of signatures (121 on the first list – hence the name, which would persist, 'Manifesto of the 121') on 'the right to rebellion in the Algerian war'. Lengthy preambles affirmed that the war was unjust, both absurd and criminal, and that public-spiritedness was on the side of those who, in all honesty, refused or would refuse to 'take up arms against the Algerian people', or who 'reckoned it their duty to bring aid and protection to the oppressed Algerians in the name of the French people'. Some of the most famous names in France (at that time and still today) followed, not only Sartre and Simone de Beauvoir but also, for example, Pierre Boulez, Marguerite Duras, Jean-François Revel, Nathalie Sarraute and dozens of others scarcely less well known. Naturally, its effect was considerable and provoked in reply on 6 October a 'Manifesto of French Intellectuals', the fundamental reasoning of which lay in stating that 'the fight was forced upon France by a minority of fanatical, terrorist and racist rebels . . . armed and financially backed by foreigners.' As usual, the whole question boils down to knowing on which side to put the passive and 'silent majority' of people who bow before the storm. The celebrity of the signatures was by no means inferior: Marshal Juin, Jules Romains, Daniel Halévy, all the Académie française and *Le Figaro* side of literature, not to mention a considerable number of famous university men, from the Sorbonne in particular, behind Roland Mousnier, Charles Picard and Pierre Chaunu.

The sociology of the intellectuals, that had its grounding in the history of Dreyfusism, can carry out some fine analyses today of the comparative proportions of cultural institutions, arts, disciplines and aesthetics on either side.[6] One analogy is missing, however, in relation to the Dreyfus Affair. General de Gaulle refused to install Sartre in Émile Zola's old role, and there were no showy legal proceedings taken against the 'master' who had turned subversive.

The most professionally vulnerable of the '121' suffered some slight harassment. In contrast, the police and the law concentrated their pressure on those – and there were some – who set up clandestine networks of 'direct aid' to the FLN and chiefly its metropolitan *wilayas* (zones of action in, for example, Paris, Marseille, Lyon).

---

[6] Jean Sirinelli, *Intellectuels et passions françaises*, Fayard, 1990.

In that radicalized sector of opinion, they detested de Gaulle and his government, likewise the Molletist left; they feared and hated the OAS right and reviled the PC for its reluctance, at the same time trying to draw it along with them.

Above all that, de Gaulle undoubtedly benefited from the division between the oppositions, who hated one another even more than they opposed the government. For, between the OAS and the determined anticolonialists who declared themselves friends of the rebels, matters had gone beyond the stage of moral civil war and were about to tip over into physical battles; the OAS, by 'planting' plastic explosives in this or that apartment, crossed that line on several occasions.

De Gaulle was also favoured by the contact he maintained with a middle-of-the-road popular opinion that yearned to see an end to the affair and was not completely infiltrated by the passions of political circles, notables and militants. Let us remember that, in the referendum of 8 January 1961, the free hand sought by the General for his Algerian policy had received a 75 per cent 'yes' vote.

It was a curious regime, however. De Gaulle and the Debré government, and its leading servants – Frey, Minister of the Interior, and Papon, Prefect of Police – having taken the stand of giving up Algeria, and being thus obliged to fight against the French Algerian camp and its formidable supporters, had also to fight to the very end on the other front, so to speak, against the FLN and opponents on the extreme left. The former front was all the better held because the administrative and police machinery serving the government, long since prepared for anti-Arab and anti-red hostility, proved more than zealous.

On 17 October 1961, the FLN organized its members and sympathizers among the immigrant working-class population to hold a procession in the streets of Paris in protest against police harassment and, chiefly, the imposition of a curfew. This peaceful demonstration was repulsed with murderous savagery; no precise toll of deaths was available, many of the corpses having been thrown into the Seine.

Then there was 'Charonne': the OAS having carried out a particularly glaring outrage (a bomb intended to kill Malraux succeeded only in wounding and blinding his concierge's little daughter), the anticolonialist, pacifist and antifascist extreme left (the word 'fascism' was starting to be used again in the face of the OAS phenomenon) called for a procession in Paris on the evening of 8 February 1962. Actually, the anti-OAS procession was, indirectly, tending to follow the government path, but that did not prevent the government from having them attacked by the police, who made a charge against the unarmed crowd, brutal enough to result in eight dead against the closed grille of the Charonne métro entrance. The name remained to signify the episode.

Consequently, it was a month of mourning and fury! Meanwhile, negotiations were going on. In the final stage, France, represented by Louis

Joxe, Robert Buron and Jean de Broglie, concluded with the representatives of the future independent Algeria the Évian agreements. The date was 18 March 1962.

Near Algiers, at the 'Black Rock', a provisional executive (Abderrahman Farès) prepared the transition. The agreements stipulated Algeria's prompt achievement of independence, the ways and means of extensive co-operation with France and the maintenance of a French presence: they had even stipulated the number of seats to be reserved for deputies of European origin in the Algerian Assembly to be elected.

But that arrangement soon proved obsolete, when the unleashing of violence organized by the OAS in Algeria raised the drama and tension between communities to such a degree that the European population, almost in its entirety, flung itself into the simple and desperate policy of mass exodus. In the space of a few weeks, French Algeria poured into mainland France, but there was not the slightest corresponding movement of Arabs back to Africa. Only the FLN leaders released from captivity took the plane for Algeria. Ben Bella, on landing, cried 'We are Arabs.' He was saluting a victory, not a compromise peace.

In France itself, the affair had a triple epilogue. On 8 April the Évian agreements, submitted to referendum, were approved by a 90 per cent 'yes'. On 14 April de Gaulle thanked his Prime Minister, Michel Debré, and to demonstrate clearly that another page in history had been turned, handed the government to a new man, Georges Pompidou. But on 22 August, at the Petit-Clamart crossroad on the route leading to the military airfield of Villacoublay, his car caught in a hail of machine-gun fire, the General escaped death only by a miracle. Colonel Bastien-Thiry and his men had wanted to punish the abandonment of 'French' territory, and the distressing fate of the uprooted pieds-noirs. Their anger, they explained, had been exacerbated by the spectacle of mainland French opinion's massive consent, and a government already turning its attention to other schemes.

What schemes? Before we watch Georges Pompidou institute the policies of a Gaullism delivered – dare one say – from Algeria, we must recall the general conditions to which the fate of that territory had been subordinated.

De Gaulle, as we know, wanted France to be strong and independent. Strong through its political institutions, strong through the modernization of its economy.

What about independence? After 1958, as between 1940 and 1944, the external policies of Gaullism were defined on two levels, unequal and complementary: an overall attachment to the camp of liberty, that is, loyalty to the American alliance, above all at critical moments (the incident of the U2 in 1960, the Cuban crisis in October 1962), but refusal to be placed under supervision in the heart of that camp. As early as September 1958 the General, in his first diplomatic initiative, had proposed that NATO should be headed by a tripartite directorate (United States, Great Britain, France). Following the polite refusal of General Eisenhower and Prime Minister Macmillan, de Gaulle had felt empowered unilaterally to give France the means of its independence: that presupposed regaining complete control of the French army by coming out of NATO (very quickly done: American bases and headquarters moved out), and committing France to a nuclear deterrent by building the atomic bomb (the first French atomic bomb test took place in February 1960 at Reggane, in the heart of the Sahara).

Thus had been defined the framework of the foreign policy still in force today. The rest was merely a corollary.

Towards the USSR there was a great, abiding mistrust that ruled out friendship, but relations were inspired by the same spirit of counter-insurance and freedom to manoeuvre that had already motivated the journey to Moscow in December 1944. Courtesy therefore. Contacts. Trade encouraged. At the beginning of 1960 Khrushchev was even received in France.

With regard to Europe, the Common Market was accepted as a *fait accompli* and its advantages recognized, but there was a refusal to complement it by any confederal political initiative which might subject France to a superior body.

At the occasion of a press conference on 15 May 1962, de Gaulle presented the idea of European unity as a ridiculous utopian dream; the Head of State even went so far as to overwhelm it with one of his scathing comments, referring to it as a Europe where people would speak 'heaven knows what sort of integrated Volapük'. That jibe, offensive to any real European conviction, brought about the instant resignation of the MRP members of Pompidou's brand new government. De Gaulle's Europe was the Europe of nation-states, and its unity was derived from the common leadership, one might almost say the institutional friendship, that the General established between France and Germany by welcoming Chancellor Adenauer.

In one sense, the Franco-German reconciliation, vainly attempted by the men of Locarno, was a European operation which succeeded. But it was also a piece of French power politics because, in the pair created by France, erstwhile victor, and Germany, erstwhile vanquished, France had some right of seniority, whereas other small Europeans (Italy, Benelux) could only follow and the other western European nations remain separate.

Even better than independence, France must gain additional strength from its position as leader in western Europe and beyond, if possible. Why not leader of those parts of the world unwilling to be dependent on either Moscow or Washington? But that nonaligned world (before the term was in use) was the same as the one emerging from decolonization. It could not be friendly to France until the latter had shed its colonial image. Perhaps that contributed to the peace of Évian being regarded as serving some greater design. And yet another aspect: the cost of the traditional war waged by France in Algeria was scarcely compatible with that of forming a modern army, based on the atomic bomb and the machines that carried it. There again, Évian cleared the ground for the strike force.

Thus it is possible to reconstruct an overall picture and a coherence in Gaullist policy. That does not mean to say that everyone at the time was prepared to rally to it. The year 1962 would remain shaken by the war throughout, and owe several unexpected and worrying repercussions to that drama.

After Algeria, beyond the historical phase that it marks, when the Fifth Republic changed its programme it also changed its leading player. Few government transformations can have been as significant as the one which, a month after Évian, brought Georges Pompidou to the Hôtel Matignon.

Georges Pompidou was born in 1911 in Montboudif, a Cantal village where his parents were schoolteachers. Rural roots and – as they say today – a meritocratic career. A brilliant student at the Albi *lycée*, prizewinner in the open competitive examinations, a *khâgne* in Paris, he then attended the *École normale supérieure* in the rue d'Ulm, gained his *agrégation* in literature and a teaching post in a *lycée*, and during the occupation sympathized with the Resistance. At the Liberation, de Gaulle needed a good colleague 'who knew how to write' in order to make up his civilian cabinet. René Brouillet, a *normalien*, Resistance member and already a member of the General's cabinet, brought along his comrade Georges Pompidou. Thus began, between the General and the former teacher, a career of work in common which would endure because the two men had more than esteem for each other, they found each other captivating.

Everything in his origins steered Georges Pompidou towards the left; he may even have belonged for a time to the SFIO in his student days. It was his realization of the naivety and weakness of the pacifist and parliamentarist left in the face of the Hitlerian menace that disabused him and led him towards the anti-Munich republican right to which Gaullism would one day form a natural extension. Gaullist before he met de Gaulle, Pompidou, like so many others, could not but be fascinated by the great man seen at close quarters. And de Gaulle was capable of valuing the gifts that Georges Pompidou possessed to a high degree: intelligence, the most refined literary and artistic culture, together with the ability to grasp the driest and most complicated matters, the will and the power to work and, in short, the inner strength that allowed the man to be at ease in every ambience. When he left the government in January 1946, de Gaulle, according to custom, had his colleague rehoused in the Council of State. From there, Pompidou went to the Rothschild bank, while discreetly busying himself with the RPF. On 1 June 1958 the General, who had not lost sight of him, took him back into his cabinet where he underwent a new training course of seven months.

But the transition from the junior and unobtrusive office of a statesman's principal private secretary to a major governmental role appeared, in 1962, as a sensational novelty. It was viewed, and with reason, as the result and almost the symbol of the personal nature assumed by the regime: was the rank of Prime Minister therefore open to a man who was neither a deputy elected by the people, nor a top civil servant, nor a former *grand résistant* – nothing more than a worthy man whom the President had noticed and chosen? Looked at more widely still, the appointment expressed the first manifest application of an institutional reversal within the spirit of the Fifth Republic.

Before, a politician began by getting himself elected; if he became a prominent deputy he could become a minister, and if he proved to be a good minister he could later become the first among them. Such had been the case with Michel Debré (or Jacques Chaban-Delmas or V. Giscard d'Estaing and others).

Henceforth, in contrast, it would be possible to see a young man make his way upwards in the discreet surroundings of political circles and government offices, achieve renown one day as a minister and then, possibly, look around for a constituency in which to 'implant' himself, have his 'home ground', make sure that he had a base where he could withdraw and wait; in short, become a deputy after being famous and powerful. The list of examples started by the Pompidou case is well known, inexhaustible and, moreover, multi-party.

The Fifth Republic, continuing thus to define itself, gradually established its unwritten laws.

About that time also, the para-constitutional idea of the 'private domain' became completely clear. The Constitution described only vaguely, in legal terms, the respective shares of the Head of State and Prime Minister in the running of affairs. But unofficially it appeared that internal, social and economic matters closely concerned the Prime Minister, and more loftily or distantly, the 'Château'. On the other hand, the Head of State considered as essentially of closer concern to himself (the 'private domain') those old 'affairs of state' – one might almost say 'royal' matters – diplomacy and national defence. Foreign affairs were thus steadfastly managed, between 1958 and 1968, by M. Couve de Murville, with a specialist's competence but in the General's shadow. It was also said that General de Gaulle paid particular attention to a third field in the famous 'domain': African and Madagascan affairs, allocated to a special secretariat established in the Élysée, which was also thought to cover the secret services. Jacques Foccart was its powerful and unobtrusive quasi-minister.

If police matters assumed so great an importance, it was because of the important role they had played on the fringes of the Algerian war, in successive combats against the FLN and the anticolonial networks and then against OAS activism.

They were obscure, dramatic and painful affairs, from which a spectacular trial emerged from time to time. Matters of political subversion were dealt with by a special jurisdiction, the Court of State Security.

One of the generals of the 1961 putsch, Jouhaud, who had disappeared underground, was finally captured, tried and sentenced to death. He had not yet been executed when the police, in April 1962, seized General Salan. Tried in his turn, brilliantly defended by an expert barrister, Maître Tixier-Vignancour, whose old extreme right-wing convictions made him the OAS's natural choice of advocate, Salan escaped capital punishment and was sentenced only to life imprisonment. Consequently, it was necessary to commute Jouhaud's sentence, as the two men had held the same responsibilities. De Gaulle, so it is said, resigned himself to it reluctantly, furious that the rebellion was eluding the supreme punishment.

But several weeks later, the trial of the conspirators in the Petit-Clamart attempt revived the tragic problem. The court pronounced punishments that were carefully graded according to the degree of responsibility that had been established: three death sentences, life sentences, limited period sentences, etc.

The Head of State commuted two of the death sentences and let the third be carried out. Colonel Bastien-Thiry was shot on 11 March 1963 in the name of the principle of inflexibility for crime against the state, which had already been harshly employed in 1943 and 1945.

The Petit-Clamart attack had taken place in August 1962. In September of the same year de Gaulle and Pompidou commenced a procedure of revision of the Constitution to alter the method of election of the Head of State: turning his electoral body into one of universal suffrage.

Thus, four years after the French had been persuaded to adopt institutions that were at last sound (which had justified the overturning of the Fourth Republic), these were now deemed sufficiently imperfect to warrant some alteration! It could be argued that they were being adapted to meet the circumstances, and that after the Petit-Clamart attack the executive needed some moral reinforcement through the sanction of the popular vote. In reality, it is hard to see how democratic unction could form a shield against hatred and bullets, the authors of assassination attempts generally being those who most scorn the ballot box. More probably, it must be considered that presidential election by the entire nation was part of the logic of the regime, and the relevant point here is that in 1958 it had drawn back from that logic. Since 1958, referenda, frequently in the nature of giving a free hand to general policies, had accustomed people to the plebiscitary vote. So one could go further. The difficulty arose with regard to procedure. The Constitution anticipated (was it premeditation?) two possibilities for using the referendum: one (article 89) for a constitutional revision, the other (article 11) for the adoption of certain bills that might bear notably on 'the organization of public authorities'. The procedure of article 11 was convenient, since the Head of State, on the proposal of the government, in this case submitted the bill directly to a referendum, whereas that of article 89 required that, before the popular vote, there should be the double deliberation of the parliamentary Assemblies. De Gaulle and Pompidou had therefore opted to get round the parliamentary obstacle by referring to article 11, but the greater part of the deputies and almost all the lawyers considered that the procedure of article 89 should have been used, since it was a matter of changing the Constitution and not ordinary legislation.

Certain Gaullists also suggested that the government could act as it pleased, since it could still make use of the special powers that had been granted to it for combating the disturbances associated with Algeria. True, the duration of the special powers had not yet lapsed. But to employ, for a matter of constitutional revision, exceptional powers accorded for quite another purpose represented a procedural deviation. At least, the lawyers who were consulted thought so, as did the majority of deputies. On 5 October 1962 the National Assembly passed a motion of censure against Pompidou's government; the numerous right-wing deputies who, Gaullist in 1958, had become anti-Gaullist after the watershed of decolonization, were obviously making the government pay for having abandoned Algeria.

Pompidou reacted, as was his right, by asking the Head of State to dissolve the Assembly. The people would thus be the arbiters, in two successive votes, on 28 October, with the referendum on the revision of the Constitution, and on 18 and 25 November, with the legislative elections to choose a new Assembly.

That referendum of 28 October 1962 assumed an extreme importance. Directly at stake was the election of the President by the people. Part of the left declared itself against by reason of anti-Bonapartist tradition; as for the other opponents, they joined the opposition because they no longer appreciated de Gaulle. Because, in reality, the General and Gaullism constituted the ultimate, if implicit, stakes in these consultations. Lastly, there was the matter of the law: the procedure was irregular, and that deserved disapproval. On that basis of formal legalism, the understanding that extended from the left to the extreme right and had succeeded in getting the motion of censure carried, was rediscovered in the campaign calling for a 'no' vote. It formed the '"no" cartel', which the Gaullists tried to discredit by pointing out that this coalition, from Pinay to Mollet and Mendès France, was too heterogeneous to be honest. Yes, but what about the law? Well, the law, if it was in question, would be defeated!

There were about 13 million 'yes' votes, against 8 million 'no' votes. That plebiscitary victory for Gaullism was confirmed a month later by the result of the legislative elections. Of course, the left-wing parties won votes and seats, but the liberal right (those who had played the liberalism card in order to 'punish' Gaullism, the 'no' right wing) was eroded, and the UNR regained the majority.

Pompidou therefore formed a new government. Power triumphed, and even with some arrogance. A key man in the 'no' cartel had been Gaston Monnerville, president of the Senate, a radical and lawyer in the old republican tradition. He had publicly used the words 'abuse of authority' to describe Pompidou's conduct in the affair. General de Gaulle, meeting Monnerville at the funeral of the former President René Coty, refused conspicuously to shake his hand. Worse still, the entire Senate would for years be boycotted by the ministers.

As for the republican tradition, it had not gone down very well with the country as a whole. The defeat of the 'no' of 1962, slightly mitigating but still confirming the 'no' of 1958, marked the end of certain political ethics defined by the republicans of the previous century, and opened the way to a quest for a revision of systems of values.

Internal politics, after Algeria and after the plebiscitary reform of 1962, was dominated by the prospect of the next presidential election.

The left-wing parties gradually recovered from the impact of 1958 and began to win back the wavering fringe of their electorate, those who had felt the driving force of de Gaulle as historic hero, as prestigious and protective leader, as miracle man in the colonial imbroglio. Subsequent events had partly broken the spell. Moreover, despite the overall forward leap in prosperity, enough critical sectors and social conflicts remained for the parties and trades unions to capitalize on working-class dissatisfaction with the government (miners' strike in 1963). The PC continued to set the tone and the line in the CGT, which was still the biggest workers' union. The liberation from religious ties in Christian trades unionism also assisted the dynamism of protest: certainly, it expressed itself in a split, because a Catholic group kept going, with the old title CFTC, while a new one appeared, the CFDT (Confédération française démocratique du travail, Democratic French Labour Confederation), led by Eugène Descamps. But this one succeeded in inspiring in wage-earners reluctant to embrace Communism the spirit of battle that the old CGT-FO, enclosed within its corporate bastions, had not been able to arouse or extend. All in all, the working-class movement was not doing badly!

Meanwhile, the opposition had to adapt itself to the new method of ballot and seek a 'good candidate' for an 'American-style', personalized, televisual campaign, a candidate who could be a plausible challenger for someone of de Gaulle's stature. A difficult undertaking! In 1963 *L'Express*, a Mendèsist organ, caught the public's interest by setting up a portrait of this *rara avis*, Monsieur X, who eventually turned out to be none other than Gaston Defferre. According to these somewhat naive prognostications, Defferre – known for his imperious disposition as mayor of Marseille, and for his love of sports in private life – must be doubly 'dynamic' . . . But a programme was needed, as well as an 'image'. The old logic of the Resistance, of the French version of Labour philosophy, of the 'third force' and of the Fourth Republic, pushed socialists and Christian democrats to form a coalition. It appeared that what they shared in common – the taste for a democratic and humanist Republic, the sense of social justice and of liberty, European aims – was far more considerable than what divided them. The union stumbled, however, at the final hurdle: would the great federation call itself 'socialist' or merely 'social'? It came to grief over the insurmountable conflict between those who wished to keep in mind, or at least on paper, with the '-ist', a prospect of state-controlled economy and collectivism, and those who were against it.

That setback was all to the good of the Communists, because the failure of the great federation, which would have been a centre-left alliance around the MRP and the SFIO, left no other possible alliance open to the socialists except left-wing union, thus union with the Communists. But for a presidential ballot of the new kind, they had nobody to propose. Their leader, Maurice Thorez, who had been ill and had really gone downhill, had died in August 1963. Neither his successor to the general secretaryship, Waldeck Rochet, nor the veteran Jacques Duclos, seemed a likely candidate. The former, a self-taught peasant, compelled esteem and liking, but his dreary and rustic appearance and speech 'didn't go down well'. In contrast, the second had all the glamour possible, and vitality and eloquence, but his long past as a Stalinist and manoeuvrer, because he had shone in the most conflicting roles, vehement or bland and ingratiating, rebel or patriot, demagogue or 'responsible' leader, made him a man who was as much dreaded outside the party as he was popular among his own partisans.

François Mitterrand then came on the scene to exploit this deal of the cards: the non-Communist left could ally itself only with the PC, and it alone could find in its ranks a candidate capable of being popularized – himself. Long and astute negotiations followed. Waldeck Rochet ended by accepting that the PCF did not have a candidate, the SFIO ended by giving up its own, rivals in any case and thus cancelling one another out. Meanwhile, François Mitterrand had managed to federate in a Convention of Republican Institutions the amorphous mass of clubs and small parties that continued the UFD of 1958, left-wing intellectuals and young people, Mendèsists, dissident socialists, etc. In a new stage, he then brought together the Convention, the SFIO and the Radical Party under the name 'Federation of the Democratic and Socialist Left' (FGDS). 'Left' well expressed what he meant, 'democratic' marked the distinction with regard to the PC, which still had a reputation for being authoritarian, and 'socialist' indicated the separation with regard to the Christian democrats, who were merely 'social' without the '-ist'.

Mitterrand would bear the colours of the FGDS. The Christian democrats, the debris of the MRP, rechristened Democratic Centre, presented Jean Lecanuet, a philosophy professor, as their candidate.

On 5 December 1965, General de Gaulle, a candidate for his own succession, obtained only 10,000,000 votes, thus failing to get an absolute majority. Mitterrand won 7,500,000, Lecanuet 4,000,000, Maître Tixier-Vignancour 1,000,000, and two outsiders a negligible number. There had to be a second round, which the law confined to the two strongest competitors in the first round. On 19 December, the General was re-elected, with 12,500,000 votes, François Mitterrand gaining 10,000,000, a result which constituted a more than honourable failure since he outstripped not only the votes he had received in the first round but even the number of 'no' votes in the referendum of October 1962. In short, the progress of the left tended to nudge the General towards the situation of leader of the conservative section of the country.

For his part, he refused to be enclosed in that role, since he laid stress on the originality of his foreign policy plans.

Between 1962 and 1967, rid of the Algerian hindrance, Gaullist policies were freely unfurled.[7] The strike force could be developed by economizing on traditional military forces and armaments (and, since France had lost its testing grounds in the Sahara it set them up on Mururoa atoll, in Polynesia – South Pacific), and at the same time friendship with the Third World could be cultivated, now that France could pride itself on having decolonized.

Europe remained a limited project, even if the country was deriving economic advantages from it. To the initial industrial market, the Brussels agreement added the agricultural Common Market (June 1962). But the General's diplomacy gave rough treatment to the inevitable conflicts of interest that arose (the crisis of June 1965, with the – French – policy of temporarily boycotting participation, known as the 'empty chair' policy), and he refused to allow Britain to join, despite its desire to do so. Of course, it was not so much a matter of emphasizing the quality of the union as of extending it geographically. The European impetus was brought to an abrupt halt.

With the USSR and its eastern neighbours, the policy of counter-insurance was continued.

With the United States, while the finishing touches were put to France's disengagement from NATO, Paris passed gradually from waspish friendliness to criticism. At the end of 1962 (Cuban crisis), France and the United States still stood together. But in 1964 France recognized the People's China – which the British had already done while Washington still hesitated.

General de Gaulle travelled about, and was chiefly acclaimed where the Yankees were not liked (Mexico, for instance). In 1966 he visited Cambodia

---

[7] It is odd to recall that the argument had already been used by Sirius, (Hubert Beuve-Méry) in *Le Monde* on 22 July 1954, to congratulate Mendès France for making peace in Geneva: 'The cessation of hostilities in Indochina was the prerequisite for any French recovery . . . It was as if the whole of national life had been poisoned, made gangrenous by that suppurating wound.' This type of reasoning was easy to transpose.

and, in a remarkable speech made in Phnom Penh, berated the colonial war which the United States was keeping up in Vietnam.

In 1967 he made the trip to Canada, and his famous address from the balcony of Montreal's town hall, finishing with the cry 'Vive le Québec libre!' That improvised outburst created a diplomatic incident and naturally chilled relations between France and Canada, where the General had ignited an internal conflict. But he was appreciated by many Québecois, and all anti-British, anti-American, 'anti-imperialist' Third Worldism. As he went through the continents, in addition to his highly coloured image as the hero of the pretty extraordinary adventure of Free France, de Gaulle won acclaim for himself in two interwoven roles, wherein he represented republican France, the exporter of liberty, and proud France, that dared to defy America.

The summit of Gaullist Third Worldism appeared to be reached in June 1967 when, during a new episode in the permanent Arab–Israeli conflict, de Gaulle and his government seemed clearly to incline toward the Arab cause, instead of the customary support for Israel, a democratic republic and refuge for the survivors of Nazism.

With regard to Israel, de Gaulle had mixed feelings and was perhaps once betrayed by his solemn and occasionally emphatic language. Did he not one day, at a press conference, describe the Jewish people as 'imperious, cocksure and masterful'? The phrase could be taken as homage to the vital force of this people who had become a nation and a state, but maybe it also revealed an echo of the old theme of Jewry seeking to conquer the world. The description lingered on, both because it had created a sensation and because it had created a problem.

Where was all this leading? National independence was undeniably the central inspiration. But could it be achieved in the face of Europe and America? If de Gaulle wanted to free the West from the single supervision of Washington, was not the best way to consolidate Europe? And if the aim of making France into a kind of leader of the nonaligned countries was to be achieved by the rejection of NATO and a united Europe alike, to what other contradictions would it be exposed?

The General's foreign policy towards the end of the 1960s thus bred anxiety and opposition. Certainly, it won him, if not the liking, at least the interested attention, and almost the neutrality, of the PC. But those 'positive aspects' of the foreign policy, which the Communists periodically acknowledged as such, were interpreted negatively by the more numerous sectors of opinion, on both right and left, the friends of the United States and the free world, those loyal to Europe, defenders of Israel and enemies of Communism.

Furthermore, the General's global views seemed to have as a counterpart in his domestic policies both the absence of any profound reforms (where was the capital–labour association?) and his rather haughty disregard of certain sordid and brutal happenings. In 1965, it had to be admitted that a Third World combatant, the Moroccan Medhi Ben Barka, legitimately opposing the King for greater democracy, had in the middle of Paris been lured into an ambush, carried off and killed by henchmen of the King of Morocco, in collusion with French police and special agents. The General had no hand in the affair, but it clearly appeared, on this occasion, that under its panache a certain sector of the state's apparatus had retained their devious procedures and reactionary inspirations.

Left-wing propaganda made the most of it, but the right wing was also worried. It was V. Giscard d'Estaing who one day dared to speak of 'the solitary exercise of power', and a classic and wise political science handbook described the General as 'on an increasingly personal path'.

It was no surprise that, in the regular legislative elections in March 1967, the forces of opposition should make a fresh advance. Pompidou only just obtained a legislative majority. The movement of 1968, then imminent, would depend to a certain extent on those disenchantments. But there would be many other, perhaps deeper, causes and in order to understand them we must tackle the last section of the work of the Fifth Republic, its economic operations.

During the Algerian war, that heavy burden on the budget and heavy hindrance to the economy, the situation went downhill: deficit, resumption of inflation, increased disequilibrium in the balance of payments. The Debré government, with Pinay in Finance, assisted by the liberal economist Jacques Rueff, had used the classic means. The budget deficit had been reduced by new or increased taxes or by cutting down expenditure: certain economic subsidies were decreased, and aid was removed from the Coal Board and the SNCF (railways), which had to try to make themselves profitable, and an attempt was even made to attack certain social budgets; the system of administering social security funds was altered to the disadvantage of trades unions; even war veterans' pensions might have been affected if the idea had not roused such an outcry. In the matter of foreign trade, various relaxations favoured the entry of foreign products, which was in keeping with European Common Market policy, and was through competition to help hold French prices. Lastly, a slight monetary devaluation had been accompanied and completed by a spectacular measure. French money was reformulated: starting on 1 January 1960, the new franc (or 'heavy' franc that we know today) was worth one hundred old francs. Thus values expressed in francs lost two noughts at a stroke, and regained parity with strong currencies – dollar, mark, Swiss franc.

After that psychological shock, the stringency and austerity, and soon the end of the war, had combined their effects to produce good results. The budgetary deficit began to decrease again, the balance of payments to recover, and the Banque de France's gold reserves to swell.

It must be added that, in the background, the worldwide economic situation was favourable: it was the era of the 'thirty glorious' years, already mentioned, which had appeared around the start of the 1950s. This expansion, which became evident and even spectacular in the years we are now retracing, therefore properly belonged neither to France nor to the 'Fifth Republic'. Gaullist propaganda attributed credit for it to the regime, which was excusable and, moreover, traditional (the Second Empire had also given Napoleon III the credit for the superb growth in the period 1850–73). The Fourth Republic had already put in a great deal of work on it, but with less talk. It must be admitted, however, that de Gaulle and his followers knew how to notice and encourage these changes and modernizations, linking them with the 'grand design' of a strong France: they are to be thanked for having implanted the idea that in the twentieth century a great country can no longer be the harmoniously balanced country of Méline (even less the utopianly rural country of a certain Vichy), but must be, or become, an advanced industrial country.

The Gaullist plan for a strong France thus progressed along the right path. The no less Gaullist plan for a just society was not so evident. The idea of overcoming the respective drawbacks of socialism and capitalism by capital–labour association or, as it more frequently came to be called, 'participation', was realized to only a limited extent by such means as encouragement of workers' shareholding.

Was the still-capitalist French economic system so modern after all? The government requested a report from a committee of great experts, the Rueff –Armand report, in order to make an inventory of 'the inflexibilities which hinder France's economic expansion'. Many were listed and very few abolished. In fact, it was entering an era of 'stop–start' economic policies, when a few years of expansion led to an inflationist upsurge, which needed the brakes to be applied to expansion in order to halt it, and then meant starting anew later (thus the 'stabilization plan' of September 1963, the 'relaunch' of autumn 1965). The government influenced the system by exerting control on the deficit, on prices and, above all, on credit.

Overall, the situation remained expansionist, but was not without a few ups and downs. As for the social consequences (and more than social, as we shall see) of expansion, they were most impressive. France was metamorphosed.

First, the population increased, or rather, continued to increase. In 1967 statistics showed that the population had reached 50 million. Without staying at the high post-war rate (an average 21 per thousand between 1946 and 1950, 18 per thousand in 1961–5), the birth rate remained very adequately above the death rate (11 per thousand in 1961–5). That population was increasingly urban because agriculture was employing ever fewer people. The primary sector which had still represented 36 per cent of the working population in 1946, and 32 per cent in 1954, was down to 19 per cent in 1962. Towns therefore grew as never before, in particular medium-sized towns of between 20,000 and 200,000 inhabitants. This urban growth was visibly, even spectacularly, written into the geography: new suburbs, new districts, 'housing schemes', etc.

Industry was boosted by the requirements of the new urban construction, of the new transport systems (more and more airports were beginning to be constructed, and motorways to be mapped out), and above all by the need for new consumer goods.

A process made up of natural aspirations and wants stimulated by advertising (still a booming sector) made familiar and desirable to the entire population the enjoyment of articles which pre-war generations had not known, or believed to be inevitably reserved for the rich: a car, a refrigerator, a washing machine and a television. Those were the four objects, now accessible, without which the average French family of the 1960s would have felt poor and frustrated. The active industries which produced them offered employment and wages; people worked hard (they did overtime, and more and more women went out to work), families' purchasing power increased in consequence, and in its turn their appetite as consumers stimulated production. An ascending spiral thus brought about production and consumption, the expansion of industry and a change in lifestyle.

That expansion needed workers, all the more so because the quest for productivity in the factories, long since rationalized, still rarely went as far as automation. The transfer of the labour force that had come from the countryside was far from sufficient. France therefore took in, legally or not – not much heed was paid to it in those days – numerous contingents of immigrants. Muslim Algerians might well now be nearly all foreigners, their numbers none the less continued to grow. The old immigrant sources, Polish, Spanish, Italian, had more or less dried up, for reasons peculiar to their countries of origin. In contrast, the increase in the number of arrivals from Morocco and Portugal, as well as from the West Indies, was staggering. The advent of Africans from countries south of the Sahara had hardly begun. As for the West Indians, who were certainly legally French citizens, their arrival in France was no different, for example, from that of Corsican islanders. But their dark skin often caused them to be regarded as 'foreigners' in the instinctive sense of the word, because there is a commonplace perception of difference which has more to do with noticeable appearance than official status. Similarly, the mainland Frenchman had a vision of 'Arabs' (or 'Maghrebis') that made no distinction between the Muslim Frenchman (*harki* or son of a *harki*, the auxiliaries attached to the French army, therefore a French citizen and former combatant on the French side) and the Algerian Muslim (foreigner and ex-enemy). Those difficulties of perception and that widespread mistrust were still only latent, because there was no unemployment yet to ignite them. Expansion offered such advantages . . .

It presented another, considerable, one: prosperity had fortunately facilitated the assimilation of the pieds-noirs, repatriated from Algeria, into mainland society and economy. Painlessly? That would be an exaggeration! For the vast majority of the Europeans in Algeria, it had been a little homeland, and not their prey. Their more or less enforced exodus had therefore left them with a sense of injustice, at the same time as quite understandable feelings of nostalgia. Furthermore, they received compensation for the loss of their possessions only extremely slowly. But the surrounding prosperity, well and truly exploited by their undeniable dynamism, had allowed them very quickly to rebuild their situation, sometimes even their affluence, in all sectors, chiefly the tertiary, but also on occasion the primary (farming in the Midi or in Corsica).

As for ordinary migrants, notably the massive groups of Algerians, Portuguese and Moroccans, they too fitted themselves in, chiefly in industry (building, metallurgy, chemicals, mechanical engineering) and in the less skilled jobs in urban public services (cleaning). But in contrast to the situation before the war, they were no longer to be found in the coal-mining industry, where recruitment had virtually stopped.

For the shift in importance of sources of energy was another aspect of the economic changes of the 1950s to the 1970s. Coal was thenceforward considered outmoded, attention was on oil (imported from Algeria or the Near East), natural gas (from Aquitaine), hydroelectricity and, finally, building was started on power stations using atomic energy.

Taken as a whole, the geography of industrial France remained stable. The stagnation of the old regions (Nord and Lorraine) had not yet begun. More noteworthy were the places that were thriving, or new: the Parisian region, large towns in general, the south-eastern quarter of the country, the Rhône valley and what would henceforth be called the Rhône-Alps region, and the Pyrenean Midi, with Toulouse, the aircraft capital.

In the latter domain, specifically, French industry succeeded in regaining the front rank by producing, in association with British industry, the extraordinary supersonic intercontinental commercial aircraft known as Concorde (first flight on 2 March 1969). The Head of State and the government saw it as proof of the success of their 'grand design' for a France once more pioneering and powerful. Certain opposition circles pointed out that the commercial study had not been as successful as the industrial study, since the cost of the machine was prohibitive for ordinary passengers as well as for the foreign airlines that were supposed to purchase it. Concorde was more of a technical than a commercial triumph and, despite the fine name which had been chosen for it, did not manage to bridge the polemical gap separating Gaullists and anti-Gaullists. Nevertheless, it would seem that, in wider opinion, feelings of national pride had been stirred.

All this modernization could not proceed at the same rate. Not to mention the difficulties continually created by working conditions or wage levels, branch by branch, even factory by factory – for the class struggle had by no means been chloroformed – problems existed even in the euphoric area of consumerism. The spread of the car, and the desire to use it during the summer, raced ahead of motorway construction. The idea of, and the taste for, easy communications likewise surged ahead of the telephone industry. Delays on motorways, the wait for a telephone remained the usual causes of recrimination, whereas the food industry grew more sophisticated and the housing crisis was reduced.

Industry was doing well, the building trade going along nicely, business was prospering and with them, sometimes, 'affairs' where speculation on the stock market or property gave rise to criminal acts revealed in the press. Occasionally, influential civil servants or deputies were mixed up in them. The Fifth Republic thus had its scandals, just like the ones that had gone before. Formerly, politico-financial scandals had been blamed on 'the Republic' and there had been calls for an authoritative regime to make a clean sweep. Now that the authority was there, the opposition, on the left and extreme left (extreme right, as well, but it had less weight) denounced the strong power in whose shelter networks and shady associations could go about their dubious affairs. Some would go as far as talking about 'real-estate Gaullism'. The term, insulting to the General's name, might well express, though somewhat excessively, a reality of the times: with the victory of the Fifth Republic, a new political personnel was installed in administrative offices, constituencies, town halls; with expansion as well, a great wave of entrepreneurs and businessmen flowed towards labour and towards profit; and it happened that the two movements, the two waves and the two groups huddled together rather too closely.

Economic development posed many other problems, chiefly that of the future of farming, which was affected simultaneously by the rural exodus and the prospect of the opening of the agricultural Common Market. Modern methods were there, too: everywhere the tendency was to go over to intensive production, for an enlarged commercial market, with peasant workers reduced in number, younger and more competent. The state encouraged that development (laws aimed at farming in 1960 and 1962), and on the other hand, in Brussels, saw to it that French interests were defended, at the cost – as we have seen – of putting a sharp brake on Europe. That did not mean, however, that peasantry and government were always on good terms. Firstly, there were regions where the dominant political tradition among the rural population was hostile to Gaullism (left or extreme left in some places, ultra-conservatism in others). Then, certain aspects of the general policy shocked and annoyed: imports of wines coming from the independent Algeria that France was treating so considerately. Lastly, even where, at the expense of former political notables, young executives of an agricultural trades unionism frankly set on modernization and with little political commitment were beginning to increase their influence – a situation which should have favoured good relations with the regime – agreement was not always easy. In some places an increased and rationalized production did not sell well for lack of means of transport and suitable distribution networks (Breton artichokes); in others, peasants who had turned to new ventures, such as large-scale poultry rearing, found themselves rivalled by entrepreneurs who were strangers to the rural world; elsewhere, the burden of debts contracted for equipment and modernization crippled the rewards of labour as soon as prices dropped. In short, the peasantry became economically bold, and soon competitive, without being completely reassured.

In certain regions at least, it suffered competition within the very setting of its daily life. In former days the village or the countryside had been essentially given over to agriculture. Now another use had been found for them: residences for town-dwellers thirsty for the wide open spaces and tranquillity; pensioners coming to end their days near their 'roots'; holidaying public servants coming to spend a month in their 'second home'; even blue- or white-collar workers, as permanent residents if the town where they had their job was near enough for them to get to it by car in the morning and return in the evening to sleep peacefully. These new villagers of town origin were warmly welcomed as long as their numbers remained small, but the feeling was that the numbers were destined to grow. What would happen when the townsman using the country as supplement to his creature comforts would have sufficient weight to challenge the farmer for control of the land, the choice of local amenities and majority on the municipal council?

If towns were beginning to overspill into the countryside, it was because, more generally, life was changing everywhere. What has been said about articles of domestic comfort, which in a few years reached the status of mass (or popular, or at least majority) consumer goods, proved equally true about the changing scale of many ways of life. Travelling by car now occupied so many people that living with the car (traffic, parking, insurance, safety, taxation) became a daily worry, a major municipal problem and almost a state matter. Taking a plane was no longer a millionaire's luxury. Taking holidays involved nearly half the French, getting out of town for the weekend even more, and having mini-breaks in summer and winter – the long weekends and extra days off between public holidays, arising from the chance of the calendar – were events to be considered seriously. Summer holidays caused enormous migrations that required more police than a hundred uprisings, and the great 'normal' lethargy in the month of August put the brakes on the economy just as much as weeks of general strike. In the towns themselves, the car even had an effect on daily trade. In the new faubourgs, thanks to their guaranteed parking space, vast supermarkets allowed people to come and stock up with provisions, selected at leisure from 'self-service' shelves, and then pack them into the car boot. Consequently, the small grocery or household goods shop in the old town streets complained because of being deserted, or rather reduced to a clientele of 'carless' citizens: the 'left-overs' of the poor, Arab workers and elderly ladies living on their own.

In contrast, other trades were thriving – leisure goods, semi-luxury items or cultural artefacts. For this or that trade or craft, formerly utilitarian, reappeared for use of a cultural kind, the daily life of yesteryear becoming, like rural life, something which satisfied the tastes and desires of the sophisticated.

Some common object, a hand-operated coffee grinder, a wooden horse from a children's roundabout, a cartwheel, well worn and still in use around 1950, resurfaced fifteen years later amid the second-hand dealers as a curio. As everyday life became futuristic, taste, to keep the balance, became 'way out' and, for bourgeois holiday-makers, snobbery turned rustic. The wealthy person who heated his luxury town apartment at the mere touch of a switch delighted in using bellows on his wood fire in the crumbling village where he had restored his country cottage. And his neighbour, a permanent resident, an old local peasant, for whom progress once meant exactly that transition from a wood fire to a butane stove, shrugged his shoulders uncomprehendingly. It was a curious mix-up which added a touch of paradox to the general upheaval in habits.

There are other examples of the same trend. Until around 1950, workers and schoolboys went to work by bicycle. Then progress enabled them to swap that useful machine for other less tiring ones, various kinds of motor cycles. Around 1960, in spite of the Tour de France, bicycle production was on the verge of disappearing. Now it was reborn, but as a machine for pure enjoyment or physical fitness for a comfortably-off public which also owned a car. The same applied to horses. Around 1950 there were still some in the countryside, used to pull a cart or a plough. They too had been eclipsed in favour of the car or tractor. If they were now to be seen again in the village, it was a certainty that there would be some 'ranch' in the vicinity where holidaying upper and middle classes were doing some riding. The horse, like the bike (or the manual coffee grinder), had to some extent changed social class in the space of twenty years! For classes still existed. Employers and employees, tradesmen, liberal professions, etc. But rich and poor as well.

For prosperity was not total. If the optimist can show that the majority of workers and peasants attained a material standard of living not far removed from that of the middle classes, the pessimist can point out that social inequality was intensely polarized at either end of the hierarchy. On large-scale, prosperous businesses, on property speculation, in the upper layer of the financial, political and administrative world, lived an opulent and very obvious oligarchy. Not that it was defiantly ostentatious, but simply because a whole industry, also typical of our times, made a living out of its display; glossy magazines, show business news constantly kept the great and the fortunate in full view. At the other end of the scale, there was a 'poor France'[8] made up of peasants who had not adapted and were almost 'left-overs', old people on small or nonexistent pensions (that still happened), workers in small industrial centres that were in difficulties, the unemployed when there were any (still very few), and above all, immigrants. The latter, who had started from zero in the economic race, often

---

[8] Title of a work by P.-M. de la Gorce, a Gaullist publicist.

did the work requiring few skills; certainly, they were sober and thrifty, but as they had usually come to France alone they sent part of their wage to a family who had stayed in their native land, which obviously reduced their own resources to a minimum. Thus the 'consumer society' was composed. It tended to turn France into a huge market for uniform products and habits. Was it for that reason that France, whose metamorphosis we are trying to follow at the same time as its entry into the Gaullian era, also witnessed the rebirth of regionalism?

The movement reappeared at that time with an unexpected force. Certainly, regionalist movements went back a long way, and the nineteenth century had experienced them, but they were then more backward-looking, more noticeable on the right (less than is said, however) and, above all, almost exclusively literary and folklorish. Aspirations of this kind, at the time of the Third Republic, sometimes called for decentralization but hardly ever mentioned the economy.

After the Liberation gradually, and then in the 1960s quite conspicuously, new regionalisms arose which were more often left wing, even extreme left, and which, above all, dared to include economic grievances in the more general analyses and to speak more loudly. Henceforth, when an industry went to the wall in a southern region, it was easy to blame the 'colonial' state in the north, Paris; when a farming business got into difficulties, the Parisian government was again blamed for having opened the frontiers to this or that foreign competition; when old, picturesque and history-laden sites were spoilt by tourist resorts catering for well-to-do Germans, or by the intrusive dwellings for Parisians and Dutch people, again 'colonial' control was denounced.

The clearest example is obviously to be found in Corsica, which was enriched during the 1960s by the exploitation of the eastern plain (vineyards and orchards) and the development of tourism. Now, that fortune was not regarded as beneficial because it was accompanied by a migration of capital and men that threatened to place the islanders in a minority in their own land. A borderline case, but typical. Economic changes were greater and faster than in former times, and were better analysed and less well received when they were accompanied by too many drawbacks.

The major disadvantage, to be sure, was related to cultural uniformity. What remained of regional dialects and local customs – and there were some remnants – disappeared in the great alteration, and for two connected reasons. On the one hand, the traditional peasantry and old ways of farming, together with the old ways of life, which formed the backbone of language and customs, were tending to collapse and, in their wake, the culture associated with them. On the other, modern methods of communication imposed far more deeply than before a knowledge and imitative use of words and habits from the urban, national and cosmopolitan world. In brief, it was now that the agricultural revolution and television succeeded where Jules Ferry's school had failed (is it even certain that it would have wanted to?): in dealing the fatal blow to regional languages. All that rendered regionalisms more anxious and more bitter than before.

The regional question, moreover, numbered among the government's preoccupations. Even the 'Jacobins', who had no desire for a rebirth of the provinces as historical entities, accepted the idea of re-establishing geographical regions in order to have available frameworks of economic development capable of balancing the magnetism and gigantic overexpansion of the Parisian region. The comparative merits of small regions (mostly historic and cultural) and large regions (chiefly geographic and defined around a 'counterbalancing city') was one of the arguments of the time. In the end, in 1965, the twenty-one (afterwards twenty-two) present regions were created, all in all closer to the 'large region' concept, despite notable exceptions (Limousin, Corsica). In any case, there was a chasm between the government's idea, limited to an empirical restructuring of French economic space, and that of the more radical regionalists, passionately keen on history and culture, and wanting to work out their development for themselves.

The resurgence of the regionalist phenomenon was thus very probably connected with the economic, social and cultural metamorphosis of the era. Was it also linked with the other great contemporary event, Algeria, and its consequences? It is possible.

In 1965, at one of those conferences where the intellectual left tried to rebuild its forces by updating its doctrines, much note was taken of the report presented under a pseudonym by a young civil servant (actually Michel Rocard); it was entitled 'Decolonizing provincial France'. 'Provincial France' and not 'the provinces'; the plural would have been revolutionary, likening Lorraine or Brittany to colonies such as Vietnam or the Congo. If 'provincial France' in general was meant, thus the whole of the country outside Paris, 'decolonize' could only be a synonym full of imagery for 'liberate'. In fact, it meant only 'decentralize'. But that provocative title showed that 'decolonize' could be understood as something positive, and decolonization taken in good part. For others, as we know, the word more bluntly meant loss or abandon of the empire, thus defeat and grief.

So the question inevitably arises: what connection did the Algerian drama, the final paroxysm of decolonization, have with French national feeling?

Defeated and bitter, the partisans of French Algeria henceforth joined cause with the best adherents of traditional nationalism. They retained the justifications inherited from the Third Republic, or even further back, adding the tense rigidity naturally inspired by defeat and the sense of being betrayed, misunderstood and hated. That French nationalism in its turn hated de Gaulle, and the mass of French people who agreed to follow him.

De Gaulle and his men had no shortage of arguments, however. They tried to convince opinion that France was not necessarily diminished or humiliated by its retreat to what was then beginning to be known as the 'hexagon' (everyday use of this word dates back to that time). Letting go of subject peoples who were obviously too different from the French to be capable of assimilation had proved inevitable, in relation to the way things were going in the world generally. The cost of maintaining control and of waging war would be better invested in mainland France. Perhaps decolonization (the 'Cartierist' argument)[9] might represent an economic relief? France would remain a strong power by virtue of its own development and by maintaining a new type of influential relationship with its former colonies, which had become allies and were often sisters in the French language.

Could that powerful, coherent but also austere reasoning erase all the negative opposing viewpoints? For those who needed some uplift, the 'hexagon' was less exciting than the great pink splotches, representing a far-flung empire, that had been splashed across the world map.

The difficulty became worse for those who needed justification for their patriotism. For decolonization had caused French patriotism to lose not only the pride it had derived from the strength and extent of the empire, but also the good conscience it had derived from colonial legitimacy. If it must be admitted that decolonization was part of the order of things, and stemmed from the idea of liberty, then it must also be conceded that colonization belonged to the order of oppression. This old theme of revolutionary propaganda thus became a public truth!

In that case, had everything in the 'civilizing mission' been a mistake? Of what worth was the old idea associating France's moral identity with justice and liberty? That idea, which had allowed the left to be patriotic for so long, an idea already shattered by pacifist criticism following 1918, slightly reinvigorated in the antifascist fight of the Resistance, suffered a further blow after a colonial combat not only lost but, above all, discredited. So, anyone who loved justice would seek it elsewhere and find moral references in the new territories where they were being asserted. It was in the Third World that he would henceforth find the stormers of Bastilles, it was in the far continents where the last wars of national liberation were rising that the new revolutionary romanticism would find its sustenance.

Those were the feelings that were fairly clearly held, and which at that time were gaining ground in the France of republican tradition. They probably go some way towards explaining the increase in 'hexagonal' regionalisms, that upsurge being the counterpart of the weakening of the French patriotism which had contained or repressed them for one and a half centuries.

And without doubt, those same feelings help to throw some light on 'May'.

---

[9] From the name of the journalist Raymond Cartier, who did much to popularize this argument (in *Paris-Match*).

'The May Movement', or 'May–June 1968'? It certainly seems as if 'May' is preferred if attention is focused chiefly on the young, the cultural and the libertarian, and 'May–June' if trades unionism and general politics are not to be forgotten. 'May' or 'May–June', therefore, stemmed from a multiplicity of causes. And there had to be a convergence of causes, even heterogeneous ones, to provoke such a strong and extraordinary upheaval.

First of all, France, in that time of industrial growth and social change, was not without its class struggles or protest movements, to which prosperity at any time is fairly vulnerable. Next, the Fifth Republic suffered from the ferocious resentments aroused by the Algerian tragedy, and the power of the old General fell victim to that vague yet very real 'wear and tear' that comes with time. Thirdly, the 'consumer society', with the cultural changes it brought in its wake, by favouring both hedonism and uprooting had prepared the ground for the quest for innovation, or even a 'crisis of values'. Between all those elements, which may appear rather vague, intuited rather than demonstrable, a fairly plausible correlation may be established. Fourthly and lastly, from the restrictions of a 'hexagon' that was not very exciting and all the more inclined to look for points of reference in distant countries – countries, moreover, which had become better known through easier travel and the cosmopolitanism of the mass media – foreign libertarian movements were followed with approval. People knew about Berkeley, Berlin, China: Berkeley, the starting point for world-wide young people's anti-establishment protest; China where, under the admirable title 'cultural revolution', something held sway which would later stand revealed as an anti-intellectual and anti-scientific counter-revolution; Berlin, where the young leader Rudi Dutschke 'fought death' in the hospital bed where a fascist's bullet had put him. The sustained unrest that this distant drama aroused in French universities gives some measure of the new permeability of frontiers to international waves of feeling.

Let us add that world revolutionary romanticism was no longer channelled and almost monopolized, as it had been during the cold war, by the French Communist Party. This found itself undeniably weakened, notably in young and intellectual circles, where it paid the price for its 'Stalinism' (its completely negative reaction to the jolts of 1956), and even more for its circumspect attitude at the time of the Algerian war. The groups, tendencies and personalities calling themselves revolutionary and claiming to be 'further left' than the PCF no longer formed an almost negligible marginal fringe, as they had in the Fourth Republic. It was in order to designate this sphere of influence (anarchists, Trotskyists of various allegiances, Third Worldists, etc.) that the words 'leftism' and 'leftists', themselves borrowed from Leninist vocabulary, were to become familiar to public opinion. The leftists, in any case very divided among themselves, maintained a ferocious rivalry with the Communists, but all that created a climate of emulation and overreaching that was favourable to protest.

It goes without saying that those last factors were at work chiefly in the universities, where the crisis was to take off. Student numbers were greatly on the increase: democratization and the demographic rise gradually swelled the total numbers of the young clientele of the education system. Prosperity had rendered the entry of children of modest families into higher education slightly less rare. And even if less fuss was made than today about the idea that, in a developing economy, new jobs call for higher qualifications, that conviction was not completely absent. In short, everything encouraged the increase in student numbers at the very time when the growth that should have accompanied it had undeniably fallen behind. There were neither enough premises nor enough teachers. The number of 'lecturers' properly speaking, that is to say, faculty professors, eminent educationalists, highly qualified and well paid, could of course grow only slowly. In order to fill the widening gap between their low number and their vast audiences, the university had therefore had to recruit – and in vast quantities – cohorts of assistant and junior lecturers culled from among young *lycée* teachers. Thence arose an almost entirely new category of teachers in higher education, who assumed a large share of the teaching work while being regarded as statutorily and symbolically minor. From that came a feeling of frustration among its members that was to turn many of them – perhaps the majority – into active trades unionists and allies of the student anti-establishment movement. A shortage of teachers, therefore; also a shortage of premises despite busy construction work, the amount of teaching space available always lagging slightly behind the amount needed. The old Sorbonne in the Latin Quarter, for its scientific side, had already been relieved by the d'Orsay and Halle aux Vins buildings. In order to ease the literature faculty, the Nanterre annexe had just been built, and it was there that the movement would have its birth.

Much has been said of the soul-destroying atmosphere of Nanterre where, in a poor, working-class and at that time awkward-to-reach suburb, a new faculty still surrounded by muddy tracks was squeezed in between a hospice and a shanty town. This again is an imponderable part of the explanation, if it is one at all. Doubtless much more significance lies in the incidents that took place, after the start of the academic year in 1967, still in Nanterre, in the student halls of residence. They threw light on another contemporary conflict, which set the strict and traditional nature of disciplinary regulations in the student halls against the aspirations for complete freedom of movement among the young of both sexes.

In the spring two things emerged from that flood of minor incidents. A date, first, 22 March, that was to give its name to the most progressive of the anti-establishment organizations – if one can apply the term organization to a group which set its spontaneity and permanent self-regulation against the wiser trades unionism of the students' union, the UNEF – the Movement of 22 March. Then a person, Daniel Cohn-Bendit, a very young sociology student, of leftist tendency, eloquent, expansive and endearing in appearance, of German origin (Jewish, what is more, which would one day have a relevance).

The movement would rise between 3 and 27 May, get involved in a political crisis between 27 and 30 May, and ebb in June.

Events in Paris, May 1968. Demonstrators throwing paving stones, Boulevard Saint-Michel. (Photo: Roger-Viollet)

On 3 May, the students from Nanterre, in a state of permanent unrest since the beginning of the spring, and prevented from holding a meeting in their establishment, came to do so in the courtyard of the Sorbonne in the heart of the Latin Quarter. The principal of the Académie de Paris summoned the police to have them ejected. That violence, more symbolic than physical, provoked a call for a general strike launched by the UNEF, the 22 March Movement and also by a teachers' union attached to the powerful secular group FEN, the SNE-Sup. The leaders of these organizations, Jacques Sauvageot, Daniel Cohn-Bendit and Alain Geismar respectively, would soon be seen by opinion (that is, telespectators) as the guiding trio of the movement.

Between 3 and 10 May the strike spread, unevenly but in the main successfully, to the universities of Paris and the provinces, and was already assuming an unusual character: not only did work stop (courses were no longer attended), accompanied by a demand that examinations be postponed (they were imminent), but also time was spent in meetings to challenge and debate organization, educational methods, the school system, and so on.

On the evening of Friday 10 May, a procession of students in the Latin Quarter crossed swords with the police and matters turned sour. The students fought, defended themselves; it was the first 'night of the barricades', when once again, between Sorbonne, Panthéon and Luxembourg, streets were to be seen with their cobblestones torn up and cars put crosswise on the roads like the tipcarts in Louis-Philippe's time. Of course, the students had no weapons other than paving stones and other improvised missiles. Some Molotov cocktails, as well, which caused several cars to be burnt.

The police overcame them easily as soon as they received the order. On their side, they were well armed: helmets and shields against the missiles, truncheons and tear gas for the attack. The students soon learned the drill: wear sneakers in order to run fast, put a handkerchief round your nose to cut out some of the gas. Each side soon had its familiar outline, one might almost say its uniform. As for the May-night-in-the-Latin-Quarter (others would follow that of 10 May), that too acquired its characteristic image; and it would be less one of barricades than of overturned cars, sometimes set alight, and clouds of gas. A legend about the night of rioting was soon born: peaceable residents in the attacked streets threw water from their windows: on the movement's side it was asserted that their intention had been to dissipate the clouds of gas, thus to help the students, thus to demonstrate the solidarity of the people in the Quarter. Others stated, however, that the primary aim of the jets of water was to protect the houses against fires arising from the burning vehicles, a view which stemmed from a more classic and probably more widespread attitude of mind. There was also controversy – let us say it once and for all – on the subject of police brutality. Unaccustomed to being its victims, the students were horrified by it and launched a highly successful slogan: 'CRS equals SS'. They were often reproached for that naive comparison, which even backfired on them, so obvious was it that the professional roughness of a police officer of the Republic could in no way be compared to the murderous cruelty of Hitler's elite troops. Today one is struck more by the perfection reached by the forces of order in the art of restraining without killing, or even seriously wounding. Grimaud, the Perfect of Police, would later publish a convincing book[10] on the feat achieved, on the part of the institution of which he was head, in gaining control of the area without causing any serious harm. It was not completely idyllic, however. It turned out that the truncheon blows which had rained down behind the reconquered barricades had also continued in the holding centres to which arrested students were taken on the night of 10–11 May. In short, there were some severe beatings-up. Police brutality was thus real, even if exaggerated. Stories about it spread very rapidly and provoked an immediate and decisive effect.

Left-wing opposition, quite naturally, showed itself more favourable towards the young people and the strikers in the universities than towards the 'Gaullist government'. There was no cause for surprise when on the 11th, the workers' trades unions called for an all-out, 24-hour strike, on Monday 13th, in protest against police excesses.

That strike took place successfully on 13 May, for the first time involving the world of labour alongside the student world. Now, it happened that,

---

[10] *En Mai, fais ce qui te plaît . . .* (In May, do as you please . . .), Stock, 1977.

planned for twenty-four hours, it repercussed in an unexpected way, and that the movement became social in the most classic sense of the word. On the 15th, the whole of France learned that workers in certain provincial factories had not only failed to resume work but were also occupying the buildings. A sit-down strike, a spontaneous action by the workers, reminiscent of June 1936, it was quite a different kettle of fish from disturbances in the Latin Quarter!

Quickly taken in hand by the unions, the general strike was extended and it was against a background of generalized class warfare that the university anti-establishment challenge continued, not without deriving a higher degree of elation and revolutionary hopes from that populist backdrop. Then, in the second fortnight of May, the whole of France was to find itself in an unprecedented situation: a workers' strike, which in itself was not without precedent, but this time complete enough to slow down the activity of millions of people, virtually to give them a holiday, which was far more rare; and finally a strike and 'holiday' during which leisure time was used to discuss the situation and seek reforms. The universities set up the educational system again with new bases in general assemblies and mixed working committees (students, lecturers, staff of all levels and types of work), and a key word emerged from it – 'co-management'. That demand, which was both libertarian (fewer central regulations) and egalitarian (management bringing together teachers and students), formally characterized the 'spirit of May', and was to be found to a greater or lesser degree in other professions on strike. It sometimes inspired the most unexpected circles since, for example, there was a 'May' of professional writers, who were also seeking new and fair statutes.

Out of those occupied premises, where discussions went on endlessly, came a torrent of newspapers, tracts, posters and pamphlets; assemblies, shows, 'happenings' were held, and political preachings abounded. The general strike provided leftism, notably in university circles (for it was less easy to express oneself so freely in working-class circles, which were more under the control of trades union headquarters), with an extraordinary sounding board.

It was at that point that uninitiated France learned of the existence of hitherto marginal doctrines and aspirations aimed at nothing less than 'changing people's lives'.

Changing people's lives? A vast programme which, from a distance, one can only affirm that the whole of striking and anti-establishment France had conceived the ambition to undertake. Among my own memories I recognize that two less grandiose wishes coincided: a change of government – a fairly classic aspiration to see a conservative power give place to another more sympathetic to the social forces at work – and a change in universities, chiefly through co-management. To change one's *own* life, therefore, by some specific reform, and by so doing to change the course of politics. However, as regards the movement, a certain solidarity and a whole range of intermediate theories and aspirations brought together a wide spread of participants whose wishes went from the most ordinary reformism to the most exuberant and utopian anarchism.

As for the large number of French people who were hostile to all this turmoil because they did not know how to react to it, they barely voiced an opinion, and their temporary tactfulness created for the movement an illusion of strength that encouraged it still further.

For, at the very top, the essentially conservative strength of the government seemed to be wavering.

During the crisis of 10–13 May, quite by chance, the Head of State and the Prime Minister were both away. On their return the General fulminated and Pompidou manoeuvred.

The General's wrath could be expressed verbally, and yet effectively. The 'Volapük' had been a real blow for the Europe of the MRP, and the 'quarteron' (quartet) the first offensive against the rebel generals in 1961. But the 'chienlit' (almost archaic term for 'bloody shambles') fell flat. The students did not feel affected by a word so outmoded and peculiar that its cutting edge was blunted. Far more apparent was the huge gap between the old leader and the whirlwind that was going on.

As for Pompidou, he climbed down; he had the Sorbonne evacuated by the police, hoped for (one dare not say begged for, but he obtained) the freeing of some students who had been charged, and looked for a point of contact in order to negotiate with the workers' unions.

The primary consequence was that the Sorbonne was immediately re-occupied by protesting students, and it was then that it became the headquarters so frequently described. Space for speeches, meetings, studies; staff offices, arsenal, infirmary; a yard where each group or subgroup had its stand for propaganda and literature. And amid all that, a courageous and skilful order-keeping force in the fortress, policing a protest which they approved or disapproved according to the infinite variety of the shades of opinion among them, top-ranking intellectuals made it their duty constantly to do the rounds, watching over fire prevention and keeping the libraries safe.

Let us come back to the Prime Minister. Only the economic strike represented a threat to the state. The universities could wait. Pompidou therefore had first to give his attention to the former, and he had some reason to think that the workers' unions, in control of the factories, were not, as they say, 'on the same wavelength' as those occupying the faculty premises. It was well known that the student delegations who had come from the Sorbonne to fraternize romantically with the working class had not been let in to the Renault factory. There was no need to be a great expert in Communism to know that, on principle, the PC preferred a modest movement that it could control to a powerful and radical movement over which it had no say. At the beginning of May, *L'Humanité*, in an article by Georges Marchais himself, had expressed its distrust regarding the 'German anarchist' Cohn-Bendit.

The Communists displayed as much tenacity in stigmatizing the 'irresponsibility' of the leftist 'splinter groups' as they used in legitimizing the workers' protest action and organizing its fight.

The government therefore had little difficulty in setting up a conference in the Ministry of Labour for all the influential social forces, from both employers and trades unions, a meeting which brought to mind the one which Léon Blum had convoked at the Hôtel Matignon in June 1936. The 'Grenelle' discussion was long and hard but classic, and resulted in proposals to give very substantial satisfaction to the embattled workers.

Meanwhile, the movement had again experienced some violent episodes in the Latin Quarter and Paris had been crisscrossed by gigantic processions. On 23 May, in particular, beginning to regain his sang-froid, the Minister of the Interior had decided to expel Cohn-Bendit from France, as a foreigner and agitator. The protest procession heard the famous cry of solidarity shouted: 'We are all German Jews' – a moving stroke of inspiration.

The PC had had nothing to do with it. It became evident that the battle was being played out between not two but three camps: the government of the state, the Movement (vast, diffused, undefinable, 'leftist') and lastly the PC (or, according to its own saying, 'the working class').

The left-wing political opposition remained silent and perplexed. At the end of the month, it seemed destined to take advantage of not only the other two, but the other three. It was then that the drama started and the denouement followed very shortly afterwards.

On the morning of Monday 27 May, while reporting back to the Renault workers on the benefits obtained at the close of the Grenelle meetings, the general secretary of the CGT in person was forced to the conclusion that the rank and file wanted more and intended to continue the strike. Georges Séguy and his friends gave assurances that it was not a setback for them but only a fact which they had noted, and that they had not come to call for a resumption of work. At the time, however, everyone immediately drew a conclusion from that surprising piece of news: Renault repudiated Grenelle, and the working class had 'outflanked' its customary representatives; a prospect opened out there for leftism.

And so it happened that, on the afternoon of the same day, the presence of Pierre Mendès France and several left-wing worthies was noted at the meeting of the student movement held in the Charléty Stadium (Paris University student centre). Was there a prospect of union between the Movement, at the summit of its power, and the left-wing opposition, which would offer a political way out of the crisis? That impression was confirmed when, at a press conference the following day, François Mitterrand declared, in substance, that such an outcome was possible, with no clash; that if General de Gaulle had to resign, there would be elections, in which he himself would stand as candidate, and that he would invite Pierre Mendès

France to join the government. There was nothing outrageous in all that, and his speech was astute rather than scandalous. If it did appear scandalous, however, it was because the televised broadcast of the scene, by its selective photographic shots and cutting, gave an 'over-the-top' version of the speech. There was to be much argument over this point subsequently.

For the moment, the prospect of the moderate left pretending to government by virtue of the general strike provoked two categorical responses, one from the PC, the other from Gaullism.

On the following day, 29 May, the PC and the CGT launched a powerful procession through Paris under the slogan 'Popular Government'. That expression assumed a revolutionary note, since there was no power vacuum, and 'popular' bore connotations that were known. But the oracle was not mistaken: 'Popular Government' expressed a 'no' to Mendès France just as much as a 'no' to de Gaulle. The PC was saying 'no' to a parliamentary way out of the crisis from which the men of the moderate left would profit, to whom it was bound by no agreement and over whose policies it would therefore have no influence.

As for the General . . . he vanished. Accompanied by Mme de Gaulle and his aide-de-camp, but without warning anyone, even Georges Pompidou, he took the helicopter and, overshooting his stated destination, Colombey-les-Deux-Églises, went on to land at Baden-Baden, the general headquarters of the French garrisons in Germany, under the command of General Massu. He would return the next day, doubly bewildering France, because the extraordinary confusion aroused by the announcement of his mysterious absence was compounded by the shock of his miraculous reappearance. What had been going on?

Three hypotheses have since vied to explain that trip. Firstly, the pure and simple 'staging' of the double emotion and his triumphal return. Secondly, an appeal to the army. And lastly a temptation to get away from it all. At first sight, hypothesis number one would seem highly unlikely because of the excessive Machiavellism it presupposes. The second is a little less so: de Gaulle may have thought that matters could take a revolutionary turn and that, should the need arise, he must be sure that the army would conduct itself as a loyal auxiliary of the government – but there is no explicit testimony to such a pact, only an indirect assumption (the pardon granted shortly afterwards to the OAS generals and the Petit-Clamart conspirators could pass for the price paid by de Gaulle to bring back military sympathies to his side). The third has two strong arguments in its favour, the direct and formal testimony of General Massu and the conclusion which Pompidou himself reached, in a posthumous work. Yes, de Gaulle might for a moment have believed the situation impossible to put right, and could have been tempted to opt for resignation and exile, from which the faithful Massu was able to dissuade him. Is that unlikely? The General had certainly experienced the temptation even in London (he mentions it incidentally in his *War Memoirs*), and he had already given up power without being obliged to do so in January 1946; and would do so again in April 1969. Why could he not have had such an inclination on 29 May 1968?[11] Whatever path may have led him to his decision (the psychology of a man of de Gaulle's importance is not irrelevant to the history of France, or superfluous in its narration), the General came back, rejoined his men and prepared for action.

Militant Parisians of the UNR, for their part, had judged the time ripe to express themselves. As long as it was a matter of protest movement, general strike, an unaccustomed cultural and social ensemble, Gaullism could have no obvious influence. But when that turned to politics, and there was talk of the PC, Mitterrand, Mendès, it became possible to mobilize precise feelings against the left. Hence arose the idea of a demonstration, on the Champs Élysées, as befitted a following whose social and symbolic affinities were rather those of western Paris.

In a radio broadcast message, de Gaulle asked his faithful to join this supportive demonstration, and announced that he would appeal to opinion by pronouncing the dissolution of the National Assembly (in which, let us remember, the majority elected in 1967 were only a little ahead).

The Gaullist procession from Concorde to the Arc de Triomphe was a huge success. And the opening of an electoral prospect caused an explosion in the Movement, or the various combinations starting up in its wake.

In fact, the moderate and Mendèsist left immediately launched into an electoral campaign, and the PC as well, whereas leftism, that is the simultaneously dynamic and 'fuzzy' part of the forces engaged in the struggle, considered itself betrayed by this too classically bourgeois outcome. From then on, the Movement would wage a rearguard campaign on the theme: 'Elections–betrayal' – a watchword sometimes translated in more modern terms as: 'Elections–idiot-trap'. 'Idiots' or not, there was not a majority in France who would opt for boycotting the ballot box.

In June, while voting preparations were being made for the 23rd and 30th, the strikes tapered off. It was during this phase of resistance without prospects that victims died, at least victims among ordinary people (for a police commissioner had died in Lyon in May), two workers in Sochaux and a schoolboy in Flins. As the Movement had never achieved unanimity and, furthermore, appeared not to have obtained any of what it had been demanding (there had been no 'change of life' or change of government), the opposition, which had broadly sympathized with it, was severely punished by the electorate. The majority won 358 seats, including 293 for the UDR alone (the new initials of the old UNR) and 64 for its right-wing allies, the independent republicans. Facing them, 127 opponents, very much divided because among them were centrists, FGDS (the Mitterrand coalition of 1965) and Communists.

---

[11] One who was close to the General, Bernard Tricot, secretary general at the Élysée, is not convinced, however. According to him, Massu could in quite good faith have taken at face value one of those half-provocative, half-probing conversations to which the General was given when reflecting aloud about a difficult problem. But is that not to return to the Machiavellian thesis? (Conversation with the author, 20 June 1990.)

Was it a Pyrrhic victory? De Gaulle's presidency would not survive the events of May by as much as a year . . .

On 10 July 1968 the Head of State asked Georges Pompidou for his resignation, and appointed his loyal Minister of Foreign Affairs, Maurice Couve de Murville, as Prime Minister. That decision provoked fresh controversy. Was it the ritual of turning over a new leaf, like the replacement of Debré with Pompidou after Évian? When a matter is settled, life goes on and there is an amicable change of man? Or was it something more serious, de Gaulle unhappy that Pompidou had upset him by making a better job of analysing and gaining control of the May disturbances? No one knows.[12]

In the Couve de Murville government, Michel Debré was for a while in charge of the Economy, once more weakened by the exodus of bourgeois capital fleeing the 'revolution'. There was no question of devaluing the franc.[13] Raymond Marcellin came to the Ministry of the Interior, and wiped out the last after-effects of the movement (the police cleared the Odéon and the Sorbonne). Edgar Faure received the crushing responsibility of National Education, and it was there, through him and in the most unexpected way, that 'May' at last obtained its most tangible success: Edgar Faure's law reorganized the universities and introduced, notably, a system of elected councils on which all categories of teachers, students and other staff were represented. On the whole it was very akin to the co-management for which the struggle had taken place. Gaullism saved face by assuring that the system involved participation and was thus in keeping with its doctrine. That last argument presented the government with the advantage of introducing a rift into the camp of the university left. In fact, the leftists boycotted the new institutions because they had been 'granted by the Gaullist government', whereas the Communists and a section of the moderate left participated in the proceedings because they represented a 'May asset'.

Pompidou, who was no longer Cantal's deputy, was travelling. On 17 January 1969, in Rome, he was led to say that if, one day, General de Gaulle should give up power, he would naturally stand as a candidate. It seemed quite a banal statement; after all, the old President had just entered his seventy-ninth year, and Pompidou had shown himself to be enough of a statesman to be able to aspire to the Élysée. Nevertheless, it must be accepted that this declaration seems to have had the effect of an act of hostility, or at least disloyalty, to the General. Pompidou defended himself. Official statements were exchanged, supposedly soothing, but cold. As if

---

[12] According to the witness quoted earlier (A.P.), de Gaulle did not approve of the flexible policy effected by Pompidou in May. Had he been present in France on 11 May, he would not have ordered the clearing of the Sorbonne by the police. Would what followed have been changed? Let us just say that it is not demonstrable.

[13] The Minister of Finance was then F.-X. Ortoli, but the decision was taken by the General, on the advice of J.-M. Jeanneney and R. Barre.

by chance, after several weeks, Pompidou was the target of a stupid and cruel slander campaign (the Markovitch affair), the origin of which he had to impute not to the General (very much above all that sort of thing, of course), but to over-zealous men on his side.

De Gaulle, however, as if he felt defied either by Pompidou or by the May upheavals, wanted to set the regime off again in its reformatory vocation. He had a study made of a daring regionalization law that would have serious constitutional implications (the Senate's method of recruitment would undergo change). And chiefly, he announced that it would be subject to a referendum, and he would make that referendum a personal test of French confidence. In short, he put his mandate at stake.

The bill was too complicated to be popular, the reform of the Senate awoke anxieties among 'old republicans', and the regime seemed to be more in search of an expedient for gaining popularity than at the forefront of a clear intent. Above all, V. Giscard d'Estaing swung the balance by declaring himself for the 'no' vote. Apparently he believed that the General had had his day, and that a new generation with fresh methods should take over. Pompidou, faithful to Gaullism, obviously called for a 'yes' vote.

But on 27 April 1969, the 'noes' won the day and the General immediately announced his resignation. As laid down in the constitutional rule, the interregnum of the Republic's presidency was assured by the president of the Senate, Alain Poher, a centrist (ex-MRP).

Alain Poher had succeeded Gaston Monnerville in 1968, and started to patch up relations between the Senate and the Élysée. Centrist, thus Catholic, European, and liberal in the true sense of the word (committed to the principles of law, liberalism and humanism), he was then in the opposition and could stand as the man who could offer an alternative to Gaullism, in the spirit of the 'no' cartel of 1962. Moderate opposition, but opposition all the same. As he was still moderate, and had become noticed, if not famous, by virtue of his office as interim Head of State, he might seem the ideal candidate to defeat what was authoritarian in strict Gaullism, to which Pompidou was the obvious heir. He let himself be persuaded.

In the first round, on 1 June 1969, the Gaullist candidate Pompidou confronted the moderate opposition candidate Poher, together with a veritable profusion of left-wing candidates, whose spread revealed the disarray and bitterness caused by the May failure. Mitterrand had reckoned that he had no card worth playing in those conditions (besides, his declaration on 28 May 1968 could be taken as a *faux pas* best forgotten). The following had thus entered the lists: the socialist Defferre with the active support of Mendès France; the PSU Rocard; the Trotskyist Krivine; and most importantly, the Communist Duclos. The latter, with 4,800,000 votes, outclassed all his left-wing rivals, but did not manage to get ahead of Poher who, as the only credible candidate in the second round, gained second place with 5,200,000 votes. Pompidou came first with 9,800,000.

In the second round, on 15 June, all the non-Communist left rallied to Poher. But the PC defected. Declaring that Pompidou and Poher were 'six of one and half a dozen of the other', the PC advocated abstention and, at the same stroke, ensured an easy success for the Gaullist candidate: 10,700,000 votes against the 7,900,000 of his rival. Pompidou would not deny that this singular decision had been to his advantage, adding nevertheless that, even if the PC had called for a vote for Poher, he, Pompidou, would have been elected just the same. It is possible, but not demonstrable.

The fact is that the PC had preferred to renew the lease of the most faithfully Gaullist policies, those of Pompidou. No doubt it feared that Poher's policies might include a European and 'Atlantic' shift and might abandon the famous 'positive aspects' of the General's diplomacy. For in the PC's political determinations, 'worldwide' continued to be of more moment than 'hexagonal'.

The General, meanwhile, quit the political stage. He lived at Colombey, contemplated and wrote, or else travelled in the old countries, Ireland in 1969 and Spain in 1970, where his presence bore scant risk of giving rise to wrong interpretations or political movements. For he abstained completely from any intervention in public life, only letting it be known that he had approved of the election of Georges Pompidou.

And it was at Colombey, on 9 November 1970, that death overtook him, suddenly and swiftly, at the end of the day. At Colombey again, on the 12th, he was buried, according to his wishes, in the cemetery adjoining the church, in the presence only of his intimates, Compagnons de la Libération and villagers. Meanwhile, in Paris, in Notre Dame Cathedral, at the head of a numerous and glittering gathering of monarchs and heads of state, Pompidou attended a funeral ceremony held *in absentia*.

That distinction between a family burial and a ceremony of public homage is tending to become more common these days, and replace the traditional solemn state funeral. It was fairly new in 1970, fresh evidence of the General's inexhaustible originality. In him, the historic hero could not be spared the great Parisian organ, but the man, perhaps disappointed in what he saw as national ingratitude, withdrew into intimacy. No one could have challenged his right to the Panthéon, among the great defenders of liberty, or the Invalides, alongside the nation's great soldiers. Eluding this sharing of history and symbol, by electing to be buried in the village, he made a most ambiguous choice: an acceptance of the utmost humility, or the creation of a new 'Mecca' around himself alone?

In Colombey-les-Deux-Églises, the main street witnessed the growth of many tourist 'souvenir' shops, full of nasty and vulgar rubbish. La Boisserie would become a museum after Mme de Gaulle's death (which occurred in 1979). With that, two opposite poles of attraction draw the contemplation of the visitor. The pole of humility is to be found at the cemetery, where the headstone, quite flat and without decoration, simply bears the words 'Charles de Gaulle 1890–1970',[14] in the same size and lettering as those of

---

[14] To which, of course, have been added the name and dates of his wife. A cross, also of stone, towers over and links the two graves.

the next stone, that of his sick daughter, 'Anne de Gaulle 1928–1948'. The pole of grandeur lies beyond the village, on a nearby hill which has entirely become a garden of remembrance, and at the summit of its tree-covered slopes towers an immense cross of Lorraine. The new emblem with which the epic of Free France and the Resistance had enriched national symbolism thus received its fullest consecration in that corner of the countryside which the hero had made his own.

12

Between Gaullism and Mitterrandism 1969–1983

Georges Pompidou wanted to carry on the General's work faithfully. It was a faithfulness without useless imitation, for Pompidou was sufficiently astute to know that the inimitable cannot be reproduced, and sufficiently strong to be his own man and assume his own character. There was quite a distance between his physical chubbiness and smiling face (smiling with *joie de vivre* or mischievous mockery) and the solemn countenance and imposing figure of his great predecessor. His liking for literary and artistic modernity extended as far as a friendly curiosity with regard to the creators, the 'stars', their amusements and their parties, their sociability. Pompidou was on familiar terms with a *Tout-Paris* that the General, though not scorning it, had viewed from further away and a loftier level. He would leave his name and his mark on the capital, between the Halles and the Marais, in the gigantic Cultural Centre at Beaubourg, an audacious piece of architecture, its metal structure fully visible, deriving its attraction from the simple and powerful functional regularity of its beams and tubes, its sole artifice being the use of many colours.

That the edifice brought machinery to mind (an oil refinery, for the most . . . refined detractors) may not have displeased the President. For in Georges Pompidou a taste for novelty in art (it quickly became known that the Élysée apartment had been refurnished in 'design centre' style and adorned with abstract paintings) converged with the design (inherited from de Gaulle) for the economic modernization of the country. Had he not used Concorde as his emblem in the 1969 electoral campaign? Another sign: we have already had occasion to cast an almost indiscreet eye on the collection of presidential medals, and know that in 1959, with de Gaulle, the cross of Lorraine had broken the long line of feminine Republics. In 1969, Pompidou took care not to resuscitate the Marianne of yesteryear or to prolong the life of the cross of Free France.

He thus invented – or approved – for his own accession medal a singular monogram, a bunch of semicircular segments attached by one of their ends

Leonid Brezhnev on the Champs Élysées with Pompidou, 26 October 1971. (Photo: Roger-Viollet)

to a common axis, like petals to the centre of a wilting flower. The impression of a turning wheel is conveyed to the eye. How could one fail to see in it the happily combined homage to abstract art and industrial dynamism? Taking on this modern civilization which presented itself as both a revolution in ways of life and a commercial opportunity for France, Pompidou was an automobile man; he accepted the adaptation of the town to meet the new traffic (the 'express' way which runs along the right bank of the Seine in Paris bears his name), the residential and office tower blocks; he inaugurated, in person, at the wheel of a Renault, the last section of the A6 motorway which up until then had fallen short of a complete Lille–Paris–Marseille linkup.

Gaullist, therefore, but futuristic in style far more than keeping an eye on history. He was acquainted with power, had a taste for it, had learnt, from the inside, the unequally bicephalous management of the Fifth Republic, and now from the Élysée it was his turn to appoint and guide the Matignon man.

His first choice fell on Jacques Chaban-Delmas, who stayed as Prime Minister from June 1969 to July 1972. Chaban-Delmas, a deputy and mayor of Bordeaux, combined many reasons for suitability. A likeable and charming man, a great sportsman who had held a highly responsible position in the Resistance (one of only three who, when they came out of hiding, received the equivalent rank of general), a former minister under Pierre Mendès France, he was able to (and did) have friends well beyond the confines of the Gaullist movement. So his government included three members (Pleven, Fontanet, Duhamel) who came from the centrist opposition. Above all, he surrounded himself with a determinedly modern and reformative brains trust, in which Jacques Delors figured (he later became a socialist, as we know).

Chaban-Delmas and his men adopted social analyses which, for all that they were functionalist rather than Marxist, were none the less undeniably critical. Speaking of a 'blocked society', arguing the case for a 'new society' – here was a new language making itself heard. It was nevertheless at variance with the mostly conservative tendency of the presidential electorate.

So there were no drastic changes. There remained meanwhile some useful legal reforms on marriage settlements, the rights of married women, those of natural offspring, and some social progress, for example the encouragement to put hourly paid workers' pay on a monthly basis. The limitations of this liberalism were even more obvious in the political sphere. In 1970, the 'anti-crook' law extended the notion of responsibility, the better to get at those who committed damage and looting during street demonstrations. In 1971, with the same intent, government and majority would even have blunted the edges of the right of association if the Council of State had not blocked the plan.

In July 1972, Pompidou dismissed Chaban-Delmas and appointed Pierre Messmer to the Matignon, a man who had been regarded until then as a minister specializing in colonial and military affairs rather than a politician.

This appointment created waves and eddies, as had the similar changes effected by de Gaulle, of which Pompidou had been the beneficiary in 1962 and the victim in 1968. On each occasion people wondered if it was a matter of conflict or custom. Conflict? Pompidou was suspected of being socially conservative, and irritated by the reformism of Chaban's team. Custom? An unwritten law of the Fifth Republic was believed to be emerging, by which two prime ministers per seven year term were 'worn out', because Matignon, with the tough job of confronting daily tasks and conflicts, was the more vulnerable element of the diarchy. Chaban, however, seemed far from 'worn out' since he had obtained from the Assembly, several weeks earlier, a massive vote of confidence given by an intact majority. That Élysée–Matignon dialectic, as it was called by a rather esoteric and cumbersome official political study, formed part of the repertoire, and indeed the heritage, of de Gaulle. Just like the referendum, which Pompidou had equally believed he could use.

Pompidou, who watched the union of the left make progress and considered it dangerous for his policies, looked for an opportunity to thwart it. Britain's entry into the Common Market provided him with just that opportunity.

In April 1972, Pompidou put its ratification to the French people, which was by no means legally essential. He thought that the non-Communist left, favourable to Europe and for a long time attached to friendship with Britain, would answer 'yes', thus combining its votes with those of the majority, which it would swell come election time, while the Communists and implacable chauvinists would be isolated. But the socialists eluded this blatantly obvious trap by advocating a blank vote. The Communists voting 'no' as expected, the 'yes' obtained only those votes normally gained in the majority, and the effort had been pointless.

In the face of this complicated management, despite its fundamental internal division over Europe, the left gave an impression of dynamism, as if the overall élan of the movement of May 1968 counted for more than the electoral defeat in the following June. The big trades union affiliations had young leaders, whose features were popularized on television as frequently as those of the party leaders. The leader of the CGT, Georges Séguy, and the leader of the CFDT, Edmond Maire, were both attractive figures by virtue of their evident generosity, warmer and more familiar in the one, more tense and didactic in the other. The continuing flagrant social inequality, the rapid economic changes, a good many political abuses or politico-financial scandals, both large and small, continually fuelled their calls to battle. Those were relayed by the political parties, Communist and socialist respectively, even though their situations relative to the trades unions were not the same.

Despite periodically protesting their independence, the PC–CGT coupling remained a stable fact. In contrast, the Socialist Party were not, and never would be, affiliated to a single trades union. Socialist employees and officials were to be, and would be, found in *Force ouvrière*, the CFDT, some even in the CGT (not to mention the teachers who, in the FEN, were shoulder to shoulder with Communist teachers).

The Communist Party, now led by Georges Marchais, was not doing badly. May 1968 appears to have boosted its fortunes. The 1956 drama seemed a long way off, Algeria had receded into the past, and now memories were only of the roles played by the Communists in 1968, among the working class, by fulfilling their traditional function of providing impetus and training, and in university circles in the newer job of offering a reasonable counterweight to leftist turbulence.

They were able once more to recruit militants. But their great rival was also forging ahead in its own quite different way.

The key idea (and that of François Mitterrand first and foremost) had been to build a new political force by amalgamating the SFIO with the nebulous mixture of Mendèsism, the new left and *clubs de réflexion*[1] in a union of the entire non-Communist left, such as the Union of Democratic Forces (UFD) had modestly prefigured in 1958. At the end of complicated procedures, the detail of which matters little here, the SFIO had at first given place to a new party, which called itself quite simply 'socialist' (abandoning the old initials, SFIO). Then, in June 1971, at the time of the famous and already almost legendary Congress of Épinay, François Mitterrand had become its first secretary, strategist and indisputable leader. He based his strategy on the supposition that France would have available a potentially very wide left-wing body of opinion; that this opinion had veered away from Guy Mollet's SFIO because of its moderatism and colonialism; that the Mitterrandist clubs which, though well oriented, were not very popular or deep-rooted, had not been able to capture it; and that, in order to mobilize this opinion, there was need of a new party in which would be associated young intellectual executives and old notables of the red regions who had remained republican at heart. That party, genuinely in opposition, genuinely democratic and social, would be able to challenge the traditional hegemony of the Communist Party.

For France, a developed country with a liberal tradition, a strong Bolshevik-type party was indeed an anomaly, and the normal situation would be to have a party involving democratic socialism. But, in order to challenge the PC for its voters, it was better to be on the same side of the barrier. Mitterrand's PS thus joined the PC in its unitarian policy, although with some different and even antagonistic ulterior motives. The PC, for its part, remained loyal to the policies of the Popular Front. Certainly, it mistrusted Mitterrand, but thought that the image of severity habitually linked with Communism would always be more attractive than the image of opportunism indissociable, in its view, from any 'social democracy'.

Thinking along those lines, the stage had been reached in June 1972, of agreeing the Common Programme of government, signed by the Socialist and Communist Parties, which the left half of the old Radical Party (MRG) naturally joined. Despite this union, the opposition lost, albeit by little, the 1973 legislative elections. The Messmer government carried off the victory by only a tiny majority, obtained chiefly thanks to reinforcement in the second round from a last-minute flood of centrist supporters led by Jean Lecanuet. The PS had advanced and was virtually on equal footing with the PC.

Those elections in March 1973 gave Pompidou and Messmer the chance to reshuffle the government slightly. Michel Debré came out of it.

For the presidency of the Assembly, the Élysée influence caused Chaban-Delmas to be set aside in favour of Edgar Faure. It was as if the veteran

---

[1] (Note to English translation) These were true clubs (in the British sense of the word), the principal being the 'Club Jean Moulin'. They comprised political men with innovatory minds, intellectuals, top civil servants, reflecting on ways to renovate politics, restore republican public-spiritedness and civic conscience etc.

Gaullists were losing ground to the advantage of other conservative allegiances. During these years, two men increasingly appeared, after Pompidou, to be the key men of the regime; two independent republicans, firmly ensconced in their posts since 1969, for the Interior, Raymond Marcellin, the man who maintained order unsubtly and inflexibly, and for the Economy, Valéry Giscard d'Estaing. The latter, who had already shown proof of his competence and astuteness,[2] became popular, with the help of television, by playing on two very distinct but complementary talents: sometimes being very obviously a man of the people (seen playing football, or playing his accordion), sometimes marvellously taking a teaching role (the clear mind, blackboard and piece of chalk). As for Raymond Marcellin, the installation by his service of a bugging device in the offices of the *Canard enchaîné* would raise a lasting commotion.

In the autumn of 1973, tension between left and right reached its peak under the effect of the distant events in Chile (the overthrow of Salvador Allende's legal socialist government by a military putsch that unleashed a veritable white Terror). The left became impassioned over the memory of Allende, the victim of a cruel and retrograde militarism. The right did not go quite so far as to extol Pinochet, but held that a 'Marxist' government which had wanted to dictate the economy and failed, had met its more or less inevitable fate. Rather as at the time of the Spanish War, the French did not fight each other, but took a moral stance and supported the cause of the sides who were actually exchanging blows. Cross-frontier right and left, so to speak.

In this atmosphere, President Pompidou's last great political project – to reform the Constitution in order to reduce the term of presidency to five years, then a referendum, of course – took on an outdated air, to the point where even its promoters soon abandoned it.

Must this wrong manoeuvre be interpreted as indicating a flaw in his judgement and capability? He had been known to be seriously ill since the end of 1972. The frequency of his rest periods; changes in his appearance and even his face, made puffy by remedies only too well known, changes that were pitilessly revealed on television; little confidences passed on; there was no doubting the presence of a pernicious and fatal illness.

Georges Pompidou died in Paris on 2 April 1974. About his demise, which has to do with biographical chance and could thus for propriety's sake be left aside, history must nevertheless record two details. First, the stoicism of the sick man who, informed of his condition and its fatal prognosis, nevertheless continued to work in his sufferings right to the end, adds a new and more than respectful touch to his portrait. Next, and less venerable in our eyes, the reason of state which, to the last day and against

---

[2] In 1962 he did not follow the mass of Independents (right) in the 'no' cartel, and remained loyal to the de Gaulle–Pompidou majority.

all the evidence, let it be declared through official channels that the President was well. Some years later, the infinitely less threatened health of President Ronald Reagan would offer the astounded world the opposite example of a sincerity of information verging on exhibitionism. The recurring theme of the antagonism between French and American temperaments or national traditions (or 'Latin' and 'Anglo-Saxon'? or 'Catholic' and 'Puritan'? or royal and democratic?) received fresh fuel there.

Like de Gaulle, Georges Pompidou had made his funeral arrangements by separating the intimate ceremony at Orvilliers from the solemn Mass in Notre Dame in Paris. But he had made no arrangements for his political successor.

Pierre Messmer, the Prime Minister in office, having declined, Chaban-Delmas stood as candidate for the UDR, then Valéry Giscard d'Estaing. Believing, not without reason, that the latter had more of an audience in the country and was thus a better candidate, Jacques Chirac took the risk of persuading some of the UDR deputies to declare for Giscard against Chaban!

The left, united in its near entirety behind Mitterrand (for there were numerous 'little' candidates, with various motives and improbable chances), saw victory within its grasp.

On 5 May 1974 the first round gave 43 per cent of the votes to Mitterrand, 33 per cent to Giscard d'Estaing and 15 per cent to Chaban-Delmas. In the second round, on 19 May, Giscard d'Estaing, with 51 per cent of the votes, carried the day and became President of the Republic.

The right thus kept the power, but at its heart a veritable turnabout had occured, with the tendencies furthest from Gaullism beating the official heirs of the General.

It could be said that, if Pompidou had still practised 'Gaullism without de Gaulle', 'après-Gaullism' was about to begin.

The new President was a young man (born at the beginning of 1926, he was still only forty-eight, which is not much for the Head of State of an old nation). 'Young' meant modern and 'relaxed'. He inaugurated his official function by going along the Champs Élysées on foot (and not by car), and posing for the official photographs in a lounge suit (and not a formal dress suit). Of course, those acts were deliberate. In essence, Giscard d'Estaing was no less conservative than de Gaulle or Pompidou, but he apparently thought that order gained nothing by being defended in tradition and stiffness; that it might be opportune, even clever, to defend society by adapting to the movement of the age. The left still being kept away from power, the 1974 election thus substituted a modern right for a more conventional right.

For there really was a movement of the age. The 'after-de-Gaulle' period was also and chiefly an aftermath of May. The profound social and cultural aspirations which had formed some of the general causes of the explosion in spring 1968, had not been erased by the political failure of the movement; they had even been strengthened, since May's 'time to speak' had broadly had the result of formulating and popularizing their arguments. The 'May revolt', defeated at the ballot boxes, channelled within the Faculties, had thus continued even harder in the press, in bookshops and in artistic expression. The crisis in traditional civilization that was going on fed a whole range of protests: against industry, wage exploitation, piece-work, oversized production units; against school and university, private coaching, competition, the hierarchy; against the army, discipline and war; against Parisian centralization, against state control and going further, against the state, and even further still, against the nation; against the inequality of the sexes and the oppression of women; against all harshness and brutality, against modern industries that harass human beings, plunder resources and pollute the planet; against prison; against towns; against laws and regulations, to which the wily and powerful adapt while the weak, the ignorant and the handicapped of all kinds are overwhelmed; against organ-ization, against order and, with even greater reason, against order that defends itself, that is, against repression (the key concept) – there is no end to the reasons for the all-embracing indictment brought by the sixty-eighters' anti-establishment protest.

Certainly, the catalogue was not a recent one, and nearly all its slogans are to be found in the indictments of socialism and anarchism against the reign of capital. But the spirit of May could not be reduced to that resur-rection or resurgence. In fact, it no longer called industrial society into question because it was in the hands of capitalists, but because it was . . . what it was. It no longer called power into question because it might be in the hands of the bosses, but because it was power. Its analysis no longer concerned only the economy, it no longer harked back to Marx, and what was known of the poor functioning and aberrant phenomena of 'socialist' countries thus no longer affected it. If that spirit had to be symbolized, at a first rough estimate, by a philosopher, one would need to think of Herbert Marcuse, or perhaps better still, of Michel Foucault, or at least of that part of his work which the public at large has retained. It takes as its target the system of powers, not inasmuch as they are the powers of any one man or class, but inasmuch as they are power, pure and simple.

Here we are touching on the common root of all sorts of heterogeneous movements, some of which took the form of updated and reputedly sym-pathetic social protests (regionalism, feminism, ecology, pacifism, hedon-ism, etc.), while others may be said to have had antisocial effects. For if in essence authority and the law inspire suspicion, how, without appearing repressive, can even the most elementary social rules be inculcated? All 'morality' would in effect be 'police morality', all 'cops' hateful, and every delinquency regarded sympathetically inasmuch as it was a deviation from the norm. It was because they intuitively sensed that kind of relationship that many conservatives unhesitatingly ascribed the obvious increase in delinquency and criminality to a sort of mental perversion peculiar to May 1968. We will not take up that simplistic analysis here; it is well known that troubles in social and civil behaviour have deep and ancient causes in economic injustice, overhasty urbanization, culture shock, before being hit by depression and unemployment. But it may well be that those troubles were aggravated by the general enfeeblement of all forms of moral and civic teaching, at a time when many leaders of opinion, above all on the left, became libertarians for fear of being taken for *normalisateurs*[3] or 'Moral Order-ists'.

For the general tendency of the right wing was to oppose that spate of ideas, feelings and sensibilities, while that of the left was to accept and harness it.

Certainly, not all the left had taken on board everything about the intellectual revolt. Part, but only part, of those aspirations had been inte-grated into the socialist analyses of the 'Common Programme left' (femin-ism, moderate versions of ecology, regionalism); another part tended rather to feed an impatient revolutionism which found expression in the new extreme left (Workers' Fight, Communist League) or in certain splinter groups of the PSU, the CFDT, even the Churches; yet another part re-mained frankly uninvolved in the political sphere. But the difference be-tween post- and pre-May 1968 lay in the fact that socialists, Communists, radicals and even certain circles within the majority had learnt to become more attentive and receptive to the movements and ideas of the rebels. Even if only partial, that 'tuning-in' would probably play a role in the increasing influence of the young Socialist Party.

With but a few exceptions, which will soon be mentioned, the right exhibited a negative attitude that would accentuate the bipolarization and confrontation between right and left. As they squared up to each other, their positions became more general and more tough. When all the pro-cesses of civil and social breakdown first got under way, and then worsened under the pressure of the economic crisis (various types of indiscipline, including the potentially lethal one of traffic violations, rejection of collect-ive regulations, vandalism, delinquency, mental evasion of the law through drug abuse – with, as counterpart, the rise in xenophobic and 'anti-youth' harassment, the often over-rough 'self-defence' of shopkeepers and property owners), the most summary speeches were heard from either side.

On the right, the overall reaction would stigmatize burglary in the same breath as sexual freedom, under the all-embracing heading of 'laxity'. On

[3] (Note to English translation) In this sense the word dates from 1968, when the Soviet armed forces entered Czechoslovakia to put down Dubček's democratized Communism. They said they had come to 'normalize' the situation – a cynical euphemism for repression and counter-revolution. The cynicism of this choice of word created a scandal which ensured its wide use. 'Normalization' quickly became synonymous with the restoring of order – thus a word seen as pejorative.

the left, there would be many who, in return, would feel obliged to turn completely libertarian, as if thefts in supermarkets or fraud on the métro were mere 'facts of society', unavoidable, even understandable revolts against 'bourgeois morality'. What we have now learnt to call 'society's problems' well and truly constituted a new ideological stake in the game.

In the presence of this philosophical polarization, which reinforced the political polarization, those voices capable of speaking in favour of a respect for law, property and person (the only alternative to the law of the jungle) faded to a murmur. It was not one of the least signs of the enfeeblement of the profoundest and most legitimate aspects of the old republican culture.

This climate of reciprocal hatreds and widespread contempt for social rules gradually altered public habits. Protest action itself was no longer satisfied with the traditional forms of petition, demonstration and strike. In order to speak ever more loudly and strongly, it was an easy transition from the spectacular to the brutal, and from symbolic action to activism. Premises were taken over and occupied (the printing-works of the *Parisien libéré*, the church of Saint-Nicolas-du-Chardonnet), roads were barricaded, foreign lorries were looted. Formerly unusual and extreme methods, such as hunger strikes or use of explosives, became less rare.

As national interest and the nation itself had been knocked from their pedestals just as much as society and the law, protests aimed at them would in their turn reach the critical threshold of activism. When the police tried to face up to it, blood flowed and there were deaths (in Corsica at Aleria and Bastia in August 1975, at Creys-Malville in July 1977). That was how things stood with civil society and the political world, in which the young President spotted several blemishes and made it his first task to try to put right.

The man was showered with blessings. Coming from a rich family which for several generations had divided its time between business and public service, he was outstanding for his intellectual and physical abilities, had been a high-flying student (Polytechnique, then École nationale d'administration), after gaining honours as a very young volunteer in a war campaign in 1944–5. Then he had had experience of top-level financial administration, of ministerial cabinets (with Edgar Faure), and of parliament (elected in 1956 as deputy for Puy-de-Dôme on the retirement of his maternal grandfather, Jacques Bardoux). He had distinguished himself everywhere and had thereby acquired an ease and assurance which, seen on television, would later be taken for haughtiness or pretentiousness, once the initial spell had been broken. But in 1974 the charm had worked, making him a sound and effective candidate.

Having become Head of State, he was the target of many attacks. In France it is not easy to have a name with a 'de' in it (a recent 'de' and a fictitious kinship, as it happens), any more than it is to belong so obviously to the world of 'beaux quartiers' and châteaux, and to have a liking for it. Neither Vincent Auriol nor René Coty, nor Georges Pompidou had been perceived as distant by the French man-in-the-street. Charles de Gaulle, yes, but that was because of his age, his past and his singular genius. Valéry Giscard d'Estaing (people said Giscard, or sometimes VGE) was just as foreign to the common run of French people as de Gaulle without – and by a long chalk – as many ways of getting himself accepted.

He tried, however, with an insistence that an oversevere press would call demagogic, but which could just as easily be seen as likeable and touching.[4] For instance, from time to time he would go and dine with an ordinary French family. He certainly needed that artificial process to enable him to meet the people, because in the natural course of events, the people were very far removed from him. But after all, he need not have met any of the people, except in 'his' villages in the Auvergne, of course.

Perhaps it was also simplicity, initially, that caused him to make much display of his family (wife, children, relatives); one cannot blame individuals any more than the mass media for excessive indiscretion, since the customs of the time increasingly urged in that direction. All the same, public man or in private life, man alone or with a society entourage, Giscard was an extremely easy target for the satirical press, wrongly perhaps as much as rightly, but it would count in the end, as we shall see.

Meanwhile, the beginning proved to be simple, humane and liberal. The President went about, let himself be seen, analysed problems from close at hand. One day, in Lyon, he even visited the prison and shook hands with an inmate. He involved government and majority in voting for two laws of democratic and humanistic inspiration, one lowering the age of legal majority to eighteen years, and the other legalizing contraception and 'the voluntary interruption of pregnancy' (*interruption volontaire de grossesse*, abortion, thus rechristened IVG).

This law, known for the name of Simone Veil, the Minister who prepared and got it passed, totally overturned the policies of the French right wing, which since 1920 had been clerical and supported a rising birth rate. Being unfamiliar with contraception (because of that very law of 1920), many French women had resorted to abortion, although it was illegal; but the secrecy surrounding it had made it impossible to supervise and very often lethal. Experts would easily prove that the combination of contraception and IVG would cause fewer victims than clandestine abortion. Undeniably social and consequently humane, Veil's law, accepting that it was dealing a blow against life, was no less surely anti-Christian.

It therefore encountered (and kept) vigorous opponents on the right, and managed to get through thanks only to massive support from the

---

[4] *Le pouvoir et la vie*, a book of memoirs published in 1988, is certainly clever and justificatory, but often reveals the accents of an undeniable and endearing sincerity.

parliamentary left. This was an exceptional case. The politicians would draw from it the conclusion that Giscard had played against his own side. The historian or political scientist would see it rather as an exemplary case of the complexity of the right–left phenomenon: normally, the majority that had elected Giscard was held to be the right, and the opposition the left; but in a law so crammed with principles as Veil's law, the philosophical left, which passed it, extended far beyond the confines of the political left. The ideological landscape did not always coincide with the institutional landscape, a truth which we shall meet again.

The President's initial goodwill was revealed by still further signs. Attached to fundamental liberties, a constitutional regime, a law-based state, he had the good sense to note that the whole political world shared those options and that, since there was thus agreement on the essentials of the rules of the game, political debate could well do without the accents of civil war. Hence arose the appeal for 'defusing' political life, and the other appeal for recognition of a 'consensus' on some fundamental liberal values; and again that sensible axiom that France must be 'governed at the centre'. All those frequently repeated phrases became famous, but most often only to be mocked, and they produced hardly any results.

It is true that Giscard – despite his good intentions – remained a prisoner of his own side; from the majority which supported him, from the very ministers he had created, voices were often raised speaking a crusading language rather than one of 'consensus'. In all fairness, it must be said that the calls for consensus and defusing the tension were no better heeded by the opposition, with the exception of Robert Fabre, the leader of the left-wing Radicals, who was somewhat disappointed by his partners.

The President himself chose his ministers and other colleagues, opening up a political career to some strong personalities: Simone Veil, already appointed, and Raymond Barre. Some other discoveries were less fortunate . . .

There was one man, however, who had not needed to be chosen, so necessary did he seem. The Prime Minister of the seven-year term was in fact Jacques Chirac, whose rallying, it may be recalled, had ensured the success of Giscard's candidacy at the time of the presidential election. The Giscard–Chirac collaboration lasted only two years and ended in what was a novelty in the political customs of the Fifth Republic: in August 1976, the Prime Minister took the initiative over the change by tendering his resignation, without disguising the fact that a conflict had set him at odds with the President. Its nature remained vague, apart from the allegation that the Élysée did not allow Matignon 'the means of governing'.

The major weakness of the Constitution – uncertainty about who was really managing current policies – revealed its disadvantages when neither of the two partners could gain mastery over the other by obvious superiority of age or stature.

Giscard d'Estaing next entrusted the office of Prime Minister to Raymond Barre, a university man, professor of political economy who, in Chirac's government, had the Foreign Trade portfolio.

The economy was indeed in question, as we shall shortly see.

The Giscardian right was at that time stronger than ever, since the Gaullist party had lost Matignon. It was deeply conservative, because it was attached to the values of order, property, authority, deference to religion and the maintenance of the established legal and economic system. It gladly described itself as 'liberal', however, first in connection with its partial opening up to the way customs were changing, but also and chiefly, because of its attachment to free enterprise and everything that set liberalism against socialism in the economic sphere. There then began a period of equivocation and confusion in French political language. French citizens, increasingly informed about American politics, began to learn that in the United States a right-wing man was called a 'conservative' and a left-wing man, a 'liberal', and those equivalents were gradually adopted in higher education and the French quality press. But at the same time, the right in France proclaimed itself 'liberal', by clear reference and opposition to a left identified with socialism, collectivism and state control. So there were two contemporary and contradictory language conventions.

Nobody disputed that the right which we are speaking of was both 'conservative' in the American (and all-embracing) sense of the term, and 'liberal' in the French (and more specialized) sense of the word.

As the right was very generally preferred by rich people, big property owners and heads of industrial or financial enterprises, the traditional and almost inevitable encounters between money and power periodically got into the news. They ranged from the osmosis between political, administrative and economic circles and personnel to more precise and criminal 'affairs' of influence or corruption. Some were eventually cleared up and the guilty parties punished or pushed into the background; others remained at the stage of suspicions or polemics in the press. The details matter less than the general conditions, which were complex. For not everything could be explained by the fact that the 'bourgeoisie' was in power. The importance of official regulations in the economy (customs, taxation, controls of all kinds) on the one hand, and the role of the state, diplomacy and the army, local communities, industrial plant and equipment, as large-scale purchasers on the other hand, contributed just as much to explaining these problems.

Lastly, other 'affairs' raised the more serious question of the relations between politics and speculation deals rendered frankly odious, either by their international links or their connections with the underworld. To put it clearly, was there a shady political life, with underground domains where political coteries rubbed shoulders with and made use of bunches of crooks, and vice versa? The question was often raised in the 1960s and 1970s, in relation to episodes that are far from being clarified today. Of course, accusations of inadmissible practices were chiefly hurled by the opposition against the government, thus by the left against the right. But sometimes also within the bosom of the majority, by Giscardians against Gaullists. It was a Gaullist who was targeted in M. Poniatowski's famous statement on 'pals and rogues'. This partiality obviously had to do with the fact that Gaullism had been in power for fifteen years, and must have had recourse – for reasons already mentioned – to some fairly peculiar people. Whatever the reasons, the affinities, the networks, the motives, the end result in those years was an appreciable number (for a non-revolutionary period) of political murders, the perpetrators of which are still unknown and their motives still partly obscure – Judge Renaud, Jean de Broglie and perhaps even Robert Boulin and Joseph Fontanet. To which must be added the deaths of Henri Curiel, Pierre Goldmann and François Duprat.

This many-sided crisis of state and society, and perhaps of an ancient culture, could only deepen, for want of an appropriate remedy. Worse still – and a stroke of bad luck for V. Giscard d'Estaing's term of office – it was aggravated by difficulties arising from the world situation.

With the second oil shock of 1974,[5] France entered a grave economic crisis. The rise in the price of liquid fuels upset the balance of payments. In the same era came competition from recently industrialized Asian countries (South Korea, Taiwan, Hong Kong, Singapore), in addition to that from Japan. National industries (iron and steel, textiles, shipbuilding, etc.) were shaken by this shock wave.

The economic and social crisis sometimes took on the air of a veritable geographical alteration. In the Nord and Pas-de-Calais (setting aside the coastal area), or in Lorraine in the Moselle valley, when there was a simultaneous closure of coal and iron ore mines, blast furnaces, rolling mills and wireworks, the workers' housing estates would be home only to pensioners, 'pre-pensioners', the unemployed with some kind of assistance; the young moved away; and the entire life of the people – the mainstay of a genuine micro-regional culture – became ossified or was offered up to nostalgia and erudition. In the same way, deteriorating buildings and factory chimneys, for want of a now defunct output, survived only as a focus of interest for the rather sad upsurge in industrial ethnology and archeology. The landscapes of modernity formed around the end of the nineteenth century were being effaced, together with their legends.

The phenomenon was not unknown, moreover, in the very capital, since Citroën left the quai de Javel and Renault had to resign itself one day to quit Billancourt. It was not unknown even in the south of France, despite

---

[5] The first, as it is usually called, rather forgetting the Suez crisis of 1956.

the general tendency – familiar in America – for business enterprises to drift towards the sunshine. The Mediterranean coast was very far from completely becoming a French California, and a shipbuilding town like La Ciotat would one day have to resign itself to turning back into a seaside resort.

In floods, coming from entire disaster-stricken regions, or in dribs and drabs coming from all towns and all branches of work, the ranks of the unemployed began to swell until they became the massive fact and major problem that everyone knows today.

The economic history of France in the 1970s and 1980s, very complicated in its detail, at all events imposed a simple choice: defend the apparatus of production or reconvert it by adapting it.

Defensive action, by means of state intervention to bolster branches in difficulty, had been the rule for a long time, even in de Gaulle's era. It had failed, to the point where it could find almost no supporters except among the Communists, whose voluntarist, interventionist policies rejected the capitalist criteria of profitability and market forces and who, in their hatred of Europe, would easily return to national protectionism. On the other hand, all the other parties admitted, with a variety of nuances of opinion, that opening the Common Market out to Europe, to begin with, and beyond that opening out to trade in the world market, was irreversible and might prove advantageous. Competition was stimulating. And, in that competition, France was capable of developing strong, even dominant, economic sectors, in any case well able to compete: aircraft, automobile, aerospace, perhaps electronic, industries, as well as the manufacture of all sorts of modern machinery for military use. It was more worthwhile, so it was said, to boost 'performance' sectors than to keep propping up 'lame ducks'.

Such a choice, however, was not the answer to everything. Although, if need be, the progressive and exporting sectors could make up for the deficiencies in foreign trade, they did not seem able to fill the gaps in employment. Electronics and aerospace would never absorb all the work-force lost from coal-mining and textiles. Performance industries were auto-mated, and the more they were perfected the fewer workers they required.

It was now more or less accepted that employment would not grow in the secondary sector, but in the tertiary, and that the solution to unemploy-ment would come from the invention of new types of roles, not only in commerce and classic administrative posts, but in all kinds of new social and cultural services to meet unprecedented collective needs. Those ser-vices were yet to be invented, so the problem of jobs remained in its entirety.

To that structural difficulty must be added others, even more complex, connected with the state of currency and international circulation of capital. More than ever, the franc suffered the repercussions of American financial policy, speculative use of oil revenues, and in short a universal capitalist and stock market anarchy, from which not even Europe could protect France, since it numbered as many currencies and economic policies as countries that composed it. That economic stagnation would thus weigh ever more heavily on French diplomatic choices.

An optimistic thesis, fairly widespread in today's opinion, attributes to General de Gaulle the honour of having imparted some impetus that one no longer dares dispute. Domestically, there would be consensus on the institutions of the Fifth Republic, and externally, consensus on the policy of national independence (diplomatic autonomy, France's own defence through the nuclear deterrent and strike force). That is true, but might it not have been because the cold war, in the shape of East–West confrontation, was outdated?[6]

With the exception of the PC and other elements of the revolutionary extreme left, everyone accepted, with varying nuances, that, with regard to the United States, France must be an ally but not a vassal and, with regard to the USSR, both vigilant and 'open to dialogue'.

But were not the problems of Europe and relations with the Third World by now more important and more difficult than the Russo-American problem? The consensus on Europe (setting aside the PC) belonged more to the post-Gaullian era than to the Gaullist heritage. As for the heart of the matter, everyone admitted that Europe could form a new diplomatic pole of some considerable weight in the face of Washington and Moscow, and a sound economic pole in the face of Japan and other competitors, but that it could fill those roles only by taking additional and decisive steps forward in its monetary, legal and institutional unity. But it could also be foreseen that those steps would in France rub interests and sensibilities the wrong way, perhaps aggravating the crisis in this or that locality or sector. A profound and hitherto unknown division, as yet latent, between those who were to varying degrees in favour of Europe, was certainly part of the foreseeable future.

Above all, the importance of the problem of French policies regarding the Third World, already perceptible at the end of de Gaulle's presidency, continued to grow. With V. Giscard d'Estaing, the custom spread of presenting it in terms of 'North–South'. The East–West symbolism which had signified collectivism–liberalism would be replaced by another cosmic symbolism in which the 'North' would be the camp of the rich, developed and powerful countries, and the 'South' that of the poor countries, barely decolonized, economically underdeveloped but dynamic in so many other respects. It was only too obvious that it was necessary to have more equitable relations with the South, because the poor had been overexploited

---

[6] These lines, written before the great crisis in the Soviet system and empire in the autumn of 1989, have become even more plausible since then.

and their very poverty aggravated the world's overall poor state of health. France, after de Gaulle and Pompidou, with Giscard and soon Mitterrand, had its own area in the South requiring vigilance, assistance and possible intervention: Africa. That tropism was scarcely disputed. But the 'South' embraced more than the plaintive cries of black Africa, it also comprised the Arab world, which was much more restive. And, beyond, a whole ensemble of countries aware of forming a Third World: this bloc was steadily gaining weight in the United Nations, and had snatched the romantic banner of 'anti-imperialist' revolution from the USSR. To put it clearly, hatred for America was henceforth less ardently fomented in Moscow than in the Middle East.

Now, a number of very varied factors impelled France to interest itself closely in the South in its Arab form: the desire to maintain cultural and economic ties with Algeria, Morocco and Tunisia, the tradition of longstanding links with Egypt, Syria and Lebanon; the fact that Arab oilproducing countries sold oil; and lastly the fact that with such wealth they were good customers for French export industries, especially military supplies and equipment.

With all these reasons, there is no need to look for an explanation by suggesting a pro-Arab 'lobby', even if influential groups operating in that direction did exist. Indeed, it was countered by the solidarity that linked France with the free countries (the 'imperialist' side denounced, after the Stalinists, by advocates of the Third World, was nevertheless the one with secular, tolerant, liberal democracies whose behaviour was reasonably civilized); another influence was the fear of deliberate demographic invasion by religious fanatics, the vanguard and expression of which were seen in terrorist acts (rue Copernic, 1980). Lastly – but it was the same thing – solidarity with Israel had some bearing on the matter, that island of liberal civilization in the 'complicated Orient'.

Was France in the 1970s Israelophile or Arabophile? That was without a doubt the most sensitive problem for its diplomacy and the true dividing line in public opinion, in so far as that looked beyond the sea. It seems possible to say that the pro-Arab, and more generally pro-Islamic, antiAmerican, anti-Israeli, option found greater favour during the seven-year term of V. Giscard d'Estaing. At least, that would appear to have been the case, with the spectacular hospitality accorded to Ayatollah Khomeini who, during the winter of 1978–9, openly had his operating base at Neauphle-leChâteau.[7] In comparison with that, François Mitterrand in 1981 could easily give the impression of restoring balance to the trends in French foreign policy. But not in any complete or definitive way, however, because of the weighty matters already mentioned and also because the great dividing

---

[7] In his book of memoirs quoted earlier, V. Giscard d'Estaing defends himself against any charge of complicity, and argues that it was at the express wish of the Shah of Iran, who was anxious not to annoy the Islamic opposition, that he refrained from expelling Ayatollah Khomeini from France.

line (Third World or free world) split the PS just as it split other sectors of opinion.

Since, however, external events only rarely occupied first place in national politics, on the surface a normal electoral life carried on and could still be described in terms of classic politics.

Never had France appeared so geometrically divided into four quarters, two on each side of the barrier.

On the right, there was but one solid party, that of the Gaullist tradition, soon taken in hand by Jacques Chirac. He had begun by a sort of betrayal regarding the UDR, because in 1974 he had dropped its official candidate, Chaban-Delmas, in favour of Giscard d'Estaing. Despite that divergence, he was able very quickly to regain leadership of the movement which, at its refounding, received its umpteenth baptism. It was now called the RPR (Rassemblement pour la République, Union for the Republic), a cleverly chosen set of initials, since it began like the RPF of 1947, and ended with the word 'Republic'. It was a party of deputies, militants, active men, with younger leaders, in which the veterans of the Resistance (the 'barons' of Gaullism) saw their influence wane.

After his resignation from the government, Chirac had plenty of time to busy himself with the party. In 1977, he won a resounding success. A recent law, liberal in the true sense of the word, had brought Paris back into common law by restoring its central town council. Giscard launched his friend Michel d'Ornano to conquer that most prestigious of town halls. Chirac stood as candidate and won, against d'Ornano and against the left. One knows how much additional authority, prestige and means of influence he was to derive from it.

In comparison with this vigorous partner, the 'Giscardian' component of the majority might well be the President's party, but it did not have the same force. It was organized under the name UDF (Union pour la démocratie française, Union for French Democracy), but that boiled down to a federation of three pre-existing (and surviving) parties, the Republican Party (of Giscard, Poniatowski, d'Ornano, heirs of Antoine Pinay's Independents, in short, the rich notables and hardline conservatives of the classic right), the CDS (heir of Christian democracy, via the MRP, with Lecanuet, Barrot, Diligent, Stasi, Méhaignerie) and the Radical Party (a right-wing portion of the old Radical Party of which the MRG had been the left-wing breakaway, rejection of Communist alliance being the touchstone between them).

The unity of the UDF, as may be seen, was defined in a totally negative manner. It brought together those sections of the right who rejected, or had rejected, Gaullism. But what did that refusal of Gaullism or the memory of de Gaulle consist of? For some, perhaps, a nostalgia for Vichy, intensified by that for French Algeria; for others, a regret for the legalist and parliamentary republicanism that the 1958 Constitution had harmed; for yet others, an attachment to the Europe that the 'Volapük' had knocked on the head. Various and sometimes contradictory tendencies, therefore. In the UDF, all that was most conservative, even fascist-sympathizing, in the presidential majority coexisted with all that was most democratic, humanistic and social. No true homogeneity, so no likely future, only the empirical solidity of a number of entrenched electoral positions in the provinces.

On the left, setting aside the MRG and PSU, which were being increasingly eroded by the rise in socialism (the most active part of the PSU, behind Michel Rocard, had joined the PS in 1974), and if one also excepts the fragmentary survival of Trotskyist parties, there were only socialists and Communists. The latter, still under the leadership of Georges Marchais, were in principle more and more drawn to the aims of a socialism 'bearing French colours', even going so far as to give up the idea and the prospect of a 'proletariat dictatorship'. But they made no progress, for all that, and the effects of bathing in the 1968 'waters of youth' were dwindling. For the falling-off in industry weakened their sources of recruitment, and the presence of a Socialist Party, henceforth resolutely . . . socialist, prevented them from attracting people as they had formerly by using the bogeyman of a caricaturized SFIO. Their history therefore became pretty chaotic, alternating, with regard to the USSR, between keeping their distance and demonstrations of attachment while, with regard to the PS, between fraternization and quarrels. It was as if the PC, aware of its inevitable loss of influence and desirous at least of slowing it down, was attempting to discover by trial and error whether the better tactic was to stimulate

Meeting of the Left-wing Union on 3 March 1978. G. Marchais, F. Mitterrand and R. Fabre; C. Fiterman, M. Crepeau and Y. Roudy. (Photo: Roger-Viollet)

single-minded enthusiasm for the Common Programme or to blacken the PS in order to increase its own standing at the other's expense.

As for the PS, it had the wind in its sails. As it had no pretension to monolithism, and was not in government, it was not really handicapped by the sometimes conflicting plurality of its components, its tendencies, and the networks of influence connected with its various leaders.

The following of François Mitterrand, the undisputed founder and author of this improbable renaissance, formed a very strong tie; it was further strengthened by the many and eminent qualities of the first secretary: authority and charm, eloquence and skilfulness, a refined culture and Machiavellian *savoir-faire*, the society allure of the town and the rustic allure of the countryside . . . he had it all, and was unsurpassable. To point out that he was no longer young (born in 1916), that he had twice failed to get elected (in 1965 and 1974), that he had in his past the Fourth Republic and two or three *faux pas*, or that his economic training was weak, almost smacks of committing sacrilege. Sometimes one ventures to do so by making the comparison with Michel Rocard who, some fifteen years younger, was well versed in economy, and whose 'image' borrowed austerity from that of Mendès France and cerebral virtuosity from that of Giscard. The party would seem to hesitate in his favour in 1980 before choosing Mitterrand for its candidate in 1981. Before reaching that decisive election, the country had had other chances of expressing its views.

It was in the legislative by-elections in September 1974 that socialist progress, at the expense of both the right and the PC, had really begun to attract attention. Hence arose a flood of Communist polemic against their invasive ally. But the two parties soon had to strengthen their ties, which the bipolarization of political life made inevitable. Together they had won considerable success in the 1977 municipal elections, chiefly remembered for the return to the left of large towns in the west of France: Rennes, Angers and Nantes, as if the regional nature of the distribution of the great political forces were tending to die down to the advantage of more directly sociological rationales.

The right, however, still won the general legislative elections in March 1978, though by a fairly short head. The campaign had been an opportunity to reopen the everlasting constitutional debate: what would become of the famous 'institutions of the Fifth Republic' if by chance the friends of the President in office no longer had a majority in the Assembly? To avoid that experience, Giscard had launched himself into battle by indicating 'the right choice', and he had been followed.

In the following spring, June 1979, the first European elections by universal suffrage, with national lists and proportional representation, showed exactly the development of the forces. The list closest to the government, led by Simone Veil, obtained 27.39 per cent of registered votes, the socialist list 23.73 per cent, the Communist list 20.59 per cent, and the Gaullist list

16.09 per cent, the remainder shared between minor formations. Right and left were thus almost equally balanced (43 per cent and 44 per cent). But in each camp the most European list (UDF, PS) was clearly ahead of the least so (RPR, PC).

By that date, the end of Giscard's term was in sight. It closed on a vastly different note from the one on which it had begun. The President, who had formerly been censured for not being sufficiently solemn, now found himself reproached for being too much so. He was no longer accused of affected simplicity, but of arrogance; people dissected the details of the almost monarchic ceremonial with which he caused or allowed Élysée protocol to be burdened. It seemed as if the Head of State had retreated into solitary loftiness, since his relaxed air had disappeared.

On top of all that came one more 'affair', which concerned him in person, and that bore the name 'Bokassa'. The president of the Central African Republic, Jean Bedel Bokassa, was a former NCO in the colonial army, an uneducated and flimsy person, whose head had clearly been turned by power. But he 'ruled' over virgin forest and Giscard, a great sporting type and hunter, had a predilection for spending his lesiure time on safari. He allowed himself to be called the friend and even 'relative' of this odious and ridiculous petty tyrant; he let the French Treasury foot the bill for the imperial coronation of Bokassa I, a painful parody, in which it is hard to say whether the idea of the Republic or the memory of Napoleon brought the most humiliation. Then, when the 'emperor' had gone beyond the bounds of megalomania and cruelty, Giscard casually had him punished by a coup d'état, stage-managed behind the scenes. In the meantime, he had received and accepted presents – the all-too-famous diamonds.

For months, the satirical press and the left-wing political press had talked about jewels, and it is by no means ruled out that these equatorial blunders contributed to the electoral swing in 1981.

The President had been, at the very least, imprudent and clumsy. Furthermore, as he had failed to gain the upper hand over the economic crisis, social paralysis, or the new international setup, it may well be that his image, additionally tarnished by the affair, tipped the balance, and that more than one citizen voted for Mitterrand more in order to 'punish' the outgoing President than to give a socialist society a try.

For the President stood as candidate for his own office. Against him was Mitterrand, of course. And Jacques Chirac (but he was not alone in representing historic Gaullism, as Michel Debré and Marie-France Garaud were also candidates). And Georges Marchais, since the PC felt that absence from presidential competition would be bad for it. And a few other 'small-time' candidates. In all, ten.

In the first round, on 26 April 1981, Giscard gained 28.31 per cent of the registered votes, Mitterrand 25.84 per cent, Chirac 17.99 per cent and Marchais 15.34 per cent.

One is struck by the classic fall of the Communist Party, with its 15 per cent (hitherto, the PC had always wavered between 20 and 25 per cent). Struck too, in other respects, by the slowness and half-heartedness with which Chirac announced his withdrawal in favour of Giscard. The PC, for its part, raised votes for Mitterrand without any reluctance and, on 10 May, the socialist leader was elected President of the Republic by 51.75 per cent of the votes against 48.24 per cent.

He was to resolve the constitutional problem of the homogeneity of power by dissolving the Assembly. According to his wish, and in any case in keeping with precedent, the legislative vote confirmed the presidential one, and swelled it: in June, 54 per cent of the votes went to the left in the first round and revealed at the outset a crushing majority of 285 socialist deputies (including a few radicals), flanked by 44 Communists, dominating the 152 right-wing representatives.

A new management could now commence.

The election of François Mitterrand filled his electors with more enthusiasm than an ordinary victory.

It is difficult to know how many of those who celebrated, quaffed champagne or danced in the place de la Bastille in Paris in May 1981 were thinking of building a socialist France; how many simply wanted to restore to the norm a Republic that de Gaulle had drawn into new ways; or how many – doubtless the most numerous – were simply congratulating themselves because, after some twenty-five years, the left had overcome its seemingly inevitable fate of being kept out of power.

It is not possible to trace even a summary outline of the phase of history marked by François Mitterrand's presidency and a socialist government, since it is not yet over. At the most, one may comment on some striking signs that will remain instructive, and report some immediate gains that are likely to last.

First of all, the period May–June 1981 was striking for three outstanding features: François Mitterrand visited the Panthéon, assumed full presidential power and took on Communists in his government.

Thus, on 21 May, at the end of the afternoon, at the head of a vast crowd, to the strains of the 'Hymn to Joy', the new President went up the rue Soufflot then, alone, entered the secular temple of Liberty to go to the crypt and lay roses on the tombs of Jean Jaures, Victor Schoelcher and Jean Moulin – thereby paying homage to the values of socialism,[8] antislavery and the Resistance.

As it was difficult to be scandalized by such noble thoughts, people preferred to poke fun. The Panthéon, indubitably, had a Third Republic

[8] It may be recalled that this symbolism was discussed in chapter 6.

aspect; reference to great ancestors was no longer popular, and even respect for the dead 'wasn't what it used to be'. The first, most insistent and perhaps most effective of the grievances of the opposition (henceforth the right) against Mitterrand was that he was a commemorator, 'backward-looking' and even a 'necrophile'. It is not failing history's neutrality to point out the frailty of that accusation. Under the Arc de Triomphe in the Étoile, or at the funeral ceremonies of great veterans in the Invalides, political men of all sides (and notably those of the right) were perfectly capable of commemorating and calling on the dead. And on 21 May, Mitterrand himself had not missed the ritual visit to the tomb of the unknown warrior. The novelty, on his part, lay simply in thinking of the Panthéon *as well*, the Invalides of Liberty. In doing so he renewed the link with the oldest tradition, the one which, across Paris, united the cults of the west and the cults of the east, the dead of the National Defence and the dead of the Revolution.

To restore the Panthéon to the memory and respect of the nation was, for a Head of State, the smallest of matters. As regards the Panthéon, sectarianism did not mean going there, but *not* going there! On the first symbol, therefore, the grievance was a poor one.

The second sign, or feature, more diffuse and less immediately perceptible, was the full and entire exercise of power, not only in its constitutional measures, but in all the informal and customary authority that de Gaulle and his first two successors had added. 'Republican tradition', from Jules Grévy to René Coty, had favoured an unobtrusive presidency. The Fifth, on the other hand, wanted it to be strong, almost monarchic, from the most careful details of protocol to the extension of prerogatives.

It would soon be known that, on this point, Mitterrand did not share the reaction of traditional republicans, but that he would continue the desire for the total and attentive management, combined with an impressive etiquette, inaugurated in 1959.

A few years later, like Valéry Giscard d'Estaing, he would have to face the complaint – outrageous of course, but still significant – that he had transformed the 'Château' into Olympus.

The third sign, this time with an immediately noticeable fuss: in the government over which Pierre Mauroy was to preside after the legislative renewal in June, four Communists were appointed ministers.

It was not much (four out of forty) and they did not exactly hold key posts (Transport, Health, Professional Training and Civil Service). And it was not even parliamentarily useful, since the PS on its own enjoyed absolute majority in the Assembly. It was more a matter of theoretical usefulness. The operation involved the PC in boldly reforming policies, but under socialist management, so that it was not in control of them but lost its specific character of belligerently radical anti-establishment protest.

Thus, the 'Communist people' no longer had any reason to be distinct from the immense electorate of democratic socialism; they would continue to be reabsorbed and, eventually, France would be gently cured of Bolshevism.

'I embrace my rival, but only to stifle him', the President might say, quoting not Machiavelli but Racine.[9]

After that, the socialist government (which the right would rather improperly call 'socialo-communist', to turn it into a bugbear) would go through two years of triumphalism.

They are ridiculed today, because of the backward turn that was soon to come. Let us nevertheless admit that out of them came three serious, generous and probably lasting things, with which the names of Jean Auroux, Gaston Defferre and Robert Badinter respectively will always be connected.

A series of laws – the Auroux laws – improved social relations in businesses in favour of the employees. Another law, ambitious and complex, but indisputably inspired, realized administrative decentralization. Another finally abolished the death sentence. The first was socialist in the most precise meaning of the term, the second is, properly speaking, liberal, and the third is humanitarian – the complete philosophical spectrum.

The Mauroy government had undertaken to be socialist also in its management of the economy. Hence a policy of expenditure[10] to improve the incomes of the poor, with the hope of revitalizing the economy by consumer demand; and a policy of nationalization of large industrial and financial enterprises. It was this policy that would fail, for want of having taken sufficient account of an international environment that was barely socialist, and the constraints of a world market that was not socialist at all.

In the spring of 1983, it was necessary to straighten up and return to more classic systems, that is to say, more strictness in the running of things and less socialism in the aims.

The important point is that this change in policy was clearly and consciously made. Since that date, it is agreed that French socialists no longer sought to build a socialist France (which would inevitably mean a protectionist, isolated, barricaded France) and confined their ambition to a Europe, unavoidable or necessary, that would be as social as possible.

The party was thus no longer a theoretically revolutionary party (collectivist and dirigiste), but a progressive liberal party, the main line of a humanist left with, as they say, a 'vocation' to be the leaders in a developed society such as that of France.

It is what the PS sometimes call substituting a 'government culture' for an 'opposition culture'.

It is important enough to justify our halting at that date this account of the last avatars of the French Republic. One last word, however, since Republic is also a word!

---

[9] Racine in *Britannicus*, I, 1. Nero to Narcissus, speaking of Britannicus.

[10] Direct or indirect: under the latter heading could be included the reduction of the working week (thirty-nine hours).

The 'Republic'. During the two years from spring 1981 to spring 1983, and despite the homage rendered at the Panthéon, the socialists hardly mentioned it, preferring to talk 'Socialism'.

That was to lower the old flag, and the opposition hastened to hoist it again. Between 1981 and 1983, with the socialists in power, posing as fighters who would change society, the right naturally assumed the role of those who wanted to keep society as it was, that is, as a . . . republican state. 'Republic', 'republican', just as much as 'liberty', 'liberalism', were thus much bandied about *against* the astonished PS by an opposition as astute as it was vigorous. Would the old word 'Republic' have to change sides? In periods of innovation, it does indeed happen that words change place, just like things, and sometimes more so. The PS would later try to regain its footing on this point.

However, the PS had not succeeded in extending the 'government culture' to all domains of political life.

The constraints of government had not caused it to abandon all its previous convictions; for example, careful and even zealous running of the army, the strike force and nuclear testing grounds had not stifled its pacifist sensibilities. In fact, the PS ruled and existed amid multiple tensions between opposing poles: French interests or strengthening the European Community, national defence or pacifism, Third Worldism or defence of Israel, old secular France or France as a mosaic of religious cults, republican tradition or libertarian aspirations, there is no end to the alternatives, which revealed themselves in vacillation or which fuelled conflicting 'trends'. The question of whether this diversity is a strength or weakness for French socialism, or if clarifications will soon be found, still has no obvious answer. Here, indubitably, beyond the decisive turning point towards integral reformism in the summer of 1983, even the boldest history can but give place, either to the chronicle that will recount day by day, or to speculation that would suggest preferences.

Its own task is temporarily achieved.

Conclusion:
The Republic, *La Patrie*, Liberty

The conclusion of a historical account, when the history is very recent, poses a particular problem: its nearness to, and partial confusion with, reflection on the present time. Many people are worried by this because they clearly perceive a change of genre. Now, while one is dealing with history one is in the scientific, or at least academic, genre – lofty and dignified – but when speaking of the collective present one is talking of politics, a practice that many question, fear or despise. Much could be said, moreover, on the subject of this aversion with regard to politics that remains so widespread in France, while by definition the democracy on which we pride ourselves invites every citizen to be concerned with it.

Let us, however, leave aside that possible reflection and content ourselves with recalling this elementary truth: what we are presently experiencing as politics (for example, the election of a new President – theoretically in 1995) will appear in next century's history books; and, vice versa, what we read today in history books (for example, the election of General de Gaulle in 1958) was, thirty or thirty-five years ago, at the very heart of politics.

History, and above all political history, on which this collective work[1] especially set its sights, is thus of no other nature or other content than politics. But that does not mean that they can be treated in the same fashion.

The account that is qualified as historical always has a somewhat rationalized construction, an ordered arrangement so that it may be better understood; such rationalization is possible only because it is dealing with a definite account, in other words, a sequence that has come to a close and is therefore observable as a whole. By contrast, a sketch of the present (of

Unlike the preceding chapters, this Conclusion does not reproduce but replaces that contained in Hachette's edition of *Histoire de France*.

[1] I am speaking of the five works that make up the overall *Histoire de France* (Hachette, then Pluriel) of which my *République* forms the last volume. However, this conclusion has been written by myself (M.A.) and I take sole responsibility for it. The 'conclusions' arrived at and stated here in no way commit my friends and colleagues Duby, Le Roy Ladurie and Furet.

necessity including the most recent past and the nearest future, since pure present is by definition transitory) is open-ended, indefinite, unforeseeable; it is impossible to suggest some guiding theme as there is no way of knowing how it will end. It must therefore be constructed differently, in the form of a thematic essay, an exposition of problems rather than a recital of events; moreover, the latter are still sufficiently alive in people's memories to need no recounting, unless by allusion.

Having settled that in principle, there remains the necessity to make a concrete choice: at what date should the account claiming historical objectivity halt in order to pass on to a more problematic reflective essay?

It may be seen above, at the end of chapter 12: rejecting the facile solution presented by making the break in 1981 (first election of M. Mitterrand, the beginning of a socialist experiment), I looked for an alternative in 1983, when the men in power, choosing the 'path of austerity', renounced a complete change in the economic and social system and opted for the constitution in France of a social democrat type of reformism, limited to amending and humanizing the market economy, without doing away with it entirely.

Even protected by this prudent statement (this is a reflective essay with no claim to be historical) such an exercise is not without risk. My conclusion in the Hachette edition of the present work had received its final touches in July 1990, therefore before the explosion of the 'Gulf crisis'. The summer having been spent in making up (in the typographical sense of the word), the book appeared in the shops in November and was distributed during the winter, thus during that crisis, soon to be extended into war! Apart from its other infinitely more harmful effects, has this drama rendered unreadable and obsolete the sketch of France that I had outlined before its eruption? I do not think so. It seems to me that the argument I had put forward – French Communism is not as dead as people like to say it is, because Third Worldism is vigorously taking up its baton – was rather confirmed by observation of movements of opinion relating to the Gulf War.

I am writing this Conclusion in January-February 1992, thus after the end of the Gulf War, with Israeli–Arab talks under way, the USSR completely obliterated, Yugoslavia torn apart, the Maastricht agreements signed, and the Rocard government replaced by the Cresson government; but before the electoral consultations in March . . . and all the unforeseeable probabilities of this spring, which my first readers will already have behind them.

Under these conditions and within these limitations, what can be said of political France, taking a bird's-eye view today of the as yet incomplete era of the Mitterrand presidencies? In this fleeting and unstable present, how are the various problems that have served as guiding threads in the foregoing chapters to be presented?

In a history of France, the fate of the French nation is the principal subject and the principal matter at stake. Is it an exaggeration to say that this theme has never been so conspicuous as it is today? It has to be said that never have so many works on the national past been written permeated by nostalgic yearning for the good old days. As if people were preparing to witness the end of France. Two questions feed that hypothesis. The first, official: will France be integrated, at least partially, in a European super-state, and thus at least partially suppressed? The other, unofficial: could the nature of France be changed from within by immigrants who are not easily absorbed into the melting pot of French historical identity? We shall return to these questions, merely noting here that they are without any precedent.

On the other hand, a more relative conclusion presents itself: though it may not mark the absolute end of France, the last decade of the twentieth century at least confirms its end as a front-ranking world power. From the grandson of Charlemagne up to and including Charles de Gaulle – and with the latter, at the price of a slightly artificial and all the more praise-worthy voluntarism – France had always been one of the two or three leading actors on the European stage, and in the world in relation to Europe. Today, that preponderance no longer exists. Legally, France certainly remains one of the five permanent members of the UN Security Council, thus one of the five official 'great powers'. Economically, it still holds comparable rank as a member of the (informal) club of the seven most industrialized countries. But the demographic basis for these inherited pre-eminences is fragile.

Valéry Giscard d'Estaing surprised and rather wounded the French when he dared to remind them that out of every hundred men in the world 'there was only one Frenchman', which was exact, as there were about 55 million French among five or six billion human beings. Can France at least make up for it in quality? The French, and above all their political rulers, are happy to believe so, notably thanks to culture. But might it be that the sacrosanct culture evoked under this heading could also act as a handicap? Is it not because French elites, inspired by prestigious historic traditions, have a predilection for cultivating legal and literary disciplines and profes-sions and seek the excellence of pure science, arts and crafts, that French society has such difficulty in extricating from its bosom the generations of industrialists and businessmen, although it is daily assured that their per-formance is essential for national survival? As for consoling itself by turning the France of 55 million inhabitants into the leader of a French-speaking entity that would be widespread and numerous enough to form a new, respectable global 'empire', well . . . The French language is also a pretty frail force. I will not digress here to recall the difficulties encountered by the French-speaking African countries, the peoples of Quebec or Lebanon, the Walloons, or the old bourgeoisies cultivated in the French style now growing old in central Europe or South America. Suffice it to recall that in contemporary France itself Franco-English bilingualism is admitted to be the required cultural minimum, while everyday and commercial French is becoming insidiously anglicized.

As a last resource there remains the 'spirit' that France is deemed to represent in the world. Yesterday 'the oldest daughter of the Church', today certainly liberated from that 'mother', it would always be the missionary of a faith, a secularized humanism, the official philosophy of the free world. But is not this ultimate primacy also challenged? Decidedly, the task of the political rulers of the country is overwhelming.

These rulers are, at the present time, socialist, for the most part affiliated to the party of that name. President Mitterrand, by reason of his high office, is no longer formally a member, but no one would dare to deny that he is in fact its inspiring and unifying force.

This party governs. Mention has already been made (chapter 12) of its first achievements, its alliance with the Communists, then the great turn towards market economy (Mauroy governments, 1981–3 and 1983–4).

The socialists tried to have done with the old education argument by the plan to create a 'great unified public service' of National Education. The immense movement of opinion that succeeded in imposing, in opposition to them, the maintenance of the status quo (1984) demonstrated at the same time that religious conflicts were being presented in new terms. We will come back to that. Let us remember here that this crisis was the occasion of the replacement of M. Mauroy in the Hôtel Matignon by M. Fabius, at the head of a government this time without any Communist participation. Like his predecessor, M. Fabius governed, shouldering the obligations of power and thereby subjected to the specific contradictions that caused him to gather together in his ranks not only bank administrators and trades unionists, but also pacifists and military men (the affair of the secret services against *Rainbow Warrior*, 1985).

A prisoner of those contradictions, doubtless inevitable but not at all appreciated by its electorate, the Socialist Party suffered a setback in the legislative elections of 1986, and this for the first time put the Constitution to the test of 'cohabitation' between a left-wing Head of State and a right-wing head of government, M. Jacques Chirac. From this brief phase, optimists were able to draw the conclusion that the Constitution was strengthened, as it proved its ability to adapt to an unprecedented situation. Pessimists insisted rather on the painful political guerrilla warfare to which it gave rise: that prospect, however, was pushed aside for several years because, re-elected easily in 1988 against the same Jacques Chirac, François Mitterrand immediately managed to obtain the election of an Assembly with a relative socialist majority, allowing the re-establishment of a socialist government, under Michel Rocard.

Seen from a distance, two salient points emerge from Rocard's management (1988–91), one a success: the negotiated compromise which nipped in the bud a seemingly imminent colonial rebellion in New Caledonia; and one a failure: the policy of opening out towards the centrists, which would have enabled him to compensate for the absence of an absolute majority. In the end, President Mitterrand considered the government to be worn out, and replaced M. Rocard with Mme Édith Cresson at its head. That kind of 'law' making two governments per seven-year term 'necessary' had already been seen at work.

Doubtless the 'wearing-out', or rather the report ordered on the wearing-out of M. Rocard, had its own particular reasons . . .

To the problems created by what is actually happening, official memory sometimes adds its own. The year 1989 witnessed the unfolding of what is usually described as 'the splendours of the Bicentenary', in which the optimists greeted an appreciable success among a national and international audience, while the pessimists were struck chiefly by the sharpness of the debates and the bitterness of disagreements. Right-wing French were seen to refuse to have anything to do with the Bicentenary and to denigrate the Revolution the better to attack the government; left-wing French to use the Bicentenary to relaunch their own ideological offensive against the right; French of both right and left trying to keep to a civic, patriotic and unitarian version of this enlarged national festival; and lastly others, disconcerted by the interplay of these three rival political lines, contenting themselves with promoting in their own little corner, since it was required of them, anodyne blends of carnival and local history.

The French festival of historic liberty was hardly over when, in the autumn of 1989, there was an explosion of real liberty, the fall of the Communist system in the USSR and eastern Europe. It was nothing more than a coincidence that the 1989 of the French festivities and the 1989 of the Soviet break-up came together. The latter owed everything to *perestroika*, which had begun before the Bicentenary. Moreover, it seems unlikely that many were thinking of the walls of the Bastille when the Berlin Wall was being torn down. It should rather be considered that, between the Great Revolution of the French eighteenth century and the present revolutions of eastern Europe, there came the intermediary of an ideology, the cosmopolitan vulgate of the free world – that of the Rights of Man. As if the France of 1789 were the grandmother, rather than the mother, of revolutions . . .

Much comment has been made on the part taken by the Communist Party in the 'Jacobin' festivities. That contribution, if there was one, did not prevent it from seeing a reduction, at each electoral consultation, in its influence, the number of its elected members and the groups that it administered, at the same time as a shrinkage in its organization and a loss of both efficiency and coherence. There were two probable causes for this decline, which it would be trite to describe as historic; one was French and social, the dwindling of that working class and urban proletariat whose indefinite expansion had been Marx's dream, and which our futurist capitalism, on the contrary, has learnt to manage without.

The other cause is international, and that is the resounding failure, the economic, political, cultural failure, the overall human failure and finally, in 1991, the self-abolition of regimes of the Soviet type with which the PCF had remained in solidarity. Let us add the habits of internal intellectual discipline which, by preventing 'Italian-style' discussion, have until the present day prevented it from considering ways of adapting, and consequently from finding them.

Not everything is dead or moribund, however, in the heritage of the potent French Stalinism of the years 1934–56. Or, if there is a death, perhaps it is that of the seed in the biblical parable ('Unless the seed dies . . .'): to rot in the soil in order to be reborn as a new shoot.

To take a single example, forty years ago the PCF alone in France preached – and in what language! – hatred for the United States of America. Today, though the furious preacher may be discredited, his 'anti-imperialist' message has gained wide acceptance: all the leftist sphere of influence, all the intelligentsia impassioned by decolonization, and whole sections of the Socialist Party itself, vie with one another in vituperating against the West, the Atlantic and the 'North'. That is why the end of the PC in France does not mean the disappearance of every anti-Western extreme left. Revolutionary hostility towards the prosperous West has perforce ceased to be based on a Communism installed in the East, but it can find equivalent backing in a widespread Third Worldism. Between one and the other there is a fine relay system, as was revealed by the size of resistance to the Gulf War. The latter, ordered by the UN against Iraq, guilty of annexing Kuwait, was in essence waged and won by the American army. France made its contribution, as we know, not without some traces of official reluctance, and with at least one resounding rejection (M. Chevènement resigning from the Ministry of Defence).

There are – it is true – those, chiefly intellectuals and especially on the left, who wonder, sometimes with distress, whether France's ideal vocation summons it to the camp of the free world, of the United States, western Europe, Israel, where broadly speaking the demands of liberty, democracy and modern law are respected, or to the camp of the rebellion of the wretched, that of the Third World, whether that rebellion be fundamentalist or neo-Bolshevik.

The poorest and least cultivated French, who are also the most numerous, tend to think 'hexagonal', that is to say, first and foremost in terms of economy and society.

Socialist governments were at first able, with the help of favourable world circumstances, to improve the economic situation. Production took off again, currency was strong, but external trade remained weak and unemployment not only did not diminish but, recently, has started to grow still further. It is of course understood that market economy, engaged in since 1983, cannot be completely individualist or liberalist, as the maintaining of a state duty of social aid to poor and dependent elements constitutes an additional demand that is just as imperative as that of liberty. In order the better to satisfy that demand, must the state retain control of at least a sector of economic production and financial networks? The debate goes on over this point, and the running of the economy remains an issue in the political battle between right and left. The latter would like the state to retain a certain stake, and the former would like to reduce it. At present, the mixed economy in the hands of socialist management is working and even prospering. As it remains essentially integrated in the overall and even world capitalist system, it fails to escape the law of unequal development; the poor, and even the impoverished, continue to exist. The socialist-run state feels bound to intervene to help them, but at the same time avoiding an excess of regulatory or fiscal interventionism that might scare off the powers of big money – the moving force of growth. Its present policy thus walks the narrow tightrope between two possible dangers.

As for realizing full employment once again . . . It is obvious that, however prosperous one may imagine them to be, neither the agriculture nor the industry of tomorrow will ever absorb as much labour as the fields, mines and factories of yesteryear. To put an end to an unemployment that has become endemic would presuppose the massive creation of new types of work, such as 'close-to-home' jobs in the social tertiary sector, to cite but one example, and that still very vague. It is a distant prospect.

It is to unemployment that the socialists tend to attribute at least indirect responsibility for another social evil of the times: a crime rate that is becoming enormous in urban areas, notably in the form of theft. One may wonder whether this simplification does not purely and simply counterbalance the pronouncements of the extreme right which, for its part, attributes delinquency and the consequent fear of crime to foreign immigration. It can hardly be disputed that social difficulties provide fertile ground for all criminal inclinations. But is that ground solely to blame? There would without doubt be fewer thieves if it was repeated everywhere, with as much emphasis as in former days, that it is wrong to steal. The question of thieves thus brings us directly to a question of . . . values, as that is how morality is sometimes termed these days, when it is not called 'ethics' to make it sound loftier. The question of morality – an almost unmentionable word nowadays – is undeniably a sensitive public question and even a stake in the political game, since it is debated among opposing party extremes.

As for the facts, right-wing propaganda tends to exaggerate the scale of crime and fear while that of the left on the other hand tends to play it down. When it comes to solutions, on the right there is a tendency to recommend an overall return to the conservative morality of last century, often of Catholic inspiration, while on the left, for fear of such a return, there is a tendency to reject all moralizing, with the risk of pushing the libertarian spirit almost to an acceptance of anomy. The middle-of-the-road idea that a republican and secular social morality might exist, capable of saying 'no' to burglars and puritans alike, is certainly today the least widespread of political utterances. Perhaps in no other domain is the spirit of Jules Ferry so far from our own time.

There are thieves and thieves, it is true. From the crook who carries out a robbery on a security vehicle to the schoolyard 'racketeer' by way of the 'mugger' who snatches an old lady's handbag, these all come under the heading of 'everyday events in society at large'. With white-collar crime, politics is involved more directly. The long tradition of illicit 'get rich quick' speculation, business affairs giving rise to 'Affairs', has been polarized in recent years on speculation set up for the benefit of political men and parties for the financing of propaganda. It is obvious that the ultra-perfected modern media make party political propaganda astoundingly costly. This immorality is at least in theory destined to be eliminated, as the socialists have passed a law regulating, limiting and controlling the financing of the parties and electoral campaigns. But the cancellation of practices prior to that law, which were criminal, and the trials already under way relating to them, contribute not a little to worsening the atmosphere, both by sharpening polemics in the bosom of the political class and, as in the old days of the 'Fifteen thousand', by adding fuel to its public discredit.

This ill-loved political class, moreover, finds itself increasingly numerous and conspicuous, if only because the law of 1982 gave a powerful boost to its regional level, without in any way diminishing that of the *départements*.

Decentralization was the great event of 1982. Symbolically, a blow was struck at the old state control tradition and, more concretely, a response was made to the aspirations of regions wishing to see their problems dealt with closer to home. The upheaval proved slightly less significant than had been foreseen, however, because the state did not relinquish as much authority as certain people would have liked. In any case, matters are still feeling their way on this subject.

But decentralization was not limited to these administrative aspects. It also wore a political garb: the Socialist Party, in 1982, had desired the new Republic to have a more open attitude with regard to regional, or even regionalist, aspirations. It has to be noted that good intentions came up against the diversity of situations. There is a whole central France for which the patriotisms of area or province have only historical relevance, and whose inhabitants feel only French; and a peripheral France in which, on the other hand, the rebirth of regional quasi-patriotisms is not inconceivable. These, in their turn, take on vastly differing aspects and forms of expression, to the point where in some places they are repressed (Basque country) while in others they are treated considerately (Corsica). Is France a happy family of regions? Or a single entity threatened by ungrateful dissidents? The question has not really been settled.

In addition, it is all the more complicated because it interferes with the problem of Europe, whose consolidation the present government desires. Some years ago, the logic of a certain political extremism could hold that the 'Jacobin' French national state was equally disastrous for regionalisms, based on old, deep-rooted feelings, as for Europe, an imminent reality, and that it could happily be abolished by the conjunction of the two: that was the ideal of a 'Europe of regions'. Today when Europe is getting into position, after a fashion, it is noticeable that in French regions, especially in the poorest and most rural, Brussels is just as constricting, not to say irksome, as Paris. The Europe of the technocrats may perhaps reconcile 'Jacobin' France and the regionalist provinces in opposition to it!

If the regional problem has some links with that of Europe, it also has some kinship with another problem of minorities (these without any territorial concentration), that of immigrant groups. They come chiefly from overseas. The overseas *départements* and territories all have their own distinct problems: there is no room to list them here. As a whole, however, they suffer to a greater extent from the contradiction that can be seen in certain poor French regions, such as Corsica, between the need for aid and the need for an identity. The absence of local work opportunities leads young people to come to mainland France, thus creating 'immigrants' who are not foreigners. This collective exile brings material relief, at the same time as moral exasperation: they cling to France, the dispenser of assistance and employment, while blaming it for having been colonial. French governments have been aware of this sad situation for several years, and know that in theory the solution lies in a policy that will bring about economic prosperity overseas. But the recipe for replacing the financing of aid with that of development does not appear to have been found.

There is also an influx of migrants, who have even greater reason to leave their native land, from the independent states of black Africa, formerly French and still French-speaking. France keeps some interests and feels some obligations there. But chiefly they present some problems that are not offered – and with cause – by the Antilles or Réunion: independence obliges France to engage in diplomatic dealings which are due to all states; it also allows the states to provide themselves with political regimes *sui generis*, frequently dictatorial, which France is as embarrassed to uphold as it would be to overturn them (or let them be overturned). Thence arises an empirical status quo, hardly different in these last years from what it was under de Gaulle or Giscard d'Estaing, but which seems to have reached its limits.

The poor of the former colonies tend to make their way to mainland France, where they thus create a new problem – immigration. Is it really new? That is sometimes disputed. Fifty years ago, the Poles, the Kabyles (already) and the Italians (chiefly) together formed a contingent of foreigners of the same kind and size as that of today. The novelty of the problem is qualitative rather than quantitative. Today's immigrant is said to be more of a nuisance because he swells the ranks of unskilled labour, already in excess; because he comes from far away, sometimes bringing unacceptable customs (polygamy, excision), and because he sometimes comes from Islamic lands, whose religion is both exotic and absolutist. As a bogeyman the sharia (Islamic Law) thus takes over from the abandoned *Syllabus*, with the aggravating circumstance that it could have the support not, like the *Syllabus*, of a captive pope, but of states that are very much alive and ill-intentioned.

Everything depends on where the emphasis is placed in these analyses. The difficulties just listed tend to be undervalued by the left – caught up with humanity, and often with a systematic Third Worldism born of remorse for a colonial past – and overemphasized by the right, through nationalism. As in the case of crime, mentioned earlier. These exaggerations exacerbate each other in such a way that immigration poisons French politics less by its very real inconveniences than by the polemics it arouses. It is immigration in particular that has given a veritable rejuvenating boost – and a far from negligible potential electorate – to an extreme right that was very much in a minority when it was reduced to its barest nucleus of intransigent traditionalists and convinced fascists. It is this new avatar of the 'revolutionary right', under the name of National Front and under the guidance of a leader both vehement and clever (Jean-Marie Le Pen, former leader of the student right in the Latin Quarter, former officer in Algeria, former Poujadist deputy), that has marked out its place in the French political field shared out between the 'gang of four'[2] – held in contempt all together. Le Pen is simultaneously a man of the present and a man of the past. A man of the present in that, as a French nationalist, his xenophobia is anti-immigrant, thus above all anti-Arab; but a man of the past in that, counter-revolutionary by tradition, he is equally anti-Semitic. This last factor prevailed at the time of the Gulf War, which he opposed. Thus, the man who made his mark in internal politics for his anti-Maghrebian phobia found himself Arabophile at world level, a fine example of the contradictions that seethe in impassioned politics – more than one precedent has been pointed out.

Beyond these political effects, and considered in itself, the immigrant problem is very real. The nuisance is that it is situated at several levels. Sociologically, it results from the daily cohabitation, in a climate of unemployment and in run-down urban environments, of populations that differ in race and culture. There are distressing tensions but, as I have just defined them, it might be thought that a social and specifically urban policy endowed with very great resources could bring them to an end.

But the philosophical aspect remains – that of defining the national community which will need to be welded together after it has been pacified. Will it be a community of communities, France becoming a mosaic of

---

[2] In Le Pen's words (taken up in ridicule of the Chinese polemics against the clique who superseded Mao Tse Tung), the 'gang of four' (parties) comprised the PC, the PS, the RPR and the UDF.

groups each with an ethnic–religious definition, who will retain a certain aloofness in the name of their particular values? Or on the other hand, will it stay as a community of individual citizens united by taking on a modern, republican French loyalty, agreeing to return religious faith to the domain of private life, and special historical traditions to the domain of optional folklore?

If too much is made, however, of the problem of immigrants of Muslim faith or tradition, it might be thought that the secular struggle now had Islam as its principal target, while the hatchet had been buried as regards Roman Catholicism. That would be only partly true. Of course, the majority of the faithful and Catholic clergy have broken their erstwhile links with the political counter-revolution, so that, as a quite natural consequence, the secular spirit and anticlericalism have greatly diminished in comparison with what they were a hundred years ago.

But is this pacification on the basis of an accepted status quo definitive? On the Catholic side also there exists a 'religious revival'. The schismatic fundamentalism of the faithful who reject the directions taken by the Second Vatican Council displays the well-known ardour of all passionate minorities. Its proselytism animates that of the official clergy, whom Pope John Paul II, not resigned to reducing religion to the private sphere, summons to the conquest of society. And that zeal reaches out to meet the aspirations of a good many simple people, who are frightened by the very real demoralization around them and can no longer be satisfied by over-discreet secular morality (without a doubt the popularity of private Catholic schools, which was the great revelation of 1984, had no other cause). Briefly, the religious question of today is no longer what it was in the time of Jules Ferry or Émile Combes, it is quite a bit different, but is none the less with us. However, the way it will influence political combats, as it inevitably will, is hard to predict, since it has not yet been settled at the time when these lines are being written.

The seriousness of these tensions and fundamental choices does not prevent political France from paying particular attention, which many consider disproportionate, to the regulating of its internal affairs. Institutions continue to occupy a leading place. The present Constitution, of the Fifth Republic, worked out in 1958, has already been retouched on several occasions. It has not yet attained the record for longevity established by the constitutional laws of 1875 (sixty-five years). The latter, and more generally the political practices of the Third and Fourth Republics, form a constantly evoked bugbear for the present epoch. No one doubts that the Fifth Republic has succeeded well in suppressing the abuses of parliament-arianism, government instability, a too feeble executive and repeated crises. The question is increasingly asked whether it may not have succeeded too well, and if a parliament that is too easily kept in check and an over-invasive executive may not also be inconveniences. Other features are also being challenged. The election of the president by universal suffrage, the fairly logical outcome of democracy, has been able to snatch the choice of Head of State from the power of parliamentary notables. Was it in order to give it to the professional 'image-makers', and would it end in splitting the parties into new kinds of coteries who prepare too far in advance to launch their 'presidential material'? Let us add that, even technically, the famous strong executive, with its allocation of power shared in a very ill-defined fashion between a President and Prime Minister, introduces into politics a truly French sort of difficulty which neighbouring states, friends as well as rivals, have the good fortune not to experience.

No one, however, dares to call for too profound a revision. In 1991–2 the debate tended to concentrate on two main points: the duration of the presidential mandate – and resorting to a referendum. For the adjustments rendered inevitable by European integration (complete or partial) will certainly have to be ratified.

A political system, in any case, is not reduced to its constitutional mechanism. There are other structures and other authorities. The parties, for example, constrained by presidential election through universal suffrage to 'bipolarization', as has been said. Now, the French system of political formations is antiquated, and thus esoteric. The ideological and moral division between right and left does not really coincide with the political division, that has become almost institutional between majority and opposition.[3] Many Christian democrats, today in the opposition and therefore classed in the political right, are nearer to the left than to the rest of the right.

In the heart of the left, it has already been suggested with what degree of difficulty the Socialist Party amalgamates genuine republicans and quasi-revolutionaries. On matters of social morality, foreign policy, the regions, perhaps Europe tomorrow, differences lie just below the surface. They are forced into concealment by allegiance, for form's sake, to the carefully weighed choices made by the Élysée, and have no obvious connection with the patent divisions between the trends.

This distortion between profound differences of opinion and visible organizations similarly affects the right wing. The latter still lives on the separation between RPR and UDF, formerly a very clear-cut division between those who were Gaullists and those who were not, but that split has little meaning any longer for its young electorate and young elected. The right comprises Europeans and anti-Europeans, convinced democrats

---

[3] Perhaps this non-coincidence is unavoidable, since it is not unknown outside France. In the United States, *institutional* bipartism differentiates Republicans and Democrats, whereas an *internalized* moral sensibility puts Conservatives against Liberals. They are by no means perfectly superimposed, however. Most Republicans are conservative, but not all; most Democrats are liberal, but not all.

Demonstration by schoolchildren and students against 'Devaquet's Law' (the reform of higher education) in Paris on 27 November 1986, Boulevard Saint-Germain. (Photo: Roger-Viollet)

and those nostalgic for authority, those who extol unbridled capitalism and quasi-social-democrats, but none of those divisions really matches the one that distinguishes RPR from UDF.

Now, the difficulty of attributing, on either right or left, intellectually coherent definitions to differences in affiliation renders the business of making an informed political choice scarcely comprehensible to the public at large, and forces people to judge by appearances – of personalities, their rivalries and their networks.

Beyond these obscurities, at ground level, a long-term tendency can be discerned: the electoral map is evolving, and is beginning to escape from the stability of those regional traditions, records of which have been the marvel of political science since the times of André Siegfried. The Mediterranean Midi, for example, is no longer the private hunting ground of the left, and the Armorican west, on the other hand, is no longer out of bounds to it. It is the effect of social and cultural intermingling accelerated by industry and, to be more exact, the result of the effacement of the peasantry, who were the principal support of regional particularisms.

The recomposition of internal politics is thus in full swing while at the same time being diagnosed as in crisis. But it is not the least paradoxical aspect of the present era to see Western democracy take a turn for the worse at the very moment when it is becoming a hope for that part of the world which shakes dictatorships.

In France, the time has passed when the main beneficiary of disillusion with the political system was the French Communist Party. It is no longer even capable of capitalizing electorally on discontent of economic and social origin. The counterpart of its effacement is quite clearly the upsurge, most impressive in 1991 and 1992, of the newcomers to the political arena – on the one hand, the National Front (already mentioned), and on the other, the ecologists. It is very significant that the latter are no longer locked into defending nature against pollution, but are beginning to make room in their programme for criticism of more abstract nuisances.

Such, it would seem, might the national political landscape appear in the winter of 1991–2.

At this point, and to draw to a close, one must ask what has become of the great ideals, Republic, France, Liberty, whose evolution has served as leading strands in this volume.

The Republic. The year of its bicentenary, where we are now, will probably give rise to very confused and contradictory utterances on the subject. There will be argument about the essence of the Republic, as if that essence had not been born of history, and by history ceaselessly amended. At least there will be agreement that the Republic is a positive value. In fact, it remains sturdy, since what is most commonly understood today by 'Republic' – a system without king or dictator, a law-based state, a liberal democracy – receives an almost unanimous acceptance. It is also admitted that the French Republic has lived in the form of numbered incarnations, not one of which is absolutely unworthy of the name. To put it plainly, no one would dare to maintain today that the 'Republic' was given the death blow in 1958 by the return of General de Gaulle and the changing of the Constitution. Such pessimism has been given the lie. In other words, no one today would any longer dare to challenge the description of de Gaulle and the Fifth Republic as 'republican', except to give 'republican' a *historical* definition, like that applied to the period from Jules Ferry to Mendès France but these days embraced only by historians and a small number of militants. Some people go still further and maintain that the post-1958 Republic was even more republican than its predecessors because, with the Constitutional Council, it had the advantage of controlling the constitutionality of laws. One cannot follow them as far as that, however, as one would then have to admit that political liberty in France between 1875 and 1958 had been no more than a precarious state, which is an extremely harsh judgement. Nevertheless, the widening of the scope of the Constitutional Council is being studied, which forces the conclusion that the present Constitution may be fairly easily returned to the drawing board!

So there is one thing of which General de Gaulle did not manage to cure France – that historical tendency towards constitutional perfectionism, in other words, the constant search for political good by refining the mechanism, as if the mechanism counted for more than the spirit of the citizens!

Perhaps it would be more worthwhile to watch over the forming of that spirit and not, for example, allow the (eminently republican) idea that the law must be respected to wither.

What about the Patrie? It has been the subject of an even more spectacular alteration than that of the Republic, and national feeling has entered a more serious crisis than that of the politico-institutional system.

Pre-1914 France was almost entirely patriotic, through the convergence in favour of this value of the principal political philosophies that were antagonistic in all other regards. This patriotism enabled the war to be won in 1918, but everything seems to suggest that it was dealt a death blow by that very victory, and by the horror aroused by the sufferings endured in order to obtain it. Since 1918, it has no longer been possible to be a patriot as in 1914, with as much absolutism and good conscience. 'All things considered, the history of France seems to me today to have stopped at that sublime and absurd adventure, the First World War', as the best historian of French nationalism recently put it.[4] Can it be that for over three-quarters of a century France has merely been in a state of survival? And did de Gaulle and the Resistance only succeed in procuring temporary remission for the dying? In fact, though the conflict between 1940 and 1945 served to reassert the value of *Patrie*, liberty and even the idea that there could be 'just wars' to defend them, that moral revival scarcely outlived the doubts awakened by decolonization, or those aroused by the many-sided criticism of our way of life.

The flight of some into a radical individualism, the withdrawal of others into more restricted territorial or cultural attachments, the aspiration of yet others to build in Europe a *Patrie* on a superior scale, are all tendencies that French patriotism used to smother or contain. It is no longer in a position to do so today. Must a hard line be taken to reconstitute it? Or must one reconcile oneself to this fading away of France in order to transfer the collective will-to-live to Europe? Or wait until a future as yet difficult to give a name to extricates itself from a confused and chaotic present? That is probably one of tomorrow's choices.

Liberty, lastly? Nowadays the idea that traditional French systems, the right and the left if you will, of respectively Christian and rationalist origin, allow a sort of 'humanist' common denominator – humanitarian, demo-cratic, liberal, juridical (the Rights of Man) – has become commonplace. That would be the common basis and consensus of official France if it survives, or of programmed Europe if it consolidates its position. Is that an optimistic deduction?

There is indeed some truth in the idea that a certain philosophical civil war is in the act of being pacified. One may wonder only whether this civic code of ethics, proclaimed by the great majority of leaders of opinion, finds any deep resonance among the vast mass of citizens, seeing that is is

[4] Raoul Girardet, in *Le Figaro* of 30 April 1990 (literary page) on the occasion of the publication of his work *Singulièrement libre*, Perrin, 1990.

impossible, and undesirable, to catechize them as in former days. One may wonder above all what aim should be allotted, in the present-day world, to the moral and political good conscience that would unite the French. Who is to be designated as the counter-model, ideological adversary, bogey-man and target? 'Fascism', whose resurgence is constantly being revealed? 'American imperialism', which still has its obsessive denouncers? Or the 'South', which encompasses all the miseries but from which arise also all the fanaticisms? This is the final subject of choice for the citizens, and of contemplation for readers of history.

Chronological Survey of the Dreyfus Affair

1894

20 July Major Marie Charles-Ferdinand Walsin-Esterhazy presents himself to Colonel Maximilien von Schwarzkoppen, military attaché to the German Embassy.

1, 5 and 6 September Esterhazy brings Schwarzkoppen the five items listed in the *Bordereau* (covering note).

24 September The *Bordereau* comes to the notice of Major Hubert Joseph Henry, assigned to the Secret Intelligence Section (counter-espionage). Torn across in two places, this sheet of 'flimsy', with no heading, date or signature, is part of a delivery of several interesting pieces of information. Neither folded nor creased, it purports to 'have been discovered in Schwartzkoppen's wastepaper basket by Marie Bastian', a cleaning woman in the German Embassy and an agent of the Intelligence Service.

6 October the name of Alfred Dreyfus, a captain in the army general staff, is given by Major A. du Paty de Clam, of the Deuxième Bureau.

13 October Invited to give a judgement on the handwriting on the *Bordereau*, Alphonse Bertillon, head of the Prefecture of Police's anthropometric department, expresses some reservations.

14 October Threatened by a campaign in *La Libre Parole* (Édouard Drumont's anti-Jewish newspaper) denouncing 'the great Jewish plot that would deliver us into the enemy's hands', General Auguste Mercier, War Minister, signs the order to arrest Dreyfus.

15 October Following a dictate from the Minister's office, du Paty de Clam arrests Dreyfus.

2 November Colonel Alessandro Panizzardi, military attaché to the Italian Embassy, sends his superior in Rome a telegram in which he implicitly admits that he has had no relations with Dreyfus.

3 November On Mercier's orders, General Félix Gustave Saussier, military governor of Paris and vice-president of the Senior Military Council, signs the order to start inquiries concerning Dreyfus.

3 December Report of Major d'Ormescheville, who has been given the task of carrying out the investigation decided upon by the Council of Ministers.

19 December First hearing of the Dreyfus case, ordered to be held in camera. The first court martial of Paris consider a 'secret file', which Mercier has had passed to them by du Paty de Clam, illegally, not in the presence of the accused and his defence counsel, Edgar Demange. Among the 'secret documents', the item 'that scoundrel D—': a letter addressed to Schwartzkoppen by Alexandrine (the pseudonym used by Panizzardi when writing to his German colleague). Written in 1892 or 1893, this document has been falsely dated March 1894. It will be discovered that D— is a certain Dubois.

22 December The court martial sentences Dreyfus to be stripped of his military rank and deported for life to a fortified prison.

31 December Du Paty de Clam visits Dreyfus in the Cherche-Midi prison to try to force a confession and obtain evidence from him.

1895

5 January Dreyfus is degraded.

13 April Dreyfus on Devil's Island, Guiana.

1 July Lieutenant-Colonel Georges Picquart is appointed Chief of the Intelligence Section.

1896

March Picquart discovers the *Petit Bleu* (express letter transmitted by pneumatic tube in Paris). Addressed to Esterhazy and dictated by Schwartzkoppen (a feminine handwriting never having been identified), this telegram-letter had been torn up and thrown in the wastepaper basket; the thirty-two fragments had been 'lifted' from the German Embassy.

5 August Picquart notifies General de Boisdeffre, chief of the army general staff.

3 September London's *Daily Chronicle* publishes the false news of Dreyfus's escape.

8 September *La Libre Parole* invents, publishes and comments on an interview with a sailor who states that 'Dreyfus has certainly got away.'

15 September In a long article, entitled 'The Traitor', *L'Éclair* attempts to demonstrate Dreyfus's guilt.

26 October Picquart is sent on an inspection mission in the East.

1 November The announcement of interpellation in the Chamber by Castelin, the Aisne deputy, provokes the fabrication of the *Henry forgery*: a letter addressed to Schwartzkoppen and signed Alexandrine 'found, torn up, in a paper bag belonging to Marie Bastian'.

6 November Bernard Lazare's pamphlet: 'A judicial error. The truth about the Dreyfus Affair'.

10 November *Le Matin* publishes the facsimile of the *Bordereau*, passed on by the expert Teyssonnières.

18 November Castelin's interpellation.

21 November Picquart has to continue his mission 'without a break'.

1897

6 January Picquart is 'temporarily' assigned to the Fourth Infantry Regiment in the south of Tunisia.

31 May Henry sends a threatening letter to Picquart.

29 June Picquart confides in the lawyer Louis Leblois, an old schoolfriend.

13 July Leblois confides in Auguste Scheurer-Kestner, vice-president of the Senate.

17 August Esterhazy is suspended from duty.

30 October Letter from Esterhazy to the President of the Republic. Scheurer-Kestner goes to see his friend General Billot, War Minister.

7 November Threatening letter from Esterhazy to Picquart.

9 November Official communiqué from the War Minister: 'Dreyfus has been legally and justly sentenced.'

10 November To discredit Picquart, Henry makes up false telegrams *Speranza* and *Blanche* using unsealed correspondence addressed to Picquart.

14 November In the morning, Vidi (pen-name of Emmanuel Arène) gives an analysis in *Le Figaro* of Scheurer-Kestner's file. In the evening, in *Le Temps* dated the 15th, an open letter to Senator Arthur Ranc by Scheurer-Kestner.

15 November In a letter addressed to the War Minister, Mathieu Dreyfus, Alfred's brother, denounces Esterhazy as the writer of the *Bordereau*.

16 November Esterhazy asks the War Minister for an inquiry to be held, which is entrusted to General de Pellieux.

20 November Du Paty de Clam sends Esterhazy the *Note on the two handwritings*, in which he comes to an agreement with him over his deposition. ('Get firmly fixed in your mind everything I have marked in red, and destroy it. You realize how important it is for us to agree . . . for your sake as much as mine.')

26 November Picquart in Paris.

27 November On Scheurer-Kestner's request to Pellieux, seizure of Esterhazy's letters to one of his former mistresses, Mme de Boulancy.

28 November Next to the *Bordereau*, *Le Figaro* publishes the 'Letter from the uhlan', in which Esterhazy declares that he would be perfectly happy to be killed as a captain of the uhlans, putting the French to the sabre.

3 December Pellieux files a report condemning Picquart and concluding, subject to an evaluation of the handwritings, that there is lack of proof against Esterhazy. On Pellieux's advice, Esterhazy asks to go before the court martial, 'who can do nothing but acquit him'.

7 December On the refusal to review the trial, interpellation in the Senate by Scheurer-Kestner, seconded only by Ludovic Trarieux, former Keeper of the Seals. Reply by Jules Méline, president of the Council: 'there *is* no Dreyfus Affair.'

13 January Emile Zola publishes a first pamphlet: 'Letter to young people!'

24 December The experts state that the *Bordereau* is not in Esterhazy's handwriting.

1898

2 January Order for Esterhazy's trial.

7 January Zola's second pamphlet: 'Letter to France'. In *Le Siècle*, Yves Guyot publishes the bill of indictment of 1894 signed d'Ormescheville.

10 January Esterhazy's trial.

11 January Esterhazy is acquitted.

13 January in *L'Aurore*, run by Clemenceau, open letter to the President of the Republic by Émile Zola: 'J'accuse'.

17 January Government statement on 'the existence of confessions made by Dreyfus to Lebrun-Renault' (Captain in the gendarmerie, given the task of guarding Dreyfus on the day he was degraded).

19 January *Le Siècle* publishes the 'Letters of an innocent man', which Dreyfus has been sending to his wife for three years.

22 January Godefroy Cavaignac questions the government over 'Dreyfus's confession'.

17 February At Zola's trial (Paris Assize Court), Pellieux states that the government is in possession of a 'document of undisputed origin' (the *Henry forgery*).

20 February The moderate republican Trarieux founds the League for the Defence of the Rights of Man and the Citizen.

23 February Zola is sentenced to the maximum penalty: one year's imprisonment and 3,000 francs fine.

25 February The savant Grimaux is placed on leave from the École polytechnique until his retirement. Lieutenant Chapelain is taken off active service for having congratulated Zola.

26 February Picquart is discharged for 'a serious act of administrative negligence'.

15 March For his connections with Scheurer-Kestner, Leblois is suspended for six months.

2 April The Court of Appeal quashes the sentence on Zola.

8 April The Military Council lodges a complaint against Zola.

23 May The Zola affair at Versailles.

4 June First meeting of the League for the Defence of the Rights of Man and the Citizen.

15 June Méline's resignation.

16 June The Court of Appeal refuses Zola's suspensive appeal.

28 June Formation of Henri Brisson's government.

7 July In the Chamber, speech by Cavaignac, War Minister, presenting his proofs of Dreyfus's guilt: the *Henry forgery*, the 'confessions' and the *liberating Document* (the item 'that scoundrel D—', 'stolen from Picquart and delivered to Esterhazy by the *Veiled Lady*'). The Chamber acclaims Cavaignac and his speech is publicly displayed.

9 July *La Petite République* (Alexandre Millerand's press organ) publishes the letter sent the evening before to Cavaignac by Jean Jaurès protesting against the 'so-called confessions'. In a letter to the president of the Council, Picquart issues a protest concerning the *Henry forgery*.

12 July Esterhazy is arrested for swindling.

13 July Accused of having fabricated the *Petit bleu*, Picquart is arrested.

18 July Maximum sentence imposed on Zola, who leaves for London.

28 July Bertulus, the examining judge in charge of the Esterhazy affair, declares himself unable to investigate a complaint by Picquart against du Paty de Clam, accused by Henry of having composed the false telegrams.

5 August The Court of Arraignment quashes Bertulus's order referring Esterhazy to the Assize Court for forgery and making use of forged items.

13 August A captain in the War Minister's office, L. Cuignet, discovers and unmasks the *Henry forgery*.

30 August Interrogation, confession and arrest of Henry, who is sent to the fort at Mont-Valérien, where he is left in possession of his razors.

31 August Henry's suicide. Esterhazy is discharged. Resignation of Boisdeffre, who is against a revision of the trial.

3 September Resignation of Cavaignac, also opposed to revision. Request for a revision by Lucie Dreyfus.

5 September General Émile Thomas Zurlinden is War Minister.

12 September Du Paty de Clam suspended from active duty.

17 September Declaring his solidarity with his predecessors, Zurlinden resigns. General Jules Chanoine becomes War Minister. The government empowers the revision commission.

20 September Order to start inquiries into Picquart, accused by the general staff of having falsified the *Petit bleu*.

23 September The revision commission reaches a negative conclusion.

26 September The government refers to the Court of Appeal. Jean Jaurès publishes *Les Preuves* (The Proof).

25 October Questioned by the nationalist Paul Déroulède, Chanoine invokes 'respect for what has been judged' and resigns. The Chamber passes the order of the day affirming 'the supremacy of civil over military authority'; but an addition proposed by the opposition, 'inviting the government to put an end to the campaign of abuse organized by the newspapers against the army', is carried by 296 to 243 votes and provokes the withdrawal of the Brisson government.

29 October The request for a revision is declared acceptable. An inquiry is decided upon.

31 October Charles Dupuy government. Charles de Freycinet is War Minister.

7 November Joseph Reinach accuses Henry of complicity with Esterhazy.

28 November Raymond Poincaré states in the Chamber: 'I am happy, on this platform, to grasp the long overdue opportunity to relieve my conscience.'

2 December Prosecuted by both the civil and military courts, Picquart requests the procedure of 'ruling on the judges' by the Court of Appeal.

1899

January Accusations against the criminal court judges made by Jules Quesnay de Beaurepaire, president of the civil chamber of the Court of Appeal.

7 January The Minister of Justice gives the task of holding an inquiry to the first president of the Court, Mazeau.

15 Jaunary Closing of the subscription (131,110 francs, 15,000 subscribers, including 1,000 officers and 300 priests) launched by *La Libre Parole* 'for the widow and orphan of Colonel Henry against the Jew Reinach'.

27 January Report of president Mazeau who, despite a negative inquiry, concludes that, his colleagues having worked for three months 'amid an unprecedented unleashing of opposing passions', 'responsibility for a definitive judgement cannot be left to the criminal court alone'. Dupuy proposes to the Council of Ministers a plan for removing the case from the criminal court, the revision judgement having to be rendered by the Court of Appeal as a whole, with all courts united (approved by eight votes to three).

10 February The Chamber passes the plan by 324 votes to 207.

16 February Death of Félix Faure.

18 February Émile Loubet is President of the Republic.

23 February Attempted coup d'état by Déroulède.

1 March The Senate passes the law withdrawing the case from the criminal court.

3 March The Court of Appeal allows the 'ruling on the judges' asked for by Picquart.

31 March *Le Figaro* publishes the secret inquiry of the criminal court.

27 April Confrontation between Maurice Paléologue, diplomat, and Cuignet, casting doubt on the good faith of the diplomats in deciphering Panizzardi's dispatch of 2 November 1894.

5 May Resignation of Freycinet, replaced by Camille Krantz.

12 May At the request of Théophile Delcassé, Minister of Foreign Affairs, Cuignet is relieved of active duty.

31 May The jury of the Seine court acquits Déroulède, charged with inciting soldiers to disobedience.

3 June The Court of Appeal orders a revision, quashing the sentence passed on 22 December 1894.

5 June Zola returns to Paris.

12 June Challenged over the role of the police, Dupuy is overthrown.

13 June Benefiting from the withdrawal of the case, Picquart is released.

22 June Pierre Waldeck-Rousseau's government of 'Republican defence'.

30 June Brought back to France on the cruiser *Sfax*, Dreyfus lands at Quiberon.

30 July In *L'Écho de Paris*, Quesnay de Beaurepaire publishes his own inquiry, damning Dreyfus.

7 August First hearing of the court martial in Rennes. Mercier affirms his 'absolute conviction' of Dreyfus's guilt.

14 August An unknown man fires a revolver, hitting Fernand Labori in the back (Zola's and Dreyfus's barrister in Rennes).

9 September By five votes to two, the court martial declares Dreyfus guilty, but with mitigating circumstances, and sentences him to ten years' imprisonment.

19 September Dreyfus is pardoned.

21 September Order of the day of General Gaston Auguste de Galliffet, War Minister: 'The incident is closed!'

6 November Fleeing to London, Esterhazy is condemned in his absence to three years in prison.

1900

At the start of the year, the Senate, assuming the function of High Court, sentences Déroulède to ten years' banishment for plotting against state security.

1 January Waldeck-Rousseau presents a bill granting amnesty concerning the events connected with the Dreyfus Affair.

28 May Resignation of Galliffet. General Louis André becomes War Minister.

24 December The amnesty law is passed.

1903

6–7 April In the Chamber, Jaurès asks for an inquiry on the 'annotated *Bordereau*'. Shortly before the Rennes trial, Mercier had claimed to be in possession of this 'ultra-secret document'. The *Bordereau* is supposed to have been traced by Esterhazy from the real one, which was not 'divulged because it bore annotations in the margin in the hand of Wilhelm II'. André agrees to undertake the task of proceeding with the administration necessary for an inquiry, a proposal rejected by the Chamber.

May–October André's inquiry, assisted by his aide, Captain Targe. Item 26 (note from Alexandrine to Schwarzkoppen concerning railway organization) bears in red ink, in Henry's hand, the date: April 1894. André discovers that the letter sent containing this text from the Intelligence Section to the chief of general staff bears the date 1 April 1895, and that the date given on the copy of Alexandrine's letter, which was enclosed, is 28 March 1895, 3 p.m.

19 October André presents his report to the president of the Council: 'I have been able to establish that important pieces of evidence, favourable to the accused, were not produced and that, on the other hand, certain items in the file were subjected to either material alternations or erroneous commentaries that distorted their significance.'

26 October   Petition for a revision by Dreyfus.

1904

5 March   The criminal court orders a new inquiry.

1905

2 November   Amnesty law passed. Déroulède returns to France.

1906

12 July   Decree of the Court of Appeal, overturning the Rennes sentence, clears Dreyfus's name.

13 July   Vote on bills to rehabilitate Dreyfus and Picquart. Dreyfus is promoted to major, and Picquart to general.

20 July   Dreyfus is made a Chevalier of the Légion d'honneur.

25 October   Picquart becomes War Minister.

1908

4 June   Zola's ashes transferred to the Panthéon. Grégori, in charge of the military press, fires two revolver shots at Dreyfus, wounding him in the arm.

Principal source: *L'Affaire Dreyfus* by J. Kayser, 1946.

Chronology
1879–1983

1879

5 January The Senate election gives a strong republican majority (174 to 126). Mac-Mahon turns down General Farre, Gambetta's candidate, as Minister of War.

16 January Declaration of the Dufaure ministry, read to the Chamber, and interpellation.

28 January Mac-Mahon refuses to apply the decree limiting the length of command for army corps commanders.

30 January Resignation of Mac-Mahon. Election of Jules Grévy to the presidency of the Republic by 563 out of 713 votes. End of the Dufaure ministry.

31 January Gambetta is elected president of the Chamber.

4 February Waddington government. Jules Ferry in charge of Public Education.

7 February Jules Grévy's first message (giving up the right of dissolution).

14 February A decree of the Minister of War officially makes *La Marseillaise* the national anthem (following the decree of 26 Messidor Year III).

April Complementary elections bring nineteen republicans and two monarchists to the Chamber.

April–May Pardon and amnesty (partial) of 3,500 Commune prisoners.

14 June The Senate agrees to the meeting of the Congress to vote on transferring the public authorities to Paris.

19 June The Congress repeals the article in the Constitution establishing the seat of the authorities in Versailles.

20 October The Third Workers' Congress at Marseille adopts the name Socialist Workers' Congress of France.

November The Assemblies are once more installed in Paris.

16 December Challenged over the application of the amnesty, the Minister of Justice resigns.

21 December Shaken by the resignation of the Ministers of War and Justice, the Waddington government steps down without having been overthrown.

28 December The Freycinet government ('reshuffling of the reshuffle of 4 February').

1880

20 February   Adoption of the Ferry bill reforming the Upper Council of Public Education.

12 March   Ferry bill on the conferment of university degrees.

29 March   Two decrees charge all unauthorized *congrégations* to ask the state for authorization within three months, and order the dissolution and dispersal of the Society of Jesus within three months.

April   The Chamber adopts the free trade that has been under discussion since February.

3 May   Interpellation in the Chamber by Lamy, a Catholic republican.

16 June   Gambetta proposes a general amnesty.

21 June   The Senate rules out of order petitions against decrees.

July   Amnesty for the Commune exiles.

9 July   The Chamber passes Ferry's bill on higher education, restoring to the state the exclusive right of conferring university degrees (330 votes to 164 on article 7).

14 July   The Fourteenth of July is instituted, and celebrated for the first time, as a national festival.

18 August   Freycinet's speech on the *congrégations* at Montauban.

16–17 September   The government adjourns the execution of the decrees on unauthorized *congrégations* pending the decision of the jurisdictional court.

18 September   Three ministers of the Republican Union resign.

19 September   Circular from Constans (the resigning Minister of the Interior) to the leaders of unauthorized *congrégations* prohibiting them from any activity. Resignation of Freycinet.

23 September   Jules Ferry, president of the Council, stays as Minister of Public Education.

October   The government carries out the decrees expelling unauthorized *congrégations*.

1 October   In his speech at Marseille, Clemenceau reproaches Gambetta for exercising a 'hidden power'.

14 November   The collectivists excluded from the Le Havre national congress form themselves into the Workers' Socialist National Congress.

21 December   Law instituting public and secular secondary teaching by women and creation of the Sèvres *École normale supérieure* for young women. Founding of *lycées* for girls.

1881

January–February   The Chamber votes on the bill relating to the press.

12 May   Treaty of Le Bardo: the Bey of Tunis accepts the French protectorate.

30 May   The Chamber rejects Gambetta's bill on the list ballot.

9 June   The Senate does likewise.

16 June   Law on free primary education.

30 June   Law on public meetings (no authorization, as long as notice is given in advance).

28 July   Abolition of the denominational nature of cemeteries.

29 July   Law on the freedom of public meetings and of the press.

21 August and September   General legislative elections: 467 seats go to the republicans against 96 to the monarchists.

10 November Placed in a difficult situation over the Tunisian expedition, Jules Ferry withdraws.

14 November Gambetta's 'great cabinet'. Paul Bert goes to Education and Religions.

1882

8 January Renewal of the Senate: the republicans obtain twenty-four additional seats (out of seventy-nine).

19 January Crash of the *Union générale des banques*.

27 January Fall of Gambetta's government over the question of revision of the Constitution.

30 January Freycinet government. Jules Ferry to Public Education, Léon Say to Finance.

28 March Law on compulsory primary education.

29 March Law on the neutral nature of teaching.

May Foundation of the League of Patriots (Henri Martin president).

29 July The Chamber refuses new funds of 9 million to send troops to occupy the Suez isthmus. Fall of Freycinet's government.

7 August Duclerc's 'sea-bathing government'.

September At the Saint-Étienne Congress, split of the Socialist Workers' Party.

29 September During their banquet in Paris, the legitimists ask the Comte de Chambord to return to France.

31 December Accidental death of Gambetta.

1883

15 January Prince Napoleon calls for a plebiscite.

21 February Jules Ferry president of the Council and Minister of Foreign Affairs.

July The Chamber ratifies the agreements with the railways.

24 August Death of the Comte de Chambord.

29 September Visit of Alfonso XII of Spain to Paris. Demonstration by Parisian radicals.

13–14 October In Rouen and Le Havre Jules Ferry makes two speeches against his left-wing adversaries.

1884

21 March Law on workers' and employers' professional trades unions.

5 April Law on municipalities, stipulating notably the election of mayors by municipal councillors (except for Paris).

27 July Naquet's law on divorce.

4–13 August The Congress, constituted into a National Assembly, votes on the definitive republican form of the government, the abolition of public prayers at the opening of parliamentary sittings, and the gradual removal of permanent senators.

1885

January Renewal of the Senate: Sixty-seven republican seats out of eighty-seven.

27 March The Chamber votes for a departmental list ballot for the election of deputies.

30 March Clemenceau's interpellation over the failure of Lang Son (Tonkin) brings about the fall of Ferry's government. Paul Déroulède obtains the presidency of the League of Patriots.

6 April China gives up Tonkin and Annam. Brisson's 'waiting' government.

22 May Death of Victor Hugo.

31 May–1 June Victor Hugo's funeral ceremony.

11 October The second round of legislative elections gives the definitive result of 383 republican seats to 201.

24 December Funds for Tonkin are voted for with a majority of four.

28 December Re-election of Jules Grévy to the Presidency of the Republic.

1886

7 January Freycinet's 'reshuffled' government. Recommended by Clemenceau, Boulanger becomes Minister of War.

26 January Incidents during the miners' strike at Decazeville.

10 April First socialist interpellation (over the Decazeville incidents).

22 May The Chamber votes on a counterplan prohibiting the heads of the two royal and imperial families from entering France, and banning the princes from any office or elective mandate.

14 July The Parisian crowds acclaim Boulanger.

1 August Elections of general councillors: conservative gains.

October Bartholdi's *Liberty Enlightening the World* (1884) is inaugurated in the bay of New York.

18 October Interpellation by the radicals on the use of troops in the Vierzon strike.

30 October Final law on secular primary education, complementing the laws of 1881 and 1882.

3 December Dispute over the budget provokes the withdrawal of the government.

12 December Goblet's 'Freycinet government minus Freycinet'.

1887

Creation of the Indochinese Union, comprising the protectorates of Annam, Tonkin, Cambodia and then Laos (1893); Cochin-China is a colony and Tonkin will gradually become one.

20 April Frontier incident between French and German police: arrest of the French police commissaire Schnaebelé.

18 May Fall of the Goblet government (and of Boulanger).

24 May Mackau, president of the Right-wing Union, pays a visit to Jules Grévy.

30 May Rouvier's government (without Boulanger).

24 June The League of Patriots acclaims Boulanger.

June–July The Chamber votes on the principle of three years' service.

8 July Appointed commander of the 13th army corps in Clermont-Ferrand, Boulanger leaves Paris. In order to escape the crowds demonstrating on his behalf, the General is forced to climb on to the locomotive.

11 July Interpellation by the radicals on 'clerical and monarchist machinations'.

14 July The crowds demonstrate with cries of 'Long live Boulanger! Down with Ferry!'

24 July Jules Ferry's speech at Épinal on the 'foreigners' party'.

15 September Instructions from the Comte de Paris to the 'representatives of the monarchic party'.

25 October   Start of the affair of trafficking in the decorations of the Légion d'honneur (in which Wilson, Grévy's son-in-law, is implicated).

27 October   Wilson sends a cheque to the Treasury.

5 November   Parliamentary commission of inquiry.

10 November   The government orders a judicial inquiry.

17 November   The Chamber authorizes legal proceedings to be taken against Wilson. Clemenceau's interpellation.

28–9 November   During the 'historic nights', Clemenceau has interviews with the leaders of the Boulangist party, Déroulède and Boulanger.

30 November   Grévy announces his resignation.

2 December   Grévy resigns.

3 December   Election of Sadi Carnot as President of the Republic.

12 December   The 'business government' of Tirard (independent senator).

1888

Wilhelm II King of Prussia and Emperor of Germany.

January   Partial renewal of the Senate: conservative gains.

14 March   The government pensions off Boulanger.

20 March   Interpellation by an imperialist deputy on the measures taken against Boulanger.

31 March   Pensioned off, Boulanger becomes eligible to stand.

8 April   Election of Boulanger in the Dordogne.

15 April   Election of Boulanger in the Nord.

21 April   The municipal council of Paris votes for an agenda against the 'plebiscitary and Boulangist campaign'.

24 April   The Comte de Paris gets into position.

27 April   Boulanger declares himself for an 'open Republic'.

23 May   Under the presidency of Clemenceau, the 'possibilist' federation creates the Society of the Rights of Man and the Citizen in order to defend the Republic.

12 July   Boulanger resigns as deputy and is wounded by Floquet, president of the Council, in a sword duel.

19 August   Triple election of Boulanger.

15 October   Floquet proposes the revision of the Constitution.

1889

27 January   Elected in the Seine constituency, Boulanger refuses to march on the Élysée.

9 February   The Chamber votes for a return to single-name ballot by 268 to 222 (law of 13 February).

14 February   Adjournment of the debate on the revision called for by Floquet, who resigns.

22 February   Tirard government, which declares itself ready for 'wide-ranging, tolerant and wise policies, in order to ensure the success of the Universal Exhibition'.

23 February   The government announces that it wishes to ensure the maintenance of law and order and the respect due to the Republic.

24 February   Constans, Minister of the Interior, orders prefects not to receive workers' delegations. Only a petition to the Chambers is permitted.

2 March   Dissolution of the League of Patriots.

17 March Boulanger–conservative alliance at the Tours banquet.

1 April Boulanger flees to Brussels.

12 April Boulanger, Dillon and Rochefort are condemned in their absence.

5 May Opening of the Universal Exhibition.

17 July Constans' law forbidding multiple candidacies.

18 July Law establishing three-year military service 'the same for all' (reduced to one year for those with 'exemption').

14 August Boulanger and his two fellow accused are sentenced in their absence to deportation to a secure and guarded place.

15 September Boulanger's 'appeal to France'.

6 October Second round of the legislative elections. Definitive result: 336 seats to the republicans against 172 to the conservatives.

1890

1 March Resignation of Constans, Minister of the Interior.

13 March Resignation of the Tirard government.

17 March Freycinet government. Ribot to Foreign Affairs, Constans to the Interior.

18 March Resignation of Bismarck.

May Visit of the Grand Duke Nicholas to Paris.

10 May In the Chamber, statement by Étienne, Under-Secretary of State for the colonies, on the development of the French colonial empire in Africa.

7 July Law on the creation of elected delegates for the protection of non-adult workers.

5 August Franco-British declaration recognizing French rights over Madagascar and a British protectorate over Zanzibar.

30 September Suicide of Boulanger in Brussels.

6 November In reply to Delcassé's interpellation, Ribot declares that 'France does not conceal the efforts it has imposed on itself for the past twenty years to rebuild its army, which is the safeguard of its independence.'

12 November The toast in Algiers by Cardinal Lavigerie, the first sign of a *rapprochement* between Catholicism and the republican regime.

1891

18 February The 'incognito' visit of the Dowager Empress of Germany to Paris provokes incidents.

1 May The French Workers' Party (Jules Guesde) organizes a general demonstration in favour of an eight-hour working day. Several deaths following demonstrations at Fourmies.

15 May The encyclical *Rerum Novarum* of Leo XIII, to the development of which Albert le Mun has contributed.

16 July Giers, Russian Minister of Foreign Affairs, has talks with Laboulaye, the French Ambassador, about his desire for an *entente*.

18 July The Chamber votes for a general protectionist tariff by 385 votes to 111.

20 July Law creating the Employment Office.

23 July Arrival at Kronstadt of French naval division.

27 August A diplomatic agreement creates the Franco-Russian *entente cordiale*.

1892

11 January Law on the return to protectionism.

20 January Common declaration by the five French metropolitan cardinals on the opposition between the Republic and the Catholic faith.

17 February In an interview with the journalist Ernest Judet, of the *Petit Journal*, Leo XIII states that 'the Republic is as legitimate a form of government as the rest, and the Constitution must be accepted in order to change legislation.'

19 February Forced into a minority over a bill concerning associations (and indirectly religious *congrégations*), the Freycinet government resigns.

20 February Publication of the encyclical *Inter Sollicitudines*, written in French.

27 February Loubet's government of 'republican concentration'.

29 February In Paris, the anarchist Ravachol's first bomb attempt.

27 March In Paris, fourth attempt to create an explosion.

30 March Arrest of Ravachol.

August Strike in the glassworks at Carmaux.

17 August French and Russian top officials sign an agreement plan for reciprocal aid.

2 November The maximum length of the working day for women and adolescents is reduced to eleven hours; a weekly day of rest is compulsory.

21 November Interpellation by Delahaye, affirming that 150 members of parliament have misappropriated public funds in the Panama affair, leads the Chamber to appoint a commission of inquiry.

28 November Fall of the 'Loubet–Ribot' cabinet.

6 December 'Ribot–Loubet' government.

20 December Vote to lift parliamentary immunity from five deputies. Déroulède's attack on Clemenceau.

1893

As a 'French' reaction against Wagner's dominating influence, Debussy composes the *Prélude à l'après-midi d'un Faune* dedicated to Mallarmé.

January Before the first chamber of the Court of Appeal of Paris, lawsuit for swindling and abuse of trust against the leading members of the Panama Company, as well as Eiffel the entrepreneur. Prison and fines for all the accused (sentence quashed without further reference some months later).

February In *La Petite République*, Millerand proposes a 'coalition of the left-wing parties against all conservative parties'.

8 March Before the Assize Court of the Seine, opening of the corruption trial of five members of parliament and the directors of the Panama Company.

20 March Sentence: Charles de Lesseps guilty with mitigating circumstances; acquittal of the other accused with the exception of Baihaut, former Minister of Public Works.

30 March Following a conflict between the Chamber and the Senate over the reform of the tax on beverages, fall of Ribot's cabinet.

4 April Dupuy government. Raymond Poincaré to Public Education.

31 May At the banquet of the *Journal des débats*, Léon Say (centre-left) rejects an *entente* with the socialists.

3 June In the republican club of Toulouse, Constans proposes to the republican centre groups an alliance with the conservatives over a programme of practical interests.

3 September Second round of the legislative elections. Government republicans have 278 seats, against 140 for the radicals, 45 for the socialists, 76 for the right and 27 for the *ralliés*.

3 October   Treaty between France and Siam recognizing the sovereignty of Annam over Laos.

13 October   Visit to Toulon of Admiral Avellane's Russian squadron.

25 November   Fall of Dupuy's government as a result of a socialist interpellation.

3 December   Moderate government of Casimir-Perier.

9 December   The anarchist Vaillant throws a bomb at the Chamber.

11–12 December   Law on criminal association.

1894

4 January   Definitive conclusion of the Franco-Russian Alliance.

7 February   Vaillant goes to the scaffold.

22 May   Following a conflict over the right of state employees to belong to a trade union, the Casimir-Perier government resigns.

30 May   Dupuy's cabinet, 'guaranteeing public order in the face of all disturbances and ensuring the observance of republican laws'. Poincaré goes to Finance.

24 June   Sadi Carnot is assassinated in Lyon by the anarchist Caserio.

27 June   Casimir-Perier is elected President of the Republic.

28 June   The Chamber finally adopts the bill on press offences (exceptional law against anarchists).

September   The Congress of the Trades Unions Federation votes for Briand's proposal on a general strike.

24 September   Start of the Dreyfus Affair. (See separate detailed chronology.)

1895

15 January   Fall of the Dupuy government.

16 January   Casimir-Perier, President of the Republic, resigns.

17 January   At Versailles, the Congress elects Félix Faure to the presidency of the Republic by a majority of sixty-nine votes.

26 January   Ribot's 'republican union' government.

13 February   The Lumière brothers patent their invention.

22 March   Projection of the first cinematographic film in Paris: 'Workers coming out of the Lumière factory'.

10 June   Interpellations by the radical Flourens and the socialist Millerand reproaching the government for heading for a *rapprochement* with Germany.

September   The Workers' Congress in Limoges decides on the constitution of a General Workers' Confederation (CGT).

1 October   Treaty of Tananarive: Queen Ranavalona III recognizes the French protectorate.

28 October   Fought by the clergy and attacked by the socialists, Ribot's government resigns.

1 November   Léon Bourgeois's homogeneous radical cabinet. Combes to Public Education and Religions. Doumer to Finance.

1896

18 January   The government notifies foreign powers of its 'taking possession' of Madagascar.

23 February   At Châlons, the Minister of Trade argues for a wise and practical socialism.

26 March Vote in principle for a general income tax.

21 April The Senate refuses to place confidence in the government.

23 April Without a majority in the Chamber or the Senate, Léon Bourgeois's cabinet withdraws.

29 April Homogeneous moderate government of Méline, who takes the Agriculture portfolio.

24 May The Christian Workers' Congress of Reims creates a Christian Democrat Party.

30 May During a banquet of socialist mayors in Saint-Mandé, Millerand makes a speech outlining his programme.

29 June The revelations of Arton lead the Chamber to elect a commission of inquiry into the Panama scandal.

21–4 July The Congress of the French Workers' Party in Lille recommends the socialist doctrine as a rule of the electoral discipline.

6 August Law annexing Madagascar to France.

24 August Ecclesiastical Congress.

5 October Arrival at Cherbourg of Tsar Nicholas II and Tsarina Alexandra.

1897

May Burning of the Bazar de la Charité.

August The Tsar receives Félix Faure at Kronstadt.

September The Masonic Assembly invites Freemasons in parliament to replace the 'reactionary and clerical government'.

10 October At Remiremont, Méline rejects anticlericalism and resumes the formula of appeasement.

14 October The 'airplane' of Clément Ader succeeds in making a leap of 200 metres.

1898

Pierre and Marie Curie discover polonium and radium.

9 April Law on accidents at work.

17 April At Remiremont, Méline's speech outlining his programme: 'Neither reaction nor revolution'.

22 May Second round of legislative elections. The moderate republicans have 250 seats, against 170 for the radicals, 50 for the socialists, 45 for the pure right and 20 for the 'revisionists'; the *ralliés* gain 10 seats. Law on mutual aid societies.

30 May Report of the commission of inquiry on the Panama scandal. The Chamber blames the shortcomings of the magistrature.

14 June Interpellation by Millerand, who promises unconditionally 'the backing of socialists for a left-wing government that will prove by its actions its determination to bring republican forms to fruition'. The proposal of an exclusively republican majority made by the radical Ricard brings about the withdrawal of the Méline cabinet (on the 15th).

28 June Brisson's radical government.

25 October The Brisson cabinet resigns over an order of the day inviting the government to repress attacks on the army.

1 November Dupuy's 'balanced' government.

7 November The government telegraphs the order to Major Marchand to evacuate Fachoda.

1899

12 June Fall of Dupuy's government.

22 June Waldeck-Rousseau's 'Republican Defence' government. The socialist Millerand enters the government as Minister of Trade and Industry (Labour). Delcassé keeps Foreign Affairs.

14 July 'Manifesto to working class and socialist France' by the Guesdists and Blanquists: 'The Socialist Party . . . could never become . . . a government party.'

August Decree on working conditions for works carried out for the state, *départements* and communes.

19 November Inauguration of the *Triumph of the Republic* by Dalou, in the place de la Nation.

1900

January Dissolution by sentence of the *congrégation* of the Augustinians of the Assumption (Assumptionists).

28 January Partial renewal of the Senate: the left obtains eighty out of ninety-nine seats.

15 March First performance of Edmond Rostand's *L'Aiglon*, starring Sarah Bernhardt.

30 March Law shortening the working day for industrial workers to ten hours, to be effected within a period of four years.

11 April To the interpellation of a Catholic, Waldeck-Rousseau replies that there are 'too many monks who are members of leagues, and too many monks dabbling in business'.

14 April The President of the Republic inaugurates the Universal Exhibition in Paris.

28 April The Vatican nullifies the Organic Articles.

May The Paris municipal council elects a nationalist to be its president.

22 May Waldeck-Rousseau obtains a vote of confidence to 'pursue a policy of republican reforms and the defence of the secular state'.

28 May Resignation of Galliffet, Minister of War.

July New extensions of the Franco-Russian Alliance: joint establishment of protocols on French and Russian mobilization in the eventuality of an attack by Britain.

16 July The first line of the Parisian métro comes into service, between Vincennes and Porte Maillot.

September In Paris, the national socialist congress and the international socialist congress discuss the 'Millerand case'. The Guesdists quit the party.

22 September 20,777 mayors attend a banquet given by the government in the Tuileries gardens.

28 October In Toulouse, Waldeck-Rousseau gives a fighting speech in which he talks of the *'congrégations'* billion' and the opposition between the 'two kinds of youth'.

12 November After welcoming its visitor number 50,860,801, the Universal Exhibition closes.

29 November Law compelling shop employers to place chairs for the use of the sales ladies.

December Franco-Italian agreement on Tripolitania and Morocco.

1901

15 January Opening of the debate in the Chamber on the freedom to form associations.

21 January Death of Queen Victoria; accession of Edward VII.

February Protocols of Franco-Russian military agreement concerning the role of Great Britain.

April Visit of an Italian squadron to Toulon.

May The French government approves the Franco-Russian military protocols. The dissident progressive Adolphe Carnot founds the Democratic Republican Alliance (moderate). Socialist congress in Lyon, new split.

23 June First congress of the Radical and Radical Socialist Party in Paris.

1 July Law on associations.

17 September Tsar Nicholas II and Tsarina Alexandra land at Dunkirk.

1902

Renewal of the *Triplice* (Triple Alliance). Clemenceau senator for the Var.

30 January Alliance treaty between Britain and Japan.

March Creation of the French Socialist Party at Tours.

8 May The sudden eruption of Mount Pelée completely destroys Saint-Pierre and Martinique.

11 May Second round of legislative elections: the left-wing coalition has 350 seats (including 110 radicals, 100 radical socialists and 45 socialists) against 230.

Third week of May The President of the Republic visits the Tsar.

28 May Ill, Waldeck-Rousseau withdraws without having been placed in a minority.

1 June Léon Bourgeois president of the Chamber.

15 June Combes forms a cabinet including seven radicals and radical socialists and three moderates. The president of the Council takes the Interior and Religions portfolio, Delcassé keeps Foreign Affairs.

28 June Prinetti, Italian Minister of Foreign Affairs, and Barrère, French Ambassador, exchange letters limiting Italy's role in the *Triplice*.

6 August Cambon, French Ambassador in London, informs Lord Lansdowne, British Secretary of State for Foreign Affairs, that France now deems it possible to conduct its policies 'in accord with Great Britain'.

September Creation of the Socialist Party of France at Commentry.

22 October Cambon–Lansdowne talks on Morocco.

2 November Fresh Cambon–Lansdowne talks on Morocco.

23 November The government has all unauthorized schools closed, except in areas lacking a secular school. Issue in France of a loan intended to finance the completion of the trans-Siberian railway.

28 March By 304 votes to 246 the Chamber rejects all the requests for authorization made by the fifty-four unrecognized *congrégations*.

8 April Lansdowne affirms to Cambon that he wishes to deal with the Moroccan question with Spain and France.

May Official visit of Edward VII to Paris.

25–6 June By a majority of sixteen votes, the Chamber rejects *en bloc* requests for authorization made by eighty-one unrecognized women's *congrégations*.

27 June In a speech to the Senate, Waldeck-Rousseau denounces Combes's sectarianism.

July   Garin wins the first Tour de France cycle race.

6 July   Official visit of Émile Loubet to London.

11 July   Law on hygiene in workplaces.

20 July   Death of Leo XIII.

August   Election of Pius X.

13 September   Combes inaugurates the statue of Renan in Tréguier.

October   Official visit of King Victor-Emmanuel III to Paris.

18 December   The president of the Council presents a bill withdrawing the right to teach from all *congrégations*.

1904

6 January   Breaking off of diplomatic relations between Japan and Russia.

8 February   Japanese torpedo boats sink the Tsar's ships in the harbour of Chemui Po (Korea).

March   By 316 votes to 269, the Chamber votes for Combes's bill, with an amendment exempting from its provisions the noviciates on the staff of French schools in the colonies and abroad.

24–9 March   The official visit of Émile Loubet to Rome upsets the Vatican.

8 April   The Franco-British agreement on the colonies lays the foundations for the *Entente Cordiale*.

18 April   First issue of *L'Humanité*, founded by Jaurès.

May   On the occasion of municipal elections, Paris evades the nationalists and the radicals win several big towns.

27 May   The Chamber rejects the proposal to denounce the Concordat.

5 July   After ratification by the Senate by 167 votes to 108, the law is passed withdrawing the right to teach from all *congrégations* (with amendment).

29 July   The Council of Ministers decides to withdraw the embassy to the Vatican.

30 July   The Chamber votes for breaking off diplomatic relations with the Vatican.

August   At the Congress of the Workers' Internationale in Amsterdam, the 'Amsterdam resolution' condemns any policy of support for a bourgeois government.

30 October   *Le Figaro* denounces the existence of files kept in the War Ministry's *Corinthe* and *Carthage* dossiers.

4 November   Guyot de Villeneuve brings up the 'affair of the files' in the Chamber.

15 November   Resignation of General André.

9 December   Interpellation in the Chamber concerning the prefect's 'delegates' by Millerand, who speaks of the government's abject domination. A vote of confidence is passed by 296 to 266.

1905

10 January   Doumer is elected president of the Chamber.

14 January   Challenged on his general policies, Combes replies that his fall would be a disaster for the Republic and again receives a majority of six votes.

18 January   Resignation of the Combes government.

24 January   Rouvier's cabinet of 'realist policies'. The president of the Council takes the Finance portfolio and Delcassé keeps Foreign Affairs.

4 March   Final vote for the law fixing military service at two years without exemptions.

31 March   Wilhelm II lands at Tangiers. Charles Maurras founds the French League of Action. Marc Sangnier begins to transform *Le Sillon* (magazine founded in 1894) into an organized social and political movement.

April The French Socialist Party and the Socialist Party of France merge into a single party: the Unified Socialist Party or French Section of the Workers' Internationale.

19 April Challenged in the Chamber over the Tangiers affair, Delcassé offers his resignation, but then withdraws it.

15 May Rouvier directs Cambon not to continue Franco-British negotiations regarding German aims in Morocco.

30 May The adviser to the German Embassy in Paris asks Rouvier for 'a change in the conduct of French foreign policy'.

4 June The official visit to Paris of King Alfonso XIII of Spain provokes an assassination attempt.

6 June The decision of the Council of Ministers not to pursue talks with Britain causes Delcassé to resign.

19 June Law limiting the working day of those who work underground to eight hours.

26 June Clemenceau declares to the British Embassy: 'If Germany wants war, well then, we will fight!'

1 July Rouvier rallies to the plan for a Moroccan conference.

3 July By 341 to 233 votes, the Chamber passes the bill on the Separation of Churches and State.

24 July In Bjoerkoe (Finland), secret German–Russian treaty of defensive alliance.

28 September Franco-German agreement on the programme for the international conference on Morocco.

November The War Office in London assures the French military attaché of immediate aid in the form of 115,000 men in case of a German attack.

9 December Adopted by the Senate, the law instituting the Separation of Churches and State.

1906

7 January Partial renewal of the Senate.

16 January Opening of the Algeciras conference on Morocco.

17 January Armand Fallières is elected President of the Republic by the 449 left votes against the 371 votes of the centre and right for Paul Doumer.

1–2 February Incidents in Paris over the inventories affair.

11 February The encyclical *Vehementer Nos* of Pius X condemns the Separation law.

18 February Entry into office of the new President of the Republic.

24 February The Chamber votes for the bill on workers' pensions.

3 March The Algeciras conference gives responsibility for the organization of the police in Morocco to France and Spain.

7 March The death of a demonstrator in Boeschepe brings about the resignation of the Rouvier cabinet.

10 March The Courrières catastrophe provokes a strike of 70,000 miners.

14 March The Sarrien government. Clemenceau enters government as Minister of the Interior; Briand to Public Education and Religions.

7 April The final Act of the Algeciras conference guarantees independence to the Sultan, the integrity of his state and 'perfect equality' of all nations in the Moroccan 'economic domain'.

20 May Second round of legislative elections: the former 'Bloc' has 414 seats (including 130 radical socialists) against 175 seats for the opposition.

30 May The French episcopacy meet in Paris.

1 June Meeting of the new Chamber.

21 June The Chamber gives the Sarrien government a vote of confidence.

12–13 July Acquittal, clearing and reinstatement of Dreyfus.

13 July Law re-establishing the compulsory weekly day of rest.

15 August The encyclical *Gravissimo officii* rejects religious associations.

13 October The CGT congress approves the Amiens Charter.

19 October Ill, Sarrien withdraws.

25 October The Clemenceau government. Joseph Caillaux to Finance, Picquart to War. Creation of the Ministry of Labour, headed by the independent socialist Viviani. Clemenceau keeps the Interior portfolio.

5 November In a government statement Clemenceau affirms: 'Before philosophizing one must *be!* That is why we intend to maintain our military forces in a fit state to deal with all eventualities, without any hiccups.'

8 November The creation of the Ministry of Labour is approved by the Chamber.

22 November The Chamber and Senate adopt the new rate for parliamentary salaries fixed at 15,000 francs per annum.

7 December The Chamber votes to repurchase the Western Railway Company.

12 December The Separation law comes into force.

1907

7 February Caillaux's plan for income tax.

March The Chambers adopt Flandin's proposal quashing the obligatory notice of public meetings.

8–9 March Strike and demonstration of electricity workers in Paris.

12 March In the port of Toulon a series of explosions destroy the battleship *Iéna*, causing the death of 200 victims.

20 March First big meeting in favour of electoral reform. After the murder of a French doctor, General Lyautey's troops occupy Oujda.

6 April In a letter to the teachers' union Clemenceau states his hostility to civil servants' associations.

7 April The government dismisses the signatories to a notice issuing from the teachers' and postal workers' unions.

23 April The Toulon arsenal is destroyed by a fire.

12 May–9 June Demonstrations by wine-growers in the Midi. In several towns the troops refuse to ensure the maintenance of order.

14 May The Chamber approves Clemenceau's hostility to associations of civil servants.

9 June 700,000 people demonstrate at Montpellier.

16 June Tsar Nicholas II dissolves the Second Douma (legislative assembly).

19 June The demonstrating wine-growers burn the sub-prefecture of Narbonne and the prefecture of Perpignan.

21 June The 17th infantry regiment mutinies and marches on Béziers.

29 June Law suppressing fraud in the wine industry.

July Wilhelm II receives Eugène Étienne, head of the French colonial party.

20 July Resignation of the Generalissimo, General Hagron.

27 July (and 4 August) Elections to the general and *arrondissement* Councils. Success for the radicals and radical socialists.

31 July Massacres of French workers in Casablanca.

August In Nancy, Fourth Congress of the Unified Socialist Party. At the International Socialist Congress in Stuttgart, Jaurès pledges himself to getting a motion carried recommending a struggle against war by all possible means.

7 September Antimilitarist speech by Jaurès in the Tivoli-Vaux-Hall in Paris.

10 October The Radical and Radical Socialist Party Congress in Nancy condemns antipatriotism and antimilitarism, but does not agree to break with the Unified Socialist Party.

November Wilhelm II goes to England.

21 December The Chamber adopts the bill on the devolution of church possessions.

1908

24 January In the Chamber Jaurès calls for the withdrawal of French troops from Morocco.

10 and 24 February The Chamber approves government policy in Morocco.

18 and 20 February The Senate approves government policy in Morocco.

1 March First issue of the daily *Action française*.

10 March Reinstatement of Joseph Reinach as officer of the general staff of the territorial army.

14 March In the Chamber the radical socialist Maurice Berteaux attacks the Clemenceau government.

5 April In response to their workers' demands, lock-out by the building firms in Paris.

7 April The Senate modifies the law on devolution voted for by the Chamber.

13 April Law on devolution of church possessions.

3 and 10 May Municipal elections: victory for the radicals and radical socialists and left-wing republicans.

17 May In a letter to French cardinals, Pius X disapproves of the terms of the law on devolution.

25 May The Chamber votes for a tax on state bonds.

1 June Incidents in the strike of sand quarry miners at Draveil.

26 June The Senate votes to buy back the Western Railways Company.

27 July Meeting of the Tsar and President Fallières at Reval.

30 July Bloody demonstrations at Villeneuve-Saint-Georges.

31 July Arrest of the leaders of the CGT and judicial investigation.

14 September Franco-Spanish note to the Sultan of Morocco, Moulai Hafid.

23 September The German government backs the Franco-Spanish note.

26 September Franco-German incident of Foreign Legion deserters in Casablanca.

7 October The Austro-Hungarian Empire annexes Bosnia and Hercegovina.

10 October At the Dijon Congress the radicals oppose a break with the socialists.

19 October Challenged in the Chamber, Thomson, Minister for the Navy, resigns.

8 December The Chamber votes for the retention of the death penalty.

1909

3 January Senatorial elections. Success for the radical socialists.

11 February Clemenceau wins the confidence of the Chamber against extending the amnesty to dismissed civil servants and those sentenced for antipatriotism.

15 March Postal strike. Troops ensure a replacement service.

21–2 March Clemenceau receives a strikers' delegation.

26 March Resolved to give civil servants a legal status, the Chamber formally excludes the right to strike, by 470 votes to 63.

May Strike of registered sailors.

22 May The judgement of the Hague goes in France's favour in the affair of the Foreign Legion deserters.

28 May   The Chamber refuses an amnesty for the dismissed postal workers.

11 June   The Chamber adopts the plan for the reform of military justice.

15 June   The Senate refuses to extend the amnesty to postal workers dismissed for strike activities.

3 July   End of the registered sailors' strike.

20 July   The Chamber overturns Clemenceau by 212 votes to 196.

24 July   Briand president of the Council and Minister of the Interior. Millerand to Public Works, Post and Telegraph. Law relating to ordnance.

25 July   Louis Blériot crosses the Channel by aeroplane in one and a half hours.

27 July   Government statement: a policy of reforms and progress and, abroad, loyalty to the alliances and friendships contracted.

10 October   In his speech in Périgueux Briand condemns the *arrondissement* ballot.

13 October   The execution in Barcelona of the anarchist Ferrer provokes a riot in Paris.

8 November   On Briand's intervention, the Chamber rejects the principle of proportional representation.

23 November   The Chamber approves France's policy in Morocco by 433 votes to 67.

1910

14 January   Interpellation in the Chamber on scholastic neutrality.

28 January   The Seine floods Paris.

29 March   Increase in customs duties. Law on the new system for the elimination of *congrégations*.

5 April   Law organizing workers' and peasants' pensions (adopted by the Senate on 22 March and the Chamber on 31 March).

8 May   Second round of legislative elections. The radicals and radical socialists lose seventeen seats.

28 June   The new Chamber gives the Briand government a vote of confidence by 404 to 121 votes.

30 June   Briand presents a bill on electoral reform: list ballot, with representation for minorities (proportional representation).

1 July   Interpellation on the Rochette financial scandal and constitution of a parliamentary commission of inquiry.

11–12 October   General strike on the railways; conscription of employees by militarization.

18 October   End of the strike.

29–30 October   Before the Chamber, Briand defends the measures taken to break the railways strike and wins a vote of confidence by a 146 majority.

2 November   Briand overthrows his own government.

3 November   Second Briand government, eliminating the two independent socialists Millerand and Viviani.

10 November   Confidence is voted by a majority of eighty-seven.

1911

17 January   In the Chamber, a madman fires two revolver shots at Briand.

27 February   Having a majority of only sixteen, Briand resigns.

6 March   The Monis radical socialist cabinet obtains a vote of approval by 309 to 114, with 126 abstentions.

11 April   Wine-growers' riots in Champagne. The government imposes military occupation on the entire Marne *département*.

21 May At the takeoff for the Paris–Madrid race, at Issy-les-Moulineaux, Train's aeroplane badly wounds the president of the Council and kills Berteaux, the War Minister. Arrival of the French expeditionary force at Fez.

15 June Bill ending delimitation (wines). Agreement between the wine-growers of the Aube and the Marne.

19 June By declaring to the Senate that there is no generalissimo, General Goiran, the new War Minister, brings about the fall of the Monis cabinet four days later.

22 June The Chamber proves in favour of proportional representation.

27 June Caillaux government.

1 July The German warship *Panther* at Agadir.

28 July Reorganization of the Senior Military Council. General Joffre is appointed chief of the army general staff.

4 November Franco-German Treaty of Berlin on Morocco, the Congo and Cameroon.

28 November The cruiser *Berlin* (replacing the *Panther*) receives the order to return to Germany.

20 December The Chamber ratifies the Franco-German Treaty by 393 votes to 36.

30 December By 312 votes to 140, the Chamber refuses to reinstate striking railway workers.

1912

7 January The senatorial elections call a halt to the progress of the left. The Caillaux–Clemenceau incident concerning secret bargaining for the Franco-German Treaty. Resignation of the Minister of Foreign Affairs, de Selves.

11 January Resignation of the Caillaux government.

13 January Poincaré president of the Council and Minister of Foreign Affairs, Millerand to the War Ministry.

16 and 18 January Two French liners are arrested near Sardinia by an Italian torpedo boat.

10 February The Senate approves the Franco-German Treaty by 212 votes to 42.

30 March Treaty of Fez instituting the French Protectorate in Morocco.

5 and 12 May The municipal elections bring few changes.

14 May Second decree reorganizing the military high command.

22 May Paul Deschanel replaces Brisson (who died on 14 April) as president of the Chamber.

9 June New strike of merchant navy crews (until 23 August).

1 July The Chamber ratifies the French Protectorate Treaty for Morocco.

10 July The Chamber adopts the government electoral reform bill ensuring the representation of minorities by 339 votes to 217.

11 July Opponents of electoral reform, Clemenceau and Combes found the Committee for the Defence of Universal Suffrage. The Senate ratifies the French Protectorate of Morocco Treaty.

15 August At Chambéry the congress of teachers' trade unions declares its solidarity with the CGT and approves the 'Soldier's Sou' created by the trades union centres.

15 October Treaty of Lausanne between Italy and Turkey.

27 October In his speech at Nantes, Poincaré evinces concern over the state of the Balkan peninsula.

4 November Renewal of the *Triplice*.

22 November Franco-British agreement on the strengthening of the *Entente Cordiale*.

3 December   Armistice between Turkey and the Balkan belligerents.

1913

In the Champs Élysées Theatre, *The Rite of Spring* causes uproar.

13 January   Resignation of Millerand (the affair of the reinstatement of du Paty de Clam).

15 January   Encouraged by Clemenceau and Combes, the radical socialist groups in the Chamber and Senate oppose Poincaré's candidacy for the presidency of the Republic.

17 January   Raymond Poincaré is elected President of the Republic by 483 votes out of 870. He takes up office on 18 February.

21 January   Third Briand government.

February   Hostilities resume between Turkey and the Balkan belligerents.

6 March   Bill re-establishing three-year military service.

7 March   The Chamber finally approves the Franco-Spanish Treaty on Morocco.

18 March   By a thirty-three vote majority the Senate turns down electoral reform and overturns the Briand government.

22 March   Barthou's cabinet.

29 March   The Senate approves the Franco-Spanish Treaty.

15 May   The Chamber approves by 322 votes to 155 the maintenance of a dischargeable class under military service. Riots by soldiers in Toul and Rodez.

30 May   End of the first Balkan war.

10 June   The Senate adopts an electoral reform: small list ballot without representation for minorities.

19 June   The Chamber's Commission on universal suffrage rejects the Senate's proposal.

20 June   The Chamber rejects Jaurès's counterproposal to the three years' service, putting forward notably a system of militias.

11 July   The Chamber rebukes the soldiers' demonstrations.

14 July   Law on assistance to families with many children.

30 July   Law on rest for women in childbirth. Law on the secrecy and freedom of the vote (creation of polling booths).

9 August   The three years' service law (adopted in the Chamber on 19 July and in the Senate on 7 August).

10 August   The Treaty of Bucharest puts an end to the second Balkan war.

September   In Saverne (Alsace) serious incidents between a German officer and the Alsatian population and soldiery increase Franco-German tension.

16–18 October   At the Paris Congress, the Radical Socialist Party is unified.

18 November   The Chamber again votes for its electoral reform plan in opposition to the Senate's, by 333 votes to 225.

2 December   The Chamber overthrows the Barthou government on the fiscal immunity of French state bonds.

9 December   Doumergue forms a government of radical socialist tendency and takes the Foreign Affairs portfolio. Caillaux goes to Finance.

1914

13 January   Constitutive meeting of Briand and Barthou's Left-wing Federation.

3 February   Amid 100,000 people, Briand, Barthou and J. Reinach attend Déroulède's funeral.

25 February   The Senate turns down Perchot's amendment (income tax).

13 March   The Senate rejects a tax on state bonds. Attacks on Caillaux in *Le Figaro*.

17 March   Mme Caillaux murders Calmette, *Le Figaro*'s editor. Caillaux resigns.

18 March   Delahaye challenges on the Rochette affair. The Chamber decides to reopen the inquiry. Monis resigns from the Naval Ministry.

2 April   The Chamber reproves the improper intervention of finance in politics and of politics in justice (Rochette affair).

10 May   Socialist success after the second round of legislative elections. Re-election of Caillaux.

12 June   Formed on 9 June, Ribot's cabinet is overturned.

13 June   Viviani government.

16 June   Interpellation by Jaurès on the three-year law.

20 June   Law authorizing the National Defence loan (805 million; 3.5 per cent).

28 June   The Sarajevo assassination.

July   In Paris Jaurès gets the special congress of the Unified Socialist Party to agree to a general strike as a means against war.

3 July   The Senate adopts the institution of general income tax by 230 votes to 54.

20–9 July   Trial of Mme Caillaux before the Seine jury; she is acquitted.

31 July   Jaurès is assassinated by Villain in Paris. German ultimatum to France.

1 August   General mobilization in France. President Poincaré's call to the French nation. Germany declares war on Russia.

3 August   Germany declares war on France.

4 August   At Jaurès's funeral, L. Jouhaux gives the CGT's backing to National Defence. Funeral eulogy in the Chamber. The Chamber and Senate vote for war supplies and adjourn *sine die*. The violation of Belgian neutrality puts Britain in a state of war with Germany.

5 August   Law on censorship.

8 and 14 August   The two offensives in Alsace.

19–23 August   Frontier battle.

25 August   Victory of the Charmes breakthrough.

26 August   Viviani's 'sacred union' government. The unified socialists J. Guesde and M. Sembat enter the government. Briand is vice-president of the Council, Malvy to the Interior, Delcassé to Foreign Affairs, Millerand to War, Ribot to Finance and Sarraut to Public Education.

26–9 August   The Germans beat the Russians at Tannenberg.

29–30 August   Battle of Guise.

2–3 September   The government and parliament leave Paris for Bordeaux.

4 September   In London, Britain, France and Russia engage not to conclude a separate peace.

4–12 September   Battle of the Grand-Couronné at Nancy.

5 September   Joffre's order of the day: 'this is not the time to look back . . . attack and make the enemy retreat . . . get killed on the spot rather than withdraw.'

6–12 September   Battle of the Marne.

13 September   Issue of National Defence bonds.

15 September–15 November   The race to the sea and the Battle of Flanders.

October   Poincaré and Millerand go to Paris and visit the fronts.

29 October   Britain decides on a blockade of Germany.

November   The government ministries return to Paris.

3 November   France and Britain declare war on Turkey.

10 December   President Poincaré returns to the Élysée.

22 December   The Chamber and Senate meet in Paris. Government statement: 'the imperishable union of parliament, the nation and the army'.

1915

1 January   End of the moratorium on bank deposits.

13 February   Issue of National Defence bonds (ten years, 5 per cent tax-free).

16 February–10 March   First French offensive in Champagne.

18 March   Failure of the Franco-British attempt to force the Dardanelles.

26 March   The Senate adopts the proposal for a law instituting the *Croix de guerre* decoration (voted in the Chamber on 4 February).

25 April   Franco-British landing at Gallipoli.

26 April   Secret treaty in London: the Allies promise Italy Trentino and Istria.

7 May   The torpedoing of the liner *Lusitania* by a German submarine causes 1,447 deaths.

9 May–16 June   First French offensive in Artois. Battle of Arras.

23 May   Italy enters the war against Austria-Hungary.

2 July   Beginning of the campaign calling on the public to hand in their gold coins (in return for banknotes).

14 July   Transfer of the remains of Rouget de Lisle to the Invalides.

14–15 July   The national council of the Unified Socialist Party declares itself for continuing the war until the victory of the Allies and the ruin of German militarist imperialism.

4 August   Agreement between the Chamber and the president of the Council defining parliamentary control over National Defence: 'temporary missions' and 'with a specific intent'.

5 August   General Sarrail is appointed chief of the Eastern army.

21 August   In the Chamber Millerand replies to the criticisms of socialists and radical socialists: the freedom of action of the Generalissimo is exercised under the authority and control of the government.

25 September   Second French offensive in Champagne and Artois.

6 October   French troops land at Salonika.

17 October   France declares war on Bulgaria.

29 October   Briand is president of the Council and Minister of Foreign Affairs. Gallieni is War Minister, and A. Thomas Under-Secretary of State for Munitions.

12 November   The Chamber unanimously adopts the issue of the first war loan in 5 per cent permanent bonds.

14 November   Clemenceau in *L'Homme enchaîné*: 'We must give money so that our men may have the right to spill their blood.'

2 December   Decree appointing Joffre as commander-in-chief of the French armies (North-eastern and Eastern).

1916

16 January   Sarrail is commander-in-chief of the Franco-British troops in Salonika.

29 January   Zeppelin raid on Paris.

21 February   Start of the German offensive at Verdun (artillery).

25–6 February   Loss of the fort at Douaumont. Pétain is given overall command at Verdun.

16 March   Resignation of Gallieni through illness, replaced by General Roques (on 17th).

9 April Failure of a German attempt at a general offensive on the whole front at Verdun.

22 April The Chamber votes for the law on rents by 308 votes to 5, with 141 abstentions.

May Passing to the command of the group of armies of the Centre, Pétain yields command of the Verdun army to Nivelle.

26 May Death of Gallieni.

31 May Battle of Jutland.

7 June Fall of the Vaux fort.

16–22 June First secret committee of the Chamber (German attack on Verdun). Replying to a radical deputy Briand declares: 'The government is running the war, the command is carrying it out, in full independence, under the supervision of the government . . . responsible to you . . .'

23 June German offensive at Thiaumont and Souville.

1 July Franco-British offensive on the Somme.

9 July First secret committee of the Senate (Verdun and the Balkans).

28 July After modification, the Senate unanimously adopts the law on rents.

5–25 October Second National Defence loan (5 per cent).

24 October Recapture of Douaumont.

2 November Recapture of the Vaux fort.

21 November Second secret committee of the Chamber (registration for service of the 1918 class).

28 November–7 December Third secret committee of the Chamber (eastern affairs, Joffre's high command and situation). The government gets a vote of confidence by 344 (– 100) to 160.

12 December Reshuffle of Briand's cabinet. Lyautey to War. Thomas to Armaments and War Production. Creation of a War Committee (Briand, Ribot, Lyautey, Lacaze, Thomas).

13 December Briand rejects German offers of peace made on the 12th and gets a vote of confidence for vigorously pursuing the conduct of the war (314 votes).

17 December Nivelle is appointed commander-in-chief of the armies of the North and East.

19–23 December Second secret committee of the Senate (peace proposals made by the central powers).

26 December Joffre is promoted to marshal.

1917

25–7 January Fourth secret committee of the Chamber (foreign and military policy in Macedonia and Greece).

1 February Germany resumes submarine war to excess.

14 March Fifth secret committee of the Chamber (military aviation) provokes the resignation of Lyautey, and of Briand (17th).

15 March Abdication of Tsar Nicholas II. Russia becomes a republic.

17 March Start of the German withdrawal to the Hindenburg line.

20 March Fourth Ribot government. Painlevé to War (unanimous confidence of the Chamber on 21st).

3 April The United States enters the war.

16–21 April Failure of the Chemin des Dames offensive.

28 April Pétain is chief of the army general staff.

May   Strike movements.

15 May   Pétain commander-in-chief. Foch chief of the army general staff.

20 May   Beginning of mutinies.

1–4 June   Sixth secret committee of the Chamber (Russian Revolution and international socialist congress in Stockholm). The government refuses to allow socialist deputies passports to attend the Stockholm conference.

6 June   Third secret committee of the Senate (Stockholm socialist congress). Unanimous confidence.

13 June   General Pershing arrives in Paris.

29 June–7 July   Seventh secret committee of the Chamber (responsibilities for the offensives of March and April).

19–21 July   Fourth secret committee of the Senate (failure of the April offensive).

22 July   Public sitting of the Senate. Clemenceau reproaches Malvy (Minister of the Interior) for 'betraying France's interests' (with regard to pacifists and antipatriots).

31 July   Voted for in the Chamber on the 18th by 462 to 1, then by the Senate, income tax is finally adopted.

20 August   Victory of the Mort Homme.

31 August   The Almereyda affair brings about Malvy's resignation.

7 September   Collective resignation of Ribot's cabinet.

13 September   Painlevé is president of the Council and War Minister. The socialists refuse to participate.

16 October   Eighth secret committee of the Chamber (relations between Briand and Baron Lancken, the German governor of occupied Belgium).

23 October   Barthou replaces Ribot in Foreign Affairs.

23–6 October   Victory of Malmaison.

6 November   The Bolsheviks take power in Russia.

13 November   The Chamber overturns the Painlevé government.

17 November   Clemenceau is president of the Council and War Minister.

20 November   Government statement: 'The war will be conducted with redoubled efforts.' Confidence is voted by 418 to 65, the socialists refusing to vote.

26 November–16 December   Third National Defence loan (4 per cent).

15 December   Armistice of Brest-Litovsk between the Bolsheviks and the central empires.

22 December   By 306 votes to 2 and 115 abstentions, the Chamber votes to lift parliamentary immunity from Loustalot and Caillaux (the Bolo affair and defeatist conversations in Rome). The Senate votes unanimously for the law on war damages.

24 December   The Chamber votes for the bill postponing all elections until the cessation of hostilities.

27 December   In the Chamber, discussion on policy with regard to Russia. The government refuses to enter into official relations with Petrograd.

1918

8 January   The fourteen points of President Wilson.

11 January   Clemenceau's government obtains a vote of confidence by 377 to 113.

14 January   Arrest of Caillaux (the 'Rubicon' affair).

18 January   Clemenceau tells the Chamber: 'We are determined to prosecute all antirepublican manoeuvres.'

28 January   Meeting in High Court, the Senate decides to investigate the Malvy affair.

14 February   The Third Council of War in Paris sentences Bolo to death for having secret dealings with the enemy.

21 February   The Chamber's final vote for the law on rents.

8 March   Socialist attacks on Clemenceau, who retaliates and wins confidence by 374 votes to 41. Bombardment of Paris by German long-range cannon.

21 March–7 July   The five great German offensives.

26 March   The Doullens conference gives Foch the task of co-ordinating the action of the allied armies on the Western front.

14 April   Foch is commander-in-chief of the allied armies.

15 May   The Third Council of War in Paris passes the death sentence on Duval (editor of the defeatist newspaper *Le Bonnet rouge*, subsidized by Germany).

30 May   The Germans reach the Marne.

6 June   Paris is put back into the army zone.

18 July–4 August   The second Battle of the Marne marks the beginning of the Allies' victorious offensive.

6 August   Foch is made a Marshal of France.

8 August   The High Court sentences Malvy to five years' banishment for abuse of authority.

12 September   American offensive of Saint-Mihiel.

15–30 September   Victorious offensive of Franchet d'Esperey in Macedonia.

17 September   In the Senate, Clemenceau's speech: 'Civilians and soldiers, governments and assemblies of the Entente, all had a duty to perform. They will continue until that duty is accomplished. All are worthy of victory, because they will honour it.'

25 September   Artillery major at Verdun and the Chemin des Dames (20th Artillery Company), Dreyfus is made lieutenant-colonel and an officer of the Légion d'honneur.

6 October   Germany asks President Wilson for an armistice.

10 October   In Paris, Socialist Party Congress. The leaders are overthrown by minority members in favour of the Russian Revolution.

17 October   Recapture of Lille and Douai.

20 October   The Belgians liberate Bruges.

20 October–25 November   Fourth National Defence loan (4 per cent).

4 November   The heads of the allied governments approve the armistice terms drawn up by Foch and the leaders of the allied armies on 25 October.

7 November   By acclamation the Senate adopts the proposal declaring that the armies and their leaders, the government, Clemenceau and Foch have deserved well of their country.

8 November   Germany capitulates.

9 November   Wilhelm II relinquishes power.

11 November   The Rethondes armistice is signed at 5 a.m.

15 November   Decree appointing three Commissaires of the Republic for Alsace-Lorraine.

17 November   Hirschauer enters Mulhouse.

19 November   Pétain enters Metz and is made a Marshal of France.

22 and 25 November   Entry of troops into Colmar, Strasbourg and Brussels.

7–8 December   Government and parliament trip to Strasbourg and Metz.

11 December   The Americans enter Koblenz, the French enter Mainz and the English enter Cologne.

13 December   President Wilson's arrival in Paris.

29–30 December   In the Chamber, debate on the Allies' foreign policy and relations with Russia.

1919

18 January   Opening of the peace conference at the Quai d'Orsay.

19 February   The anarchist Cottin wounds Clemenceau with a revolver shot.

6 April   100,000 demonstrators against the acquittal of Villain, Jaurès's killer (29 March).

19–21 April   Incidents on French ships in the Black Sea.

23 April   Adoption of the law on an eight-hour working day.

1 May   General strike. Incidents in Paris.

28 June   Treaty of Versailles.

8 July   The Chamber retains censorship.

14 July   Victory parade.

22 July   Clemenceau wins the confidence of the Chamber.

10 September   Treaty of Saint-Germain with Austria.

26 September   Clemenceau: 'The Treaty is a bloc.'

1 October   The Chamber discusses the status of Alsace-Lorraine.

2 and 12 October   The peace treaty and treaty of alliance with the United States and Great Britain are ratified by the Chamber and the Senate.

3 November   Clemenceau in Strasbourg: 'National union' and 'the threat of Bolshevism.'

7 November   In Paris, Millerand's programme-speech: union, work, solidarity, economic liberalism, religious pacification, increase in the powers of the Head of State.

16 November   Legislative elections: the republican National Bloc obtains two-thirds of the seats.

1920

16 January   Clemenceau informs L. Bourgeois of his definitive withdrawal from the political scene.

17 January   P. Deschanel is elected President of the Republic (734 votes out of 868). He takes up office on 18 February.

20 January   Millerand is president of the Council and Minister of Foreign Affairs.

10 and 12 February   The Chambers vote on Barthou's bill: 'President Poincaré has deserved well of the country.'

25–9 February   Strasbourg Socialist Congress: abandonment of the Second Internationale.

28 February–2 March   Railway strike.

7–10 March–25 May   General strike of miners in the Pas-de-Calais and the Nord.

19 March   The American Senate rejects the Treaty of Versailles.

5 April–17 May   In response to the penetration of German troops into the demilitarized zone of the Ruhr, French troops occupy German towns. Lloyd George disagrees.

23 April   The High Court sentences Caillaux for 'secret dealings with the enemy'.

15 May   Meeting of Lloyd George and Millerand in Hythe on the disarmament of Germany and reparations.

24 May   P. Deschanel evinces the first signs of mental derangement.

4 June Treaty of Trianon with Hungary.

6–17 July Spa Conference (Allies and German delegation) on German disarmament, compensation and 'the coal arrangement'.

30–1 July The Chamber and the Senate approve the Spa inter-allied protocol.

11 August Millerand recognizes the government of the anti-Bolshevik General Wrangel (Poland).

5 September Franco-Belgian military agreements.

21 September The Chambers accept P. Deschanel's resignation.

24 September Election of A. Millerand to the presidency of the Republic (695 votes out of 786).

25 September Leygues renews the Millerand cabinet and obtains a vote of confidence.

20 October New loan (28 billion, not redeemable).

11 November Celebration of the Republic's fiftieth anniversary. Placing of the unknown soldier under the Arc de Triomphe and transfer of Gambetta's heart to the Panthéon.

30 November The Chamber re-establishes the funds for the embassy to the Vatican by 397 votes to 209.

20–6 December At the Congress of Tours, split of the Socialist Party (birth of the Communist Party).

1921

24–9 January Paris Conference. Briand accepts the British principle of fixing the amount of reparations in proportion to Germany's ability to pay. Guarantee against Bolshevism (Lloyd George), the 400,000 paramilitary civil guards are a threat to France (Briand).

1 February Germany refuses to hold discussions on the bases established in Paris.

27 February–3 March The London Conference strengthens the Franco-British *Entente*. Lloyd George's reprimand to the German delegation.

8 March The allied troops occupy Duisburg, Ruhrort and Dusseldorf.

27 April Lloyd George has the intention of associating with France to extend coercive measures in the Ruhr.

30 April The amount of damages imputed to Germany by the Reparations Commission (CDR) is estimated at 132 billion gold marks; France agrees to a new cut in its claim.

5 May The 'state of payments' established by the CDR reduces 'in actual value' the sums owed by Germany to 75 billion.

11 May Berlin accepts the Allies' decisions.

16 May Jonnart is Ambassador to the Vatican, Mgr Cerretti the Nuncio to Paris.

7 June The Chamber ratifies the Treaties of Trianon and Saint-Germain (constitutive acts of the new central Europe).

July CGT Congress in Lille: split between majority and minority members.

20 October Peace of Angora between France and Mustapha Kemal.

29 October Start of the Washington Conference on disarmament and the Far East.

8 December Briand in the Senate: 'The re-establishment of the embassy to the Vatican is in keeping with republican tradition' (approved on the 16th by 169 votes to 123).

13 December Treaty of the four powers (Washington): status quo in the Pacific.

26 December Creation of the CGTU.

1922

6–12 January Economic and financial conference in Cannes (France, Britain, Italy, Belgium, Japan and American observers). Millerand intends to supervise negotiations.

12 January 'Others will do better than I.' To the surprise of the Chamber, Briand withdraws.

15 January Poincaré is president of the Council and Minister of Foreign Affairs.

6 February Treaty of the five powers on the limitation of naval armament (Washington).

21 March The CDR grants Germany a moratorium.

10 April Genoa Conference. Negotiations with the Russians over debts and confiscated possessions. Favourable view on an international loan intended to refloat the German economy.

16 April Treaty of Rapallo: Germany and Soviet Russia mutually renounce war debts and reparations.

15 May German–Polish agreement on Upper Silesia.

16 June–20 July Hague Conference: unity of the Europeans in the face of the Soviets.

25 June–1 July First CGTU Congress at Saint-Etienne.

8 July Vote for the law of amnesty for all military delinquents, with the exception of deserters.

12 July Berlin asks for a reduction in coal deliveries and a two-year moratorium to which Lloyd George is favourable.

1 August The 'Balfour' note to Great Britain's European debtors. Poincaré gives Germany an ultimatum.

3 August As Germany declares its inability to pay, reprisals are taken against German private interests in France.

7–14 August London Conference. Disagreement between Britain and France; the latter resumes its freedom of action.

1 September Replying to the 'Balfour' note, Poincaré points out the difference between the inter-allied debts and those of Germany.

20 October Reynaud advises a Franco-German economic *entente*. For Poincaré the best solution remains an international loan to Germany, if not, France will return to seizing securities.

9–11 December At the London Conference, rejection of a German request for a four-year moratorium (14 November).

30 December Clemenceau in the *Petit Parisien*: 'I am against the occupation of the Ruhr.'

1923

2–4 January Paris Conference: Franco-British split.

11 January Under the protection of French and Belgian troops, the International Mission to oversee mines and factories (French, Belgian and Italian engineers) is installed at Essen (Ruhr).

15 January The German government organizes 'passive resistance'.

22 January General strike in the Ruhr; the Reichstag votes funds to help the strikers. Occupation is extended to the whole basin. The anarchist Germaine Berton assassinates Marius Plateau, general secretary of the League of French Action and the Camelots du Roi.

February   Customs cordon around the Ruhr.

12 March   After the killing of two French soldiers, 15,000 men go into the Ruhr.

31 March   In the Krupp factories, serious incidents over a requisition. Krupp is put in prison.

1 April   Law on eighteen months' service.

21 April   Lord Curzon (Foreign Office): 'Germany has only to take the first step for the Ruhr conflict to be settled.'

May   At the Hamburg Congress, with Blum's impetus, birth of the Workers' Socialist Internationale (headquarters in London).

2 May   Germany demands the evacuation of the Ruhr. Protest in Paris and Brussels.

3 May   Bérard's decree on the reform of secondary education, strengthening the humanities.

22 May   Poincaré: 'We entered the Ruhr in order to get payment.' Criticism by Herriot. Vote for funds by 481 to 73.

24 May   The Senate (High Court) declares that it is not competent to give a ruling on the fate of the Communist leaders arrested on the eve of entry into the Ruhr.

25 May   Millerand refuses to accept the resignation of Poincaré's government.

26 June   Pius XI condemns the Ruhr occupation.

27 June   Protests by Herriot and Poincaré. Blum sees the Pope as an 'august accomplice' of the SFIO.

14 July   Amnesty measures. The freeing of Marty (an officer who rebelled in the Black Sea in 1919) is greeted as a victory for the left (Communists and radicals).

20 August   Lord Curzon having taken Germany's side over the occupation of the Ruhr, Poincaré shifts the responsibility for the European economic crisis to German industrialists.

24 September   In Düsseldorf, French troops protect a congress of Rhineland autonomists. *L'Humanité* and *Le Populaire* support German nationalists.

14 October   The 'Évreux Bombshell': Millerand defends the National Bloc.

24 October   Germany is ready to resume coal deliveries.

26–7 October   Poincaré is ready to engage in talks and accepts the plan for a meeting of experts to settle Germany's capacity for payment.

8 November   In Munich, Hitler proclaims himself head of a provisional national government.

30 November   Abandonment of the *gage productif* ('lucrative pawn' in the game, that is, the Ruhr mining basin): Poincaré agrees to the reform of German finances and the Dawes Committee limiting reparations.

31 December   In the space of a year, the franc has lost more than 50 per cent of its value.

1924

3 January   The publication of the balance sheet of the Banque de France provokes a new lowering of the franc.

14 January   Exchange reaches record rates.

18 January   The encyclical *Maximam gravissimamque* approves diocesan associations.

8 February   Granting full powers to Poincaré, the Chamber adopts the statutory orders for making savings in the economy.

12 February   Twenty-seven Rhineland separatists are massacred at Pirmasens (non-intervention of French soldiers).

23 February   The Chamber votes for the 'double tenth' (20 per cent increase on all taxes).

9 March   'Historic meeting at the Élysée'. Lasteyrie, Minister of Finance, summons all the directors of the Banque de France. Millerand supports all his demands.

22 March   Adopted by the Senate (forty-four vote majority), the finance law is promulgated.

29 March   Resigning on the 26th (seven vote minority on pensions), Poincaré forms a new cabinet.

12 April   Adoption of the law on civil and military pensions.

23 April   The dollar and franc reach their lowest rate. France rebuilds its exchange reserves.

11 May   Legislative elections. The Left-wing Cartel obtains 327 seats (104 SFIO, 44 socialist republicans (Briand), 139 radical socialists, 40 radical left).

31 May   Resignation of Poincaré's government.

10 June   The Chamber refuses to enter into relations with the François-Marsal cabinet formed the previous day.

11 June   Having refused to accept the government's resignation, President Millerand resigns.

13 June   G. Doumergue is elected President of the Republic by 515 votes against 309 for Painlevé.

15 June   Radical government. Herriot president of the Council and Minister of Foreign Affairs.

1 September   The Dawes plan comes into force.

28 September   The assembly of the League of Nations adopts the Geneva protocol (arbitration, security, disarmament).

28 October   France recognizes the USSR.

November   Amnesty for Caillaux and Malvy.

2 November   National Council of the Socialist Party: refusal to support a majority and conditional backing for the radical government.

23 November   Transfer of Jaurès's remains to the Panthéon.

29 November   Sarrail replaces Weygand as the Republic's High Commissioner in Syria and Lebanon.

1925

7–14 January   Paris conference on the inter-allied debts.

11 January   The National Republican League (Millerand) launches a propaganda campaign against the Cartel.

28 January   Herriot gathers a National Union majority on security and launches an appeal in favour of a United States of Europe.

February   The Catholic leagues (1,800,000 members) unite in a Catholic National Federation.

2 February   The Chamber votes to cancel funds for the embassy to the Vatican.

11 March   The manifesto of the cardinals and archbishops of France again calls into question the principle of state secularism.

12 March   Herriot sets his religious policy against the ultramontanism of the majority of the Catholic clergy.

8 April   Herriot gets approval by only 290 votes to 246.

10 April   In the Senate, François-Marsal and Poincaré overthrow Herriot.

17 April   Painlevé president of the Council and War Minister. Briand to Foreign Affairs. Caillaux to Finance.

12 July Break-up of the Cartel: a changed majority (with centre and right-wing votes) votes for a tax on business turnover (Caillaux plan).

16 October Pact of Locarno: Great Britain and Italy guarantee Belgium and Germany the maintenance of their frontiers (Treaty of Versailles) and the observance of the clauses stipulating the demilitarization of German territories on the left bank of the Rhine.

17 October Hostility of Herriot to Caillaux's financial rehabilitation plan.

27 October In order to get rid of Caillaux, Painlevé makes the cabinet resign.

29 October Painlevé president of the Council and at the Treasury.

30 October Sarrail is relieved of his office.

22 November The radical left breaks up the Cartel and provokes the fall of Painlevé's government.

3 December The Chamber votes for the financial plan by a majority of twenty-eight: Briand's eighth government is very fragile.

1926

10 January Socialist Congress of Belleville: support without participation.

27 January–16 February In the Chamber, discussion on the plan for 'financial rehabilitation' confirms the rupture of the Cartellist majority.

31 January Having obtained complete evacuation of the Ruhr basin, Stresemann gets it for the Cologne zone as well.

February The Senate rejects the Cartel's fiscal innovations.

6 March In a shared hostility to taxation on all trading operations, 131 votes of the former Cartel and the right bring down the Briand government.

18 March Briand's 'concentrated left-wing' government (Malvy to the Interior) receives a Cartel majority.

4 April Finance law, including taxation on turnover.

9 April Resignation of Malvy.

25 April Poincaré: 'The moral obligation of each of the allied nations to help France obtain damage reparation'.

29 April Washington agreement on war debts.

18 May Speculation against the franc brings the pound to a record rate of 178 francs.

25 May Socialist Party Congress in Clermont-Ferrand: against participation in the government.

26 May Abd-el-Krim submits (Rif).

2 June Exclusively preoccupied by putting the franc to rights, the government chooses a policy of financial confidence, disapproved by the Cartel.

15 June The resignation of the Minister of Finance brings about that of the cabinet.

20 June After trying to effect a left-wing republican union during a 'mad night', Herriot gives up forming a government.

24 June Tenth Briand government. Caillaux dismisses Robineau, governor of the Banque de France.

12 July Caillaux–Churchill agreement reducing French debts to Great Britain by 63 per cent.

16 July The drop in the franc leads Caillaux to demand full powers.

17 July Herriot overturns the Briand–Caillaux cabinet.

21 July Formed the previous day, Herriot's second government is overthrown (fifty-three votes).

27 July Poincaré's 'great ministry' of National Union obtains confidence and is urged to proceed immediately with its financial plans.

6 August The Chamber votes for Queuille's bill creating a Bread-making Cereals Bureau.

9 and 13 August Decrees on administrative reform (savings and rationalization in the administration).

10 August The National Assembly adopts the constitutional law creating the autonomous sinking fund.

8 September Germany enters the League of Nations.

17 September Talks between Stresemann and Briand at Thoiry. Reluctance of Poincaré.

20 December Stabilization: the purchase of foreign currency prevents an excessive rise in the franc and keeps the pound at about 120 francs.

1927

8 March Auriol attacks Poincaré over the debt to the United States (Washington agreements). The Chamber accepts the provisional agreements on war debts to Britain (£6,000,000).

22 April Confronted with Communist agitation in the army and the colonies, Sarraut declares in Constantine: 'Communism – that is the enemy!'

12 July By 320 votes to 234, the Chamber votes for electoral reform: a return to a single-name, *arrondissement* ballot in two rounds.

27–30 October Radical Congress: rejection of the National Union for elections (Daladier).

26 December Socialist Congress: criticism of financial policy, hostility to Communist principles, withdrawal at the second round in favour of the radicals.

1928

19 January The Chamber votes for one-year military service by 410 votes to 23 (Communists): socialists abstain.

February The Senate rejects the bill on the organization of the country in time of war.

22 February The Chamber adopts the raising of import duties on various agricultural products.

22 and 29 April Legislative elections; victory for the National Union.

14 June Division of the radicals at the legislature's first vote.

25 June The monetary law defines the 'Poincaré franc': 65.5 mg of gold, with a purity of 900 per 1,000. The gold standard replaces bimetallism.

7 July Loucheur's law on cheap housing.

27 August At the Quai d'Orsay Germany and the Allies sign the Briand–Kellogg pact renouncing war.

14 September Creation of the Air Ministry.

4 November Radical Socialist Congress in Angers: break-up of the National Union (articles 70 and 71 of the finance law threaten secularism). Resignation of the radical ministers.

6 November Resignation of Poincaré's cabinet.

8 November The Chamber votes for the removal from office of two autonomist deputies for the Upper Rhine.

11 November Fifth Poincaré government (minus the radicals).

14 December The scandal of the 'Gazette du franc' leads the Chamber to vote for an act restricting the extra-parliamentary activities of deputies.

1929

11 January Poincaré obtains a vote of confidence by 325 to 251.

24 January–7 February In the Chamber, debate on the Alsatian problem.

31 May In Paris, signing of the Young plan for German reparations (37 million gold marks). Commercialization of the German debt.

20 July In the Chamber, ratification with reservations of the agreements on inter-allied debts (eight votes).

26 July The Senate ratifies with no reservations the London and Washington agreements.

27 July Ill, Poincaré resigns.

29 July Eleventh Briand government brings back the Poincaré cabinet.

August Conference at the Hague on reparations and the early evacuation of the Rhineland.

5 September At the League of Nations, Briand puts forward a proposal for a United States of Europe.

22 October The Chamber overthrows the Briand government for its foreign policy (ten votes).

2 November Tardieu's moderate government. Briand to Foreign Affairs. Maginot to War.

7 November For his 'policy for prosperity' Tardieu obtains confidence by 332 votes to 253.

1930

3–20 January Second Hague conference (the application of the Young plan).

21 January London conference on naval disarmament.

17 February The intransigence of Chéron (Minister of Finance) brings about the fall of the cabinet (five votes).

2 March Second Tardieu government, without the radicals. Paul Reynaud to Finance.

24 April Adoption of the correction to the law on social insurance (March 1928).

25 April Naval Treaty of London (United States, Britain, France, Japan and Italy).

30 June French troops evacuate the third Rhineland zone (Mainz) five years ahead of time.

1–22 August Strike in the metal and textile industries of the Nord. Violent incidents.

4 December In the Senate, the Oustric financial scandal causes Tardieu's fall (eight votes).

19 December Formed on the 13th, Steeg's government just manages to obtain confidence (seven votes).

1931

22 January Speculation on corn brings about the fall of the government (ten votes).

27 January Laval government, supported by the former Tardieu majority.

3 and 5 March The Chambers approve Briand's foreign policy.

19 March Protocol of Austro-German economic agreement.

8 May Herriot in the Chamber: 'The *Anschluss* is inadmissible.'

13 May Presidential election. First round: Doumer – 442 votes; Briand – 401. Second round: Doumer obtains 504 votes out of 874 (Briand 12).

18 May Germany accepts the postponement of the application of the agreement of 19 March.

5 June Germany can no longer pay reparations.

20 June The Hoover moratorium: adjournment for a year of payment of all inter-governmental war debts.

4 December To halt unemployment, the Chamber votes unanimously for the bill on national equipment.

1932

12 January The death of Maginot and Briand's state of health bring about the resignation of the government.

14 January Third ministry of Laval, who replaces Briand in Foreign Affairs. The radicals refuse to participate.

23 January Laval obtains only a frail majority.

16 February Hostile to the single-name one-round ballot (voted for by the Chamber on the 12th) the Senate overturns the government (twenty-three votes).

23 February Formed on the 20th, the third Tardieu government obtains a majority of forty-seven votes.

6 April Opening of the electoral campaign. In the Bullier Hall Tardieu makes a vain appeal to the radicals.

10 April Blum at Narbonne: 'Change the majority'; proposal of alliance with the radicals.

5 May First broadcast address by a president of the Council (Tardieu).

6 May At the Rothschild Foundation, Paul Doumer is assassinated by Gorguloff.

8 May Second round of legislative elections. The left has 356 seats.

10 May The president of the Senate, Albert Lebrun, is elected President of the Republic (633 votes out of 826).

7 June Formed on the 3rd, Herriot's radical socialist government obtains confidence.

9 July The final act of the Lausanne conference annuls reparations.

23 July Disarmament conference in Geneva: general arms limitation (rejection by Germany and the USSR).

26 November The Council of Ministers approves the nonaggression pact with the USSR.

14 December The Chamber refuses to pay the debt to the United States and overturns the Herriot government.

18 December Paul-Boncour government (left orientated). Refusal of the socialists to participate.

22 December Paul-Boncour obtains confidence by 379 votes (including socialists) to 166.

1933

28 January By 401 votes to 171, Paul-Boncour's cabinet is brought down over its plans for budgetary rehabilitation.

30 January Hitler becomes Chancellor.

31 January Daladier's radical socialist government. Paul-Boncour to Foreign Affairs. The president of the Council to the War Ministry.

5 March   Hitler abolishes the Weimar Constitution.

31 May   The finance law institutes the national lottery.

7 June   Four-power pact (France, Britain, Germany, Italy).

12–18 July   London international economic conference.

October   Radical Congress in Vichy. The need to act according to the demands of the moment prevails over left-wing union.

14 October   Germany quits the disarmament conference.

16 October   Germany quits the League of Nations.

18 October   The socialists oppose a levy on civil servants' salaries (article 37) and refuse to negotiate with the radicals.

24 October   The Daladier government falls because of article 37, by 329 votes to 241 (including 28 Renaudel socialists).

26 October   Sarraut's radical cabinet.

5 November   National Congress of the SFIO Party. Excluded, the Renaudel tendency creates the Socialist Party of France.

12 November   Hitler's policy gets a 95 per cent plebiscite.

23 November   By 321 votes to 247, Sarraut's government falls over the article relating to civil servants' salaries.

26 November   Chautemps's radical cabinet.

12 December   The Chamber adopts the financial plan by 280 votes to 175.

18 December   Memorandum from Germany to France: army of 30,000 men and ten-year pact of nonaggression.

1934

January   Stavisky financial scandal. Demonstrations by Action française in Paris.

27 January   Resignation of the Chautemps cabinet.

30 January   Second Daladier government, radical widened towards the centre.

3 February   Changes in high officials (including the Prefect of Police, Chiappe). Paul-Boncour agrees to replace Fabry, the resigning War Minister.

6 February   Uproar in the Chamber. In Paris, violent antiparliamentary demonstrations (twenty-nine dead) and resignation of the cabinet (on the 7th).

9 February   Communist demonstrations in Paris (four dead). Doumergue forms a 'National Union' government.

12 February   General strike and demonstrations by the Socialist and Communist Parties. Blum: 'All united to defend the Republic.'

16 February   The government obtains the creation of a commission of inquiry of forty-four members on the Stavisky scandal.

22 February   By 368 votes to 185, the Chamber authorizes 'statutory orders' (full financial powers) to maintain the stability of the franc.

5–15 and 20 April   Statutory orders: administrative reform, repression of multiple posts, deductions from salaries.

7 April   The 'workers' States General' call for the dissolution of the leagues and protest against deflation.

20 May   Thirty-first Congress of the SFIO Party. Adoption of the centrist resolution: battle against fascism, measures at the farthest extreme from deflation, the conquest of power.

June   Social troubles and disturbances.

26–9 June   Debate on fiscal reform. Reynaud is favourable towards devaluation. The reform is voted.

4 July Not having solved the question of responsibility, the 'commission of 6 February' disbands.

15 July The National Council of the Socialist SFIO Party adopts a motion of action in common with the Communist Party.

4 August The Congress of the National Teachers' Trade Union rises up against the statutory orders.

20 August The Communist Party launches an appeal to the Radical Party.

9 October In Marseille, a Croatian assassinates Alexander I of Yugoslavia and Barthou, Minister of Foreign Affairs.

22 October The democratic left of the Senate opposes the planned reform of the state (Doumergue's speech on 24 September).

8 November The departure of the radical ministers brings about the resignation of the Doumergue cabinet. Flandin's 'truce' government. Herriot Minister of State.

1935

7 January Laval agreements (Foreign Affairs) with Mussolini (with which Britain will be associated).

13 January The inhabitants of the Sarre territory declare themselves *en masse* for attachment to Germany.

25 January Flandin stands out against devaluation.

15 March The Chamber votes for the two-year military service law by 350 to 196 (including 32 radicals).

16 March Hitler re-establishes compulsory military service in Germany.

20 March At Herriot's instigation, the government wishes to have recourse to the League of Nations.

14 April Stresa agreements between France, Britain and Italy.

2 May Franco-Soviet pact of assistance.

12 May Second round of municipal elections. The results reveal political stability. Retreat of the right in Paris, and Communist surge in the Parisian suburbs and the Nord.

31 May On his plan for 'extended powers' Flandin is overturned by 353 votes to 202.

4 June Formed on 1 June, the Bouisson government is overthrown on the request for full powers.

18 June Anglo-German naval agreement.

14 July Organized by the Committee of Popular Assembly (V. Basch), a large antifascist republican demonstration brings together the leaders of the Radical Party, the SFIO Socialist Party and the Communist Party.

16 July The publication of the first nineteen of Laval's statutory orders cements the unity of the left against them.

6 and 8 August Serious incidents in the Brest and Toulon arsenals in reaction to the statutory orders.

8 August Promulgation of eighty-three statutory orders.

3 October Italian troops penetrate Ethiopia.

24–7 October Radical Congress in the Wagram Hall. Against the leagues (La Rocque's Fiery Cross) and Laval's foreign policy, decision to join with the 'Popular Front'.

29 November The government obtains confidence on its financial policy, but seventy-three radicals have voted against.

6 December By 351 votes to 219 the Chamber gives its confidence to the government to dissolve the leagues.

7 December The Hoare–Laval (Foreign Office) plan hands over two-thirds of Ethiopia to Mussolini, who rejects the plan. Protests from British opinion.

18 December Herriot resigns from the presidency of the Radical Party.

28 December Keenly attacked on his foreign policy, Laval still obtains a majority of twenty votes (ninety-three radicals against).

1936

19 January Daladier president of the Radical Party.

22 January The departure of the radical ministers brings about the resignation of the Laval government.

31 January Formed on the 24th, Sarraut's 'waiting' government obtains a vote of confidence.

13 February Some Camelots du Roi attack L. Blum. Sarraut's decree on the dissolution of the leagues (Action française).

16 February Maurras is accused of inciting to murder (article on Blum in *L'Action française* of 9 April 1935). Arrest of Action française militants. Over 500,000 Popular Front demonstrators in the streets. Electoral victory of *Frente populare* in Spain.

6 March At the Toulouse Congress, merger between the CGT and the CGTU.

7 March Hitler reoccupies the Rhineland.

8 March Government hesitation. Sarraut's broadcast speech: 'We are not prepared to let Strasbourg be placed under German cannon fire.' No concrete consequences.

10 March Britain and Belgium advise against any military action. Italy remains silent.

12 March The Senate approves the Franco-Soviet pact (voted in the Chamber on 27 February).

21 March Maurras is sentenced to four months' imprisonment.

17 April Broadcast electoral speech by Thorez: the dictatorship of banks and the '200 families', and a 'hand extended to the Catholic worker'.

3 May Second round of legislative elections. The Popular Front has 376 seats: 72 Communists (+ 62), 147 SFIO socialists (+ 49), 106 radicals (– 43), 51 from various left-wing groups. The other camp obtains 239 elected members.

9 May Mussolini annexes Ethiopia.

10 May National Council of the SFIO. Azaña is elected president of the Spanish Republic.

11 May At Le Havre, a strike and occupation of the Bréguet factories mark the start of an important movement.

24 May Demonstration by the Popular Front at the *Mur des Fédérés* ('600,000 at the Wall').

30 May Agreement at Renault's.

3 June Trades union organizations invite delegates to reach special agreements and show evidence of reconciliation.

4 June Herriot is elected president of the Chamber. The strikes spread to new sectors.

6 June Blum cabinet: sixteen SFIO, fourteen radicals, two USR.

8 June Matignon agreements between the CGPF and the CGT.

13 June Beginning of the evacuation of the factories.

18 June Decrees dissolving seditious leagues.

20 June Law on paid holidays.

21 June Law on the forty-hour working week.

24 June Law on collective agreements.

26 June End of the strikes (except for 10,000 salaried employees).

July Beginning of the civil war in Spain.

1 July Blum's speech to the League of Nations.

20 July Telegram from Giral (Spanish Communist Party) asking Blum for arms and aeroplanes.

24 July Nationalization of the Banque de France.

2 August Delbos, Minister of Foreign Affairs, obtains from the Council of Ministers a decision to stop all arms deliveries to Spain.

11 August Zay's law on extending compulsory schooling (from 13 to 14 years). Law nationalizing war industries.

7 September Strike in the metal industry to protest against the 'blockade' applied to the Spanish government.

30 September Franco becomes 'Spanish Head of State'.

1 October After much resistance in the Senate, Auriol's bill for devaluation is finally adopted.

5 October Blum's government proposes an international commission of nonintervention (in Spain).

14 October Blum receives Colonel de Gaulle, a supporter of the creation of an armoured corps.

31 October Colonel de la Rocque creates the French Social Party (replacing the Fiery Crosses). Its motto: Work, Family, Homeland.

18 November Germany and Italy recognize *de jure* General Franco's government.

24 November After Salengro's suicide (18th), Marx Dormoy becomes Minister of the Interior.

5 December The Communists abstain from a vote of confidence in government foreign policy.

22 December The Franco-Syrian Treaty confirms the end of the French mandate and proclaims Syria's independence (not ratified by parliament).

30 December Blum–Violette plan on reforming the status of the Algerian peoples.

1937

3 January Anglo-Italian agreement on the Mediterranean.

30 January The Reichstag grants Hitler four years of full powers.

February Aggravation of the situation in Algeria. Creation of the National Union (800,000 Europeans).

3 February Auriol, Minister of Finance, declares himself against a new devaluation.

11 February Blum's speech delivered while on a visit to the building sites of the International Exhibition in Paris.

13 February Blum announces a 'pause' in the social programme.

2 March The fascist Grand Council meets in Rome.

10 March The Senate votes for the National Defence loan.

16 March Serious incidents at Clichy between Communists and members of the French Social Party (Colonel de la Rocque) leave seven dead.

28 April Before the Chamber's Finance Commission, Auriol clarifies the financial situation.

7 May Constitution of the Liberty Front at the instigation of Jacques Doriot, head of the French Popular Party and dismissed mayor of Saint-Denis.

24 May Originally planned for 1 May, inauguration of the Universal Exhibition (incomplete) by President Lebrun.

15 June By a 99-vote majority the Chamber grants full financial powers to the government.

21 June The Senate's hostility to full powers causes the retreat of the Blum government.

29 June Chautemps's Popular Front government with radical leadership. Blum vice-president of the Council. The radical G. Bonnet (adversary of the Popular Front) to Finance.

30 June In the Chamber, the government wins full powers with the support of Communist votes. The plan is adopted by the Senate.

July The Marseille Socialist Congress declares itself for socialist participation.

28 August The Council of Ministers approves the creation of the National Railways Company (31 August).

7 September Nuremberg Congress: Hitler proclaims the Rome–Berlin Axis.

11 September Terrorist attacks against the CGPF (rue de Presbourg) and the Union of Mechanical Industries (rue Boissière), condemned by the CGT.

10–14 September Conference of Mediterranean coastal dwellers.

23 November Communiqué of the Minister of the Interior instancing a monarchist plot aiming at the republican form of the government.

December Hardening of the strikes. Tension on the exchange market (the franc placed at 33.5 mg of gold).

11 December Mussolini announces the withdrawal of Italy from the League of Nations to the Italian people.

24 December Pius XI protests against religious persecution in Germany.

1938

8 January The building up of Italian naval forces constitutes a threat to the French fleet.

14 January The resignation of socialist ministers brings about the withdrawal of the cabinet.

19 January After his own refusal and that of Daladier, and the attempts of Bonnet and Blum, Chautemps forms a Popular Front government without the socialists.

5 February Hitler takes over the running of the Reich's foreign and military policy.

12 February Hitler orders Chancellor Schuschnigg to admit the head of Austrian Nazism, Seyss-Inquart, to his cabinet as Minister of the Interior.

March The commission on universal suffrage adopts article 1 of the Violette bill granting the right to vote to 200,000 native Algerians. Opposition from the Europeans in Algeria.

10 March The refusal of full powers and the gravity of the international crisis precipitate the resignation of Chautemp's cabinet.

13 March The *Anschluss* is approved by plebiscite.

14 March Backed by the Communists, Blum's second government contains only socialists, radical socialists and members of the socialist and republican union. Daladier to War, Blum to the Treasury, Paul-Boncour to Foreign Affairs, Frossard to Propaganda.

6 April The Chamber adopts Blum's financial projects by a mere 61-vote majority (exchange control, deductions on capital, mobilization of bank holdings).

10 April The Senate overturns Blum's government by 214 votes to 47. Third Daladier government, radical widened towards the right.

1 May First Daladier decrees. An 8 per cent rise in state taxes.

4 May Devaluation of the franc.

28 June Statutory orders for the defence of currency. Ratification of the agreement between the state and the Banque de France on the ceiling for temporary advances. Creation of the 'open market' policy.

11 July Law on general wartime organization. General Gamelin is head of the National Defence staff.

12 August Dockers' strike in Marseille, refusing extra work. Replacement by Senegalese soldiers.

21 August Daladier's speech on the length of the working week (forty hours) provokes the resignation of Frossard (Public Works) and Ramadier (Labour).

15 September K. Henlein asks for the joining of Sudeten Germans to the Reich.

29 September Munich conference between Hitler, Mussolini, Daladier and Chamberlain on Czechoslovakia. Hitler obtains the territories claimed without granting any guarantee to the Czech state.

4 October The Communists break the Popular Front. A new majority grants full powers to Daladier (331 votes to 78 with 203 abstentions).

5 October The Senate votes for full powers by 280 votes to 2.

28 October At the Radical Congress in Marseille, Daladier breaks with the Communists.

1 November Hostile to exchange controls, Reynaud replaces the resigning Marchandeau in Finance.

30 November A fresh attempt at a general strike fails. The government exacts serious penalties (the secretary of the CGT, Jouhaux, is deprived of his mandates).

2 December The Senior Military Council decides on the creation of two armoured divisions.

6 December Franco-German agreement in Paris: recognition of the frontier.

9 December Daladier obtains a majority of seventy-five votes. The socialists, Communists and Ramadier are in the opposition.

1939

10 January Opening of the parliamentary session. Discussion between those pro- and anti-Munich (the Communists).

14 January Blum asks Daladier to intervene in Spain.

27 January The Council of Ministers recognizes Franco's government.

2 March Marshal Pétain is appointed France's ambassador to Burgos. Election of Pius XII.

6 March The National Council of the SFIO votes against union with the Communists and condemns Daladier's foreign policy.

16 and 31 March The Chamber and Senate adopt the bill offering assistance to Spanish refugees.

18 March By 321 votes to 264, The Chamber grants Daladier full powers for the defence of the country.

20 March The Senate votes for full powers.

21–4 March President Lebrun's official visit to London strengthens the *Entente Cordiale*.

5 April Re-election of Albert Lebrun to the presidency of the Republic.

28 April Before the Reichstag, Hitler reckons that all territorial problems between France and Germany in Europe are over, and denounces the German–Polish Treaty of 1934.

12 May The Council of Ministers approves the additional draft to the Franco-Polish agreement on mutual assistance obligations.

17 May Franco-Polish military agreement.

5 June Arrest of those running *Je suis partout*.

23 June In Paris, Franco-Turkish mutual assistance agreement.

27 June The Chamber adopts proportional representation by 339 votes to 234.

1 July Statutory orders authorizing 4.4 billion francs for National Defence.

2 July In Lille, Weygand states that 'the French army now has a greater value than at any other time in its history.'

14 July Celebration of the 150th anniversary of the tricolour.

28 July The Cabinet Council decides on the prorogation of the Chamber for two years.

29 July Statutory order establishing government control of information and broadcasting. Statutory order on the external security of the state. Statutory order on the Family Code.

23 August German–Soviet pact of nonaggression. Meeting of the permanent committee for National Defence.

24 August Requisition of establishments working for National Defence.

25 August Seizure and suspension of *L'Humanité* and *Ce Soir*.

26 August Letter from Daladier to Hitler: '. . . a final attempt at a peaceful settlement . . . between Germany and Poland.'

28 August Establishment of censorship.

30 August Inquiry into the leaders of the Communist Party.

31 August The Council of Ministers decides unanimously to uphold France's commitments.

1 September The Wehrmacht invades Poland. General mobilization in France.

3 September France and Great Britain declare war on Germany. Daladier's appeal to the French nation.

13 September Government reshuffle: Daladier takes the portfolios of War and Foreign Affairs.

26 September Decree on the dissolution of the Communist Party.

27 September German–Soviet Treaty of Moscow.

28 September Capitulation of Warsaw.

4 October Thorez leaves France for Moscow.

5–10 October Incarceration of Communist members of parliament.

11 October France and Britain reject Hitler's peace proposal.

30 November Extraordinary session of parliament.

1 December Law granting the government full powers for the duration of the war.

1940

4 January Franco-Polish agreement for the reconstitution of the Polish army.

20 January Law deposing Communist members of parliament who have not broken with the Third Internationale.

15 and 20 March The Russo-Finnish armistice (12 March) provokes debates in the Chamber and Senate, in secret committee, on the running of the war.

20 March A vote of confidence wins only 239 to 1 and 300 abstentions. Daladier resigns.

21 March After Daladier's refusal, Paul Reynaud forms the new government and takes the portfolio of Foreign Affairs. Chautemps vice-president of the Council.

Daladier to War. Socialist participation. Creation of a War Cabinet (three meetings per week).

28 March   Franco-British agreement: neither peace nor armistice to be made separately.

19 April   Landing of French troops at Namsos (in Norway invaded by the Germans on the 9th).

10–27 May   German thrust to the centre of Belgium and encirclement of Belgian troops.

10 May   Churchill becomes Prime Minister of Great Britain.

18 May   Second government reshuffle: Reynaud to National Defence and War; Pétain Minister of State, vice-president of the Council; Daladier to Foreign Affairs. Weygand replaces Gamelin.

28 May   Capitulation of Leopold III.

5–24 June   Battle of France.

5 June   Government reshuffle: Reynaud to Foreign Affairs; de Gaulle Under-Secretary of State for Defence.

9 and 16 June   In London, de Gaulle and Churchill work out a plan of indissoluble union between France and Britain.

10 June   Italy declares war on France. Transfer of the government to Tours.

12 June   Treaty of nonaggression between France and Thailand.

13 June   In Tours, meeting of the Supreme Franco-British Council (in the presence of Churchill).

14 June   German troops enter Paris.

15 June   Installation of the government in Bordeaux. Weygand refuses to order a cease-fire. Chautemps proposes to ask Germany for its armistice conditions.

16 June   Pétain affirms the necessity of asking for an armistice. Hostility of Reynaud, who resigns at 8 p.m.

17 June   Pétain government. Chautemps vice-president, Weygand to National Defence, Darlan to the Navy. Baudouin, Minister of Foreign Affairs, gets Spain and the Vatican to ask Hitler and Mussolini for their armistice terms. The British and American ambassadors are informed. Having returned from London to Bordeaux the previous evening, de Gaulle goes back to the English capital.

18 June   General de Gaulle's appeal on BBC radio.

19 June   Communist militants ask the Germans for authorization to bring out *L'Humanité* again.

19, 22 and 23 June   More broadcast appeals from General de Gaulle.

22 June   Signing of the Franco-German armistice agreement at Rethondes. Laval enters the Pétain government.

24 June   Signing of the Franco-Italian armistice in Rome.

28 June   Churchill recognizes de Gaulle as leader of the Free French.

30 June and 2 July   Transfer of the government to Clermont-Ferrand, then to Vichy.

3 July   At Mers el-Kebir the British fleet sinks several French warships (1,297 victims).

5 July   The Vichy government breaks off relations with Britain.

6 July   Author of the first anti-German sabotage (20 June), Achavanne is shot in Rouen.

9 July   The Chamber (by 385 votes to 6) and the Senate (by 229 votes to 1) vote for the revision of the constitutional laws of 1875.

10 July   By 569 votes to 80 with 18 abstentions, the Vichy National Assembly gives full powers to the Pétain government for the promulgation of a new Constitution of the French State.

11 July   Promulgation of the Constitutional Acts making Pétain Head of the French State (Nos I and II) and adjourning the Chambers (No III).

12 July   Government reshuffle: Laval vice-president of the Council.

16 July   Law relating to loss of French nationality (affecting mainly Jews fleeing Nazism).

17 July   Law on the increase of public agents' and magistrates' offices.

22 July   The rallying of the New Hebrides to de Gaulle marks the birth of Free French forces (FFL).

2 August   In Clermont-Ferrand de Gaulle is condemned to death in his absence.

7 August   The Chequers agreement assures de Gaulle of British financial aid for the FFL.

19 August   Decree on the dissolution of the Grand Orient and Grande Loge de France.

29 August   Creation of the French Legion of Fighters.

8–16 September   Daladier, Reynaud, Gamelin, Mandel and Blum are interned in the château de Chazeron (Puy-de-Dôme).

20 September   Daladier and Gamelin are charged (Riom).

28 September   Thailand planes bomb French troops in Indochina.

2 October   Arrest of Jouhaux, general secretary of the CGT.

3 October   Law on the status of Jews. Dismissal of Jewish and Freemason officials.

19 October   Blum, Mandel and Reynaud are charged (Riom).

23 October   Laval–Hitler interview.

24 October   Pétain–Hitler interview at Montoire.

27 October   De Gaulle places all the rallied territories under the authority of an Empire Defence Council (Brazzaville).

9 November   Decree on the dissolution of the CGT, the CGPF, the Ironworks Committee and the Coalmines Committee.

11 November   The Germans quell a procession of patriotic students and school-children along the Champs Élysées.

14 November   Arrests of Daladier, Blum and Gamelin, imprisoned at Bourrassol.

17 November   In Brazzaville, institution of the Order of Liberation (Free French).

1 December   Constitutional Act No VI regarding the deposition of members of parliament.

13 December   Arrest of Laval, replaced by Flandin in Foreign Affairs.

15 December   The Germans restore the mortal remains of the Duc de Reichstadt (l'Aiglon) to France.

17 December   Brinon is appointed the Vichy government's general delegate in the occupied territories.

1941

4 January   The *Journal officiel de la République française* becomes the *Journal officiel de l'État français*.

15 January   Churchill accepts de Gaulle's currency (176 francs to the pound).

19 January   Pétain–Laval interview at La Ferté-Hauterive.

22 January   Law instituting the National Council.

27 January   Constitutional Act No VII on the responsibility of secretaries of state and top civil servants.

28 January   Cessation of hostilities between Indochina and Thailand.

1 February   In Paris, constitution of the Popular National Union (RNP) by Marcel Déat.

9 February   Resignation of Flandin; Darlan vice-president of the Council and Minister of Foreign Affairs.

10 February   Quater's Constitutional Act No IV entrusts to Darlan the replacement and succession of head of state.

25 February   Government reshuffle: Darlan takes the portfolios of the Interior, Navy and Information. Pucheu to Industrial Production.

11 March   Franco-Thailand Treaty of Tokyo fixing new frontiers between Indochina and Thailand.

19 March   De Gaulle–Churchill treasury agreement (advances for expenses incurred by the Free French).

1 April   Saint-Étienne speech on the social, paternalist and corporatist regime.

10 April   The Gannat court martial condemns General Catroux to death in his absence.

18 April   Notification of the departure of the 'French State' from the League of Nations.

1 May   At Commentry, speech by Pétain on the significance of the First of May.

11–12 May   Darlan–Hitler meeting at Berchtesgaden.

14 May   The Parisian police arrest 5,000 Jews of foreign origin.

27 May   Darlan and Warlimont sign the Paris Protocol allowing the Germans to make use of the naval bases in Syria, Dakar, Casablanca and Bizerta, as well as Tunisian communication routes.

2 June   New law on the status of Jews.

3 June   Weygand protests against the application of the Paris Protocol.

4 June   Pétain institutes the Committee of Professional Organization to work out the Labour Charter.

8 June–14 July   In Syria, the FFL fight Vichy troops.

22 June   The Wehrmacht invades the USSR.

30 June   The Vichy government breaks off diplomatic relations with the USSR.

11 July   Creation of the Legion of French volunteers against Bolshevism (LVF).

14 July   Anglo-Vichyssois convention of Saint-Jean-d'Acre ending the war in Syria.

18 July   Pucheu Secretary of State for the Interior.

24 July   Declaration of the cardinals and archbishops of France: loyalism 'without allegiance'.

26 July   Marx Dormoy is assassinated in his enforced residence in Montélimar.

29 July   Franco-Japanese agreement of Vichy on 'common defence' in Indochina.

12 August   Pétain's broadcast speech: 'A real malaise . . . London radio and certain French newspapers add to this confusion of minds . . . The activity of political parties . . . is suspended until a new order in the unoccupied zone.'

14 August   Institution of the Service d'ordre légionnaire (SOL). Law repressing Communist or anarchist activity. Constitutional Acts Nos VIII and IX imposing the oath of loyalty to the Head of State on top civil servants, magistrates and military personnel.

21 August   At the Barbès-Rochechouart métro station, Pierre George (Colonel Fabien) kills a German officer. At Versailles, an attempt on the lives of Laval and Déat by Paul Colette.

28 August   First execution of militant Communists, sentenced to death by the Special Tribunal of the Seine.

2 September Only Paul Didier (magistrate in the Paris Appeal Court) refuses to take the oath of loyalty to Pétain.

7 September Law instituting the State Tribunal.

23 September De Gaulle announces on the radio the constitution of the French National Committee.

26 September The USSR recognizes the French National Committee.

October In London, de Gaulle creates the Central Bureau of Information and Action (BCRA), a link with the Resistance.

4 October Promulgation of the Labour Charter: professional groups supported by single, compulsory trade unions.

6–10 October 1,600 people are arrested in Paris for anti-German propaganda.

15 October The German authorities arrest Paul Langevin.

22 October Following attempts on German soldiers, there are reprisals in Nantes, Châteaubriant and Bordeaux: ninety-nine hostages are executed.

12 November Internment of Daladier, Blum and Gamelin in the fort of Portalet (decided by Pétain on 16 October).

20 November The retirement of Weygand provokes reaction from the United States.

8 December The National Committee of Free France declares war on Japan.

14 December Following murder attempts, serious punishments inflicted on the Jews. The Vichy government 'regrets this massive repression'.

15 December Handed over to the Gestapo by the Vichy police, G. Péri is executed.

31 December Daladier, Blum and Gamelin are transferred to the Bourrassol prison.

1942

January Appearance of the first maquis at Maurienne.

20 January The Paris police swear the oath to Pétain.

19 February Opening of the Daladier, Blum and Gamelin trial before the Supreme Court of Justice in Riom. In Vichy, the oath of twenty-one regional prefects of metropolitan France.

28 February The United States recognizes the authority of the French National Committee over the French territories in the Pacific.

7 March Algerian civil servants take the oath before Pucheu.

26 March Pétain–Laval talks at Randan.

3 April Darlan to the press: 'Centralize the conception, decentralize the execution.'

10 April Hitler makes Laval's return a matter of principle.

11 April Suspension *sine die* of the Riom trial.

18 April Return of Laval: head of government, Minister of the Interior and Foreign Affairs.

20 April Broadcast speech by Laval: 'At Montoire . . . a victor who agreed not to abuse his victory and offered France, in the new Europe, a place worthy of its past.'

23 April The South African Union breaks off diplomatic relations with the Vichy government.

5 May The SS chief, Heydrich, wants a closer collaboration between the Gestapo and the Vichy police.

10 May German ordinance forcing Jews to wear a yellow star (as from 7 June).

26 May–11 June Koenig contains Rommel's German–Italian offensive in Cyrenaica (Bir Hakeim).

17 June Broadcast message from Pétain: 'By no means do I close my eyes to the feeble response to my appeals.'

22 June Broadcast speech by Laval: 'I want victory for Germany because, without it, Bolshevism would be everywhere tomorrow.'

23 June Publication in all clandestine newspapers of de Gaulle's condemnation of the Vichy government.

28 July Arriving in London on the 25th, A. Philip (SFIO) enters the French National Committee (Interior and Labour).

7 August The French National Committee protests against the deportation of Jews from the unoccupied zone.

15 and 25 August Arrested in the unoccupied zone, several thousand stateless Jews are handed over to the German authorities.

25 August Law ending the activity of the offices of the two Chambers.

30 August The Archbishop of Toulouse, Mgr Salièges, protests against the government's anti-Semitic measures. In a letter to Pétain, Herriot protests against decorations awarded to legionnaires; he sends back his Légion d'honneur cross.

31 August The president of the Senate, Jeanneney, and president of the Chamber, Herriot, protest against the unconstitutional and illegal nature of the government.

4 September Law instituting compulsory labour (to supply Germany with a work-force).

15 September Washington considers that sending French workers to Germany constitutes giving help to an enemy of the United States.

17 September Arrival in London of Ch. Valin, vice-president of the French Social Party.

20 September On the 150th anniversary of the First Republic, German sanctions following attacks carried out at the Rex cinema and Marbeuf station.

30 September Herriot is placed under house arrest in Brotel.

5 October Cardinal Gerlier (Archbishop of Lyon) at Lourdes: 'Providence has given France a leader around whom we are proud to gather.'

2 November Giraud–Murphy agreements (exchange of letters).

5 November Armistice agreement and cessation of hostilities between the French and British in Madagascar.

8 November The Allies land in Morocco and Algeria. Message from Roosevelt to Pétain breaking off his diplomatic relations with the United States.

9 November Giraud's arrival in Algiers. Talks between Laval and Hitler at Berchtesgaden.

10 November Cease-fire in the whole of North Africa, concluded by Darlan.

11 November German troops occupy the free zone. The Vichy government stays.

13 November Darlan–Clark agreement allowing Africa's entry into the war on the Allies' side (on the 19th).

14 November Pétain orders the African army to take no action against the Axis forces.

15 November Darlan appoints Giraud commander-in-chief of French troops in North Africa. Pétain orders Giraud to refuse to obey.

16 November Pétain declares Darlan stripped of all office.

17 November Constitutional Act No XII: the head of government alone can promulgate laws and decrees.

19 November Broadcast message by Darlan: 'The liberation of France by its empire'.

20 November Arrest and transfer to Germany of Weygand, Reynaud and Mandel.

21 November De Gaulle protests against the Allies' compromise with pro-Vichy authorities.

22 November   Clark–Darlan agreements on the relations of French and American authorities in North Africa.

27 November   Occupation of Toulon by German forces and scuttling of the French fleet.

28 November   At German request, Darlan is deprived of French nationality by Pétain.

4 December   Darlan states that he is taking on the office of head of the French State in Africa and commander-in-chief of the military, naval and air forces, with the assistance of an Imperial Council (including Giraud).

14 December   Acting on behalf of the French National Committee, General Legentilhomme receives the administration of Madagascar.

24 December   In Rennes, the execution of twenty-five French people for blowing up the offices of the LVF and recruitment bureau of French workers for Germany. The monarcho-Gaullist Fernand Bonnier de la Chapelle assassinates Darlan in Algiers.

26 December   Execution of Bonnier de la Chapelle. Giraud replaces Darlan.

28 December   Juin is commander-in-chief of the French troops in North Africa.

1943

9 January   The State Tribunal sentences de Lattre de Tassigny to ten years' gaol.

14–26 January   Churchill–Roosevelt conference at Casablanca.

24 January   In Casablanca interview between de Gaulle and Giraud: complete agreement on the liberation of France.

30 January   Law constituting the SOL into a French militia. Darnand is secretary general.

16 February   Law creating the Compulsory Labour Service (STO) (workforce for Germany).

20 February   Having escaped from the Châteaubriant concentration camp, F. Grenier (Communist deputy) arrives in London.

March   Spread of the maquis. Creation of united Resistance movements (MUR).

18 March   Publication in North Africa of eight ordinances leading to the re-establishment of republican legislation.

4 April   Broadcast message by Pétain: 'The rebel leaders have chosen emigration and a return to the past. I have chosen France and its future.'

5 April   Announcement of the handing over to the Reich by the Vichy government of Gamelin, Daladier, Blum, Reynaud and Mandel, and of their transfer to Germany.

27 April   Queuille (radical socialist), Viénot (socialist), Buisson (CGT) and Poimboeuf (CFTC) rally to fighting France.

6 May   Giraud dissolves the French Legion of fighters in North Africa.

12 May   After the liberation of Tunisian towns, Giraud's official entry into Tunis.

15 May   Jean Moulin founds the National Resistance Council (CNR).

19 May   Message from de Gaulle to the CNR: 'A coherent, organized, concentrated entity'.

27 May   The CNR decides to entrust the management of French interests to de Gaulle and the command of its forces to Giraud (appointed on 31 July).

30 May   De Gaulle lands at Boufarik.

3 June   In Algiers, constitution of the National French Liberation Committee (CFLN), with de Gaulle and Giraud as co-presidents.

21 June In Lyon, Jean Moulin is captured, tortured and put to death. He will be replaced by G. Bidault.

14 July In Algiers, de Gaulle speaks of the 'Fourth Republic'.

25 July Fall of the fascist regime in Italy.

26 August The Anglo-Americans and the Russians recognize the CFLN.

3 September De Gaulle's speech in Algiers: 'The recognition of the CFLN by the twenty-six united nations is the outstanding proof of our solidarity.'

12–13 September–5 October Liberation of Corsica, under Giraud's responsibility.

17 September In Algiers, creation of the provisional Consultative Assembly (Resistance, reorganized and rallied political parties). On-the-spot liberation of the Communists.

21 September The CFLN announces to the Corsican population the abolition of Vichy legislation.

29 September Having constituted the fascist republican government, Mussolini announces his intention of assuming the office of head of the new Italian fascist state.

3 November In Algiers, first meeting of the provisional Consultative Assembly.

9 November Giraud resigns from co-presidency of the CFLN but remains as commander-in-chief of the French forces.

29 November In a letter to Pétain, von Ribbentrop denies the representativeness of the National Assembly and affirms the role of the Wehrmacht in maintaining order.

6 December In Algiers, an ordinance instituting a Purging Commission.

18 December Arrest of Flandin, Peyrouton and Boisson.

22 December Having escaped from Riom, de Lattre de Tassigny arrives in Algiers.

24 December Broadcast message by Pétain: 'Listen to a man who loves you like a father . . . think of the risk of death our country would run if a hideous civil war should swoop down on it, or if Communism and its pagan barbarism should triumph.'

30 December Darnand secretary general for the maintenance of order.

1944

30 January In his Brazzaville speech, de Gaulle promises the men of the empire the possibility of 'participating in their own country in the running of their own affairs'.

February Beginning of operations to wipe out the maquis in Haute-Savoie by the Vichy police and the Wehrmacht.

20 March In Algiers, execution of Pucheu (sentenced on the 11th).

25 March 20,000 Germans and militiamen attack the 460 French on the plateau des Glières.

26 March Repression in the Dordogne by German troops.

30 March Amount of occupation expenses: 381 billion francs.

1 April The Ascq butchery (eighty-six inhabitants).

15 April Transfer of Giraud's family to Thüringen.

21 April De Gaulle's ordinance on the organization of public authorities in liberated France: regions to be managed by Commissaires of the Republic. The electorate is extended to include women.

3 June De Gaulle transforms the CFLN into a provisional government of the French Republic (GPRF).

6 June   Landing of the Allied forces in Normandy.

10 June   The Oradour-sur-Glane massacre.

14 June   De Gaulle visits Bayeux.

26 June   Ordinance creating courts of justice.

28 June   The Resistance executes Philippe Henriot.

July   In Algiers, debate on the aid given to Vercors. The Communist ministers threaten to leave the de Gaulle government.

5 July   Militiamen shoot G. Mandel, J. Zay and V. Basch.

21 July   German assault in the Vercors.

27 July   Ordinance quashing the Labour Charter and restoring trades union freedom.

30 July   American breakthrough at Avranches.

10–15 August   In Paris, strike of railway and transport workers, postal workers and police.

12 August   Herriot–Laval interview in Paris.

15 August   Provence landing.

19 August   Insurrection in Paris.

20 August   Pétain and Laval leave Vichy for Sigmaringen.

22 August   Resistance newspapers appear openly.

23–8 August   Liberation of Marseille.

24 August   At 9.30 p.m. the first parts of Leclerc's division reach the Porte d'Orléans.

25 August   At Montparnasse station Leclerc receives von Choltitz's surrender (3 p.m.), passed to de Gaulle (4 p.m.). De Gaulle at the War Ministry then the Hôtel-de-ville (7.30 p.m.).

26 August   De Gaulle goes down the Champs Élysées.

31 August   Assessment of the occupation in Alsace-Lorraine: 520,000 deported and 140,000 incorporated into the German army.

8 September   Publication in the *Journal officiel* of the ordinance of 9 August (Algiers) annulling the Acts of the French State.

9 September   De Gaulle reshuffles the GPRF: government of 'national unanimity'.

12 September   At the palais de Chaillot, de Gaulle's speech on France's new institutions.

14 September   Ordinance on the raising of salaries.

14–17 September   De Gaulle makes a tour of Lyon, Marseille, Toulouse, Bordeaux and Orléans.

15 September   Liberation of Nancy.

16 September–19 March 1945   Battle for the liberation of eastern France.

12 October   Ordinance on the functioning of the Consultative Assembly (248 seats).

18 October   Ordinance on the confiscation of illict profits.

23 October   Roosevelt recognizes the GPRF, as do the United Kingdom, the USSR and Canada.

28 October   The government orders the dissolution of patriotic militias.

November   Christian democrat Catholics and Christian trades unionists give a definitive status to the Popular Republican Movement (MRP) created clandestinely under the name Republican Movement for Liberty.

4 November   Decree on the Liberation loan (3 per cent perpetual loans).

7 November   First meeting of the Consultative Assembly.

11 November   France enters the European Consultative Commission.

17 November   The Council of Ministers approves a price freeze (Mendès France).

18 November   Ordinance creating a High Court of Justice.

23 November   Liberation of Strasbourg.

27 November   Amnestied, Maurice Thorez, secretary general of the PCF, lands in Paris.

28 November   Ordinance creating the Civic Chambers ('national disgrace').

4 December   Common meeting of socialists and Communists in Paris.

10 December   In Moscow, Molotov–Bidault Franco-Soviet pact (in the presence of de Gaulle and Stalin).

14 December   First ordinance on nationalization: National Coal-mines of the Nord and Pas-de-Calais.

15–18 December   National Assembly of the Departmental Liberation Committees.

18 December   Nationalization of the Merchant Navy. First issue of *Le Monde*.

21 December   The radical 'little congress' excludes thirty-four members of parliament and gives de Gaulle its confidence.

31 December   Ordinances on the reform of insurance and social security institutions.

1945

16 January   Ordinance on the nationalization of the Renault firm.

25 January   De Gaulle: 'The Rhine means French security and . . . a large part of the security of the rest of the world.'

27 January   Condemnation of Maurras to life imprisonment and national degradation by the Lyon Court of Justice.

9 February   Wiping out of the Colmar pocket.

20 February   France is officially informed of the results of the Yalta Conference (from 5th to 12th, between Churchill, Roosevelt and Stalin).

22 February   Ordinance instituting enterprise committees.

2 March   Programme-speech of de Gaulle before the Consultative Assembly: the re-establishment of freedoms, of suffrage (extended to women), the birth rate, multi-party system.

27 March   Franco-British financial agreement: the financing of trade exchange between the franc and sterling zones, reciprocal liquidation of debts originating since the start of the war.

28 March   Motion of the provisional Consultative Assembly on the suppression of allowances to private schools (realized at the end of the school year).

31 March–2 April   Paris Congress of the Federation of Communist Youth, which becomes the Union of Republican Youth of France.

2 April   De Gaulle passes the cross of the Liberation to the city of Paris.

6, 12 and 19 April   The Communist Party decides to be known as the Anti-fascist Republican Patriotic Union and brings the question of secularism to the fore.

7 April   Decree on the composition of the honorary jury given the task of ruling on the cases of members of parliament who had voted for delegating powers to Pétain.

21 April   Entry of the First French Army into Stuttgart.

25 April   Pétain surrenders to the judicial authorities.

27 April   First ordinances fixing the new prices.

1 May   The GPRF adheres to the London agreement of 14 November 1944 (Great Britain, United States, USSR) on the allocation of controls to the Allied Authority over Germany after its surrender.

8 May   Near Berlin, the German act of capitulation. Rioting in Setif during a nationalist demonstration.

13 May   Second round of municipal elections. In Paris, a decline of the radicals and moderates; 15.3 per cent to the MRP.

24 May   De Gaulle makes a peace speech on the radio.

29 May   Nationalization of Gnome et Rhône (aircraft construction).

4–15 June   Exchange of bank notes.

21 June   Constitution of the United Movement of French Renaissance (MURF, a branch of the PCF).

22 June   The Consultative Assembly adopts the plan for reforming public office and the creation of a National School of Administration.

25 June   Constitution of the Democratic and Socialist Union of the Resistance (UDSR).

26 June   Nationalization of air companies. Signing of the United Nations Charter (San Francisco).

28 June   Ordinance regulating rents.

30 June   Ordinance regulating prices. France recognizes the Polish government.

16 July   In the minority, the MURF breaks away from the National Liberation Movement (MLN) which has refused to merge with the FN.

27–8 July   The Consultative Assembly rejects the plan for an ordinance on the referendum, and declares itself in favour of a sovereign Constituent Assembly.

31 July   Seven moderate parties create the Republican Entente for Liberty and Social Progress.

2 August   The Consultative Assembly adopts a proportional share-out using the remainder on the national level.

3 August   Final meeting of the Consultative Assembly.

11 August   In Paris, opening of the conference of Tangier (France, Great Britain, United States, USSR).

12–15 August   The 37th Socialist Congress rejects the French Workers' Party (united with the PC).

15 August   Death sentence for Pétain (accompanied by a request that it should not be carried out).

17 August   Ordinance on the imposition of a direct, exceptional and temporary tax.

19 August   Ordinance on the double referendum and elections for an Assembly.

23 August   The CGT convokes the Left-wing Delegation (co-ordination of protests from various left-wing groupings).

1 September   De Gaulle refuses to receive the Left-wing Delegation.

2 September   The Viet-minh proclaims Vietnam's independence.

4 September   Tangier again becomes an international zone (1923 status).

4–5 September   Meeting of the confederal committee on the political role of the CGT. The Socialist Party protests.

12 September   De Gaulle's reply to the left-wing memorandum of the 8th: 485 deputies, proportional system with a minimum of 2 deputies per *département*. No integral proportional share-out using the remainder on the national level.

29 September   The moderates resign from the MURF (Mauriac).

2 October   De Gaulle visits occupied Germany.

4 and 19 October   Ordinances for the reorganization of the whole of Social Security (the inclusion of accidents at work).

15 October   Execution of Laval.

21 October   Double referendum and election of the Constituent National Assembly. 96.4 per cent 'yes' for a new Constitution; 66.3 per cent 'yes' to limit the Constituent Assembly's powers. Over 73 per cent of votes for the MRP, socialists and Communists.

9 November   Opening of the conference on reparations in Paris.

13 November The Assembly unanimously elects de Gaulle head of government.

21 November Formation of the government: five Communists, five socialists, five MRP, three UDSR, one moderate, one radical socialist.

29 November The Constituent Assembly appoints the Constitution Commission.

12 December Civil servants' strike.

13 December Franco-British agreement on regrouping forces in the Levant. The second national congress of the MRP declares itself against the Liberation Committees keeping the last traces of political autonomy.

26 December Devaluation of the franc. The Assembly approves the Bretton Woods agreements (22 July 1944).

28 December Decree re-establishing bread coupons.

29 December Franco-Russian trade agreement.

1946

1 January Nationalization of the Banque de France and the big deposit banks. De Gaulle is nearly brought down over military funds.

3 January Decree creating the general commissionership for the Plan (General Commissioner: J. Monnet).

10 January Opening of the first general assembly of the United Nations Organization in London.

20 January To the surprise of the Council of Ministers, de Gaulle resigns.

24 and 26 January After the election of Gouin on 23 January, protocol of agreement between socialists, Communists and MRP allows the formation of his government.

26 January–1 February Press strike in Paris.

29 January Government statement: 'Work, produce and organize'. Budgetary cutbacks and fiscal measures. Freeze on salaries, wages and agricultural prices. Confidence is voted by 503 to 44.

3 February First meeting of the National Credit Council.

14 February A. Philip (Finance) before the Assembly: effort on behalf of agriculture, pursual of the policy of nationalization.

25 February Re-establishment of the forty-hour week.

6 March Franco-Vietnamese agreement between Ho Chi Minh and Sainteny: France recognizes Vietnam as a free state making up part of the Indochinese Federation and the French Union.

16–19 March Meeting of the Plan Council. Report by Monnet.

25 March Strike of executive staff.

6 April Vote on electoral law: proportional with national allocation of the remainder and rule of the strongest average. Each *département* has at least two deputies.

8 April Nationalization of electricity and gas.

9–19 April The Assembly examines the bill on the 'institutions of the Republic'. MRP opposition to 'Assembly government'.

12 April In Essen, Franco-British conference on German coal.

16 April Law on staff delegates.

17 April Final evacuation of Syria by French troops.

19 April Franco-Vietnamese conference in Dalat.

25 April Nationalization of insurance.

5 May Referendum: 53 per cent of votes reject the Constitution ('Assembly government').

17 May Law on nationalization of credit.

22 May Law on the generalization of social insurance.

28 May Franco-American economic agreement (Blum–Byrnes): war debts and claims, commercial policy, credit.

2 June Election of the second Constituent Assembly: success for the MRP, Communist stability, socialist losses, stability of the union of left-wingers and moderates.

16 June De Gaulle's speech in Bayeux: sovereignty of the state, French Union, separation and balance of powers, presidential regime.

23 July Bidault government: eight MRP, seven Communists, six socialists, one UDSR. The CGT office demands a general increase of 25 per cent in salaries.

6 July–14 September Franco-Vietnamese conference at Fontainebleau: failure.

22 July The national economic conference on prices and wages recommends a 25 per cent increase in salaries from 1 July without consequences on the cost of living, setting farm prices in order and maintaining subsidies.

29 July Order relating to salaries: average increase of 18 per cent.

3–15 August Second Dalat conference: light federal system, elaborate economic organization, safeguarding of French culture.

5 August Serious Franco-Vietnamese incident on the road from Hanoi to Lang Son (in violation of the agreement of 6 March).

28 August UN Security Council.

31 August Final evacuation of Lebanon by the French army.

September The Gaullists intensify their propaganda.

13–14 September Franco-Vietnamese *modus vivendi*.

13–20 September General strike of Treasury employees.

20 September By 537 votes to 12, an order of the day of confidence in the refusal to allow a new rise to the civil servants.

22 September In Épinal, de Gaulle criticizes the plan for the Constitution: no separation of powers, not enough power for the President of the Republic and the omnipotence of parties.

26 September Agreement of the three major parties on the plan for the Constitution.

30 September The Assembly adopts the Constitutional plan by 440 votes to 106: compromise between a purely parliamentary regime with a strong executive power (MRP) and an Assembly regime (SFIO and PC).

13 October Referendum: a slight lead in the 'yes' votes puts the Fourth Republic's Constitution in place. Heavy abstentions.

1 November Before the press, de Gaulle condemns the 'absurd and out-of-date system' of the new Constitution.

10 November Election of the National Assembly. The PC gets ahead of the MRP. Big socialist setback.

13 November The European Coal Committee proposes a new reduction for December and January (Ruhr).

17 November Franco-Siamese agreement: Siam restores the territories seized by virtue of the treaty of 5 May 1941.

20–1 November Violent Franco-Vietnamese engagements at Haiphong (Tonkin).

24 November Designation of the large electorates (cantons). Success for the MRP.

30 November Franco-Italian agreement on the immigration of Italian workers to France.

3 December Franco-British financial agreement in London on the outstanding trade debt and the settlement of war debts and claims. V. Auriol is re-elected president of the Assembly.

8 December   Appointment of the councillors of the Republic by the large electorates, deputies and general councillors. The MRP comes first.

12 December   The Council of Ministers adopts a programme of restrictions (coal crisis).

16 December   Blum's homogeneous socialist government. Abolition of the Ministry of Food Supply.

19 December   Large-scale attack of Vietnamese troops and 'Tu-Ve' militias.

22 December   The Sarre is removed from the French occupation zone.

23 December   Policy of firmness in Indochina: negotiation once order is restored. General Leclerc is given the task of carrying out a military inspection. Law on collective agreements (tight government control).

27 December   The MRP Champetier de Ribes is elected president of the Council of the Republic.

1947

1 January   The social security plan comes into force.

2 January   First decree on a 5 per cent lowering of industrial, commercial and agricultural prices. (Second stage: 5 per cent on 1 March.)

7 January   Adoption of the Monnet plan (equipment and modernization).

8 January   Creation of control-shops (to prevent abuses).

8–15 January   Strike of Parisian newspapers.

14 January   Re-election of Auriol to the presidency of the Assembly, and Champetier de Ribes to that of the Council of the Republic.

16 January   In Versailles, parliament elects V. Auriol in the first round to the presidency of the Republic (452 votes to 242 for Champetier de Ribes). Resignation of the Blum government.

21 January   Herriot is elected president of the National Assembly.

22 January   Ramadier's government 'of general agreement'.

24 January   French memorandum on Germany: economic unity, political decentralization.

1 February   Law on the reform of public office: reduction in personnel, adjustment of salaries, 48-hour week. Provisional compensation.

3 February   French memorandum on the Ruhr: economic control by an international authority.

5 February   Talks between Ramadier and the CGT on prices. Strike of dockers in the west.

6 February   Following on from the CGT, the PC demands the minimum living wage.

8 February   Decree on the organization of National Defence: pre-eminence of the president of the Council.

10 February   At the Quai d'Orsay, signing of peace treaties with Germany's former satellites (France, Italy).

14 February   The Minister of Agriculture, Tanguy-Prigent, obtains 200,000 tons of American corn.

14 February–15 March   Strike of Parisian newspapers.

16 February   Speech by Ramadier at Decazeville on the lowering of prices and the wage freeze.

20 February   The National Assembly gives a vote of confidence on price lowering and wage freezing.

1 March   New 5 per cent price lowering (decree of 24 February).

6 March   F. de Brinon sentenced to death. Demise of Champetier de Ribes.

10 March   Opening of the Moscow conference on German and Austrian problems.

13–16 March   The MRP Congress finds the confusion of politics and economics in the state serious (both judge and judged in social conflicts).

17 March   The Minister of the Interior, Depreux, refers to the 'plot of the monasteries' and the Joanovici scandal (on the 20th, suspension of the Prefect of Police, Luizet).

18 March   Election of Monnerville (radical) to the presidency of the Council of the Republic. In Moscow, Bidault sets out the French argument on German coal, reparations and the Sarre.

22 March   Military funds for the war against Vietnam are voted unanimously; the Communists abstain, but Communist ministers vote.

30 March   Legislative elections in the Drôme: victory for the MRP. De Gaulle at Bruneval: 'The day will come when . . . the vast mass of the French will gather together with France.'

31 March   In Avignon, Ramadier justifies the parliamentary regime. Referring to Boulangist attempts: 'There is no supreme saviour, neither God, nor Caesar, nor tribune' (line from *L'Internationale*, 1871).

2 April   The Council of Ministers decides to refuse military honours to de Gaulle outside official ceremonies. The government decides on a reduction of the daily bread ration to 250 g (1 May).

7 April   In Strasbourg, de Gaulle criticizes the parties and the Constitution, and announces the founding of the Union of the French People (RPF) (reform of the Constitution, presidential regime).

10 April   Bidault proposes the internationalization of the Ruhr and the political and economic separation of the Rhineland with permanent military occupation. Hostility from Bevin and Molotov. Marshall and Bevin are favourable towards the economic attachment of the Sarre to France.

14 April   Report of the 'hatchet commission': elimination of 50,000 jobs in the public sector.

17, 19 and 27 April   The PC, SFIO and MRP take up their position against the RPF.

21 April   Anglo-Franco-American agreement on the sharing-out of coal from the three western zones of Germany.

23 April   The Council of Ministers decides to reduce public expenditure by 7 per cent.

24 April   The Moscow conference closes: failure, but a Franco-Anglo-American *rapprochement*. Election of the administrative personnel of the Family Allowance Office and the first Social Security offices (CGT 59.27 per cent; CFTC 26.36 per cent).

25–9 April   At Renault's, the CGT takes responsibility for a spontaneous movement making wage claims.

30 April   The Communist ministers withdraw their support from the government's wage freeze policy.

4 May   Dismissal of the Communist ministers.

13–14 May   Reduction in food rations provokes violent incidents. Launch of the 'corn crusade'.

19 May   The small and medium businesses react against the planned economy.

23 May   The government settles the wages problem: minimum living wage, collective productivity bonuses.

25–6 May The first National Congress of the UDSR (Paris) authorizes dual membership of the UDSR-RPF.

June Large strike movements in key sectors.

21 June In *Le Populaire* Blum considers that the price-lowering experiment is over.

27 June–2 July In Paris, Franco-Soviet-British conference on Europe's needs in response to the Marshall proposals (5 June). Molotov refuses the working out of a combined plan.

2 July The Minister of the Interior refers to the 'blueprint' plot directed against the Fourth Republic.

27 July In Rennes, de Gaulle's speech of indictment against the PC.

6 August The government rejects the CGT-CNPF agreement (1 August) on raising of wages and general revision of prices.

14–17 August Thirty-ninth Socialist Congress in Lyon: state economic control and austerity.

20 August In the Assembly, constitution of a cross-parliamentary group of 'action for a true democracy' (agreement with de Gaulle).

27 and 31 August Vote on the status of Algeria by the Assembly and Council of the Republic.

28 August Vote for the law on the collection of corn. Protest by the General Agricultural Confederation (CGA).

9 September Creation of a committee to fight inflation.

18–21 September Radical Congress in Nice: agreement with the RPF.

20 September Decree confirming the decisions of the 'guillotine committee' (June): reduction of jobs in the Ministries of Labour and Health.

5 October 87 per cent of the electorate in the Sarre choose economic attachment to France.

19 and 26 October Municipal elections: success for the RPF (+ 38 per cent in the large towns). Fall of the MRP (10 per cent). The PC wins 30 per cent.

27 October De Gaulle proposes the dissolution of the Assembly.

28 October Ramadier condemns social agitation (PC) and political agitation (RPF).

30 October Ramadier obtains a majority of only twenty votes.

31 October Creation of a committee for the improvement of food supplies (CGT, CFTC, CGA, CNPF).

November Large strike movements.

8 November In Paris, first national conference of the Workers' Force (CGT minority): against the politicization of trades unionism.

10 and 12 November In Marseille, the rise in tramway fares provokes a seious riot.

14 November The Assembly authorizes the government to introduce the franc as legal tender in the Sarre.

19 November Disowned by the MRP and shocked by G. Mollet's declaration ('L. Blum has in principle accepted the presidency of the Council'), Ramadier defers the government's resignation.

20–1 November Designated president of the Council, Blum attacks the PC and personal power. Despite the support of the MRP and all the socialists, he lacks ten votes.

24 November Schumann government (eleven MRP, eight SFIO . . .) René Mayer (radical) goes to Finance and Economic Affairs.

4 December The Assembly votes for the plan for the defence of the Republic and freedom to work by 413 votes against the 183 Communists who reject these 'blackguardly laws'.

10 December 'Strategic withdrawal' of the central strike committee (28 November).
At Versailles, first sitting of the French Union Assembly.

19 December Second national conference of the Workers' Force: split with the
CGT.

1948

2 January In Paris, signing of the Franco-American agreement on interim aid (284
million dollars).

7 January Final vote for the law on the exceptional levy on all unsalaried incomes.

16 January The SFIO excludes the 'Socialist Battle' tendency (unity of action with
the Communists).

19 January Inauguration of the Génissiat dam.

25 January Decisions of the Council of Ministers: devaluation of the franc (80 per
cent), freeing of gold (4 February), free exchange market, fiscal amnesty.

28 January Franco-Anglo-American agreement on coal from the Sarre.

30 January By 308 votes to 288, adoption of the plan to withdraw 5,000 franc
notes.

19 February The radical parliamentary group rejects the calls for dissidence launched by Blum to enlarge the 'third force'.

5 March De Gaulle establishes the relations between the RPF and Gaullist cross-
parliamentary groups.

13 March The UDSR approves Pleven's proposal for a *rapprochement* between the
'third force' and the RPF.

17 March The SFIO reacts against Pleven's proposal.

1 April Lowering of industrial prices affecting family budgets.

3 April Foreign Assistance Act of 1948 (Marshall Plan).

4 and 11 April Election of an Algerian Assembly. Success of Algerian Union and RPF
lists in the first college, and absolute majority of 'independents' in the second.

12–13 April In Paris, first constitutive congress of the CGT-FO (Force ouvrière,
Workers' Force), with Jouhaux as president.

16–17 April In Marseille, first RPF Congress.

22 April Strike in the mines of the Nord and Pas-de-Calais.

1 May RPF festival of labour at Saint-Cloud.

13 May Vote for a new fiscal law increasing income tax.

15 May In the Assembly, a regrouping of the SFIO-PCF radicals allows the adoption of the Deixonne plan (nationalization of the mining companies' schools).

22 May The Poinso-Chapuis decree entitles family associations to receive subsidies. The PC protests against this 'attack on secularism'.

4 June London agreements (Western Allies) on the organization of western Germany. France aligns its position with that of the United States (Germany, the
rampart against Communism). Ratification on the 17th by an eight-vote majority.

5 June In the Bay of Along, Bollaert-Xuan agreement: independence of Vietnam
which adheres to the French Union.

19 July In a minority over military funding, the government resigns.

22 July The CGA and the CFTC come closer to the CGT on wages and prices.

26 July André Marie government (enlarged towards the right): eight SFIO (including Blum), eight MRP, return of the radicals (seven).

27 August The opposition of socialist ministers to Reynaud's plan for putting
finances in order brings about the government's resignation.

31 August   After Ramadier's failure (reservations of the radicals on the 29th), the Assembly appoints Schuman.

September   Strikes at Renault, Air France and in the Paris metal industry.

7 September   Failure of the 'third force': despite the participation of the SFIO (who had at first refused), Schuman's government fails to win confidence.

12 September   Queuille government. The president of the Council (radical) goes to Finance and Economic Affairs.

20 September   Definitive vote on the law on the renewal of the Council of the Republic (elimination of the 'co-opted members').

9 October   The 15 per cent granted to salaried workers (24 September) is extended to civil servants and old age pensioners.

10 October   J. Moch at the national council of the SFIO: 'French Communist agents have received a sum of 100 million to wage their campaign of disruption against our economy.'

7 November   Elections of the new councillors of the Republic. Success for the RPF and the RGR.

20 November   French memorandum on the Ruhr, in reply to a unilateral ordinance of the military governments of the bizone (on the 10th).

29 November   End of all the social conflicts.

9 December   Scission of the UDSR: constitution of an RPF parliamentary group for 'democratic and social action'.

16 December   The councillors of the Republic take the title of senators.

1949

19 January   Abolition of the bread ration card.

22 January   Launch of a loan of 100 billion for reconstruction.

20 and 27 March   Cantonal elections: the PC and RPF lose ground.

8 April   Anglo-Franco-American agreement in Washington creates the German Federal Republic (23 May).

5 May   Creation of the Council of Europe (Strasbourg).

10–12 June   The UDSR Congress condemns dual membership (Mitterrand position).

5 July   In Paris, opening of the Joanovici trial, 'the Stavisky affair of the Liberation' (Depreux).

27 July   Ratification of the Atlantic Pact.

8 September   The cardinals recommend Catholics to leave Communist bodies. (Condemnation by the Holy Office.)

19 September   Devaluation of the franc (2.545 mg of gold).

6 October   Public disapproval of the wages and prices policy by D. Mayer, SFIO Minister of Labour, causes the resignation of the Queuille government.

16 October   Municipal elections: decline of the PC and RPF.

17 October   J. Moch (appointed on the 14th by one vote) steps down, as do F. de Menthon and H. Queuille.

22 October   Appointed on the 20th, R. Mayer (radical) steps down (SFIO difficulties).

28 October   Bidault government (participation of the socialists and radicals).

1950

25 January   The President of the Republic denounces the anticonstitutional nature (political strike) of the social agitation conducted by the PC.

27 January Ratification of the agreements with Vietnam, Laos and Cambodia. Dockers refuse to load cargo ships for Indochina.

4 February Collective resignation of the socialist ministers.

7 February Bidault steers his government towards the right. Diplomatic recognition by the United States of the state of Vietnam, the kingdom of Laos and the kingdom of Cambodia as independent states within the framework of the French Union.

12 February Law on collective agreements (salaries). The state intervenes in the fixing of the SMIG (guaranteed minimum wage).

3 and 11 March The Assembly and Council of the Republic vote for the law on attacks on state security. Communist opposition.

31 March Report of the commission of inquiry on the affair of Generals Revers and Mast (Indochina).

15–17 April Serious incidents in Brest (strike of building industry workers). Arrest of two Communist deputies.

23 April 200,000 people defend independent Roman Catholic schools.

28 April Dismissal of Fr. Joliot-Curie, high commissioner for atomic energy (declarations to the PCF Congress from 2 to 6 April).

24 June The Assembly overturns the Bidault government by 352 votes (including 98 socialists) to 230.

27–9 June In the face of hostility from the socialists over social policy, Pleven, Mayer and Bidault decline responsibility.

4 July Formed on the 2nd, Queuille's centre-right government fails to win confidence (socialist hostility towards Paul Reynaud, Minister of Associated States).

13 July Pleven's government wins confidence (by 329 votes to 224). Participation by the socialists and support from the right.

10 October Law on eighteen months' military service.

19 October Mendès France to the Assembly: 'Choose between the defence of Europe and that of Indochina.'

26 October In response to the German rearmament recommended by the Americans, Pleven presents his CED plan (integration of German contingents into a European army). Hostility of the Communists and the right. Division of the majority.

28 November Vote on the Communist motion sending J. Moch (National Defence) before the High Court (the affair of the generals). V. Auriol rejects the collective resignation of the government, which wins confidence on the 29th.

1951

15 February Creation of the National Centre of Independents and Peasants (CNIP).

28 February The debate on electoral reform brings about the resignation of Pleven's government.

6 March The Assembly refuses to appoint G. Mollet.

10 March Queuille government (little change in relation to the Pleven government). Bidault, Mollet and Pleven vice-presidents of the Council.

14 March The Executive Committee of the Radical Party condemns 'bigamy': the dual radical and Gaullist membership.

7 May Twice rejected by the Council of the Republic, the plan for electoral law is adopted definitively by the Assembly (332 votes to 248): law on the grouping of electoral lists (departmental list ballot with a majority).

17 June Legislative elections. The 'third force' keeps the majority (400 elected). Clear decline of the MRP and PCF. The RPF obtains only 117 seats.

July Creation of the Parliamentary Association for the Freedom to Teach (200 deputies).

10 July The schools quarrel provokes the resignation of the Queuille government.

8 August After the failure of R. Mayer and M. Petsche, and G. Mollet's refusal, Pleven is appointed by a large majority (289 votes).

11 August Pleven government: MRP, radicals, moderates; no socialists.

4 September By 361 votes to 236, adoption at the first reading of Marie's plan extending grants to deserving students from private schools.

10 September By 313 votes to 255, adoption of Barange's law: allowance paid to public and private establishments. End of the 'third force': the MRP is for the law, the SFIO against; division of the radicals.

1 November L. Jouhaux gains the Nobel Peace Prize.

12 December The Assembly ratifies Schuman's plan for a Franco-German coal and steel pool (9 May 1950). Opposition from the PC and RPF.

1952

7 January The Pleven government is overturned on the budget debate.

20 January Edgar Faure is president of the Council and Minister of Finance.

February Extraction of gas at Lacq.

29 February The Assembly's rejection of tax increases brings about the resignation of the Faure government.

8 March Pinay's 'defence of the franc' government obtains confidence by 290 votes to 101 with 229 abstentions.

1 and 12 April Finance law ('the Pinay experiment') is voted for by the Assembly (311 votes to 206) and the Council of the Republic.

20 April Pinay spells out his prices policy: persuasion and refusal to take authoritarian measures.

20 May The Pinay loan (3.5 per cent indexed to gold, exempt) is voted for by the Assembly (324 to 206) and the Council of the Republic.

26 May Bonn agreements and Treaty of Paris on the CED (the German Federal Republic obtains external sovereignty).

28 May Violent Communist demonstration against the arrival of General Ridgway (NATO). Charging of J. Duclos (29th) and search of the PC headquarters (31st).

3 June Adoption of the law on a sliding salary scale (42-vote majority).

12 July Constitution of Republican and Social Action (ARS) (rebellion of the RPF parliamentary group).

25 July The CECA comes into force (Treaty of Paris of 18 April 1951).

5–6 August Peasant areas protest against the fixing of corn prices.

11 September Decree on price freeze (inadequacies of price lowering).

25 October V. Auriol inaugurates the Donzère-Mondragon dam.

6 November The Finance Commission refuses to examine the plan for tax reform.

10 November At the UN, R. Schuman (Foreign Affairs) defends his record on the Maghreb.

7–10 December Riots in Casablanca. Numerous arrests and dissolution of the Istiqlal (Moroccan national party).

22 December Attacked over his foreign policy (radicals) and economic policy (MRP and SFIO), A. Pinay resigns.

1953

7 January   After refusals of G. Mollet, J. Soustelle and G. Bidault, R. Mayer (radical) is appointed by 389 votes (MRP, radicals, independents, ARS and RPF).

18 February   Full and complete amnesty for the sentenced Frenchmen in Morocco (319 votes to 211 with 83 abstentions).

25 February   De Gaulle condemns the CED.

1 March   The president of the Council pronounces in favour of ratification of the treaties on the CED.

26 April and 3 May   Municipal elections. Success of the RGR and MRP. Failure of the RPF. The SFIO makes some progress. G. Defferre is mayor of Marseille.

6 May   De Gaulle gives the RPF members of parliament their freedom.

20 May   In Paris, signing of the Franco-Sarrian agreements.

21 May   The Assembly overthrows the Mayer government (328 votes to 244). (Defection of the Gaullists and role of the Agricultural Parliamentary Association.)

26 May   P. Reynaud does not obtain appointment.

4 June   'To govern is to choose.' Giving priority to settling the Indochinese problem, Mendès France fails to obtain appointment (202 abstentions).

10 June   The radicals' hostility over the schools question prevents Bidault's appointment by one vote.

19 June   Meeting at the Élysée of former presidents of the Council and leaders of parliamentary groups.

23 June   In the face of hostility from the MRP and URAS (ex-RPF), Pinay steps down.

26 June   The independent J. Laniel is appointed by a large vote (government on the 30th).

2 July   Commission of inquiry into the traffic in Indochinese currency. Paul Auriol, son of the President, is implicated.

21 July   Adoption of the Navarre plan for Indochina.

4–25 August   Large strike movements in the public services, extended to the private sector on the 13th.

20 August   The Sultan of Morocco, Ben Youssef, is deposed and replaced by Ben Arafa.

4 November   After his condemnation of worker priests (23 September) Pius XII authorizes craft work. Prohibition of political or trades union activities.

29 November   In Cahors, P. Poujade creates the Union for the Defence of Shopkeepers and Artisans (against taxation).

23 December   Meeting since the 17th, Congress elects René Coty to the presidency of the Republic (477 votes at the 13th ballot).

1954

6 January   V. Auriol having refused the constitutional resignation of his government (on the 2nd), J. Laniel seeks the Assembly's confidence, won by 319 to 249 votes.

1 February   Radio broadcast appeal by the Abbé Pierre on behalf of the homeless.

4 February   Adoption of the eighteen-month expansion plan (E. Faure).

1 March   J. Laniel: 'Settle the Indochinese conflict by the path of negotiation.'

7 April   De Gaulle: 'I see (Europe) extending from Gibraltar to the Urals, from Spitzberg to Sicily and not limited to a Franco-German group . . . under a Germanic hegemony.'

10 April Vote for VAT (M. Laure).

7 May Fall of Diên Biên Phu.

4 June Treaties of independence and association between France and Vietnam (Laniel–Bun Loc).

9 June The report against the CED (J. Moch) is adopted by the Foreign Affairs Commission.

12 June The Laniel government falls because of its European and Indochinese policies (306 votes to 293).

18 June Mendès France is appointed by a very large majority (372 votes) and refuses to take account of Communist votes.

20–1 July Geneva agreements on Indochina. French forces leave Tonkin (deadline: 15 May 1955); partition: 17th parallel. Laos and Cambodia independent states. Ratification on the 22nd.

31 July In Cathage, Mendès France recognizes the internal self-government of the Tunisian state.

13 August Resignation of the Gaullist ministers, Chaban-Delmas, Koenig and Lemaire (disagreement over the compromise on the CED).

30 August In the Assembly, the anti-CED members win by 319 votes (including 53 socialists) to 264 (including the MRP).

19 September Investigation into the 'affair of the leaks'.

23 October Paris agreements on the Sarre, and the German Federal Republic, which obtains external sovereignty, enters the Western European Union (WEU, whose forces replace the CED) and NATO.

1 November Insurrection in Algeria.

4 November Dissolution of the MTLD (Messali Hadj).

12 November Mendès France: 'Algeria is France and not a foreign country that we are protecting.'

30 December With some reservation, the Assembly adopts the WEU.

1955

5 January The Mitterand plan (Interior) for a better integration of Algeria.

25 January Soustelle is appointed governor general of Algeria (1 February). Hostility of the radicals.

6 February The government is overturned on the problems of North Africa.

23 February After attempts by Pinay and Pflimlin, and Pineau's failure, E. Faure's government is voted in by 369 to 210. General Koenig goes to National Defence.

30 March The Assembly votes for special powers in economic matters (303 votes to 268).

2 April The Assembly votes for a state of emergency in Algeria (decreed on 21 March).

4–5 May The reformist ideas of Mendès France win the day at the extraordinary Congress of the Radical Party. Herriot leaves the presidency (on the 7th).

3 June E. Faure–T. ben Ammar agreement: recognition of Tunisia's internal autonomy, Bourguiba comes back to Tunis.

30 June–3 July The SFIO National Congress readmits the seventeen excluded anti-CED deputies.

20 August Insurrection in Morocco. Philippeville massacre and reprisals.

23 August Call-up and retention of active troops.

15 September Wages agreement in the Renault firm with the Workers' Force and CGC. The CGT will not sign.

26 September The sixty-one Muslim elected members reject integration.

8 October In Rouen, violent incidents between the forces of order and soldiers called up for North Africa.

9 October The Assembly approves the Aix-les-Bains agreements with Moroccan nationalists (26 August) by 477 votes (Communists, socialists, MRP) to 140.

3–6 November At the Radical Congress Mendès France opposes E. Faure.

6 November At La Celle Saint-Cloud, talks between Pinay and Mohammed Ben Youssef: independence in interdependence (Morocco).

25 November The UN General Assembly withdraws the Algerian question from the agenda (30 September). Return of the French delegation.

29 November The Assembly refuses its confidence to E. Faure's government (318 votes to 218).

2 December Decree on the dissolution of the National Assembly (art. 51).

1956

2 January Legislative elections. Victory of the Republican Front (centre-left): socialists, Mendèsist republicans, majority of the UDSR, some ARS. Success for the Poujade Movement (12.5 per cent). The PC obtains 146 seats.

14 January In Algiers, creation of a Committee of Action and Defence of French Algeria.

16 January The executive committee of the Radical Party rejects E. Faure's National Union (of socialists with moderates) and falls into line with Mendès France's position.

31 January Declaration of the appointment of G. Mollet: priority for the Algerian problem (cease-fire, elections to a single college, agrarian reform). His government is backed by the Republican Front, the Communists and the MRP.

2 February The Europeans in Algeria bemoan Soustelle's departure.

6 February G. Mollet is very badly received in Algiers.

9 February R. Lacoste resident Minister in Algiers.

28 February Three weeks' paid holidays.

7 March Independence for Morocco.

12 March A strong majority (including the Communists) grants special powers for the settlement of the Algerian problem.

20 March France recognizes Tunisia's independence (Bourguiba–Pineau agreement).

11 April Three decrees on Algeria: recall of reserves, compulsory purchase of land, dissolution of the Algerian Assembly.

20 April Creation of the Union for the Safety and Revival of French Algeria (Violette, Soustelle, Debré, Bidault, Marie, Morice).

23 May Resignation of Mendès France (Minister of State): inadequacy of Lacoste's reform plan.

28 May Franco-Indian agreement on the transfer of trading posts in India.

5 June G. Mollet–K. Adenauer agreement on the Sarre after the victory of the pro-German parties (18 December 1955). Confidence on Algerian policy, but 200 abstentions.

19 June In Algiers, the first execution of members of the FLN (two).

22 June Defferre's outline law on the development of Overseas Territories is adopted by 446 votes to 98.

29 June–2 July In Lille, the SFIO Congress declares itself against the rebels and ultras of colonialism (Algeria).

1–5 September In Rome, secret negotiations with the FLN.

30 September In Algiers, first FLN bomb attacks.

22 October Inspection of a Moroccan aircraft carrying five FLN leaders (including Ben Bella).

5–6 November Franco-British Suez expedition.

15 November Salan is commander-in-chief in Algeria.

24 December Discovery of General Faure's plot (setting up a military dictatorship in Algeria).

1957

7 January General Massu receives police powers over the Algiers region.

9 January Guy Mollet: 'France will never desert Algeria.' Unconditional ceasefire, single college elections, autonomy of management.

16 January An ultra group uses bazooka fire against Salan.

28 January–4 February FLN general strike.

3 February Semi-autonomous status for twelve black African territories.

25 March Treaties of Rome (EEC and Euratom).

27 March M. Faure (Secretary of State for Foreign Affairs) gives Tunisia and Morocco a warning (neutrality in the Algerian affair).

5 April Creation of the Commission for the Safeguarding of Individual Rights and Liberties.

5–7 April In Asnières, first Congress of the dissident Radical Party. A. Morice criticizes the abandonment policy (Tunisia, Morocco, Indian trading posts).

4 May At the Congress of the Radical Party of Valois, Mendès France criticizes the Algerian policy: 'The reforms have been mystifying . . . Who is in command in Algiers? . . . M. Lacoste or that handful of seditionaries? . . . It is fascism that rules in Algeria.'

21 May The Mollet government falls because of its financial plans (new taxes for the war in Algeria).

28–9 May At Melouza, 300 people are massacred by the FLN.

12 June After refusals of Pleven, Pflimlin and Mollet, appointment of the Bourgès-Maunoury government (enlarged towards the right) by 240 votes to 194 with 150 abstentions.

10 July Ratification of the Treaties of Rome by 342 votes (including all the socialists and the MRP) to 239.

30 September The Bourgès-Maunoury government comes to grief over Lacoste's outline law.

16–18 October The socialists, MRP, Valoisian radicals and ARS refuse to take part in Pinay's public safety government, which is not appointed by the Assembly.

28 October The Mollet government (socialists, radicals and MRP) is not appointed.

5 November Acceptance of the Gaillard government. The Mendèsists abstain.

29 November The government refuses Moroccan and Tunisian proposals to use their good offices.

16 December Failure of Mendès France in the executive committee of the Radical Party.

1958

16 January The government obtains only a twenty-vote majority on the plan for constitutional revision and the deferment of veterans' pensions.

31 January   Definitive vote for Lacoste's blueprint law (modified) by the Assembly (292 to 249).

8 February   French aircraft bomb Sakhiet (Tunisia).

25 February   F. Mauriac: 'This daily ration of shame . . . de Gaulle would give us back our honour.'

10 March   The budget deficit is reduced by 600 billion francs (reduction in military funds and investments).

23 March   R. Frey (ARS): 'The sooner he (de Gaulle) is appealed to the sooner will the nation regain confidence in itself.'

2 April   Following the strikes in the public sector, F. Gaillard says on the radio: 'Wage increases would be nothing but a deception.'

15 April   The failure of the Anglo-American mission (to use their good offices with regard to Franco-Tunisian relations) places the government in a minority.

8 May   Failure of Pleven's government before appointment: refusal of the socialists to participate and resignation of the Valoisian radicals.

9 May   The FLN announces the execution of three French soldiers.

13 May   In Algiers, taking of the general government headquarters by P. Lagaillarde. F. Gaillard delegates civil and military powers to General Salan. Creation of a military and civil Committee of Public Safety, with General Massu as president.

14 May   At 2 p.m., appointment of the Pflimlin government (tendency towards the right), supported by the SFIO. Abstention by the Communists. The Committee of Public Safety appeals to de Gaulle.

15 May   Enlargement of the government (SFIO Mollet and Moch). De Gaulle: 'I hold myself in readiness to assume the powers of the Republic.'

16 May   The two Assemblies vote for a state of emergency.

17 May   Soustelle flees to Algiers.

27 May   De Gaulle: 'Yesterday I initiated the regular procedures necessary for the establishment of a republican government.' The SFIO (less three votes) refuses to rally to his candidacy.

28 May   Resignation of the Pflimlin government. Left-wing demonstration for 'the defence of the Republic'.

29 May   Called by R. Coty, de Gaulle agrees to form a government.

1 June   De Gaulle is appointed by 329 votes (including 42 SFIO and 24 radicals) to 224 (including Mendès France and Mitterrand). G. Mollet is Minister of State.

3 June   Vote for three government bills: renewal of special powers in Algeria, full powers for six months, preparation of a new Constitution.

4–7 June   De Gaulle in Algiers ('I have understood you'), Constantine, Bône, Oran and Mostaganem.

9 June   Salan general delegate in Algiers.

17 June–5 July   De Gaulle–Pinay loan.

1–5 July   De Gaulle's second trip to Algeria.

7 July   Soustelle Minister of Information.

20–9 August   De Gaulle in black Africa. In Conakry, speech on the Community.

4 September   De Gaulle and Malraux present the new Constitution in the place de la Republique.

15 September   FLN murder attempt on Soustelle in Paris.

16 September   D. Mayer and E. Depreux found the Autonomous Socialist Party (PSA).

19 September   In Cairo, formation of the provisional government of the Algerian Republic (GPRA) (Ferhat Abbas).

24 September Creation of the Union for the New Republic (UNR) (president: J. Soustelle).

28 September Referendum: 79.25 per cent 'yes' votes for the Constitution (a massive 'yes' in Algeria and black Africa, with the exception of Guinea).

3 October De Gaulle in Constantine: plan for Algeria's economic and social development.

10 October Adoption of the single-name two-round ballot for the next legislative elections.

20 October Eisenhower rejects the three-man directorate of NATO sought by de Gaulle (17 September).

25 October The FLN rejects the 'peace with honour' proposed by de Gaulle on the 23rd.

23 November First round of legislative elections. Moderates and CNI: 19.90 per cent. Gaullists: 17.6 per cent. Defeat of the left. The PC loses 30 per cent of its votes.

30 November Second round: Seats: 198 UNR, 133 CNI, 44 SFIO, 23 radicals and UDSR, 10 PC.

9 December J. Chaban-Delmas is elected president of the Assembly.

19 December P. Delouvrier is the general delegate in Algeria. General Challe is commander-in-chief.

21 December General de Gaulle is elected President of the Republic (77 per cent).

26 December Resignation of G. Mollet.

28 December Devaluation and creation of the new franc.

1959

1 January France enters the EEC.

6 January School-leaving age is extended to sixteen.

8 January R. Coty hands over power to General de Gaulle.

9 January Michel Debré government. The SFIO does not participate (decision of 4 December 1958). A. Malraux is Minister of Culture.

March The French Mediterranean fleet leaves NATO.

14 April The left-wing Gaullists create the Democratic Labour Union (UDT).

18–19 June Publication and seizure of *La Gangrène*, which denounces torture in Algeria.

27–30 August De Gaulle's 'canteen tour' in Algeria.

16 September Speech by de Gaulle on Algeria's self-determination after peace is restored.

19 September Creation of the Union for French Algeria (RAF) (Bidault–Duchet).

30 December Debré law on the contractual regulations for private education.

1960

1 January The new franc goes into circulation. Independence of Cameroon.

13 January A. Pinay leaves the government.

19 January General Massu is recalled to Paris.

24 January–1 February Week of barricades in Algiers.

1 February The trades unions decide to have an hour's stoppage of work (support for de Gaulle).

2 February The government is authorized to make some ordinances.

5 February A government reshuffle sets aside supporters of French Algeria (Soustelle and Cornut-Gentille), P. Messmer replaces P. Guillaumat at the Army Ministry.

13 February Explosion of the first French atomic bomb, at Reggane.

3–5 March Second 'canteen tour'. De Gaulle speaks of an 'Algerian Algeria'.

1–2 April Talks between de Gaulle and Khrushchev at Rambouillet.

3 April Foundation of the Unified Socialist Party (PSU).

23–4 April FLN murder attempts in France.

25 April Soustelle is excluded from the UNR.

10 June Si Salah (*Wilaya* 4) is received in secret at the Élysée.

14 June De Gaulle proposes negotiation to the leaders of the uprising.

25–9 June Failure of Melun discussions (France–FLN).

26 June Independence of Madagascar.

30 June Joint text of the CGT, CFTC, FEN and UNEF calling for negotiations.

July Law on improvement of agricultural incomes.

5 September 'Manifesto of the 121' on the right to insubordination in the Algerian war. Before the military tribunal in Paris, opening of the trial of the Jeanson network of aid to the FLN (discovered on 24 February).

6 October Manifesto of intellectuals in favour of French Algeria.

27 October In Paris and the provinces, demonstrations for peace in Algeria.

4 November De Gaulle refers to the 'Algerian Republic'.

22 November L. Joxe Minister of Algerian Affairs.

9–13 December De Gaulle travels to Algeria. In Algiers, violent demonstrations by Europeans; the FLN organizes its first large demonstration.

1961

8 January Referendum: 75 per cent 'yes' for the principle of Algerian self-determination (72 per cent 'no' for Alger-ville).

February Constitution of the Secret Army Organization (OAS).

2 March Acquittal of the accused in the barricades trial (opened on 31 October 1960).

11 April At his press conference, de Gaulle uses the expression 'sovereign Algerian state'.

22–5 April In Algiers, putsch of the generals (Challe, Zeller, Jouhaud, Salan).

25 April One hour's general strike against the putsch.

20 May Opening of the Évian negotiations. Cancellation of the French army's offensive operations.

29 May Sentence of Generals Challe and Zeller to fifteen years' imprisonment.

31 May–2 June Official visit to France by President Kennedy.

13 June Suspension of the Évian negotiations.

12 July Bourguiba asks France to evacuate the naval base at Bizerta.

18–22 July Violent confrontations in Bizerta.

20–7 July Failure of the Lugrin discussions (France–FLN).

August Further and more serious terrorist attacks by the OAS in Algeria.

27 August Ben Khedda president of the GPRA.

5 September De Gaulle accepts the 'Algerian Sahara'.

9 September In Pont-sur-Seine, de Gaulle escapes an OAS assassination attempt.

17 October In Paris, Algerians demonstrate against the curfew (numerous deaths).

6 December Anti-OAS day in France.

1962

January OAS terrorist attacks in France and Algeria (until March).

18 January   V. Giscard d'Estaing Minister of Finance.

8 February   In Paris, a demonstration against the OAS. Eight dead at the Charonne métro.

11–19 February   Les Rousses meeting between French and Algerian ministers.

7–18 March   Second Évian conference.

18 March   The Évian agreements (France–GPRA). Liberation of Ben Bella.

19 March   Cease-fire.

26 March   In Algiers, demonstration by Europeans. Firing in the rue d'Isly causes fifty-four deaths.

29 March   Setting-up of the provisional Executive.

April–May   OAS murder attempts.

8 April   Referendum: 90 per cent 'yes' votes for the Évian agreements.

13 April   General Jouhaud sentenced to death.

14 April   G. Pompidou is Prime Minister.

20 April   Arrest of General Salan in Algiers.

15 May   De Gaulle rejects European integration. Resignation of the MRP ministers.

23 May   General Salan is sentenced to life imprisonment.

17 June   Local FLN–OAS agreements.

1 July   Referendum in Algeria: 99.72 per cent 'yes' votes for self-determination.

2–9 July   Chancellor Adenauer visits France.

3 July   Independence for Algeria.

22 August   De Gaulle escapes the Petit-Clamart assassination attempt.

4–9 September   De Gaulle's official visit to the Federal German Republic.

5 October   Censure against the Pompidou government (280 votes).

10 October   De Gaulle dissolves the Assembly.

28 October   Referendum: 61.75 per cent 'yes' votes for election of the President of the Republic by universal suffrage. Abstentions: 22.76 per cent.

25 November   Second round of legislative elections. Big success for the UNR: 42.1 per cent of the votes and 233 elected members. The extra help of the 36 independent republicans (V. Giscard d'Estaing) gives it an absolute majority.

29 December   Renault workers get four weeks' paid holiday.

1963

14 January   De Gaulle vetoes Great Britain's entry to the EEC.

23 January   At the Élysée, de Gaulle and Adenauer sign the treaty of Franco-German co-operation.

March–5 April   Miners' strike.

June   The French Channel and Atlantic fleets withdraw from NATO.

July   Law regulating the right to strike in the public sector. Creation of the Franco-German Youth Bureau.

3 August   Creation of secondary modern schools (CES).

19 September   *L'Express* launches Monsieur X.

25 November   Demonstrations against the strike force.

1964

27 January   France recognizes Communist China.

2 February   The SFIO Congress approves G. Defferre's candidacy for presidency of the Republic.

14 March   Creation of twenty-one programme areas.

May Adoption of the ORTF statute.

7 June Constitution of the Convention of Republican Institutions (president: F. Mitterrand).

12 July Following the death of M. Thorez, Waldeck Rochet becomes general secretary of the PCF.

6–7 November Extraordinary Congress of the CFTC. The majority (70 per cent) decide on the secularization of the affiliated group of trades unions and produces the CFDT. A strong minority preserves the name of the confederation and the Christian reference.

1965

14 and 21 March Municipal elections: success for the opposition.

25 June Withdrawal of G. Defferre after the failure of his plan for a great Democratic and Socialist Federation (on the 18th).

1 July In Brussels, France employs the 'empty chair' policy.

9 September Candidacy of F. Mitterrand for the presidency of the Republic.

10 September Constitution of the Federation of the Democratic and Socialist Left (FGDS): SFIO, Radical Party and clubs of the Convention of Republican Institutions.

23 September The PC backs F. Mitterrand's candidacy.

19 October J. Lecanuet, president of the MRP, stands as democratic, social and European candidate.

29 October The Ben Barka affair.

4 November De Gaulle's candidacy, against the representatives of the parties ('me or chaos').

5 December First round in the presidential election. De Gaulle has to undergo a second ballot (45 per cent). F. Mitterrand obtains 32 per cent of the votes.

19 December De Gaulle is re-elected President of the Republic with 54.5 of the votes.

1966

7 January Creation of University Institutes of Technology (IUT).

2 February Constitution of the Democratic Centre, regrouping the MRP and part of the CNIP (president: J. Lecanuet).

4 March France leaves the integrated Command of NATO.

May F. Mitterrand forms a 'shadow cabinet'.

22 June Fouchet's reform of higher education.

1 September Speech by De Gaulle at Phnom Penh.

December Law on professional training and social advancement.

20 December FGDS–PC agreement of reciprocal withdrawal in the second round (the PSU will join in).

1967

10 January The 'Yes, but . . .' of V. Giscard d'Estaing.

3 February Compulsory schooling is increased from the age of fourteen to sixteen.

5 March First round of legislative elections. The Union for the Fifth Republic obtains 38 per cent of the votes. The PC gets 22.5 per cent.

12 March Second round: the Gaullist coalition just manages to win (thanks to overseas).

1 April Evacuation of American and Canadian bases in France.

26 April The Council of Ministers asks for special powers. Resignation of the Minister of Agriculture, E. Pisani.

17 May General strike against the special powers.

June V. Giscard d'Estaing creates the Federation of Independent Republicans.

16 June The Assembly grants G. Pompidou the right to legislate by making ordinances (economic and social reforms) until 31 October. G. Séguy is general secretary of the CGT.

12 July Ordinance instituting unemployment insurance and creating the ANPE (National Employment Agency).

26 July De Gaulle in Montreal: 'Long live free Quebec!'

17 August V. Giscard d'Estaing denounces the 'solitary exercise of power' and wants the restoration of parliament's rights. Ordinance on workers' participation in the firm's achievements.

22 August Ordinances reforming the organization of Social Security.

November In Lille, conference of the UNR, which expands and takes the name Union of Democrats for the Fifth Republic (UD V^e).

19 December Vote for Neuwirth's law authorizing contraception.

1968

26 January Incidents at the university faculty of Nanterre.

22 March The Council Hall of the literature faculty at Nanterre is occupied by extreme left-wing students (D. Cohn-Bendit). Creation of the Movement of 22 March.

2 May Closure of the Nanterre faculty. G. Pompidou leaves Paris for a ten-day trip to Afghanistan.

3 May Fighting in the Latin Quarter.

10–11 May The night of the barricades.

13 May Combined student–trades unions procession from the République to Denfert-Rochereau.

14–18 May De Gaulle visits Romania.

22 May A general strike paralyses France.

27 May The 'Grenelle agreements' (not signed, and rejected by the rank and file): increase of the SMIG (guaranteed minimum wage) by 35 per cent, 10 per cent increase in salaries (in two stages), trades union section in firms . . . Meeting in the Charléty Stadium.

28 May F. Mitterrand proposes the formation of a provisional government.

29 May De Gaulle with General Massu at Baden-Baden.

30 May Address by General de Gaulle, dissolving the Assembly. Procession of Gaullists along the Champs Élysées.

31 May The government reshuffle excludes ministers who have had any responsibility in the events.

June The UD V^e takes the name Union for the Defence of the Republic (UDR).

30 June Second round of legislative elections. The UDR holds an absolute majority of seats (293 out of 487) with 38 per cent of the votes.

10 July M. Couve de Murville becomes Prime Minister.

12 November Definitive adoption of E. Faure's blueprint law on improvement of university management through participation.

23 November De Gaulle refuses to devalue the franc.

1969

22 January De Gaulle announces his intention to continue to the very end of his mandate.

3 February The president of the Senate, A. Poher, rejects the reform of the Senate.

11 March Strike of the public sector after the failure of the 'Tilsitt conference' (the government wants to 'hold wages').

27 April Referendum on the creation of regions and a reform of the Senate. The 'no' vote wins (53 per cent).

28 April Resignation of General de Gaulle. A. Poher takes care of the interim period.

15 June G. Pompidou is elected President of the Republic by 57.58 per cent of the votes (against A. Poher).

22 June J. Chaban-Delmas government. M. Debré to National Defence. M. Schumann to Foreign Affairs. V. Giscard d'Estaing to Finance.

11–13 July At the Issy-les-Moulineaux Congress, a new Socialist Party replaces the SFIO. G. Mollet is set aside.

8 August The franc is devalued by 12.5 per cent.

16 September In the Assembly, speech by J. Chaban-Delmas on the 'new society'.

10 December By 285 votes to 91, the Assembly adopts the Fontanet plan replacing the SMIG with the SMIC. At the EGF progress agreement between management and trades union federations (with the exception of the CGT).

1970

8 February At the 19th Congress of the PCF the new assistant general secretary, G. Marchais, commits the PCF to a policy of opening up the political spectrum. R. Garaudy is removed from the central committee and the political bureau.

30 April Adoption of the law against demonstrators who wilfully cause damage (collective responsibility).

27 May Dissolution of the Proletarian Left.

August Demonstration by the Women's Liberation Movement.

1971

5 April Manifesto of 343 female personalities in favour of abortion.

11–13 June At the Épinay Congress, the Convention of Republican Institutions (F. Mitterrand) joins the Socialist Party. F. Mitterrand replaces A. Savary in the post of first secretary.

12 July 'Presence and action of Gaullism' (P. Messmer), a reproach to the government for neglecting its parliamentary majority.

16 July Law on further career training and training leave.

3 November At Saint-Germain-en-Laye the radicals (J.-J. Servan-Schreiber) and the Democratic Centre (J. Lecanuet) create the Reform Movement.

1972

23 April Referendum on the enlargement of the EEC to include Great Britain, Denmark and Ireland: 68 per cent 'yes', but heavy abstention (40 per cent).

25 May The Assembly gives a vote of confidence on the general policies of J. Chaban-Delmas by 368 to 96.

26 June The Socialist and Communist Parties sign a Common Programme of government.

27 June G. Pompidou gives up the idea of dissolving the Assembly.

5 July Resignation of J. Chaban-Delmas, replaced by P. Messmer. Vote for the law instituting regional responsibility for economic questions.

4 October Dissident radicals create the Radical Socialist Left Movement, which adheres to the Common Programme.

1973

4 March First round of legislative elections: the majority (URP) loses votes; PC, 21.3 per cent; Union of Socialist and Democratic Left (PS and MRG), 20.4 per cent; Reform Movement (opposition centrists), 12.5 per cent.

11 March Second round of legislative elections. Very heavy participation (82 per cent). The majority loses the absolute majority: 257 seats (– 97, including 90 for the UDR). The left obtains 176 seats (including 100 for the PS).

3 April In his message to the new Assembly, Pompidou announces that he intends to change the duration of the presidential mandate to five years.

28 June Dissolution of the Communist and New Order League.

26 August Demonstration against the extension of the Larzac military camp.

October First oil shock: the price of a barrel quadruples.

16 October In the Assembly, the text of the revision of the Constitution (presidential mandate reduced to five years) is adopted by 270 deputies to 211 (including M. Couve de Murville).

19 October The text is adopted by 162 senators to 112.

23 October The Chairman and Managing Director of the ORTF, A. Conte, is dismissed from office and Ph. Malaud is relieved of Information.

24 October G. Pompidou abandons the constitutional reform (the 432 votes do not represent the three-fifths necessary for Congress).

1974

19 January The government decides to let the franc float.

28 February Resignation of P. Messmer, immediately reappointed, J. Chirac to the Interior.

2 April Death of G. Pompidou. A. Poher looks after the interim period of the Republic's presidency.

8 April From Chamalières, V. Giscard d'Estaing announces his candidacy for the presidency of the Republic.

13 April Forty-three deputies (including thirty-five UDR) sign Chirac's motion for a combined candidacy (V. Giscard d'Estaing).

5 May First round of presidential election. Very heavy participation (84.23 per cent). F. Mitterrand, 43.2 per cent; V. Giscard d'Estaing, 32.6 per cent.

11 May The morning after their televised debate, Mitterrand and Giscard are on equal footing in the opinion polls.

19 May Second round of presidential election. Record participation (87.3 per cent). V. Giscard d'Estaing is elected with 50.81 per cent of the votes.

28 May Chirac government. S. Veil is the first woman to have a ministry of her own (Public Health).

30 May   V. Giscard d'Estaing's message to parliament stresses presidentialism.

9 June   Openly hostile to atomic explosions, the Minister of Reforms, J.-J. Servan-Schreiber, is relieved of his duties.

5 July   The age of majority is lowered to eighteen years.

7 August   Abolition of the ORTF, replaced by seven companies.

October–December   Postal strike.

21 October   At Versailles the Congress adopts the parliamentary members' bill requiring the Constitutional Council to pronounce on the constitutionality of proposed laws.

1975

17 January   The Veil law on the liberalization over five years of voluntary termination of pregnancy. Against 184 votes, 284 deputies vote in favour: the left, a third of the UDR, a quarter of the RI (Républicains indépendants) and half the reformers.

11 July   Law on more flexible divorce procedures.

22 August   In Aleria (Corsica) two anti-riot police are killed.

September   Plan to relaunch the economy.

20 September   The European Council of Ministers decides that the election of European representatives shall be effected by universal suffrage.

16 December   In Paris, opening of the conference on international economic co-operation: North–South dialogue recommended by Giscard.

31 December   Law abrogating the exceptional status of Paris, which will have its own mayor.

1976

14 March   France comes out of the European currency snake.

17 March   The left carries off the presidency of fifteen general councils.

March–May   Students' strike against reform of Finals year.

6 and 10 July   Adoption of the law strengthening the majority ballot: the minimum for keeping in the second round goes from 10 to 12.5 per cent of registered electors.

25 August   Resignation of J. Chirac. The Minister of Foreign Trade, R. Barre, is appointed Prime Minister.

22 September   R. Barre presents a corrective Finance Bill for 1976 (the Barre plan against inflation).

15 and 26 October   Adoption by parliament of the Barre plan (utilization of article 49, paragraph 3).

5 December   The UDR is transformed into the Union for the Republic (RPR) under the presidency of J. Chirac.

30 December   The Constitutional Council decides on the suitability of the plan for European election by universal suffrage.

1977

19 January   In response to the candidacy of M. d'Ornano (12 November 1976), J. Chirac announces his candidacy for the office of mayor of Paris.

13 and 20 March   Municipal elections: success for the left, particularly in the west. In Paris, success for J. Chirac (elected mayor on the 25th).

26 and 28 April   Hostile reaction from the CGT and CFDT to Barre's second plan (including the national employment pact). The FO and CGC have some reservations. The CNPF is satisfied. Drop in prices on the Paris Bourse.

30–1 July   Ecologists demonstrate at Creys-Malville (one death).

14 and 21 September   Split in the Left-wing Union.

1978

January   At Verdun-sur-le-Doubs, speech by the President of the Republic on the 'right choice'. Giscard announces that he will not resign and will exercise his constitutional prerogatives.

1 February   Creation of the Union for French Democracy (UDF): Republican Party (ex-RI), Centre of Social Democrats (ex-Democratic Centre) and Radical Party.

19 March   Second round of legislative elections: narrow victory for the right (50.47 per cent). Heavy participation (84.76 per cent). Seats: RPR, 154 (– 29); UDF, 24; PS, 113 (+ 11); PC, 86 (+ 13).

19 May   Intervention of French parachutists at Kolwezi.

June   Giscard asks the Prime Minister to hold discussion with the opposition on the limitation of multiple mandates, the financing of the parties and the introduction of proportional representation into municipal elections.

12 August   Freeing of bread prices.

6 December   In the 'Cochin appeal', J. Chirac denounces the 'foreigner's party'.

1979

Second oil shock: the price of a barrel doubles.

6–8 April   Socialist Congress of Metz: to eliminate the Rocardians from the management committee, F. Mitterrand joins forces with the CERES (J.-P. Chevenement).

10 June   First European elections by universal suffrage (proportional national list ballot.) Weak participation (61 per cent). Majority–opposition equality (44 per cent). The UDF is ahead (27.6 per cent), the RPR obtains only 16.24 per cent.

10 October   *Le Canard enchaîné* unleashes the 'affair of the diamonds'.

27 and 29 November   In the face of the hostility of the majority of the RPR, R. Barre has recourse to article 49, paragraph 3 for the renewal of the Veil law.

December   The RPR deputies refuse to vote for the 1980 budget.

1980

30 April   Peyrefitte's bill on 'Safety and liberty'.

5 June   Faced with the anxiety of south-western farmers, Giscard opposes membership of the EEC for Spain and Portugal.

3 October   Attack on the synagogue in rue Copernic.

19 October   From Conflans-Sainte-Honorine, M. Rocard puts forward to the socialists his candidacy for the presidency of the Republic.

December   Inflation reaches 13.6 per cent. Adoption of Peyrefitte's plan (use of the block vote).

1981

26 April   First round of the presidential election. Giscard, 28.31 per cent (– 4); Mitterrand, 25.8 per cent; Chirac, 18 per cent; Marchais, 15.34 per cent.

May More than one and a half million unemployed in France.

10 May François Mitterrand is elected President of the Republic with a lead of 1.1 million votes over V. Giscard d'Estaing.

21 May P. Mauroy forms an almost homogeneous socialist government. François Mitterrand dissolves the Assembly.

21 June Second round of legislative elections: the Socialist Party obtains an absolute majority of seats (285 out of 491).

23 June P. Mauroy is reappointed Prime Minister. Four Communists enter the government (Transport, Public Health, Public Office, Career Training). J. Delors goes to Economy and Finance.

8 July In the Assembly, P. Mauroy's speech on the 'new citizenship' (plans for government reforms).

17 September Abolition of the death penalty.

4 October The franc is devalued by 3 per cent, the mark revalued upwards by 5.5 per cent.

18 December After rejection by the Senate, the Assembly adopts the plan for nationalizations at its final reading.

1982

13 January Ordinances on the 39-hour week and a fifth week of paid holiday.

17 January Legislative by-elections: success for the opposition.

18 January The Constitutional Council quashes some terms of the law on nationalization.

28 January First Defferre law on decentralization: suppression of supervision by the state representative over the deliberations of municipal and departmental councils.

26 March Renewal of half the general councils: the left loses eight presidencies, the opposition holds fifty-nine out of ninety-five. Law transferring executive power over the departmental community from the Commissioner of the Republic (ex-prefect) to the president of the general council.

April New devaluation of the franc (5.75 per cent) and revaluation of the mark (4.25 per cent).

29 July Law on audio-visual techniques, notably instituting the High Authority on audio-visual matters.

20 October The law on electoral reform for municipal elections combines majority voting with proportional representation.

1 November End of the wage and price freeze (four months).

1983

13 March Second round of municipal elections: success for the opposition. In Paris, the Chirac lists carry off the twenty *arrondissements*.

22–3 March F. Mitterrand brings back P. Maurroy and comes down in favour of a rigorous policy.

April Devaluation of the franc by 2.5 per cent, and revaluation of the mark by 5.5 per cent.

11 April The Assembly authorizes the government to legislate by edicts.

Bibliography

Publication is in Paris, unless otherwise indicated.

REFERENCE WORKS, REVIEWS

Articles, lists, verifications and chronicles of general French political history of the past century are to be found in all the major historical reviews, *Revue historique, Annales (Économies, sociétés, civilisations), Revue d'histoire moderne et contemporaine, Historiens et géographes*, to name only the best known and best established. The period 1880–1932, however, is more often dealt with in publications covering a limited chronological field, such as *XXe Siècle, Le Mouvement social* and *La Revue française de science politique*; whereas the recent past is naturally dealt with more in *La Revue d'histoire de la Deuxième Guerre Mondiale*. A 'laboratory' responsible to the Centre national de la recherche scientifique, the Institute of Present-day History specializes, as its name indicates, in the recent past, and publishes *Cahiers*.

The *Année politique* is a valuable chronological record, in an annual volume launched in 1874 by André DANIEL (pseudonym of Georges BONNEFOUS), interrupted in 1905, then continued by Georges BONNEFOUS (and Édouard BONNEFOUS) in *L'Histoire politique de la Troisième République* (7 vol., PUF, 1956ff). Relaunched in 1945 by André SIEGFRIED, and continued after him by Édouard BONNEFOUS, Jean-Baptiste DUROSELLE, etc., soon taking the title *Année politique, économique et sociale* (ed. PUF).

Famous people figure in the *Dictionnaire de biographie française*, by PRÉVOST and Roman d'AMAT, though necessarily selective as the work is incomplete (having today reached letter J).

On the other hand, all members of parliament are noted, before 1889, in the *Dictionnaire des parlementaires* by BOURLOTON, ROBERT and COUGNY (5 vol.), and from 1889 to 1940 in JOLLY's work of the same name (8 vol., ed. PUF).

For the most part, actors on the political scene in the wider sense, not necessarily members of parliament, may be found, according to their tendencies and spheres of action, in either the *Dictionnaire biographique du mouvement ouvrier français* founded by Jean MAITRON (Ed. ouvrières), which actually comes up to the present period, or G. JACQUEMET's encyclopaedia *Catholicisme* (ed. Letouzey).

Lastly, consult François GOGUEL, *Chroniques électorales* (Presses de la FN des sciences politiques); and his *Géographie des élections françaises de 1870 à 1951*, A. Colin, 1951; *Les Élections sous la Ve République* by A. LANCELOT (PUF, 1983).

MEMOIRS AND RECOLLECTIONS

The *Mémoires* and *Souvenirs* of political men and actors participating in events rarely have a comparable source value with archive documents, but at the very least they are informative about the personality of their author, are evocative of the climate and atmosphere of their era and, like all contemporary writings, can recreate for younger readers the flavour of the epoch. For that reason they are very valuable.

LAVERGNE Bernard, *Les Deux Présidences de Jules Grévy 1879–1887*, Fischbacher, 1966.

CAILLAUX Joseph, *Mes Mémoires*, 3 vol., Plon, 1942.

POINCARÉ Raymond, *Au service de la France*, 10 vol., Plon, 1926ff.

PAUL-BONCOUR Joseph, *Entre deux guerres. Souvenirs sur la IIIe République*, 2 vol., Plon, 1945.

HERRIOT Édouard, *Jadis*, 2 vol., Flammarion, 1948.

REYNAUD Paul, *Mémoires*, 3 vol., Flammarion, 1959–63.

Obviously without parallel are General de GAULLE's *Mémoires de Guerre*, 3 vol., Plon, 1954–9, followed by *Mémoires d'espoir*, 2 vol., Plon, 1970–1, *Discours et Messages*, Plon, 1970, and finally *Lettres, notes et carnets*, Plon, 1980–1.

President Vincent AURIOL kept a journal, the subject of a partial edition in a volume *Mon Septennat*, Gallimard, 1977; the complete journal, edited by Pierre NORA and J. OZOUF, is published as *Journal du Septennat*, 7 vol., Armand Colin, 1970–80. President René COTY left no memoirs.

Under the Fifth Republic, after de Gaulle, Georges POMPIDOU left two fragmentary and posthumous works, *Le Nœud Gordien*, Plon, 1974, and *Pour rétablir une vérité*, Flammarion, 1982.

Those of Valéry GISCARD d'ESTAING are in course of publication: *Le Pouvoir et la Vie*, Compagnie 12, Book 1, 1988; Book 2, *L'Affrontement*, 1991.

The works of François MITTERRAND (*Œuvres complètes* in 13 volumes, Éditions Rencontre, Lausanne, 1988) are contributions in the nature of polemics, chronicles and commentaries and not memoirs. Recommended, *Le Coup d'État permanent* (Plon, 1964).

Ministers and top functionaries who publish memoirs and recollections are too numerous to be quoted in detail, as the list grows daily. Mention must at least be made of Jules MOCH, Louis JOXE, Jean MONNET, Jean CHAUVEL (diplomat), Edgar FAURE, Michel DEBRÉ.

Among the writers of memoirs who had no major responsibility but who were observers and commentators, two stand out: Raymond ARON for his *Mémoires* (Julliard, 1983) and above all Marc BLOCH for *L'Étrange défaite* (ed. Franc-Tireur, 1946, republished Armand Colin, 1957, and a new Gallimard edition, 1990).

Lastly, a new genre has appeared, as if to resolve the following contradiction: the public at large is avid for accounts, but professional historians, who like to stand back, take their time and await the opening of archives, are slow to provide them. So along come the journalists, who make enquiries, bring evidence to light and sketch out temporary syntheses, of a history sometimes called 'immediate'. This genre flourished particularly about 13 May and decolonization, and it prospers, with J. LACOUTURE, J. FERNIOT, Cl. PAILLAT, M. BROMBERGER, Ph. ALEXANDRE and many others. Especially productive and interesting is J.-R. TOURNOUX, published by Plon.

GENERAL HISTORICAL ACCOUNTS

Among the the general historical accounts that are more detailed than mine, and well up to date, the best are those of the *Nouvelle histoire de la France contemporaine* (ed. Seuil, 'Points-Histoire' series in paperback), all of which are provided with extensive bibliographies:

MAYEUR Jean-Marie, *Les Débuts de la IIIe République 1871–1898*, Book 10, 1973.

REBÉRIOUX Madeleine, *La République radicale? 1898–1914*, Book 11, 1975.

BECKER Jean-Jacques and BERSTEIN Serge, *Victoire et frustrations 1914–1929*, Book 12, 1976.

DUBIEFF Henri, *Le Déclin de la Troisième République 1929–1938*, Book 13, 1976.

More cursory, but regularly re-edited and updated, *La Troisième République 1871–1914* by Georges BOURGIN (continued by Jean NÉRÉ), Armand Colin, 1967

The great dramatic 'events' of the period have naturally given rise to specialized works, thus for the Dreyfus Affair, *L'Affaire*, by Jean-Denis BREDIN, Julliard, 1983, and for the Great War, *La Grande Guerre 1914–1918* by Marc FERRO, Gallimard, 1969, and *L'Histoire de la Première Guerre mondiale* by General GAMBIEZ and Colonel SUIRE, 2 vol., Fayard, 1968–71.

Popular Front

LEFRANC Georges, *Histoire du Front Populaire*, Payot, 1963.

Second World War

MICHEL Henri, *La Seconde Guerre mondiale*, 2 vol., PUF, 1968–9.

Vichy, Occupation

DURAND Yves, *Vichy 1940–1944*, Bordas, 1972.

AZÉMA J.-P. and BEDARIDA F., *Vichy et les Français*, Fayard, 1992.

LABORIE Pierre, *L'Opinion française sous Vichy*, Seuil, 1990.

Resistance

NOGUÈRES Henri, *Histoire de la Résistance en France*, 5 vol., Laffont, 1967ff.

Liberation

La Libération de France (Coll. Actes du Colloque de 1974), ed. CNRS, 1976.

Fourth Republic

WILLIAMS Phillippe, *La Vie politique sous la IVe République*, Armand Colin, 1971.

JULLIARD Jacques, *La Quatrième République (Naissance et mort)*, Calmann-Lévy, 1968.

Algerian War

DROZ Bernard and LEVER Évelyne, *Histoire de la guerre d'Algérie 1954–1962*, Seuil, 1982.

Fifth Republic

VIANSSON-PONTÉ Pierre, *Histoire de la République gaullienne*, 2 vol., Fayard, 1971–2.

May 1968

DANSETTE Adrien, *Mai 68*, Plon, 1971.

GREAT BIOGRAPHIES

More in-depth studies of a political nature usually centre around a person or an organized collective force. As regards, biographies, I would highly recommend the following:

GAILLARD Jean-Michel, *Jules Ferry*, Fayard, 1989.
GARRIGUES Jean, *Le Général Boulanger*, Olivier Orban, 1991.
LEVILLAIN Philippe, *Albert de Mun*, École française de Rome, 1983.
GOLDBERG Harvey, *Jean Jaurès*, Fayard, 1970.
DUROSELLE Jean-Baptiste, *Georges Clemenceau*, Fayard, 1988.
MIQUEL Pierre, *Raymond Poincaré*, Fayard, 1961.
BERSTEIN Serge, *Édouard Herriot ou la République en personne*, Presses de la FN des sciences politiques, 1985.
KUPFERMAN Fred, *Pierre Laval*, Balland, 1987.
COLTON Joel, *Léon Blum*, Fayard, 1967.
MAYEUR Jean-Marie, *L'abbé Lemire*, Casterman, 1968.
SORLIN Pierre, *Waldeck-Rousseau*, Armand Colin, 1966.
JULLIARD Jacques, *Fernand Pelloutier*, Seuil, 1971.
ALLAIN Jean-Claude, *Joseph Caillaux*, Imprimerie nationale, 1981.
OUDIN Bernard, *Aristide Briand*, Laffont, 1987.

The principal and most recent biographies of leading political figures are by Jean LACOUTURE in the Seuil editions: *Léon Blum* (1976), *Pierre Mendès France* (1979) and the important *Charles de Gaulle* (3 vol., 1984–6).

Among numerous works on *Pétain*, that of Marc FERRO (Fayard, 1987) should be kept in mind.

With reference to the workers' movement:

ROBRIEUX Philippe, *Maurice Thorez, vie secrète et vie publique*, Fayard, 1975.
BRUNET J.-P., *Doriot*, Balland, 1986.
GEORGES B., TINTANT D. and RENAULD M.-A., *Jouhaux*, PUF, 1962.
GIRAULT Jacques, *Benoît Frachon, communiste et syndicaliste*, Presses de la FN des sciences politiques, 1989.

Lastly, for heads of state after de Gaulle, the life of Pompidou has been retraced by E. ROUSSEL (Lattes, 1984) and, as had already happened in the case of de Gaulle himself while he still lived, there is already a biography of Valéry Giscard d'Estaing by Michel BASSI (Grasset, 1968), and of François Mitterrand by F.-O. GIESBERT (Seuil, 1977) and Catherine NAY (*Le Noir et le Rouge*, Grasset, 1984). There is also a *Jacques Chirac* by F.-O. GIESBERT (Seuil, 1987).

GREAT POLITICAL FORCES

The pioneer in the scientific approach to studying political forces was André SIEGFRIED, with his *Tableau politique de la France de l'Ouest sous la IIIe République*,

A. Colin, 1913. Today such studies abound and it becomes increasingly difficult, for a period that is so close, to distinguish history from analyses of political science and circumstantial or apologetic works. In our times, historical literature has been dominated by a work which has swiftly become a classic in its turn, René RÉMOND's *La Droite en France de 1815 à nos jours*, Aubier, 1954, constantly reprinted since (new edition entitled *Les Droites en France*, 1984).

Valuable works on the various components of the right (or, if preferred, the various forms of the right) are more recent and only just beginning to emerge from its wake. Because it challenges most strongly, albeit implicitly, Rémond's famous tripartite breakdown, Zeev STERNHELL's *La Droite révolutionnaire*, Seuil, 1978, should be noted. That sound work was followed by a less convincing *Ni Droite ni Gauche* (new edition, Brussels, ed. Complexe, 1990). See also Raoul GIRARDET, *Le Nationalisme français 1871–1914*, A. Colin, 1966, and François-Georges DREYFUS, *Histoire de la démocratie chrétienne en France*, Albin Michel, 1988. A synthesis on *L'Extrême droite en France, de Maurras à Le Pen* has been produced by A. CHEBDEL d'APOLLONIA, Brussels, ed. Complexe, 1988.

For the left, it is the opposite. Works on each of its components have a good historiographic tradition, while an essay synthesizing left-wing elements, which would form an honourable counterpart to Rémond's *La Droite*, is still awaited, despite several attempts. I would just draw attention to:

LEFRANC Georges, *Le Mouvement socialiste sous la Troisième République*, Payot, 1963, completed by the same author with *Le Mouvement syndical sous la Troisième République*, Payot, 1967.

DUBIEFF Henri, *Le Syndicalisme révolutionnaire*, A. Colin, 1969.

KRIEGEL Annie, *Aux origines du communisme français 1914–1920*, 2 vol., Paris and the Hague, Mouton, 1964.

BRUNET Jean-Paul, *Histoire du PCF*, PUF, 'Que sais-je?', 1982.

ROBRIEUX Philippe, *Histoire intérieure du parti communiste*, 4 vol., Fayard, 1980–4.

MAITRON Jean, *Histoire du mouvement anarchiste en France*, Sudel, 1951.

BERSTEIN Serge, *Histoire du parti radical*, 2 vol., Presses de la FN des sciences politiques, 1980–2.

KAYSER Jacques, *Les Grandes batailles du radicalisme (…) 1820–1901*, Marcel Rivière, 1962.

However, the left cannot be reduced to the sum of its components, any more than the right. Masses of 'republicans' (the word was then chiefly used by the left) were not organized into parties, which is not to say that they were negligible. Really, the leading actor of the earlier epoch was not a physical person, but the Republic and the way it was seen. History has recently taken on board this singular reality through two works that have made their mark:

RUDELLE Odile, *La République absolue*, Publications of the Sorbonne, 1983;

NICOLET Claude, *L'Idée républicaine en France*, Gallimard, 1982. Also:

AGULHON Maurice, *Marianne au pouvoir. L'imagerie et la symbolique républicaines de 1880 à 1914*, Flammarion, 1989.

Gaullism, in power since 1958, has given birth to a whole literature. The most recent, complex but naturally very rich, comes from the Proceedings of the Symposium *De Gaulle en son siècle*, in the process of publication by Documentation française.

On social movements most closely linked with the right, see:

BARRAL Pierre, *Les Agrariens français de Méline à Pisani*, Armand Colin, 1968.

BORNE Dominique, *Petits bourgeois en révolte, le Mouvement Poujade*, Flammarion, 1977.

On socialism, after G. LEFRANC, Roger QUILLOT has given an account of the period 1944–58 in *La SFIO et l'exercice du pouvoir*, Fayard, 1972.

The synthesis on the *Gauche française*, at least for the period of change from 1958 to 1973, has been attempted, under this title, by Jean POPEREN, 2 vol., Fayard, 1972–3. On the subject of the extreme left, mention must be made of Hervé HAMON and Patrick ROTMAN for *Génération*, 2 vol., Seuil, 1987–8.

OTHER AREAS

To penetrate more deeply into those areas of history that lie further from the main theme of the present work and may have been merely alluded to, the reader is directed to the following books (and their bibliographies).

Foreign Policies and Relations

RENOUVIN Pierre, *L'Histoire des relations internationales*, Parts VI, VII and VIII, Hachette, 1955ff.

GIRARDET Raoul, *L'Idée coloniale en France 1871–1962*, La Table ronde, 1972.

DUROSELLE J.-B., *La Décadence*, Imprimerie nationale, 1979, and *L'Abîme*, Imprimerie nationale, 1982, 1986.

GOSSER Alfred, *La IVe République et sa politique extérieure*, A Colin, 3rd edn. 1972, and *La Politique extérieure de la Ve République*, Seuil, 1965.

Economic and Social History

BRAUDEL F. and LABROUSSE E., *Histoire économique et sociale de la France*, Book 4, PUF, 1980, and Book IV-3, PUF, 1982.

DUBY G. and WALLON A. (eds), *Histoire de la France rurale*, Books III and IV, Seuil, 1976ff.

DUBY G. (ed.) *Histoire de la France urbaine*, Book IV, Seuil, 1985.

DUROSELLE Jean-Baptiste, *La France de la Belle Époque. La France et les Français 1900–1914*, ed. Richelieu, 1972.

ASSELAIN Jean-Charles, *Histoire économique de la France*, Book II, Seuil, 1984.

FOURASTIÉ Jean, *Les Trente Glorieuses*, Fayard, 1979.

MALINVAUD E., CARRÉ J.-J. and DUBOIS P., *La Croissance française*, Seuil, 1972.

Colonies

MARSEILLE Jacques, *Empire colonial et capitalisme français, histoire d'un divorce*, Albin Michel, 1984.

Institutions and Political Life

CHEVALLIER Jean-Jacques, *Histoire des institutions et des régimes politiques de la France de 1789 à nos jours*, Dalloz, 1971.

Religion

CHOLVY G. and HILAIRE Y.-M., *Histoire religieuse de la France contemporaine*, Book 2 (1880–1930) and Book 3 (1930–1988), Toulouse, Privat, 1986 and 1988.

Daily Life and Customs

ARIÈS Ph. and DUBY G. (eds), *Histoire de la vie privée*, Books IV and V, Seuil, 1987.

VINCENT Gérard, *Les Français de 1945 à 1975*, Masson, 1977.

PROST Antoine, *L'Enseignement en France 1800–1967*, Armand Colin, 1969, and *Histoire général de l'enseignement et de l'éducation en France*, Book IV, Nouvelle Librairie de France, 1982.

Intellectual and Cultural Life

ALBERT Pierre, *Histoire générale de la Presse française*, Book III (1871 to 1940), PUF, 1972.

CRUBELLIER Maurice, *Histoire culturelle de la France XIXe–XXe siècles*, A. Colin, 1974.

MAYEUR Jean *et al.*, *La France bourgeoise devient laïque et républicaine*, Book V of *Histoire du peuple français*, ed. by L. PARIAS, Nouvelle Librairie de France, 1964.

ORY Pascal and SIRINELLI Jean-François, *Les Intellectuels en France de l'Affaire Dreyfus à nos jours*, Armand Colin, 1986.

ORY Pascal, *L'Entre-deux-mai: Histoire culturelle de la France mai 1968–mai 1981*, Seuil, 1983.

WORKS OF FICTION

The daily life, the atmosphere, the ways of thinking belonging to an era – the many and diffuse realities that history is only just beginning to analyse and reconstruct – are made accessible by fictional works of a realist or naturalist nature. Can they help the reader (or viewer) to get a better understanding of and feel for a time he has not experienced, and which history delivers to him in a dissected form? Yes, without a doubt, bearing in mind that those novels recognized as great by literary judgement have only very secondarily the merit of reflecting reality, whereas those most faithful to the task of chronicler or photographer are no longer elevated to the heights, as were Balzac, Zola or even Jules Romains.

Jules ROMAINS, *Les Hommes de bonne volonté* (27 volumes, published between 1932 and 1946), covers the period 1907–33 with an explicit, and perfectly successful, documentary ambition. Two other sagas have the same ambition and cover the same epoch: *La Chronique des Pasquier*, by Georges DUHAMEL (10 volumes published between 1933 and 1945), and *Les Thibault*, by Roger-Martin du GARD (8 volumes from 1922 to 1940).

The Great War is present in each of these famous novel-type ensembles. But in itself and by itself the war gave rise to a whole literature of testimony, totally bald and blunt or clad in a fictional form. The best known are: *Le Feu*, by Henri BARBUSSE (1916, Prix Goncourt), *Les Croix de Bois*, by Roland DORGELÉS (1919 Prix Fémina), and *Ceux de 14*, by Maurice GENEVOIX.

I would not hazard even a selective list from the vast amount of literature of rural and provincial realism. Let us just remember that the presence of politics in village life has never been as strong and deep-rooted as at the height of the Third Republic. Two celebrated works at least recall it: *La Guerre des boutons*, by Louis PERCAUD (1913), and, more of a caricature but one that has passed into the language, *Clochemerle*, by Gabriel CHEVALLIER (1934).

Need it be said that the series of novels by Marcel PROUST, *À la recherche du temps perdu* (1913 to 1927), though much narrower as regards social and historical observation, outdoes and transcends the tradition of realism through its other merits?

What has been said of Proust may also be applied to CÉLINE, *mutatis mutandis.* *Le Voyage au bout de la nuit* (1932) and *Mort à crédit* (1936) are today perceived far more as a revolution of subjectivity and writing than as witness to the life of the people in the Parisian urban area at a time of crisis, but to a certain extent that is what they are.

Similar remarks could be made about the works of MAURIAC or BERNANOS, which are very precisely situated, but whose underlying meaning goes widely beyond their situation.

On a more modest note, the Popular Front may be relived through *La Maison du peuple*, by Louis GUILLOUX, or *La Galère*, by André CHAMSON; life under the occupation in *Au Bon Beurre*, by Jean DUTOURD, or *Mon village à l'heure allemande*, by Jean-Louis BORY; captivity in *Les Grandes Vacances*, by Francis AMBRIÉRE, etc.

The evocation of the political and social climate through a work of fiction still remains a recurring ambition, as it has tempted ARAGON (*Les Beaux Quartiers, Aurélien, Les Communistes*), SARTRE (*Les Chemins de la Liberté*), Simone de BEAUVOIR (*Les Mandarins*) and Maurice DRUON (*Les Grandes Familles*).

However, since it became 'talking', an industry and popular, it is above all the cinema that has tended to take over from the novel as the provider of historical fiction. That is not to say that the relationship of the work with reality is simpler in the cinema than in the contemporary novel. The public does not go to the cinema to study history, either old or modern, and even less does the director see himself as teacher or witness (with a few exceptions as, for example, René CLÉMENT's *La Bataille du rail* in 1945, on the Resistance). In spite of that, it is generally agreed that the Parisian people of the Popular Front are to be found in certain films by René CLAIR, Jean GRÉMILLON or Marcel CARNÉ, the provincial France of the occupation in CLOUZOT's *Le Corbeau*, etc. Whatever the nuances of their conception of reality may be, when the cameras are turning the creators of films are bound to capture urban or village settings, clothes, customs, ways of doing things and ways of speaking, and they pass on the memory of them and record their development. To borrow an example from a recent publication, 'three films would have been enough (for Jacques TATI) to portray the evolution of post-war France: rural, somewhat archaic but already fascinated by America in *Jour de fête*, 1948; timidly opening up to the civilization of leisure activities in *Les Vacances de Monsieur Hulot*, 1953; and in *Mon oncle*, 1958, torn between the plastic and chrome world of dawning consumerism and the still lively disorder of the old popular quarters' (Claude-Jean PHILIPPE, in the article 'Cinéma' in the *Encyclopédie de la culture française*, Eclectis, 1991).

Index of Names

Index of Subjects